THE WONDERLAND OF KNOWLEDGE

AN
UP·TO·DATE
ILLUSTRATED
ENCYCLOPAEDIA

Edited by
ERNEST OGAN

VOLUME 1

S. van Abbe

ODHAMS PRESS LIMITED. LONG ACRE. LONDON.

*Printed and Bound in Great Britain by the
Greycaine Book Manufacturing Co., Ltd., Watford, Herts.*

CONTENTS OF VOLUME I

THE STORY OF THE NATIONS

	PAGE		PAGE
Just Before History Began	1	The History of the Chaldeans	279
The History of Egypt (Part I)	53	The History of the Phoenicians	325
The History of Egypt (Part II)	101	The History of the Hittites	353
The History of Egypt (Part III)	157	The History of the Jews (Part I)	389
The History of the Sumerians	199	The History of the Jews (Part II)	429
The History of Babylonia and		The History of Persia	471
Assyria	243	The History of the Cretans	497

MUSIC THROUGH THE AGES

	PAGE		PAGE
How We Came to Have Music	5	Music Begins to Sound Modern	269
The Childhood of Music	64	Seven Giants of Music	375
Music Comes of Age	185	Mighty Music for Our Modern Age	459

THE ROMANCE OF EXPLORATION

	PAGE		PAGE
Marco Polo	13	John Cabot	291
Amerigo Vespucci	15	Jacques Cartier	293
Bartholomeu Diaz	16	Sir Francis Drake	383
Vasco Nuñez de Balboa	17	Sir Walter Raleigh	386
Ferdinand Magellan	85	Samuel de Champlain	419
Vasco Da Gama	87	Henry Hudson	421
Christopher Columbus	119	Jacques Marquette	495

GREAT NAMES IN ENGLISH LITERATURE

	PAGE		PAGE
The Venerable Bede	32	Richard Steele	222
Geoffrey Chaucer	33	Joseph Addison	222
Sir Thomas Malory	37	Alexander Pope	319
Sir Thomas More	39	Samuel Richardson	322
Edmund Spenser	95	Henry Fielding	323
Sir Francis Bacon	96	Samuel Johnson	367
Christopher Marlowe	99	James Boswell	370
William Shakespeare	145	Oliver Goldsmith	372
Ben Jonson	175	Laurence Sterne	402
Izaak Walton	207	Tobias Smollett	403
John Milton	208	Edward Gibbon	405
John Bunyan	212	Edmund Burke	406
Samuel Pepys	214	Thomas Gray	505
John Dryden	215	Thomas Chatterton	507
Daniel Defoe	217	Richard Brinsley Sheridan	508
Jonathan Swift	219	Jane Austen	510

MARVELS OF INVENTION

	PAGE			PAGE
The Steam-engine	19	Spinning and Weaving . . .	229	
The Reaping-machine . . .	89	Weights and Measures . . .	312	
The Sewing-machine . . .	141	The Work of the Diver . . .	355	
The Cotton-gin	195			

WONDERS OF THE INSECT WORLD

Swarms of Midgets with Six Legs .	41	The Queer Ways of the Lowly Beetle	331
Like Flowers on the Wing . .	109	Insect Fiddlers	407
Clever Insect Actors . .	165	The Horrible House-fly . . .	441
Insects Armed with Stings . .	257	Insect Armies	481
The Busy Life of the Ant . .	283	Ogres of the Insect World . .	501

MISCELLANEOUS

What We Need to Build a House .	73	How We Learned to Tell the	
The Boy Scout Movement . .	128	Time	295
Where Our Pearls Come From .	177	The Story of Buttons . .	362
The Seven Wonders of the World .	225	The Story of the Gipsies . .	424

STORIES RETOLD

Tansy and Bobbles on Fable Island	47	The Story of Beowulf . . .	238
180, 252, 347, 451			

THINGS TO MAKE AND DO

THINGS TO MAKE: How to Draw to		THINGS TO MAKE (continued)	
Scale	27, 480	Ice-boat, Pop-gun, and Whistle .	428
Clothes-hanger, Telephone		Passe-partout Frame . .	440
Screen, Waste-paper Basket,		Batiked Glass	494
and Lampshade . .	278	Alligator, Igloo, Algernon Pea-	
Sled, Hockey-stick, Barrel Stave		nut, Kangaroo, and Dodo .	512
Skis, and Dutch Jumper .	311	PUZZLES . . 63, 108, 118,	366
Silhouettes . . .	330	TRICKS . . . 174, 194,	346
How to Make a Rose . .	418	MAGIC	450

COLOUR PLATES IN THIS VOLUME

(The page number is that which the plate faces)

	PAGE
Special painting by Charles Robinson, R.I. . . . *Frontispiece*	
Some Typical British Insects . .	41
Hawks, Tigers and Other British Moths	109
Nursery Rhymes: Jack and Jill, Three Blind Mice, Little Boy Blue .	185
Familiar and Lesser Known Butterflies	257
Brightly Clad Beetles of Many Lands	331
Moths in Gaily Coloured Clothing .	407
Flitting Flowers of the Insect World	481
Nursery Rhyme: Simple Simon .	497

SPECIAL COLOUR SUPPLEMENTS

What Happens at Broadcasting House and Wild Animals in their Native Homes . *Following page* 224

Marvels of the Modern World and Little People of Many Lands

Following page 352

KEY TO PRONUNCIATION

To help readers to pronounce difficult technical words and proper names appearing in "The Wonderland of Knowledge," the following phonetic system, or scheme of pronunciation, is adopted. It is framed on simple but adequate lines, and no attempt has been made to cover the complicated method required to give the more delicate distinctions of the science of vocal sounds.

ā as in māte
å as in senăte
â as in hâir
ă as in hăt
ä as in fäther
ch as in chest
ē as in ēve
ė as in rėlate
ĕ as in bĕnd
ē as in hēr
g as in go
ī as in bīte
ĭ as in ĭnn
j as in join
K the guttural sound of ch, as in the German *ach*, or the Scottish *loch*

N indicates the French nasal sound, as in *bon*
ō as in bōne
ȯ as in Christȯpher
ô as in lôrd
ŏ as in hŏt
oi as in toil
ōō as in sōōn
o͝o as in bo͝ok
ou as in shout
s as in so
sh as in ship
th as in thumb
th as in thus
ū as in cūre
û as in fûr
ŭ as in bŭt

ü a sound formed by pronouncing ē with the lips in the position for oo, as in the German *über* and the French *une*
z as in maze
zh as in azure
' an indication that a vowel sound is elided or cut off, as in apple (ăp''l)
An accent (') follows a syllable receiving stress, and a heavy accent (') the principal syllable when more than one is stressed

To those about to make this Great Adventure

YOU are now standing at the gateway to the Wonderland of Knowledge. This land—more wonderful than any fairyland of ancient story—is yours. It is yours for the asking. For here, in your hands, you hold the key to the gate—the right of entry to the Wonderland of Knowledge.

✦ ✦ ✦

You will find that this new world has no forbidding boundaries or limitations. You may wander where you will, and yet, should you wish to keep to the highroad, following on from chapter to chapter, you will find the journey smooth and pleasant, with each new volume revealing more and yet more wonders.

You will see the story of the Earth on which you work and play unfold before your eyes in living pictures. You will

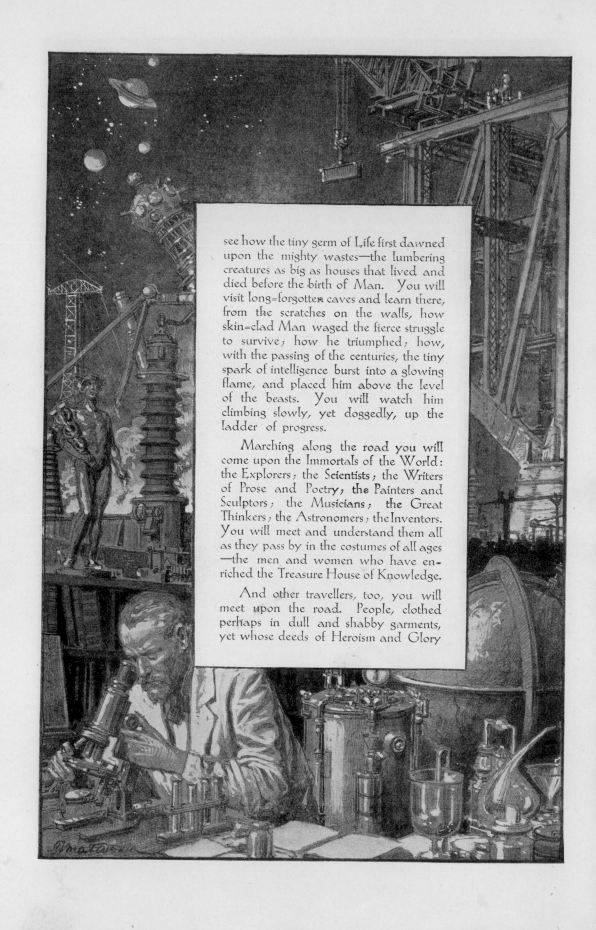

see how the tiny germ of Life first dawned upon the mighty wastes—the lumbering creatures as big as houses that lived and died before the birth of Man. You will visit long=forgotten caves and learn there, from the scratches on the walls, how skin=clad Man waged the fierce struggle to survive; how he triumphed; how, with the passing of the centuries, the tiny spark of intelligence burst into a glowing flame, and placed him above the level of the beasts. You will watch him climbing slowly, yet doggedly, up the ladder of progress.

Marching along the road you will come upon the Immortals of the World: the Explorers; the Scientists; the Writers of Prose and Poetry; the Painters and Sculptors; the Musicians; the Great Thinkers; the Astronomers; the Inventors. You will meet and understand them all as they pass by in the costumes of all ages —the men and women who have en= riched the Treasure House of Knowledge.

And other travellers, too, you will meet upon the road. People, clothed perhaps in dull and shabby garments, yet whose deeds of Heroism and Glory

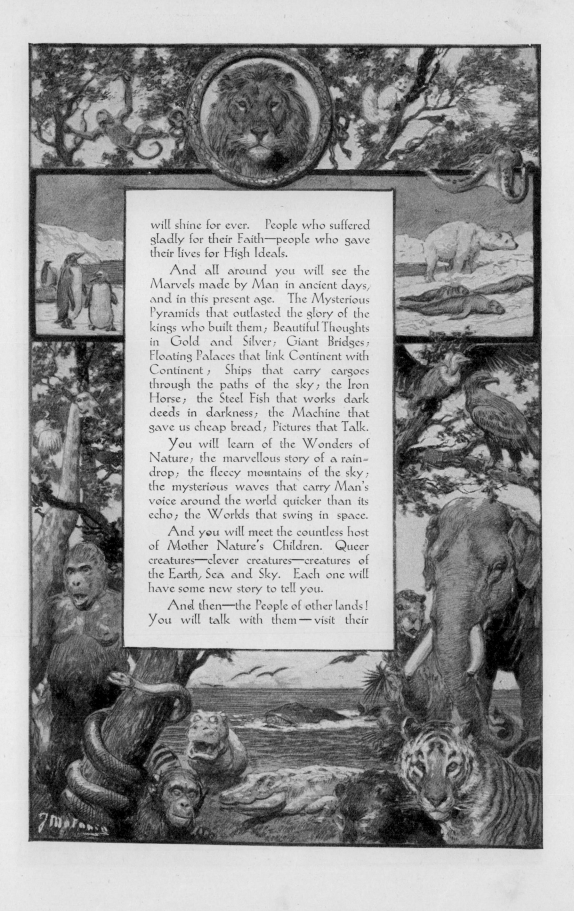

will shine for ever. People who suffered gladly for their Faith—people who gave their lives for High Ideals.

And all around you will see the Marvels made by Man in ancient days, and in this present age. The Mysterious Pyramids that outlasted the glory of the kings who built them; Beautiful Thoughts in Gold and Silver; Giant Bridges; Floating Palaces that link Continent with Continent; Ships that carry cargoes through the paths of the sky; the Iron Horse; the Steel Fish that works dark deeds in darkness; the Machine that gave us cheap bread; Pictures that Talk.

You will learn of the Wonders of Nature; the marvellous story of a rain= drop; the fleecy mountains of the sky; the mysterious waves that carry Man's voice around the world quicker than its echo; the Worlds that swing in space.

And you will meet the countless host of Mother Nature's Children. Queer creatures—clever creatures—creatures of the Earth, Sea and Sky. Each one will have some new story to tell you.

And then—the People of other lands! You will talk with them — visit their

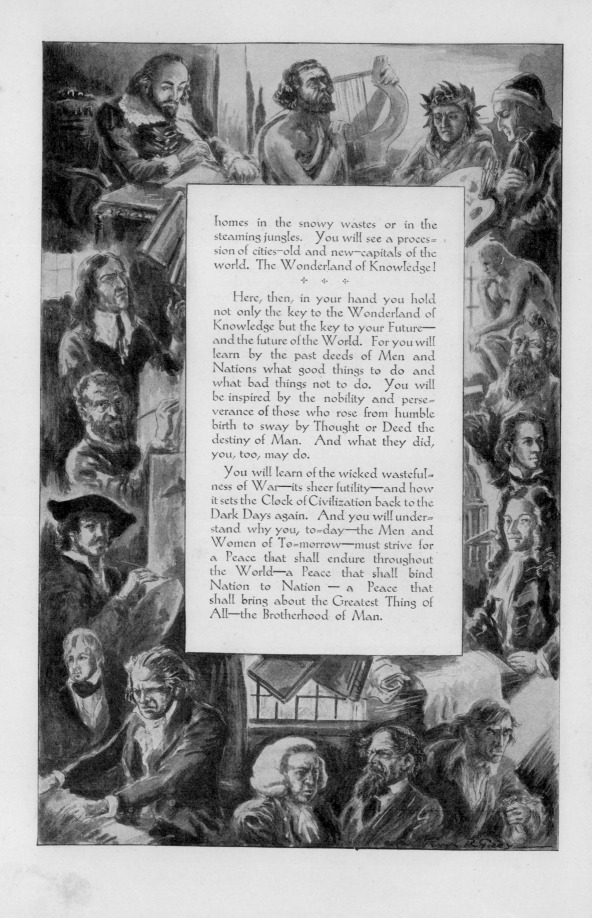

homes in the snowy wastes or in the steaming jungles. You will see a procession of cities—old and new—capitals of the world. The Wonderland of Knowledge!

✢ ✢ ✢

Here, then, in your hand you hold not only the key to the Wonderland of Knowledge but the key to your Future— and the future of the World. For you will learn by the past deeds of Men and Nations what good things to do and what bad things not to do. You will be inspired by the nobility and perseverance of those who rose from humble birth to sway by Thought or Deed the destiny of Man. And what they did, you, too, may do.

You will learn of the wicked wastefulness of War—its sheer futility—and how it sets the Clock of Civilization back to the Dark Days again. And you will understand why you, to=day—the Men and Women of To=morrow—must strive for a Peace that shall endure throughout the World—a Peace that shall bind Nation to Nation — a Peace that shall bring about the Greatest Thing of All—the Brotherhood of Man.

Long, long ago, before mankind learned how to read and write, the world was peopled with men who looked a good deal like these. We may think of them with scorn, perhaps, yet to their bravery and dogged endurance we owe the very foundations of our civilization, together with many extremely useful inventions, such as the wheel.

JUST BEFORE HISTORY BEGAN

Where were All the People, and What were They Like? And How Did What We Know as History Begin?

IF YOU think about our great earth with all the different countries upon it, and if you remember that almost all of those countries for thousands of years back have had people living in them, it makes you wonder about the way in which history starts in your books. For history begins about six thousand years ago with a few people living in two little countries not far away from each other. There was Egypt, a tiny country in Africa, and Sumeria (sū-mē′-rĭ-ȧ), a still smaller land a little way off in Asia. Why do we forget all the rest of the world and begin with these two small areas on the map?

The answer is that these were the places where people began reading and writing. Before people can read and write they are called barbarians, and before they can even make clay pots in which to keep things they are called savages. When they can read and write they are said to be civilized, and the first civilizations about which we have any knowledge began in Egypt and in Sumeria, the two little countries whose story you will soon hear.

You see, when people learn to read and write they can put down the interesting things that happen, so that they may not be forgotten. They can tell us the names of their kings, the stories of their fighting, and all about the way in which they lived. Before we know these things we cannot learn much of the story, or the history, of those people.

The Influence of Writing on History

Writing was invented about six thousand years ago, but only a few people knew how to write at first. As writing spread, so did history. We find more and more countries being drawn into the magic circle of civilization, until to-day, though there may be some backward nations, very few people can be called really uncivilized. Nearly all the peoples of the world can now read and write.

History begins with what we call the white race of men. Both the Egyptians and the Sumerians were of this white race, and so were the Greeks,

On this page are examples of the four great races of mankind. Below is Captain R. F. Scott, a typical representative of the white race, which is now the strongest of the four, and has spread to nearly every corner of the globe.

Above is a Chinese, a member of the yellow race, to which the Japanese also belong. This race has a very ancient civilization, and is highly cultivated.

the Persians, the Hebrews, the Assyrians, the Romans, and almost all the other people whose stories are told in these books. But you must not think that the white race is the only important one in the world. It is important for the beginning of history, because it was the white race that first recorded history. But the other races are important, too.

Who Are the Mongolians?

Those other races are the brown, the yellow, and the red. The brown race lives mostly in Africa, and its members are called negroes. It did not invent reading and writing by itself, but learned them from the white race; so one may say that it borrowed its civilization.

The yellow, or Mongolian (mŏng-gō'lĭ-ăn), race lives in China and Japan, and in several other countries. It invented its

own reading and writing many thousands of years ago, and it has a very long and honourable history, of which you will be able to read later.

The red, or Indian race, is believed by some historians to be the same as the yellow race, but this is not at all certain. The Indians, who live in North and South America, did invent a sort of writing, so that they cannot be called barbarians. Some of them were highly civilized, but most of them borrowed so much from the white races that their civilization is not all their own.

These four races — white, yellow, brown and red—

On the left is a member of the brown, or black race; and to the right a member of the red race, otherwise known as the American Indian.

are divided from one another by the colour of their skins and eyes, the shape of their features, and the places where they live. Since the white race has the oldest known history, and is therefore most important for us at this moment, you will want to know a little more about it.

While there are probably more than three big divisions of the white race, we usually speak of three great branches: Hamites, Semites, and Aryans or Indo-Europeans. The Hamites (hăm'īte) were the white people who lived in the northern part of Africa. The Egyptians were Hamites, and

2

so were the Libyans, who lived next to them to the west, in the territory lying between the Mediterranean and the Sahara and extending to the Atlantic Ocean.

The Semites (sĕm'ĭte) were the people of the great deserts which partly cover Arabia and the country to the north and east. The Phoenicians (fĕ-nĭsh'ăn), Assyrians, Babylonians, and Hebrews were all Semitic (sĕ-mĭt'ĭk) peoples, and their stories make delightful reading. The Hittites also may have been Semitic. Among modern people the Jews and the Arabs are Semitic.

It is from the Semites that we get the Jewish, Christian, and Mohammedan religions, and also the alphabet which we use. It is these gifts to mankind which cause us to rank the Semitic race as one of the greatest in the world.

The Greatest White Race

Then we come to the Indo-European race, which is also known as the Aryan (är'yăn). This is the greatest white race of all. Almost all the people we call white—Hindus, Persians, Greeks, Italians, Spaniards, Scandinavians, Frenchmen, Germans, Englishmen and Americans — all these great nations belong to the Indo-European race.

We believe that the Indo-European race began in Western India, and that its tribes pushed westward farther and farther until they had practically circled the globe. People sometimes divide Indo-Europeans into two groups: the fair-haired, blue-eyed Nordics, who settled in Germany, Denmark, Sweden, Norway and England; and the dark-haired, brown-eyed southern race, the Italians, Spaniards, Portuguese and others.

It cannot be expected that races of men will always remain the same. People of different races, if they live near together,

Here are representative types of the three main divisions of the white race, as they are found in the modern world. At the left is a modern Arab, a member of the Semitic race, which once ruled in Asia Minor. In the centre is an Englishman, a representative of the Indo-European race. And at the right is a present-day Egyptian, a representative of the Hamitic race, which has now greatly declined in importance.

will often fall in love and marry one another; and then their children will be of mixed race. In the thousands of years of history, the Indo-European peoples have come to be so mixed that very often we cannot say with any degree of certainty to what race they belong.

Take Englishmen, for example. When the fair-haired German tribes came to England they found there a dark-haired people called the Britons. Many of the British men were killed, but many of the women married Germans, and there was the first mixing of races. Then the Danes and the Normans came to England, and two more mixings took place, so that the Englishman of to-day

3

is really a mixture of Briton, German, Dane, and Norman.

We know something about these Indo-European peoples as separate races, however, and of how they moved about to cover the earth. They came by waves westward from India. Each wave was an army, but very often with the army came the soldiers' wives and children, all ready to stay and settle down. Some of these armies, such as the first one that came to Greece, arrived so long ago that by the time their descendants began to read and write they had forgotten that they had ever lived anywhere but in Greece. Others, like the Germans who came to England, could read and write when they arrived.

Many of the stories you will read—stories of the Assyrians, the Phoenicians, the Hittites, the Greeks—are stories of such waves of travelling armies. They are tales of how a new, strong kingdom would rise somewhere within the magic circle of civilized history; how it would grow in power and riches until it was the greatest nation on earth; and how it would then gradually lose its power and grow weak once more, or perhaps split up into a great many little districts, or possibly come under the rule of another kingdom.

This rise and fall of kingdom after kingdom, this westward marching of waves of Indo-European peoples, is the fascinating story you will read. You will read, too, how people lived in those far-off times, what they thought, and what became of them.

All through history you will see this rising

Here the two great groups of the Indo-European race are clearly contrasted. The girl in the oval is a Spaniard, with dark eyes, smooth black hair, and clear olive skin. She belongs to the southern race. Above are two Norwegian girls, whose blue eyes, light hair, and fair white skin stamp them as Nordic types, or members of the race from Northern Europe.

and falling of kingdoms, with a country becoming powerful for a time and then weakening and passing away. What is the reason for their rise and fall?

The reason seems to be that so long as people were poor but lived hard, free lives, they were strong and brave and could fight well, so that they conquered many other people and grew very rich. Then for a long time—perhaps several hundred years—they enjoyed their riches and power. But little by little they came to dislike hard work and careful thinking. They grew lazy and careless, and when a new, free, energetic nation came along, it found them easy to conquer.

This is one of the great lessons of history—that it is through hard work, careful thinking, and healthy living that nations, like individuals, may become great. The real enemies of civilization are not people, but luxury, greed, laziness and hate.

Some people tell us that the nations of to-day will, in the course of time, go downhill just as did the great nations of centuries ago. They tell us that another war, with poison gas and other terrible weapons, might easily wipe out whole nations. Will our modern world last?

The modern world is not like the old world. In the first place, we can keep in touch with the whole world and its people now, and an enemy country cannot take people by surprise as it could long ago. In the second place, most of the great nations have agreements or pacts in an effort to keep peace. We must make every possible effort to see that these agreements and pacts are kept, and thus ensure lasting peace.

4

How WE CAME to Have MUSIC

The Birds, the Waves, and the Winds were Man's First Music Teachers, and the Scales He Learned from Them were Only Three or Four Notes Long

WHO was the inventor of music, and when did it actually begin?

If you will think a moment, you will realize that there never has been a time when there were not sweet sounds upon the earth. For even in the twilight past, there must have been a grand surging of the waves and, as they broke on the bare shores, a sounding like the beating of great drums, and whenever the lightning played it was followed by the majestic rolling of the thunder. Later, when life began to quiver all around, there was the soft murmur of leaves, the lapping of waves, the ripple of little streams, the pleasant hum of insects, and the song of birds. All this is Nature's music—music which our greatest composers try hard to imitate with flutes and horns and strings.

But where, you will ask, did our kind of music come from—man-made music to

The harp, the lute and the lyre, all played by plucking the strings, were among the earlier instruments of musicians.

which we can sing and dance, and which we make with our own fingers and lips? Why, it came from Nature's music, which is as old as the earth; it came from the very winds and waters and birds about which we have been talking.

Have you ever seen a little child try to imitate the kitten's mew, or the dog's big bow-wow? It is as natural for him to copy the sounds around him as it is to learn to talk. And he works hard at it, too! That is just what early men tried to do. They copied, as best they could, the sounds of the animals round them, and particularly the singing of the birds. For men have by nature a beautiful device for making lovely sounds. It is their bird-like whistle.

One can imagine how, gathered into the cave at night or on a cold winter's day, they would beg some talented member of the tribe to give the various bird calls—or a whole concert, perhaps, made up of his imitations of the song of the nightingale.

Thunder of the Drums

But there were also other sounds that they liked—the distant drums of the thunder and the steady swish of the waves. Those were harder to imitate, but men learned from them how to beat time and to listen for beautiful rhythms. Finally, when someone had the happy notion of stretching a sheep-skin over a frame, he could produce the thunder's majestic roll in a way to fill everybody with delight. Naturally, they used so marvellous an instrument in their religion. They felt it was of untold value in frightening demons away! And savage tribes to this day delight in the tom-tom.

Then, too, early men learned the pleasant sounds you can get by plucking at a string, and the lovely tones a reed or pipe will give if you know how to stop it up at the proper lengths. Even before that, perhaps, they had discovered that if you blow on a blade of grass held between your two thumbs you can produce musical sounds. When the curtain first rises on the drama of history, between four and five thousand years before Christ, the people discovered on the stage possess drums and instruments fitted with strings, and before very long they will add to those the pipes, or "wind instruments." Both along the Nile and on the banks of the Tigris and Euphrates, in Mesopotamia, men were experimenting with these three kinds of instruments, and some of their lyres and other instruments were often very quaint although well and beautifully made.

The two amusing little affairs at the top are whistling jars from Peru. In the square are musicians who whiled away the hours for Assurbanipal, who lived more than six hundred years before Christ and was the most magnificent of all Assyrian kings. One would give a good deal to know the kind of sound those strange-looking instruments made. The group adorned the wall in Assurbanipal's great palace. At the right is a native African drum, made from a hollow log.

But early men did not usually think of music as a thing to be enjoyed by itself. Instead, it was an accompaniment to poetry and dancing, and its tones were sad or merry according as their mood was grave or gay. It was this companionship with dancing which gave to music the beautiful thing that we call "rhythm" (rĭth'm) —that exciting accent or stress that falls on regular beats. It is a delight in rhythm that makes us like to dance or march, or keep time with music in any other way.

At first early men had probably just tapped or beaten on their instruments—blow after blow after blow. But when they began to make up dances the music naturally divided itself up according to the kind of dance it had to follow— into twos or threes or fours. *Tum*, tum, tum; *tum*, tum, tum; *tum*, tum, tum! And that regularly accented string of beats is what makes rhythm. How much more interesting it is than just a tum, tum, tum, tum, tum, tum, on and on and on without any variety at all!

We shall never know the sound of the music that was played by the dark-skinned people along the ancient Nile. But perhaps it is just as well. For it is almost certain that it would be somewhat disappointing to our ears to-day. Those ancient musicians had not invented a way to write their music, but some of the instruments on which they played it have come down to us, and a few lucky persons have heard those ancient harps and flutes yield up their sounds.

The result has nearly always been un-pleasant to our ears. Perhaps the Egyptians who played them could do better than we can to-day; certainly their poets loved to hear them, and the Egyptian lute was popular until not very long ago. But it is hard to think that the sounds it yielded, even when it was new, could have been very beautiful in comparison with the tone of our modern instruments.

Instruments Played by the Wind

But crude as they were, those simple contrivances were very dear to men. The use of them spread through Asia as far as China. And other kinds were invented, too. Some clever person in Asia Minor ages ago found that the wind passing over strings stretched upon hollow boards would make music of its own. So he invented an instrument upon which the wind could play as long as it would. It was named after Æolus (ē′ŏ-lŭs), the Greek god of the winds. We call it the Æolian (ē-ō′lĭ-ăn) harp.

There were various other instruments on which the breeze would play. We have the story that King David's harp would sing at midnight in the boisterous north wind as it hung above his bed. It is also on record that St. Dunstan, Archbishop of Canterbury, was at one time accustomed to following King David's example, and that the practice led to his being regarded as a sorcerer. He was charged with committing wrongful acts and punished with banishment. The East Indians and Chinese knew how to cause the wind to make music in some such way; and even to-day the Chinese fly kites with vibrating strings stretched across them, and so snatch musical sounds out of the air. The Malays amuse themselves with a bamboo cane pierced with holes; they stick it into the ground and let the wind play at its own sweet will.

Playing to the Gods

There is one ancient instrument that is common in our own time, though, of course, it has been very much improved. It is the timbrel, or tambourine. It is often to be seen in the carvings of the Assyrians and other ancient peoples. In fact the Incas of Peru and the earliest inhabitants of Greenland, Britain, and Northern Europe all

The tambourine, cymbals and pipes accompanied early dances in honour of the gods. Frequently it was the custom for the dancers to continue until they sank down from exhaustion.

enjoyed its lively tones. It was used everywhere in the religious ceremonies in which music played a part; it even kept time for the famous dances in honour of the god Bacchus (băk′ŭs) in ancient Greece. For its music was thought to please the gods so much that they would become quite obliging, and could then be persuaded to answer all sorts of prayers. A mighty instrument—the little tambourine!

Different races have different thoughts to express in musical sounds; and, of course, their musical languages, like their spoken words, have come to sound very different. The songs and chants of China and Japan are so unlike ours in the West that we can hardly feel they are music at all, though they probably have come straight down from the old songs and dances of Egypt and Asia Minor—just as ours have done.

It was the ancient Hebrews and the Greeks who passed the early music on to us—and in doing

Above are two famous early instruments—at the left the Pan-pipes of the Greeks, the favourite instrument of shepherds, and at the right the Hebrew shofar, which sounded the signal at the fall of the walls of Jericho. In the square is Miriam, with her maidens, celebrating the passage of the Children of Israel through the Red Sea.

so they did a great deal to make it more interesting and more beautiful. Anyone who reads the Book of Exodus in the Bible can learn the words of one of the oldest songs in the world, the song of Miriam, which she sang when the children of Israel saw their enemies the Egyptians swallowed up in the Red Sea. We have lost the music to which she sang it, though some people think it may have come down to us without our knowing it. But whatever it was, it almost certainly was Egyptian, for the Israelites had lived in Egypt for a long, long time, and had learned the arts of the Egyptians.

When they started on their long march to the Promised Land, the Hebrews took with them the instruments of their taskmasters, for Miriam and her maidens offered up their thanks "with timbrels and with dances." The marching host had drums, cymbals (sĭm′băl), flutes, harps, lyres and trumpets; and later they learned to use the Pan-pipe—a kind of mouth organ—and the bagpipe. All those instruments were played in religious services; and many of the words that they used to accompany have come down to us as the Psalms in the Bible.

If you look just under the number of the Psalm, you will see, in many cases, the name of the person who was believed to have written it, and sometimes the very occasion upon which it is thought to have been written. Often you will see the words, "To the Chief Musician." For the later Hebrews had a magnificent Temple service with four thousand singers and a large orchestra. The chorus was composed of men and women divided into two great choirs, who stood on the Temple steps, and at a signal from the trumpets chanted their hymns in unison or alternately, each answering the other in what we call antiphony (ăn-tĭf′ŏ-nĭ) —or "sound against sound."

Three times a year the people came up to the Temple from all over the land, and then there was tremendous rejoicing, the whole nation forming the congregation.

"I will lift up mine eyes unto the hills: from whence cometh my help," the choir on one side would intone.

"My help cometh even from the Lord, Who hath made Heaven and earth," the second choir would answer.

"He will not suffer thy foot to be moved:

and He that keepeth thee will not sleep," the first choir took up the chant. And in that way they would sing the well-known Psalm through to the end. It is thought that the word "Selah," which we meet in many Psalms, may have been some sort of direction to the musicians, but we do not know exactly what. Besides religious music, the Hebrews are known to have had a large number of harvest and vintage songs.

all sounded together, must have been the trumpets that gave the signal for the fall of the walls of Jericho. And it was the shofars, too, that sounded the attack for Gideon's valiant army.

How Solomon's Music was Preserved

The Hebrews composed a great deal of music for their Temple services, but nearly all of it has been forgotten. It would hardly

APOLLO MAKES SWEET MUSIC FOR THE DAUGHTERS OF THE GOD ZEUS

The lyre was the instrument of Apollo, the god of music and poetry. Here he is playing it for the delight of the Muses, of whom he was leader. It was their duty to preside over the various arts. You will often hear of them, and so should know their names. They are Urania, with her globe, Muse of astronomy; Thalia, Muse of comedy—she is usually shown with a comic mask; Calliope, with her wax tablet, Muse of epic poetry; Melpomene, with tragic mask and wreath, Muse of tragedy; Erato, Muse of love poetry; Terpsichore, with her lyre, Muse of choral song and of the dance; Euterpe, with her flute, Muse of lyric poetry; Clio, Muse of history, and grave Polyhymnia, the Muse of sacred song. The Muses were the daughters of the god Zeus.

One of those ancient Temple instruments has been used in Jewish worship down to this very day. It is a horn called the shofar (shō'fär), which is blown in the synagogue with great solemnity during the service on the Day of Atonement. It was always part of the Temple orchestra at Jerusalem.

Now, early peoples had to make their musical instruments out of whatever was handy. The Hebrews made their shofar out of a ram's horn. And if they had a very large twisted horn they could blow a mighty blast upon it. No wonder they were used to call men to battle! A number of those horns,

be true to say that it was lost, since it is certain that very many of the melodies that came to be used as hymns in the early Christian Church were taken, either in part or note for note, from those very Hebrew chants that were sung so expressively in Solomon's beautiful Temple.

For when people have learned a tune and love it, they never care to let it go, but set new words to it if the old ones get out of date, and hand it down to their grandchildren century after century. Some of our tunes to-day go back a very long way indeed. But we must not think of them as dull and musty, just because they were sung so long ago. Instead, we must try to remember that they were hummed by gentle maidens bending over great embroidery frames inside a castle tower, or were trolled by lusty knights in armour as they rode to joust or tournament.

In Europe, the beauty-loving Greeks were the first nation to do much with music. Before their time it had been just a hand-maid to help out at various ceremonies; but the Greeks made of it an art. Their instruments were borrowed from Asia, and were of different sorts. The syrinx (sĭr'ĭngks)—a row of seven little reeds bound together in the order of their pitch—was loved by shepherds and simple country folk. It was called the Pan-pipe, for it was thought to be an invention of the great god Pan, who ruled over flocks and pastures, forests and all wild things, and was especially dear to shepherds and those who led a life in the open air.

The story is that Pan fell in love with a beautiful wood nymph named Syrinx, who, being frightened at his advances, begged the water nymphs to help her. So they saved her from his embrace by changing her into a clump of rustling reeds. But her ardent lover plucked the reeds to press them to his lips, and as he kissed them he sighed. The force of his breath in the hollow stems awoke sweet music, which so delighted the love-lorn god that he bound the little reeds together and used them ever after to play upon. Our own mouth organ is a descendant of the little syrinx.

But the instrument the Greeks loved most was the lyre, which, as we have seen, had been used by the Egyptians. In shape and size it was between a harp and a lute or

Centuries ago these two strange old instruments gave forth tones that listeners felt were quite entrancing. The Greek lyre, on the left, was used only for striking chords by way of accompaniment to singing. It was never played alone.

By courtesy of the British Museum

One hardly knows how this harp was used. David, of course, knew how to play the harp as a solo instrument. But that was long after the day of the strange and beautiful instrument shown here. For this harp was first strung in Ur, the city of Abraham's birth, and is at least five thousand years old.

guitar, and was played upon by plucking its strings. This was the instrument of Apollo, the Greek god of music.

The Greeks Invent the Scale

It was the Greeks who invented the scale—but they had a number of different scales, called "modes," and even those came about after a long, slow growth. To us, who are used to hearing our modern music almost from the day of our birth, it seems absurd to think that there could be any other scale than the one we know. We feel that our seven notes are as bound to follow one after another as sunrise is bound to follow the dawn. It seems to us to be the way the world is made.

But our scale, as we have it to-day, is one of the latest products of civilization. Large parts of the world—China, India, and Japan—do not use it at all; and in its present form it did not come into common use in Europe until the eighteenth century.

It all comes from the fact that early men did not have ears trained to carry a tune—so, of course, they had no tunes. By slow degrees they learned how to be sure of two notes that should be always just the same distance apart—or, as we say, at just the same "interval" in the scale. It is thought that, in many tribes, those were the first and fourth notes, or *do* and *fa*, in our modern scale; as you may possibly know, they are the first two tones in the hymn "Lead, kindly light." In other tribes those first notes were *do* and *sol*, the next note above *fa*.

Primitive men to-day have to do their best with whatever instruments they are able to invent—just as our own forefathers did, thousands of years ago. These native Africans seem to have got together quite an orchestra, but one wonders if, perhaps, it is not just as agreeable to look at in the picture as it is to listen to.

Now, the learning of those two notes was a great advance. How much better to have two notes with which to make up tunes than to have only one! It is possible to do a good deal with two notes. Some of the tunes of savages to-day do not have any more than that. And then, of course, once those two tones have been firmly fixed in mind, one can put a note or two in between them. And then one has a scale! It is not a very long scale—only three or four notes—and it has no sharps and flats; but it is quite long enough and will do very well for the simple tunes that its inventors will be able to make up.

All their tunes will be made out of those same three or four notes, and those alone. It will just be a matter of arranging them in as many different ways as possible, and varying their length. If you take the first four notes in our scale and arrange them in every order you can think of, you will be doing exactly what the early musicians did.

But the first four notes of our scale would probably not be just the same ones upon which early men hit. The first scale we know of among the Greeks was only three notes long, and very nearly corresponded to our E, F, and A—or *mi*, *fa*, and *la*, the third,

11

fourth, and sixth notes of our scale. It seems a queer scale to us; but the people who used it had never heard any other, so it sounded natural enough to them. And at first its three notes were all they needed to make up their tunes.

Some Queer Scales

Later they added a fourth note—G, or *sol*—between F and A. And then they learned how to repeat the little scale from A up and from E down, so that they had quite a range of notes in which to sing or play. But they never went so high or so low as we do. All their music lay within a range of about two octaves. They probably felt that very high or very low singing was strained, and bad art.

It was in this way that the Greeks finally worked out a scale of seven notes. But many peoples—among them the Chinese and Japanese—have scales of only five notes, and curious notes at that! It makes their music sound very strange to us. The Scottish bagpipers, too, have an unusual scale; and so have the people of India and of Persia.

In Persia an octave is divided into twice as many notes as we have in ours. Only think how highly trained the ear of a musician must be to hear all those tones! If you try to put an extra note exactly between the third and fourth notes of our scale, you will see how hard it is to do.

There were other Greek "modes," or scales, besides the one we have just mentioned, which was the oldest and was called the Doric. Altogether there were nine, each one differing from the rest according as the space between those first two precious notes had been filled up in one way or another.

One mode—called the Lydian (lĭd′ĭ-ăn)—became our major scale of to-day; and another—the Hypodorian (hĭp′ō-dōr′ĭ-ăn)—became our minor scale.

You can see how the old Greek modes sounded if you play a series of scales using only the white keys on the piano and beginning each scale on a different white key. If you begin on E, you are playing the Doric mode; if on C, the Lydian; if on A, the Hypodorian. And if you make up a little tune using only the notes in one of those modes, you will have some idea of the way a Greek air in that mode sounded.

For the Greeks never used notes from any other mode than the one in which they were playing or singing—they never had any sharps or flats. So far as we know, their music consisted of nothing but little airs. There were no chords at all. All singing and playing was probably in unison—or sometimes on the same note an octave apart.

Music's Effect on Character

Those different modes had very strongly marked traits for Greek ears. The boys of Sparta might sing and play only in the Doric mode, for it was thought to be full of manliness and dignity; and airs in the Lydian mode were felt to be very emotional, and therefore weakening. Indeed, music in general was thought to have a powerful effect in forming character.

Between 400 B.C. and A.D. 500 the Greeks did a great deal for music. They perfected the airs that they had borrowed from Asia, they wrote words for them and chanted them on important occasions, they developed skill in singing and playing, and they also invented a way to write music.

(CONTINUED ON PAGE 64)

This strange horn is one of the oldest instruments known in Europe. It is called the alpenhorn, and its mellow tones may still be heard in out-of-the-way places in Switzerland and the Scandinavian countries.

Photo by Swiss Federal Railway

MOST FAMOUS *of* ALL TRAVELLERS

The Stories That Marco Polo Told about His Voyages were so Strange That for a Long Time People Would not Believe Them

THIS is one of the strangest stories in the world. So strange indeed is it that for many years after it was first told, about six hundred years ago, it was usually considered to be a fabrication. Then it was proved to be absolutely true.

For many a long century before any European ever attempted to sail across the sea to China, the trading ships of Italy, especially those of Venice, had been finding their way into the eastern harbours of the Mediterranean and along the shores of the Black Sea. There they would buy the spices and silks, the rich carpets and precious stones, such as we still obtain from the Far East; only in those days these were brought west by caravans. Venice had long controlled the profitable trade and so had roused the ill will of other states. So the envious kings of Spain and Portugal sent mariners south and west hoping to discover a navigable route to Cipango (sǐ-păng′gō) and

When Marco Polo returned from Cathay his own household did not recognize him and, as you see here, refused to let him enter.

Cathay (kǎ-thā′), the two lands of the mysterious East that we now call Japan and China. The wealth and wonders of those lands had already been made known to the Western world by a Venetian merchant, Marco Polo, who had made his way afoot into them, returned laden with riches, and then written an account of his travels which gave us the strange story that we are now going to relate. It is just as enthralling as a page from the famous "Arabian Nights."

While on a trading expedition along the coast of the Black Sea, about 1260, Marco's father, Nicolo Polo, a nobleman and wealthy merchant, accompanied by his brother Maffeo, had continued travelling inland to the east until he finally reached Cathay, or China. There the brothers were cordially received by Kublai Khan (kōō′blī kän), the emperor, at whose court they remained for two years. Then they returned to Venice, bearing letters from the great Kublai Khan to the Pope and to many of the rulers of Europe, but not before they had promised Kublai Khan that they would return and bring with them missionaries who could teach his people their religion and tell them about the art and science of the Western World.

When Nicolo and Maffeo reached Aere in April, 1269, they found that the Pope was dead, and that no new Pope had yet been elected. They accordingly returned to Venice to await the re-election; but after two years, there having been no new Pope appointed, they resolved to set out again for the East, taking with them Nicolo's son Marco, now a youth of some seventeen years, having been born about 1254. Soon after they had started, a new Pope was at last elected, who, according to the wish of Kublai Khan, provided the adventurous Polos with two friars belonging to the order of St. Dominic.

In their fear of the dangerous trip, which

was finally undertaken in November, 1271, the Dominicans whom the Pope had asked to go soon deserted and turned back; but the Polos continued on their way. Passing through Persia and Tartary, and crossing the great Desert of Gobi (gō'bē), where they suffered all kinds of hardships, they finally reached China and were welcomed by the emperor. At once Kublai Khan took a fancy to young Marco. The boy, in turn, liked the people and their country, and at once began to master some of the strange and difficult languages he heard there. Then, indeed, the emperor showered favours on him. He sent Marco on many diplomatic missions from one end of the empire to the other, and Marco talked with all kinds of influential persons living there, and with many merchants and travellers from places that he himself had not visited. Always he made notes of what he saw and heard. At last he was made governor of the great city of Yangchow, and loaded with honours and riches; for now that the Polos were back in China, the old emperor hoped that they would spend the rest of their lives there.

But such was not to be the case. The Polos had always looked forward to going home again, and they patiently awaited their chance. It arrived when Kublai Khan gave a lady of his court in marriage to the king of Persia. Because they were such experienced travellers, the three Italians were appointed to take charge of the expedition to conduct the bride to her future home. From inner Cathay the party went southwestwards to the sea, then by boat among the islands of the Indian Ocean and along the coast of India, until after more than two years of difficult voyaging they finally reached their destination. After a stay

While Marco Polo was in prison he told his strange tale to a fellow-prisoner, who wrote it down, and thus preserved a most remarkable story.

there the Polos travelled on, but this time northwards of the Black Sea, where they once more took ship and returned to Venice, which they reached about the end of 1295, after an absence of nearly twenty years.

Great Riches and Wonderful Stories

With them they brought such riches in gems and such a wealth of marvellous tales as their countrymen had never before seen or heard. Many of their stories were doubted, but not their wealth, for Marco came to be popularly known as "Marco Millioni." His riches brought him high positions in Venice, and in hostilities with Genoa in 1298 he served in the capacity of "Sopracomito" or gentleman commander. A battle ended in victory for Genoa, and Marco Polo was captured by the enemy and imprisoned for nearly a year. There he helped to pass the time by telling his story to a fellow prisoner named Rusticiano, of Pisa, who wrote it down from his dictation and made a book of it. Marco survived until 1324.

The book has ever since been one of the most famous in the world. Marco had been to many places that no other man from Europe had ever seen, or was ever going to see for many a year to come—indeed, to places where we are still sending explorers to this very day. He was the first man to travel right across Asia, visiting many countries on his way and leaving descriptions of them. Peking, China, Tibet, Burma, Laos, Siam, Japan, Java, Sumatra—these are only some of the many places of which he tells us. And most people would not believe his tale until much later, when explorers in the East proved without a doubt that his amazing story was just as true as was the existence of his enormous riches.

HALF *the* WORLD *was* NAMED *after* HIM

Yet the Name of America Was an Error; the Continent Should Have Been Called Columbia, in Honour of its Discoverer

IN the past a man who wrote a book would often have two names—one in his native language and the other in Latin. For his book would almost certainly be written in Latin, in which case his name would be translated into Latin too. That is why the man after whom America is named is sometimes called Americus Vespucius (vĕs-pū′shŭs) and sometimes Amerigo Vespucci (ä-mā′rē-gō vĕs-pōōt′chē).

Amerigo knew he was intended to be a merchant when he grew up, but still he spent a great deal of time in his early days poring over old maps and charts of the world. No one would have been more surprised than he to know that the time would come when two new continents would appear on those maps of the world and that they would be named after him. Yet that is what actually happened.

Born on March 9, 1451, at Florence, in Italy, Vespucci was educated by his uncle, a Dominican monk, who taught him the mathematics and astronomy that were later to be of so much use to him. As a young man he entered the great commercial house of the Medici. Then, in 1492, he left his native land and went to Spain. At Seville he established for himself a good position as a merchant, and finally undertook the business of furnishing supplies to the sailors engaged in trade with the West Indies.

His interest in the New World continued to grow, and in 1497 he claimed that he had made a voyage to South America. We are

Photo by Alinari

"America" is the feminine form of "Americus," and here is the Americus from whose name the word was taken. Yet if Americus Vespucius had not been such a clever writer and had not spread his knowledge abroad, it is extremely unlikely that he would have had two great continents named after him.

doubtful whether he made this trip, but we do know that he made another two years later. On his return to Seville he met Columbus and talked with him about the new lands in the west. It has sometimes been thought that the two men were rivals; but it is believed that Columbus wrote to his son about his worthy countryman, stating that Vespucci had done all he could to help him.

Later, Vespucci received an invitation from the king of Portugal to join an expedition to the New World. The voyage was made in 1501, and was followed by another with the Portuguese in 1503.

On his return to Spain Vespucci wrote some interesting accounts of his voyages and of the things he had seen, of which the most important was the "Mundus Novus," or "New World." Because he told so much about the new lands and the people who inhabited them, it was decided that they ought to bear his name. So they were called America, and America they have remained to this day. They might more aptly have been christened Columbia.

Most of Vespucci's accounts of his travels are now lost, and we are not sure exactly what lands he explored. It is believed, however, that he visited a great part of the northeastern coast of South America. Certainly he amassed a good deal of valuable information and wrote the first reliable description of the new land.

Vespucci became a naturalized citizen of Spain in 1505, and spent his last years there, dying at Seville, on February 22, 1512.

Who FOUND the CAPE of GOOD HOPE?

And do You Know Why it was Given that Name?

IT was not to be wondered at that young Bartholomeu Diaz wished to become a sailor. For several centuries his ancestors had been renowned for their seamanship and for their daring. And Bartholomeu had been born at a time when his countrymen thought and dreamed of nothing but discoveries in other lands.

In the belief that India, with her great wealth, could best be reached by sailing round the south of Africa, the Portuguese sailors had slowly pushed their way down the African coast. For nearly a hundred years they had worked patiently, charting the shore line and seeking the southern extremity of the continent. Finally, one expedition crossed the Equator and reached Guinea. Soon afterwards the ivory and gold obtained from there made Portugal one of the wealthiest countries of Europe. This spurred the Portuguese on in their search for the even richer shores of India. The entire country hummed with the talk of her great sailors and their brave deeds on uncharted seas.

In Search of Gold and Ivory

We do not know the exact date of his birth, but we do know that this was the world into which Diaz (dē'äzh) was born. He set out to sea when he was very young. At first he made several voyages to Guinea in search of gold and ivory. On these trips he displayed such bravery and skill that King John II placed him in charge of an expedition to explore the western coast of Africa farther south than any European had yet penetrated. Leaving Portugal in 1481, he sailed southwards for months, exploring the coast, making charts and gathering information. Upon his return the king rewarded him for his splendid work by making him a member of the royal household and granting him an annuity for "services to come." But this was only the beginning of the great sailor's success.

In 1486 he was chosen to command another expedition that was to search for a route round Africa. After several months of preparation he set sail from Portugal in command of three ships. Making his way southward, he sailed into unknown seas. The weather grew colder each day and his men were afraid to continue. But Diaz would not turn back.

Then one day the little vessels ran into a terrible storm. For nearly two weeks they were tossed about as though they had been made of paper. Although Diaz tried to hug the shore, the gale blew his ships far out to sea. When the storm passed and he finally sighted the coast again, he discovered that the land no longer stretched southward in front of him. Instead, it inclined to the north-east.

Rounding the Cape of Good Hope

Although this made him think that he might have rounded Africa, he continued on his course for some weeks. To his amazement the land continued to run in a northerly direction. This made him practically certain that he had accomplished the great task upon which he had set out. Overjoyed with his success, he determined to make for home. When he had again passed the stormy cape, he knew that he really had found the most southerly point of the "Dark Continent."

In December, 1488, Diaz reached Portugal again. On the charts that he placed before the king, so it is said, the cape at the southern extremity of the continent was named the "Cape of Storms." This the king changed at once to the "Cape of Good Hope," for he knew that the finding of that cape would bring Portugal great power and wealth.

Two years later Diaz returned to Africa and carried on trade again much as he had done before his famous voyage. After the discovery of America, he went to Brazil on another trading expedition. This was his last voyage, for on his way home, some time in the early autumn of 1500, he was shipwrecked and was never heard of again.

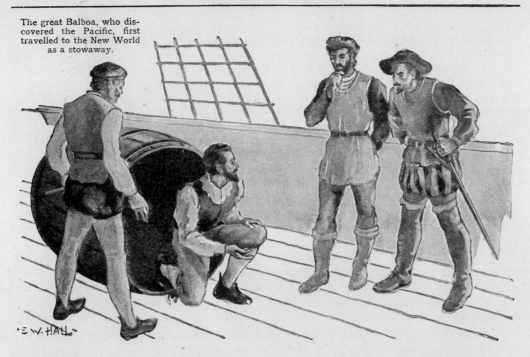

The great Balboa, who discovered the Pacific, first travelled to the New World as a stowaway.

He DISCOVERED the PACIFIC OCEAN

And That was Only One of the Many Exciting Incidents in the Life of Vasco Nuñez de Balboa, Who Finally Met His Death by the Headsman's Axe

THE life of Vasco Nuñez de Balboa was simply one adventure after another. Born of a good Spanish family about 1475, he early entered the army and fought against the Moors. Soon, however, he had spent all his money and was deeply in debt. Like many another young Spaniard of his day, he decided to go to the New World in search of riches. In San Domingo he tried farming, but he was not successful. Before long he was even deeper in debt than he had been at home. When he learned that his creditors were planning to have him arrested, he determined to escape them. How was this to be done? Balboa (băl-bō′à) was accustomed to finding his way out of tight corners and he knew he must do it once again.

His plan was a clever one. He had himself hauled in a closed cask from his farm, to a vessel that was about to sail for Panama, under Enciso, a lawyer, with provisions for the new settlement of San Sebastian. Since the cask was supposed to hold provisions, he was soon at sea. Imagine the astonishment of the sailors when he emerged from his hiding-place. At first the captain threatened to have him put ashore, but finally allowed him to remain aboard.

In Panama, Balboa's adventures became even more exciting. Soon after landing he cunningly contrived to have himself made governor of Darien (dā′rĭ-ĕn′), a small settlement on the coast of the Isthmus. This, of course, did not please Enciso, who went back to Spain to inform the king of what had occurred. Not wishing to be without a friend at court, Balboa sent another man to plead his cause there. With him went a gift of gold for the king. This, the crafty Balboa thought, would so please the king that he would not hesitate to allow him to continue as ruler of the rich little colony.

While he waited for news Balboa spent his time making friends with the Indians, exploring the country, and collecting what riches he could find. Before long he had so won the friendship of the natives that they told him of a great body of water that lay to the west. On its shores, they said, were wonderful golden temples. Naturally, Balboa was eager to see whether their stories were true. But he did not wish to leave Darien until he had heard from his friend in Spain.

At last a letter came saying that the friend had not been successful. King Ferdinand had decided against Balboa, and had ordered that he should be brought back to Spain and punished for his misdeeds. Balboa knew that there was only one way to save himself. He must find the fabled ocean. If he could report such a discovery to the king, he felt sure he would be pardoned.

Although he could muster only about two hundred followers, apart from native attendants, he set out at once on the journey that was to prove the greatest adventure of his life. Travelling over steep mountain crags and through dense tropical forests the little party suffered terribly from the intense heat. The Indians of the region were not at all pleased to see him, but Balboa forced them to guide him. The first shot from his guns and the sight of the ferocious bloodhounds he had brought with him were usually all that was needed to obtain anything he required.

On the Shores of the "Southern Sea"

At last he was told that he could get a view of the great sea from a neighbouring peak. Leaving his men behind, Balboa hurried on alone. When he reached the summit of the mountain he saw what no European had ever seen. Before him lay another vast ocean. He called his men, and at the sight of the great expanse of water they burst into cheers and song. After setting up a cross on the spot they hurried on to the sea coast.

Several days later they stood on the shores of the ocean. Balboa named it the "Southern Sea"; to-day we call it the Pacific. Wading into the water to his knees, Balboa drew his sword and claimed the sea and all the lands washed by it for the king of Spain.

While Balboa was resting there, the Indians told him of another rich land far to the south. It was the land that we now call Peru. The ambitious adventurer wanted to visit it, but he had no ships. Besides it was necessary for him to return to Darien as soon as possible.

Upon his return he was hailed as a great explorer. At once he sent a report of his discovery to King Ferdinand and with it a great quantity of gold. When Ferdinand saw this he regretted having sent another governor to take Balboa's place; but before he could send word to Darien the new governor had made peace with Balboa by offering him his daughter in marriage.

Sailing the Pacific Ocean

While the explorer waited for the girl to be brought from Spain, he began to build two ships for his voyage to the rich land to the south. And this was no mean task. Hundreds of Indian slaves perished in their attempt to carry the heavy timbers across the rugged mountains to the "Southern Sea," on whose shore the ships were to be built. When at last the work was completed, Balboa launched the vessels on the waters of the Pacific. The first Europeans to sail that sea, he and his men started southwards. But a violent storm arose and drove them back.

Balboa then decided that iron and pitch would be needed for his ships, so he returned to Darien for them. Before he reached the settlement he was met by a messenger who informed him that the governor desired to see him. Believing that all was well, he hurried on, only to be taken prisoner as he neared the town. The governor had lent a willing ear to false charges made against the bold explorer, and had determined to put him to death. So Balboa was charged with treason and beheaded (1517). Thus the great adventurer met his death. But the people of Darien grieved for the daring man who had done so much for their country, and, even to-day, we gratefully remember Balboa as one of Spain's greatest and most heroic explorers.

The MACHINE that CHANGED the WORLD

James Watt Saw the Possibility of Converting Steam into a Powerful Driving Force and so He Set to Work to Invent a Practical Steam-engine

JUST suppose that one of our ancestors two or three hundred years ago had had to lift a ton of stone a foot high, how would he have done it? He would have had to get a dozen or so men with long levers to pry it up by might and main.

And then suppose we had come along with a tiny cup of water and said, "Let the water lift your rock for you!" We can imagine how he would have laughed at our nonsense. Lift a rock with a few spoonfuls of water?

Yet a cubic inch of water, if we put it to work in the right way, will lift a ton of rock twelve inches. To make it do so we must first change it into steam, and a cubic inch of water will make about a cubic foot of steam. And then we must have an engine that will put the tremendous power of the steam to work.

Now steam is simply the gas into which water turns when we boil it. And its power comes from the fact that the steam expands

Photo by Rischgitz

James Watt's parents do not yet realize that their son is a genius, though it is clear that they think he is uncommonly curious. They are waiting for the lid to fly off the kettle, for James is preventing the steam from coming out of the spout. They will laugh at James's surprise, and then the incident for them will be over. But for James it will only be the beginning of a train of thought that will change the lives of all mankind.

about sixteen hundred times, or needs about sixteen hundred times as much room, as the water from which it came. If we boil the water in a pan the steam will merely flow off into the air, and will seem to have no power at all. But if we boil it in a bottle or a sealed vessel made of tin, we shall need to get out of the way in good time, for there will be an explosion.

But if we are going to use the steam, we must not let it float away in the air, and we must not allow it to cause an explosion. We must keep it compressed in a strong steel box, from which it will try to escape by exerting great pressure, pushing in all directions with a force of two hundred pounds or more to every square inch. And there must be one place where it can get out, but only by pushing something ahead of it. Then the thing it pushes with such great force is connected with the machine we want it to run —in the case of a locomotive, for instance, with the wheels on the track. The force of the escaping steam is such that it makes the wheels go round. And that is the secret of the steam-engine.

It took us a long time to find out how to make use of the secret. We have had steam-engines only for about a hundred and fifty years. And in that short time they have practically changed the world for us.

Of course, we knew something about the great power of steam long before we found out how to put it to work. A good many

The picture in the oval shows a model of Hero's little steam apparatus. Water in the big cauldron was brought to the boiling-point by a fire underneath. The only way of escape for the steam was through the two pipes leading into the hollow globe above, which was provided with two little spouts. The force of the steam rushing out of the spouts set the globe spinning. This device was never put to any useful work.

In the square is a model of an engine made in 1629 by an Italian named Giovanni Branca. The big wheel at the top was turned by a jet of steam. The steam rushed out of a pipe on to numerous little blades set on end along the edge of the wheel. This made the big wheel turn; and the big wheel turned other wheels that might have accomplished some sort of work if the device had been big enough, and if a strong enough jet of steam had been applied. The modern steam turbine operates on the principle of Branca's engine.

By courtesy of the Science Museum

men were at work on the subject, and as long ago as 150 B.C. a Greek, named Hero of Alexandria, is said to have made a sort of steam-engine. It was only a kind of whirligig, little more than a toy, and it was never put to work.

For many centuries there was nothing better. Stories are told of steam-engines invented three or four hundred years ago, but we are not sure how true they are. A Spaniard is said to have built a steam-boat about 1543, and to have sailed it across the Bay of Barcelona. And about 1629 an Italian blew steam from a pipe on to a wheel and made it turn like a windmill. But the mill was not strong enough to do any real work.

By 1698 steam was finally set to work by an Englishman named Thomas Savery, though in a fashion very different from the way we use it. When you drink lemonade through a straw, what you do is to suck out the air in the straw, and leave a vacuum, or empty space, in it; then the lemonade flows up into the empty straw, for "Nature abhors a vacuum." The weight of the air pressing down on the surface of the lemonade in the glass forces the liquid up into the vacuum. Now that was precisely the way in which Savery's steam-engine worked.

Savery wanted to draw water up into a tank without pumping it, so he first filled the big copper tank with steam. Then the steam cooled and changed back into water, converting most of the tank into a vacuum. And into this vacuum, through a pipe, came

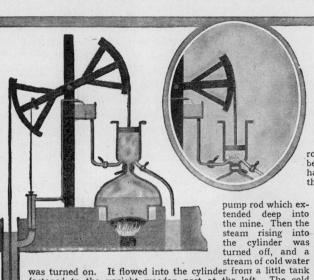

Left: Newcomen's engine, for pumping water out of mines. Water in the boiler, heated by the fire underneath it, gave off steam which rose into the cylinder above and pushed up a sliding disc called the piston. Attached to the top of the disc was a piston-rod which was connected with a rocking beam. As the piston-rod rose, the right-hand end of the beam rose with it, and the left-hand end of the beam sank, at the same time pushing down a pump rod which extended deep into the mine. Then the steam rising into the cylinder was turned off, and a stream of cold water was turned on. It flowed into the cylinder from a little tank fastened to the upright wooden post at the left. The cold water condensed the steam in the cylinder, and so a vacuum was formed. Since there was now nothing to hold up the piston, it sank to the bottom of the cylinder—as shown in the oval—pulling the right-hand beam end down with it and raising the left-hand beam end and also the pump rod in the mine. The cool water in the cylinder ran off through the pipe at the right. Then the whole process began again. Water was pumped into the tank by a second pump rod on the left-hand beam end.

HOW A MODERN STEAM-ENGINE WORKS

Right: Boiler and cylinder in a modern double-acting steam-engine. At the top you may see how tubes running through a boiler full of water carry heat from the fire below and so keep the water at boiling-point. The steam gathers in the boiler under great pressure. Then, when a stopcock is opened in the pipe at the right, the steam rushes through the pipe to the cylinder, which it enters at A, as shown in the centre picture. The pressure of the expanding steam forces a sliding metal disc, called the piston, along the cylinder to the right; and the piston-rod, attached to the piston, pushes a metal shaft connecting with a wheel. So the wheel is turned. When the piston reaches the right of the cylinder, as shown in the lowest picture, a neat affair called a slide-valve is at the same time automatically slipped to the left across the left-hand entrance to the cylinder, and the right-hand entrance is opened for the steam to rush into the right-hand end of the cylinder B and push the piston to the left. The returning piston drives the used steam out of the cylinder through the opening in the centre of the slide-valve. In both pictures the slide-valve is shown just above the main body of the cylinder, for the two views are both pictures of the same cylinder. On top of the boiler is a safety-valve which lets steam escape if the pressure inside the boiler becomes too great for safety. We measure an engine's power in "horse-power," because early buyers of an engine wanted to know how many horses it would save them. A one-horse-power engine must supply the power to raise 33,000 pounds one foot per minute.

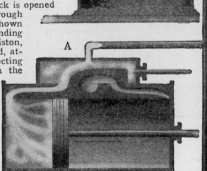

A

B

the water from below, in the same way as the lemonade fills the vacuum in the straw. For a long time this kind of engine was used to draw the water out of mines.

We may regard it as a steam-engine that worked backwards. Instead of making water expand into steam and push something out, it made the steam condense into water and draw something in. And nearly a hundred years were still to pass before James Watt discovered a way to reverse the process, so that the steam worked with a push instead of a pull.

In the meantime Savery's engine had been improved by Denis Papin (pä-păN′), a Frenchman, and by an Englishman, Thomas Newcomen. They gave the engine a cylinder and piston—two parts that are found in every steam-engine to-day. The steam that enters the cylinder pushes the piston back and forth and so operates the machinery.

In Newcomen's engine the steam pushed the piston out, and then cold water was squirted into the cylinder to condense it and to leave a vacuum which would pull the piston back. Then more steam would be let in to push it out again, and so the process would continue at the rate of some sixteen strokes a minute. The modern steam-engine commonly makes about ten times as many strokes.

The first Newcomen engines could not run by themselves. Someone had to stand by and open valves to let the steam and water in and out of the cylinder. The story goes that a clever boy named Humphrey Potter thought of a better way. He was hired to open and shut the valves, and he grew tired of the tedious work. So he just tied some strings to the handles and bars and beams of the engine, and so made it open and shut its own valves at the right moment. In this way the boy is said to have invented the slide valve, which is now an important part of every steam-engine.

The Newcomen engine slowly pumped the water out of English coal-mines all day long for many a year. But it often gave trouble. It would spring a leak or become jammed, or find some other way of going wrong. But its chief defect was that it consumed so much coal. Never did an engine need so much coal to generate enough steam to do its work. For heating the cylinder with steam for every stroke and then immediately cooling it again was far from being satisfactory.

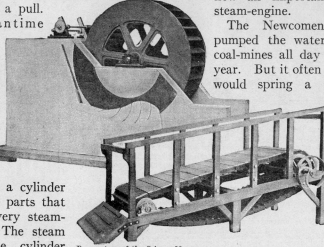

By courtesy of the Science Museum

BEFORE WE TURNED OUR WHEELS BY STEAM

Here are two ways by which men turned their wheels before they put steam to work. The upper picture shows an undershot water-wheel invented by Jean Victor Poncelet, a Frenchman. The wheel was hung inside a narrow wheel-pit. The water, which was on a level with the top of the pit, at the left, was held back by a movable sluice. When the sluice was raised, a stream of water, flowing down an inclined channel at the bottom of the wheel-pit, hit the curved blades of the wheel and pushed them forward to the right. This sent the wheel round. The outline of the wheel is here shown painted on the outside of the wheel-pit, together with the position of the water as it pushes against the bottom of the wheel. This was the kind of wheel best suited to a shallow stream.

A horse furnished the power for the lower device. The unlucky animal was driven up the inclined plane of the movable platform. All day long he walked and walked on the platform, which his steady tread pushed out behind him. So the plane passed under the horse and round, under and round, and turned the wheel shown at the right.

Yet the engine managed to pump water, and for some time no one thought of anything better. Indeed, there was not much machinery to run in those days, as nearly everything was done by hand. The Newcomen engines were never used for any other purpose than pumping water, and so there were not very many of them in use. Even blacksmiths and machinists knew

By courtesy of the Science Museum

This is a picture of James Watt's workshop, as it has been reconstructed in the Science Museum, London. It was in this workshop that his steam-engine came to life. In the oval is a portrait of the great inventor.

little about them. We may be fairly certain that James Watt, who was later to produce a far better machine, never saw one of the Newcomen engines when he was a boy.

Experiment with a Kettle

There is, however, a story about the boy Watt that we always love to tell. It is about his listening to the kettle singing, watching the vapour pouring out of the spout, and wondering what would happen if the spout were stopped up. So he just tried the experiment, and found that the steam pushed off the lid of the kettle at once. And that, according to the story, is the way James Watt got the idea of the power of steam and started thinking about his engine.

The fact is that when Watt was a boy in Greenock, where he was born in 1736, he had other things than kettles and steam-engines to think about. He had his lessons and his games, and his rambles over the Scottish hills. He was also a great reader, and never so happy as when he had a book.

But he was a sickly boy, and sometimes he had to stay away from school for weeks at a time. Then he often found his father's shop the best place in which to play.

His father's business was that of a ship-chandler, so the store-house was full of rope and canvas, with a strong smell of oakum. But best of all, there was a carpenter's shop, where all sorts of things were turned and shaped for use on board ship.

Valuable Workshop Experience

In the shop the boy learned how to make many things out of wood and metal. He liked to build models of machines, and soon grew to be an expert with every tool in the shop. By the time he was fifteen the good folk in his native town had begun to think that Jamie was something of a genius.

He intended going to college, but unfortunately his father lost most of his money, and James had to find employment. The natural thing for him was to become an instrument maker. That was easy work for him, and he would like it.

So he set out for London, with a friend, and on his arrival he had little trouble in finding work as an apprentice to a maker of instruments. In those days anyone who wanted to be a skilled worker had to serve seven years as an apprentice, and to work very hard for very little pay. At the end of his first year young Jamie found that the long hours and the poor food were telling on his health, so he had to return home.

As soon as he was well again he went to Glasgow and began making instruments for the university there. That was in 1756, and for the following eight years he was busy making mathematical instruments and working at engineering problems.

At last came the great day when he started on the work that was going to change the world. There was a model of the Newcomen engine in the museum of the university, and Watt was called upon to do some minor repairs.

Thinking out an Ideal Engine

The work gave him no trouble, but the more he studied the engine, the less he liked its crude construction. It wasted too much heat and generated too little power; and it worked too slowly. Couldn't he manage to make something better? He wanted an engine that would keep hot all the time instead of cooling off at every stroke. He wanted one that would not have to wait for a vacuum to form. If he could build one, it would work faster and better than the old Newcomen contrivance.

For three years Watt pondered and experimented without making much headway. But he knew there was an answer to his problem, and he felt sure he could find it. When he was walking in Glasgow one day, the right idea flashed across his mind, and he at once began to build a model.

But even with an inspiration, a great invention is not finished in a day. For many years Watt had to struggle against discouragement, failure, and occasional despair. He made a little model that worked well enough; then he built a big engine on the same model, with money he had borrowed, but it did not work at all. It had been so badly made that it was full of leaks.

Success Comes at Last

Then Matthew Boulton, of Birmingham, offered to join Watt as a partner. Together they found better ironworkers and mechanics, and built a new engine that was a success.

In its general method of working, their engine was very much like the engine of to-day. In the pictures you may see the parts that the genius of Watt invented. Notice especially the condenser, the slide valve, and the governor. All of these he thought out and perfected.

The condenser was one of his great triumphs. With it he could draw out the steam when it had been used, without cooling or stopping the engine, which could thus run faster and exert more power. The governor is a neat little device to keep the engine from running too fast or too slow. It has two little iron spheres that hang down when the engine is at rest, but fly out like balls on a string when it is running. The faster the engine goes, the faster the governor whirls and the higher the balls fly. But they are attached to the machine in such a way that when they get too high they will operate so as to turn off some of the steam and in that way slow the engine up slightly; and if they fall too low they will likewise speed it up a little by turning on

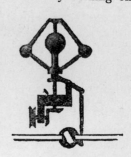

HOW A GOVERNOR WORKS

If you swing a stone tied to a piece of cord you will find that the faster you swing it, the higher the stone will fly. This is the principle that controls the governor on an engine. Those two small metal balls hang on arms that are hinged to the top of an upright spindle, and the spindle is turned by the engine. So when the engine is working fast it turns the spindle very rapidly and whirls the balls through the air at a great rate. This makes them fly outwards. Now they, in turn, are attached to a metal collar by their lower arms. This is pulled up when they fly out, thus operating a lever which closes a valve in the steam pipe that supplies the engine. This regulates the speed of the engine.

Photos by the Deutsches Museum, Munich

The powerful giant in the large picture is a modern steam-engine. Together with thousands of its fellows it helps to drive our modern world. In the oval is its primitive little ancestor, James Watt's first steam-engine.

more steam. Thus they always keep it going at a steady speed.

James Watt continued to work at his engine, improving and perfecting it, till he was sixty-four years old. Then he retired to enjoy his many hobbies. He thought out a way of copying sculpture. He made a study of the gas that we burn in stoves; and he tried to discover of what water is composed. He continued making experiments right up to the time of his death in 1819. He was one of the greatest inventors of all time; and we often use his name without thinking of it, for we employ the word "watt" as the name of a measure for electricity.

If Watt had lived just a little longer, he would have seen greater wonders performed with his engine than even he had ever dreamed. He could have watched it hauling heavy trains across the continents and driving immense ships across the oceans. He could have seen it whirling the wheels in a million factories, and doing nearly all the hard and heavy work of the world. For his steam-engine was responsible for the advent of the Machine Age. And because of it we can have and do thousands of things that would otherwise have been impossible.

The Marvellous Turbine Engine

Even Watt's invention, great as it was, was not the last word in the use of steam. Another kind of steam-engine was made in 1884 by an English engineer named Parsons. In this engine the steam is made to rush out of a pipe with tremendous force. Then it strikes upon a wheel with many little blades, and makes it whirl round at the rate of two thousand revolutions a minute. There is a number of the wheels, and the steam goes from one to another until they are all spinning with tremendous power.

Such is the turbine-engine that is used to drive big ships over the water and to turn electric dynamos on land. Nowadays electrically-driven engines are gradually displacing those driven by steam, but the world will always remember the miracle that James Watt performed with a little steam.

If you will read the text and follow the directions carefully, you will learn how to enlarge the animals shown in this page, and in several later pages of this work, and to make them into an amusing farmyard or zoo. We have mentioned the rocking rabbit on page 29. The squirrel can be turned into a telephone cover, the cat may be coaxed to serve in a pair of book-ends, and the frog will do excellent duty as a paper-weight. A little thought will enable you to turn every one of these creatures into some useful and attractive article for the home.

Here Benjamin West, the famous eighteenth-century painter, is seen earnestly taking the first steps along the road that was to lead him to fame. It is a long road and a hard one, but one that is always interesting. Some of you who read these pages will one day be artists probably—and perhaps become famous like Benjamin West. So you may as well begin your career now by learning how to draw to scale. Whether you decide to become an artist or not, you will find it splendid fun to try. With practice you will be able to draw quite well.

HOW *to* DRAW *to* SCALE

By This Simple Art You Can Easily Learn to Make Animals That Will Run or Roll or Rock—and Many Other Pretty and Useful Things

NOT all of us can visit the big zoo in London or Whipsnade, but anyone with patience can have a zoo at home—and the making of it will give many more hours of fun and profit than the longest visit to the living animals. The first step in the setting up of your menagerie is to buy a few sheets of artist's tracing-paper, though tissue paper or any other very thin paper will do quite well. Now, on the tissue paper, trace in pencil the animals illustrated here and elsewhere in this work, and, before you remove the paper, be sure to trace the vertical and horizontal scale-lines over the animal, as shown in Fig. 1, on the next page.

The next step is to enlarge your animal to the size that will best fit your zoo. Suppose you decide that he should be twice the size given here. You will follow the same process as shown in the case of the pelican in Fig. 1. You must first number every line on your traced pattern at both ends, as in the figure. Then draw a frame twice as long and twice as wide as the frame in which your small animal stands. The frame round the small pelican is $\frac{7}{8}$ of an inch wide and 2 inches high, so the frame for the enlarged pelican is twice as wide and twice as high—or $1\frac{3}{4}$ inches by 4 inches.

Now divide your large frame into squares with just the same number of horizontal and vertical lines as there are in the small frame, and number them in just the same way. You will find it helpful to make the

Figure 1

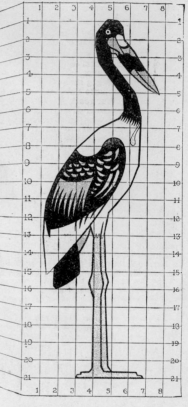

enlargement on the same sheet of paper, and to connect the two frames with lines, as shown in the illustration.

The hardest part of the job is now over, and the more interesting work begins. Suppose we start the enlargement with the animal's feet. The feet of the pelican in the little frame extend from line 3 to line 7 along horizontal line 21. A line drawn from line 3 to line 7 along horizontal line 21 on the big frame gives the bottom of the big pelican's feet. And in the same way, by exactly reproducing the lines in each small square of your pattern, you will fill in your large squares and have a nice big animal when you have finished.

If you want to enlarge your pattern three times, you can do so by making your frame and squares three times as large as your pattern—and by the same kind of multiplication you can enlarge it to any size you like. And, of course, you can reduce your picture in a similar way. Just draw your frame and squares half or a third or a fourth the size of those in the pattern, and your finished copy will be only half or a third or a fourth as large. If you take care to draw the lines and squares exactly right, and count the numbers correctly, you will not need to trace the small pattern, but can draw your big frame and fill it in with the figure without any preliminaries.

Now that you have made your animal the right size, you can transfer him to the paper or wood on which you want him, by placing carbon paper between the enlarged pattern and the substance to which it is to be transferred, and tracing the pattern with a pencil. When you have done this you can colour him with crayon or paint him in natural and becoming colours, just as you wish.

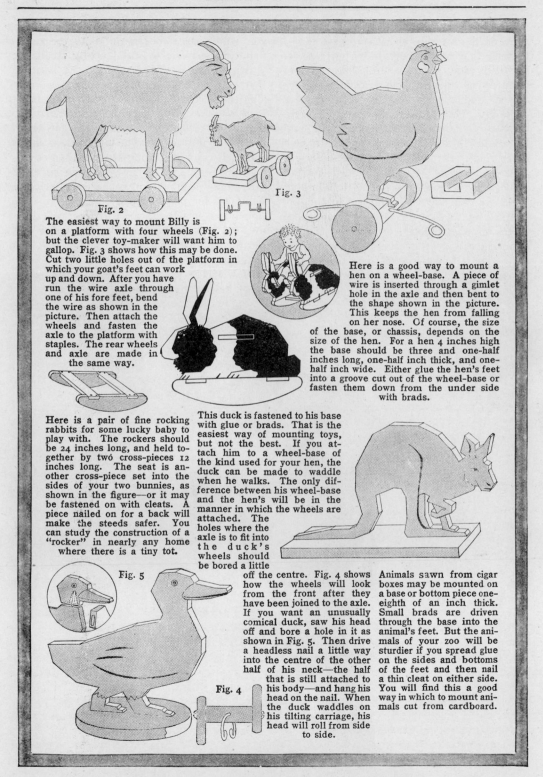

Fig. 2

Fig. 3

Fig. 5

Fig. 4

The easiest way to mount Billy is on a platform with four wheels (Fig. 2); but the clever toy-maker will want him to gallop. Fig. 3 shows how this may be done. Cut two little holes out of the platform in which your goat's feet can work up and down. After you have run the wire axle through one of his fore feet, bend the wire as shown in the picture. Then attach the wheels and fasten the axle to the platform with staples. The rear wheels and axle are made in the same way.

Here is a pair of fine rocking rabbits for some lucky baby to play with. The rockers should be 24 inches long, and held together by two cross-pieces 12 inches long. The seat is another cross-piece set into the sides of your two bunnies, as shown in the figure—or it may be fastened on with cleats. A piece nailed on for a back will make the steeds safer. You can study the construction of a "rocker" in nearly any home where there is a tiny tot.

Here is a good way to mount a hen on a wheel-base. A piece of wire is inserted through a gimlet hole in the axle and then bent to the shape shown in the picture. This keeps the hen from falling on her nose. Of course, the size of the base, or chassis, depends on the size of the hen. For a hen 4 inches high the base should be three and one-half inches long, one-half inch thick, and one-half inch wide. Either glue the hen's feet into a groove cut out of the wheel-base or fasten them down from the under side with brads.

This duck is fastened to his base with glue or brads. That is the easiest way of mounting toys, but not the best. If you attach him to a wheel-base of the kind used for your hen, the duck can be made to waddle when he walks. The only difference between his wheel-base and the hen's will be in the manner in which the wheels are attached. The holes where the axle is to fit into the duck's wheels should be bored a little off the centre. Fig. 4 shows how the wheels will look from the front after they have been joined to the axle. If you want an unusually comical duck, saw his head off and bore a hole in it as shown in Fig. 5. Then drive a headless nail a little way into the centre of the other half of his neck—the half that is still attached to his body—and hang his head on the nail. When the duck waddles on his tilting carriage, his head will roll from side to side.

Animals sawn from cigar boxes may be mounted on a base or bottom piece one-eighth of an inch thick. Small brads are driven through the base into the animal's feet. But the animals of your zoo will be sturdier if you spread glue on the sides and bottoms of the feet and then nail a thin cleat on either side. You will find this a good way in which to mount animals cut from cardboard.

We have suggested that you make a copy of the animals shown in these pages, because they are already drawn on a scale, but it is easy to draw scale-lines on any picture you like—a house a landscape, a flower—and so enlarge it to fit a score of purposes. Only be sure that your lines run perfectly straight, that the vertical and horizontal lines are at right angles to each other, and that the squares are the same size.

And now that we have learned how to make our zoo, how are we going to house it? Well, we can make an amusing scrap-book by pasting the animals on the plain white leaves of a notebook—or we can transfer them directly to the page, and paint them on it. It is fun to try to think of a rhyme for each animal and write it underneath him. If you paste your animals on cardboard and

cut it out neatly round them with scissors, you will have some quite noble creatures that can be made to stand up by means of a strip of cardboard pasted on the back.

If you want your animals to last a very long time—and you know how to use a fret-saw—your exhibits may be transferred to the lid of a cigar box, which you can then saw out round them. The illustrations show many ways of mounting these creatures on bases, wheels, or in cages. A clever boy can paint them in convincing colours and sell them for pocket-money. And the boy who has a few tools can turn out practical toys for little tots to rock or ride—like the rocking rabbit seen in the illustration on page 29.

You will be told later how to make many other interesting and useful things.

By enlarging these animals on stiff cardboard and then cutting them out with scissors, you can have a farmyard full of interesting live-stock. To these you can add chickens, ducks, turkeys, and other fowls shown elsewhere in this work. By sawing the horse's head out of wood with a fretsaw and nailing it to a stick, you can make a dashing hobby-horse. For real speed you may add a wheel at the end of the stick. The Dutch maid is suitable for a telephone cover or book-ends, or for embroidering on linen.

The FATHER of ENGLISH LEARNING

As Simple as a Child, the Venerable Bede was One of the Wisest Men of His Day, and the Old Monastery at Jarrow is Still Famous because of Him

AN OLD man lay dying in an English monastery. Outside, it was spring-time. Easter had come and gone since the man had fallen ill. But it was the scenes inside that the old monk loved. On one side of the room was the place where he had offered up his prayers year after year, and near it was a chest where he kept the few little things he owned. Around his bed were the possessions he loved most—his little collection of precious books.

Bede (bēd) was the old man's name—and because of his saintly life we often speak of him to-day as "the venerable Bede." He lived long ago—twelve hundred years—when English people had not found it necessary to have more than one name. His parents had been born heathens, but they had been so glad to see the land become Christian that they had brought their boy, at the age of seven, to live in the beautiful new monastery. Here he was happy for

Photo by Autotype Fine Art Company

"There is yet one sentence unwritten, dear master," the little scribe said.
"Write it quickly," said Bede, giving him the words.

"It is finished now," at last the boy announced.
"True," said the master, "all is finished now." And chanting the Gloria, he breathed his last.

32

the rest of his life (672–735). At an early age he had become a teacher, and people had come to the monastery from far and near to learn from the gentle scholar. He had been a good monk and a good teacher, but every spare moment he could get he had spent in studying and in writing books.

The greatest book that Bede wrote was a history of the English race—not of its great kings and warriors, but of its leaders and teachers in the Church. Bede was very careful to put down nothing except what he knew to be a fact, and his history has therefore been very valuable. He also tells us of Caedmon, the earliest English Christian poet, a Yorkshire herdsman who wrote religious verses.

At last Bede had grown too old and too ill to handle a pen. But even so he had dictated his works to one of his pupils. Now, as he lay on his death-bed, there remained still to be finished his translation into English of the Gospel of St. John.

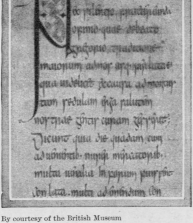

By courtesy of the British Museum

This is a page from Bede's famous history of England. The copy is upon vellum, and was made within a century after Bede's death; it is now in the British Museum. The particular passage shown here relates, in Latin, the story of how Pope Gregory came to send Augustine to England to convert the people to Christianity.

The boy scribe said, "There is still a chapter wanting, and it is hard for thee to question thyself any longer."

"It is easily done," said Bede. "Take thy pen and write quickly."

So the work went on until Bede remembered that he had a few little things in his chest that he wanted to give to his fellow priests. While they wept, he gave out his simple treasures—pepper, napkins, and incense—and asked his friends to pray for him.

Then the little scribe said, "There is yet one sentence unwritten, dear master."

"Write it quickly," said Bede, giving him the words.

"It is finished now," at last the boy announced.

"True," said the master, "all is finished now."

And then he asked to be held up with his face turned towards the place where he had been used to pray. Then he chanted, "Glory be to the Father and to the Son and to the Holy Ghost."

As he uttered the well-known words he breathed his last and fell back dead.

The WITTIEST and WISEST of OUR POETS

It is Well Worth While Spending a Little Time Learning How to Read the Quaint English of Geoffrey Chaucer

NEARLY six hundred years ago (1359) an English boy of nineteen joined the army to fight for his king in France. He had already been a page to one of the king's sons, and he had heard many a story of the glorious things that Englishmen were doing overseas. Only a little while before, the famous Black Prince had won a victory for his father and had become the model of bravery and chivalry for every English boy. And our young warrior must have hoped to be a hero too. But instead he met the cruel fate—or such it must have seemed—of falling captive to the French. Yet even in his misfortune there was a little touch of romance. For when the ransom came to set the boy free, a large part of it had been paid by no less a person than the king himself.

This boy grew up to be the famous Geoffrey Chaucer, the greatest of our poets before Shakespeare. All through his life he remained in the service of the king, and that is how we obtain the greater part of

3

This is the gay company that under an April sky set out from the Tabard Inn to journey to Canterbury. Here are many types living in England in the Middle Ages; you may meet them all in "The Canterbury Tales."

our knowledge of him. But he was always busy also on the poems that have remained a delight for all the world to our day.

Chaucer was born about 1340, and his father was a well-to-do wine merchant who had a certain influence in his time. To fit the boy for a career, the father placed him at the court of King Edward III, and for some time after his adventure in France, the young man lived in the king's own household. King Edward called him his "beloved yeoman" and granted him a pension for life.

Friend of the Famous John of Gaunt

But Chaucer's special friend at court was the famous son of Edward, whom we know as John of Gaunt. One of the early poems from Chaucer's pen was written on the death of this prince's wife. The good and beautiful young lady had been a victim of a terrible plague that had carried off a third of the people of Europe in a single year. She was the Duchess Blanche, and the poem was called "The Book of the Duchess."

It must have been at the court that Chaucer met and married his wife Philippa, one of the queen's ladies of the chamber. For their services to him, both Geoffrey and Philippa received pensions for life from John of Gaunt.

Chaucer often went abroad on secret business for the king. In this way he travelled in France, in Flanders, and in Italy. On the journeys he kept his ears open for the new poetry that was being written in these lands. During the middle period of his life he was mainly interested in the poetry of the French, but in the last period he turned largely to that of the great Italians. To their influence we owe one of his finest poems, the long story of "Troilus and Cressida."

But his love of poetry never made him neglect the business of the king. Chaucer was the kind of poet who was also a good business man; no poet ever kept a more level head. And after every trip the king would give him a reward. Once he granted him a pitcher of wine every day—which Chaucer probably turned into a convenient money payment.

He also served his king at home. For more than ten years he helped to keep the accounts in the customs offices. In one of his poems he complains that his days are so full of these accounts that he has to do all his studying and writing in the night. So it must have been a great relief when he was given a helper in the office work.

Chaucer and the Boy King

By this time King Edward had died, and King Richard II, son of the Black Prince, had come to the throne at the age of eleven, and was under the guidance of John of Gaunt. Richard grew up to be a wayward ruler. In one of his poems Chaucer was bold enough to urge the boy king to rule more firmly. But the king seems to have taken no offence, for he, too, gave the poet a life pension. In the very last years of Chaucer's life there was still another king—Henry IV, the son of John of Gaunt. Our poet at once addressed him in the

CHAUCER READING TO THE KING AND HIS COURT

This painting by the artist Ford Madox Brown shows the poet Chaucer reading before King Edward III and his court. The picture is modern, but it is full of the colourful splendour of the Middle Ages. In those days, when there were no theatres or cinemas, no gramophones or wireless sets, no newspapers or books or magazines, the skilful teller of tales could hold the attention of the proudest and most critical of audiences for hours on end.

amusing verses called "The Complaint of Chaucer to His Empty Purse." Four days later the king filled the purse by increasing some of the poet's pensions.

Characters Taken from Real Life

Thus Chaucer prospered. To the very end he was busy with his offices and with his poems. He was knight of the shire of Kent, and he served as clerk of the works—a sort of engineering office—and as a royal forester. In following his duties he came to know many kinds of people, and that had a great deal to do with his poetry. Into his finest work he put nearly all the kinds of people that he knew, and the result is not only a great and most amusing poem but also a matchless picture gallery of the people all over England in those far-distant days.

That work is the famous "Canterbury Tales." A whole troop of people, queerly mixed, are riding on a pilgrimage from London to the shrine of Thomas Becket at Canterbury. There is a famous knight and also a common inn-keeper. There is a merry friar and also a rascally miller. There is a worldly woman from Bath, a dainty prioress and a devout nun. There are a doctor and a merchant, a parson and a ploughman, and many more widely differing characters.

Above all, there is a portrait of Chaucer himself. As he rides along on his nag he remains silent and seems always to be looking down at the ground. Of course, he did not really think of his stories on a journey with pilgrims to Canterbury. The idea is just a device to connect them together. Many of the old story-tellers joined their stories together in a similar way.

All the pilgrims tell stories as they ride along, to pass away the time. When it is Chaucer's turn to tell a story, he plays a trick on them. He, the one great story-teller in the whole troop, begins to tell such a ridiculous tale that nobody will listen to him. They cut him short and tell him to give them something better. Then he puts them to sleep with the dullest and most uninteresting story that was ever heard.

A Poet of Great Humour

One of the five greatest English poets, Chaucer is the most comical of them all. He has a profound sense of humour. He is also probably the wisest of them all, if by wisdom we mean abounding in knowledge. From this you may realize the place he holds among the poets. Chaucer appears to have made little or no provision for his later years of life, and had it not been for the various pensions granted to him—part of which was often received in advance to pay off debts—he would have passed his declining years in a state akin to poverty. When he died in 1400, it was very fitting for him to be the first poet buried in the famous nook of Westminster Abbey that we now call the "Poets' Corner."

By courtesy of the British Museum

If you had been living in England in the decades following Chaucer's death, you would have had to read his poetry from this beautiful manuscript, or from one much like it. The passage above is taken from what is known as the Lansdowne Manuscript of "The Canterbury Tales," a copy made, so it is thought, about the middle of the fifteenth century. When William Caxton brought the first printing press to England, one of the earliest books he printed upon it was this much-loved poem, which probably appeared in the year 1478.

Photo by Rischgitz

Sir Tristram is being admitted to the fellowship of the Round Table. He was never a regular member of King Arthur's court, for he served his uncle, King Mark of Cornwall. But he visited the court of Arthur from time to time, and became a rival of Sir Lancelot. Of all the knights he was the most perfect in knightly accomplishment. Besides being a master of horseman-ship and sword-play, he excelled at chess, was con-versant with the lore of the chase, spoke a number of languages, and was, in addition, a skilled musician.

The HISTORIAN of the ROUND TABLE

Sir Thomas Malory, Himself as Chivalrous as the Knights of King Arthur's Court, Gave Us Some of Our Most Famous Stories of the Knights of Old

WHEN Sir Thomas Malory was a young man, he served in the French wars in the retinue of Richard Beauchamp (bē′chăm), earl of Warwick, a knight so gallant and dashing that he was called the Father of Chivalry. Many were the brave deeds that this chivalrous warrior and noble-man placed to his credit. One day, in 1411, when it appeared that the French were not going to attack the English at Calais as they had been expected to do, Warwick determined to hold a joust, or tourney, "to put in practice some new point of chivalry." So he challenged three French knights to combat, sending each challenge under a different name. And coming to each fight in a separate disguise, he won them all. Then he feasted all the people, and returned to the city with much honour.

Sir Thomas Malory never forgot the lessons of chivalry he had learned from his lord and commander, and many years later he introduced them into his great book, the "Morte d'Arthur." Between the tales he borrowed from other books he even slipped in the story of the triple combat with the French knights.

We do not know much about what Malory did in the later campaigns of the Hundred Years' War—indeed, we do not know much about what he did at any time. He must have seen much fighting. He may have seen Joan of Arc, perhaps have been present when she was burned as a witch. We know that when he returned to England, about 1445, he entered Parliament, as representative for Warwickshire. He came from a very old Warwickshire family, whose seat was Newbold Revell, not a long distance from modern Rugby and Coventry.

When we catch another glimpse of our knight, he has just escaped from prison. It was, as a man of that day remarked, a "right wild" time. So we need not be surprised or shocked to find our student of honour and chivalry mixed up in some kind of local brawl.

Some say that later Malory put on the red rose and fought for the House of Lancaster in the Wars of the Roses, which began about this time. It would seem that twice in the year 1468 he was excluded by name from a pardon granted to many Lancastrians and other political prisoners. For some reason or other, the unfortunate knight seems to have been always in trouble, and frequently in prison. It is probable that, before his death in 1471, he had been continually in prison for something like twenty years. If so, small wonder that at the end of his great romance he begs the reader to pray "that God send me good deliverance."

Opposite Newgate Prison, where Malory spent these bitter years, was the great library of the Grey Friars. Doubtless his wife Elizabeth—in whose honour he changed the name of a lovely lady in his romance—or some of his friends would bring him books from there. At least he had what he calls a "Frensshe Booke," made up, it seems, of many long French tales about Arthur and the Knights of the Round Table. Out of these, translating and cutting and condensing and changing to suit his taste, Malory composed his book.

He called it the "Morte d'Arthur"—the "Death of Arthur"—but it is really the whole fascinating story of Arthur and his knights from first to last—of Merlin, the great magician; of Lancelot, the flower of

Photo by Anderson

This painting shows us Malory as a dashing knight when he followed his noble lord to France and learned of the famous exploits of which he told in his tales of Arthur and the Round Table.

chivalry, and his great love for Guinevere, the queen; of Gawaine and Gareth and their doings, and of the lovers, Tristan and Iseult; of the quest for the Holy Grail, and Galahad's finding of it; and last of all, of the black treason of Modred, and the king's sailing to the Isles of the Dead. It is all there, written down for the first time in English prose. It is told so simply and charmingly that it is still very good indeed to read; it is the earliest of all masterpieces of English prose. And as for the way in which Malory tells these age-old stories—nearly all the poets who have told them after him have used him as a guide.

As he wrote his great book, the old knight must have looked back across the years to the days of his youth, when the old-time chivalry which he imagines flowering in Arthur's court was still alive in the gallant Warwick. Then he must have looked about him at the four walls of his prison, and through them with his mind's eye to a disturbed England, and longed for the "good old days." For, even while he was writing his perfect story of the days "when knighthood was in flower," the Middle Ages were passing away.

His book was one of the very first, for example, to be *printed* in England. And Caxton, the printer, in choosing this book for production by his press, certainly made a very good choice.

It is interesting to remember some other famous books that have been written in prison: "Pilgrim's Progress" by John Bunyan and "The History of the World" by Sir Walter Raleigh; and in modern times "The Ballad of Reading Gaol" by Oscar Wilde.

The story of King Arthur has a moral behind it. It is this: Seek good and shun evil if you wish to leave a good name behind you. It is better for a man to leave a good portrait of his character behind him than a finely painted portrait of his face.

The MAN *Who* WROTE "UTOPIA"

A Great Statesman, Sir Thomas More was also a Scholar and a Wit, Even in the Last Moments before His Death as the Chief Victim of Henry VIII

HAVE you ever sat and dreamed of some green island in the sea where you and a few of your best friends could live an ideal life, far from the pressing cares and troubles of this confusing world? Nearly every man who is worth his salt has had a few brief dreams of this kind.

A good many men have kept on dreaming until they have thought out a whole new scheme of life for the little group on their imaginary island. A hundred or more of these dreamers have made the dream into a book—to explain the ideal commonwealth they would build up if they could have their own way freely in constructing it. But probably the most famous of all the books of this kind is the one written by Sir Thomas More (1478–1535). It is called "Utopia";

and how well Sir Thomas knew it was a dream is shown by the fact that "utopia" (ū-tō′pĭ-ā) is just a Greek word meaning "nowhere."

To-day, after four hundred years, the immortal "Utopia" is the main thing that everybody mentions in connection with Sir Thomas More. But in his own day this product of his wit and fancy, though widely read, was only one of the many diversions in a very important life; for More was one of the most prominent men in England in the troublous times of Henry VIII, and in the end the most glorious martyr to his religious faith.

Even as a boy, More had shown that he was going to make a mark in the world. After a little schooling he was placed in the

Photo by Rischgitz

From a barred window in the dreaded Tower of London, where he is imprisoned, Sir Thomas More and his daughter Margaret are watching four monks on their way to execution for having refused to swear that Henry VIII was the sole head of the Church. It was for a similar refusal that More was thrown into the Tower.

house of the Archbishop of Canterbury, who said at once that More would "prove a marvellous man." The archbishop sent him to Oxford, and his father made him study law; so at twenty-two More was admitted to practice. He soon had a large number of clients, and gained high renown for his legal skill and wisdom.

Adoption of a Simple Life of Prayer, Fasting and Penance

Then he entered public life for a time, as a member of Parliament. But he soon found himself in disagreement with the king, Henry VII, and in those days it was dangerous indeed to disagree with the king. So More returned to his legal and literary studies, and to a stern and pure religious life. Indeed, he very nearly became a monk. He spent much time in prayer and fasting, and always wore a hair shirt next his body as a penance. He had given up all idea of a public career, and desired only to lead a quiet and studious life, like his famous friend Erasmus.

In Favour with the King

But now Henry VIII came to the throne, and More's retirement was over. Although he did not wish to emerge from his quiet life, the new king induced him to return to politics, diplomacy, and to all the cares of high office in the State. More now rose rapidly in glory, and in due time he became chancellor. He had all the trust and affection of the king, who used to walk up and down the garden with his arm round More's neck. But More well knew how deceptive is glory, and how fickle the favour of a tyrant.

"Master More," the duke of Norfolk said one day, "it is perilous striving with princes; the revenge of princes is death." "Is that all, my lord?" More answered with a smile; "then, in good faith, the difference between your Grace and me is that I shall die to-day and you to-morrow."

Strife with Henry VIII arose over various matters, but two were by far the most important. The king had put away his wife, Catherine of Aragon, and married the pretty Anne Boleyn (bōōl′ĭn); and neither by entreaty nor by force could he get More

to say that the act was right or legal. The king had also broken with the Pope and set himself up as the head of the Church in England; but nothing could persuade More to accept the king as head of the Church. Then the doom of More was sealed. He was tried for treason, and beheaded. His death has been called "the blackest crime that has ever been perpetrated in England under the form of law."

It would be hard to find a nobler example of the way in which a man ought to behave than the conduct of Sir Thomas More during his trial and while he was waiting for the axe to fall. For a parallel men have often looked back to the story of Socrates during his trial and death in Athens, and More has often been called the English Socrates.

If he resembled Socrates in his heroism, and even in his gaiety under persecution, he was a little like him also in his way of thought. For More was a scholar and a philosopher, and the ideas that circulated in his brain are more important to us now than are his actions as a statesman. He lived at a time when the old world of the Middle Ages was breaking up, and when the great movement known as the Renaissance (rĕ-nā′sȧns) was opening the door to the modern world.

Facing Death on the Scaffold with a Smile and a Joke

Like a good scholar of the Renaissance, like a good disciple of the philosophers of old, More was also a wit. When he had given his fervent blessing to his weeping children and his servants just before his death beneath the axe, he accepted his fate with the smile of a gentleman and a philosopher. As he mounted the scaffold to his death, he said to one of the officers, "I pray thee, see me safe up, and for my coming down let me shift for myself."

When the man with the axe hesitated a moment, More did what he could to give him courage. "Pluck up thy spirits, man," he said, "and be not afraid to do thine office." And then, with his head on the block, he pushed his beard away to bare his throat, saying, "Stay till I have moved my beard; that at least has not committed treason."

(CONTINUED ON PAGE 95)

Reading from the top left-hand corner across the page the British insects shown above are the spotted frog-hopper, flat-bodied dragon-fly, shield bug, caddis fly, lace-wing fly, great green-spotted dragon-fly, hornet, queen bumble bee, may-fly, common brown grasshopper, and saw-fly.

"Stop, stop!" said the grasshopper, as he planted his foot firmly in the face of the newcomer. "This is my blade of grass!"

SWARMS *of* MIDGETS *with* SIX LEGS

Creeping, Crawling, Flying, or Digging, They Breathe Through the Slits in Their Sides

NOT so very long ago it was the fashion for ladies to scream at the sight of a little worm. Not that they thought it could hurt them! They were merely trying to show how refined they were—for all little creeping things were thought disgusting, however gentle, and were always stepped on by ladies who were unusually brave.

Nowadays we know better, and little Miss Muffet's behaviour has come to be a joke. We have found out that she was only ignorant and silly, for spiders are among the most interesting and useful of all the tiny creatures that inhabit the earth—as knowing as the ant or the bee, or the busy blustering wasp who is such a capable carpenter and constructional engineer.

So our great-grandmothers missed a good deal by not knowing what was going on around them. Anyone with his eyes open and his wits about him can find more to interest him in watching a spider building a web than in a builder erecting a house for someone to live in. And the little creatures that creep and hop and fly and burrow are often among the most beautiful and interesting of living things.

They are mostly so very small that we may pass them by without ever seeing them. But, tiny as they are, they are very important; and there are such vast armies of them that they far outnumber all other kinds of animals living on the earth. No one knows exactly how many different kinds of insects there are, for new ones are always

41

being discovered; but there must be at least a million different kinds.

They creep and fly and hum in the forests, lanes, and meadows, crawl and swim in the pools and streams, and dance over the surface of the water. All day long butterflies flit from flower to flower; bees bustle about gathering honey and pollen; fussy

light up their lamps under the hedgerows, and fire-flies dart like shooting stars through the dark forests and over the meadows. For Nature never rests. When the sunshine lovers are sleeping, the shy creatures who have slumbered away the hot hours wake up and move about busily in the stillness of the night.

Did ever a child change more as it grew? From one of those tiny eggs in the oval there hatched the hairy caterpillar you see just to the left of the eggs. He is dressed for protection, for his strong bristles break the force of many a fall and lead a hungry bird to think twice before eating him.

As a caterpillar, he eats and eats and grows and grows; and when he has done all the growing he ever intends to do, he makes for himself the hairy cocoon that you see just below him. In that he shuts himself up and turns into the strange, smooth affair shown at the right of the cocoon; it is called a chrysalis. In two or three weeks he will be able to step out into the world as the muslin moth that you see below at the right.

little beetles run very fast over the ground and climb up and down the tall grass stems; grubs and caterpillars without number munch away at the green leaves on the plants and trees; and gauzy-winged flies buzz gaily about in the sunshine.

When evening comes, the insect folk who have worked and played and fed all through the long summer day settle themselves for the night. Flies stop buzzing and dancing, butterflies fold their wings and go to sleep among the flowers, and the busy bees cease their daily toil and hurry home to bed.

Night Owls of the Insect World

Then the night-flying moths and beetles and all sorts of queer little creatures come out and flit about in the dark. Glow-worms

Nearly everywhere in the world there are some of these wonderful little beings scrambling for a living. Only in the Polar regions, where from year's end to year's end the snow and ice never melt, and in the heart of burning deserts, where every living thing is shrivelled up by the scorching sun, are there no insects at all.

Swarms of winged insects fly over the frozen seas to the ice-bound coasts of the far north, where they tease the reindeer and worry the Eskimos. Some even spend the best part of their life buried deep under

Here is an enlarged view of a queen humble bee. Her furry body is covered with feathered hairs for catching the pollen from flowers. The pollen is cleaned off by special brushes and combs on her legs, and carried home in large masses on the pollen carriers. On the right is a worker humble bee collecting nectar from a clover flower.

the snow on the tops of high mountains. But it is in hot, tropical lands that the little creatures are found in the greatest numbers. There, too, they are bigger and more brilliantly coloured than in the more temperate climates; for insects revel in warmth and sunshine, and many of them compete successfully with the gorgeous tropical flowers in the remarkable splendour of their varied colouring.

The Wise and the Foolish

There are all sorts and conditions of insect folk. Each little fellow goes about his business and lives his life in his own peculiar way. Some are idle and some are industrious; some are wise and some are foolish—just as human beings are. Some build wonderful cities in which they live and work together in a most intelligent way. Fierce insect clans make war on one another, and the victors not only carry off the children of their defeated foes but they also keep them in captivity as slaves.

Some kinds of insects are terribly troublesome. They bite us and sting us, worry our cattle, ruin our crops, and damage our property; and worse still, they carry the germs of diseases wherever they go. Others are friendly little fellows, always working, though they may not know it, for our good. They help to fertilize the soil, clear away decaying rubbish, check the growth of plants that would choke the ground, and are our most valuable allies in fighting and keeping down the vast number of our insect foes.

But most important of all are the busy little insects that all through the spring and summer fly from flower to flower carrying the precious pollen dust needed to form seeds—for the seeds of many flowers cannot ripen without the pollen from another flower of the same kind. Some of the pollen is carried by the wind. But the wind is a

which only the long tongues of the bees can reach. When a blossom unfurls its bright petals and gives out a sweet scent, the bees know it has honey to give. So they come hurrying up, dive into the flower to sip the honey, and then fly away with their hairy little bodies dusted with the golden pollen to other flowers, where some of it is bound to be rubbed off.

Some of the flowers, however, are not quite so careful. They keep their supply of honey in open cups from which all

Insects vary enormously in form, size and appearance. Here are three examples from the vast multitude of different types—a brimstone butterfly, a ground beetle (on the right) and a sand wasp (below).

careless worker. It scatters the pollen far and wide, so that a great deal is wasted and never reaches the blossoms for which it is meant.

How Insects Help the Plants

If it were not for the help of our insect friends we should have few bright flowers and very little fruit. Butterflies and moths, and certain of the flies and little beetles, all assist in the good work of taking pollen from one blossom to another. But the chief carriers are the bees. They are most industrious, trustworthy little creatures. They can always be counted on to do their work right. So some of the plants do all in their power to attract the bees and induce them to act as their messengers. It is to catch their eye that the flowers put on their vivid colours, and it is to reward them for their services that the buds keep stores of sweet nectar hidden away in secret cups or pockets

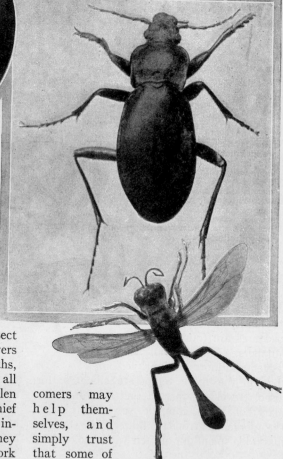

comers may help themselves, and simply trust that some of the pollen will be carried to the right address. Honey is the favourite food of a host of little insects, and pollen is another; so flowers and insects are about equally necessary to each other. Bees and many other insects could not live without honey and pollen, and many of the pretty flowering plants would die out if there were no insects to help them make their seeds. Neither the insects nor the flowers understand what they are doing. They work together unconsciously, helping, all the same, to keep the earth fertile and beautiful.

Now, before we venture closer to the strange little beings of the insect world, it will be just as well to make sure that we know an insect when we see it. For there are many other small creatures we might easily mistake for insects if we had not some way of telling them apart. But if we remember that a true and "perfect" insect, no matter of what sort or size or shape it may be, always has six legs, and only six, we shall not often make a mistake. Spiders and scorpions have eight legs worms have none, and centipedes may boast a hundred legs or more. This tells us at once that the creatures are not insects. So the first thing to do when you meet with a puzzling little animal and are not quite sure whether it is an insect or not is to count its legs. Caterpillars, grubs, and maggots may have more than six legs or may have none at all, but they are baby insects, not "perfect" insects. When they grow up into butterflies, bees, beetles, or flies, they will all have six legs—no more and no less.

Insects are really very curious little animals. For one thing, they have no bones. They wear their skeletons outside, so to speak, in the shape of a number of stiff, horny plates or rings. These rings slightly overlap one another, forming a complete suit of jointed armour that covers its owner from head to foot. Beetles are clothed with very strong armour-plating, but butterflies, bees, and many other insects are clad in much lighter suits.

The body of an insect is always divided

Here is a part of one of the most dangerous insects known to man—the common house-fly. This front view of its head is from an enlarged model. Note the two enormous eyes with their innumerable lenses.

into two distinct parts—a fore body and a hind body. Indeed, the word "insect," which comes from the Latin, means "cut into." The two halves are joined by a waist. You can see this very clearly if you look at a wasp, which has such a delicate, thread-like waist that you may wonder why it does not break in two. Other insects, such as the cockchafer, have waists so thick as to be hardly noticeable, but the division is there all the same.

The six legs and the wings of an insect are attached to the fore part of its body—never to the hind part. There may be one or two pairs of wings, or, in some cases, none at all; but no insect ever has more than two pairs.

On its head an insect always has a pair of feelers, called antennae (ăn-tĕn′ē). They are most useful to the little creature; they act as organs of touch and smell, and sometimes even of hearing. Some are long and thread-like, others are short, stout clubs; and some may even be fan-shaped or like beautiful feathery plumes.

On the insect's head, too, are a pair of very large eyes, called compound eyes. They are made up of a number of separate lenses, set side by side like the facets of a diamond, each one at a slightly different angle; so the owners of these wonderful eyes are able to keep a look-out in all directions without troubling to turn their heads. Between the great compound eyes most insects have three lenses, called simple eyes, or ocelli (ŏ-sĕl′ĭ), but these are so small that you would seldom notice them.

Insects do not breathe through a nose as we do, but through tiny openings, or breathing pores, placed at intervals all along their sides. These little openings are connected with a wonderful network of air tubes which carry supplies of oxygen throughout the insect's body. Spiral fibres like fine wires

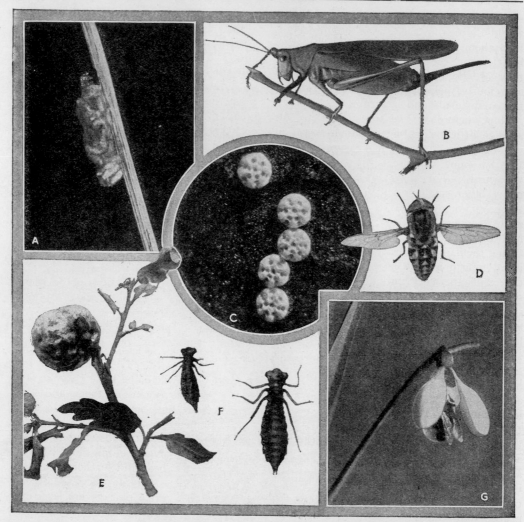

THE GRASSHOPPER, THE GADFLY AND OTHER INSECTS

Some of the strange little creatures whose acquaintance you are going to make in later chapters of this story of insect life are shown here. At A is a caterpillar covered with the cocoons of an ichneumon (ĭk-nū′mŏn) fly. It is a peculiarity of this beautiful, gauzy-winged insect to deposit its eggs in or on the eggs, larvae or pupae of various other insects. When its larvae hatch out they eat their way into the larvae of the other insects and gradually kill them. For this reason the ichneumon fly is regarded as a friend of the farmer, since it helps to destroy many insects that do great harm to the crops. A great green grasshopper is seen at B; and at C are five highly magnified eggs of the large copper butterfly, which the mother fixes to a plant leaf of the baby's favourite food. The insect marked D is a gadfly, about natural size. The pretty "oak apple" at E is the work of the gall-fly, which lays an egg inside the tender leaf; when the caterpillar hatches and begins to eat, the leaf swells like a great blister. At F are two dragon-fly nymphs, which live in the water for two or three years, until they arrive at the adult stage; they feed chiefly on small water insects. At G is shown a honey-bee paying a visit to a snowdrop. In his effort to reach the luscious nectar he has almost disappeared from view.

inside the tubes prevent them from collapsing under pressure, while tiny valves regulate the supply of air passing through the breathing pores.

So you see insects are not at all like the little four-footed animals of the earth in the way they are formed or in the way they breathe—or even like the birds, although they often have wings and are able to fly. But all this we shall see for ourselves if we set forth on an exploring expedition to study the habits and customs of the insects.

(CONTINUED ON PAGE 109)

TANSY *and* BOBBLES *on* FABLE ISLAND

If You Think It Would Be Fun to Talk with All the Animals, You Will Like Reading This Story of What Two Children Learned from Their Four-footed Friends, Instead of Going to School

TANSY and Bobbles were fairies. They were not good fairies, or bad fairies, but just middling fairies.

They lived long, long ago, on Fable Island, which was full of woods and streams and mountains and quiet valleys, and which lay out in the ocean just about where the sun dips down at sunset into the water.

No one can land a boat there now, for on a certain glorious night Fable Island rose up from the sea, stretching out her arms to the sky. If you chance to look at the right moment, when the western sky is full of glory, you may see Fable Island, floating up among the clouds. She takes a different shape each time you see her; but, whatever her shape, she is always beautiful,

and the children all over the world can point upward and cry, "Look! Look! There is Fable Island!"

The animals and trees and plants on Fable Island could all talk, and that made life very interesting for Tansy and Bobbles. They did not go to school, for Father Fairy and Mother Fairy had explained that fairies were of no use unless they could find out the meaning of things for themselves.

So each day Tansy and Bobbles darted about, finding out the meaning of things; and great fun they had, especially as they could make themselves invisible by just linking their little fingers together and putting out their tongues.

Of course, Tansy and Bobbles could

Through the long sunshine of the summer days Tansy and Bobbles pried with their inquisitive eyes and ears and fingers and noses into the Meaning of Things. For even though they were fairies, with all sorts of fairy tricks to play, they had to use their wits to find out what the world is all about. They worked hard, and had a jolly time, for the best way to enjoy yourself is to keep your wits at work. Their adventures will make you feel quite envious.

always see each other; and when they wanted anyone else to see them, they had only to exclaim "Booh!"—which was sometimes rather startling.

One morning, as they sat astride a farm fence—they were watching an old cock scratching about to find tit-bits for his pet hens—when suddenly a young hen screamed with joy.

"What's that? What's that beautiful thing?" she cried, pointing with her toe to a shining jewel.

"Pooh!" mocked the cock. "If you swallowed that, it would give you a terrible pain. I only wish it were good honest wheat!" and he scratched the dirt over it.

But Tansy was off the fence like a shot, with Bobbles after her.

"Booh! Booh!" they both shouted, and how the farmyard creatures scattered!

Tansy laughed, and poked about till she found the jewel.

"Silly old bird!" she said to Bobbles. "He only sneers at this jewel because he's too ignorant to know its real value!" and she popped it into her pocket.

But Bobbles wasn't listening, for he had darted off and was now calling to her excitedly.

By the tall trellis surrounding one side of the farmer's garden a fox was jumping and jumping, vainly trying to reach some lovely bunches of grapes which were hanging just above his head.

The fairies giggled with joy at the funny sight, and just as the fox was lying down exhausted, Tansy cried out:

"You'll soon make yourself too tired to gallop home!"

The fox was a little vexed at this, for he hated to be laughed at; so he answered back, gruffly enough:

"As if I wanted the silly grapes! They're sour, anyway!"

"Only because you can't get them!" cried Bobbles. Then he unfolded his wings and

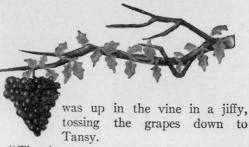

was up in the vine in a jiffy, tossing the grapes down to Tansy.

"They're sweet enough! Try for yourself!" cried Tansy.

But the fox would not do it, for he was a proud beast, and he trotted off, with his elegant brush sweeping the ground.

Tansy and Bobbles slept under the ferns in the summer. Early one morning they were startled greatly by a tremendous crashing through the underwood, as though all the animals on the island had gone mad.

"What's happened?" cried Bobbles.

"Fairies shouldn't ask about things they can find out for themselves!" answered the owl. "Can't you hear the mountain? Not that the mountain matters to me. I'm off to sleep!" And he shut his eyes up tight.

"The mountain!" growled the lion as he plunged past, followed by his wife and cub.

"The mountain!" cried the wolf, the fox, the deer, the sheep, the hare, and lots and lots more of the animals, as they started running towards it. Even the tortoise sprinted at a marvellous pace.

Tansy and Bobbles made themselves in-

Suppose you saw some delicious grapes that were just out of reach. Would you go off in a huff, or would you pass on the secret to someone else who was tall enough to pick them?

This is a nice mouse, but nothing much for a mountain to make a great fuss about. It must be with mountains very much as it is with people—the ones that boast most are they who nearly always make the poorest showing.

visible and flew high over the trees towards the mountain, where they looked round in astonishment at the great crowd of animals, birds, insects, men, women and children, who had all gathered to know why the mountain was groaning so.

"Booh!" said Tansy and Bobbles in a breath, as they alighted on the mountain's crown. "Tell us all the news!"

"No impudence!" said the mountain. "I'm going to do something BIG! Go down below, and watch me doing something BIG!"

"You conceited old blusterer!" mocked Bobbles.

But at that the mountain gave the most fearful groan of all. Tansy and Bobbles flew down into the valley, where the trumpets were sounding, for lo, the king and queen and all the royal family had come in state to watch the mountain do something BIG.

"I hope he will send out a dragon," said Bobbles.

"Or a witch," said Tansy.

"Or a giant," said a boy called Jack; "then I can kill him."

"Booh!" said Bobbles suddenly, and Jack's hair stood up straight, and then went down with a flop.

"Fairies," cried Jack; "and my father says they've all flown away!"

"Silence!" called a trumpeter. So everyone kept silence.

A terrific sound of thunder awed them.

"The mountain is opening," whispered Bobbles. All the crowd saw Tansy and Bobbles and Jack run forward, and shouted to them to come back.

But they only laughed and ran on, expecting something BIG.

The mountain opened a wide rocky mouth, and everyone rushed back screaming. Only the brave three stood their ground.

And then, out of the mouth of the mountain, there came a tiny mouse. He looked round, wondering what the fuss was about, and then squatted on his haunches and began to clean his whiskers.

"You darling!" cried Tansy, as she picked him up.

"Only a mouse, after all that bluster!" said the king to the queen, for he was very much annoyed.

"Only a mouse!" said all the rest; and, since the mountain had closed up again, they all dashed off for the breakfasts they had missed.

"Next time," said Tansy to the mountain, "I hope you won't promise to do something BIG and only do something LITTLE!"

But the mountain refused to answer, and only laughed in his inside.

"Why, the mouse has gone, too!" said Tansy, looking into her empty hands.

The Lion and the Mouse

"Look!" said Tansy, as she crept close up to the snoring lion. "I do believe that's the very mouse that came out of the mountain."

And so it was, for the mouse looked at the fairies and waggled his whiskers at them by way of greeting.

But, alas! he forgot where he was going, and ran right across the lion's nose. When the lion felt the tickling, he put up his paw and seemed about to crush the poor little mouse.

"No, no, King Lion!" squeaked the mouse. "Please have pity upon me. Do not stain your glorious paws with my poor, insignificant blood!"

"Of course he won't! Of course he won't!" cried Tansy and Bobbles, as they skipped up quite close.

The lion looked round and nodded at the fairies, for he had taken them for many a wonderful ride as they clung to his mane. Then he gave a roaring laugh as he glared at the terrified mouse.

"Mind you look where you're going next time!" he said.

Then he lifted up his paw, and the mouse ran off.

"Mind you look where you're going yourself, Sir Lion," said Bobbles. "The hunters have been setting their nets in the wood."

"Pooh!" said the lion, "I'm too old to be caught by any silly hunter!" And he began washing his face like a cat.

The Tortoise and the Hare

Now Bobbles and Tansy had an engagement to watch a race between the hare and the tortoise, so they darted off.

It was a very good thing for the lion that he did not think the mouse too insignificant to be worth a little kindness.

It would be a very dull race, they thought, for the hare would be sure to win from the creeping tortoise.

50

However, they had promised to referee, so they had to be there.

The hare and the tortoise shook each other's paws before they started, and the fairies gave the signal by clapping.

But they were astonished to see that although the tortoise toddled off, the hare only laughed and lay down for a nap.

"The race has started," warned Tansy.

"I know! I know!" said the hare. "But it's a long way to the ancient oak tree. It will take the tortoise all the morning."

So Tansy and Bobbles followed the tortoise, and kept looking round to see if the hare was coming. But he had not started yet. And at last the tortoise poked out his head and cried: "Hello! There's the oak tree."

He was very much ex- hausted with crawling through the grass and over the stones, but he pulled himself together for a final spurt.

"Here comes the hare!" whispered Tansy. And there he came, but still far away, just on the brow of the hill.

It was too exciting for words as the hare came nearer and nearer, in great galloping bounds. But he was too late! The tortoise touched the ancient oak just before him, and the hare had lost the race.

But now there came an awful roaring through the wood, and the fairies raced off to find that the lion had, after all, been caught in the hunter's snare. The more he tried to get out of the net, the worse he was entangled.

"We must help him!" said Bobbles valiantly.

"No! No! Look!" whispered Tansy.

There was the mouse once more. But this time he was nibbling hard at the knots in the net. He worked so quickly that in a few minutes the lion was free.

"One good turn deserves another," said the mouse delightedly, as he scampered away to his dinner.

"And even the little can help the big sometimes!" said Tansy.

Tansy and Bobbles were feasting on wild raspberries and wondering what meanings they would find out for themselves on this lovely day, when the tortoise, who was resting after his great race with the hare, heaved a terrible sigh.

"If only I could fly!" he groaned. "I'm tired of groping on the ground."

"My father says people ought to be con- tented to be what they are," said Tansy.

"That's all very well for you," said the disgruntled tortoise; "you can run and fly. But, hello! Here's my chance!"

For a giant eagle had come swooping down and now stood with folded wings on a rock close by.

If this unhandsome tortoise had refused to do his best, because of his slow legs, things might have turned out very differently. But the good old lumbering fellow had one great advantage over the boastful hare. He had the priceless gift of common sense—and the pluck to keep plodding steadily along.

"Sir Eagle," said the tortoise respectfully, "please teach me to fly."

"Who's speaking?" asked the eagle, as he stared downward.

"Me! Only me! The tortoise who won the race against the hare. Teach me to fly, Sir Eagle, and I will give you all the treasures of the ocean."

"Now don't be silly and conceited," warned Bobbles.

But the tortoise refused to be warned, and kept on begging to be taught to fly. So at last the eagle took him in his talons, and mounted up and up into the sky.

"Now!" said the eagle, "away you fly! It's quite easy!" And he let the tortoise go.

"Oh! Oh!" gasped Tansy, as she clung to Bobbles. "Look!"

And as the fairies looked, the tortoise came spinning down from the sky and was dashed to pieces on the rock.

"I suppose," said Bobbles, "the meaning of this is that the tortoise was foolish not to remember that he was not an eagle."

Why the Wolf Got the Sheep

Just then Jack the shepherd boy came rushing towards them, as though in terror.

"Wolf! Wolf!" he cried. "The wolf is among the sheep!"

But Tansy and Bobbles only laughed. They had heard Jack pretending that the wolf was among the sheep so often.

"But he really, really is!" cried Jack frantically.

Alas, the fairies did not believe him, and neither did the farmer, nor the folk in the village.

But when Tansy and Bobbles flew across to the meadow, they were dismayed to find that the wolf was really there, tearing at the poor sheep. They flew off to tell the farmer that Jack had spoken the truth this time. But, alas, it was too late.

"I hope we shan't see any more dreadful things to-day," said Tansy, as they hurried off to tell Father Fairy and Mother Fairy their adventures.

A Frog That Burst with Pride

They could not help stopping at the pond, however, for a little frog was telling its mother how a great ox had nearly trodden his little brothers and sisters to death.

"Was the ox as big as this?" asked the mother, as she swelled herself out.

"Bigger! Bigger!" cried the little frog.

"Not bigger than this?" and mother frog swelled herself still more.

"Far, far bigger!" cried the little frog.

But at that the mother frog was so offended that she swelled out more and more until suddenly—Pop! She had burst.

"Oh, dear," cried Tansy. "Do let's go away. I wonder what was the meaning of that. The third horrible thing we've seen to-day."

"That's easy enough," said Bobbles. "Trying to be BIG when she was only LITTLE."

(CONTINUED ON PAGE 180)

For thousands of years the Sphinx has gazed in silent calm upon the doings of the little race of men. The mighty Alexander left him unperturbed; great Caesar came and went, and also the conquering Napoleon, and still he held his peace, as mysterious as the ancient men who carved him there out of the solid stone. All this the artist Elihu Vedder had in mind when he painted this picture of "The Questioning of the Sphinx."

In the DAYS of the PYRAMIDS
How the History of Man Began in a Crumpled Ribbon of Country Running through a Desert

IF YOU look at the map of Egypt in your geography book you will see an irregular oblong area in the north-east corner of Africa. But no map can convey to you what the real Egypt is like. The country has changed considerably since the period of which we write, when its shape could have been likened to a crumpled ribbon with a small bow or knot at one end.

Imagine yourself a farmer living upon the bank of a great river. For a few miles—from five to fifteen—east and west of the river, the land is the richest farm land you could possibly desire. It will grow such splendid crops that all by yourself you can raise enough wheat and barley to feed many people.

The reason why this land is so good is that every year the river overflows its banks;

the precious waters cover your farm and fill all the many canals which you and your friends have dug to help carry the supply; and when this flood slowly goes down again there is left on your land a thin layer of new, black, fertile mud—the gift of the Nile River to your farm. How plants love to grow in that mud!

A Vast Desert Expanse

But just behind this rich river country, on both sides of the Nile, is an enormous sandy desert, so vast that no one can tell with certainty what lies on the other side of it. You never venture far into this desert, because if you did there would be danger that you might never come back to tell what you had seen. You have never seen anyone, friend or foe, coming across it to visit you. To you there are only two directions that matter—up-stream and down-stream.

Egypt was just a ribbon of country 750 miles long and from ten to thirty miles wide.

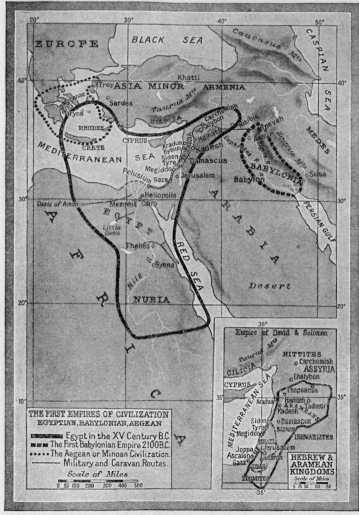

THE FIRST EMPIRES OF CIVILIZATION
EGYPTIAN, BABYLONIAN, AEGEAN

▦▦▦ Egypt in the XV Century B.C.
▦▦▦ The First Babylonian Empire 2100 B.C.
•••• The Aegean or Minoan Civilization.
—— Military and Caravan Routes.
Scale of Miles
0 50 100 200 300 400 500

HEBREW & ARAMEAN KINGDOMS
Scale of Miles

Later in life some of you who read this book may sail for many sunny days up the blue waters of the Nile. Then you will feel the charm of this strange land of Egypt, where history began, and will visit for yourselves the ancient pyramids and temples standing, like outposts of the past, along its palm-strewn shores.

It began at what is called the first cataract of the Nile, that is, the first place where the river is full of rocks which boats find difficult to pass. From there Egypt stretched northwards along the Nile as it flowed to the sea, until at the mouth of the river there was the knot or bow we mentioned. This is what is known as the Delta of the

Nile. A delta consists of land that has been built up by the mud which a river carries to the sea.

So if you can imagine a sunny and peaceful land where it scarcely ever rained, a land which was just a green ribbon unfolding its wavy length between yellow sands, with the river a blue stripe down the centre of the green, you have imagined Egypt. In ancient times seven million people lived there.

If we say that history began in Egypt, we do not mean that it was the first place in which human beings lived. People were living in the world many thousands of years before history begins, and we can discover a good deal about these people, too, from the tools, the weapons, and the other things they left lying about where they lived. Often such things are found in caves or buried under layers of dirt, and now we are able to dig them out and study them to learn their story.

But stories such as those are not exactly history; they are called anthropology (ăn'thrō-pŏl'ō-jǐ). To possess a knowledge of history we must know not only what happened but when it happened. It is not history to say that men used flint axes many thousands of years ago in France, but it is history to say that William the Conqueror invaded England in 1066.

Every day in Egypt men of our own times are earnestly and diligently engaged in digging up history. They are removing the dust and dirt of centuries which covers the story of these old forgotten days—a story

In the Vatican Museum at Rome is this splendid ancient Roman sculpture of old Father Nile. It represents the great river of Africa that by its yearly floods nourished its children—the people who lived along its banks.

written on walls, on doors, even on pins and other trinkets. Every year we are learning more about the history of Egypt, but it is not likely that we shall ever be able to go back beyond the Egyptian year one, the beginning of the story of Egypt.

The Egyptian Year One

This Egyptian year one is the year we call 4,241 B.C.—that is, the year which was 4,241 years before the birth of Christ. This was actually the year one for the Egyptians, for it was then that they began their calendar. Hundreds of years before the Chinese and the Hebrew calendars began, the Egyptians knew enough to start counting time; and their year one is the oldest date in known history.

What sort of people lived in Egypt in this "year one"? We know that they were Hamites (hăm'ĭt), and so belonged to the white race; that they had dark hair; and that they often wore a few clothes, made sometimes of skins and sometimes of linen. They were great makers of jars and vessels, first in clay and later in stone also. They knew how to write and to count—their calendar shows that. They could hammer gold thin enough to make handsome handles for flint knives.

And above all they were great makers of pictures. Everything they made—knife handles, pots, jars, even the walls of their houses and their tombs—they covered with pictures of all the pleasant things which interested them, such as boats, birds, and gazelles, as well as of events like the opening of a new canal. It took a happy, active people to draw so many designs and pictures of their life and surroundings.

Of course, the river meant everything to these early Egyptian farmers. In their religion the Nile was one of the chief gods. The crocodile in the river was a god, too, and so were many other animals and birds. Seeing the river flow past every day, always in the same direction, people imagined that it must flow back continually through underground caverns. The sun, they felt, must go round in much the same way. He was a god, too; and every night he tunnelled under the earth and came up again in the east.

Curious Belief About the Sky

Such were the simple beliefs of these first Egyptians. The sky they imagined to be a great cow, or sometimes a woman lying across the heavens. Or it was a blue sea across which the sun god rowed his boats. Always the boats and the river came into the story somewhere.

In their year one this 750-mile-long country was probably split into a great many little towns or districts, each with its own chief

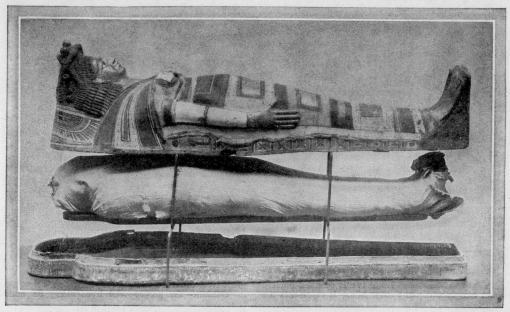

No people has ever cared for its dead so skilfully as did the ancient Egyptians, for they thought it necessary to preserve the body as a home to which the soul could return some day. The photograph above shows an opened mummy case with the mummy suspended between the top and bottom. The body has been wound in yards and yards of linen bandaging, after having been carefully treated with resin and spices—and numerous charms, as well! A mask of linen and stucco often helped to preserve the outlines of the face; and the dry air of the desert did its part in the process of mummification. The outside of the case—the shell of this huge chrysalis—was often carved or moulded to look like the face of the dead man, and was painted in brilliant colours. To have all this done might take as long as seventy days, and was very expensive. Only the rich could afford it. But sacred animals—cats, birds and crocodiles—were often made into mummies.

or ruler, and even its own special local gods. But soon after that time chiefs who were a little stronger than their neighbours began to conquer the districts next their own and bring them under their own rule. This conquering went on until soon there were just two kingdoms in Egypt; but these two kingdoms lasted separately for many hundreds of years.

One of these kingdoms was called the Upper, or Southern, Kingdom, because it was farther from the ocean and therefore farther up the river. It was long and thin, covering about six hundred of Egypt's 750 miles.

The other kingdom was called the Lower, or Northern, Kingdom, and this contained the Delta of the Nile.

Long before Egyptian history began, men in the Nile Valley were making fine pottery; sometimes a polished ware in red and black and sometimes pieces decorated with figures or geometrical designs, as shown above.

It was in this delta, by the way, that the calendar began.

At last there came a king strong enough to join the two kingdoms together and make one Egypt out of the two. This was Menes (3400 B.C.), the first Egyptian king about whom we know much. Menes (mē'nēz) was called the "Lord of the Two Houses," because he had succeeded in uniting the Upper and Lower Kingdoms into a single realm.

For hundreds of years afterwards the kings of Egypt were known by this name. As the memory of the two kingdoms grew dim, the name changed to "Lord of the Great House," or just

ANCIENT TOOLS THAT MAY HAVE HELPED TO BUILD THE PYRAMIDS

For thousands of years the hands that carved and wielded these tools have been dust, but their handiwork has come down to us. In many of the crafts the early Egyptians worked with great skill. Here are mallets, wedges, chisels, a wooden dipper, and a plasterer's float, such as is used to smooth the plaster before it is left to set. In the pyramids there is plaster that has stood for nearly five thousand years and is still firm and hard. Some of it is better in composition than the kind used by the ingenious builders of to-day.

57

Beside the River Nile at Gizeh are these famous pyramids, the only one of the seven wonders of the ancient world remaining to this day. Each one of these gigantic tombs of the Egyptian pharaohs took many years to build.

"the Great House," which in Egyptian was the word *pero*; and this word *pero*, meaning "great house" or "king," is the same as the word "pharaoh," which we use to-day as the title of each of the kings of ancient Egypt.

Menes and the kings who followed him lived at Memphis (mĕm'fĭs), at a place they called the "White Wall." They built their palaces in duplicate, and in front they often had two gates, one bearing a red crown and one a white. At first there were separate officers and separate accounts for red and white, but finally these were merged into one. The double crown, too, became one crown, and Egypt was one country.

A Missing Page in Egypt's History

All this took hundreds of years to bring about. There were some seventeen kings following Menes who took part in the slow process of merging the two kingdoms. We know very little about these kings, not even the names of some of them. We do know that they often had trouble keeping the Upper and the Lower Kingdoms together, and that the people of the Delta, especially, rebelled again and again, and had to be punished. But we know very little of the years that come between Menes (3400 B.C.) and Zoser (2980 B.C.).

A Wise Vizier and His Many Duties

Zoser (zō'sẽr) was himself a good and wise king, but he is remembered mostly because of his vizier, or chief counsellor, Imhotep (ēm-hō'tĕp). The vizier (vĭz'yẽr) of the king had to be his architect or builder, his engineer, his judge or lawyer, his scribe or writer, and his secretary; so you can see that Imhotep had many duties to perform. In two of these offices he was one of the greatest of the Egyptians. He wrote down many wise sayings, so that his books and his wisdom were the model for future ages; and also he planned the first pyramid as a tomb for his master, King Zoser.

Now, it would seem to you very queer for a man to spend twenty years of his life in building a magnificent house to hold his body

BUILDING THE GREAT PYRAMIDS

We are sometimes puzzled to know how the Egyptians constructed the pyramids with the simple tools they had. We know that they built an incline leading to the top of the structure, and that the stones were dragged up this causeway and set in place. The feverish activity with which the work was carried on is here seen. The nation must have been well organized and prosperous to have undertaken so gigantic a project.

after its death, would it not? Yet, since the pyramids are merely enormous tombs, that is what the Egyptian pharaohs (fär'ō), beginning with Zoser, spent their best energies in doing. Before this, pharaohs had built great tombs, but they were poor affairs of brick or stone, nothing like the tremendous structures of Zoser and the kings who followed him. Imhotep planned and directed the building of the first pyramid, which is called the "terraced pyramid," because it is built with zigzag edges, like steps, and is not finished off so neatly as are the later pyramids.

The Egyptians did not believe that death was the end of a man. They believed that there was life after death, and around that belief they built a whole religion, the religion of Osiris (ō-sī'rĭs), the god of the hereafter, and of the "ka," the vital force or spirit of man. To take care of the "ka" (kä) after the body's death, the body itself must be preserved, and this was done so skilfully that the mummies, or preserved bodies, of the Egyptian kings and queens still show us very clearly what the rulers looked like. This belief in the continuance of life after the body's death was the reason for the pyramids, and for all the elaborate burial customs of the Egyptians. There was even a "Book of the Dead," intended to direct the soul as to its conduct in the world to come, and to

SOME OF THE GODS OF ANCIENT EGYPT

The ancient Egyptians drew these pictures of the gods they worshipped. It was their belief that in the beginning there had been only a great ocean, but that finally upon it an egg appeared which hatched into the god Re, who is shown at 5. He was also thought of as a hawk, and was represented by a disk with outspread wings, a design one often sees to-day. Re, they believed, gave birth to the earth and the heavens, who in turn produced the gods Isis and Osiris. Osiris, shown at 2, was god of the dead and of the life-bringing Nile, and to him his wife Isis, shown at 1, bore a son Horus, who ruled the earth. He is shown at 3, and his bird, too, was the hawk. Ptah was the god of artisans and artists; he is shown at 6. At 4 is the god Khnemu, the creator of gods and mankind.

give it certain charms to use in the event of meeting with danger.

But the pyramids also show us that Egypt was at last really one country. It took the work of a whole united nation to build such royal tombs, and for nearly two hundred years after Zoser the Egyptian people lent themselves to this pious task. The years from 2980 to about 2800 B.C. saw the setting up of the pyramids we see and marvel at to-day. The Greeks saw them and marvelled at them over two thousand years ago. They placed the pyramids among the seven wonders of the world; and they are the only one of the seven that we still have to-day. The others have all disappeared, except for a few fragmentary remains, but the pyramids will stand for ages to come, to remind us of the Egyptians' faith in a life after death.

If Zoser and Imhotep began the building of pyramids, it was Khufu (2900 B.C.) who built the largest of them. The Greeks called this man Cheops (kē'ŏps), and perhaps you have heard of him by this name; but his real Egyptian name was Khufu (koo'foo). His great pyramid covered nearly thirteen acres. Khufu called it "Khut" (koot), which means "Glory," and it certainly deserves its name. It is much higher than any building in London and is 7,745 feet square at the base. A hundred thousand men had to work for twenty years to build up the huge pile. No

The Great Sphinx dates from the time of the pyramids and is known to have been the portrait of one of the pharaohs, though of which one we do not know. It was given the body of a lion by way of showing the ruler's power, and is thought to have been set up to guard the Nile Valley. The statue is 189 feet long, and is carved in the solid rock. The picture above shows the conqueror Napoleon regarding this great and impressive figure that has outlived so many empires—the monument of an Egyptian king whose very name is lost.

other building in the world is so heavy. And yet the stones are so beautifully fitted together that we can barely see where they are joined.

Khufu Changes Engineers

Students of history nowadays think that Khufu changed engineers when his pyramid was half built, because the top half is not quite so beautifully done as the lower half. But the very greatest engineers of our day marvel at the skill and patience which are shown in the building of this mighty mass of stone, in days when no modern machinery had been invented.

Was Khufu's pyramid building a waste of time? In some ways it seems so, for in itself no tomb, however splendid, could be worth all the mighty effort this Egyptian king gave to it. But in building the pyramid many good results were achieved. Roads were opened up; mines and quarries were sought out and worked; trade with other countries was carried on; and Egyptian artists and skilled workmen were given a chance to develop and to display their skill. So we cannot say that Khufu was a waster of his country's wealth, even if the chief aim of the work was not worth all the labour that was expended on it.

Altogether nine pyramids, at Gizeh (gē′zĕ), mark the resting places of the bodies of Khufu and the kings who reigned before and after him in Egypt. Near them is the famous Sphinx (sfĭngks). This is simply a huge rock measuring 189 feet in length and 70 feet in height, which was carved—no one knows by whom—into a stone lion with the face of a man, and with a shrine between its two paws. At one time the Sphinx was painted red.

When Priests Ruled Kings

You remember that the sun was a god in Egypt. His name was Re (rā), and soon after the reign of Khufu his religion became more and more powerful, until finally the priests of Re were able to tell the king what he might or might not do, and even sometimes to say who should be king.

Each king, these priests said, must take a new name of which the name Re was a part, and before this name must be placed the title "Son of Re." Beside the royal palace, which was still at the "White Wall" near the city called Memphis, was to be a magnificent temple to the sun, where the god could be worshipped with due ceremony. Since the king was called "Son of Re," he became in a way a god, and was to be worshipped in much the same way as Re himself. At this time the sun god gained a political power in Egypt which lasted for many years.

When the Sun God was Challenged

Many kings came and went during this period of sun worship, but they were not very strong rulers, or they would not have let themselves be governed by the priests of Re. The chiefs or rulers of the towns or districts, who since the time of Menes had been nothing but king's officers, began to feel therefore that now was a good time to recover some of the power which they had lost. They became stronger and stronger, until finally they were able to establish a new king who would not be so completely ruled by Re.

Among these later rulers of the Old Kingdom, whose story you are reading, were Mernere (mûr′ně-rā) and his half brother Pepi II. Pepi (pěp′ē) is interesting because he was king for ninety-four years—the longest reign in the history of any country. Mernere ruled only four years, but the two reigns together saw an undertaking which you may think better than building pyramids. It was that of exploring new and distant countries.

You remember that Egypt ended—or began—at the first cataract on the River Nile, and so, about 2575 B.C., Mernere built a canal through which boats might pass up and down safely. Near this first cataract was the island we call Elephantine (ěl′ě-făn-tī′ně), and it was Uni and Harkhuf, two of the lords of this island, who became the earliest explorers in history, first under Mernere and later under Pepi II.

Both of these explorers, Uni and Harkhuf, have left us the story of their adventures, which must have been as thrilling as any we read about to-day. They pushed eastward into the countries beyond the Red Sea, and beyond the first cataract they went southward into the heart of Africa, bringing back loads of treasures to delight the heart of the king.

The present which most pleased the little boy king, Pepi II, was an African pigmy, or dwarf, brought by Harkhuf from one of these trips. When Harkhuf wrote to tell the child pharaoh of the prize, Pepi II wrote back, "My majesty desires to see this dwarf more than the gifts of Sinai and of Punt." There was much more in this letter, which pleased Harkhuf so much that he had it inscribed on his tomb on the island of Elephantine.

Altogether the Old Kingdom lasted a thousand years, from Menes in 3400 to about 2400 B.C., when it fell into decay. Perhaps the kingship was made weaker by the long rule of Pepi II, who in his old age cannot have been a very strong king. Anyhow, the Old Kingdom with all its glories passed away about 2400 B.C., and Egypt again became a series of separate districts lying one after another along the Nile.

(CONTINUED ON PAGE 101)

The mummy of Mut-em-Mennu, priestess of Amon-Re at Thebes. A heavy curse was laid by the Egyptian priests upon anyone who should disturb a dead man's grave.

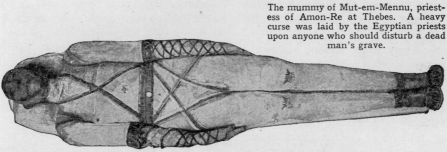

By courtesy of the British Museum

(THE SOLUTIONS TO THESE PUZZLES WILL BE FOUND ON PAGE 100 OF THIS VOLUME)

THE PUZZLED FARMER
No. 1

Once upon a time a farmer set out to market with a goose, a fox, and a basket of wheat. When he came to the river he found there only an empty tub, so small that he could carry but one of his articles across with him at a time. Now if the fox was left alone with the goose, he would surely devour her, and if the goose was left with the wheat, she would eat it up. How did the farmer get them all across safely?

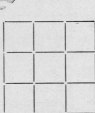

THE MAGIC SQUARES
No. 2

Can you rub out eight lines of this figure and leave only two squares?

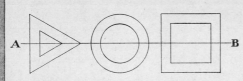

THE DISAPPEARING DOT

Hold this book about a foot away from your eyes. Close your right eye and look at the X — with your left eye. Now move the book slowly towards your eyes. At first you will see the black dot, too, though you are looking at the X — but at a certain point the black dot will disappear. This is because there is a blind spot in each of our eyes, and the dot disappears when it is in focus with that spot. As you move the book towards your eyes, the dot will appear again.

THE PUZZLING MATCHES
No. 3

Take six matches and break two of them into equal halves. Now by using the four unbroken matches and the four halves of the two broken ones, make three squares of equal area.

A ▷ ◯ ▢ B

CAN YOU DO THIS TRICK?
No. 4

With a pencil start at point A, above, and trace a route to point B without going over any line twice or lifting your pencil.

THE ORCHARD FENCE
No. 5

Can you fence off this orchard by drawing two straight lines in such a way that there will be four plots all of the same size and shape with three trees in a plot?

The CHILDHOOD of MUSIC

The Early Christian Church was Like a Cradle in Which Music Grew Until It Could Sally Forth and Travel Through Europe on the Lips of Minstrels and Troubadours

(CONTINUED FROM PAGE 12)

WHEN little knots of brave and earnest people gathered together, some nineteen centuries ago, to worship God in the way that Jesus Christ had taught them, they had no choirs and organs, no priests and ministers, no churches or cathedrals. Sometimes they had the sky for a roof; at other times they crowded into some-

THE PATRON SAINT OF MUSIC

Artists have always loved to paint St. Cecilia, patron saint of music and of the blind. She is usually shown with some musical instrument, and often is crowned with flowers. Legend tells us that she was a beautiful and talented Roman maiden who became converted to Christianity when to be a Christian was very dangerous. Her father betrothed her to a noble Roman named Valerian, and Cecilia's heart longed for his conversion. On the evening of her wedding day she is said to have asked Valerian to take a walk along the Appian Way, a magnificent road leading out from Rome. Here the young man met the aged Bishop Urban, and suddenly was granted a marvellous vision. He was instantly converted to Christianity, and was baptized by the bishop. The legend tells us that upon his return to Cecilia both she and her husband were crowned with flowers by an angel. But soon the emperor's officers sought them out, and put them to death, in about A.D. 180.

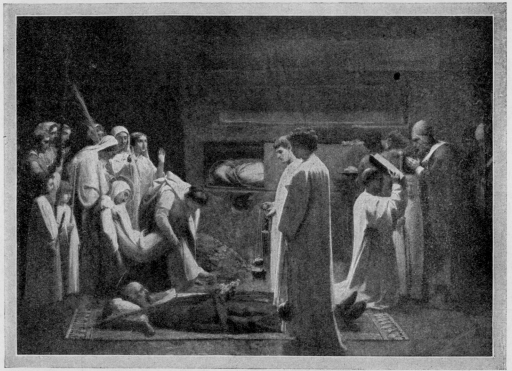

It was upon occasions like this one that the early Christians sang their noblest hymns. The artist has shown the touching burial of some Christians. In an underground chamber of the catacombs friends have gathered to bury their remains in little niches which have been hollowed out in the wall for the purpose.

one's house; and all too often they had to hide in caverns underground to save their very lives.

But they were full of faith and deep joy at the new meaning life had taken on for them, and so no fear of danger could keep them from bursting into song. For if you are very glad, you find an air upon your lips almost before you know it. And if you are just a little frightened, or are in fear of something which you are expecting to take place, there will be nothing quite so good to keep your courage up as a noble tune. Soldiers have always known this. And the persecuted Christians were likely to sing whenever they found themselves gathered together.

The First Church Music

But what were the hymns in which they voiced their joy and faith and resolution? Certainly none of those we sing to-day. For our church music, like all our religious ceremonies, has a long history behind it. No, they had to do just what we should have to do if we were starting a new religion. They took the tunes they knew and wrote new words for them.

Old Greek Modes Employed

Now, wherever Christians met—in Rome, in Greece, in Asia Minor—the only music they knew was the music the Greeks had invented. No other people in the ancient world had understood the art so well; the Romans had never done more than borrow Grecian music. So all the old Greek "modes," or different kinds of scales from which tunes could be put together, were used to make up the tunes the early Christians borrowed and those they invented later. Those hymns were no more than airs, chanted in unison, or perhaps an octave apart—no one had ever heard of chords, or of our modern part singing. Like all the early songs, they would probably seem very queer and meaningless to us, for they rambled about without ever getting anywhere, and could end at almost

4

any point. This was because the singers did not think of the music apart from the words, and the rhythm of the music, therefore, was that of ordinary speech. It was little more than a kind of melodious talking. But we may be sure that those early worshippers sang with as much fervour as we put into the singing of our own hymns.

As the centuries passed, the church service was growing more and more complex. Certain songs had come to be a fixed part of it, and new music was being written all the time. Naturally some of it was not so good as the rest. In order that it might be kept at as high a level as possible, certain very strict rules for it were laid down by Bishop Ambrose of Milan in the fourth century; and again by the famous Pope Gregory I about the year 600.

Gregory established fourteen "modes," or scales, and all the church music had to be written in some one of those modes. He thought he was reviving the old Greek modes, and called them by the Greek names, although we now know that he read them upside down, and gave every mode a name that was exactly the opposite of the one the Greeks had given it. Like the Greek

This musical score may look strange to us to-day, but it was a great advance on earlier methods of writing music. Of the first of these, probably invented by the peoples of the East, we know very little. But when music became a part of the church service, various schemes of notation were invented. These were all systems of dots and crooks written just above the words of the song. They were called the "neumes," and on the next page you will see a chart of various styles of neumes. But such systems were most unsatisfactory, and many improvements were tried. Different colours were used to indicate different letters, and gradually lines were added to show the pitch. You will notice that the staff above has only four lines. At one time four lines were used for sacred music, and five for other kinds. You will notice, too, that no measures are indicated, for that was never done before the twelfth century. All the music up to quite a late date was in triple time, which was thought to be perfect because it was the number of the Trinity. By the end of the fourteenth century the strange-looking neumes had entirely given way before the square black notes which you see in this page from an old antiphonary (ăn-tĭf'ŏ-nă-rĭ), or book containing the responses sung in church. In the fifteenth century lozenge-shaped notes were added, and tails showed the time value. It was not long then before our modern system was developed.

modes, they called for music that was always just an air and nothing more. No air might make use of notes outside the mode, or scale, in which it happened to be written—there were no sharps or flats. But the scales were themselves quite varied. Only one was like our major scale to-day. The airs, which we call "plain-song," were always sung to Latin words by men's and boys' voices.

The instrument in the picture below is a lyre, the favourite instrument of the Greeks, who had it from the Egyptians and passed it on to many later nations.

Many of those fine old Gregorian (grē-gôr'ĭ-ăn) chants may be heard in the Catholic Church to this day, and most of our modern music has descended from them. If an ancient Greek could wander into a service to-day where those old plain-songs were being sung, he would find in them music that he understood. Our modern music, on the other hand, would completely bewilder him.

The rules of Gregory the Great were so strict that music changed very little for at least three hundred years. For, although the people always sang songs, which sprang up no one knew whence, those "folk songs," as we call them, were felt to be immoral, and were often forbidden by the Church. So they did not help much in the growth of music, except that

Elements	Name of Neume
Grave accent	Punctum
Acute accent	Virga
Acute and grave accent combined	Clivis or Clinis
Grave and acute accent combined	Podatus or Pes
Two grave and one acute accent	Scandicus
Acute accent and two grave accents	Climacus
Grave, acute, and grave accents	Torculus
Acute, grave, and acute accents	Porrectus
Grave, acute, and one or more grave accents	Podatus subpunctis or sub-bipunctis
Acute, two grave, and one acute accents	Climacus resupinus
Two grave, one acute, and one grave accents	Scandicus flexus
Two grave, one acute, and two grave accents	Scandicus subpunctis or sub-bipunctis
Grave, acute, grave, acute accents	Torculus resupinus
Acute, grave, acute, grave accents	Porrectus flexus
Acute, grave, acute, and two grave accents	Porrectus subpunctis

Column headings (for the notation examples, left to right): Elementary Form · St. Gall IX Cent. · North Italy X Cent. · Germany XI Cent. · Lombardy XI Cent. · Aquitaine XI Cent. on one line · Germany XII Cent. · Gothic XIII Cent. · Sarum Gradual XIII Cent. on four lines · Gothic XIV Cent. · South Italy XV Cent. · Ratisbon 1889 · Solesmes 1902

Reproduced from Grove's "Dictionary of Music" by permission of the Macmillan Co.

By following this chart from left to right, you will see how the strange dots and crooks called neumes gradually developed into our present musical notation.

67

the Church occasionally borrowed a tune from them.

In those early times none of the musical instruments was of much use for anything except accompaniment; and nearly all the trained musicians were to be found singing and composing for the church services. So the Church ruled the world of music. Under its guidance the system of writing music was greatly improved. During the earlier Middle Ages music had been set down in a sort of system of musical shorthand known as the "neumes" (nūmz). It was very complicated and very vague, and was hard to read even in those days. Many specimens still survive that we cannot puzzle out at all. But about the year 1000 an Italian monk named Guido of Arezzo (gōō-ē′dō of ä-rĕt′sō) perfected a method of writing music that is— with some improvements— virtually the one we use to-day. Since it was now comparatively easy to write and easy to read accurately, music immediately began to progress faster than it had ever done before. Great choruses were formed, and more and more people began to compose.

And gradually those big choruses of men's and boys' voices grew impatient of always singing in unison. For one thing, it was not easy to manage. The sopranos and the heavy basses could always sing an octave apart, but even that did not help the voices in between the two—the altos and the baritones. Everything was too high or too low for them.

So at last the choristers hit upon the idea of making some of the voices sing at a pitch between the high and low—usually five notes

Photo by Alinari

This picture of the Virgin and Child is by the famous Venetian painter Bellini (bĕl-lē′nē), who lived in the latter part of the fifteenth century. He has shown us three musicians of his day, all playing upon their instruments. The one at the left is holding a rebeck, an ancestor of the violin. This little instrument could trace its descent back through an early stringed instrument used in the East to a thousand years before Christ. This was called the rebab, and was brought into Europe by the Moors, though it may also have come in by way of Constantinople. The other two instruments are lutes, popular throughout the Middle Ages and tracing their ancestry back to the rebabs that were the ancestors of the rebeck. The lute, however, was not played with a bow, as was the rebeck. It was plucked, after the manner of our modern mandoline and guitar.

above the tune. For at first it was the bass only that kept the air, not the soprano, as to-day. And then voices were added at still another level.

The result would have been unsatisfactory to our modern ears, for although every effort was made to avoid discords, some of the sounds were quite unpleasing; and there never was anything that we should think of as a fine re-sounding chord. We should not have liked it at all! The singers simply sang their parts together, each part sawing away at the tune in another key, and trying as well as it could to keep out of its neighbour's way. Sometimes they were horribly out of tune and sometimes they got along quite well; but there were always several parts singing, each one on its own separate level, or "register," instead of each part doing its share to make up a harmonious whole, as in our own part songs.

But how amazing it must have sounded to the congregations, who had never heard anything but an air of unison before! People were so patient with the discords that the composers were encouraged to make every sort of experiment, just to see how things would sound. They tried letting the various voices sing the same air, but with each one coming in a little late, one after the other. That was known as a "canon." A very famous one called "Sumer is icumen in" was written in England in the thirteenth century and is sometimes sung even to-day. And we still follow the canon plan in the "rounds" we sing—such, for example, as "Three Blind Mice."

Then those earnest experimenters tried the

A SCENE FROM WAGNER'S FAMOUS OPERA, "THE MASTERSINGERS"

This is a scene from Wagner's famous opera, "The Mastersingers of Nuremberg," which takes place at a time when the old-fashioned music of the Middle Ages was giving way before the richer music that was to follow. The young knight Walter is in love with Eva, but her father has said that no one may marry her save a mastersinger, that is, one who is master of all the complex and foolish rules of musical composition then in fashion. Walter is seen here undergoing a test to prove that he possesses this special knowledge.

startling plan of making their choirs sing two different tunes at once. Now, it is true that there are a few tunes that will go together very well. "The Spanish Cavalier" and "Solomon Levi" sound quite charming when sung at the same time. But when this was tried for the first time, in the Middle Ages, the tunes did not harmonize at all. They were just rammed together, and if one singer saw a discord ahead, he hurried up to get past that danger spot before the other singer should have arrived there. Words, tune, time, everything was different for each voice. In fact, there was very little sense of time in those care-free days. Singers were more eager to keep out of one another's way than to keep together.

But gradually men were learning. They were still tied down to those old-fashioned Gregorian modes, and each part had its own separate tune, whilst one of the lower parts carried a more important tune than the rest. But their ears were getting used to hearing two, three, or four sounds of different pitch at the same time, and they were learning when such combinations were pleasant and when they were not. In other words,

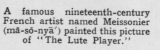

A famous nineteenth-century French artist named Meissonier (mā-sō-nyā′) painted this picture of "The Lute Player."

they were beginning to understand what "harmony" is. And it is harmony that makes our magnificent modern music possible —our choruses, our operas, and our great symphonies. The discovery of its laws brought about the greatest revolution of all in the history of music.

And men were finding out other things, too. As they learned to fit several parts together, they had to find some way for all to arrive at the end at the same time, or to arrive at a given chord together. It was not an easy thing to do, when each part was singing its own separate tune. You need only try it to see how hard it is. But gradually they learned how to divide their

songs up into short lengths, or "measures," each lasting a certain length of time, which they told off in beats, and allowed for each measure. Then all the parts could march along abreast and all keep in step. In that way "time" came to be an important feature in all music. For nowadays a piece may be almost lacking in "rhythm," or swing, but it is always played in some kind of "time."

And besides all this they were gradually getting rid of those old modes—and it was high time. While the modes had been most useful as a beginning, and had helped to give a delightful variety to the old Greek and church melodies, they were now a kind of strait-jacket in which music found itself confined. For harmony could not develop freely while it was against the rules to use sharps and flats in your piece. It was almost as if a painter should decide that he must never make use of certain colours.

These changes took place quite naturally and gradually. As various tunes, or "voices," were sung together, the singers discovered that by using sharps and flats discords could often be avoided. No mode had ever contained any written sharps or flats, and when these were added the modes began to merge and vanish, until composers found that all they needed was one "major" scale and a "minor" scale. It happened that the scale they found most suited to their purpose was the same as the old Greek Lydian (lĭd′ĭ-ăn) mode; and the "minor" scale was the same as the old Hypodorian (hĭp′ō-dōr′ĭ-ăn) mode.

When Several Tunes were Sung Together

Towards the close of the Middle Ages some very beautiful music was being written, for a great deal had been learned about the art. All church music was of the kind we have

Not only was John Milton a great poet, he was also an accomplished musician, an art he acquired from his father, who was prominent in the world of music. He is here seen playing the organ at Hampton Court, while Oliver Cromwell, the lord protector of the Commonwealth, and his family listen with rapt attention.

described—several tunes, or "voices," going along together. It was called "counterpoint," for when a second voice was added to the main tune, it had to be made to fit, note by note—or "point against point"—which explains why that style of composition was so named.

Music Spreads Beyond the Church

But the musicians were now no longer found only in church choirs. The folk songs had been growing more and more beautiful, and the Church ceased frowning upon the singing of them. In the south of France the aristocratic poets and musicians called troubadours (troo′bȧ-door) delighted the knights and ladies with original songs. It was not beneath the dignity of kings to compose in this way; Richard the Lion-hearted was one of the troubadours.

In the north of France the "trouvères" (troo-vâr′) were not so highly born, and perhaps for that reason they took their music more seriously; they were more like our professional musicians. One of the greatest of them was a hunchback named Adam de la Hale (about 1230–1288). He

wrote a great many little three-part songs called "rondels" (rŏn′dĕl) and "rondeaux" (rŏn′dō), and was considered a learned musician. The Englishman John Dunstable, some two centuries later, was one of the great musicians of his day; and he was followed by a whole group of able composers in the Netherlands, of whom a man named Josquin des Prés (zhŏs-kăN′ dā prā) was the best. He has been called the first great composer.

Germany's "Singers of Love"

And so music spread. England had her wandering minstrels, who sang in noble hall or in the market-place. Germany had her "minnesingers" (mĭn′ĕ-sĭng′ẽr), highborn musicians who, like the troubadours, sang their own poems to while away the heavy hours for knights and ladies. The name means "singers of love"; and for accompaniment they used the romantic harp.

Wagner, in his great opera "Tannhäuser" (tän′hoi-zẽr), shows how the minnesingers held their "Tournaments of Song" at famous castles in the twelfth and thirteenth centuries, and gives us a portrait of the greatest of them, Wolfram von Eschenbach (vŏl′främ fŏn ĕsh'ĕn-bäK). And in another opera, "The Mastersingers," Wagner shows us Hans Sachs (zäKs), a famous cobbler-poet who lived in the early sixteenth century and belonged to one of the musical guilds. These had grown up among the humbler people in the German cities and had taken the place of the minnesingers.

Musicians Become More Important

A guild was a good deal like a trade union; and the mastersingers were members of various guilds of musicians. They held vocal competitions in the schools and churches and in the open meadows, and their contests were governed by very strict rules. You see, as the people learned to love music more and more, the musicians grew to be more and more important persons. Before 1550 we have names of men who were writing or singing music in all the countries of Europe—among them Martin Luther himself.

It is easy to see that all these hard-working musicians would not long be satisfied with their existing instruments. They soon set to work to improve the ones they had and to invent new ones. They greatly improved the lute, a very old instrument somewhat like a guitar; its blunt little notes accompanied the songs of the troubadours and of the love-lorn maidens who are always represented at the windows of frowning castle towers.

What the First Organs were Like

But men worked hardest to perfect the organ, for the lute was used only by individual musicians, while the organ was used in the church services. We have some very amusing old fifth-century pictures of various kinds of organs. How quaint and strange those little instruments must have been! The pipes, made of wood or metal, were bound together in every possible shape, and the wind was sometimes supplied by as many as four sets of bellows, each set blown by a different man, who had to wear iron

shoes, for he trod the bellows down. Before the keyboard was invented each organ often needed two players; and when an instrument did have keys, it sometimes took the whole of a man's fist to force one down.

When Organists were Strong Men

A writer on music has given us an amusing account of what it must have been like to play on the organ built about 957 in Winchester Cathedral: "We can imagine the organists—all men picked for their physique—darting madly to and fro at the keyboard, screwed up to the excitement of smiting the right key at the right moment, and attacking it with all the force of their bodies gathered into their thickly-gloved hands; the toiling, moiling crowd of blowers behind, treading away for dear life to keep the wind-chest full; the frightful din of the heavy timber mechanism, creaking and groaning like a four-decker in a heavy sea."

And yet many of the people living at that time thought that the tone of those awkward instruments was very sweet and pure.

Music's Greatest Messenger

In the ninth and tenth centuries organs were wonderfully improved, and the big churches and cathedrals everywhere in Europe began to install the best that could be made. It is hard to imagine what a service must have been without them, for no other instrument can compare with them for richness and solemnity of tone. It is probably true that the organ has done more than any other instrument to spread the knowledge and love of music.

And now we shall bid farewell to the Middle Ages, with its music-loving monks, who were the teachers; its romantic troubadours and minnesingers, who made music the fashion; and its great contests of song. It laid the broad foundation for the fine music that was to come. It was, indeed, in the days that followed that the great art flowered into what is known as the Golden Age of Music, about which you will read later.

(CONTINUED ON PAGE 185)

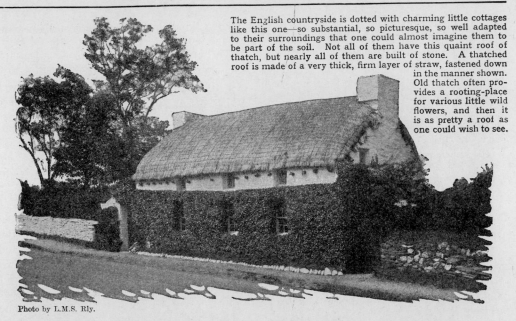

The English countryside is dotted with charming little cottages like this one—so substantial, so picturesque, so well adapted to their surroundings that one could almost imagine them to be part of the soil. Not all of them have this quaint roof of thatch, but nearly all of them are built of stone. A thatched roof is made of a very thick, firm layer of straw, fastened down in the manner shown. Old thatch often provides a rooting-place for various little wild flowers, and then it is as pretty a roof as one could wish to see.

Photo by L.M.S. Rly.

What WE NEED *to* BUILD *a* HOUSE

We Have to Dig and Melt and Bake and Saw to Get the Things of Which Our Homes are Made

WHAT would you do if you were caught out in the woods some rainy night without a tent? If you had a hatchet, you could cut branches off the trees and try to make a roof over your head; and you can make a fairly good roof in this way, if you know how.

Long ago, before our ancestors had any tents or houses, they often adopted this method. Of course, they lived in a cave when they could find one, and they often dug their own cave when they did not have one ready-made. But in time they also learned to cut off branches from the trees and build crude huts with them. Yet they were a long time learning how to build and what materials to use for building.

At first they just used poles and branches laced together and sometimes covered with mud that dried in the sun. Slowly they found out how to make use of other materials. After very many years they had learned how to utilize the four chief materials—wood, stone, brick, and straw. Much later still, in Roman times, they also possessed tile, cement, plaster, and other useful materials.

In the early days before the dawn of history, men had to use the wood just as it came from the tree, in logs and poles. We still follow this method whenever we build a log-cabin. But long ago there was no way of sawing out such planks as we have now, for the best tools to be had were nothing but pieces of sharpened stone. Many centuries later men were making saws of bronze or copper, and with these they could cut out planks, though it was hard work and took a long time. Only within the past two thousand years have we had saws made of steel; and only in the past century or so have we operated them with anything but our own hands. And stone is far more difficult to saw than wood.

In a rocky country it was easy to pick up enough stones and pile them into some sort of wall, but to make a house the stones had to be fitted close together, and that meant chipping them until they were smooth, or "dressed." Yet without any steel or iron chisels the patient men of old would sometimes shape their stones as smoothly as if they had been cut by the best machinery.

4*

73

In many parts of the world there are ruins of great stone-works made by the hands of men long since forgotten.

The most useful of all the old materials for building was brick. Bricks were small and light, and easy to handle. They were made of clay mixed with sand

Like other savages, an Apache made his house of materials that lay close at hand and were easy to gather. Here is one of his houses under construction, from the first rude framework of slender boughs to the finished te- pee, or tent. It is clear that such a home was more picturesque than com- fortable.

and baked until they were hard. In Bible times the workers put chopped straw in the bricks to hold the clay together.

Bricks are found in many of the oldest buildings. Six thousand years ago the houses and walls of great Babylon were built of brick. Wherever stone was hard to find, brick would be used instead.

Savages would often use branches of trees, and straw and big leaves in making their huts. Some of them do it to this very day. And they would often make small houses out of clay baked by the sun into what we call "adobe" (ă-dō'bĕ). The Arizona Indians still build houses of that material.

How We Make Our Brick

If a man from the olden time could see one of our great buildings of to-day, or even one of our modest dwellings, he might find it hard to believe that they were made out of the same materials that he used to have. Although we have many new materials, most of our building is done in wood and brick and stone. And yet our brick, or even our wood and stone, is so different from the

ancient kind as to seem almost like some- thing new.

The bricks of early times were long, thin, uneven slabs of clay, and often poorly baked. The bricks we have now are always well baked, and of a standard size and quality, though there are many different grades and kinds.

The clay for bricks can be found almost any- where. In England there are brick factories near most large cities. When the clay comes to the factory it is mixed with sand and water until it makes a stiff mud. The mixing is done in a machine with a queer name—the "pug-mill." It is something like a great churn, with blades that whirl round and round through the mud to do the mixing.

Then the mud is forced through a small tunnel just the size of a brick. So out at the other end comes a long stream of stiff mud which needs only to be cut off into the right lengths for bricks. And the cutting is done by little wires that come down and go through the stream of mud at the right moment. The whole operation is done so quickly that a single machine can turn out 100,000 bricks in a day.

There is another kind of machine that

74

In the upper part of the picture is a modern brick-yard, showing the dome-topped kilns in which the bricks are baked. Along the bottom may be seen four bricks which were made several thousands of years ago in Ur, Abraham's birthplace. The tablet-like marks that you can see stamped into their sides tell us their age.

presses the mud into moulds, a hundred or more at a time, and turns it out as brick.

But it is not very good brick yet. It would turn into mud again in a heavy rain, and wash away. That was the trouble which the first men to use brick had with it. By and by they learned that it could be made to stand any storm if it were well burned first.

When the bricks are first cut they are carried by long belts to sheds where they are piled to dry. After a few days, or possibly a few weeks, they must be burned in a kiln to harden them. A kiln is really just a great hot oven. In it the bricks are stacked with little spaces between to let the heat get to every part of them, and there they stay to burn for a week or more. Common bricks are burned to a red heat; fire-bricks—the kind that we use in furnaces which smelt iron—are made white-hot.

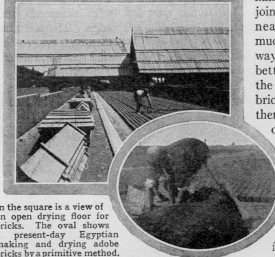

In the square is a view of an open drying floor for bricks. The oval shows a present-day Egyptian making and drying adobe bricks by a primitive method.

When this has been done, the bricks are ready to start out on their career of usefulness.

Bricks are laid with mortar to make walls. Every brick should lie half-way across the joint of the two beneath it—they are much stronger in this way, and they look better. We may make the whole wall out of brick, or we may put them only on the outside, to look well, while the real wall behind them is made of wood or steel. In many a modern building the steel frame stands all the strain of the walls, and the bricks are put on for appearance and protection from the weather. That is called a "curtain" wall.

Brick is not the only form of clay we use in building. Since the early days of Greece, tile has also been employed for roofs and floors and decorations. Nowadays we sometimes make whole buildings out of tile, or "terra cotta," as we call it; the words are Italian and simply mean "cooked earth." And our tiles may be made in rough, hollow blocks to use inside the walls and under floors, or they may be carefully moulded and shaped into designs for the outside ornament of houses. For ornamental work the tiles are made to order; they are often coloured and are always given a hard, glazed finish. The rougher tiles are made by machinery, more or less like bricks, several thousands at a time.

The Tiles on Our Bathroom Wall

The tiles on a bathroom wall are commonly made of white clay and given a glazed surface. All clay tiles have to be burned, just as bricks are, for five or six days. If they are to be glazed in addition, they are then painted with a glazing mixture and baked again. The glazing mixture is made out of chemicals that form a shiny film over the tile as it is baked.

Of stone there are many kinds that we can use in building—marble, limestone, granite, sandstone, and slate. All of these come out of quarries. Often the quarries follow the stone ledges for hundreds of feet into the ground.

It is still heavy work to quarry stone, although we now have electrical machinery to make it easier. We take out great blocks of granite or marble by drilling holes all round them and cutting them loose. Then we haul them out of the quarries with electric cranes. We have taken out blocks weighing over sixty tons, but commonly they weigh about fifteen. Imagine the labour it must have required to dig out stone enough to build a pyramid!

Giving Stone its Shape

When the rough stones have been lifted out of the quarry, they are carried off to a mill. There they are worked into any shape that may be wanted. If a long round column is desired, the block of stone is put into a great lathe and turned round and round. As it turns, the rough corners are gradually ground completely away until a smooth round shaft is left.

If thin slabs are wanted, the stone blocks must be sawn into strips. The saw we use for cutting stone has no teeth. It is a band of steel that works back and forth on the stone while sand and water are poured on it. The gritty sand rolls between the iron and the rock, and cuts a groove just as cleanly as a knife.

Still more remarkable for cutting stone is the diamond saw. This is a disk of steel with diamonds set all round its cutting edge. There is nothing that will cut like a diamond; and as this saw whirls round some six hundred times a minute, it shaves through the hardest marble as if the stone were mere wood.

Then there are machines for smoothing

Here is a photograph of a model that shows how an Eskimo's igloo is built out of snow. This type of snow tent can be built in a very short time, and with care can be made quite weatherproof and reasonably comfortable.

1—Laplander's deer-skin house for summer weather.

2—Native hut of reeds and straw, West Africa.

3—The Nigerians, West Africa, have learned to make mud-plastered houses.

4—Pioneer log cabin, with hand-made shingles and ladder leading up to loft.

5—West African native hut, made of reeds, straw, vines, and other dried vegetation.

6—Laplander's winter cottage, made of mud over a wooden framework.

blocks of stone, for polishing them, and for cutting figures and designs in them. But any special design, such as you may see at the top of a column or over many church doors, has to be carved in the stone by hand. In the old days the sculptor did the carving with a chisel and a mallet. Now he has a patent chisel that is operated by compressed air.

Where Our Stone Comes From

A great deal of our granite comes from Aberdeenshire, Cornwall and Cumberland; marble from Devonshire, Yorkshire, Wales and Ireland; and limestone from Durham and Northumberland. Sandstone is obtained from various parts of the British Isles. From the quarries at Portland and Purbeck, in Dorsetshire, we get Portland stone, which is largely used in the construction of public buildings in this country. St. Paul's Cathedral is built of this stone. In Italy there are famous quarries at Carrara (kär-rä′rä) that furnish beautiful marble. And there are other quarries in every country of the world.

Tiles Cut from Stone

There is still another valuable stone used in building. This is slate, the stone we use so much for roofing.

The important thing about slate is that it splits easily into thin strips. It would not be very good for holding up a wall, but is excellent for making a light stone roof. For that purpose the slabs are cut to a small, convenient size, and have two holes drilled in them for the nails that attach them to the wooden framework. They are really just stone tiles, and are usually made to overlap one another to make them watertight.

There is no better roof than one of slate. It never rots or warps, nor is it affected by rain and snow. There is nothing that lasts longer or looks better.

The best quarries are in Wales, but there are others in many other countries of the world. A good deal of stone is wasted in the quarrying, and it takes six tons of rock to yield enough slate to cover a small house.

Houses and Bungalows of Wood

Brick and stone are the best materials for building, because they cannot burn and because they last so long. But in Japan many houses and other buildings are made of wood, and so are many small houses and bungalows in other countries. And very pretty houses can be built of wood.

In our story about lumber we have told how the trees in the great forests are felled and floated down the rivers to the mills where they are sawn into smooth beams and planks, or turned into special shapes for staircases and all kinds of woodwork. Even a wooden house can be built sound and strong enough to last for several centuries.

Steel Bones of Big Buildings

In our great modern buildings very little wood is now used. It would never have the strength to hold them up. For this purpose we need steel and concrete.

Steel is a comparatively new thing for the

It was stone, the most lasting of all construction materials, that the builders chose for this castle centuries ago.

Photo by L.M.S. Rly.

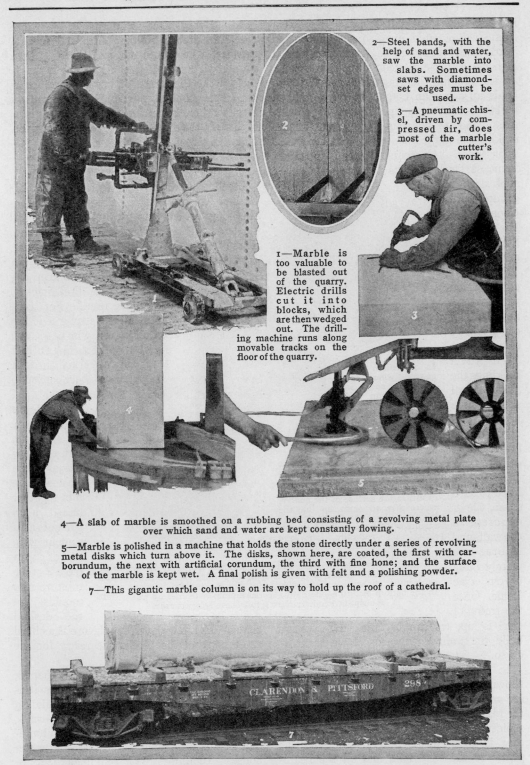

2—Steel bands, with the help of sand and water, saw the marble into slabs. Sometimes saws with diamond-set edges must be used.

3—A pneumatic chisel, driven by compressed air, does most of the marble cutter's work.

1—Marble is too valuable to be blasted out of the quarry. Electric drills cut it into blocks, which are then wedged out. The drilling machine runs along movable tracks on the floor of the quarry.

4—A slab of marble is smoothed on a rubbing bed consisting of a revolving metal plate over which sand and water are kept constantly flowing.

5—Marble is polished in a machine that holds the stone directly under a series of revolving metal disks which turn above it. The disks, shown here, are coated, the first with carborundum, the next with artificial corundum, the third with fine hone; and the surface of the marble is kept wet. A final polish is given with felt and a polishing powder.

7—This gigantic marble column is on its way to hold up the roof of a cathedral.

builder. The first tall house with a steel frame was erected in 1886; yet nowadays nearly every new building over four stories high has a frame of steel. The frame holds up the building just as the frame of bones holds up a human body. So we now have buildings eight or nine stories high with glass windows all round the ground floor, making the whole building look as if it rested upon glass. Of course it really rests on immense steel columns sunk deep into the ground. In Canada and the United States there are buildings of similar construction with as many as eighty or ninety stories.

In such buildings the great steel skeleton goes up first and carries all the load. The other materials — the brick and stone, tile or concrete in the walls and floors—are merely hung upon the frame. Once the frame of steel is up, we can begin at the top and build the walls downwards if we want to do so.

In the story of steel and iron we have shown how the strong steel beams and girders are made and shaped. When we draw up the plans for a big building, we have to make a picture, or "print," of every piece of steel that is going into it. Then we send the prints to the steel mill, and all the beams are made exactly the size and shape we need. Every piece is numbered when it is delivered at our building site; and so they can easily be sorted out and lifted to their proper places. Then the riveters begin to put all the thousands of beams together as the frame mounts up into the sky. And the steel worker, balancing himself on a girder high up in the air, has one of the most exciting and dangerous of all trades.

Making Stone to Suit Our Needs

Steel is used in other forms besides big beams. In most of our fire-proof buildings the floors are held up by thousands of small steel rods that run from column to column. These rods are all buried in the cement, or "concrete," that makes the floors, but it is the rods that keep the concrete from breaking up under its load. For concrete is very strong if it has something on which to rest, but it will break in two if it is only stretched through space between two columns.

Concrete is a stone that man himself has made. When we need it we mix together sand and gravel and cement with water, and pour the mixture into moulds of the desired shape. In a few days the mixture is as hard as stone, and the blocks are ready for the builder.

Natural stone needs to be cut and shaped, but concrete gets its proper shape as it is made. We can even make a whole building out of concrete in one solid piece—walls, floors, and roof. And we often put up buildings in this way, such as factories and warehouses. In almost all big buildings the foundations and the floors are made of concrete.

In a modern slate quarry, where the age-old rock is taken from the ground, a wire is used for cutting down into the stone. This leaves a smooth, clean surface. Blocks weighing six or seven tons apiece are then cut and wedged out of their resting-place, as shown in the top picture. Next they are hoisted by chains to the surface of the quarry, where they are sawn up into the lengths and split to the thicknesses required. This is easily done, for slate slits naturally, and the workers are so highly skilled that they have no trouble in splitting a large block, as shown in the centre picture, into slabs only the thickness of a blackboard. After the slate is split, its surface is smoothed and finished in various ways until the slab is ready for the purpose it has to serve. In the bottom picture is one of the carborundum machines by which slate is shaped when its surface is to be bevelled or curved.

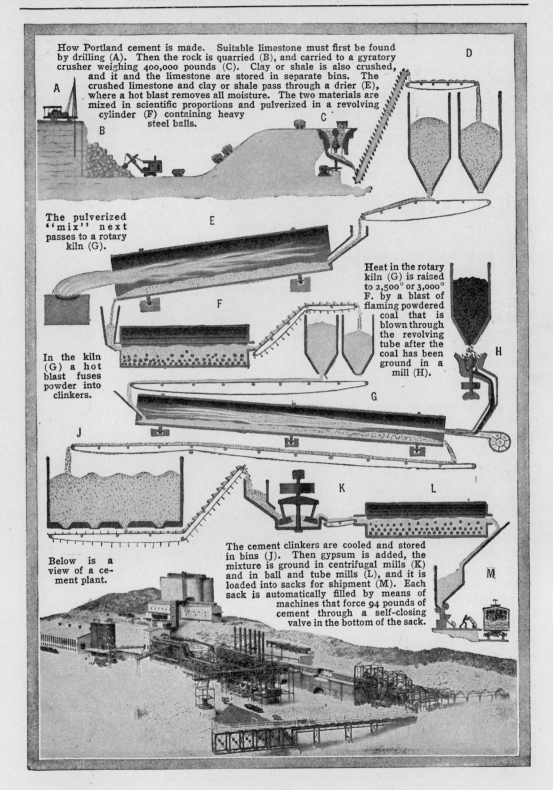

How Portland cement is made. Suitable limestone must first be found by drilling (A). Then the rock is quarried (B), and carried to a gyratory crusher weighing 400,000 pounds (C). Clay or shale is also crushed, and it and the limestone are stored in separate bins. The crushed limestone and clay or shale pass through a drier (E), where a hot blast removes all moisture. The two materials are mixed in scientific proportions and pulverized in a revolving cylinder (F) containing heavy steel balls.

The pulverized "mix" next passes to a rotary kiln (G).

In the kiln (G) a hot blast fuses powder into clinkers.

Heat in the rotary kiln (G) is raised to 2,500° or 3,000° F. by a blast of flaming powdered coal that is blown through the revolving tube after the coal has been ground in a mill (H).

Below is a view of a cement plant.

The cement clinkers are cooled and stored in bins (J). Then gypsum is added, the mixture is ground in centrifugal mills (K) and in ball and tube mills (L), and it is loaded into sacks for shipment (M). Each sack is automatically filled by means of machines that force 94 pounds of cement through a self-closing valve in the bottom of the sack.

This is the way a lime factory would look if we could take pieces out of its walls to see what was going on inside—for it is a model that is shown in the photograph. Limestone, which was formed ages ago from the shells and skeletons of very tiny sea animals, is crushed and burned in a kiln till it gives up part of its substance. What is left we call "quicklime," a material which is used in making plaster and mortar.

The sand and gravel and water, however, would never stick together and make stone all by themselves. It is the cement that holds and hardens them. Long ago the Romans had a kind of cement and used to make concrete — t h e best that we have ever seen—but after their day the world forgot all about it. It was only a little over a century ago that the secret of cement was discovered again, and a new great industry was begun. And now many millions of barrels of cement are made in England every year.

Our modern cement is a powder made of clay and lime. The lime may be obtained from oyster shells, chalk, limestone, and various other things containing lime. The clay and lime are heated in a special kiln until they nearly melt. They come out of the kiln in clinkers, and are then broken up into the powder we use.

Even with all these materials, we should still have poor houses without glass to let in the light and plaster to make the walls white and smooth.

Of the two, plaster is much the older. It was used four thousand years ago in building the pyramids. If you watch a plasterer at work to-day you will notice that he puts on three coats of his material. The first two are rather rough, but the last one, made of different materials, is smooth and white. The first two coats are made of gypsum (jĭp′sŭm) mixed with sand and wood fibre, while the other is made of fine lime mingled with a little plaster of Paris.

Gypsum is a mineral that is usually whitish as it comes out of the earth. Plaster of Paris is gypsum that has been specially heated, dried, and powdered. When we add a little water to it, we have a plaster which may be moulded to any form we like, and which will dry and harden in about ten minutes. The mould-

When we are going to plaster a wall we nail up narrow strips of wood, called laths, with a small space between each strip. Then the plaster is applied to the surface of the laths. It sinks in between the strips, and when it hardens, it holds tight to the laths. This sectional view of a wall is cut down through the laths so that you may see the plaster face securely anchored in the spaces between them.

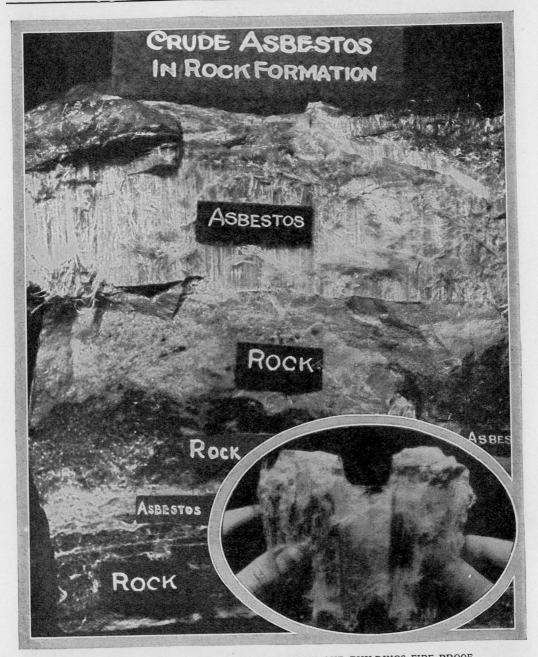

CRUDE ASBESTOS IN ROCK FORMATION

ASBESTOS

ROCK

ROCK

ASBESTOS

ROCK

ASBES

THE STRANGE, SILKY ROCK THAT WILL MAKE OUR BUILDINGS FIRE-PROOF

Asbestos is one of the most remarkable of minerals. Millions of years ago it was made in the earth under terrific heat and pressure. Men in ancient times knew a little about what they thought to be its magical qualities, but it was not until 1870 that people began to realize the value of this strange, silky rock that resists the action of moisture and of many chemicals, and will not catch fire. To-day asbestos is used for a large number of purposes and is of the greatest value as a building material. Roofs made of it are fire-proof. A single truck load of it wrapped round the steam lines in a high-pressure power plant will hold enough heat to save thirty-seven truck-loads of coal a year. Its resistance to heat and chemicals makes it a valuable packing for all sorts of machinery. It is used in the making of cement that must stand high temperatures. It is even made into clothing for firemen. Wherever heat must be preserved and danger of fire overcome, this strange fibrous rock is used. The inset above shows a piece of asbestos as it comes from the rock, before its fibres are sorted and combed and spun and woven. The largest asbestos mines are in Quebec.

ings on our ceilings and other decorations in large halls are commonly made of plaster of Paris.

We have a kind of plaster for use even on the outside of a house. It is called stucco. Usually it is hardened by the addition of cement, and may be coloured a beautiful shade.

Glass is very old, too, and beautiful things were made out of it long ago in Egypt; but its use in windows such as ours dates from comparatively recent times, for we have used it in that way only for some four centuries.

Glass is mostly made of a substance called silica (sĭl′ĭ-kȧ), which we obtain from common sand. It is mixed with lime, soda, salt, and other chemicals, and melted in a furnace for about sixteen hours. It can then be blown into great bubbles. For common window glass we blow an enormous bubble out of thirty or forty pounds of melted glass, and then cut the bubble open to let the glass flatten out on a table. It makes a great sheet, which is heated and heated again before it is ready to be cut into standard sizes for our windows.

The plate glass that we see in large windows is not blown in this way, but is poured out on a great, smooth table in a rough sheet. When it has cooled, it is smoothed and polished by being turned round rapidly against sand and emery polishers. Sometimes it is ground down to half its original thickness before it is perfectly smooth.

These are the main things we use in building. There are many others—wire laths and wire nails, brass locks and hinges, and various other devices. But these are only little things to help us in making our principal materials into what are certainly the most comfortable homes the world has ever seen.

When the white man went to North America he found that the best houses the Indians could build were pueblos. In those crude but picturesque homes constructed of stone or sun-dried brick, a whole village was housed.

Photo by Canadian Government

Four hundred and fifty years have passed, and the pueblos are no longer the pride of North American builders. Their simple forms seem unimportant beside the lofty buildings of Toronto, in Canada. And yet all this soaring modern style has been made possible by the use of just one new building material—steel.

The FIRST MAN to Sail ROUND the WORLD

Although the Gallant Magellan and His Crew were Forced to Feed on Rats and Leather During Their Voyage Round the Globe They Sailed on into the Unknown

MANY of the great explorers went to sea when they were boys, but the first one of them all to sail completely round the world was not a sailor by training. Ferdinand Magellan (må-jĕl'ån) was born, about 1480, some fifty miles from the coast in Portugal. As the son of a poor nobleman, he went to serve as a page at the court when he was fourteen. He was twenty-five before he first put out to sea. Even then he did not go as a sailor, but as a gentleman volunteer in the forces of Almeida (äl-mā'ĕ-dä), who was going to India to take up his appointment as governor of the Portuguese territories.

The voyage round the south of Africa occupied seven long months, and during the dull days Magellan passed the time in learning all he could about seamanship. Little did he dream to what great uses his newly acquired knowledge would shortly be put.

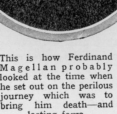

This is how Ferdinand Magellan probably looked at the time when he set out on the perilous journey which was to bring him death—and lasting fame.

In India he saw much fighting, and in the course of his journey he went as far east as the Spice Islands. During the seven years he remained in India he displayed so much courage and good sense that he was made commander of a ship.

In 1512 Magellan returned to Portugal. He went on a crusade against the Moors in Morocco, where he was wounded in the knee—a hurt which forced him to limp for the rest of his life.

But now occurred an important event in his career. He was accused of carrying on trade with the Moors and, in spite of his efforts to prove his innocence, he lost the favour of King Manoel of Portugal, and thereby all chance of serving his country—a circumstance which Portugal later had good cause to regret. Accordingly Magellan renounced his nationality, and in 1517 sought service at the Spanish court under Charles V.

In Spain he became the friend of one Diogo Barbosa, whose daughter he subsequently married, and who helped him to gain the ear of Charles and his powerful minister, and to impart to them his scheme to reach the Spice Islands by way of South America; that is, to circumnavigate, or sail round, the globe.

The young king soon gave him five ships and nearly three hundred men for his great venture.

On September 20, 1519, Magellan set sail for the west. His own ship was the "Trinidad"; the others were the "San Antonio," the "Concepción," the "Vittoria," and the "Santiago." Only one of them was destined to complete the undertaking.

The voyage started badly. Fierce storms were encountered, and the Spanish captains grumbled at their Portuguese commander. But after a time the weather cleared, and in due course South America was sighted. In December the boats were brought to anchor in the harbour that is now Rio de Janeiro.

The following month the fleet sailed into the broad mouth of the Rio de la Plata, which Magellan hoped might be a passage through to the great ocean that Balboa had seen.

But his hopes were soon dashed to the ground, and he finally put in at the harbour of St. Julian. It was March now, and in that region the winter was coming on. The fleet settled down for the cold, stormy season.

Then the Spaniards became so discontented that they started a mutiny. Magellan put it down with a firm hand, thereby establishing a reputation for strength of purpose. He sent the "Santiago" south, to scout along the coast, and it proved to be her last voyage. She was wrecked, but her sailors were rescued. It was in this land that Magellan found the tracks of what he took to be a giant race whom he called Patagonians (păt′a̤-gō′nĭ-ăn)—which means "big-footed."

Discovery of Tierra del Fuego

In August the fleet moved on to the south and waited for good weather. It was not until the middle of October that they could continue their voyage. Three days later they rounded a bold headland, and found themselves going westwards. For more than another month they fought the fierce storms as they felt their way along the bleak shores, sighting on their way the land Magellan named Tierra del Fuego, from the number of fires he saw there. Then one sunny day they finally passed the point of land which Magellan gladly named the Desired Cape, and saw another ocean stretching out ahead of them, the ocean which had first been seen by Balboa, seven years previously. Little did they think it was so much wider than the one they had just crossed.

But there were only three ships now. The "San Antonio" had turned back for Spain one night, with a story that the other boats had gone down with all on board.

Taking on fresh water and all the supplies they could obtain, the survivors set out with new courage on their last lap over the unknown sea. They had good winds to carry them, and the ocean was so calm that Magellan named it the Pacific.

But the sailors soon began to experience terrible misfortunes. The food and water ran short, and in time the men were forced to eat rats, and the leather from the rigging, dozens dying from scurvy. Magellan suffered the same privations as his men, but his strong will never wavered. He sailed on into the unknown.

After ninety-eight days of crossing the Pacific, at last, one blessed day he saw the green of a tropical island ahead. Very soon the islanders were swarming round them in canoes. They brought coconuts and other food, but they were such thieves that they carried off from the ships anything on which they could lay their hands. For that reason Magellan called the islands the Ladrones, which means "robbers." But he was grateful for food and water at any price, although he sailed away again as soon as he could. A little later, he reached one of the Philippines.

All his troubles seemed to be over. He cruised about among the Philippines, welcomed by the natives and feasted by their kings. At Cebu, the king even adopted him as a brother; and in return Magellan promised to help the king against a rebel chief in a neighbouring island. That was his great error, and it cost him his life. In the fight that followed he fell, on April 27, 1521.

Thus he never returned to Spain, but he had nevertheless sailed all the way round the world. For, on his earlier trip to India, he had been as far east as the place where he now fell dead.

End of a Three Years' Voyage

After they had lost their leader the sailors met with many other troubles, partly through the treachery of the king of Cebu. Then, on the return journey, two of their ships were lost. The "Vittoria" alone survived to see Spain again. She arrived in Seville Harbour on September 9, 1522, three years after she had set out. She brought back thirty-one men out of nearly three hundred that had started. How courageous must those have been who set out for unknown lands and seas in those far-distant days!

Yet the "Vittoria" brought back such a rich cargo of spices that they paid for the whole expedition. Her captain—Del Cano— was made a noble and given a coat of arms, and on his coat of arms appeared two sticks of cinnamon, three nutmegs, and twelve cloves.

Photo by J. and M. Lazarus

For ten long months Vasco da Gama and his weary crew have been tossed about in their little boat. At last they have reached Calcutta, and da Gama is telling the story of his perilous voyage to the Eastern king.

How VASCO DA GAMA SAILED to INDIA

It was He Who Started All the Rich Trade between the East and the West that has Gone on Since His Day

ALL Lisbon was wild with excitement. A man had at last been chosen to command the four splendid ships that lay in the harbour. That man—Vasco da Gama (väs′kō dä gä′mä)—was to sail soon on a new expedition in search of an all-water route to India. Upon him depended Portugal's glory, her wealth, and her fame.

Round Africa to the East

For more than half a century Portuguese sailors had ventured ever farther southward, and in 1488 Diaz (dē′äz) had actually rounded the Cape and sailed a short distance along the eastern coast. Yet Portugal had done little exploring during the previous nine years. In the meantime Spain had sent out Columbus and had found a path across the wide Atlantic. News of this great discovery had made the Portuguese more eager than ever to find a shorter route to the rich lands of the East. This, King Emmanuel thought, could best be done by sailing round Africa and then eastward. And so he had fitted out an expedition to undertake the difficult journey.

His choice of commander was a wise one. From the time of his birth at Sines (sē′nās), a small seaport near Palos, some time about 1460, Vasco da Gama had known the sea. He was of noble birth and he was brave. He had fought in the army; he had become a skilled sailor; and he was a favourite at the court.

On July 8, 1497, the bold explorer and his men sailed gaily out from Lisbon amid the cheers of the city. Sailing steadily for months they passed through the sweltering tropical sea, across the Equator, and finally into the milder regions to the south. When the weather began to get colder than any they had ever known and the terrific winds tossed their little vessels about, the men begged da Gama to turn back. Some of them mutinied, and da Gama put the frightened leaders of the mutiny into chains and sailed on. In November he rounded the Cape and turned northward in the direction of India. Months later he came upon a shipload of Indian traders who agreed to pilot him to their country.

Da Gama Reaches India

At last, after ten months' sailing, he landed at Calcutta—the first European to reach India by sailing round Africa. Da Gama and his men were overjoyed to touch land again, but the welcome they received from the Indian ruler was far from cordial. They did, however, see enough of the country to learn that it was enormously rich in spices and precious stones.

At the end of August, 1499, the little fleet limped back to Lisbon harbour. Many of the crew had died from the hardships of the long voyage, and their leader was weary and worn. But they had found a new trade route that was to make their country wealthy. Then indeed did Portugal sing their praises. In honour of his success Vasco da Gama was given a title and a large sum of money.

Enormous Riches from the East

In 1502 da Gama sailed again to India, founded two colonies there, and collected a great cargo of Eastern riches. Upon his return home he was given a still higher title and another large sum of money.

So rich and famous had he grown that he spent the next twenty years in luxury. In all these years he made no further expeditions. Then, in 1524, he was asked to go again to India, this time as viceroy, to set right the harm done by the misrule of the previous viceroy. A few months later the great captain died there. His body was taken back to Portugal so that it might rest for ever in his native land, for which he had won enormous riches in the golden East.

In many parts of the world the harvest field is still a place where people toil for long hours and reap a mere handful of grain in return for their labour.

Photo by Alinari

The MACHINE that MADE BREAD CHEAP

How the Wonderful Reaper Gave Us Ten Times More Wheat than We Used to Have a Hundred Years Ago

EVERY wild animal spends practically the whole of his life doing two things —sleeping, and hunting for his food.

Man, on the other hand, has leisure in which to do other things. This is because he does not have to devote all his life to the search for food—as he used to, long ago. And the reason why this no longer occupies all his time is that he has found out ways of getting so much more food than at first, and getting it so much quicker. At one period he had only the meat and fruit and grain that Nature grew for him, but now he can grow a thousand times as much as she ever supplied. And he can grow it so easily that he has a great deal of time left in which to develop himself in other directions.

This is the story of one of the great machines that he has made to help him obtain his food. It is the reaper. This machine cuts his grain for him; and the grain is probably his most important food, for out of it comes all his bread, and many of the other things he eats.

How Grain was First Reaped

The first men who ever reaped grain must have simply pulled off the heads with their hands. How long they went on doing that we do not know; but implements to help with their little crops must have been among the earlier inventions. There must soon have been some sort of knife for cutting the grain—made at first, perhaps, of stone and later of bronze. With a knife they could cut several stalks at once.

Then the knife was given a curved shape, or grew into a sickle, and still later it was made much longer and was called a scythe.

And these were the best implements available for cutting wheat for a long, long time—in fact until only about a century ago. Until that time, men were still cutting wheat in a similar way to that of the early Egyptians.

Now when wheat is ripe it has to be cut quickly. The whole crop must be cut in ten days at the most, otherwise it will break down and rot. So reaping wheat was about the hardest toil that men and women and children ever did—for they all had to go out into the sun-scorched fields and hurry along w i t h this work. Some of them went ahead and cut the grain, leaving it on the ground b e h i n d

Photo by Ollivier

Up to the last quarter of the nineteenth century great help in harvesting the corn in England was given by Irish labourers. They used to come over in hundreds for the harvesting season, just as to - day hop - pickers go down into Kent to pick the hops. These Irishmen, who brought their sickles with them, enjoyed their visit to England very much, although they used to work hard. They looked upon it as a picnic,

Here are peasants laboriously harvesting the fields of France. The man is using the old-fashioned cradle scythe, and the woman has all the work of gathering the grain into bundles and tying it ready for stacking.

for they camped out on the farms or lived in barns. At the end of the season they went back to their families with a good sum of money in their pockets.

But this method of cutting corn was very tiring and very slow, and it made corn dear, therefore the price of bread was much higher than it is to-day.

Before the long-bladed scythe was invented the sickle was the best implement men had for cutting their grain. Here is an early specimen, with its little blade well nicked with use.

them. Others followed to gather the grain and tie it into bundles, or sheaves. And still others came on and stacked the sheaves into shocks, or stooks, to keep them from rotting on the ground or through the rain.

Bread by the Sweat of the Brow

Practically the only improvement, until a hundred years ago, was the "cradle" for the scythe. This was a series of curved wooden prongs, or fingers, ranged about the steel knife of the scythe. As the grain was cut it fell in layers on these prongs, and the

This is a model of the first little reaper that Cyrus McCormick tested in 1831. There had to be one man to ride the horse and another to rake the cut grain off the machine. Six more men were required to bind the grain into bundles. The team of eight could harvest twelve acres of grain if they worked for a full day.

By 1851 McCormick had made his reaper into a thoroughly workable affair, and it was being used in many parts of the country. It now had two horses, and seats for the two workers. But the cut grain still had to be raked off the machine and bound by hand; so a team of some eight men was still needed for the work.

cutter could then lay it down in neater rows behind him. That meant less trouble for the binders who were following. But it was still terribly hard work to "bind behind a fast cradler."

And then came the reaping-machine. It made all the work much easier. It did

In this little shop near Lexington, U.S.A., Cyrus McCormick made his first reaper. Above it is a picture of the testing of one of the early machines, and at the right is a portrait of the inventor when he had won fame at home and abroad and was the head of a great business enterprise.

wheat, they gave trouble. And then the farms were too small, and often too hilly, for the best use to be made of the reaper. For a long, straight blade is difficult to use on very uneven land.

In the year 1809 Cyrus Hall McCormick was born on a farm at Walnut Grove, in what is now the State of West Virginia, U.S.A. His father was a farmer, and also something

the work ten times as fast, and so enabled ten times as much wheat to be sown. And then the price of bread became cheaper.

of an inventor, and he had a saw-mill and a blacksmith's shop on his land. For years he had set his heart on making a reaping-machine, and he put many of his ideas into wood

The First Reaping-machine

In 1826 a Scotsman named Patrick Bell made the first successful reaping-machine. It had a long blade near the ground fitted with a set of big teeth like those of a saw, and just above it was another blade with similar teeth. As it rolled along, the top teeth moved from side to side, over the lower ones, just like so many pairs of scissors, and cut down the grain. The horses were hitched behind the machine, which they pushed, so as not to tread on the wheat, which was thrown to one side by a rotating wheel.

But there were drawbacks to this machine. If there were weeds or coarse grass in the

and metal. At last, in 1831, the machine was made; though by that time the son was the inventor rather than the father. In this machine the horses were in front, but they did not walk on the corn, as the cutting blade swung out to one side of them.

But it is one thing to invent a machine and another to perfect it, and still another to get people to use it. At the very first public trial the machine failed, and the father exclaimed bitterly, "I am finished with it!" But the son did not despair. He continued to experiment, with the result that the machine began to work better, and

Photo by Ransomes, Sims and Jefferies, Ltd.

This is a modern type of mowing machine, which is capable of dealing with the most difficult crops and conditions without choking. It is drawn by horses, but a similar type, fitted with a special sliding drawbar, can be driven by tractor. An attachment consisting of a series of prongs can be used to convert it into a reaper.

after a year of improvements, it had another public test. People came from hundreds of miles around to see it.

Doom of the Scythe

At first the reaper appeared to work badly, and the owner of the field cried out, "Stop your horses—you are ruining my corn!" The onlookers began to make fun of the machine; they wanted it to fail because they were afraid it would take away their work. But just then another farmer rode up. "Pull down the fence and go into my field," he called out; "I'll give you a fair chance!" And on this field the reaper worked satisfactorily. At the end of the day it had cut six acres of corn.

McCormick immediately began making more machines. By 1839 he had made one that could cut twelve acres in a day, but even at the low cost of £10 each he found it difficult to sell them. He finally sold seven in 1842, twenty-nine in 1843, and fifty the next year.

Gradually the number of orders increased, and when requests for the new reaping-machines began to come from the western states McCormick found himself faced with the difficulty of delivering them. Eventually he decided to set up a factory in Chicago, where he could avail himself of the railways for despatching his reapers.

The machine was steadily improved, and when an invalid named Atkins, who had seen a reaper working outside his window, invented a self-raking attachment, McCormick bought the idea from him. By 1874 came the invention that enabled the machine not only to cut the grain, but to bind it into sheaves. At first it used a wire for the binding, but there were various objections to this, and when a twine-binder was invented by John Appleby, an Englishman, it was at once adapted by McCormick. This and further improvements to the machine were made, until it was finally brought to its present state of perfection.

Use of the "Stripper" in Australia

While the use of the string-binder is general in Great Britain and most of North America, a more advanced method of reaping is adopted in certain other countries, notably in Australia. Here a machine is employed which gathers the heads of the standing grain and passes them along to another part of it where the corn is extracted, deposited in sacks and thrown to the ground. This machine is called a "stripper."

With the perfection of the reaping-machine it was possible to grow and harvest enormous quantities of grain in many parts of the world, and most of the British colonies began to send us large supplies.

Wheat Lands of Canada and Australia

Canada and Australia have vast areas of land under cultivation, much of which would have been unproductive had the reaper not been invented. In Canada the area given over to wheat amounts to about 25,000,000 acres, and 400,000,000 bushels are gathered yearly. The most important crop is oats, the area cultivated exceeding 13,000,000 acres, and the yield averaging more than 400,000,000 bushels.

Nearly 15,000,000 acres are planted with wheat in Australia, resulting in the harvesting of about 127,000,000 bushels annually. Following a long way behind come oats, which cover about 1,500,000 acres, with a production of 14,000,000 bushels.

The Cornfields of England

It may surprise you to know that England possesses the most prolific cornfields in the world; that is to say, the yield per acre is greater than that of any other country. Most of the farms, however, are small compared with those of the overseas empire, the majority being under three hundred acres in extent. The total land area of England and Wales is rather more than 37,000,000 acres, and of this upwards of 4,000,000 acres are under cultivation for wheat and other crops.

The world owes a debt of gratitude to the men who invented the reaper and the binder. They completely revolutionized farming and gave the world cheap bread.

Photo by Ransomes, Sims and Jefferies, Ltd.

It is under difficult harvesting conditions, whether caused by laid or tangled crops, or crops which are fortunately very heavy, that a power-driven standard binder like this one gives full benefit to the farmer. It shows a wonderful advance on the early binders. A field of about fifteen or sixteen acres can be reaped in a day.

Photo by Rischgitz

Edmund Spenser, the great poet of Queen Elizabeth's reign, is here seen reading his poem the "Faërie Queene" to his friend Sir Walter Raleigh, who is paying a visit to Spenser at his home in Ireland.

WHO *is the* "POET'S POET"?

That is What We Call Edmund Spenser, Because so Many Other Poets Have Loved Him and Have Been Inspired by His Work

(CONTINUED FROM PAGE 40)

EDMUND SPENSER lived through the glorious days of England when Elizabeth was queen. The land was full of great men. The victory over the terrible Armada from Spain made heroes of the soldiers and sailors. The New World opened paths for bold explorers. The queen herself set a high standard in state-craft. Above all, the land was full of poets, giving voice to the brave deeds of the day. There were more great English poets then than there had ever been before or there have ever been since; and next to Shakespeare, Spenser was the greatest of them all.

He was born in London, in 1552, of a good family, that was, however, by no means rich; but he did so well at school that some wealthy men helped him to go to college— though he had to earn his education in part by waiting at table and doing other work. After he had taken two degrees at Cambridge University, he returned to London in the hope of winning fame and fortune with his pen and in the service of his queen.

He was one of a band of poets and scholars who were full of high ambition for English literature. The eyes of the world had been opened, during the Renaissance, to the glories of the poetry of ancient Greece and Rome. In every land the poets were trying now to achieve in their own tongues what Homer and Virgil (vûr'jĭl) had done so long before. The Italians had begun the movement, and the English were following bravely, and Spenser and his coterie of poets were busily engaged in this effort.

In that spirit Spenser wrote all his work. He began with the "Shepherd's Calendar" (1579), a group of poems, one for each month of the year, of the kind that we call "pastoral." In such poems, which had been written from ancient times, the poet and his friends pretend that they are simple shepherds and tell us the stories of their love, and other tales.

In the service of his queen, Spenser started as a secretary to the lord deputy of Ireland —and that, unluckily, is as far as he ever got. There was already trouble between the Irish and the English, and the Irish were full of hatred for the English overlords. So Spenser had rather an unhappy and disappointing time in Ireland.

The "Faërie Queene"

But all the while he was at work on his great poem. It was a work intended to rival the old epics of Greece and Rome, and the new ones of Italy. It was to be an allegory, teaching the lessons of the Greek philosophers in the form of a story of the bravery of the days of chivalry, and singing the glory of the queen of England. So the poem is called the "Faërie Queene," and the queen is, of course, Elizabeth—or "Gloriana," as the poet calls her. For her all the knights in the poem perform their brave deeds, and at her feet they loyally lay all their triumphs.

When part of the poem had been completed, Spenser had a famous visitor in Ireland. He was no other than Sir Walter Raleigh. He was a poet, too; and he was so charmed with Spenser's poem that he advised the author to take it to England and present it to the queen.

The queen and her court admired the poem, and Spenser may well have thought his future was now assured. But all that came to him was a small pension. The queen was old, and she was not a generous woman. So Spenser returned to Ireland a sadder and a wiser man.

But he was not the man to leave his poem untouched. For the rest of his life he was busy with it, though he died before it was finished. It was to be in twelve long books, and we have only six of them. Meanwhile, he wrote several other poems, and a beautiful series of sonnets—the "Amoretti Sonnets" —to the lady who became his wife.

Flight from Ireland

Unfortunately he had rather a hard time in Ireland. In 1598 the Irish rebels burned his home, and he and his wife barely escaped from the country with their lives. Early in the following year he died in London, in poverty and sadness.

Spenser may well have felt that his life was a failure. How could he know that his fragment of the "Faërie Queene" was going to rank as one of the greatest poems in his language? Poets love and cherish Spenser, and try to write as he did—and so he is always known as "the poet's poet."

" WISEST, BRIGHTEST, MEANEST *of* MANKIND "

In Taking all Knowledge for His Field of Interest, Francis Bacon Made Himself the Father of a Great Part of the World's Thinking from His Day to Ours

AT ONE time, three or four hundred years ago, men sometimes thought that they could learn practically everything there was to know, and even record their knowledge in a single book. And, of course, if one could learn everything one could also be an authority on everything. Sir Francis Bacon was one of the last of the great men who could say, "I take all knowledge to be my province." He succeeded in becoming a great statesman and jurist, a famous philosopher and scientist, and a most influential writer. So, whether you are reading a history of literature, of science, of philosophy, or of the English people, you are sure to come upon his name.

Before he was sixteen, Bacon had decided that he would form a philosophy of living and of government to take the place of that of Aristotle, the ruling philosopher of the world. Queen Elizabeth was calling him her "little lord keeper," and he must have dreamed of a time when he would be lord keeper of the Great Seal in fact as well as in fancy.

He came of a distinguished family; his father had himself been lord keeper, and an uncle had been lord treasurer. Born in 1561, Bacon went to Cambridge at twelve, and at fifteen was studying law at Gray's Inn, London. He spent three years in France, attached to the British embassy, but had to return home when his father died. He continued to study law, and was admitted to the Bar in 1582.

But Bacon had no intention of being an ordinary lawyer. In 1584 he entered Parliament. Almost at once he sent a wise "Letter of Advice" to the queen. His long and brilliant public life had begun.

Bacon had various plans for reforming the government of England and solving the knotty problems which later led to civil war. Some say that if he had been heeded there might never have been a war. At all events, Bacon knew from the first that, as things were, his only chance of getting the queen to listen to him was to flatter her and make use of her favourites, and in general to play the part of courtier. He did these things wisely and well, and was quite heartless as to who might be hurt in the doing of them. That is why, long after his death, the poet Pope referred to him as "the wisest, brightest, meanest of mankind."

In support of Pope's opinion, there is the story of Bacon's friendship with that brilliant, passionate, and impractical young favourite of Elizabeth's, the earl of Essex. Bacon gave Essex a wealth of good advice, and Essex tried enthusiastically to secure for him the promotion he wanted. Failing in that, Essex cried, "I die if I do not somewhat towards your fortune!" and offered Bacon a tract of land. Yet later, when Essex fell from favour, Bacon's efforts to

Here we see Sir Francis Bacon, philosopher, statesman, man of letters, and keen student of science.

save him seemed to the earl's friends but half-hearted; and, as one of the queen's learned counsel, or official lawyers, he actually consented to be the principal mover against Essex at his trial for treason.

Bacon's Rapid Rise to Fame

When James I came to the throne, in 1603, Bacon had high hopes of gaining great power for himself and a hearing for his plans of reform. And he was not disappointed. The king granted him a knighthood, and other advancements followed in rapid succession. He became solicitor-general of England, attorney-general, and lord keeper of the Great Seal. In 1618 he was appointed lord chancellor, the greatest honour of all, and was raised to the peerage as Baron Verulam; and in 1621 he was created Viscount St. Albans.

But even now, neither the king nor the Commons would listen to his advice. In spite of all his efforts, they drifted nearer and nearer to the war that was to break out a few years after Bacon's death. When he had to choose between king and Parliament, Bacon chose the king. Then Parliament began to distrust him. And in the year in which he was raised to the peerage, the pillars of his castle in the air came tumbling down about him.

He was accused of having accepted bribes from principals in law suits that came before him as lord chancellor. Though he admitted that he had accepted "presents," he said they had had no effect on the way in which he judged the cases involved. His accusers could hardly be expected to believe that, and finally Bacon, who had fallen ill, agreed to accept the judgment of his fellow peers. The Great Seal was taken from him; a huge fine of £40,000 was imposed; he was forbidden to come within twelve miles of the court; and he was to be imprisoned at the king's pleasure.

The king ordered his release from the Tower after a few days, and set aside the

5

fine for Bacon's own use; a few months later the king granted him a pardon, but his banishment from court was never fully removed, and he never again entered Parliament.

Even during the tense and busy years at court, Bacon had found time to write, and now in his retirement he became engrossed in his work. He wrote on law, government, science and philosophy. The great book

Sir Francis Bacon awaiting an audience with the duke of Buckingham. Bacon did an amazing amount of work in the course of his lifetime.

in which he tried to put down all learning and all science he wrote in Latin, believing that it would be more certain to last if written in that scholarly language. He did not live to complete the work, but he did write several shorter works which were to

form part of it. The most famous of these is the "Novum Organum"—the "New Method."

The heart of the "new method" is "in-ductive reasoning": that is, argument based on the observation of many individual cases as, for instance, when we say, "All the unripe apples I have ever tasted were sour; all the unripe apples anyone else ever tasted, so far as I can discover, were sour; so probably all unripe apples are sour." This sort of reasoning, based on the process of actually watching how things go on, developed later into what we now call "the scientific method of inquiry."

As literature, Bacon's "Essays" are his most famous work. These were the first essays written in English, and are still among the best. They are brief, pithy pronouncements on many things that Bacon had observed and pondered, such as love, friendship and marriage, truth, high position, studies, "wisdom for a man's self." They are so neatly expressed that they are as easy to quote from as poetry.

It was his devotion to science which killed him in the end. One winter day in 1626 he insisted on getting out of his coach to gather some snow. He needed it for stuffing a fowl in the experiment he was making to discover whether its flesh would remain sweet longer if it were kept cold. Already broken in health, the eager old man was seized with a chill, and a few days later died—an early and distinguished martyr to the cause of science.

Dr. Faustus, hero of Marlowe's famous play, is sitting in the chamber where he carries on his experiments for turning base metals into gold. Suddenly Satan, or Mephistopheles, appears before him and offers to give him back his youth for a period in exchange for his immortal soul, which must be surrendered to Satan at the end of the period. The play is based on the story of Faustus's decision, and the results that follow upon it.

The FATHER of ENGLISH TRAGEDY

Christopher Marlowe Was the Genius Who Disclosed to Shakespeare Many of the Secrets of His Art

WHEN Christopher Marlowe left Cambridge (where he became Bachelor of Arts in 1584) and came to London he found there the beginnings of a period that was to become the greatest in the history of English dramatic verse. Companies of resident players were attracting the people to the playhouses, and together with this growing enthusiasm there was occurring a rapid change in the basis of the drama.

The religious miracle and morality plays were giving place to imitations of the classical plays of early days, written by cultured men who were inspired by the rediscovery of Latin literature. By the Renaissance in Italy the dramas of Seneca became known to English students; and side by side with the popular play there grew up the style of drama written by Seneca, who had taken the Greek dramatists for his model.

A New Style of Drama

It was Marlowe who first took the best of each school and combined them into a whole which founded a new dramatic tradition. The racy vitality of the people's plays and the poetic possibilities of Senecan imitations were spurned by the genius of this passionate, vigorous young poet, who was murdered at the tragically early age of twenty-nine, and who yet managed in his ten years as a writer to win lasting honour as the first great English dramatist.

To those precise men of letters whose care was to adhere exactly to the Latin convention Marlowe's ardour and intensity were most deplorable; but his "Tamburlaine the Great," written and acted before he was twenty-four, proved to be an enormous success. He was charged with thinking "to outbrave better pens by the swelling bombast of blank verse," but such opposition was futile, for in Marlowe the age had found its authentic voice. The brilliance of his imagery, the rich, glittering phrases, and the resonant majesty of his line echoed superbly the changing spirit of the time. Marlowe had permanently decided the course that English drama was to take, and very soon he was quoted and imitated on all sides.

Story of Dr. Faustus

In "Dr. Faustus" (1588) he presented the story of one who, for temporal power, sells his soul to the Devil (a story which, owing to the growing interest in demonology and witchcraft, must have been peculiarly compelling). The play itself is unequal, but nevertheless it contains some of Marlowe's greatest verse, notably the famous speech beginning:

Was this the face that launch'd a thousand ships,
And burnt the topless towers of Ilium?
Sweet Helen, make me immortal with a kiss.

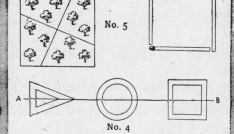

ANSWERS TO PUZZLES ON PAGE 63

No. 1. The farmer first takes the goose across the river. Next he returns for the wheat, which he carries to the other bank. Then he takes the goose back with him, and brings over the fox. Finally, he recrosses the river and returns with the goose again.

No. 3

No. 2

No. 5

No. 4

"The Jew of Malta" and "Edward II" (1593) complete his major work, although he is also considered to be author or part author of "The Massacre at Paris," "The Tragedy of Dido," and probably "Henry VI." In addition to these plays there has also come down to us "Hero and Leander," a long unfinished poem which would alone be sufficient to place its author in the front rank. This superb love poem has a freshness and passionate magnificence that are unsurpassed. In it Marlowe's delight in richness and his poetic sensibility find full expression; without any of the excessive sweetness of sentiment that marks some of the other dramatists of his day, he achieves an idyllic beauty that expresses eternally the wonderful freshness of the first glorious vision of young love.

Son of a Shoemaker

Of his life little is known. Born on February 6, 1564, at Canterbury, he was the son of a shoemaker of that city. He attended King's School, and from there passed on to Cambridge, where he took his B.A. degree in 1584. He is thought to have fought in the Low Countries, and it is certain that his conduct was gay, reckless and violent. About his death (in a tavern brawl) there is still considerable mystery, although it has been suggested by some scholars that he was deliberately murdered for certain political reasons.

(CONTINUED ON PAGE 145)

Egypt is still a land of mystery and wonder. This painting by Charles Frère represents an evening in Cairo, with a caravan passing slowly on its way, while women leisurely fill their water-jars from the stream.

In the DAYS of the PYRAMIDS

How Egypt Grew and Prospered Until She Conquered and Ruled Over Nearly All the Known World

(CONTINUED FROM PAGE 62)

THE ribbon of a country that was ancient Egypt began so far back in history that her childhood years are shrouded in mystery; but by 4241 B.C. she had learned how to read and write, and in that year she began, as it were, to keep a little diary. This simple record grew fuller and fuller as time went on, until, as you already know if you have read the first chapter of Egypt's story, it came to be an elaborate account of all the important doings of the Egyptian kings, who were busy welding their land into a single nation that should be strong and prosperous.

But eventually this "Old Kingdom" fell apart, and for about 250 years after 2400 B.C. there was no strong pharaoh in Egypt, no "Great House," no supreme pyramid builder. Instead, each small district, or nome, as the Greeks called it, along this narrow string of country had its own king or chief. Some

of these district rulers grew very proud, and built themselves little pyramids on the model of Khufu's great one. Most of them ruled wisely and well, or at least so they say in their own stories, which they wrote on the walls of the tombs they built.

But this string of separate districts did not speak very well for Egypt as a whole. To be really strong, a country needs to have a single central government which can fight enemies or cultivate friendships. To be sure, Egypt did not have many enemies. Rich as the Nile Valley was, it was almost impossible to get at. In this it was very unlike Palestine, the country to the northeast of Egypt, and north of what is now Arabia. Palestine has been fought over hundreds of times, while Egypt has generally remained undisturbed, being somewhat like a very deep and narrow pocket into which it is hard to get one's hand.

101

The first cataract of the Nile is really a rapid, and marked the southernmost boundary of early Egypt.

It was here that Sesostris III cut his great channel and opened the upper river to the passage of boats.

Again, it seemed as if a new line of kings—what historians call a "dynasty" (dĭn′ȧ-stĭ), or "ruling family"—must arise from among these district chiefs; a "Great House," or pharaoh, which would swallow up all the little houses. What Egypt was in great need of was another Menes, to combine the separate districts into one country. And that need was fulfilled.

Reign of the Theban Kings

The new king, Intef (ēn′tĕf), rose to power in 2160 B.C., that is, 260 years after the old monarchy had come to an end. Intef had been the lord of Thebes (thēbz), a city far to the south, only about a hundred miles from where Egypt ended, at the first cataract. Intef did not succeed in bringing all Egypt under his sway, but during the fifty years that he was king he extended his realm, until it included practically all the southern, or upper, half of Egypt's 750 miles of territory.

After Intef came a long line of Theban kings, and the same names are used over and over again—Mentuhotep (mĕn′tōō-hō′tĕp), Amenemhet (ä′mĕn-ĕm′hĕt), Sesostris (sĕ-sŏs′trĭs). Altogether they ruled till 1788 B.C.

And some very interesting events occurred during their reigns.

One problem of these Middle Kingdom pharaohs was how to be sure of enough grain and other supplies to meet their needs. You see, during the long time—over two hundred years—during which Egypt had again been a string of little independent districts, people had become used to paying taxes to the district ruler or nomarch (nŏm′ärk)—lord of the nome—and not to the king. Some of these nomarchs were so powerful that it was dangerous to try to take the taxes away from them. It was far better to win them as friends than to fight them as enemies, and the kings named Amenemhet and Sesostris were wise men and usually did what was in the best interests of the country.

How Egypt's Kings Grew Rich

But there were many possible means by which a king could obtain wealth. He owned all the gold, silver, and copper mines, and the quarries of alabaster and other costly stones. These were outside Egypt—to the south of the first cataract, or to the east by the Red Sea—so they did not fall into any of the nomes or districts; and a great deal of

102

money could be made from them. That was one way for a king to get rich.

Secondly, there was new territory to be conquered and taxed. In the time of the Old Kingdom a passage through the granite rocks of the first cataract had been built, but it was in bad repair. Now Sesostris III planned to make it safe for boats to pass up and down. At the most dangerous place in the cataract his engineers cut a channel in the rock 260 feet long, 34 feet wide, and 26 feet deep. Sesostris was very proud of this channel, and well he might be.

All the Nile Valley between the first and second cataracts this king conquered by means of his canal. He drove out the negroes and forbade them to pass northward beyond the first cataract, where he built two great forts. All this new Egyptian country was owned by the king and had to pay taxes directly to him. So more supplies flowed into the royal treasury.

The King Who Made the Desert Bloom

The next way in which this Theban line of pharaohs added to their income was very splendid. About twenty miles west of the Nile and sixty-five miles south of the Delta there was a low-lying region called the Fayum (fī-yōōm′), where a shallow lake was filled up every year by the flood of the Nile River. King Amenemhet III built a wall about twenty-seven miles long round the lake to hold the waters, and he also dug canals to carry the water between the lake and the Nile, a distance of about twenty-three miles.

By means of this lake and canal Amenemhet III stored up enough water to irrigate about 27,000 acres of good

farm land which before had been worthless, because it never got any water. This new farm land also belonged to the king. Amenemhet III was so pleased with his work that he built his central government building near by. This building measured about one-sixth of a mile each way, and in it there were roomy halls for each district of Egypt, where travellers from the nomes might go to worship their own local gods and so feel at home.

A Great Line of Pharaohs

These undertakings seem to us much more modern and worth while than building pyramids. They made those wise pharaohs rich and beloved of their people. One poet sang of Amenemhet III:

He makes the Two Lands verdant more than a great Nile.
He Hath filled the Two Lands with strength.
He is life, cooling the nostrils.

These wise kings had a habit of letting their sons rule with them for the last five or ten years of their reign. In this way the prince learned how to rule well, and when he came to be king he knew his work thoroughly. However, Amenemhet III, who was probably the greatest of this Theban line of kings, and one of the most capable of all the pharaohs, had no experience of ruling before his father died.

Unfortunately, by 1788 B.C. the kingdom of Egypt had broken up once more, and the pharaohs were kings in

Out of some ancient Egyptian tomb came this model of a funeral boat, such as was used to carry the dead along the Nile to their final resting-place.

name only. The real rulers of Egypt were again the district chiefs.

Two hundred years of trouble and disorder were now to come in Egypt. The Thebans still ruled Thebes, and now and then they claimed wider powers; but the central crown in Egypt was just a prize to be fought for. Some "kings" managed to reign only a few days. The crown would pass to a general of the army, then perhaps to some strong district ruler, and once it even passed to a negro king from Nubia,

At the first cataract of the Nile is the little island of Philae (fi'lé), with a number of beautiful temples built not long before the time of Christ. One of them is shown below.

Photo by James's Press Agency

far up the Nile. Our records of the period are very few, because these weak kings did not bother to record their stories. There is a story, however, and a remarkable one, about the second of these two centuries from 1788 to 1580 B.C.

In 1902 a great dam was built across the Nile at Aswan, an ancient trading post at the first cataract of the Nile. It dammed the water of the great river during the winter months and enabled it to be distributed over thousands of acres of good land in the summer. Above the dam the Nile is a lake for two hundred miles; and the island of Philae is submerged, except in summer. At the right is a winter view of the temple shown above.

During this century, we believe, Egypt and several neighbouring countries were overrun and conquered by a wandering people who may have been related to the Hebrews. We know them only as the Hyksos (hĭk'sŏs). The word Hyksos is said to mean "shepherd kings," but not all of these people were kings. The name "shepherd kings" may sound very pretty, but the rule of these invaders was anything but pleasant for the Egyptians, for the Hyksos were cruel and barbarous and cared nothing for the welfare of the Egyptian people. After these enemies were finally driven out of Egypt their memory was so hated that the Egyptians tried to erase from their records all evidence of their ever having been a conquered people.

We believe that the capital city of the Hyksos was at Avaris in the Nile Delta; and that this is one reason why we know so little about them. The Nile Delta is near the sea, and its salt air destroys buildings and other such things much more rapidly than does the dry, hot air of the Nile Valley. Thus all records of the Hyksos in the Delta are gone, and we can only guess at their story from a few scraps of evidence picked up here and there. We know the name of one of their greatest kings, Khian (kē'ȧn), whose kingdom was much larger than Egypt.

We have also the names of one or two others of these cruel kings, but we know very little else about them save that they were unlike the good kings who, in the Middle Kingdom, spread prosperity and happiness among the people. No wonder Egypt rejoiced when at last the hated invaders were forced out of the land.

Egypt Throws Off Her Yoke

Thebes, being so far from the Delta, probably suffered far less from the Hyksos than did the Delta and the lower northern regions, which were easier to reach. There were Theban rulers in Thebes even during the Hyksos invasion, and we believe these Theban princes may have played a large part in driving the enemy from Egypt. Certainly it was a Theban chief, Ahmose (ä-mō'sĕ); who became the next Egyptian king of Egypt. He assumed the kingship in the year 1580 B.C.

When great men of ancient Egypt died it was the custom to bury with them little wooden models of their servants, performing their daily tasks just as they did in life. It was believed that their spirits would minister to that of their master in the next world. Thus to-day they supply us with a picture of life in Egypt about three thousand years ago. Here you see part of a coffin, with boatmen, a granary, and various kinds of food set before it.

Ahmose had to fight both the Hyksos and the district rulers, or nomarchs. He was so successful that in the course of his reign of twenty years the barbarians were driven out, the negro kingdom beyond the first cataract was won back, and the nomarchs were not merely beaten but almost entirely wiped out. Ahmose did not have to cultivate friendship with the local lords in Egypt: not one of them was left. The whole of Egypt was crown land, and so was definitely in the hands of this powerful Theban pharaoh.

The Napoleons of Egypt

Now the Hyksos, as well as his other enemies, had taught Ahmose very thoroughly how to fight; and when a man has learned this lesson he often wants to continue to fight even when there is no real need to. So Ahmose and the pharaohs who followed him became the Napoleons of Egypt, the great war lords, who built up a vast empire which lasted for a century or more before it met the usual fate of empires. In this period, the period of the First Empire

(1580–1350 B.C.), there were three very interesting rulers—Queen Hatshepsut, Thutmose III, and Ikhnaton (1375–1358 B.C.).

After Ahmose I came Amenhotep (ä'měn-hō'těp) and then Thutmose I (thōot-mō'sĕ), both warlike kings who fought in Nubia to the south and in Syria to the north-west of Egypt, and who were generally very successful in their campaigns. And then there occurred a very remarkable thing: the first queen in history ruled over Egypt.

In those days kings had many wives, but only one of these wives was the real queen, and only her children were supposed to become rulers. The queen of Thutmose I had four children, two sons and two daughters; but only one, a daughter named Hatshepsut (hät-shĕp'sōot), was living when Thutmose himself died. Then the question arose, could a mere woman sit on the throne of the pharaohs?

Thutmose II, a son of Thutmose I by a different wife, thought she could not, and succeeded in becoming ruler himself for a little while, until he died. Thutmose III, a son of Thutmose I by still a different wife, also disliked seeing the beautiful and energetic Hatshepsut rule over Egypt, but he had to endure it, for rule she did. After her death Thutmose III did regain power —he had ruled a little while before she became queen—and you will read of his reign soon.

Queens, like many other women, are apt to care more for religion than for war; and Hatshepsut was no exception to the rule. She did not send armies of conquest to far countries; she looked after Egypt's business and left other nations free to look after theirs. She built an exquisitely beautiful temple at Thebes, and she had obelisks put up, as was the fashion of the time. An obelisk (ŏb′ĕ-lĭsk) is a very tall pointed shaft of stone; and two which this queen erected were nearly a hundred feet high.

On the Victoria Embankment, London, stands an old Egyptian obelisk known as "Cleopatra's Needle." But it really has nothing to do with Cleopatra, for when scholars learned to read the inscriptions on its sides they found that it was one of a pair that had been set up by Thutmose III, the Napoleon of Egypt. Below, you may see one as it looked when it was in its far-off home by the Nile. A picture of the needle erected in London appears elsewhere in this work.

Another unusual act of Queen Hatshepsut was to send an expedition down the Red Sea to Punt (pōōnt), which we nowadays call Somaliland, to bring back rare treasures of myrrh, or perfume, leopard skins, tropical plants, and other valuable things for her temple. She maintained friendly relations with other nations, ruled her kingdom well, and did good work repairing old temples and monuments. Altogether, the first queen in history gave a good account of herself.

While Hatshepsut ruled, Thutmose III was waiting impatiently for his chance, and finally it came. Thutmose III was a war lord through and through. No general of modern days has known better than he how to plan a war, or has been

more bold and shrewd in carrying through his plans. Thutmose III must be classed with Alexander the Greek, Julius Cæsar the Roman, and Napoleon the Corsican, as one of the world's great soldiers. He and his armies pushed southward, westward, northwestward, fighting and winning, until Egypt had conquered most of the world as people knew it then, and had placed her boundary marks beyond that other great river of the old world—the Euphrates. Thutmose III always accompanied his armies, but what he really wanted was riches, not blood. After he had captured a town or a district— and he captured 119 in his first campaigns!—he would place upon it a yearly tax of gold, grain, or some other valuable product, which it had to send to Egypt. Small wonder that Egypt now grew rich.

Indeed, under Thutmose III Egypt grew so rich that gold was weighed by the pound instead of by the grain, and all sorts of luxuries became common things. Men stopped wearing the short little linen skirts you see in the pictures, and made themselves dresses which were much more elaborate. For music at feasts there were harps twenty feet high, instead of the six-foot harps which had served in earlier ages. Egypt was becoming almost too luxurious to be a really strong nation, and some of the religious practices made matters worse. For example, the priests now had charms which they said would keep a man from being punished for his sins, and if people believe they will suffer no ill effects, many of them will do wrong things.

Three war kings followed Thutmose III, and then there came to the throne of Egypt the most remarkable of all her kings—a pharaoh who was also a prophet, or wise man. This was Ikhnaton (ĕk-nä′tŏn)—and to tell of him we shall have to relate a little more of Egypt's religion.

As you know, there were many gods in Egypt. Some were just local gods, worshipped in one district or another. Others, like Osiris (ŏ-sī′rĭs), god of the dead, were worshiped all over the country. You remember that Re (rā), the sun god, was also very powerful in men's minds. But the most powerful god of all, in this period, was Amon (ä′mŏn), called also Amon-Re.

Now King Ikhnaton thought very deeply about all these gods, and he did not care very much for any of them. He felt there must be something wrong with religions which relied upon curses and magic to make people afraid. He was sure there could not really be more than one god, a god of life and truth and beauty.

Belief in the One God

In the year 1375 B.C., when Ikhnaton began to reign, this belief was just beginning to spring up in Egypt. But Ikhnaton had the courage of his convictions. In spite of the fact that the temples and their priests were exceedingly rich and powerful, he tried to overthrow them. He sent workmen round to cut away the name of Amon wherever it appeared on stone inscriptions. He changed his own name from Amenhotep to Ikhnaton. He seized the temples and turned out the priests. He built a new city—several new cities, in fact—in honour of Aton (ä′tŏn), the One God whom he wished to worship.

Unhappily, most of the people of his time did not hear or understand Ikhnaton when he tried to tell them about the One God. A few of his courtiers pretended to, because they wanted to be in favour with the pharaoh. But almost all the other people in Egypt clung to their old fears, their many gods, their curses and magic. Ikhnaton was living in a world which was not ready for him. We can understand him to-day.

Unhappily, also, while Ikhnaton built and dreamed, Egypt's empire was falling. A new race, the Hittites, who spoke a language somewhat akin to that of the Greeks, were sweeping over Syria and Palestine, and carrying all before them. One by one the yearly tributes stopped coming to the palace of the pharaohs. Little by little the luxury faded, and the power of Egypt grew feebler. Finally, the line of great Theban pharaohs ceased, and what is called a "pretender," a man who had really no right to the position, ascended the throne.

Reign of Tutankhamen

Just before the pretender Harmhab seized the throne, there ruled for about four years a king of whom much has been heard in recent years. This was Tutankhamen (to̅o̅t′-ängk-ä′mĕn). He was not a very great king, but he is interesting to us because his is the only royal Egyptian tomb which has been found in our day with the treasures in it, just as they were left when the king died. All the other kings' tombs have long since been robbed of the precious things with which the Egyptians always filled them in order to add to the happiness of their dead, and to enable them to continue their customary existence.

Somehow the tomb of Tutankhamen escaped; and while it was not by any means the costliest of kings' tombs, it is the only one which has been found just as it had been sealed up when the young king died, nearly thirty-three hundred years before. It was opened only a few years ago.

(CONTINUED ON PAGE 157)

It was at the ancient city of Thebes that this little Egyptian mummy was taken from its age-old resting-place.

We may be sure that every one of these wrappings was regulated by a custom that could never be broken.

(THE SOLUTIONS TO THESE PUZZLES WILL BE FOUND ON PAGE 156 OF THIS VOLUME)

HOW MANY WERE GOING TO ST. IVES?
No. 6

As I was going to St. Ives
I met a man with seven wives.
Each wife had seven sacks,
Each sack had seven cats,
Each cat had seven kits;
Kits, cats, sacks, wives,
How many were going to St. Ives?

THE CARPENTER'S PROBLEM
No. 7

A carpenter has a board six feet long and three feet wide, as shown above. He wishes to cut it into two pieces which may be spliced together to make a board nine feet long and two feet wide. How can he do it?

CAN YOU MEASURE WITH YOUR EYE?

Which is larger, in the picture below, the setting sun or the wheel of the aeroplane? Don't feel sure until you measure them.

THE QUARRELSOME ISLANDERS
No. 8

Five quarrelsome families once lived on the same island, each family with a boat-landing of its own. Here is a map of the island, with each boat-landing marked with the letter of the house to which it belongs. Because these people were so silly as to be always at odds, they had to lay the paths to their boat-landings in such a way that no path crossed any other path at any point. Draw the paths that were laid out. Of course no path may leave the island.

IS THIS A STRAIGHT LINE?

Look carefully at the line crossing the two posts at the right. Is it straight? Prove your answer with a ruler.

Here you see some typical British moths. They are (left to right) the eyed hawk-moth, bee hawk-moth, elephant hawk-moth, five-spot burnet, emperor moth, wood tiger, magpie, oak eggar, scarlet tiger, cinnabar, yellow underwing, and small emerald.

If you continued to try for many years, and had the rainbow in which to dip your paint-brush, do you think you could colour a butterfly's wing as well as Nature does it?

Like FLOWERS on the WING

How a Greedy Caterpillar Can Turn into the Most Gorgeous Creature That Flies in the Air

(CONTINUED FROM PAGE 46)

WHEREVER flowers are growing, we shall surely find butterflies—the real fairies of the sunshine.

In the gardens, in the meadows, they flit lightly and joyously from blossom to blossom, fanning their dainty wings in the sunshine, sipping sweet nectar, and revelling in the warmth and brilliance of the long summer days.

Early in the spring time the first butterflies of the year come forth from the sheltered nooks in which they have been hiding all through the cold winter months. The first bright day tempts them to try their wings and warm themselves in the sun's rays. They are rather stiff and feeble, poor things, and their beautiful wings look dull and shabby. But that is not surprising, for ever since last autumn they have been tucked away in some dark corner of a dusty shed, or in some hole or crack where they could creep for shelter from the frost and snow and wintry winds. There they have waited patiently for spring to come again.

As the days grow longer and the sun grows stronger, many new butterflies make their appearance in the fresh green world—white butterflies, yellow butterflies, blue butterflies, and butterflies of many colours, all with wings as bright and fresh as the newly-opened petals of the summer flowers.

We do not see butterflies of all kinds flying about in the same place. Some of them love the flowery meadows, others the open woodland glades. Some flutter up and down the hill-side, others haunt the low marshlands. They also have their favourite plants and trees. Wherever there are plenty of nettles and thistles, we are likely to find some of the "tortoise-shells," "peacocks," and "painted ladies." The purple emperor, one of the finest of British butterflies, likes to hover round the tops of oak trees; "white admirals" love honeysuckle; and in the

Fens we may often see the "swallow-tail" with its handsome black and yellow wings.

But by no means can all the butterflies go flaunting about in the sunshine in a free and careless way. Many of the lady butterflies are intent on more important business as they move about among the plants. Watch a "peacock" as she flutters round a large clump of nettles. Every now and then she settles on a leaf, pauses for a moment or two, and appears to be examining it very carefully; then off she goes to another one.

If we look at the nettle we shall see that wherever the butterfly rested there are a number of pale green dots on the leaves. They are so small that we could cover four or five of them with a pinhead. But if we look at them through a magnifying glass—a delightful thing to carry with us when we are in the country—we shall see quite easily that they are the prettiest little things imaginable.

Fairy-like Eggs on a Nettle

As you have probably guessed, they are the eggs of my lady butterfly. When she has visited several nettle clumps and scattered a hundred eggs or so over the prickly leaves, she troubles herself no more about them, but flies off to enjoy the rest of her short life in the sunshine.

Although they are so tiny, the eggs are not all alike in shape and colour. Some are like round, flat buttons with raised and ornamented edges; others might be fairy rolling-pins of carved ivory, or tiny cups,

This is the peacock butterfly, whose life story is described. It is seen expanded, showing its full beauty, and also at rest, when its closed wings resemble a dead leaf.

caskets, or baskets, all beautifully fluted and sculptured. They may be white, yellow, or pale green, brown or almost black, while a few are splashed with different colours very much as birds' eggs often are.

Most butterflies just place an egg here or there in no regular order upon the plants they fancy; others take more pains to arrange the eggs in little clusters or neat rows or rings. But the eggs are always carefully fixed in place with a kind of glue, so that they cannot fall off the plants or blow away in the wind.

The tiny green eggs left by mother butterfly upon the nettle patch do not take long to hatch in the warm sunny weather. In about five days' time the little cases burst open and out come the babies of the "peacock." How strange that so dainty a butterfly should have such queer-looking children. They are ugly, black little creatures with shiny black heads, and their wee, wriggling bodies are covered with short stiff spines. In other words, they are baby caterpillars and not butterflies at all; and they are such tiny specks of things that at first you can hardly see them.

Caterpillars are dreadfully hungry creatures. Almost as soon as they are hatched, the baby insects begin to feed. Many of them start by eating up their own egg cases. Then without any waste of time they set to work gnawing the nettle leaves with their strong little jaws.

They eat so heartily and grow so fast that before very long the greedy young things begin to feel quite uncomfortable.

Their skin gets too tight and is all stretched and wrinkled. Presently it splits down the back, and after a good deal of wriggling and struggling the little caterpillar walks right out of its skin and appears in a nice new suit which has been gradually forming underneath the old one.

At first the new skin is very soft and tender, but it soon hardens in the warm air. Then, after a short rest, the caterpillars begin feeding again, and munch away at the nettles harder than ever. They shed their skins in this way five times, and after each moult they are a little larger and darker in colour.

When they are about two weeks old, the young caterpillars are big enough to be plainly seen as they swarm all over the nettles. We can hardly call them handsome. They are black and bristly, with spines all over their long bodies; and all are so exactly alike that you could never tell one from another.

Six Eyes and Sixteen Legs

Each caterpillar has a hard round head, with a pair of strong jaws that cut the nettle leaves as cleanly as a pair of sharp scissors. In front are a tiny pair of feelers, called antennæ (ăn-tĕn'ē), and six simple eyes, three on each side. These eyes are called ocelli (ŏ-sĕl'ī). They are nothing but small transparent spots that reflect the light, and are not much good for seeing. But since the caterpillar does nothing but eat all day long, its poor sight really does not matter much.

Behind its head the caterpillar has three pairs of legs, one pair on each of the last three body rings. They are short and stumpy, and end in stiff curved spines, with

which the insect holds tightly to the leaf on which it is feeding. These are called "true legs."

Farther along its body it has four pairs of queer, thick, soft legs that are called "false legs" or "cushion feet"; and right at the tail end is yet another pair, which are usually called "claspers." So altogether our black bristly friend has no less than sixteen legs of different sorts.

The swallow-tail, the largest and most beautiful of British butterflies; it is now found only in the Fens and the Norfolk Broads.

In four weeks the peacock caterpillars are fully grown. Then, suddenly, they lose their appetites. There are still plenty of nice young nettle leaves about, but the over-fed insects can eat no more.

When Caterpillars Get Nervous

They grow restless, too, and begin wandering all over the plants. Every now and then one of the fidgety things will stand still, raise its head, and turn it from side to side as if looking for something. And that is exactly what the insect is doing. It does not feel at all well, and is seeking a comfortable spot where it may rest undisturbed for a while.

Later on it creeps under a leaf and proceeds slowly to spin a little pad or cushion of silk, fixing it firmly to the leaf-stalk. Then, when the work is finished, the caterpillar turns itself about, grasps its silk cushion with its claspers, and hangs upside down from the leaf-stalk.

In this curious position it remains for a few hours. Then it begins to shrink and draw upward, growing shorter and stouter. Dear me! What is happening now? Ah! the caterpillar is going to moult again. Now it begins to wriggle and squirm, holding fast to its pad all the while, till suddenly its skin splits down the back once more. After much kicking and struggling it manages to free itself, and the old crumpled skin falls to the ground.

A Cradle for Baby Butterflies

But where is the caterpillar? It has disappeared. In its place hangs a pretty little shell-like thing, pale green in colour and touched here and there with splashes of gold, silver, and copper. It is a chrysalis (krĭs'ă-lĭs). In this charming little cradle the caterpillar is quietly resting, like an enchanted princess, while it is slowly changing from an ugly grub to a lovely butterfly.

For nearly two weeks, while this wonderful transformation is taking place, the chrysalis hangs from the leaf-stalk, gently rocked by the breezes. Then the little case begins to darken, and through the half-transparent walls the colours in the wings of the new butterfly can be plainly seen.

Enter the Peacock Butterfly

This is the most exciting time of all. At any moment now the peacock may break through its prison walls and come forth into the light and air, but you never can tell exactly when the wonderful thing will happen. Some butterflies are impatient to be free, and lose no time in making their escape; others do not appear until several hours after the colours of their wings are visible.

Sooner or later, however, if we watch patiently, we shall see the chrysalis suddenly begin to quiver. Then with a quick little jerk it bursts open, and the next moment the prisoner is free.

Slowly the new butterfly drags itself a little way up the nettle stem, leaving the chrysalis case empty and broken behind it.

But is this the pretty winged insect we have watched and waited for? It does not look much like a "sunshine fairy." Limp and quivering, it clings feebly to the stem, its wings all wet and crumpled and rolled up in little bundles on its back.

Magic Before Our Very Eyes

But wait! As we watch, the poor crippled-looking thing changes before our eyes. The crumpled wings unfold, showing their soft, pretty colours. Gradually, as the sun shines on them, all the wrinkles are smoothed out, and the wings are spread before us in all their fresh loveliness. The butterfly rests perfectly still for a while to allow its wings to grow quite firm and dry. Then it opens and shuts them two or three times, fluttering them gently as if to test their power. At last, growing bolder, our peacock suddenly rises into the air, and is off on its first joyous flight in the sunlight.

It hardly seems possible that such a dainty butterfly can really be the very same insect that only a few short weeks ago was greedily munching the nettle leaves.

The Sunshine Fairy Flits About

Gone is its black, bristly skin; its body is now lightly clothed with soft, downy hair, and four big, glorious wings spring from its shoulders. Gone are the stumpy little fore-legs and the clumsy hind feet; our butterfly has now six long, slender legs.

A pair of long, delicate feelers—the antennæ—wave gracefully on the top of its head, and two big round eyes have replaced the six little eye-spots. For now that it flies about, the insect needs to see where it is going.

The strong biting jaws have gone, too. In their place the butterfly has a long sucking tube, or proboscis (prŏ-bŏs'ĭs), as it is called. No longer will the insect feed on nettle leaves. For the rest of its life it will live like a real fairy—sipping nectar from the flowers and drinking glittering dewdrops from the leaves. We do not often see the proboscis, for when the butterfly is not taking a little light refreshment, the long tube is coiled up like a watch-spring, out of the way.

Here is the strange story of the birth of a butterfly. Just below at the left is the mother, the tawny-red monarch butterfly. Next to her is her egg, greatly enlarged, which she has laid on the leaf of a plant.

When he has eaten his fill the caterpillar hangs himself up by the tail, as shown below, using a kind of sticky glue which he makes himself.

After seventeen hours of hanging, our caterpillar begins to wriggle inside his skin. His head and neck swell, and finally his skin splits open, as shown below. Underneath is a beautiful green chrysalis.

The fine yellow and black and white caterpillar above is what steps out of the egg to feed on the leaf.

Out of the shapeless chrysalis comes this beautiful creature at the right. He is a black-veined, white-spotted monarch. The monarch is a North American butterfly, specimens of which have appeared in England.

Above is the light-green chrysalis of the monarch butterfly, just as it was left hanging to the midrib of the leaf when the creature shed its caterpillar skin.

The butterfly is now a "perfect" insect. It has gone through all its magic changes and reached the most wonderful time of its wonderful life.

A Butterfly's Life Cycle

First, it was a crawling caterpillar. This was the time of growth, when its business in life was to eat as much as ever it could in order to store up strength to help it pass safely through its transformations.

Secondly, it was a chrysalis. This was its time of rest, when it lay quiet in its little cradle while the last and the most amazing change of all was taking place.

Thirdly, it is now a lovely butterfly, a "perfect" insect, free to fly where it pleases, to visit the flowers and enjoy itself in the sunshine for the rest of its life.

A butterfly's wings are marvellous things. They are clothed on both sides with tiny scales, beautifully fitted together like the overlapping tiles on the roof of a house. It is these scales that give to the wings their beautiful colours and patterns. They are no bigger than specks of fine dust, yet they are shaped in all sorts of different ways and each one has a tiny stalk by which it is fastened to the wing.

Many of the scales—which are really transparent bags, very thin and flat—have a coloured layer inside them; but the flashing, changing colours we see on some butterflies' wings are caused by the rays of light striking the edges of the scales at different angles.

They are very frail and delicate, these pretty wings, and quite easily injured; yet they often carry the butterfly very long distances through the air.

The clouded yellow butterfly is one of the best known migratory butterflies in Europe. Its native home is the Mediterranean region, and from there migrations take place every spring, extending over Central and Western Europe. At irregular intervals these migratory flights reach as far as the British Isles during May or early June, but only if there are favourable winds and weather conditions just at the right time.

Thus we may go for years and hardly see a clouded yellow in England, and then one spring they are swarming all over the south of the country.

These butterflies on arrival seek for clover and lucerne fields, and there lay their eggs. The caterpillars hatch out and pupate in

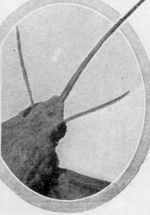

Butterflies and moths feed on the nectar of flowers, which they suck with their long tongue, or proboscis, this being rolled up when not in use. Here is shown the head of a butterfly with the tongue partly unrolled; also the remarkable tongue of the convolvulus hawkmoth, which is twice as long as its body. Notice that the antennae, or "feelers," of the butterfly are clubbed at the end, while those of the moth are not.

about a month, another brood of butterflies emerging in late July and August, and often a still later brood appears in the autumn.

Other Visitors from Foreign Lands

The cold, damp weather of the English winter is fatal to these butterflies, however, and so they all die, and we see no more clouded yellows until a fresh immigration takes place; perhaps this does not happen until a number of years later.

Clouded yellow

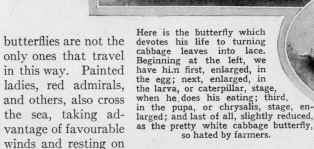

butterflies are not the only ones that travel in this way. Painted ladies, red admirals, and others, also cross the sea, taking advantage of favourable winds and resting on the ships they meet on the journey. Wherever the sun shines, some of these dainty fairies are sure to be fluttering their delicate wings. High up on bleak, cold mountains they hover over patches of Alpine flowers. Even on the borders of the great snow-fields, where dwarf forget-me-nots and buttercups open their tiny petals in the few short weeks of the Arctic summer, scores of the hardy little flutterers manage to live and find some plants on which their caterpillars can feed.

Here is the butterfly which devotes his life to turning cabbage leaves into lace. Beginning at the left, we have him first, enlarged, in the egg; next, enlarged, in the larva, or caterpillar, stage, when he does his eating; third, in the pupa, or chrysalis, stage, enlarged; and last of all, slightly reduced, as the pretty white cabbage butterfly, so hated by farmers.

Welcome and Unwelcome Guests

Painted lady, tortoise-shell, and peacock butterflies are welcome visitors to a garden. Their hungry black caterpillars like nothing so much as thistles and nettles, and do not feed on flowers and vegetables. But the white butterflies are not so welcome, although they are very pretty, with their satiny wings

and black spots. Their green-striped caterpillars are very troublesome, especially in the kitchen garden; they enjoy almost any green, juicy leaf, and often strip the poor plants of all their foliage.

The worst offender of all is the cabbage white, which is common not only in England but also on the Continent and in North America, and has become a pest to farmers.

There are beautiful butterflies in all parts of the world, but the biggest and most gorgeous live in the hottest, sunniest lands. In the great tropical forests of South America giant butterflies with wings of dazzling blue sail slowly through the green glades or soar aloft and flutter round the tops of the high trees. Some of them are as big as birds; when their glorious wings flash in the sunlight, they can be seen from a distance of a quarter of a mile.

Giant Beauties of the Tropics

Others, almost as big, are a glittering green shot with silver; and some have soft, black, velvety wings splashed with crimson or banded with bright green, rose, and orange. In the forests, too, are great owl butterflies with big spots like eyes on their wings; as they flit silently among the trees in the dusk they frighten the small birds.

There are also wonderful butterflies in the hot countries of Europe and Asia. Such are the giant bird-winged butterflies of New Guinea, whose beautiful blue-grey wings measure nine or ten inches from tip to tip. Others, almost as big, trailing long golden tails on their hind wings, or shining with rainbow hues, haunt the steamy jungles of the East Indian islands. And mysterious-looking ghost butterflies, with half transparent black and white wings, fly through the dense forests.

One of the most interesting of the Old World species is the "India leaf butterfly," which lives in hot, dry forests where the leaves on the trees are

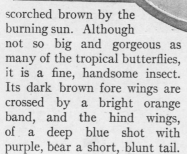

scorched brown by the burning sun. Although not so big and gorgeous as many of the tropical butterflies, it is a fine, handsome insect. Its dark brown fore wings are crossed by a bright orange band, and the hind wings, of a deep blue shot with purple, bear a short, blunt tail.

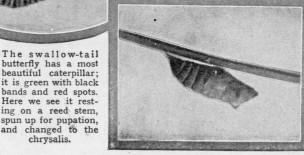

The swallow-tail butterfly has a most beautiful caterpillar; it is green with black bands and red spots. Here we see it resting on a reed stem, spun up for pupation, and changed to the chrysalis.

As it flits about in the sunshine, boldly showing off its bright wings, no one could fail to notice this striking butterfly. But if you try to catch it, or if a bird swoops down upon it, it disappears in the most bewildering way. One moment it is there, plainly to be seen; and then, as if it had donned the cap of invisibility, it vanishes before our very eyes.

Changed Into a Faded Leaf

The butterfly has simply played a trick upon us. It has turned itself into a faded leaf—at least to all appearances. Directly it is alarmed, the wily insect pops down on a branch of the nearest bush or tree, closes its wings, and at once it looks in shape and colour so like the dry leaves among which it has settled that you cannot tell the difference. Even the markings on the under side of the wings are just like the veining on the leaves; and the short, blunt tail is a perfect imitation of a leaf-stalk. As long as there is anything to fear, the leaf butterfly will keep perfectly still, with its head and antennae bent backward, quite hidden between its upright wings. There is nothing to give it away.

A Trick That Deceives the Enemy

This clever vanishing trick saves its life time and again—for hungry birds and other insect-eating creatures do not care for dry leaves. Butterflies, on the other hand, are extremely delicate things, and they have no stings, no strong jaws, nor any other kind of weapon with which to defend themselves. So they are obliged to seek safety either by hiding from the sharp eyes of their enemies or by tricking them in some cunning way.

Perhaps you have noticed that when a butterfly settles on anything it usually holds its wings close together in an upright position. On the under side the wings are by no means so brightly coloured as upon the upper surface. So, even if the insect does not give itself the appearance of a leaf, it is much less conspicuous when it is resting than when it is flying about with the sunshine throwing up the full glory of its wonderful colouring.

One of the most striking examples of this

is seen in the comma butterfly, shown on this page. The upper side is a bright chestnut brown, conspicuously spotted with black and deep chocolate; but the under surface is mottled with dull brown shades of "dead leaf" colour, while the edges of the wings are jagged in a remarkable way. Thus the butterfly looks like a dead and shrivelled leaf, and the white C mark (from which the insect takes its name) looks exactly like a crack in the leaf with the light showing through.

The swallow-tail butterfly is protected in a different way. It has such an unpleasant flavour that birds do not like it at all. They soon learn to recognize the bold colouring of its wings and leave it severely alone.

Still other butterflies rely for protection on the big eye-spots on their wings,

The comma butterfly, with wings fully spread. It can be distinguished by the C or comma-like mark which appears on its wings.

which make them look sufficiently like owls to frighten away small and timid birds.

There are no prettier things to watch than the butterflies that we may find anywhere on summer days. So felt a great poet of Nature, as he remembered how he and his sister used to chase the butterflies when they were little children and the summer days were so long. He describes it in these lovely words:

Oh! pleasant, pleasant were the days,
The time, when, in our childish plays,
My sister Emmeline and I
Together chased the butterfly!
A very hunter did I rush
Upon the prey:— with leaps and springs
I followed on from brake to bush;
But she, God love her, feared to brush
The dust from off its wings.

(CONTINUED ON PAGE 165)

Can you see the comma butterfly here? When it closes its wings it looks like a torn and withered leaf.

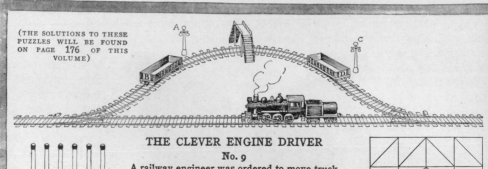

(THE SOLUTIONS TO THESE PUZZLES WILL BE FOUND ON PAGE 176 OF THIS VOLUME)

THE CLEVER ENGINE DRIVER

No. 9

A railway engineer was ordered to move truck B to lamp-post C and truck D to lamp-post A, and then to bring his engine back to the point from which it started. The picture shows the position of the engine and trucks when he received the order. He thought about it quite a time, for although the trucks would go under the bridge, the engine would not. How did he finally manage the transfer?

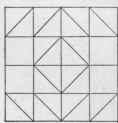

HOW MANY SQUARES?

No. 10

There are many squares of various sizes in the above diagram. How many can you count?

A TRICK WITH MATCHES

No. 11

Can you place six matches in such a way that every match touches every other match? None of them is to be cut or bent.

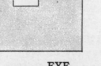

FUN WITH FIGURES

Think of a number, for example.......... 8
Double it............................... 16
Add 5................................... 21
Add 12................................. 33
Take away 3............................ 30
Halve it............................... 15
Take away the number first thought of.... 8
The answer will always be.............. 7, no matter with what number you start.

EYE MEASUREMENT

Which square is the larger? Is it the white square in the centre of the large dark square above, or is it the white square with a narrow dark border?

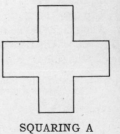

SQUARING A CROSS

No. 12

Cut a cross like the one above into four pieces of such shapes that they may be put together into a perfect square. Every cut must be along a straight line.

THE FARMER'S WILL

No. 13

Once upon a time there lived a farmer who owned a tract of land shaped like the diagram above. When he died he left a will directing that the land be divided among his four sons in such a manner that each son should have a plot of the same shape and size. How was the land divided?

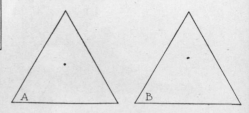

TRICKY TRIANGLES

In which triangle does the dot come nearer to being at the centre point between the top and bottom of the figure? Be sure to measure it.

Many a boy in Genoa used to sit on the shore and watch the incoming ships appear over the horizon—sails first and then the hull. And many a boy must have heard that the manner in which those ships appeared was thought by some men to prove that the earth was round. Yet of all the boys in Genoa there was only one who determined to find out if it were true. What was it in that boy which prompted him to become a great discoverer, while all the others remained at home?

This is a portrait of the courageous man who presented the world with a new hemisphere. If you have any skill in reading faces, just a glance at this one will show you that Christopher Columbus was a man not only to dream dreams, but to make them come true.

HE DOUBLED *the* SIZE *of the* WORLD

Everybody Knows That This is What Christopher Columbus Did; but What Else Do You Know about Him?

ONE evening long ago a man was trudging along a road in Northern Spain, leading his only child, a weary, worn-out little fellow of five years. They were eagerly looking for a convent, said to stand on a bleak and rugged hill, where they might find shelter for the night, and where the motherless boy might be left in charge of the monks while the father went about his affairs. Those affairs were very important to him, though they seemed very silly to most people of his time.

Assailed by Misfortunes

Not only did the way seem weary to the man, but so, too, did the whole wide world. After much travelling he was in a foreign land. Many misfortunes had assailed him. He had been shipwrecked once, and, what was even worse to him, he had been laughed at many times. He wondered whether people had once more deceived him, this time about finding shelter for his child. But after a few more miles the convent, called La Rabida, came into view, on the bleak and rugged hill-side. For once, the man had met with good fortune.

Welcomed by the Monks

The monks welcomed the traveller and made provision for him and the child. After supper some of them gathered in the great hall to hear news of the outside world, for in those days news came only by means of travellers. The monks asked all about their guest—where he came from, where he was going, what his business was, and by what name he was known.

The man had already told his story many times, but he now related it once more. He was an Italian, he said, born in Genoa about forty years before, the son of a humble wool-comber. As a boy he had worked at the weaver's trade, but in his longing for

Photo by Alinari

For many years Columbus had followed the Spanish court about, hoping for a hearing. At Salamanca, where he stayed in a monastery, his plan was at last discussed. In the picture above he is seen in despair at its rejection.

Photo by J. Ruiz Vernacci

Twice the monks of La Rabida took Columbus in when he was completely disheartened. Here is the scene in 1491 when he told them of the defeat of his plans. At once they opened the way that led him to success the next year. One wonders if his eleven-year-old son Diego, who is standing at the right, knows what it is all about.

120

adventure he had shipped as a sailor and voyaged to the eastern Mediterranean. A single voyage had given him a taste for others, and two years later he had set sail for England and the northern seas. When he arrived back in Lisbon he had settled down there for a time and married, and there the boy had been born.

Sailing Westward to the East

Dissatisfied with life ashore he sailed again in 1481, this time southward as far as the Equator. There, so he said, he made geographical measurements that confirmed what he had learned from maps and charts and voyages. He was convinced, he told the monks, that by sailing straight westward across the Atlantic he could reach those lands on the other side of the world; for like many others of his day he had come to believe that the earth was round.

The king of Portugal, to whom he had told this, had been sly enough to fit out a secret expedition without telling him. But the boat had turned back, and the sailors would not set out again. Disheartened by such treatment, the weary man had gone back to Lisbon, picked up his child—whose mother had died a year before—and set out for Spain, there to lay his plans before the king, who was much interested in finding a new route to the East. He did not know whether he could reach the king, for he had no friends at court, but he had at least reached La Rabida, where he hoped to leave the boy while he went on. The little boy was called Diego, and his father's name was Christopher Columbus.

The Monks Decide to Help Columbus

This was in 1485. After Columbus had gone to bed, some of the monks talked long and earnestly about what he had told them. They were convinced that this sailor might be right in his belief about reaching the East by sailing westward, since many other geographers held the same opinion about the shape of the earth. At any rate they concluded Columbus ought to have a chance to tell the king about his plan, for if new

Photo by J. Ruiz Vernacci

Here is Columbus at last laying his plans before Ferdinand and Isabella. The ridiculed and weary man convinced the proudest monarchs of Europe that his scheme would bring them untold wealth.

Photo by J. Ruiz Vernacci

Had it not been for Isabella, Columbus's plans would have fallen through. After he had been dismissed by King Ferdinand, the queen called him back and succeeded finally in persuading her husband to agree.

Photo by J. Ruiz Vernacci

This is the scene in the little harbour of Palos on the day Columbus set out on his most famous voyage. It is well to remember that the majority of the men who sailed with Columbus did not share his strong conviction as to the shape of the world. Many of them, indeed, feared that some day they would sail over its edge and be lost.

lands should be discovered the king would be the richer and they themselves might carry their faith to whole nations of heathen people. They decided to send Columbus to a nobleman in Seville who might be able to bring him before the king.

When Columbus heard the monks' plans he at once agreed, and soon set out for Seville, where he at once won over the nobleman. But he did not so readily convince the king, for Columbus could not even manage to lay the plan before him until some time had passed. When at last the king did hear the plan, he put off his decision for a long time, and the delay finally so disheartened Columbus that he thought of journeying on to France and trying to win the king of that land to his scheme. At length, however, the Spanish Queen Isabella prevailed upon King Ferdinand to send Columbus on a voyage, and it is said that she even sold her jewels to obtain money to fit out the ships. The agreement was made. Columbus was to be a nobleman and an admiral if he succeeded, and to become governor of all the lands he discovered—if he discovered any at all. It seems that neither the king nor queen was as yet wholly convinced that he would do so.

These are the brave little ships that set sail one August morning on the most hazardous voyage the world has ever known. The "Pinta," at the left, was a boat of fifty tons. The "Santa Maria," Columbus's flagship, was a boat of a hundred tons. And the "Niña," at the right, was a little shell of only forty tons. But with sails unfurled and pennons flying, they must have made a brave show, and certainly, when they sailed back home again, they brought the most welcome news such an expedition has ever carried.

Himself in command of the "Santa Maria," with his good friend Alonzo Pinzon commanding the "Pinta," and Alonzo's brother in charge of a third ship, the "Niña," Columbus set sail from Palos harbour on August 3, 1492, bound first for the Canary Islands, where he was to provision his ships for the great adventure. On September 6 he sailed westward across the Atlantic. As the long days passed without any sight of land, the men grew ever more dissatisfied, and talked of mutiny. But no threats could make Columbus turn back, for he was realizing a dream to which he had clung for years. The fleet kept on, ever westward, but veering just a little to the south.

After thirty-six days of sailing Columbus one night saw a light that seemed to come from a fire on land. At daybreak next morning, October 12, a sailor on the "Niña" actually sighted land, and the three small ships at once made for the shore. Columbus landed first. Bearing the flag of Spain in one hand and his sword in the other, he knelt down, kissed the earth, gave thanks to God, and claimed the land for the king of Spain. He named it San Salvador (Holy Redeemer).

The new-found land was an island of the Caribbean Sea, probably what is now known as Watling Island, and not India as Columbus thought. On this voyage the ships touched the other islands near, among them Cuba and the one now called Haiti. Columbus named it Hispaniola, and after leaving a garrison there he set sail for Spain, and arrived at Palos on March 15, 1493. Spain was filled with rejoicing. Christopher Columbus, the hero of the day, was at once made an admiral and appointed governor of the new territories, in accordance with the king's promise. Later in the same year Columbus set out on a second voyage, this time with a fleet of seventeen ships and over fifteen hundred men. When he reached Hispaniola he found that the garrison had disappeared; all the men had been killed by the natives. Undaunted, the great captain established a new settlement, which he called Isabella, and then went on an exploring expedition that lasted for the greater part of two years, finally

the eastern coast of South America, discovered the Orinoco River, and at last, with his ships in bad condition, reached the settlement on Hispaniola. Here he found the people quarrelling bitterly—so bitterly, indeed, that they had sent to Spain for a new governor. While Columbus tarried there, trying to patch up the quarrel, the new governor arrived. According to the king's agreement, made in 1492 and confirmed in 1493, Columbus still felt that he was the governor of all the lands he had discovered, so the two men at once fell into a dispute which ended by Columbus being put in chains and sent back to Spain.

When he reached Spain and was brought before the king and queen, they both pretended that they had known nothing at all

"Land! Land!" Can you imagine what it meant to the weary commander of a discouraged, rebellious crew to hear the words ring out early on that morning in October? The cry had been raised once or twice before, but it had always proved false. This time he knew it must be true, for on the day preceding the "Pinta" had hauled out of the water a cane, a pole, a board, and a stick that showed tool marks; and at ten o'clock in the evening Columbus himself had seen a light ahead. And now, on this memorable Friday, he saw the shore at last.

returning to Spain in the summer of 1496. Though the king was eager for Columbus to start at once on another voyage, two years passed before he again set sail. With a fleet of six ships he sailed in 1498, to be gone for two years. On this trip he skirted

of the affair and had had nothing to do with it, and that some great mistake had been made. Columbus was released, but he never again received much favour from the rulers. When Isabella died, his one good friend was gone. Two years later, however, the king

Photo by Underwood & Underwood

Columbus lands with members of his crew, who kneel upon the shore and kiss the ground in their great joy.

Photo by Rischgitz

Columbus presents to the king and queen a whole New World, together with the wealth he has brought home with him and some of the natives of that distant land— strange people who look upon the white men as gods.

Here is the eventful interview at which the bargain was struck between Columbus and Isabella of Spain. The intelligent and far-sighted queen must have been a good judge of men. On the soundness of her judgment she is about to stake a fortune, for in those jewel caskets lying on the table are the gems of the proudest queen in Europe at that day. We need no better evidence of the noble sincerity of the man the queen is honouring. The queen possessed the greatest confidence in the Genoese, whose implicit faith in himself and his belief that the earth was round was eventually to be so fully justified. No sovereign ever had a more faithful servant.

again fitted out an expedition, and with four miserable, leaky ships the great discoverer set sail once more. On this, his last voyage, he skirted the eastern coast of Central America, revisited Hispaniola, and at last, sick and weary, arrived in Spain.

But this time no cordial greetings awaited him, there were no friends to do him honour. The king gave him no more money. Poor, weary of life, and disappointed with his fellow men, Columbus lived on for four miserable years, dying in Valladolid (väl'yä-thŏ-lēth') on May 20, 1506. His body was sent to Hispaniola and buried in the cathedral at Santo Domingo. In 1795–1796 the remains were taken to Havana, where they rested in the cathedral until 1899. In that year, which marked Spain's loss of her last possession in the America that Columbus had given her, the remains of the dauntless Genoese were once more removed, and taken this time to Spain, where they still remain.

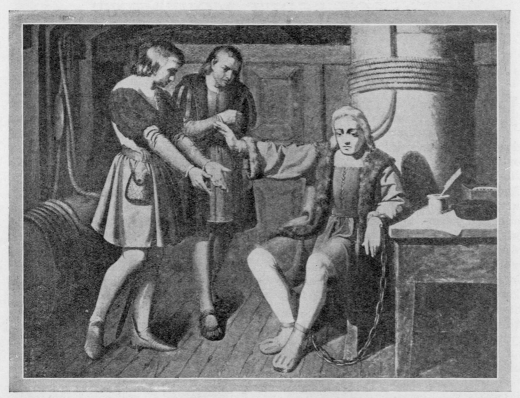

The world has a way of misusing its greatest men. From his third voyage Columbus went home in chains—which he always kept hanging in his cabinet afterwards, and which he asked to have buried with him when he died.

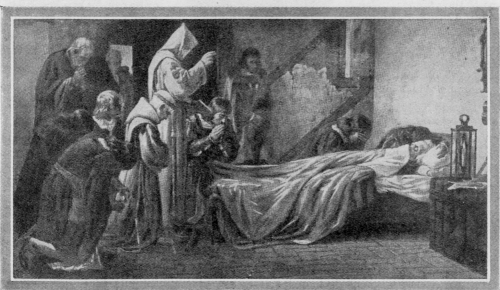

Photo by J. Ruiz Vernacci

Poor and sad, Columbus died neglected by the sovereign to whom he had given a new world. But his memory has lived on, and few ever think of America without coupling with it the honoured name of Columbus.

The BOY SCOUT MOVEMENT

It was Founded by Lord Baden-Powell, the Hero of the Siege of Mafeking, to Promote Good Citizenship Among the Rising Generation

HOW many of the grandfathers of the boys who to-day are Scouts would come home from school, and, lessons done, pore over a book by Fenimore Cooper or some other of the authors of adventure stories that used to delight boys! And how many of these boys would long to go scouting after Red Indians, to track wild animals, to sit by the camp fire and tell stories of the day's doings—and not only enjoy themselves, but be of real service to their king and country.

But for them it had all to be in the land of make-believe. The best they could hope for was a small home-made tent in the garden and a game of Indians with some of their friends. How different and how fortunate are the boys of to-day! They can really go scouting; they can engage in most of the wonderful adventures about which their grandfathers could only read and dream.

Lord Baden-Powell, in whose mind the Scout movement was born, and whom many thousands of boys all over the world regard with affection and look up to as their Chief.

stars by name and can find his way by them; he can name birds and animals and fishes, and knows the ways and dwelling-place of each.

A Scout walks through the woods with silent tread. His eyes are keen and he sees many things that others do not see. He notices tracks and signs which reveal to him the nature and habits of the creatures that made them. He knows how to stalk birds and animals, and study them in their natural haunts.

A Scout can kindle a fire in the forest on the wettest day, and he seldom uses more than one match. Even without matches he can still have a fire, for he knows the secret of rubbing sticks, like the Indians; or he can make a spark with only his knife blade and a piece of flint. He knows, also, the danger of forest fires, and he kindles a blaze that will not spread.

A Scout never flinches in the face of danger, for he knows that every faculty must be alert to preserve his safety and that of others. He knows what to do in case of fire or panic or shipwreck; he trains his mind to direct and his body to act. In all emergencies he sets an example of resourcefulness, coolness, and courage, and considers the safety of others before that of himself. He is especially kind to the helpless and weak.

What a Scout Can Do

A Boy Scout loves a hike through the woods more than a walk in the city streets. He can tell north or south or east or west by "signs." He can tie a knot that will hold; he can climb a tree that seems impossible to others; he can swim a river; he can pitch a tent; he can mend a tear in his trousers; he can tell which fruits and seeds are poisonous and which are not; he can distinguish nut-bearing trees from a distance; he can reef a sail or take his turn at the tiller, can pull an oar or use paddles and sculls; he knows the

First Aid for the Wounded

When an accident occurs a Scout does not run away or merely call for help. If a person is cut, he knows how to stop the flow of blood and gently and carefully bind up the wound.

If someone is burned, he knows how to ease the suffering. Let anyone be dragged from the water unconscious and, if a Scout is at hand, he will at once set to work to bring about his recovery.

A Scout knows his native town as well as he knows the trails in the woods. He can guide a stranger wherever he desires to go, and his knowledge of short cuts saves him many needless steps. He knows where the police stations are situated, where the fire-alarms are placed, where the nearest doctor lives, where the hospitals are, and which is the quickest way to reach them.

The Boy Scout movement was founded in 1908 by General Baden-Powell (now Lord Baden-Powell of Gilwell). The scheme of scouting had, however, been devised many years before this, and had been used by Baden-Powell in training the young soldiers in his regiments — the 13th Hussars and the 5th Dragoon Guards. In Mafeking, too, where he was besieged by the Boers for seven months during the South African War (1899 - 1902), he had made use of the boys of the place for carrying out responsible work as despatch bearers, and had convinced himself that, where trusted, they were quite capable of performing many of the duties of grown men.

This experience, coupled with the fact that his book, "Aids to Scouting," written for soldiers, was being used as a text book in boys' and girls' schools, led Baden-Powell to think that there must be something in scouting that would appeal to boys; and, while giving them an interesting and healthful hobby, could find out and develop along

useful lines such character and talents as they possessed and harness them for the benefit of the country as well as of the boys themselves.

It was on Brownsea Island, Dorset, that the scheme of scout training for boys was tried out in August, 1907. Baden-Powell went into camp there with a couple of "Assistant Scoutmasters" and two patrols of Boy Scouts consisting of boys from elementary, secondary and public schools. For a fortnight these pioneer Boy Scouts played the game of scouting for boys just as it is played in the best troops to-day. Each morning they saluted the flag, and each evening they sat round their camp fires and sang songs or listened to the yarns told by their Chief.

This first camp was a success, and showed that scouting appealed to boys of various types; while their parents, when consulted, could find nothing but praise for the new game. That it was a workable scheme had now been proved, and Baden-Powell therefore set to work and wrote the handbook "Scouting for Boys," a book which has since become world famous.

A gift from Canada. Rover Scouts with a magnificent buffalo head from the National Park, Ottawa, presented to them by the Canadian chief commissioner.

The book was issued in fortnightly parts at fourpence a copy, and before the second part was published in January, 1908, Troops and Patrols of Scouts had sprung up like mushrooms all over the country. These looked to Baden-Powell as their leader, and so heavy was his correspondence with would-be Scouts and Scoutmasters, that he was obliged to open a headquarters office and appoint a secretary to deal with the exceptionally large number of enquiries.

In 1909 the movement had become so widespread and so popular that the Chief called a gathering at the Crystal Palace of all Boy Scouts who could come. To the surprise of everyone concerned eleven thousand turned up; they had journeyed from all parts of the British Isles, and many had come from distant lands across the sea.

The King Gives Encouragement

In 1911 the king reviewed the Scouts at a rally in Windsor Great Park, giving the greatest encouragement by his approval and

Scouts from overseas enjoying a meal together outside their hut during the great jamboree held at Arrowe Park, Birkenhead, in 1929.

interest, and by 1914 the Scouts numbered 158,000 in the United Kingdom and the movement was rapidly extending to overseas dominions and foreign countries.

Then came the World War to shake it to its very foundations. Scoutmasters hurried off to join the army and navy, taking with them the older boys, and the troops were left sadly depleted. No one could have been surprised if the Scout movement had gone to pieces.

But it did no such thing. On the contrary, it made the most of a time when everybody was afire with patriotism, when service was the order of the day, and when it was much more pleasant to belong to a uniformed, dis-

ciplined body than to loaf and play about at street corners. Those who were too young to join the army or navy could, by joining up with the Scouts, carry out organized and recognized public service for the country in its time of great need.

It was the patrol system, by which six or eight boys worked under their own boy leader, that kept the troops alive through the difficult days of war. Each Troop had started life with not only a Scoutmaster and possibly an Assistant-Scoutmaster, but also with three or four Patrol Leaders, boys trained to take responsibility and to organize their own particular band of followers. Then each Patrol Leader had his "second" who could take over his duties when necessary.

In this way, even without Scoutmasters, the Troops were able to carry on and not only to keep one movement going, but also to perform work for the country, which earned high praise from the various authorities.

The war work which the Scouts did was both varied and important, and included watching the coast of England and Scotland from John o'Groats to Land's End. Thirty thousand Scouts took their turn at this coast-watching service, thus relieving the coastguardsmen for service afloat; and this went on to the end of the war.

Admiralty and War Office Work

Then at the Admiralty, the War Office, and the various ministries Scouts were taken on in large numbers to act as messengers, orderlies, and despatch riders, and throughout the country they were similarly employed by the police and municipal authorities.

In addition to these more official duties a large amount of voluntary public service was carried out, such as the collection of eggs and

Scouts spend most of their time out-of-doors, and here you see them engaged in a few of their varied activities. A. Scout setting off with his kit packed in a rucksack. B. Pitching a tent. C. Off to camp. D. Two Scouts setting off for their day's training. E. Two Scouts busy with soap and tooth-brush. "Cleanliness is next to Godliness" is a saying in which all good Scouts believe—and act upon. F. Finding their route. Every Scout includes as part of his duties a knowledge of map reading. G. A Scout with his full outfit.

131

other comforts for the wounded, the growing of vegetables for the fleet, and the collection of waste-paper, horse-chestnuts, sphagnum moss and other things, according to the requirements of the time. In Belfast the Scouts, by the systematic collection and sale of old bottles, raised the sum of £750 for the provision of a recreation hut for soldiers in France. Four other huts and two motor-ambulances were also provided in the same way, by work on the part of the boys.

One piece of war work performed by Scouts will stand out for ever in the memories of those who were in London during the German air-raids: it was their employment as buglers to sound the "all clear" when the enemy aircraft had turned homewards. These are only a few examples of the sort of work which the Scouts carried out, even in the absence of their leaders, and with the older boys constantly leaving to join the fighting forces.

The ranks were soon filled up, however, with young boys full of zeal to do something for their country. Some of these keen youngsters were well below the Scout age of eleven years, and it was at this time that the Chief Scout instituted the Wolf Cub movement for the benefit of those too young to join the Scouts. The Cubs, with their simpler training, proved a most popular branch, which has continued to flourish and increase rapidly.

Towards the end of the war the need also became apparent for a branch of the movement for those older boys who had been on service, or for those who had not previously

Photo by Boy Scouts Association

Above, a Scout making a fire by means of friction; no Scout ever lacks the means of warmth or cooking because he has no matches. Below, chip carving. Some Scouts are skilled workmen and well deserve the badges of distinction which they have been awarded.

been connected with the Scout movement. For this purpose there came into being the Rover Scouts, to carry out self-training of a more advanced kind.

In 1920 a big international rally or "jamboree" was held in London, this being open to Scouts from all countries. It had not been possible, during the war, to see much of what was going on in other countries, and it came as a surprise even to the Chief Scout himself, to realize what strides had been made. Twenty-seven countries sent representative Scouts, and these all camped together, speaking many different languages, but working and playing happily together under the same Scout Law.

Fine displays of every branch of scoutcraft were given each day for a fortnight before a large public, and on the final evening the Chief Scout of the Empire was publicly acclaimed Chief Scout of the World by those present. Thus the leader of that handful of boys on Brownsea had, in the space of twelve years, become the leader of a million and more boys throughout the world. An International Council was formed, with an office in London, and it was arranged to hold big international rallies every four years.

The Scout movement has continued to flourish and spread year by year, so that at the present time there is hardly a country in the world that has not its Scouts, all of whom live up to the same Scout Promise and Law, undergo the same training, and wear the

These seven Scouts are certain of having performed their good deed for the day. They have made a house-to-house collection of broken toys from poor children, and are seen above busily repairing them at the work-shop which they, themselves, have fitted out for this special purpose. We may be sure that their labour of love is earning real gratitude from the little owners of the toys, which will be given a new lease of life.

same uniform and badges. In 1929 the king conferred a peerage upon the Chief Scout.

What exactly is this scouting scheme which has caught the imagination of so many boys of all classes, creeds, countries and colours, and has in twenty-five years become a world-wide brotherhood? It is a form of self-education in four important things: character, health, handicraft and service.

"Man's Job Cut Down"

In the words of an eminent American professor, Dean Russell, of Columbia University, scouting is "the man's job cut down to the boy's size." It takes the best qualities of real men and holds these up to the boys as qualities which they are expected to possess.

In the Scout Law there is not a single suggestion of MUST NOT. Rather it is a statement of ten qualities which every Scout is expected to possess. 1. A Scout's honour is to be trusted; 2. A Scout is loyal; 3. A Scout's duty is to be useful and to help others; 4. A Scout is a friend to all and a brother to every other Scout; 5. A Scout is courteous; 6. A Scout is a friend to animals; 7. A Scout obeys orders; 8. A Scout smiles and whistles in all difficulties; 9. A Scout is thrifty; 10. A Scout is clean in thought, word, and deed.

Promise Taken by all Scouts

The Scout Promise, which every boy takes on joining, binds him to do his best to carry out these Laws.

On my honour I promise that I will do my best:

To do my duty to God and the king.
To help other people at all times.
To obey the Scout Law.

On these two things, the Scout Promise and the Scout Law, hangs the whole of the scheme of scouting for boys. They are the spirit underlying every part of the training.

The members of this great Scout brotherhood are graded, for purposes of training, into three sections: Wolf Cubs, from 8–11 years; Scouts and Sea Scouts, 11–17 years; Rover Scouts, 17 years and upwards.

The Wolf Cubs have a simplified Promise and Law, which is the following:—

I promise to do my best to be loyal and to do my duty to God and the king and to keep the Law of the Wolf Cub Pack.

The Law:
1. The Cub gives in to the Old Wolf.
2. The Cub does not give in to himself.

Wolf Cubs are organized in "Packs" under a man or woman Cubmaster, known to the boys as "Akela." Their training is based largely on Rudyard Kipling's Jungle Books, and appeals to the smaller boy's natural love of make-believe and dressing up. The training is quite separate from that of the Scouts, and the Cub looks up to the Scout troop as the goal for which he is aiming.

Training To Be Prepared

Boy Scouts and Sea Scouts are organized in Patrols of six, each patrol under its own boy leader. Four or more patrols form a Troop under a Scoutmaster. The ordinary training of a Scout is based on the activities of backwoodsmen and explorers. Pioneering, camping, fire-lighting, cooking, pathfinding, tracking, nature lore, astronomy—these are some of the many jobs at which the Scout tries his hand. His motto is "Be Prepared," and the number of cases where Scouts have saved lives or otherwise distinguished themselves in emergencies, prove that every member tries his level best to live up to this stirring motto.

The test of the Scout is the

The Highland fling. A Scots Rover Scout working off some of his high spirits, and at the same time entertaining his brother Scouts.

Daily Good Turn. If he performs this, he has a right to be classed with the great scouts who have served their country. The Good Turn may not be a very big thing—perhaps helping an old woman to cross the road, removing a banana skin from the pavement so that people may not slip, or giving water to a thirsty horse. Yet it is a big thing in a boy's life to wake up each morning with the thought of doing a kindness to someone.

A Scout's Brave Deed

Here is the story of one Scout who saved two other boys through his Scout training. The three boys were swimming in a river when he noticed one seize the other as though trying to duck him. He watched them closely and saw they were not playing, but were choking and unable to cry for help.

"I was fifteen feet away," he told his friends later, "and I swam towards them. I saw they were too big for me to bring them to shore, so I took several deep breaths, dived and came up under the boys, pushing them up so that they could get a little air; then I tried to swim between them so as to break their grips on each other."

But both boys clung to their would-be rescuer, pulling him down in their frantic struggles. He was practically exhausted, but he still held on like a good Scout, kicking as hard as he could, and managed to make some progress up the stream. Meanwhile, those on shore formed a human chain and at last relayed a life-belt to the Scout, who brought both boys safely to shore. A gold medal was awarded to this brave Scout, and well he deserved it.

To a Sea Scout the life of a sailor

In the upper picture are shown Scouts building a model suspension bridge in readiness for the Chief Scout's visit to their training camp. They are ex- cellent engineers and know their job thoroughly. In the lower picture a Scout is seen giving a lesson in tree felling, an art not nearly so simple as it may appear.

135

appeals rather than the life of a backwoodsman. So he does his hiking by water. Otherwise he is the same as any other Boy Scout, from whom he can be distinguished only by the cap and jersey which stamp him as a seaman. His ideals are the same;

On the left, a Scout working a backwoods lathe. Below, kit inspection. Scouts, like soldiers, must be scrupulously tidy and methodical, or there would be chaos in a large camp.

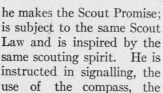

Photos by Boy Scouts' Association

he makes the Scout Promise; is subject to the same Scout Law and is inspired by the same scouting spirit. He is instructed in signalling, the use of the compass, the rule of the road at sea, distinguishing types of vessels, chart reading, sounding, nature study, the tides, the elements of astronomy and meteorology, the handling of boats, swimming, life-saving, rocket apparatus work, going aloft, knotting, sail-making, ship's carpentry, engineering, first aid and other work.

Rover Scouts generally form a "Crew" under a Rover Leader, and undergo more advanced training in scouting. Their motto is "Service," and the public services which they carry out are many and varied. The Cub Pack, Scout Troop, and Rover Scout Crew together form a complete Scout Group. Each Group has a Group Scoutmaster who is responsible for the Group as a whole, but who has assistants for each separate section.

The Cubs and Scouts train themselves to pass tests for which they receive badges to wear on their arms. Although there is a list of over sixty subjects in which Scouts may qualify for proficiency badges, no boy is expected to go in for more than a few of the subjects. He must be a "badge earner" rather than a "badge hunter," and out of the variety offered he can choose those subjects which specially interest him and which may help him to a career later on. From the following badges a Scout may select those for which he wishes to qualify: Ambulance man, airman, artist, athlete, basket worker, bee-master, bird-warden, blacksmith, boatman, bookbinder, camper, carpenter, clerk, coastwatchman, cook, cyclist, dairyman, debater, electrician, engineer, entertainer, farmer, fireman, folk dancer, forester, friend to animals, gardener, handyman, healthy man, horseman, interpreter, journalist, leather worker, marksman, mason, master-at-arms, metal worker, miner, missioner, musician, naturalist, oarsman, pathfinder, photographer, pilot, pioneer, piper, plumber, poultry farmer, printer, prospector,

Above, Boy Scouts from Ceylon rehearsing their dance in national costume, and, below, on their way to the jamboree, held at Gödöllö, Hungary, in August, 1933, where they met fellow Scouts of many other nations and made friends with them. This jamboree—the fourth —represented the twenty-fifth anniversary of Scouting.

public healthman, reader, rescuer, rigger, sea fisherman, signaller, stalker, starman, surveyor, swimmer, tailor, tracker, weatherman, wirelessman.

The Cubs proficiency badges are: Collector, observer, gardener, artist, home craft, toymaker, first - aider, guide, house - orderly, athlete, swimmer, team player.

At Gilwell Park, in Epping Forest, there is the chief training camp for Scoutmasters. For it is not only the boys who have to train themselves for their job but the Scoutmasters also. Many men are anxious to help the movement, but feel that, as they were never Boy Scouts themselves, they do not know very much about it. When they ask what they should do and how they should do it, they receive the answer—"Go to Gilwell."

At Gilwell they cease to be men for the time being and become boys, Scouts in a Troop. They go through everything that a Scout has to learn, taking turns to be Patrol Leader, Second, and so on. If they have forgotten what it feels like to be a boy they learn it over again at Gilwell, where also they are taught the best and quickest methods for training their Scouts.

Men from all over the world come to Gilwell to pass through training courses. And from Gilwell men go out and found other Gilwells, or Scouters' Training Camps, in other parts of the world, so that instead of having to come to England the Scoutmaster of the future can go to his own local Gilwell to be trained. The Chief Scout has visited "Gilwells" in Australia, New Zealand, South Africa, and many other distant places.

The Scout movement is directed by a council with the Chief Scout as chairman, and consists of a body of men specially selected for heads of the different departments of the movement, such for instance as Overseas, International, Rover Scout, Wolf Cub, Sea Scout, Equipment, Training, etc.

In each county in England there is a County Commissioner, appointed by headquarters, who is responsible for the Scouts in that county. The county is then sub-divided into districts, each under a District Commissioner who is responsible to the county commissioner. Each district again contains local associations to run the movement locally; these local associations recommend Scoutmasters, conduct badge examinations, and raise funds for the Groups in their district. Next come the Scoutmasters, each with his own Group of boys, and with Assistant - scoutmasters, Cubmasters and Assistants to help them. And so on to the Patrol Leaders, Cub Sixers, Scouts and Cubs.

Thus right through the whole movement

From Tokyo comes this picture of Japanese Sea Scouts setting out in their strange boats for a trip. They are very proud of their boats and their skill in managing them, and it is plain that they are excitedly cheering as they move down the river.

—from the Chief Scout down to the youngest Cub—everybody has responsibility for his own job, and is trusted to do his best. The Patrol Leader who has "run" his Patrol of six or eight boys is getting splendid practice towards being a Scoutmaster later on. So much for the Scout movement at home. But the Chief Scout is also Chief Scout of the *World*. So that there is also an international council, consisting of leading men of all the countries where there are Scouts. These men come together in conference not so much to represent their own countries as to work together to make the whole world of Scouting a success. Meetings of this council take place every two years, and each time in a different country.

International jamborees, or gatherings of Scouts from all parts of the world, are held every four years. The first of these was held in London, in 1920; the second in Denmark, in 1924; the third, which was postponed for a year in order to celebrate the "coming of age" of the movement, at Arrowe Park, Birkenhead, England, in 1929, when no fewer than forty-two nations and thirty-three parts of the British Empire were represented among the 50,000 Scouts in attendance.

The fourth jamboree, which was held at Gödöllö, Hungary, in August, 1933, represented the twenty-fifth anniversary of Scouting. There were 22,000 scouts in camp, and they came from thirty-four countries. The contingent from Great Britain and her dominions and colonies numbered 2,000.

The scene at the opening ceremony was one of the most impressive in the history of the Scout movement. The regent of Hungary extended an enthusiastic welcome to the visitors, and the Chief Scout gave a

Perhaps this boy is really injured and the other Scouts are skilfully dressing his wounds. But probably they are only practising—since it is so much easier in an emergency to do a thing one has often done before.

message of greeting to his followers from all over the world.

Then came the grand march past, headed by the Hungarian Boy Scouts' national flag. The long line was led by French Scouts, followed by the Belgian representatives and those of all the other countries in attendance, the British Empire contingent occupying a central position in the procession. At the end marched the Hungarian hosts, 8,000 strong.

In addition to these big occasional meetings of the Scouts of all the world, a great deal of camping is carried out by Scouts in countries other than their own. At Kandersteg, in Switzerland, the Scouts have their international Châlet, which Groups from all countries can visit and enjoy winter sports and climbing.

The movement has been adopted throughout the world with such enthusiasm that to-day the number of Boy Scouts of all ranks recognized by the International Bureau is well above 2,250,000. Of this total the British Isles claim well over 500,000, and the overseas empire is responsible for more than 400,000. In addition, British groups in foreign countries account for some 3,000.

In India and Ceylon there are upwards of 200,000 Scouts; Australia and New Zealand have some 75,000; Canada has 65,000, and there are about 18,000 in South Africa. Wherever we may travel—Nigeria or Palestine, Belgium or Brazil, Trinidad or Tanganyika Territory, Barbados or Bermuda—there we shall meet with evidence of the widespread Boy Scout movement.

In the United States of America there are nearly as many Scouts as there are in the British Empire, and it is estimated that since the movement was introduced into the country in 1910, more than four million boys have passed through the organization.

There is nothing new in the world, and the Chief Scout does not claim to have "invented" Scouting. The Scout Law, indeed, was adapted from the code of the knights of the Middle Ages, while the Scout's uniform of shirt, shorts, scarf and cowboy hat was

Boy Scouts in America dispatching and receiving messages by flag in the morse code. While one sends a message by waving the flag, another watches for the reply, which he repeats to a third Scout, who writes it down in his book.

taken from the uniform of the South African constabulary.

Much of the training was suggested by that of the Zulus, Swazi, Matabele, and Red Indian tribes; by the code of the Knights of the Round Table; by the Bushido of the Japanese; as well as by more modern methods of training in various countries, and the writings of Rudyard Kipling, Mrs. Ewing, and some others.

What the Chief Scout has done is to take the best out of these various methods and ideas and reduce them to a system of life such as boys can appreciate, wherein they can get adventure and excitement, companionship and friendly rivalry, camping and travel, to their hearts' content, and at the same time be fitting themselves for happy, healthy, efficient citizenship in the world of to-morrow.

And last but not least important is the future. Every year the numbers of Scouts increase in every country where the movement has been started; every year more boys are growing up and passing out into the world, boys who have made friends with brother Scouts in other lands, many of whom keep in close touch with each other by correspondence.

We are told that "peace cannot be forced by legislation; it must be made in the hearts of men." And in this great world brotherhood of Scouts there will be, in the future, large numbers of men whose hearts are at peace with their comrades in other countries because they know them as friends, have worked and played side by side with them, have accepted their hospitality and returned it, and have shared the same camp life in sunshine and in rain.

In a recent speech the Chief Scout said: "When one sees great international conferences failing to bring about results, while our Movement continues to progress successfully one can well believe that there is a higher power than ours helping us towards success."

An Age of Peace and Goodwill

The more this movement spreads the less likely will be the nations to go to war with one another in the future, and there will dawn in the world an age of peace and goodwill, thanks very largely to the spirit of Scouting.

Elias Howe, chief inventor of the sewing-machine; at the right is his first model. Next time you run up a seam, think how much work he has saved us all.

By courtesy of the Science Museum

TWELVE THOUSAND STITCHES *a* MINUTE

This is the Number That Can be Made by the Sewing-Machine, Which is Said to Have Been Invented as the Result of a Dream

TAKE a needle and sew a seam just as fast as you can. Count the stitches. Get your brother to hold a watch and say "Stop" at the end of one minute. You will know how many stitches you can make in a minute.

Then remember that in the big factories there are machines with several needles that sew twelve thousand stitches in a minute and you will realize what the sewing-machine has done for mankind. It will take you at least a whole day to make all those stitches; so the big machine works about five hundred times as fast as you can. Now think of how much work is saved, and how many more clothes can be made, by means of one invention.

Everything in the world was sewn by hand until about a hundred years ago. Millions of people had to sit plying their needles and straining their eyes until far into the night, to make enough clothes to cover their own backs or those of the lucky ones who could afford to have the work done for them. And then came one clever machine to do nearly all the work and set them free.

It was a long time coming, however. Far back in the dim past, when a man used to go out and kill any animal he could find to eat, he discovered that he could use the animal's fur to keep him warm. He punched a few holes in the skin and then ran a string of rawhide, also made out of the skin, through the holes. At first he must have punched the holes with a thorn or a sharp piece of bone, and run the string through with his finger; but eventually the notion occurred to him of doing both of these things at once, so he shaped a slender piece of bone or bronze to a sharp point, bored a hole in the end of it, and ran the string through the hole. Then he could punch and sew at the same time. He had invented the first needle.

141

We have found needles like that in the ruins of Egypt, and of Greece and Rome; but it was still a long way to the familiar steel needles we know to-day.

China Gives Us the Needle

These bright little needles seem to have come from the Chinese. In the Middle Ages the Arabs who swarmed into Europe brought these needles with them, and a little later the Germans were making them. By the time of Queen Elizabeth they could be bought in the shops of London, and just a little later the English were making them for themselves. To this day most of the hand needles are made in Germany and England, though the majority of the machine needles come from America.

It was an Englishman named Thomas Saint who first thought of making a needle work by machinery. He made a good many drawings, and took out a patent for a sewing-machine in 1790; but his invention never succeeded. In 1830 a French tailor named Barthélmy Thim-monier (bär'täl-mē tē-mŏ-nyā') patented a crude machine that worked well enough for him to install eighty of them in a factory. But the workmen thought he was taking away

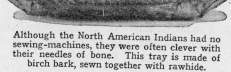

Although the North American Indians had no sewing-machines, they were often clever with their needles of bone. This tray is made of birch bark, sewn together with rawhide.

their work and they smashed his machines and nearly killed him. He continued improving his invention, but his efforts met with little appreciation.

About this time Walter Hunt, of New York, was also at work on the invention of a sewing-machine, and in 1832 he produced one with an eye-pointed needle and a shuttle to make a lock-stitch. These two inventions were of great importance, but Hunt made the mistake of never taking out a patent for his work; and all the profits went to others.

Next came Elias Howe, of Massachusetts. He was born of a family of inventors. One of his uncles is said to have built the first spring bed; another built the first truss bridge ever put up in America—the Howe Truss over the Connecticut River at Spring-field. When Howe started working on his machine he apparently had not heard of the one made by Hunt.

Howe's father was a farmer, who also had a flour mill, and in this mill the boy began to learn something about machinery when he was still very young. He was meant to be a farmer, too, but he liked machinery so well that he left the farm as soon as he could, and by the age of twenty-one had become a very good machinist. But he had his own way of doing things, and his employers did not always like them; and since he was often in poor health also, he was frequently out of work. He had married very young, and he and his family were frequently in dire poverty.

One day in Boston he heard his employer talking to a man who had invented a crude type of machine for knitting. The employer said there was a fortune waiting for the man who could make a sewing-machine. One night a little later, as Howe lay ill, he was watching his frail wife bent over her needle, for she had to take in sewing to obtain food for the family. From that moment he set himself to invent a machine.

When he had employment he worked on his machine at night, and while he was out of work he spent all his time upon it; but it was a long and difficult job. What bothered him most was the needle. He toiled a whole year before he found that a double-pointed needle with the eye in the centre would not do. But finally the idea occurred to him of putting the eye at the end of a grooved needle and of having a shuttle to carry a second thread to lock the stitch.

When a Dream Came True

The story goes that it all came to him in a dream. In his worry over his invention and the poverty of his wife and children, he is said to have dreamed that he had been brought before a great heathen king. The king ordered him to finish his machine or give up his life. The time passed and the machine was not ready, so the king's soldiers came to his cell to lead him to his death. In the head of every spear they carried was a hole like an eye.

Howe awoke and rushed to his machine. The problem of the needle was solved and the machine was soon ready to run. That was in 1844. Perhaps the story may be just one more invention, although it is a very probable dream for a man to have in such conditions.

But Howe still had a world of trouble before him. He challenged some women to a sewing race—they with needles and he with his machine. He won easily, but all he received for his pains was the enmity of the women, who thought he would take their work away. He had no money to put his machine on the market, but an old school friend came to his assistance, advancing £100 for a half share in the machine. The friend lost interest, however, and no one else considered the machine to be of value. At that period Howe had to work as a railway engineer to get bread for the family. Then his health broke down again, and he was compelled to give that up. At length, however, he was able to patent his machine, a step which was to lead to fortune.

Unable to interest anyone in America to adopt his invention, Howe decided to send his machine to England, confident that there was a future for it. The journey across the Atlantic was undertaken by his brother, who succeeded in disposing of the English rights to William Thomas, a Cheapside manufacturer. Thomas agreed to pay £250 for the machine, on condition that Howe would come over and make certain improvements —for which he offered to pay the inventor at the rate of £3 a week. So Howe and his

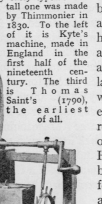

How different from our swift and beautiful sewing-machines of to-day are these three very early types. The tall one was made by Thimmonier in 1830. To the left of it is Kyte's machine, made in England in the first half of the nineteenth century. The third is Thomas Saint's (1790), the earliest of all.

By courtesy of the Science Museum

family came to England. He remained in the service of Thomas for about two years, but the machine did not prove the success that had been anticipated, and so Howe borrowed enough money to send his wife and children back to America and then worked his own passage across the Atlantic as a cook. He landed in 1849, without even enough money to reach the bedside of his sick wife. He managed to borrow sufficient for his fare, and arrived just in time to see her die.

Many things had happened while Howe had been abroad. Machines like his own had found their way on to the market, but they were infringements of his patent. He managed to raise enough money to fight for his rights in the courts, and after a long-drawn-out struggle he won his case. And before he died, in 1867, the men who were using his patents had paid him altogether about £400,000. Since that day the sewing-machine has seen all sorts of improvements, though the basic principle has remained the same, and now millions of machines are manufactured every year.

The Giant and the Dwarf Among Sewing-machines

There are a great many kinds of sewing-machines. One company makes about three thousand different kinds. Some of them are worked by hand, some by foot, and some by electricity. There is a tiny machine, weighing 2½ pounds, on which to learn how to sew; and there is a giant one, weighing 2½ tons, for sewing great machine belts as much as an inch and a half in thickness. There are machines for sewing on buttons and for cutting and sewing buttonholes. Some work with a single thread and make a chain-stitch; some with two threads and make a double chain or a lock-stitch. But the principle is always the same.

The first really successful domestic lock-stitch machine was produced in 1851. It differed widely from the modern sewing-machine, and instead of having a treadle stand it had to be fitted on to the packing-case in which it had been placed for safe delivery, and was worked by hand. Five years later, in response to a demand for a lighter and faster machine, came the machine worked by a treadle. It was fitted with a vibrating arm carrying the needle, and was worked from the treadle by means of a driving-wheel connected to the mechanism by a flat leather belt.

In 1870 a special machine was designed for the use of tailors and dressmakers, and with the introduction of the oscillating shuttle mechanism, a new era in sewing-machine construction was marked. In this model all gears were dispensed with, and less noise, increased speed, and greater thread space in the shuttle were among its chief improvements.

Various other changes were introduced in later years, and with the increasing use of electricity it was not long before it became possible to use this power for the working of the sewing-machine. For the domestic models a small motor was provided, which could be attached to the machine, and this did away with the need for pedalling or hand-turning.

Not only in the mechanism of the machines were improvements continually being made, but also in the general appearance, until to-day it is possible to purchase a sewing-machine which, when not in use, can be hidden away within a cabinet (as shown in the illustration). It is also possible to obtain a model which, when closed and with the knee lever turned up out of sight, is converted into a useful and artistic table. A variety of attachments can also be obtained that will enable you to do ruffling, binding, tuck-making, gauging, quilting, darning, pleating and other necessary and useful work, and even rugs of many patterns for the home can now be made with the aid of the domestic sewing-machine.

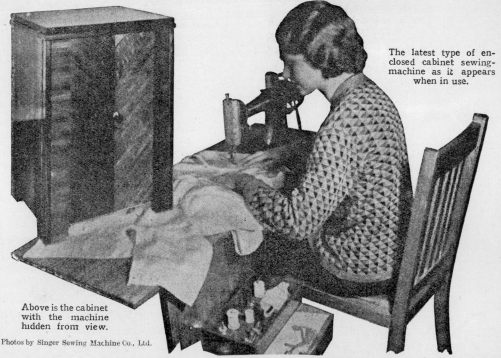

The latest type of enclosed cabinet sewing-machine as it appears when in use.

Above is the cabinet with the machine hidden from view.

Photos by Singer Sewing Machine Co., Ltd.

Photos by L.M.S. Rly. and National Portrait Gallery

In this quiet place our greatest poet, William Shakespeare, has slept for more than three centuries. Every year tens of thousands of people flock to the little church beside the river Avon to stand by the grave of the man who put their own thoughts and feelings into more perfect words than anyone has ever done—before or since.

The GREATEST POET of ALL

Mighty Shakespeare Had a Matchless Gift of Words to Paint His Glorious Vision of the Heart of Man

(CONTINUED FROM PAGE 100)

ON THE banks of a sleepy river about eighty miles north-west of London lies a town that is probably more fascinating to travellers than is any other of its size in the world. Its name is Stratford-on-Avon. Thousands of visitors wander up and down its crooked streets every year. They try to forget its noisy bustle and to think of the place as it used to be in the spacious days of Queen Elizabeth. For here in 1564 the poet, William Shakespeare, was born. Here he lived until he was old enough to go out into the world and seek his fortune. Hither he came back, rich and famous. Here he died, in 1616, and here he lies to-day in the old parish church of the Holy Trinity beside the Avon.

Even when Shakespeare was a boy, Stratford was a busy town. Although there were no newspapers in those days, and no trains, he could learn many things about the great world. Strollers and singers, acrobats and actors often came tramping over the highway from London, bringing with them all kinds of stories about the great men in the city, and about the heroes who were fighting bravely on the sea for England's honour or claiming for the flag new lands in distant countries. Sometimes a group of actors would come to the little town to present one of the very plays that had lately been acted before the queen.

Now and then the queen herself, with all her lords and ladies in gay costumes, passed through Stratford on a visit to a favourite nobleman. Once she was brilliantly entertained by the earl of Leicester at Kenilworth Castle, which was not very far away. Shakespeare was twelve years old at the time. There is little doubt that the eager boy was taken by his father to Kenilworth to see the splendour of the fireworks that night, for a description of them is given in "A Midsummer Night's Dream" in a scene between Oberon, the king of the fairies, and Puck, beginning:

"My gentle Puck come hither. Thou rememberest . . . ,"

where he refers to "certain stars" that "shot madly from their spheres."

William's father was an important man in the town. He kept a shop next door to their house, and here he sold leather, grain and wool from the farm while his thrifty wife spun warm clothing for William and his brothers and sisters, or watched the juicy roast turning on the iron spit of the great fireplace. Some day you may be able to go and see the picturesque old house where they lived, in Henley Street.

The Poet's School Days

William was not troubled by any cares heavier than the books he carried to the little grammar school, still attended by the boys of Stratford. It was a good school, and the lad was quick to learn. As likely as not, during tiresome hours indoors, his feet tapped restlessly under his hard, narrow bench, and he longed for the freedom of shadowy forests, wide meadows and quiet lanes leading across the English countryside.

A Lover of Sport and Nature

Certainly he must have been fond of fishing and swimming in the summer pools, and of all the other sports that are open to a country-bred boy. We can tell that from the poetry he wrote when he grew up. His eye never missed the delicate colouring of the evening cloud or the loveliness of the wayside flower; his ear never failed to catch the sweet note of the lark as it flew heavenwards. From childhood he loved the beauties of Nature—and that is as important in a poet as the gift of words.

As he grew older the youth's rambles often led him across the meadows to the pretty

In this dignified old house at Stratford-on-Avon William Shakespeare was born. To-day we may walk through the rooms in which he played as a child, and look upon many of his possessions. There is no authentic portrait of him as a boy, but the artist who painted the portrait above has imagined what the boy may well have been like at the age of twelve or thirteen years. Certainly he must have been a lively and wide-awake lad.

No one is able to say for certain that Shakespeare was ever caught poaching on Sir Thomas Lucy's preserves, but if he was, something like this must have happened when he was brought red-handed before the knight.

Photos by G.W. Rly. and Rischgitz

To this charming little thatched cottage in the pretty village ot Shottery the young William Shakespeare came to woo Anne Hathaway, who later became his wife. The passing centuries have not changed it very much.

147

village of Shottery, drawn not so much by the beauties of the scenery as by the bright eyes of a maiden. For here in a thatched cottage lived Anne Hathaway, whose heart the eighteen-year-old Shakespeare quickly won. When they were married the young husband brought his bride to Stratford, where within a few years their three children were born.

At first Shakespeare may not have taken his new cares very serious-ly. There is a tradition that he joined some other mischievous fellows in a wild frolic of hunting the deer on Sir Thomas Lucy's prop-erty at Charlecote, near Strat-ford, and got into trouble. Indeed, so re-lentlessly, it appeared, did Sir Thomas Lucy pursue the reckless young man that Stratford became too hot to hold him, and he was forced to leave the place of his birth.

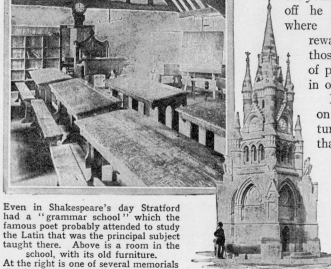

Even in Shakespeare's day Stratford had a "grammar school" which the famous poet probably attended to study the Latin that was the principal subject taught there. Above is a room in the school, with its old furniture.
At the right is one of several memorials that have been erected in Stratford, the poet's birthplace.

Many people have thrown doubt on this deer-stealing incident, although, on the other hand, there is a good deal of evidence that makes it appear possible. Colour is given to the story by the fact that Shallow, the country justice who makes his first appearance in the Second Part of "Henry IV" and again turns up in "The Merry Wives of Windsor," is almost certainly a caricature of the aggrieved knight.

In the first scene of "The Merry Wives" Justice Shallow has come to Windsor to "make a Star Chamber matter" of a poaching expedition which had been carried out by

Falstaff, and in which some of Shallow's deer had been killed. And, what makes the likeness to Sir Thomas still closer, Shakespeare makes a great point of the "dozen white luces" on Shallow's coat—and it is a fact that the Lucys of Charlecote had three luces on their coat of arms. But Shakespeare was not long in finding nobler ways in which to show his daring spirit. The needs of his wife and children were increasing. To make a fortune for them in a little place like Stratford was impos-sible. Yet fame and fortune the young man sought. So off he went to London, where there were high rewards for a few of those who ran the risk of poverty and misery in order to win them.

Before he started on this great adven-ture it is thought that he put in a little time at school-mastering, a task for which he was well equipped. At the school at Stratford Greek was not taught, but Shake-speare had been well grounded in Latin, although to such a scholar as his friend Ben Jonson his knowledge of the classics may seem to have amounted to "small Latin and less Greek."

Shakespeare Loved Good Plays

Arrived in London, it is little wonder that Shakespeare first looked for work at a theatre. From his boyhood he had loved the plays he had seen performed at Stratford. Now he found the playhouses of London doing a thriving business. On every fine day flags showing that the plays were on were flown by the two theatres—the Theatre and the Curtain, near Shoreditch—that by that time had sprung up in London. Rich and poor, well-bred and vulgar, men and women were

Photo by Rischgitz

Everyone who knows "The Merchant of Venice" will remember this scene in which Shylock, the Jewish usurer, bereft of his daughter, accuses Salanio and Salarino of having helped her to elope, and then pronounces that famous speech in which he recounts the wrongs of his unhappy and persecuted race. "Let him look to his bond!"

flocking to the theatres. Good seats on the covered balconies, or even on the stage itself, were costly, but for very little money anyone could stand on the sanded floor at the foot of the stage.

So Shakespeare found some sort of work to do at one or other of the busy theatres. At first he may have been nothing but an errand boy, or perhaps he may only have held horses for the rich men who came to the plays. It is thought that for some little time Shakespeare worked for a printer, but soon he became associated with the theatre, although in what way is not known. But genius will soon show itself, and it was not long before he became an actor.

At first he must have acted small parts in plays written by other men. There were many brilliant and witty men who had come to London from the universities to write plays for the citizens—gay comedies and gruesome tragedies such as the people liked. Some of the plays were so fine and spirited that the actors were often invited to perform them before the queen in her palace. The authors and the actors strove with one another for the chance of pleasing their sovereign. And Shakespeare had the honour of acting more than once before the queen. Though his lines were few, how proud he must have been to win the queen's applause!

But he was not the man to remain merely an actor, although he continued to act till nearly the end of his life. Very soon he was writing plays. He had an extraordinary gift of words. Now, more than ever before, he began to know his own power over them, for the great natural gift developed at an amazing pace when he entered the select world of wits and poets.

The Greatest Dramas Ever Written

So Shakespeare turned his genius for words into the making of plays for the theatre. There were scores of books from which he could obtain plots and stories

Here are the principal characters in " The Merry Wives of Windsor," and in the centre that prince of clowns, the fat, witty and boastful Sir John Falstaff, who has been described as the most agreeable knave ever portrayed.

Photos by Victoria and Albert Museum

The handsome but angry lady is Katherine, in Shakespeare's " Taming of the Shrew." She is delighted with the beautiful gown her husband has bought her, but to tame her proud spirit he is sending it back by the tailor.

—novels, histories, romances—and he dipped into many of them. There were various kinds of plays that the people liked, such as farces with country clowns, romantic comedies with love-lorn heroines, and the gloomiest tragedies of revenge and murder. He tried every kind of play that was then popular, and he soon wrote the best of every kind.

He learned his craft from the poets and playwrights around him, and it took him three or four years to master his art, for writing plays is no easy thing to accomplish. In the meanwhile he had been improving upon all the dramatists who had come before, even the great Marlowe, from whom he himself had learned the most.

And then he began to give playgoers, in the next twenty years or so, a set of plays such as England had never seen before, written in language such as Englishmen had never known. More than that: from every point of view the plays of Shakespeare are the greatest dramas ever presented, and his poetry occupies the highest place in that art since the world began. In only one of the arts have the English-speaking peoples been supreme, namely, the art of poetry. And in that art Shakespeare has no rival.

This is the verdict of posterity; but even while Shakespeare was living and working those who were in the best position to form a judgment of his powers were loud in his praises. Perhaps the most important account of his work that has come down to us from a contemporary is that of Francis

This is the merry old knight who was boon companion to Prince Hal in Shakespeare's "Henry IV." Falstaff is one of the greatest comic characters in all literature, and is as fresh to us to-day as he was to the crowds who flocked to the Globe Theatre in London when Elizabeth was queen.

Meres, a professor at Oxford and later a schoolmaster, who, in his book called "Palladis Tamia: Wit's Treasury," published twelve years after Shakespeare arrived in London, declares that "the Muses would speak Shakespeare's fine filed phrase if they could speak English," and also that "among the English he was the most excellent in both kinds [that is, tragedy and comedy] for the stage." This is high praise, indeed.

The learned and witty Thomas Fuller, who, although he was born only eight years before Shakespeare's death, lived within earshot of his living fame, bears testimony to the agility of Shakespeare's brain in an interesting comparison between Ben Jonson and Shakespeare, when alluding to the meetings of the wits of the day at the famous "Mermaid Tavern" in Bread Street.

"Many were the wit-combats," he writes in his "History of the Worthies of England," "betwixt him and Ben Jonson, which two I behold like a Spanish galleon and an English man-of-war; Master Jonson (like the former) was built far higher in learning, solid but slow in his performance. Shakespeare, with the English man-of-war, lesser in bulk, but lighter in sailing, could turn with all tides, tack about, and take advantage of all winds by the quickness of his wit and invention."

This quickness of wit showed itself not only in his writings but equally in ordinary every-day affairs, for Shakespeare was a very good

The faithful Cordelia, though disowned by her father, King Lear, has followed the heart-broken, insane old man to France, after his ungrateful daughters had shut their doors upon him.   She is shown in to him as he sleeps.

Photos by Victoria and Albert Museum and National Gallery

This merry rogue from "The Winter's Tale" is selling ballads and trinkets to all the country folk—and picking their pockets to boot.   For they are all so absorbed that he could "have filed keys off that hung in chains."

Ophelia has become insane from her father's death and the loss of the love of Hamlet; and as she scatters her flowers around, she says, "There's rosemary, that's for remembrance; and pansies, that's for thoughts."

Photos by Corporation of Liverpool and Alinari

Rather than be married to Count Paris, Juliet has taken a drug which has made her as one dead, and is being borne away for burial in the family tomb, where she will awake to tragedy too terrible for her to bear.

man of business. He had acquired a financial interest in the theatres for which he acted and wrote, and although the profits from his plays may not have been large, his pay as an actor was considerable, so that before many years had passed he had become a man of substance.

Although, during his busy life in London, it is not likely that he had been able to visit Stratford, he had not forgotten those he left behind, and one of the first tasks he undertook when his professional position was assured was to set his father, who had fallen on evil times, on his feet again.

The Shakespeare Memorial building, which was erected at Stratford-on-Avon in 1877, and was destroyed by fire on March 6, 1926. It contained a theatre, an interesting collection of the poet's books, and a fine gallery of portraits of Shakespearean interest.

This accomplished, and his father provided with a coat of arms, he proceeded to make his own status clear to the eyes of his fellow townsmen, and in 1597 he bought New Place, the second largest house in Stratford. We may imagine that as a boy he had often gazed wonderingly on the glories of this mansion—and now it was his own, although he did not actually set up house there for another fourteen years, so busy was he with his work in London. From time to time he bought more land and house property.

In 1611, shortly after his play "The Tempest" had been produced, Shakespeare retired, left London, and settled down for good at New Place, to live the life of a country gentleman, although even then he often had to go to London to attend to his financial interests. He was wise enough, however, to realize that his life work was finished, that his hold on his public was secure, and that, if he wrote any more, he might weaken that hold.

He enjoyed his house and his garden and his farm, as well as the society of those who appreciated his achievements. But this life of quiet enjoyment was not to last very long, and, indeed, long life was hardly to be expected from a man who had worked so strenuously and used his brain so unsparingly as had Shakespeare. Within five years of his retirement his health began to fail. In March, 1616, he completed his will, and on April 23 he died at New Place at the early age of fifty-two.

And now let us say a word about some of his plays. His earliest work, produced some five or six years after his arrival in London, includes the comedies "Love's Labour's Lost," "The Two Gentlemen of Verona," and "The Comedy of Errors." The first of these, a social satire, was performed before Queen Elizabeth in 1597. In it we see the princess of France and her ladies pitting themselves against the king of Navarre and his favourite courtiers, who were trying to turn the court into a kind of academy for men only, which no ladies were allowed to enter for three years. "The Comedy of Errors" is a most laughable farce, in which the fun arises out of the mistakes of identity of twin brothers and their twin servants, each member of each pair being unknown to the other.

In 1594 appeared another comedy, "The Merchant of Venice," but here the comedy in parts comes close to tragedy, in the bitter hatred shown by the Jew Shylock towards Antonio. "A Midsummer Night's Dream" was produced in the same year—a fairy comedy shot through and through with romance, fancy of the daintiest and most delicate (Titania and Oberon), and broad humour (Bottom and his merry men).

There is a tradition that Shakespeare wrote the farcical comedy "The Merry Wives of Windsor" (1598) because the queen had expressed a wish to see Falstaff in love. In Falstaff Shakespeare shows his highest powers of humour. No one can help laughing at and liking the fat and jolly knight.

This was followed, in 1599 and 1600, by those three masterpieces of romantic comedy —"Much Ado About Nothing," "As You Like It," and "Twelfth Night"— in which the practised hand of the dramatist steers the heroine and hero safely through all manner of strange trials, to be happily united in the end. His history plays —"King John," "Richard II," "Henry IV," "Henry V," and others—give a pageant of English history such as we can find in no other dramas, "Henry IV" being especially memorable, for in it we are first introduced to Falstaff.

The new Shakespeare Memorial Theatre, which stands on the site of the old building. Visitors from thirty countries attended the opening ceremony which was performed by the Prince of Wales on April 23, 1932.

Of his tragedies the earliest was "Romeo and Juliet," which was probably written and also acted about the same time as his first comedies. This clearly showed the hand of a master, of a master who was wellnigh as youthful as the star-crossed lovers he portrayed; it is the supreme tragic drama of young love.

After the year 1593 no tragedy came from his pen for some years, but all this time his genius was maturing and gathering strength. In 1600 appeared his "Julius Caesar," and after that, in quick succession, came those four tragedies which entitle Shakespeare to rank as the greatest writer of tragedy of all time—"Hamlet," the supreme tragedy of revenge; "Othello," the supreme tragedy of jealousy; "Macbeth," the supreme tragedy of ambition; and "King Lear," the supreme tragedy of ingratitude.

Of these four mighty tragedies, although "Macbeth," perhaps, contains the greatest poetry, the most popular is undoubtedly "Hamlet." For one thing, Hamlet himself is one of the most interesting characters ever conceived in the mind of a dramatist. Moreover, the play moves forward with a wealth of thrilling incident; there is plenty of comedy atmosphere to relieve the tenseness of the tragic gloom; and of all Shakespeare's plays, this is the one that most abounds in weighty and profound thoughts. "Hamlet" appeared in 1602, "Othello" in 1604, "Macbeth" in 1606, and "King Lear" in 1607. For his last two tragedies, "Antony and Cleopatra" and "Coriolanus," he returned to Roman history.

Why Shakespeare Rules Supreme

But Shakespeare did not close upon the tragic note. The very last plays are brilliant comedies again—the idyllic romances, as we may call them, of "Cymbeline," "The Winter's Tale," and "The Tempest." In the first and second comedy and tragedy are cunningly blended. In "The Tempest" tragedy has no place. All three seem like dreams, and in all there are difficulties and sorrows, but in each the difficulties are smoothed out and the ending is tranquil and happy.

It may be that these three plays were written at Stratford, far from the turmoil of London, and, indeed, the very reposefulness of their language and theme appears to point to this. And when Prospero abjures his magic, breaks his staff, and drowns his book, "deeper than did ever plummet sound," it seems as if it is Shakespeare himself who is laying to rest the powers with which he had charmed and thrilled the hearts of men.

Shakespeare's Beautiful Sonnets

Apart from the many exquisite songs and detached pieces of verse that are found scattered throughout his plays, the Sonnets are the best known of Shakespeare's purely poetic work. These were passed round among his friends long before they were actually published, for they were not given to the public until 1609, only two years before his retirement.

Not a few of the Sonnets contain some of the loveliest poetry that Shakespeare ever wrote, while some, according to the fashion of the time for this particular form of poem, are very affected and artificial. Quite early in his career, too, he had won applause with long poems based on classical legends, such, for example, as his "Venus and Adonis."

What is it that makes Shakespeare supreme as a dramatist? The secret of his supremacy lies to a great extent in the fact that he really understood both life and people. He knew what made men and women say what they said, and just why they behaved as they did. Young or old, good or bad, each of his characters behaves and speaks in a manner that appears not only natural but the only one possible in the circumstances.

In plays by some dramatists it is difficult to forget that the author has written a play and that the actors are reciting the words that he has written. But when we go to a play by Shakespeare, or even when we read one of his plays, it is as though we were listening to, or overhearing, people in real life: we forget that they are acting; indeed, we forget that it is a play at all.

A Creator of Natural Characters

But, over and above this wonderful gift of reading the hearts of men and women, Shakespeare possessed an endless fund of fancy, of imagination, and of humour. His clowns and his country yokels talk just as clowns and yokels should; his fairies speak precisely as we should expect such creatures of the imagination to speak. And, to crown all, his language, in all its beauty and power and felicity, is fitted like a glove to each of his characters in their every mood.

(CONTINUED ON PAGE 175)

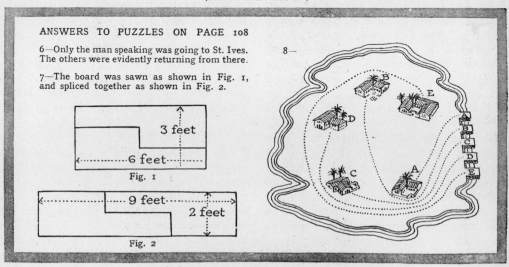

ANSWERS TO PUZZLES ON PAGE 108

6—Only the man speaking was going to St. Ives. The others were evidently returning from there.

7—The board was sawn as shown in Fig. 1, and spliced together as shown in Fig. 2.

3 feet

6 feet

Fig. 1

9 feet

2 feet

Fig. 2

8—

Towards the close of Egypt's history, when the old religion was dying, people turned to the worship of animals in which the gods were thought to reside. At that time every black and white bull was sacred, for the god Ptah was supposed to enter into one of them named Apis. At Memphis is a vast tomb where all these bulls were buried with great magnificence, and above is shown a solemn procession held in honour of Apis.

In the DAYS of the PYRAMIDS

How a Great Nation Finally Declined, and Lost Its Freedom for Twenty-four Hundred Years

(CONTINUED FROM PAGE 107)

IN THE very earliest part of the story of Egypt we see a thriving, peaceful land that had no fear of enemies from outside and no desire to conquer the world. Later, in the great period of the Middle Kingdom, the works of peace are still carried on, and Egypt remains friendly with the world outside.

And then with the Hyksos a change comes. Groaning under the humiliation of being slaves to foreigners, the Egyptians learn to fight so that they may drive out these invaders. And with the knowledge of war comes the desire for war, to treat other people as they themselves had been treated.

Under Thutmose III this desire is fully satisfied, until in 1450 B.C. Egypt is lord of nearly all the known world. Riches flow into her treasury; luxury takes the place of hard, honest work; and Egypt begins to decline. The simple virtues of justice and industry are forgotten, the priests and rulers grow greedier and greedier, and the farmer groans under his burden of taxes. Such is the tale that comes to us from the dawn of history. We must get used to it, for we are going to hear it again and again.

Peoples of Other Lands

And so the story of Egypt after 1350 B.C. is not a very happy one. But it has its bright spots. For one thing, it is in this part of the story that we hear for the first time about the people living over in Europe —the Greeks, the Sicilians, and others. Their history, so much shorter than that of Egypt, begins about the year 1000 B.C. We can also catch glimpses of the Hebrews, poor in worldly power but with untold riches in the greatness of their thoughts about God. And the story of Egypt herself is not all unhappy.

The first king of this new period was Harmhab, a general in the army who made himself pharaoh and then married a princess of the royal line to make his kingship legal. Harmhab was followed by a long line of kings, twelve of whom had the same name of Rameses (răm'ĕ-sēz). None of these kings was a fighter like Thutmose III, or a thinker like Ikhnaton, or a builder like the great Khufu. Probably the greatest of this new line was Rameses II, and even he was not so great as he thought himself.

In the early part of his long reign (1284–1225 B.C.), Rameses II fought one great battle at Kadesh, in Syria. Opposed to him were a number of kings, but particularly the ruler of the Hittites, a people who were trying to establish an empire of their own in Syria and Palestine. The battle was celebrated in Egypt as a brilliant victory for Rameses II. But what really happened was that the pharaoh, trusting two lying messengers, misled his army so that they were an easy prey to the enemy. His whole army would have been destroyed but for the curious fact that in retreating he and his soldiers left behind them their rich possessions— gold ornaments, fine robes, and other things—and the Hittite army at once stopped to pick up these things, and quarrel over the division of them among themselves.

This delay gave Rameses II the chance he needed, and he bravely charged at a weak spot in the Hittite line and kept on fighting until the rest of his army came to his support. The battle was not a complete victory for either side, but Rameses II claimed it as an enormous triumph for Egypt. Later he and the Hittite king quietly made a treaty in which they promised that neither would ever fight the other again.

Most of the long reign of Rameses II was spent in luxury at home. A favourite pastime of this ruler was the erecting of

At Luxor, in Egypt, is this enormous statue of Rameses II. The figure of a man beside it gives an idea of its size, and probably illustrates the king's estimation of himself in comparison with other men.

immense statues of himself and his wife. This was not a new idea of Rameses II; in all Egyptian drawings from the very beginning it was the custom to draw the king at least twice as tall as anybody else, and huge statues, called colossi (kŏ-lŏs'ī), had been made of nearly every king from the earliest times. But Rameses II built bigger ones. There is a broken stone colossus of this king which weighed two million pounds, or nearly a thousand tons. A tall man would not reach half way to the knee. Think of the labour of making and moving such a statue!

This proud pharaoh, Rameses II, finished the Great Hall of Karnak, the largest hall in the world, with columns greater than any we have nowadays, and stones nearly as wide as a man is tall. He is also supposed to be the pharaoh who oppressed the Hebrews, although the Egyptian records do not tell of this. We do know, however, that at about this time the Egyptian language adopted a great many Hebrew words, which show us that the Egyptians must have lived in close touch with people of this race, since that is the way in which words pass from one language into another.

After Rameses II came a long line of kings, none of them very good or strong. They gave a great deal of the wealth of Egypt to the gods, especially Amon. This was not good for Egypt, because the priests did not use the wealth for the benefit of the people, but wasted it instead.

A Foreign King on Egypt's Throne

Finally (945 B.C.) a foreigner, Sheshonk (shē'shŏnk), a Libyan from the coast of Africa to the west of the Delta, became king. This was not a bad thing for Egypt, because Sheshonk was wise and active, and did what he could to restore prosperity. But a

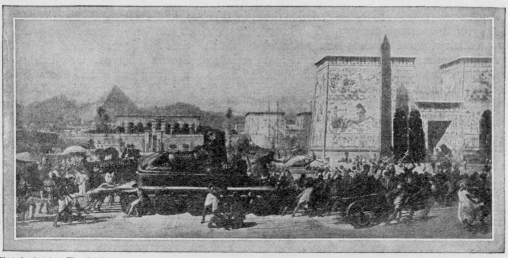

The cruel sufferings of the Hebrews in Egypt are told in the Bible. The picture above shows a number of them harnessed together to draw the chariot of one of the hated Egyptian idols, under the bite of the lash.

single king could not do very much; and Sheshonk's line of Libyan pharaohs, though they ruled for more than two hundred years (945–718 B.C.), have not left us very much worth recounting. They could not induce Egypt to renounce her thousands of little gods—animal gods, nature gods, king gods; for the king, too, was a god and was worshipped with the rest.

Sheshonk himself was the best of his line. He maintained active relations with other countries—indeed, he gave a daughter of his as a wife to King Solomon of Israel, the wise Solomon of whom you have read in the Bible. To the south of Egypt She-shonk ruled Nubia, the country of the Ethiopians, where gold was mined. He also planned to build a huge gate, called a pylon (pī'lŏn), for the Great Hall of Karnak, but he died before the work was completed, and the scaffolds and materials are lying to-day beneath the dirt which has collected on them, just as they lay when Sheshonk stopped building.

For many centuries Egypt had governed the upper Nile beyond the first cataract,

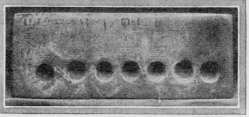

This picture shows the top of a table used for making an offering of seven holy oils in ancient Egypt. Each oil was contained in one of those small hollowed cups.

where Uni, in the Old Kingdom, and Sesostris III, in the Middle Kingdom, had built their canals. Indeed, the Ethiopians (ē'thǐ-ō'pǐ-ǎn) had become very much like the Egyptians in their religion and government. Now, as the Libyan kings became weaker and there was no lord in Egypt strong enough to rule, an Ethiopian called Piankhi (pē-ǎn'kǐ) seized the kingship, and he and three other Ethiopians following him ruled altogether for over fifty years (718–663 B.C.).

These Ethiopian kings could most easily rule the south of Egypt, which was nearest to their home. They never really obtained control of the Delta, where a city called Sais (sā'ǐs) was the seat of government. This government at Sais was under the control of Assyria, a great nation to the north-east of Egypt, which eventually ruled most of the known world. In 661 B.C., in the words of the poet Byron, "the Assyrian came down like the wolf on the fold." Egypt was plundered, and the Ethiopians were driven back to their own country. The northern, or Delta, government had submitted to Assyria and was left undisturbed.

And now we come to a strange period in the history of this strange country. You know how a stick of wood which is nearly burned up will sometimes flame with a clear fire just before it becomes a blackened cinder? Well, during the next hundred years it really seemed as though Egypt's flaming splendour might return. This was the Saitic (sā-ĭt'ĭk) period, so named from the Delta city Sais, which was the centre of its civilization.

Rebirth of Art and Industry

As you might expect, the first king in this Saitic period is also the greatest. It was necessary for him to be a great ruler, because it was he who had the task of bringing the whole country under his sway and putting the government in a position to continue its work. Psamtik I (săm'tĭk) began by being lord of Sais, and then became pharaoh. His long reign of fifty-four years (663–609 B.C.) covered more than a third of the Saitic period. He suppressed the priests and the local rulers, and encouraged the art and the trade which had once made Egypt great.

At this time the Greeks, across the Mediterranean Sea from Egypt, were just beginning to be a strong people, and Psamtik was glad for them to come to Egypt to trade and study and work. Greeks and Hebrews and Phœnicians (fĕ-nĭsh'ăn) now traded with the Egyptians in wheat, in barley, in papyrus (pȧ-pī'rŭs), or paper made from reeds by splitting them and fixing them together in sheets. There sprang up factories in Egypt, where these things were made or stored. Artists and sculptors also were busy making splendid pictures and beautiful statues, some of which we admire as much as those of earlier times.

The Last Days of Egypt

The Egyptians themselves looked back at the old glories of their land, and tried to make things resemble as nearly as possible what they had been in the past. The sayings

In magnificent splendour Cleopatra, queen of Egypt during the period when the country was under Greek rule, maintained her court at Alexandria, the capital. She is shown in the picture presiding over a festival,

Egypt to-day is a crowded land pulsing with life, in spite of the fact that everything there moves with the slow pace of the Orient.

A. This apple merchant of modern Egypt carries his wares on his back, and weighs them out on the scales he holds in his hand.

B. The old dealer in pottery has stacked his vases and plates in a convenient nook on the street, and is waiting for customers.

C. These Arab boys are at school, where they learn a smattering of useful knowledge and many texts from the Koran, the Mohammedan Bible.

At D is a family on its way to visit the cemetery. According to custom, some of the women are veiled.

of wise men like Imhotep were much read and studied, and the priests became eager students of long-forgotten lore. Side by side with the busy foreign trade and manufacture went this keen interest in the past, an interest so great that prominent Egyptians even took to copying the tombs from those of the Old Kingdom.

Unfortunately, towards the end of this period, Egypt again wasted her energies with fighting in Palestine. By this time Assyria had passed away, and Babylon and Persia had become the great powers. In 525 B.C. the Persians conquered Egypt, and dethroned its ruler.

From 525 B.C. until A.D. 1918 there had never been an independent government in Egypt. The Persians ruled it as a province until 332 B.C., when it fell to Alexander the Great, who, being a Greek himself, favoured the Greeks in Egypt. He was followed by a line of kings many of whom were named Ptolemy (tŏl′ė̇-mĭ). The later ones of these were really vassals, or underlords, of Greece or Rome. It was the thirteenth Ptolemy who had a sister named Cleopatra (klē′ṓ-pā′trȧ), who ruled for a time. You will find her story told elsewhere.

Thirty years before the birth of Christ, Egypt was conquered by the Romans, and for many years the Egyptians yielded to Rome their great stores of grain and other supplies. After the Roman empire broke up in the fifth century after Christ, Egypt was invaded now and then from the south or from the north, and in 641 it fell to the Arabs, who in that year burned the city of Alexandria and its famous library.

From that time Egypt saw many a foreign ruler. She fell into the hands of the Turks, after 1517; the French under Napoleon; and the British in our own time. In 1914, after

The great Napoleon, who visited Egypt three thousand years after the events we are now reading, never succeeded in overcoming the land of the pyramids. He came, he saw—but did not conquer. Here he is seen in command of his troops during one of his Egyptian engagements, before the British destroyed his fleet.

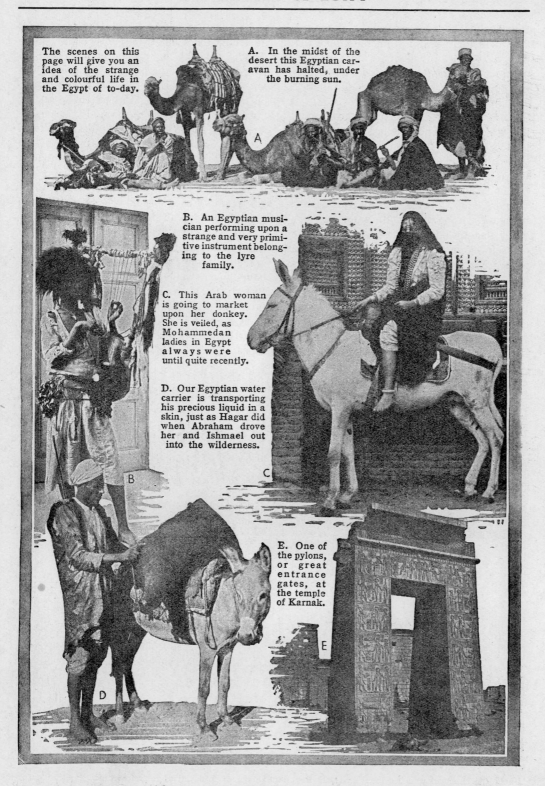

The scenes on this page will give you an idea of the strange and colourful life in the Egypt of to-day.

A. In the midst of the desert this Egyptian caravan has halted, under the burning sun.

B. An Egyptian musician performing upon a strange and very primitive instrument belonging to the lyre family.

C. This Arab woman is going to market upon her donkey. She is veiled, as Mohammedan ladies in Egypt always were until quite recently.

D. Our Egyptian water carrier is transporting his precious liquid in a skin, just as Hagar did when Abraham drove her and Ishmael out into the wilderness.

E. One of the pylons, or great entrance gates, at the temple of Karnak.

the World War, Egypt once more became an independent nation, though under British protection for a few years. In 1922 the protectorate was terminated, and Egypt became a sovereign state, the sultan being proclaimed king.

Now, as in the long ago, Egypt lives mainly by agriculture—and this in spite of the fact that less than four per cent. of the land is cultivable. The Nile is still a kindly parent to the green Egyptian fields, and under the broiling sun the date palms ripen their valuable fruit. Petroleum, phosphate rock, manganese iron ore, salt, turquoise and many other minerals are obtained. And all sorts of semi-tropical fruits—oranges, lemons, pomegranates—will grow where water is to be had. Altogether, Egypt exports thirty million pounds worth of her products every year—largely raw cotton and cotton seed, sugar, cigarettes, onions, eggs, phosphates, and rice.

So over fourteen million people manage to live to-day in this old, old land. Of these a good many are wandering Arabs whose homes are their tents and whose homeland is the desert. A fifth of the population live in towns—many of them in Cairo, the capital and largest city; in Alexandria, at the mouth of the Nile; in Port Said (sä-ēd'), at the northern entrance to the famous Suez (sōō-ĕz') Canal, which connects the Western World with the Orient. Most of the Egyptians are Mohammedans, but there are a number of Christians, most of them Copts (kŏpt)—that is, members of that ancient branch of the Christian Church which was established in Egypt not long after the time of Christ.

The Egyptians are a handsome race, with their clear, dark skin, fine features and graceful proportions; and whenever they have been well governed—as under the British, for instance—they have made rapid progress. It may be that some day this ancient country will awaken once more, and that the mighty works of earlier days will be repeated. Who knows?

Photo by Presse-Photo, Berlin

Under the shade of its palm trees this little Egyptian village of to-day tries to hide from the pitiless sun.

CLEVER INSECT ACTORS

Quick-change Artists That Can Make Themselves Invisible before Our Very Eyes

(CONTINUED FROM PAGE 117)

MOTHS are the plain cousins of the butterflies, for they mostly wear the sober clothes of dusk. There are a great many more of them, but we do not notice them so much. For although some of the moths are gaily coloured and fly about showing their bright wings in the sunlight, most of them sleep in the day-time and do not come out until evening, when the butterflies have gone to bed.

Night-flying moths are soberly dressed, as a rule in soft browns and greys; so when they are resting quite still on tree trunks or old wooden palings, or hiding in some dark corner, it is not at all easy to see them. Their dull colouring protects the weak insects from prying eyes.

We can hardly mistake a sombre, night-flying moth for a gay, sunshine-loving butterfly; but a moth that flies by day is often so gorgeously coloured that it is not so easy to know which is which. We shall always be able to tell them apart, however, if we look carefully at their antennae (ăn-tĕn′ē) —that is, the feelers on top of the insect's head.

A butterfly has long, slender antennae, like fine threads, that have tiny blunt knobs on the ends, or are swollen at the tips rather like Indian clubs. A moth has antennae that are either like feathery plumes, fine combs, or simple threads; and they never have knobs at the tip.

A butterfly usually holds its closed wings upright over its back when it is at rest. A moth either keeps its wings spread out or folds them over its back like a cloak; it never holds them upright like a butterfly.

A moth goes through just as many changes as a butterfly. But during its time of rest, the caterpillar of the moth does not turn into a chrysalis. It simply shuts itself up in a cocoon or buries itself in the ground; or it may creep into a crack in the bark of a tree or under a pile of dead leaves. There it lies, like a tiny dried-up mummy,

165

till it is ready to awake as a perfect insect. Until then it is a pupa (pū′på).

There are thousands of different kinds of moths, and they vary in shape and size much more than the butterflies. There are soft, fluffy "puss moths," all grey and white, with big heads and the prettiest of feathery antennae; "ermine moths" that appear to be wearing ermine cloaks when their white wings, dotted over with little black spots, are folded neatly over their backs; and gay yellow and red "underwings" that look as if they were dressed in dancing skirts when they flutter up and down the window - panes on warm summer evenings.

Then there are moths that disguise themselves as faded leaves on little pieces of bark, and others that mimic bees and wasps so perfectly as to deceive us completely as they hover over flowering shrubs. There are moths so small that you can only just see the wee things when they flutter their tiny wings; and giant moths as big as bats.

The largest moth of all is the great Atlas moth of India, whose wonderful wings are nearly a foot across. It is one of the silk moths, and cousin to the silkworm moths, whose caterpillars spin the threads from which our silk is made.

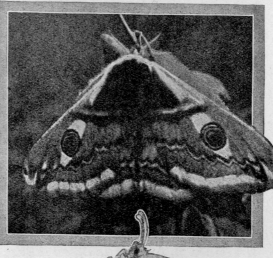

One of the most striking differences between a butterfly and a moth is the way they rest. Here an emperor moth is seen resting with its wings flattened down, showing the upper surface, and (below) a clouded yellow butterfly resting on a clover flower, with its wings closed over its back.

How Baby Moths are Born

The silk moths are a large family of handsome creatures, many of them giants of the insect world. They all make wonderful silk cocoons. Only those woven by the caterpillar of the rather plain-looking silkworm moth are of much value, although the silk spun by the huge caterpillars of the North American silk moth is sometimes used for making stockings.

The giant silk moth is a splendid fellow. Its broad body is clothed with reddish-brown hair banded with black and white. Below its big red head is a smart white collar, and its wings, which are five or six inches across, are a pale brownish colour shaded with soft pink, buff, and orange.

In late autumn, on forest trees in America may be found the cocoon of this giant silk moth. It is a big pod-shaped thing, rusty brown in colour and about three inches long.

All through the winter, while the snow whirls down and the stormy winds shake the bare branches of the trees, the pupa lies sleeping in its cosy house. This is soft and fluffy inside to keep out the cold, and has a waterproof covering against the rain and sleet. Not until the leaves are again on the trees does the pupa stir. Then one day, quite early in the summer, the tiny cocoon is shaken—not by the wind but by the insect inside. Gradually it pushes its head through a small opening that has been left on purpose at one end of the cocoon, and forces its way out into the light and air. For an hour or two the giant moth clings to the tree, while its great wings expand and dry. Then, after a trial flutter or two, it launches itself from the bough and away it goes.

The caterpillar that makes this big cocoon is a startling-looking creature, nearly four inches long. In colour it is a pale green with

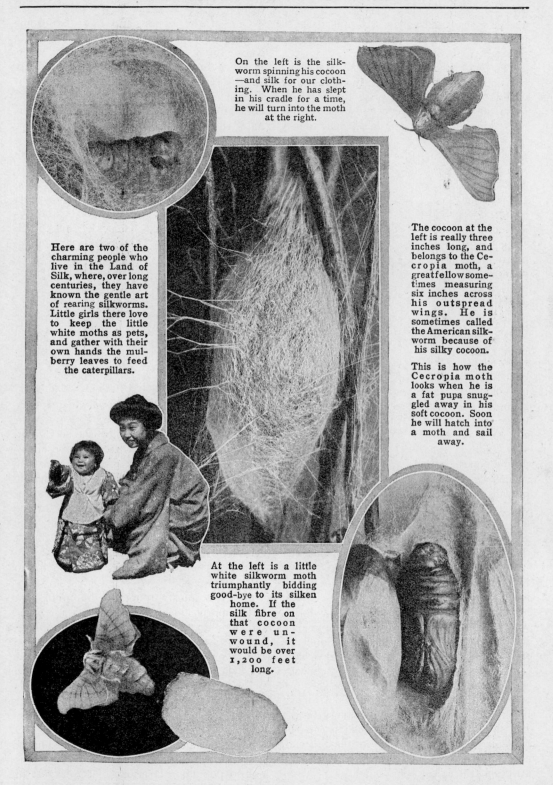

On the left is the silkworm spinning his cocoon —and silk for our clothing. When he has slept in his cradle for a time, he will turn into the moth at the right.

Here are two of the charming people who live in the Land of Silk, where, over long centuries, they have known the gentle art of rearing silkworms. Little girls there love to keep the little white moths as pets, and gather with their own hands the mulberry leaves to feed the caterpillars.

The cocoon at the left is really three inches long, and belongs to the Cecropia moth, a great fellow sometimes measuring six inches across his outspread wings. He is sometimes called the American silkworm because of his silky cocoon.

This is how the Cecropia moth looks when he is a fat pupa snuggled away in his soft cocoon. Soon he will hatch into a moth and sail away.

At the left is a little white silkworm moth triumphantly bidding good-bye to its silken home. If the silk fibre on that cocoon were unwound, it would be over 1,200 feet long.

a yellow head and yellow legs, and its back is adorned with many little coloured pimples of bright red, blue, and yellow.

The giant silk moths are very handsome; but if the moths held a beauty contest they would have to give the prize to the tailed moth of Madagascar, called by the natives the "king of the butterflies." Of course, it is not a butterfly, but it is surely the most beautiful moth in the world, and it outshines the most beautiful butterflies of tropical countries. In shape it is very much like the swallow - tailed butterflies, but each hind wing has no less than seven tails. In colour it is velvet black, splashed and banded with glowing gold, blue, and green. Its hind wings are especially gorgeous, with shot crimson and purple hues and shining gold patches. It is a day-flying moth, and as it circles the tree tops, its flashing colours are dazzling in the sunshine.

Though not quite so wonderful as this royal creature, there are many beautiful moths in the temperate countries. The hawk moths, with their long, narrow, pointed wings and torpedo-shaped bodies, are favourites with everyone. They are all noted for their swift, strong flight, and many have beautifully coloured wings painted in soft, quiet tones.

There are about sixteen different hawk moths of various sizes and colours in the British Isles. Their caterpillars can be recognized by a sharp horn at the tail end, and some have brightly coloured diagonal stripes at the sides.

The hawk moths include our largest and most beautiful insects. This is the privet hawk moth, whose hind wings and body are marked with delicate rose pink.

One of the largest and most handsome of the hawk moths is the privet hawk, whose softly shaded brown and pink wings measure fully four inches from tip to tip. In its caterpillar days it feeds on privet leaves. Many others rival this species, but the dainty humming-bird hawk moth is perhaps the most charming of them all. We know him well, for he loves to visit our gardens. During the day he may be seen hovering over the petunia bed or the honeysuckle, his quick wings vibrating so rapidly that they make a faint haze around his soft furry body.

As he hovers like a humming-bird above the flower, the moth thrusts his proboscis (prō-bŏs'ĭs), or sucking tube, which is very long, deep down into the nectar cup to reach the honey drops at the bottom. When he withdraws his proboscis some of the pollen from the flower is almost sure to cling to it. This the moth carries to the next flower he visits and so helps to form the seeds.

But the most wonderful humming-bird hawk moths live in South America. Some of them are so exactly like the humming-birds in size, shape, and colouring, and in the way they fly and hover over flowers, that it needs a very sharp eye to tell the difference between the insects and the lovely little birds they imitate.

A Moth that Robs the Bees

Everyone admires the humming-bird hawk moth, but the death's-head hawk moth is not so popular. It is one of the largest of

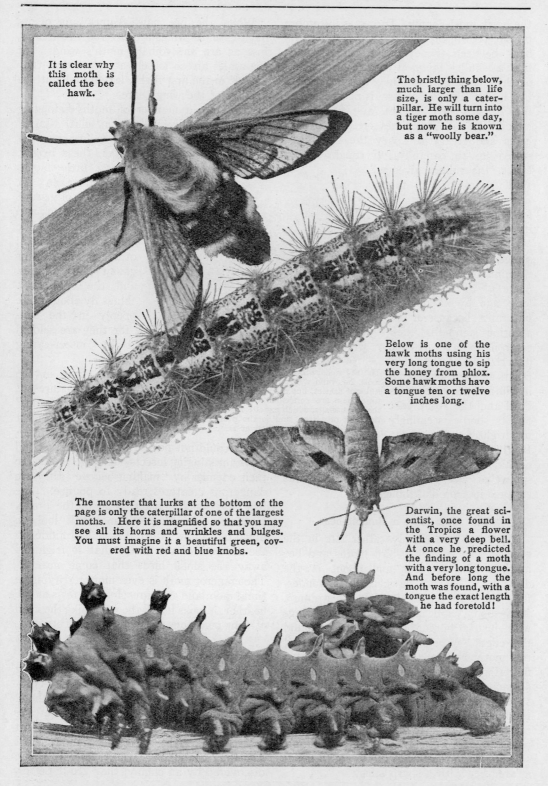

It is clear why this moth is called the bee hawk.

The bristly thing below, much larger than life size, is only a caterpillar. He will turn into a tiger moth some day, but now he is known as a "woolly bear."

Below is one of the hawk moths using his very long tongue to sip the honey from phlox. Some hawk moths have a tongue ten or twelve inches long.

The monster that lurks at the bottom of the page is only the caterpillar of one of the largest moths. Here it is magnified so that you may see all its horns and wrinkles and bulges. You must imagine it a beautiful green, covered with red and blue knobs.

Darwin, the great scientist, once found in the Tropics a flower with a very deep bell. At once he predicted the finding of a moth with a very long tongue. And before long the moth was found, with a tongue the exact length he had foretold!

the hawk moth family. It dresses in sombre purple, brown, black, and yellow, and on its back between the eyes is a curious mark like a skull. Ignorant people are afraid of this moth because they think it brings bad luck. This, of course, is nonsense; but the death's-head is not a well-behaved insect. It will sometimes creep into bee-hives and steal the honey the bees have stored up so carefully. If caught at its tricks, the robber gives a shrill squeak of a most uncanny kind, by forcing air through its long proboscis.

Hawk moths are sometimes called "sphinx moths" — a name given to them long ago by an old naturalist because of a curious habit that their caterpillars have. If you disturb one of the cater-pillars when it is feeding, it will at once rear up its head and the front part of its body—seemingly to frighten you away.

The red underwing moth has hind wings of brilliant scarlet, but in the day-time these are concealed beneath the front wings, which exactly resemble the bark of a tree, and so the moth is very difficult to see when at rest.

In this strange, stiff attitude it will often remain for hours at a time—as if, like the sphinx of the old Greek legends, it was engaged in profound thought.

The Moth Like a Bumble-bee

Most hawk moths fly rather late in the evening, but humming-bird moths and bee hawk moths are out and about in the day-time. The bee hawk moth is wonder-fully like a big bumble-bee. It has a plump, furry body, and clear, transparent wings with just a border of dark scales round the edges. When, in the early summer, the moth hovers about the sweet-scented flowering shrubs in company with a troop of excited bees, you must have sharp eyes to distinguish it from the insects buzzing round it. Its deceptive appearance is cer-tainly very useful to it. Hungry birds will pass it by; for although they enjoy a plump, soft-bodied moth, few of them care to tackle a large bee with a sharp sting.

When the bee hawk comes out of its pupa case, its wings are covered with scales, just as are an ordinary moth's wings; but the scales are so loosely attached that they fall off in the first flight, leaving all but the borders of the wings bare.

There are a number of moths belonging to another family, called the "clear wings," that have no scales, or only a few, on their wings. Like the bee hawks, these bright, quick-flying little moths are easily mistaken for other kinds of insects. Some have black and yellow bodies like wasps and hornets; others mimic bees or gauzy-winged flies, and the bold little things fly about quite openly in the sun-light, for they are seldom molested by insect-eating birds.

So you see that in the insect world "things are not always what they seem." Even some of the biggest and brightest of moths— which could not possibly pretend to be dead leaves or stinging insects—manage to deceive their enemies by "making believe" they are dangerous creatures ready to pounce. The big "eye-spots" on the wings of the pretty Canadian peacock moth makes it look so much like an owl, when it rests half hidden in the foliage of the trees, that it frightens away the small birds that come near it. The emperor moth is even more terrifying to timid moorland creatures; for as it rests on the heather, it looks for all the world like the head of some poisonous snake in the act of striking.

Baby Moths are Never Safe

It is even more important for slow-going caterpillars to have some means of pro-tection against the dangers all round them. Butterflies and moths can sometimes escape from their enemies by flying away; but caterpillars cannot. With their funny short legs they cannot even run. Once they are discovered by an enemy, they are done for.

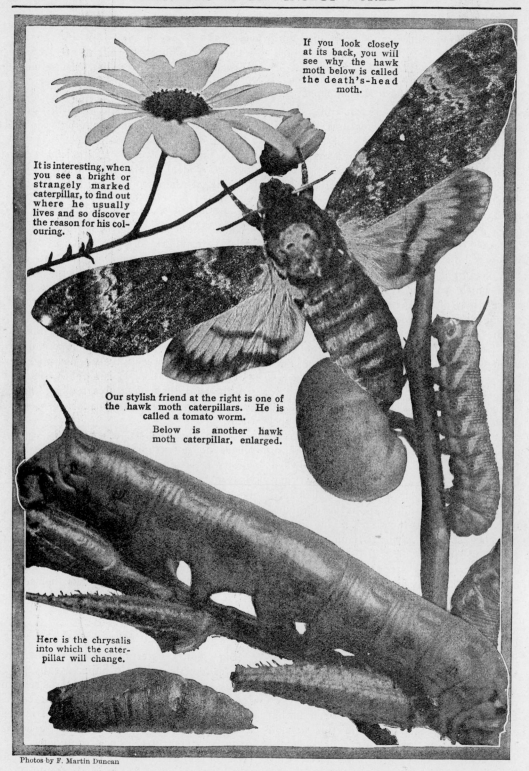

If you look closely at its back, you will see why the hawk moth below is called the death's-head moth.

It is interesting, when you see a bright or strangely marked caterpillar, to find out where he usually lives and so discover the reason for his colouring.

Our stylish friend at the right is one of the hawk moth caterpillars. He is called a tomato worm.

Below is another hawk moth caterpillar, enlarged.

Here is the chrysalis into which the caterpillar will change.

Photos by F. Martin Duncan

Yet these weak, defenceless creatures often outwit their enemies and grow up into sunshine fairies in spite of the way in which they are hunted in their young days.

How Nature Protects Her Children

The great majority of caterpillars are soft, plump, tempting creatures, greatly relished by the hungry birds. So to save their tender skins the timid crawlers strive, as far as they can, to live hidden from prying eyes. They stay under the leaves or press closely against the stems of their food plants; and since they are nearly always green enough to match the leaves, or grey or brown enough for the stems and twigs, it is very difficult to see them—so long as they keep still. The very spots and stripes with which many of them are marked only make the concealment more perfect, for they always resemble the ribs or veining of the leaves, the colours of the flowers, or the patches of light and shade that fall upon the plants.

A Game of Hide-and-Seek

The looper caterpillars, as they are often called, are especially clever at playing the game of hide-and-seek that is for ever going on between the birds and caterpillars —a game in which the caterpillars always hide and the birds always seek. When they are not feeding—and even caterpillars are obliged to stop eating sometimes—the cunning creatures grip the stems or the slender branches of their own particular plant or tree and pretend to be twigs. And so exactly like twigs are they in shape and colour, and the way in which they hold themselves, that nine times out of ten you would not be able to say which were the real twigs and which were the sham ones. Even the buds and the leaf scars of the twigs are imitated by knobs and marks on the skin of the insect actors.

These queer caterpillars are called "loopers" on account of their peculiar way of curving themselves into loops when taking a walk. They loop along in this fashion because, instead of having four pairs of false feet, as most caterpillars have, they have only one pair—right at the tail end of their long thin bodies, near the claspers.

The tiny mining caterpillars are so very cautious that they never show themselves at all in the outside world until they are ready to spin their wee cocoons. They spend their early days hidden in little green galleries which they tunnel out between the upper and lower surfaces of the leaves, or burrow into the wood of trees and often do a good deal of damage. In fact there is no end to their troublesome ways.

A Caterpillar That Lives in a Bag

Then there are bag-worms—the funny little caterpillars of the Psyche (sī′kē) moths. They have hard heads but very soft, tender bodies. So the wise insects make neat little bags, and live inside them with only their heads and their tiny forelegs sticking out of the opening at the top.

The bags are made of fine grass blades, small twigs, pine needles, or scraps snipped from leaves, all carefully fastened together with silken threads. It is a funny sight to see the odd little creatures rocking along, trailing their queer home-made bags behind them.

Woolly bears and other bristly caterpillars do not trouble to hide themselves. They are safe from the attacks of birds, who will not touch the hairy, prickly things. We may often see woolly bears, very busy among the vegetables and fruit bushes, munching away at the juicy leaves in the most impudent fashion. They hurry along the garden path as if they had not a minute to lose. Woolly bears are always in a hurry; but if you touch them, they roll themselves up at once into prickly balls that resemble tiny hedgehogs.

Insect "Bluffers"

Big, gaudy caterpillars, when they are not protected by bristly hairs, usually have a most unpleasant flavour. The birds seldom interfere with them. Some of the caterpillars that would taste better try to frighten away their foes by pretending to be fierce, dangerous creatures. The large green caterpillar of the privet hawk moth looks alarming when it rears up as if it were about to attack you. At the end of its back it also has a large curved spine.

Stranger still is the behaviour of the puss moth caterpillar. It is an odd little creature, dressed in bright green and purple. Behind its head is a bright red ring adorned with two big black spots. Its back is humped, and at the end of its body there are two absurd little tails.

We may find the puss caterpillar feeding on willow or poplar trees. It looks so plump and harmless that any bird might be tempted to snap it up. But the moment danger approaches, it rears up, draws back its head, and puffs up as if it were swelling with rage. And there, instead of a defenceless caterpillar, is a wicked-looking little hobgoblin with a round red face and staring black eyes. Above his head he brandishes two dangerous-looking pink lashers. It is enough to scare the boldest bird.

You see how the trick is done? The real head of the caterpillar is pulled back into the red ring and serves as a big nose in the middle of the hobgoblin's face; the black spots become eyes; and the pink lashers are shot out from the forked tail which the caterpillar turns up over its back. The creature spits, too—for it can spatter you with a fluid that makes your skin smart and tingle.

In spite of all their tricks and disguises, caterpillars still get eaten up in vast numbers. And a good thing, too! If they were to have everything their own way, there would soon be very few green leaves left on the trees. Nearly all our vegetables would be devoured, and our food crops would be spoiled. Fortunately, caterpillars are delicate things; cold wet weather kills large numbers of them, and the birds eat still more. In keeping down insect pests the birds are our best helpers. All through the spring and early summer they work away hunting for insects to feed all the baby birds at home in their nests.

(CONTINUED ON PAGE 257)

Here we see all the stages of the puss moth's life history. The eggs (enlarged) on a poplar leaf are shown in the circle. At the top on the left are the young caterpillars and to the right the full grown caterpillar with its curious imitation face. Next (bottom left) we see on the tree trunk the cocoon from which the moth has just emerged. and finally the fully developed puss moth. He has dried his delicate wings and is now ready to take to flight.

TRY THESE TRICKS

A SURPRISING PENNY

A card about 2 inches square is balanced on the end of the first finger, and a penny is placed on top of it, as shown in the circle. To the utter amazement of the spectators, a flip of the finger sends the card sailing across the room, while the penny is left on the tip of the finger.

FREEING THE PAPER

Turn a bottle upside down on a single sheet of paper. Pull the paper taut with the left hand, and strike the table a number of light blows with the fist of the right. At each blow the paper will slip towards you half an inch or so, and will gradually be removed from under the bottle.

THE JUMPING BALL

Place a light ball in a tapering glass goblet which you hold at an angle in your left hand, as shown in the picture. Announce to your audience that the ball is so sensitive that it will do anything to escape a draught. Then blow into the goblet containing the ball, which will jump into the goblet you hold in your right hand. The French do this trick with an egg, which they save from breaking by putting water in the right-hand glass.

RAISING A GLASS

Press the palm of your hand over the top of a light tumbler or goblet. Then lower the fingers as shown and raise them again quickly but not abruptly. When you raise your hand the glass will stick to it.

THE MAGIC GLASS

Hold a goblet of water as shown, then lift it quickly and smoothly, and swing it round as if it were empty. No water will spill.

ONE BALL OR TWO

By crossing the fingers as shown in the circle and rubbing them over a ball, you will be able almost to convince yourself that there are two balls —especially if you close your eyes. Aristotle is said to have invented this trick to amuse the little boy who became Alexander the Great.

SUGAR THAT WILL NOT DISSOLVE

Tell your friends that you will hold a cube of sugar under water for ten minutes without its dissolving. Then place the sugar on top of a cork floating in a bowl of water, and push an inverted glass down into the water over the cork. The sugar will be under, but not in, the water.

THE VANISHING SPOT

Paste a small square of black court-plaster on the back of your second finger. Tell your spectators that at your command the spot will vanish and reappear. Close your fist and say, "Go away, Jack." Then quickly extend your first finger, which has no court-plaster. Then close your fingers and say, "Come back, Jack," and extend the second finger again. All this must be done very smoothly and quickly, with the fist held somewhat downward.

THE WALKING RING

Put a ring on a perfectly smooth stick and hold the stick quite still with the ring just touching the surface of a table. Entirely of its own accord the ring will move from one end of the stick to the other.

The old alchemists, like the one shown here, have always captured men's imaginations. For centuries they handed down their lore, one to another, and carried on their strange experiments in an effort to turn less valuable metals into gold. Their efforts were in vain, but nevertheless they laid the foundation of our modern chemistry, for their discoveries have since led men on to deeper and deeper investigations. No wonder they have frequently made their appearance in literature, as in Ben Jonson's play "The Alchemist."

A BRICKLAYER *Becomes* POET LAUREATE

"Rare Ben Jonson" Who Used to Laugh and Quarrel with Shakespeare, and was Imprisoned for Killing an Actor

(CONTINUED FROM PAGE 156)

BEN JONSON of the curly hair first saw the light in the great days of Queen Elizabeth. England was growing rich and strong. The minds of men were working with a vigour they had not felt for many centuries. Imagination was overflowing and ambition knew no bounds. One of the results was the richest age of poetry and drama that England had ever seen; and one of the greatest of the poets and dramatists was the breezy Ben Jonson (1573–1637).

Ben Jonson may well have wondered whether he, too, could not win fame in such an age. He lived near Westminster Abbey, and through the kindness of William Camden, a great schoolmaster, he went to the famous Westminster School. Here the charity pupil developed one of the richest minds of his day, though his education ended in his teens. He went to work laying bricks, like his stepfather; but he hated the trade so much that he joined the army sent to support the revolt of the Netherlands against England's deadliest enemy, Spain.

When he returned he married, and soon started writing plays. He would often read late into the night or wander off for an evening with his literary friends at the famous "Mermaid Tavern." There he passed many a merry hour, and the best of all his hours must have been spent in the company of Shakespeare. So nimble-witted was the gathering that the tavern rang with mirth. And Shakespeare and Jonson soon became fast friends.

During these happy years Jonson was

fairly busy writing. At twenty-five he was the author of a rich comedy called "Every Man in his Humour" (1598), in which Shakespeare himself acted a part.

Jonson's comedies were written better and were more amusing than those that had been put on the stage before. He set out to present a true picture of his times, and this made him poke fun at various literary leaders. So, since people do not like to be laughed at, he was constantly getting into trouble. At length he killed an actor in self-defence and was sent to prison. Only by good luck did he escape hanging.

As soon as he was free again he joined a famous group of players. He had decided to write no more comedies, for he was disgusted with his former quarrels. But after an attempt at tragedy, he struck his best vein in another series of comedies, of which the two best examples are "The Alchemist" (1610) and "Bartholomew Fair" (1614).

Photo by National Portrait Gallery

Ben Jonson, a famous dramatist of the days of Queen Elizabeth and a great friend of Shakespeare.

Jonson began to achieve fame. King James I, who succeeded Elizabeth in 1603, ranked him second only to Shakespeare. Two distinguished noblemen contributed to his income, and Sir Walter Raleigh engaged him as a tutor for his son. But success went to Jonson's head. He loved to talk about himself, and as he grew older praise was ever sweeter to his ears.

When one of his plays failed, he left the stage to write only for the court. For the court he produced a number of beautiful plays called masques, and at his death he left unfinished a great pastoral play called "The Sad Shepherd," which was published in 1641, four years later. As a reward for his labours, he was appointed poet laureate, and was probably the first to hold the position officially. In his old age he was made happy by the homage of many young writers, who were known to their various friends and contemporaries as the "Sons of Ben."

(CONTINUED ON PAGE 207)

ANSWERS TO PUZZLES ON PAGE 118

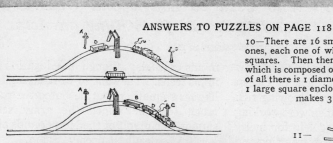

9—The engine goes forward on the main line, and then backs and pushes truck B under the bridge. Then the engine-driver comes back to the main track, backs eastwards, and enters the right end of the siding. He couples trucks D and B together and returns with them to the main line, where he uncouples truck B. Now he backs eastwards and pushes truck D up the siding at the right and under the bridge. The engine now returns to the main line, where it is coupled to truck B. Again it backs eastwards, enters the siding, and leaves truck B beside the lamp-post C. Now the engine-driver backs down to the main line, proceeds westwards, backs up the siding at the left, couples his engine to truck B, and pulls the truck to lamp-post A, where he leaves it. Then he takes his engine back to the main line.

10—There are 16 small squares and nine larger ones, each one of which is composed of 4 small squares. Then there are 4 squares each one of which is composed of 9 small squares. And last of all there is 1 diamond square in the centre and 1 large square enclosing the whole figure. That makes 31 squares in all.

11—

12 — Cut the cross as shown in Fig. 2 and the pieces will form a square when arranged as shown in Fig. 1.

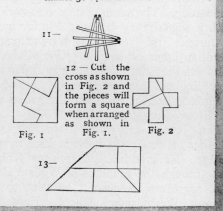

Fig. 1   Fig. 1.   Fig. 2

13—

A vision of gleaming pearls lying in the smooth curve of an oyster shell may very well rise before the mind of the Malay pearl diver as he comes to shore with his basket of oysters. But he himself will never wear the pearls. Being "of great price," they will go to the rich and great of the world, as they have gone since the beginning of history. The Mogul emperor on his throne wore an enormous rope of pearls; Cleopatra dissolved a pearl in her wine to show Antony how lavishly she could entertain him at dinner; Cæsar is said to have conquered Britain largely in the hope of finding pearls; and some robes of Queen Elizabeth were stiff with them.

The COSTLIEST PRODUCT of the SEA

In the Folds of the Ugly Oyster We Find Our Pearls of Greatest Price; and We Can Help in Making Them, Too

AMONG all the treasures of the deep there is none lovelier or costlier than the one that we get from the lowly oyster. It is the pearl. As far back as history goes, the pearl has been a prize to seek in the waters, and in olden days there were various quaint notions as to how it came to find its way into the oyster shell. Some people thought it was made by a flash of lightning striking on the shell, and others believed that if a drop of dew fell in the shell it would be changed into a pearl.

We know better now. A pearl is born when some tiny thing creeps into the oyster's shell and irritates the animal. It may be a minute sea creature, a grain of sand, or some other gritty substance. When it gets between the shell and the soft mantle of the mollusc, the oyster may protect itself by covering the intruder with the same pearly substance that lines its shell. This substance is called nacre (nā′kẽr), or mother-of-pearl. It is put on layer upon layer, and in the end it forms a pearl.

The pearl oyster is not the kind of oyster we eat. It is not really an oyster at all, but belongs to the same order as the mussel. As a matter of fact, any shell-fish that lives in a shell with a pearly lining may produce a pearl, though only very rarely; and even with the pearl oysters, one only in a thousand is likely to produce a pearl of any value. Yet the large and shapely pearls are such desirable prizes that it is worth the toil of hunting for thousands of oysters to find a single one.

Few of them are large, and even fewer are of perfect shape. If they grow on the lining of the shell itself they will be flat on one side, and then they are called "button pearls." If they are fastened to the shell by a narrow neck they are called "blister pearls." And if they are very small, growing usually in the muscles of the oyster, they are called "seed pearls." When they grow large and round in the tissues of the animals, and have a fine soft lustre without any flaw, they are the rare pearls "of the first water" that are worth a small fortune.

The strange thing is that pearl-fishers have discovered that it is the ugly shells—those which are irregular in shape or have not grown properly, or which are covered with little knobs, or holes made by tiny parasites that bore through—that are the most likely to contain the beautiful pearl.

Men have fished for pearls since ancient times around India and the Persian Gulf,

If we could watch what happens both on the water and under it, we should see something like this when the brown men dive for pearls. It makes one catch one's breath in suspense, hoping that the man on the bottom will be quick enough to escape the fierce, hungry-looking shark.

and they now fish for them in many parts of the world—in India, Japan, and China, in Australia and round many a Pacific island, in the Gulf of California and the Gulf of Mexico, and in still other places. There is commonly one fishing season every year, usually in the spring, and lasting from four to six weeks; for it would not do to keep fishing all the time—there would soon be no systems left to produce the pearls in ring or brooch or necklace.

The fishers are all divers. They go down from a boat, in which one remains, and crawl about on the floor of the ocean, gathering

the shells they find and putting them in baskets. In many parts of the world they wear diving-suits, and can stay under water a long while. But in the Far East the Japanese and Malay divers often go into the water just as they are, with a big stone to carry them down; and, even if they do not meet a shark, they cannot stay below much longer than a minute. It is a dangerous trade, and shows the risk that men will take to obtain these pearl-producing molluscs.

Sometimes the shells are opened in the boat, but usually they are taken to the shore and spread out for some days to decay. Then they are washed and carefully searched, and any pearls that may be found are taken out by hand or with special tools.

In addition to the pearls that come out of the sea, there are a good many from the streams and rivers. These are called "fresh-water pearls." They are found in many places in Europe and America, and throughout the temperate zone. They have less lustre than the ocean pearls, and are by no means so valuable; although the best of the fresh-water pearls are very beautiful and may fetch high prices.

Now if a grain of sand that strays into an oyster can bring about the formation of a pearl, why can we not put a grain into a pearl-bearing mollusc and induce it to make a pearl? We can, perfectly well; and men have been doing it, especially in China,

This photograph of a pearl diver at his dangerous work was taken from a diving-bell somewhere in the South Seas. Amid the bright coral and the startled, weird fishes, he doggedly plies his difficult and hazardous trade.

since the thirteenth century. What they do is to cut a tiny piece out of the mantle of a pearl-mussel, wrap it round a fragment of mother-of-pearl or some other substance, and then plant it in the mantle of another mussel—and the second mussel duly proceeds to build a pearl round it. These river mussels are carefully fed and protected in special beds or cages, and in time are opened for the pearls they ought to bear. The surgical operation does not always succeed— by no means; but when it does, there may be a fine pearl. Such a pearl is not artificial, for it has been made by the pearl-mussel; but, because human beings helped in the process, we call it a "culture pearl."

The artificial pearls are very different. They are made by simply coating a glass bead with a substance known as "pearl essence," or "essence d'orient," which is obtained from the silvery scales on the under side of certain little fishes—like the sardine, the herring, and the fresh-water bleak, or "ablette," found in the rivers of Europe. The pearl essence is mixed with celluloid, and several coats are put on. Although these pearls may be made cheaply they are often very beautiful, and it is difficult to tell them from the real ones. Sometimes a hollow glass bead is used; it is coated on the inside with pearl essence and gelatine, and then filled with wax.

There are some pink pearls, and yellow pearls, in addition to the creamy-white ones that are commonest; and there are black pearls that are very highly prized. A pearl needs only a little polishing to make it ready to wear, for it is never cut like a diamond or any other precious stone. But the owner of a pearl has to be careful. It must never be put in hot water, or the sheen will be ruined, and it must not be left in the dark long, or it will lose its lustre.

Pearls vary greatly in size; the largest in existence, now in the Victoria and Albert Museum, weighs about three ounces.

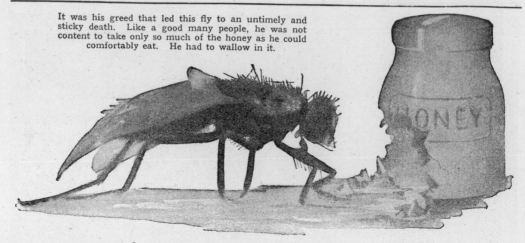

It was his greed that led this fly to an untimely and sticky death. Like a good many people, he was not content to take only so much of the honey as he could comfortably eat. He had to wallow in it.

TANSY *and* BOBBLES *on* FABLE ISLAND

A Jackdaw, a Camel, and a Greedy Dog Teach the Fairy Children That it is a Good Thing to be Satisfied with What You Have

(CONTINUED FROM PAGE 52)

TANSY was feeling very sulky. She had been thinking for several days of the fine jewel she had picked up in the farmyard, and had been teasing Mother Fairy to have it made into an ornament for her hair.

But Mother Fairy said that fine jewels were not suitable for fairy children, and that Tansy had far better give the jewel to the queen.

Now Tansy didn't want to give her jewel to the queen, so she was sulking by the royal garden when she saw a curious sight.

A jackdaw had picked up a lot of feathers which had dropped from the royal peacocks, and having stuck them about him, he was strutting around to show his finery, and mocking at the crowd of jackdaws who were watching him. Indeed, he actually pecked at them if they came too near.

"Conceited bird!" thought Tansy.

But now the jackdaw walked off to the group of peacocks, who were sunning themselves on the royal terrace. He pretended to be one of them, and waved his claw by way of greeting.

But the peacocks were very angry with the vain jackdaw, and rushing out upon him, they stripped him of his borrowed plumes and drove him off in disgrace.

Tansy watched as the jackdaw went back to his own mates. But there he fared even worse.

"No! No!" they screamed. "You don't come back among us!" And they pecked him until he ran off.

"Oh, Bobbles," said Tansy, as Bobbles discovered her ; "do look at that silly jackdaw!" and she told Bobbles the story.

"He's been punished by his betters for pretending to be as fine as they, and then by his equals for scorning them."

"I suppose," said Tansy, "I'm like the silly jackdaw. I'd better give the jewel to the queen."

At that very moment the queen advanced down the path, with seven beautiful maidens following her.

"Booh!" whispered Tansy. Then she sprang out and curtsied.

"Please, your Majesty, will you accept this jewel? My mother says it is too fine for a fairy child."

The queen lifted the jewel, and the sun laughed upon it.

Then the queen stooped and kissed Tansy; but Tansy was so shy that she linked her fingers, hung her head, and disappeared, leaving the jewel in the queen's hand.

As the fairies ran off, they came upon a broken pot of honey, all swarming with greedy flies. But, alas, the flies had trampled over the honey so excitedly that their feet were all clogged, and they couldn't get free.

"Oh, dear!" moaned a dying fly. "We've

"Silly creature!" said Bobbles. "He grasped at the shadow and lost the real thing."

The Greedy Dog and the Ponies

Bobbles loved to ride on the ponies' backs when they didn't even know that he was

This poor old dog has reason to look mournful. He had a nice juicy piece of meat, quite enough for his supper, with perhaps a little that he could save for his breakfast. But as he was crossing a stream, he chanced to look into the water and saw what he took to be another dog with a piece of meat as big as his own. Not content with his own good meal, he determined to have both pieces. He snapped at the other dog and dropped his meat, which sank to the bottom of the stream, and so he had to go supperless to bed. And all because he was so greedy!

all thrown away our lives for the sake of one gluttonous meal!"

How the Dog Lost His Dinner

"How silly!" said Bobbles. "But do look, Tansy! What's that dog doing?"

They went on tiptoe to the side of the stream. A dog was carrying a large piece of meat that he had stolen. As he crossed the water by the plank, he looked down and thought, owing to the reflection in the water, that he saw another dog with another piece of meat.

He determined to get that piece of meat, too; but when he snapped at what he thought to be another dog, he only dropped the meat he was carrying, and lost it in the stream.

there, for, when he was invisible he was just as light as the air.

He was looking at three ponies that had just walked out of a stable.

They appeared very cross as they kept nodding their heads together and talking.

"The dog's in the manger again," said number one.

"And spoiling all our food, though he can't eat any of it himself," said number two; "and snarling at us as if we had injured him."

"I wish I could get my hoof as high as the manger," said number three. "I'd soon kick him out."

Now Bobbles's father had told him that he mustn't believe all he heard, but must find

Here are the three ponies who found a dog in their manger. They were very annoyed because the dog was lying in their nice hay.

things out for himself, so he danced along hurriedly into the stable, and there, sure enough, was the dog, lying in the sweet hay.

"Booh!" said Bobbles.

The dog looked up, and when he saw Bobbles he didn't dare to snarl.

"You great greedy, disgusting animal!" said Bobbles. "If you don't get off that hay, I'll send a message to the king of the wasps. He'll know how to stir you up!"

Now the dog knew all about the king of the wasps; so he got up quickly and made at once for the door.

"So that's all right," said Bobbles to himself, "but I'll just follow him, in case he gets into any more mischief."

Sure enough the dog suddenly gave a howl and dashed off after the fox, who had been trying to get some fat chickens for his family who were waiting at home hopefully.

One glance at this fellow will tell you why he would stay in the manger even though he couldn't eat the ponies' food. This is what people begin to look like when they allow themselves always to feel envious.

Bobbles was so cross with the dog that he darted in between him and the fox, and the dog turned tail and fled. But the fox, not looking where he was going, leaped into a thorn-bush; and as the thorns stuck into him, he cried, "Thorn-bush! Thorn-bush! How can you be so cruel?"

"I only offer you the fate you offer the hens and chickens," said the thorn-bush, which refused to let go.

But Bobbles, rushing up, whispered in the thorn-bush's ear.

"Let him go this time, and we'll see if he learns to behave any better."

So the thorn-bush rustled his leaves rather grumblingly, as he opened his branches and let the wounded fox escape.

"Come on! Come on, Bobbles," cried Tansy, as she danced up to him on tiptoe. "Only come very quietly."

So they went off very quietly behind a pile of rock, and there sat a milkmaid weeping because all her milk was spilled on the ground.

"Oh, dear! Oh, dear!" she sobbed. "I was going to buy some eggs with the money I got for the milk, and get chickens from the eggs, and sell the chickens at the fair, and buy a fine silk dress, and make everyone want to dance with me; and now—now—" and she buried her face in her hands.

"Poor thing!" said Tansy. "But she oughtn't to cry so long over spilt milk."

"Or count her chickens before they are hatched," added Bobbles, thoughtfully,

Was the Satyr Right?

A satyr was squatting on a bank with his lyre at his side. He was very fond of playing the lyre.

A satyr has the body of a man, legs and hoofs like a hairy goat, two little knobs of horns on his forehead, and a tail.

Bobbles and Tansy were surprised to see a man sitting by him, for the folk in Fable Land were usually afraid of the satyrs, and avoided them.

It was a very cold day, and the man was putting his fingers to his mouth and blowing them.

"Why do you do that?" asked the satyr, as he handed him a bowl of soup.

"To warm my hands," said the man.

But in a minute the man was blowing hard at the soup.

The sad-looking maid and cow are not weeping for the same reasons. The little milkmaid has not yet learned enough to know that crying never cured anything. And the cow? Why, the cow must be sad at the sight of the maid's foolishness.

"Why do you do that?" asked the satyr.

"To cool the soup, of course!" said the man.

But the satyr leaped up fiercely.

"I thought I'd found a man sensible enough to be my friend!" he cried. "But I scorn one who blows hot and cold with the same mouth! Begone!" and he snatched away the soup.

"Booh! You needn't have been quite so rude," said Tansy, as the man disappeared.

"Oh, it's you—" and the satyr glared. "You think you can rule all the island!"

But for answer Tansy picked up the satyr's lyre and handed it to him.

"There's nothing like music for getting rid of one's temper," she said, laughing at him.

So the satyr had to laugh, too. And he made such wonderful music that a crowd of animals collected to watch Bobbles and Tansy dancing.

Then the other animals began dancing, too, and Tansy and Bobbles agreed to act as judges.

The monkey distinguished himself so much that the wood resounded with applause, and the fairies were just going to crown him with oak leaves when who should come along but a lumbering camel.

Why the Camel Looked Foolish

"I'll show you all how to dance!" he cried proudly, for he was a conceited fellow.

So the camel began to dance, and soon all the company burst into laughter. The silly camel thought they were approving and made still more ungainly efforts, but the animals rushed upon him to drive him from the ring.

"No! No! Stop! Stop!" cried Bobbles; and he went up to the amazed camel.

"My dear Mr. Camel," he said, trying to speak like his father, "never attempt to do what, by your nature, is impossible."

So Tansy crowned the monkey, and then she and Bobbles followed the camel to try to cheer him up.

"Dear, dear!" moaned the camel. "Why does everyone mock me and think me ridiculous?"

"They don't think you ridiculous when you don't try to dance," said Bobbles.

"I've a hump—and I've such short ears—"

"Yes, why *are* your ears so short?" interrupted Tansy.

"Alas!" moaned the camel, "my great-great-great-grandfather once asked Jupiter to give him horns, and Jupiter was so angry that he cropped his ears. So by asking too much he lost the little he had before."

"All the same, I like your ears," said Tansy, as she flew up and stroked them.

"Come—both of you—for a ride," cried the camel, now quite cheered.

Where the Moon's Mother Lives

No one has ever seen the moon's mother except Tansy and Bobbles.

She sits on the highest cloud in the sky and waves to the sun, the moon and the stars as they go by. She waves to Bobbles and Tansy also, for they love to go up and cool themselves after they've been having flying races with the larks.

When the larks get tired and have to drop, the fairies fly on, and the moon's mother tells them stories.

One afternoon the moon herself made a call, and tried hard to persuade the moon mother to weave her a beautiful cloak to fit her perfectly.

"You are quite as silly as any mortal child," said the moon mother with a laugh. "How could I make a cloak to fit you when you're new one day, full two weeks later, and are neither one thing nor the other in between?"

The moon couldn't help twinkling her eyes, even as she heaved a big sigh.

"It's terrible to be always growing bigger and bigger, and then getting smaller and smaller! How would you like it, Tansy and Bobbles?"

"Cheer up, moon," said Tansy. "You're always dressed in silver."

But the conversation was interrupted by a great chattering which came from close by.

It appeared that the wind and the sun were having a quarrel as to which of them was the stronger.

"Of course I am!" said the sun.

The satyr is only half a man, so perhaps he is to be excused for having lost his temper—especially as he was tired of people who always tried to evade the point at issue and never would come to a decision one way or the other.

"Nonsense!" said the wind.

"I know how we'll settle it," said Bobbles, as he sprang forward and perched on one of the wind's tempest bags.

"I do believe you two think you know everything," said the sun.

"But we don't, that's just it!" said Tansy. "That's why we wander over earth and sky to find things out for ourselves."

"Now—listen—please," said Bobbles, and he pointed far below to the high road. "There's a man walking along wearing a heavy cloak. Whichever of you can get the cloak off that man will prove himself the stronger."

"Well, that's easy enough!" roared the wind, and he began to blow so hard that Tansy and Bobbles were spun half a mile through the air.

How they laughed as they dropped like larks to the ground!

The wind blew and blew, and all the earth looked up to see what was the matter. The trees swayed, the sea around Fable Island rose up like crested horses, the animals hid, and as for the man, he frowned and wrapped his cloak closer and closer. The wind battered him and made him hold his breath, but he was dogged and plodded on, clutching at his cloak.

"Time's up!" called Bobbles. "It's the sun's turn now."

So the wind closed his tempest bags, and suddenly, on earth and sea, there was a great calm.

Out shone the sun, and the people, the animals, the birds, the insects, and all the land smiled.

As for the man on the high road, he gave a sigh of relief and flung off his cloak.

(CONTINUED ON PAGE 252)

JACK AND JILL

Jack and Jill went up the hill
To fetch a pail of water;
Jack fell down and broke his crown,
And Jill fell tumbling after.

THREE BLIND MICE

Three blind mice;
See how they run!
They all run after the farmer's
 wife.

Who cut off their tails with the carving
 knife.
Did ever you see such a sight in your life
As these three blind mice?

LITTLE BOY BLUE

Little Boy Blue, come blow your
 horn;
The sheep's in the meadow, the
 cow's in the corn.
But where is the boy that looks
 after the sheep?
He's under a haycock, fast asleep.
Will you awake him? No, not I;
For if I do, he'll be sure to cry.

Two Dutch musicians of other days contributing
to the entertainment at a family party.

MUSIC COMES of AGE

A "Golden Age" and a "New Age" Created a General Desire to Hear Music Sung and Played in Public Halls, as Well as in Churches and Palaces; and in Italy a Handful of Men Were Making Violins Such as the World Has Never Equalled

(CONTINUED FROM PAGE 72)

HAVE you ever noticed that great events have a way of happening almost at the same time? There seem to be certain periods when all the hard work men have been doing for two or three centuries past suddenly begins to bear fruit. Then everyone wakes up to the fact that the world is an amazing place, and people feel that it is a good thing to be alive.

It was during such a time that Henry VIII and Queen Elizabeth reigned over England. Exciting things were going on everywhere. The gallant Magellan was sailing round the world. On the western side of the Atlantic a whole new continent was being opened up. Shakespeare, the greatest dramatist the world has ever known, was writing plays and poetry that would make his name famous for centuries to come. In every corner of Europe a fever for action had seized men's minds. It was while all this was going on that music came into what we may call its Golden Age—its first age of perfection.

Now who were the musicians who put all those surging feelings into beautiful sounds? Mightiest of all was the great Palestrina (1515?–1594), an Italian who lived in Rome and wrote music for the choir of the Pope. Everything he composed was for the church, and was intended for choruses of male voices without any accompaniment. Palestrina (pä′lĕs-trē′nä) took the simple, elementary music of the Middle Ages and wove all those independent voices, that make up what we call counterpoint, into a whole that was beautiful, dignified and harmonious. He was one of the greatest of all writers of sacred music. Many of you know his beautiful Christmas carol, "Behold a rose of beauty from Jesse's rod is sprung."

The Age of the Folk Song

But you will remember that the world outside the church's walls was full of excitement. Men were thinking all manner of new things, and feeling very deeply. No wonder that they could scarcely keep from bursting into song. For some time musicians had been writing music that had nothing to do with religion— "secular" (sĕk′ū-lår) music, we call it—and the simple old songs of the people, or "folk songs," were on everybody's lips.

What is a Madrigal?

It was now that all this secular music came into its own. Composers tried their hand at writing madrigals (măd′rĭ-gål). These were songs of love or nature or springtime, written for several voices without any accompaniment. Anything fresher, livelier, and lovelier than some of those old madrigals it would be hard to find. The composers kept the different tunes, or "voices," all going at once—in and out and all together—in an amazing way, as a juggler keeps a number of balls in the air at the same time. And the songs were full of feeling, too. People loved them, because the common tunes that ploughboys whistled and to which boys and girls danced were woven into them.

The finest madrigals were written in Italy, the country where everyone seems to be born with a song on his lips. But

It was on the lips of simple people like these that our beautiful folk music was born. Year after year and century after century they have worn the same costumes, sung the same songs, and worshipped in the same churches as their ancestors. This particular little procession is going into a church in Sweden, but you may find similar groups everywhere in Europe, and the songs they sing are among the most beautiful in the world.

Photo by Swedish State Rlys.

A—Seventeenth-century "spinet," the English name for any small keyboard instrument that had one string to a note and was sounded by being plucked.

B—A harp played by one of the minnesingers. Though the harp is one of the oldest of instruments, and was played in Egypt and Asia Minor at least three thousand years ago, our modern harps are all descended from those like the one above which was made in Northern Europe.

C—A sixteenth-century lute, an ancestor of our modern guitars and mandolins.

D—A keyed dulcimer. The original dulcimer was a very old instrument indeed, and belonged to the East. It had ten strings, which the player struck with a long curved stick. This was the "instrument of ten strings" in the Bible. In the Middle Ages a dulcimer had from two to five strings for each note, and the player struck them with a little hammer. Finally a keyboard was added.

E—A sixteenth-century virginal, such as Queen Elizabeth might have played upon. The name was applied in England to spinets that had four or five sides. Each note had one string, plucked by means of a quill. The instrument took its name from the fact that it was often played upon by young girls.

F—A seventeenth-century harpsichord, much larger than the virginal and spinet but related to them, the strings being plucked with a quill. This ancestor of our modern piano was shaped like a harp, and had two to four strings to a note. Sometimes, as here, it had two "manuals," or keyboards, to give it variety of tone.

G—An eighteenth-century zither, an instrument somewhat like the ancient psaltery mentioned in the Bible. The player plucked the strings as the instrument lay on the table in front of him.

H—A keyboard was added to the zither in just the way in which it was added to the dulcimer and other instruments. Here you see a "zither clavier" of the eighteenth century, that is, a keyed zither.

I—A sixteenth-century clavichord, another ancestor of the piano. It developed from the keyed dulcimer, so its notes were sounded by striking the keys, instead of by plucking them. The tone was soft but very sweet.

England was not far behind Italy. Queen Elizabeth was delighted with the madrigals of Byrd (1538?–1623) and Morley (1557?–1604), which became so popular that they were sung everywhere. "A gentleman would take his part in a madrigal then as readily as he now takes a hand at bridge." And what poetry those composers had from which to choose when they wanted words to set to music! Thomas Campion, Sir Philip Sidney, and Edmund Spenser. No wonder it was the Golden Age of song!

One of the things that interests us most about these madrigal writers is the fact that many of the compositions they wrote could be either sung or played on instruments. "Apt for voices or viols" was the phrase that many a madrigal carried on its title page. And that means that instruments were being improved and at last were being used for something else besides accompaniment. Those viols, which were of different sizes, were the ancestors of our bass viols, violins and 'cellos.

Even more interesting than the viols was a little stringed instrument that the English people bought for their homes. It had a keyboard, as our piano has, and was called a virginal —or a "pair of virginals." Its little tinkle sounded very thin, for the strings were short and plucked instead of being long and struck, and so did not resound. But in Shakespeare's time the virginal was one of the noblest of instruments. Henry VIII, Queen Mary, and Queen Elizabeth were all skilled in playing upon it; and we have to this day a famous book of dainty pieces for the virginal; it is full of scales and turns, and is called "Queen Elizabeth's Virginal Book."

Ancestors of the Piano

The spinet (spĭn'ĕt), the clavichord (klăv'ĭ-kôrd), and the harpsichord were played as much as the virginals at this time. They were stringed instruments with keyboards— humble little ancestors of our own piano.

Photo by Rischgitz
This village musician is playing upon a quaint little rebeck. It was one of the forerunners of the violin, and in turn traced its descent back to the ancient Oriental rebab. Rebecks were often shaped like a boat, and some of them were so small that they could be carried in the pocket.

Orlando Gibbons (1583–1625) was another Englishman who wrote madrigals as well as fine church music; and Orlandus Lassus (1520–1594), a native of the Netherlands and one of the greatest musicians of the Golden Age, knew how to please both the priests in church and the lords and ladies in the drawing-room.

Like all other ages the Golden Age, too, passed away. Its music had been perfect of its kind, but it never had tried to voice men's stormier moods; and, after a time, its composers found they had said practically all that they knew how to say. So they sought to make music express a greater variety of things, and soon invented something new, which is what men

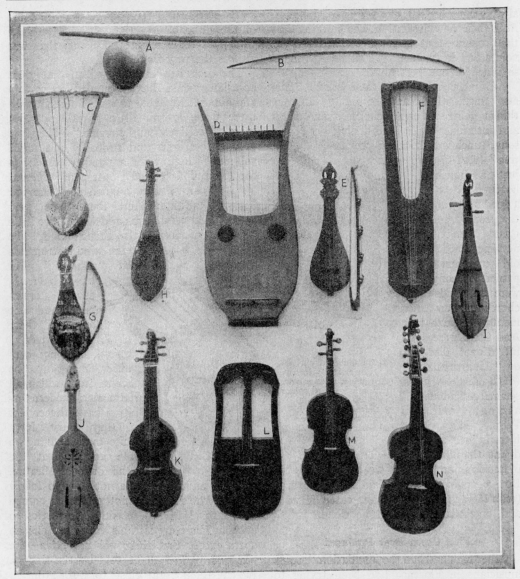

STRINGED INSTRUMENTS OF OTHER DAYS FROM WHICH THE VIOLIN HAS DESCENDED

Here are some ancestors of the modern violin, the bass viol, the viola, and the violoncello. A and B are primitive musical bows. Many an early hunter must have learned that he could get a musical sound by drawing his bow across the tense strings of various early instruments, such as the primitive African lyre at C or the Greek lyre at D, in both of which the strings were plucked. So it is not surprising to find that the Cretan "lyra" at E was played with a bow. Later came the German rotta, at F, which was plucked at first, but by the eleventh century was played upon with a bow. This developed into the Welsh crwth (krōōth), at L, which some think was an ancestor of the violin, though it was always plucked. While all these instruments were developing in Europe, they were playing in Asia a little pear-shaped affair called the rebab (rēbäb'). This was brought into Europe, bow as well, by the Arabs, and came to be known as the rebeck. To this type of instrument belong the Arabian fiddle at G, the Moorish rebeck at H, and the pear-shaped rebeck at I, which was played all over Europe during the Middle Ages. The Wends, a Slavic people of Central Europe, used to play a fiddle like that at J. And then came the viols (K). These were of various sizes; but all had flat backs, and most of them had six strings. Their place was taken by the violin (M), although our modern bass viol still survives as a form of one of those early viols. The tenor viol was the first to take on the violin shape, and was called a viola (vē-ō'lä). The viola da gamba—the "viol for the leg"—a bass viol of medium range, underwent the same change and became our modern violoncello. Because the tone of the viols was weak, the main strings were sometimes reinforced by another set of strings beneath them, which vibrated in sympathy. Such was the viola d'amore (d-ämôr'ā), or "viol of love," shown at N.

always must do, if the world is to progress. And their new invention was nothing less than opera—that mighty combination of voices and instruments which has given us so much of our best music.

At first people shook their heads. This new form, which had so many different things going at once—choruses and solos and interludes and a kind of sing song, tuneless talk called "recitative" (rĕs'ĭ-tả-tēv')—was just a horrible hotchpotch to a good many of the people who had heard nothing but the old unaccompanied part songs. There were all kinds of new chords and new arrangements of the old ones. And there were even intentional discords, or "dissonances" (dĭs'ŏ-nǎns)—which seemed ridiculous and almost wicked. People laughed or hissed, just as they do at the new styles of music in our days. But a genius named Claudio Monteverde (mŏn'tả-vâr'dā), an Italian, came forward and showed what could be done.

At the top is a curious Arabian stringed instrument played with a bow. Just below is a spinet made in Italy in the sixteenth century. And in the lower right-hand corner is a rather horrifying affair from Central Africa. It resembles a lyre in appearance, and is made from a human skull.

First Opera Ever Produced

Other men had laid the foundation. Some musicians in Florence had been trying to imitate the Greeks, who had always had a chorus as part of their tragedies and comedies. The first attempt of these Italians, and the very first opera ever produced, was Jacopo Peri's (pā'rē) "Dafne" (däf'nĕ), performed in the year 1597, at the Corsi (kôr'sē) Palace in Florence. It was a great success. So Monteverde (1567–1643), who had written his first opera—"Arianna"—in 1607, took the old Greek story of Orpheus and made a music drama of it. In it there was no spoken word; everything was sung. He called it "Orfeo," and produced it in

1608 to entertain the members of the court of the duke of Mantua. It was the duke who paid for the entertainment; that was always the way in those days.

The orchestra that played on that great occasion would have sounded very thin and almost laughable to us. To begin with there were several little portable organs, called "positives" and "regals." They had only a few keys and probably not much volume. There were a number of harpsichords and lutes—the lutes, of different sizes, were a good deal like our guitars. And then there were several harps and viols, "two little violins of the French kind," two wooden wind instruments called "cornetti," four trombones, several trumpets, and one flute. And those little piping, wheezing, scraping contrivances made up the orchestra from which all our amazing modern orchestras have descended. But they must have seemed quite overwhelming to that noble audience at the court of the duke of Mantua.

Other musicians were not slow to follow Monteverde's lead. Another Italian named Carissimi (1604?–1674) set Bible stories to music. His compositions were just like an opera except that there was no action—the whole story had to be told by the singers. We call them "oratorios" (ŏr'ả-tōr'ĭ-ō).

What is an Aria?

Carissimi (kä-rēs'sǐ-mē') had a pupil named Alessandro Scarlatti (ä'lĕs-sän'drō skär-lät'tē), who filled his operas with lovely little airs for a single voice, and so perfected what we call the aria da capo (ä'rǐ-ả dä kä'pō), or, as we now call it for short, the aria. People always love to hear those charming operatic songs, partly because the melody is pleasing and partly because they are usually so easy to remember. For an aria such as the Italians wrote mostly follows the same

This is the great Stradivari himself at work in the shop from which he turned out the most perfect violins the world has ever seen. Any one of them is now worth a small fortune to its fortunate possessor.

general pattern—first a tune in one key, then another tune leading into another key, and then a repetition of the first tune. This is known as the "binary" (bī'nȧ-rĭ) form. Though it is much too short to be an aria, "Swanee River" is a good example of the scheme. Scarlatti, with his little arias, did a great deal to help people to write music in a single key. Those old "modes" were at last left far behind, and harmony had arrived to take their place.

When Opera Left the Courts

It was during Scarlatti's day (1659–1725) that opera escaped from the courts of dukes and bishops and came to be a thing that everyone could go to hear. For in 1641 the first opera house had been opened in Venice.

And it was a friend of Scarlatti's—a man named Corelli (kŏ-rĕl'lē)—who became the first great violinist in history. Corelli (1653–1713) was the first man who really understood how to write music for the violin. And his compositions came just at the right moment, for the Italians had already begun to make those famous violins that

after two centuries and a half are still the most perfect in the world.

The Master Violin Maker

It was in the little town of Cremona (krĕ-mō'nȧ) that the most famous violins were made. Whole families of geniuses— fathers, sons, grandsons, great-nephews— worked and experimented, each maker lovingly exerting himself to fashion that magical combination of wood and catgut which is perhaps the most perfect musical instrument that we have.

Out of the clumsy viols and twanging rebecks (rē'bĕk) the early violins grew. It was the Hindus who first had the idea of playing an instrument with a bow (1500 B.C.). The Arabs brought the invention into Europe in the seventh century A.D. Then almost a thousand years had to pass before various families in Italy, like the Amatis (ä-mä'tē) and the Guarneris (gwär-nā'rē), produced the violin. But it was Antonio Stradivari (strä'dĭ-vä'rē) who was the greatest genius of them all. During his long life (1644–1737) he signed his name to instruments of such amazing beauty of tone and workmanship that the worth of genuine "Strads" is fabulous to-day.

A Master Craftsman

Stradivari was trained in his art by one of the Amati family, but after a time he learned to shape his violins after a pattern of his own, and those are the famous "Long Strads" about which we hear. Later he went back to the smaller size. It is pleasant to know that most of the great man's finest masterpieces were made when he was growing old. Each famous instrument he fashioned has a name; and it was when he had reached the age of seventy-one that he made the "Alard," the finest of them all.

We have tried hard to find out what it is that gives those old violins their amazingly beautiful tone, and have done our very best to copy them. We have reproduced to a hair's breadth every one of the fifty-seven little pieces that go to

This quaint seventeenth-century "book organ" belongs to a class of instrument much favoured in the Middle Ages. They were called "portative organs," and were small enough to be carried about by the performer. They were not all so curiously and beautifully made as this one, but they were all very small, with only a few keys; and they were pumped by a bellows which required one hand to operate it. In this portative, the bellows protrudes at the left-hand side; the performer played the keys with the right hand only. The picture at the right shows a beautiful but rather quaint old Japanese drum.

make up the permanent part of the instrument. We have chosen the wood with the greatest care, cutting the "belly" from pine and the "back" from sycamore or maple, just as the Italians did of old. We have fitted the whole together carefully and finished it in the best possible way. And yet how different it sounds! Many careful students of the matter think that the whole secret lies in the varnish, which we do not seem able to make just as the Italians did.

It was fitting that violins should have been improved in the country where opera was born, for what would an opera be without its orchestra, and what would an orchestra be without the violins? From the openings, or "overtures," that Scarlatti wrote for his operas, it was no great step to our great modern symphonies (sĭm'fŏ-nĭ). He composed short introductions, called "sinfonias," in three or more sections, grave and gay, which the orchestra played before an opera began. Other writers followed this practice, and the "symphonies" finally came to be played alone without an opera following. From that it was an easy step to composing long works for the orchestra, still keeping the three or four separate sections, or "movements."

It is not hard to see that so great an invention as opera was not likely to stay at home in Italy for very long. Its first journey was to France. Now, the French have a very lively genius that is all their own, and if there is anything that a Frenchman does not like it is a thing that is tiresome or unintelligent. He hates to be bored. So when opera fell into French hands it was shaped in quite a new way.

In Italy it had soon settled down into the most deadly monotony. Having invented a new kind of music drama, the Italians promptly forgot that it ought to be dramatic. They were carried away by the music instead. So all they did was to string together a number of empty arias that gave popular singers a chance to show off. Between those meaningless solos, full of runs and trills and quirks and quavers, were long passages of singsong prose explanation, or "recitative." But very little ever happened. It was enough to make a quick-minded Frenchman die of boredom.

The French have always had a strong feeling for the dramatic. They were not long in seeing how great an invention opera was, with its orchestra, its solos, its accompanied choruses and its thrilling situations. So they adopted it and emphasized the action. For a long time they had had little dramatic plays with songs and dancing, so they introduced dances, or "ballets" (băl'ā), into their operas. They still used plenty of arias, but at least they varied them with dancing, and made them shorter than those to which the Italians were accustomed.

They also learned the new art of writing harmonies from their neighbours across the Alps, especially from a rascally fellow named Lulli (lü-lē'), one of the few great musicians who was also a scoundrel. The poor lad had gone to France in his youth and had had rather a bad time. He had been obliged to pick up most of his musical education for himself; but he obtained an appointment as musician to King Louis XIV, and with that start forged ahead rapidly.

Writing Operas for a Court

Lulli (1633–1687) quickly discovered the French taste, and his music pleased the court so much that he was able to drive out all his rivals and forbid the production of any operas except his own. As a result, when he died there were very few good composers in France until the time of Jean Philippe Rameau (1683–1764), a writer of really fine operas, and François Couperin (frôN'swä' kōō'pē-răN'; 1688–1733), who wrote many fascinating series of dance tunes for people to play. We call such a set of separate pieces a "suite" (swēt).

To England, too, opera and the new forms of music found their way. In this country was an extremely gifted young man named Henry Purcell (1659–1695), the greatest composer of his day. He wrote music of every kind, especially a great deal of magnificent church music, for he was organist at Westminster Abbey. And it was he who composed the first great English opera, called "Dido and Aeneas." It is amusing to us to-day to know that it was written for performance by the pupils of a "boarding school of gentlewomen" near London.

A Land Where Music Throve

In Germany the exciting new music was of course getting a hearing. There a man named Heinrich Schütz (1585–1672), a famous writer of madrigals, was composing beautiful music and helping to open the way for one of the greatest composers of all time, Johann Sebastian Bach (bäK). For, by the end of the seventeenth century, it was clear that the Germans were going to be a music-loving race. Everywhere they were singing and playing. All the towns had skilled musicians as organists, and good music was growing to be necessary to everybody. It is in such soil that musical genius can be expected to bloom and flourish.

(CONTINUED ON PAGE 269)

Photo by Rischgitz

FUN WITH TRICKS

THE CANE AND THE RING

Tie a curtain ring on a string and hang it in a doorway. Present one of your friends with a cane and tell him to run it through the ring, as the boy in the picture is trying to do. It is not as easy as it looks.

LOOKING-GLASS DIFFICULTIES

Try writing or drawing pictures as the boy below is doing, keeping your eye on a mirror which reflects your hand and paper. It is a great temptation to look at the paper instead of the mirror, because everything is turned topsy-turvy, as you can see in picture No. 4.

TRY IT

Ask someone to lay a coin in the palm of his hand and brush it off with a hairbrush.

MAGIC INK

Write on white paper with a clean steel pen dipped in lemon-juice. When the lemon-juice dries, the writing will be invisible, but will reappear if you press it with a hot iron.

CAN YOU BREAK A MATCH?

It sounds simple, but if you hold the match over the first joint of the second finger and under the first joint of the first and third fingers, as you see in picture No. 3, you will find it hard to do.

SEE IT FLOAT

Put a piece of tissue paper on top of a glass of water. Place a needle on top of the paper, as in picture No. 2, without letting the needle get wet. The paper will sink but the needle will stay on top.

THE FLOATING SUGAR LUMP

Secretly place a lump of sugar in a half-filled cup of coffee. Then say that you are going to make a lump of sugar float. All you have to do is to place a second lump as shown in Fig. 5.

THE MAGNETIC HAND

Tell your audience that you have a strange power, which you do not quite understand, but which makes your hand magnetic whenever you squeeze your wrist. Then prove it to them by holding a cane as the boy in the left-hand corner is doing. Picture No. 6 will show you how it is done.

PUSHING THE TUMBLER

The boy at the left said that he could push a glass of water through a napkin ring or a tiny hole in a piece of cardboard. He is doing it too, although not quite as you expected.

The UNRULY SEEDS of a USEFUL PLANT

It was the Simple Device of a Visitor to an American Plantation that Enabled the Cultivation of Cotton to Become a Prosperous Industry

IN THE days when most of the people in Europe were still barbarians who clothed themselves in the skins of animals and in certain coarse woollen stuffs, a few wanderers from the valley of the Nile might possibly bring some fine fabrics to show them, for the Egyptians had long been skilled in the arts of spinning and weaving.

Many years later, when Alexander the Great's soldiers and travellers crossing the mountains and the deserts found their way into India, they would bring back, among other things, lengths of cloth of delicate weaving and gorgeous hue. In Europe these fine fabrics were, for centuries, almost as rare and costly as the gems and spices that came with them out of the mysterious East.

What was even more wonderful, the rare travellers in the earliest days would speak of having seen little trees bearing the "wool" that had been woven into these fabrics. In other words, they had come across the cotton plant, a discovery which brought us one of our most important industries.

Nobody knows how long the people in India had been growing cotton and making cloth out of it. Nor do we know how or when the Egyptians first discovered it. In the Bible we are told that Aaron, the high priest, wore purple and scarlet raiment, and a girdle of "fine linen" and of "cunning work."

All through the realms of King Cotton at harvest time the workers come in from the fields laden with great baskets piled high with fluffy whiteness. Here they are "weighing in," for they are paid by the pound. When it has been weighed the cotton will go straight to the cotton-gin to be combed free of its little brown seeds.

The beautiful Helen of Troy arrayed herself in garments of fine texture, embroidered by the maids of Sidon and coloured with the purple of Tyre. These might have been simply cotton fabrics, for in those days cotton was a stuff for rich and noble persons only. Until very recently, in fact, it was far too costly for any but the rich. Only for the past hundred years or so has it been cheap enough to be within the reach of the middle and lower classes of the world. And one of the main reasons why this is so is that a little over a century ago an American schoolmaster invented the cotton-gin.

But it was not the cotton-gin alone that made cotton cheap. Elsewhere we have explained how the "spinning-jenny" and the "spinning-mule" and the power-loom had come to spin out the threads and weave them into cloth much faster and more cheaply than human hands could ever do it. But cotton could never be cheap unless there was plenty of it, no matter how fast it could be spun and woven. The cotton-gin made it worth while as a big industry.

In the circle is a portrait of Eli Whitney, the inventor of the cotton-gin, and below is a picture of the first cotton-gin itself. It will interest amateur inventors to know that this famous machine's teeth were made out of bird-cage wire, and its rows of little brushes out of hearth brush.

called the "lint." And lint is what we know as cotton. Now, certain kinds of cotton have a long lint that is only loosely attached to the seeds. This cotton, probably first grown in India, was finally introduced into the southern states of America, but there it thrives only in certain places—in a few spots along the Atlantic coast and especially on certain islands near the shore. It is called "sea island" or "long-staple" cotton. But the common kind that grows all through the south of the United States and in many other countries is called "short-staple" or "up-land" cotton, because it was first grown in the rugged regions some distance from the coast. The lint from this is shorter, and it clings much more tightly to the seeds. Now, the cotton-gin is simply a machine for extracting the seeds from the short-staple cotton.

Almost from the very start, the United States began to grow a certain amount of cotton in her southern colonies. The seeds were imported from the West Indies, from Italy and Egypt, and the gin used for taking the seeds out of the lint was patterned after that which had been used in India for countless centuries. This gin looks a little like a modern clothes-wringer, and is called the "churka." It has two wooden rollers, each about a foot and a half long, placed in a wooden frame and turned by a crank. The rollers do not quite touch: there is a space between them just wide enough to allow a very heavy blotting-paper to pass through. When a lock of cotton is passed between

Queer Cousins of the Cotton Plant

The cotton plant, which is so beautiful that it was once grown in flower gardens, is a cousin of the hollyhock and milkweed—whose coarse and crinkly pods are full of delicate down. The cotton plant also bears a pod, called a "boll," and this is full of the downy fibre that is known as "seed cotton." When the petals of the cotton blossom fall, the boll grows fat with its swelling down, and finally bursts into four or five divisions. Each division holds a "lock" of cotton.

Every lock of cotton contains several little hard, brown seeds. The thick fuzz, green-grey or white, that clings to the seeds is these rollers, the lint may be pulled through, but the seeds will remain behind. Thus the cotton can be ginned, but only very, very slowly.

From the outset this kind of gin caused a great deal of trouble to the American planters. It worked fairly well with long-staple cotton, such as grows in India, but it was almost useless for ginning the short-fibre kind, the only kind that grows well in the great cotton region of the United States. The fibres were too short to be easily pulled through between the rollers, and the lint clung far too tightly to the seeds for it to come off readily. So the American planters experienced considerable difficulty in getting the seeds out of their cotton before they were able to market it.

They continued to grow a certain amount, however, because they had negro slaves to take out the seeds by hand—at night, on rainy days, and at all other times when they were not otherwise employed. But what a slow and tedious operation it was! In the evenings, after the day's work in the fields was done, the negroes would take home baskets of seed cotton to be cleaned by hand until bedtime. Sitting about in groups, singing, laughing, talking, they would pick out the shiny brown seeds one by one. And how little lint one of them could clean in an evening! Not much more than a shoeful, it was said. That would be less than a pound of lint in a day, or less than a bale of cotton for

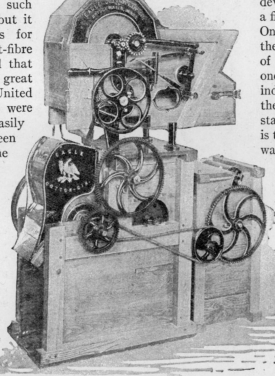

Except that it does not have to be turned by hand, this modern cotton-gin works very much as Whitney's first model did. The cotton goes into the feeder at the top, drops its seeds out through the chute at the left, and passes to the condenser at the lower right, where it is pressed into a flat band as it leaves the gin.

one person in a whole year. This was the state of affairs until the end of the seventeenth century. Then, by a mere chance, the cotton-gin, very much as we know it to-day, was invented by Eli Whitney, a native of Massachusetts. Until the year in which he invented his device he had never seen a field of growing cotton. Once he had produced it, the planting and weaving of cotton soon became one of the world's great industries, the future of the crop in the southern states of America, which is the largest in the world, was assured, and a new era began for the cotton trade.

Eli Whitney was born on December 8, 1765, and he grew up to be a skilful craftsman and a mechanical genius. On his father's farm he mended the chairs and cartwheels for the neighbours, and did all kinds of similar jobs.

After leaving Yale College, he accepted an invitation from Mrs. Nathaniel Greene, the widow of a Revolutionary general, to visit her plantation at Savannah. One day some planters from the uplands were lamenting that they could grow and clean so very little cotton. Whitney asked the reason. When he learned how difficult it was to clean short-staple cotton he said he thought he could make a machine to do the work. So he set about the task. He possessed very few tools, and he had to devise and make many that he needed. Moreover, he lacked certain materials, and for want of proper ones he had to use whatever was at hand. He even cut up a cage in which Mrs. Greene's daughter was keeping a pet bird, because he needed the wire. At last, with his home-made tools and

his makeshift materials, he carried out his plan.

The first cotton-gin was a box-like contrivance about two feet square. At the top was a hopper, with sides curved to fit over a cylinder beneath and notched into many narrow slits. The wooden cylinder, turned by a crank, was set with rows of teeth made by driving short curved wires into it, and it was so placed that one row of teeth passed through each slit in the sides of the hopper. When the gin was finished, Whitney threw a handful of seed cotton into the hopper and turned the crank. The wires tugged at the lint, carried it through the slits and dropped it into a basket below, and left the seeds behind in the hopper. This simple machine did the work of ginning rapidly and well, and from this day hence cotton was obtainable by rich and poor alike.

On March 14, 1794, Whitney patented his invention, and soon afterwards he joined with Phineas Miller in a partnership for making the machines at New Haven, Connecticut. Then his troubles began. In 1796 a native of Georgia named Hogden Holmes began to make a gin in which thin metal disks, notched like a saw, took the place of the rows of wire teeth on the cylinder of Whitney's gin. Whitney claimed that Holmes had stolen the principle of his invention, and took the matter to the highest courts of the land, but in the end, although he won his case, he lost all the profit that he might have gained from his labours. Several southern states paid him between them about £20,000 for his patent rights, but since cotton-gins were soon being produced in many parts, Whitney never made a great deal out of the machines after that. Yet he became a rich man in spite of everything. He

In these pictures we see King Cotton before and after his encounter with the cotton-gin. At the top he is riding in state to the ginnery. In the centre his hair is being skilfully combed clean of sticks and leaves and seeds. At the bottom he is waiting in snug bales ready to be shipped to the mills.

started to make fire-arms at New Haven, and was able to amass quite a small fortune before his death, which occurred on January 8, 1825.

The British Museum and the University of Pennsylvania, U.S.A., have lately been working together exploring the ancient cities of Sumeria—a land that is probably as old as Egypt, with an art that was developed earlier than Egyptian art. There the workers have toiled, in the midst of discomfort and hardship, to uncover the springs of the stream of civilization that has been sweeping steadily on down to our own day. The picture above shows natives at work digging in the sand which now covers many a populous Sumerian town.

The OLDEST PEOPLE in ASIA

How the Sumerians Lived on Mounds and Wrote Their Letters and Their Books on Flat Pieces of Clay

THOUGH you have often heard of the Egyptians and their pyramids, it will not be strange if you have never heard of the Sumerians (sū-mē'rĭ-ăn) until now. Yet they were an extremely interesting people, and they came at the very opening of history, like the Egyptians. The reason why they are not so well known is that their history has been literally dug up only in very recent years. They are the "newest" of the oldest peoples.

Their home was at one end of a very remarkable country which has no name, but which we may call the "Fertile Crescent." This ancient land lies in Western Asia, between the Mediterranean Sea on the west and the Persian Gulf on the south-east. To the north of the country there are mountains, and to the south there is the great sandy waste which we call the Arabian Desert. This desert might be likened to a huge ocean, with the fertile crescent-shaped country for its northern shore. In that fertile strip crops could be raised and people could live by farming the land. You will do well to look at the map carefully and fix the shape of that strange country in your mind, because you are going to hear a great deal about the many different peoples who once lived there.

Through the northern and eastern part of

199

the fertile crescent run two great rivers, the Tigris (tī'grĭs) and the Euphrates (ū-frā'tēz). The country between them, Iraq, was formerly called Mesopotamia (mĕs'ŏ-pŏ-tā'mĭ-å), which means "between the rivers." These rivers, overflow each year, and leave a gift of black mud when the waters go down. But farming along them cannot be really successful unless people work together to store up the flood waters for the dry season and then distribute the stored-up water by means of canals. Now when men have to work together, they are likely to think

they called Sumer (sū'mẽr), at the eastern end of the Fertile Crescent, along the lower part of the Tigris and the Euphrates. The Sumerians had not always lived there, we believe, but had come in from the hill country to the north-east. We do not know to what race they belonged. They were not Semitic (sĕ-mĭt'ĭk), like the Hebrews and Assyrians, and they were not Indo-European, like the Greeks and Persians.

Houses Built on a Mound

The Sumerians lived in houses built on great round mounds from twenty to fifty feet high and having an area as great, perhaps, as a London square. And what do you think these mounds were made of? Simply of the rubbish cast off by all the people who had lived there before.

Sumerian houses were built of clay baked in the sun. Every now and then the houses

On this map you will see one of the two ancient cradles of the civilization that you and I have inherited to-day. One of them was in Egypt, along the shores of the Nile. The other was here at the head of the Persian Gulf, where the land was watered and made fertile by two great rivers, the Tigris and the Euphrates. Here it was that the Sumerians dwelt six thousand and more years ago, and here the Flood of which we read in the Bible swept away men and flocks and left the land desolate for many a year to come. Here, too, all the little cities, Ur, Larsa, and the rest, struggled for supremacy over this eastern end of the Fertile Crescent—which, like a great bow, swept north-west from the land of Sumer, and then curved down again to end at the south-eastern corner of the Mediterranean. Since the days of the Sumerians the two great rivers have filled in the shallow waters at the head of the Persian Gulf, and now unite there to form a single stream.

together, and thinking together is one of the best ways by which they may become civilized. Perhaps that is why the Egyptians and the Sumerians were civilized so long before the rest of the world.

Four thousand years before our year one, the Sumerians were living in the country

would tumble down, and no one would bother to clear the ruins away. The people would just smooth the ground over it and build another house. And so the mounds grew. The height of the mounds and the things people now find in them show that Sumerian houses had been rising up and tumbling

Early Sumerians making pottery, which was usually buff-coloured and decorated with geometrical designs.

down for thousands of years before real Sumerian history begins.

For, as you know, history begins when people learn how to read and write. By 3000 B.C. the Sumerians could read and write very well. They had a queer and interesting way of writing, which we call Sumerian cuneiform (kū-nē′ĭ-fôrm).

As the Egyptians had done, so the Sumerians made pictures for whole words, as for the sun or the rain or an eagle. But soon they found such pictures awkward and they invented a series of several hundred signs, each of which stood for a whole syllable such as *kal* or *ur*. This syllable language was better than a picture language, although it was not so good as an alphabet.

The Sumerians did not exactly write their syllable signs. Instead, they stamped them with a writing tool into soft clay, which would harden and make a letter or even a book. There were libraries full of such clay books in some of the Sumerian mound villages, and the kings who owned the libraries had to put on their books warnings to people not to carry them off and forget to bring them back, just as we may do to-day!

At the right is a clay tablet from Ur. All those strange marks upon it are writing and were made by pressing the wet clay with a blunt instrument.

At the left is a brick from ancient Ur, the Sumerian city where Abraham was born. The Sumerians were the first people to learn how to make brick.

When Letters Were Written on Clay

A Sumerian letter was a flat piece of clay stamped with hundreds of these strange little wedge-shaped syllable signs. Often it was enclosed within a sealed clay envelope. The clay envelope would be broken off instead of being torn open like one of our paper envelopes. The seals that the Sumerian letter writers used were little cylinders, or rolls, of stone, each with a particular design or picture carved in it. When these were rolled over the soft clay the picture carved into them was stamped into the clay, and this picture signed and sealed a Sumerian's clay letters.

Life in Ancient Sumeria

Each of the mound towns or cities in Sumer was the centre of a farming district, in whose rich fields the farmers raised wheat and barley and other crops. In each town one man had charge of working and repairing the canals; and he was also the head of the town and the chief priest of the temple. Such a priest-king was called a patesi (pä-tä′sē).

The Sumerians, prosperous and civilized as they were, were not very peaceable. The towns fought among themselves, and they also fought the Semites (sĕm′ĭt), or desert folk. Those Semitic wanderers, who lived in the desert and herded sheep and goats for food, were always envious of the rich people in the Sumerian towns and desirous of obtaining some of the riches for themselves. They tried two ways of doing so—fighting and trade.

In fighting, the Sumerians could usually beat the Semites, because the Sumerians had learned how to make swords and other weapons out of metal. Then, too, as one of their pictures show, they had drilled themselves to fight in companies, while the Semites at first fought unorganized.

Trading by Peaceful Methods

When the Semites could not get the best of the Sumerians by fighting, they tried to obtain the treasures peacefully by trade. But as money had not been invented in 3000 B.C., trade was really the bartering or exchanging of goods. The Semites would bring to the Sumerian towns, cattle, ivory and

People still live in the ancient land of Sumeria, which to-day is called Iraq (ē'räk'). The camel boys at A were photographed near Kish.

Iraq is an independent Arab State. It was formerly under British mandate. At C is one of its people.

The little nurse-maids of Iraq carry their babies in the manner shown at D.

At E is a man of modern Kish, near which a Sumerian palace of 3500 B.C. was lately unearthed. To-day the chief city of Iraq is Bagdad, its capital. The country has about 3,000,000 inhabitants, mostly Mohammedans, and is 177,000 square miles in area.

B. A water carrier of Iraq, a country where water is scarce and crops can be grown only under irrigation.

F. This Arab workman of Iraq knows how to protect himself from the heat in a land where the thermometer reaches 120° F.

various kinds of valuable wood and stone, spices, jewels, and probably gold and silver. In exchange they would take grain, fruit, vegetables, clothes made of wool or linen, and especially knives and swords and tools made of metal.

You may think it was foolish for the Sumerians to let the Semites have good swords, and perhaps it was; but sooner or later the Semites were certain to make swords for themselves. For they kept trying to make their own things out of metal until at last they finally learned the way. They took up farming along the river to the north of the Sumerians.

But before the Semites settled down, Sumeria probably included all the land between the Tigris and the Euphrates. The main Sumerian cities of which we have any knowledge were Ur, Uruk, Lagash, Kish and Umma. These cities for the most part did not congregate under one king, but remained separate, sometimes quarrelling and fighting, sometimes at peace.

Now and then during the two or three thousand years of Sumer's history, one city would grow very powerful, and its king would try to assert his rule over all the other Sumerian cities as well. The first king of whom we read was called Mesilim, and at the time of his rule (about 3200 B.C.) Kish was the chief city of Sumer. Ur-Nina was also a famous king, although students of history do not think his city, Lagash (lā'gäsh), was ever quite so powerful as some of the other cities.

One of the most famous Sumerian kings

The land of modern Iraq is as fertile as it was in the great days of Sumer. About a third of the world's date palms grow there, as well as good crops of rice, barley, and wheat. This native woman and child are from Northern Iraq; she is busy harvesting—on land that saw some of man's first experiments in agriculture. Iraq is also rich in oil.

bore the name Lugal-Zagizzi. He was king of Umma and Uruk, and about 2750 B.C. he became head of all Sumer, and even sent armies out to conquer other countries from sea to sea—from the Persian Gulf to the Mediterranean. Lugal-Zagizzi was a great conqueror.

But fifty years later Sumeria had gone down before the Semites. A Semitic king named Sargon was ruling in Akkad (ăk'ăd), which was a city the Semites had built farther up the river. Sargon was a great warrior. He conquered not only all Sumeria but also much of the country to the north and west as well— a land we nowadays refer to as Babylonia (băb'ĭ-lō'nĭ-ȧ). It takes its name from a Semitic town which was near Akkad and later became the capital of the country.

When the Semitic Akkadians became lords of the Sumerians, they learned a good deal more about civilization. They took over Sumerian cuneiform writing to express their Akkadian language. Often an Akkadian prince would have a Sumerian secretary to do his writing for him. The Semitic Akkadians now made great progress in working in metals, and their merchants took their goods across to the Mediterranean coast, where they met the dark-faced traders of Egypt, whose boats had come up from the Nile.

For over two hundred years the Akkadians ruled the Sumerians, but soon after 2500 B.C. the Sumerians secured control of the country once more. After this the land was called "Sumer and Akkad." Various cities—Ur, Larsa, Isin—took the leadership one after another, but generally the country was at peace.

This Arab workman is carefully digging into the ruins of the ancient city of Ur, in modern Iraq. He has unearthed a vertical drain and two burial vases, such as were used to hold articles that were buried with the dead. All this work of excavation must be done with the greatest care and under the most expert supervision.

During this time many books were written in cuneiform, both Sumerian and Akkadian; but gradually the Sumerian language was spoken less and less in this country of Sumer and Akkad, until it became a "dead" language, as is Latin to-day. The Semitic civilization was swallowing up the Sumerian.

Near the town of Akkad, in the Semitic country north of Sumer, was the little town called Babylon (băb'ĭ-lŏn), a place of no special importance. This town was seized by a tribe of Semites called the Amorites (ăm'ō-rīt), who came from the part of the Fertile Crescent lying west of Akkad.

Hammurabi the Conqueror

The Amorites made Babylon an important city. They grew more and more powerful, and finally (about 2100 B.C.) a great king named Hammurabi (häm'oo-rä'bē) began to rule in Babylon. Like Sargon, Hammurabi was a conqueror. He made himself ruler of all Sumer and Akkad, and even conquered several neighbouring countries.

After this we hear no more about the Sumerians. For from now on all the land of Sumer and Akkad is called Babylonia, after its capital city of Babylon, and the people who lived in the land are called Babylonians. You will read their story a little later.

When you weigh an article by means of pounds you are using the old measure of the Sumerians, called a "mina." When you divide an hour into sixty minutes you are using the Sumerian way of counting, which was reckoned by sixties. Whenever you see an arch over a door or a window, you are looking at an invention of the Sumerians. So even now the Sumerians live on in the civilization of the world, and you and I still owe something to them.

When you go to a great museum you may see a quaint little figure, or perhaps a clay tablet, which has lasted the thousands of years since the Sumerians were famous in the valley of the Tigris and the Euphrates. As you look at these ancient objects that have strayed so far down the ages into a century so different from their own, you may know that you are travelling back to the very dawn of civilization. And then you will remember that civilization began when people found out how to think and work together in harmony. It is for all of us to remember that civilization will continue only in the same way.

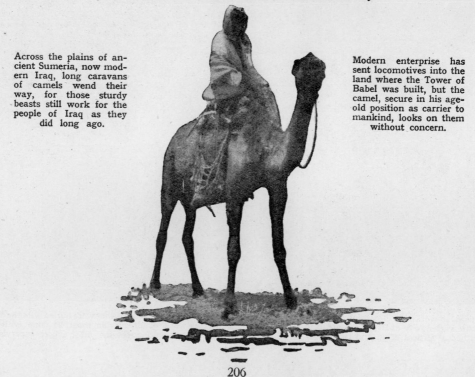

Across the plains of ancient Sumeria, now modern Iraq, long caravans of camels wend their way, for those sturdy beasts still work for the people of Iraq as they did long ago.

Modern enterprise has sent locomotives into the land where the Tower of Babel was built, but the camel, secure in his age-old position as carrier to mankind, looks on them without concern.

Good Izaak Walton was willing to share his knowledge and skill with all who loved the art of angling, so in his book he set it all down. Here he is showing a pupil how to make a fly that should lure the wariest trout.

The FATHER of ANGLING

Izaak Walton's Book on the Rod and Line is So Dear to Fishermen That It Has Been Reprinted About a Hundred Times

(CONTINUED FROM PAGE 176)

WHAT boy does not know the joys of fishing—or long to know them? If he can have a long jointed pole and a cool mountain stream in which to waggle his toes, well and good; if all he can get is a bent pin on a string and a minnow-haunted mud puddle, that will do. The attraction is the water and the sunny air, and the slippery fish themselves.

Here is a boy who, grown to be a man and getting old, still loved the noble sport of fishing—loved it so well that he wrote the most famous book ever written about it. The book is quaintly named "The Compleat Angler"—"complete" was spelt like that three hundred years ago. The man's name was Izaak Walton. He and his book became so famous that even to-day you may hear a man who dearly loves to go fishing referred to as "a regular Izaak Walton" or "one of old Izaak's staunch followers."

This beloved angler was born at Stafford in 1593, while Elizabeth still sat on the throne. We really know very little about the earlier years of his life. It is not even quite certain who his parents were, though they were probably farmer folk of Staffordshire. He seems to have gone to school for a while at Stafford, and then to have gone up to London and apprenticed himself to an iron-monger. Later he had a shop of his own in Fleet Street.

The most interesting thing about the quiet life of Walton—apart from his fishing—is his friends. He appears to have known the poet Drayton and Ben Jonson, poet and dramatist and friend of Shakespeare. But his dearest friends were among the famous clergymen of the day. Indeed, much of his later life was spent in the homes of these men of the Church, who seem always to have loved him for his gentle, charming ways. Of them all, much the most famous was John Donne, who, besides being the dean of St. Paul's Cathedral and a notable preacher, was a poet whose work is still read by many people and greatly admired.

Next to his book on angling, the finest of Walton's writings are a few short "Lives" of poets and clergymen, most of them his friends — of John Donne himself, for example, and of another well-known parson-poet, George Herbert. The stories of these men's lives he tells with rare simplicity and charm.

Like most of his friends Walton was a Royalist, and when King Charles I was beheaded by the Puritans, Walton thought it best to slip out of London and go where he might perhaps be forgotten by the authorities. But it was not very long before the dead king's son ascended the throne as Charles II, and then the Royalists, with Walton among them, thronged again into London. Walton went to live with one of his clergyman friends. But that does not mean that he

Photo by National Portrait Gallery

Though much of Izaak Walton's lore has long been discarded, the gentle old man, whose portrait is shown here, still gives the world as much pleasure as he did when Ben Jonson listened to his tales. For men who have exchanged quiet streams for the rush of city traffic still love to read his immortal work.

gave up his favourite sport. From then onwards he spent most of his time in writing and visiting, in travelling—and fishing.

"The Compleat Angler" was first published when Walton was sixty, in 1653. It is said that the book has appeared in a new edition at least once every three years since. And so this has continued for almost three hundred years.

Most of the scientific information about fishing in Walton's book was out of date long ago. People do not read it now as a treatise, but rather as the interesting story of a kindly man who loved the age-old sport, the woods and waters and the world out of doors; who had pleasant, wise thoughts, and recorded them in easy and exquisite prose.

Izaak Walton died at the home of his son-in-law at Winchester in 1683, and was buried in the cathedral of that quaint old English city. He left part of his property to the poor of his native town, and many of the books that he possessed may still be seen in the library of the cathedral where he lies buried.

GLORIOUS JOHN MILTON

In His Own Day a Leader in a National Crisis, He Is Known in Our Day as England's Greatest Poet After Shakespeare

THERE was never any doubt in John Milton's mind that he was destined for great things. As he himself hints in "Lycidas," one of his finest poems, Fame was always spurring him on "to scorn delights and live laborious days." If he had turned out to be a little man, the people of his own day would just have laughed at his confident ambition—and we might never have heard of him. But he did not turn

out to be a little man. He became one of the greatest English poets of all time, and is one of the really great men in history.

When he was born, in 1608, Shakespeare was still alive, and the Elizabethan era was only just over. He lived to see and take part in the religious uprising of the Puritans; to help execute a king for treason; to be a leader in a revolutionary government; to go into hiding when the revolutionary government fell, and to live in fear of losing his head. It was a time of bold acts and bold thinking, and Milton's own work is its grandest and sincerest monument.

John Milton, Schoolboy, Tries His Hand at Writing Verse

Milton was a man of great learning. His father, who was a London scrivener, or notary, as well as a gifted organist, put him under a tutor when he was ten. Two years later he was studying earnestly at St. Paul's School. He had even begun to try his hand at verse, writing poetic versions of two of his favourite psalms. At sixteen he went to Cambridge, and remained there, apart from a short time in 1626, for seven years.

He was a handsome and talented youth, and a great student. He was a little stiff and aloof, with much stricter ideas of morals than most of the students, and no doubt they regarded him as a prig. They certainly nicknamed him "the lady," though that may have been because he was slender and his features were delicate. They need not have despised him, however, as he knew. None of

them could have written his Latin elegies, or the sonnet "On Having Arrived at the Age of Twenty-three," or the religious ode "On the Morning of Christ's Nativity."

But to Milton seven years at Cambridge did not seem nearly enough time for study. He must be thoroughly prepared for the great work he had to do. So he studied for six years more at his father's house at Horton, some twenty miles from London, reading Shakespeare and Spenser and the ancient classics and mastering Greek and Italian.

Beautiful Poems that are Rich in Music and Adorned with Legends

Sometimes he would write an exquisite poem, stately and delicately polished, full of grave music and adorned with pleasant names and legends out of his prodigious reading. There are the charming companion poems, "L'Allegro" (läl-lä'grō) and "Il Penseroso" (ēl pĕn'să-rō'sō)—"the gay man" and "the pensive man." There is the masque, "Comus," which was written especially to be acted at a great festival at Ludlow Castle in 1634. It must have been

THE MEETING OF MARVELL AND MILTON AT CHALFONT ST. GILES

Among John Milton's friends was Andrew Marvell, a Puritan poet who was at one time assistant to Milton in Cromwell's government. Later Marvell, who had been elected to Parliament, was able to intercede for Milton when the Puritans were forced from power. The picture above shows a meeting between the two men.

a marvellous thing to see this lovely masque, with music and colour and dancing to add to its glorious poetry, when it was acted in that old baronial castle set among the green hills on the edge of Wales. Yet beautiful as it is, "Comus" is less read nowadays than the shorter "Lycidas," one of the most famous dirges ever sung by any poet. All of these, with the other short poems Milton wrote, are often referred to as his "minor poems," not because they are unimportant, but just because they are briefer than the great epics he wrote later.

In 1638 Milton broke away from Horton at last, and went on a tour of the Continent. There he found himself already famous among men of letters. He saw much and thought much, and met celebrated people—Grotius (grō′shĭ-ŭs), the Hollander who founded the science of international law, and Galileo (găl′ĭ-lē′ō), one of the most famous of all astronomers. He wrote beautiful poetry on his trip, but it was in Latin and Italian. When he had been away about fifteen months, bad news from England called him home.

John Milton, who is regarded as our greatest poet since Shakespeare.

Helping the Puritan Cause

The news was not of any trouble in his family, but of the political and religious quarrels which were soon to lead to civil war. Milton was heart and soul on the side of the Puritans and Parliament, and against the king and his followers. He saw from the first that he could best help his cause by staying at home and writing. But the writing would have to be prose. For a while there would be no more masques and lyrics, no more plans for a mighty epic that should live after him. So we come to the close of what the scholars call Milton's "first period," the time of the Minor Poems, and to the beginning of his "second period," when he was writing about public affairs in prose.

Meanwhile he was keeping a small school for the children of well-to-do friends. So when he wrote about "Education" he under-stood his subject. About this time, also, he married. Not long afterwards, however, Milton's young wife left him for two years or so, though she finally returned. Milton was a great man, but he must have made a rather trying kind of husband. He was reserved and stern and proud, and, furthermore, he had a very poor opinion of women. He could hardly have made a wife happy. Yet he was married three times, and had several children.

In 1642 the quarrel between the king and the Puritan parliament broke into civil war. Though Milton did not fight in the army, he was very active on the Puritan side. He kept on pouring out pamphlets. The most famous of them all is "Areopagitica" (ăr′ĕ-ŏp′à-jĭt′ĭ-kà), which is not nearly so hard to read as its name sounds; it is an eloquent plea that people should be allowed to say and write what they believe to be true. When the victorious Puritans beheaded the king in 1649, Milton wrote another pamphlet on "The Tenure of Kings and Magistrates," to show that the Puritans were acting within their rights.

Soon after the king's death, Milton was asked to become Latin secretary under the Puritan leader, Cromwell. It was rather like the office of secretary of state. He worked very hard at this important task, writing all sorts of treatises and state papers, all in Latin. He was having trouble with his eyes, but, believing that he laboured in the great cause of liberty, he refused to cease working, and in 1652 he became totally blind.

Milton On His Blindness

Among the majestic sonnets which are almost the only poems he wrote during this period of busy prose is one, perhaps most famous of them all, on his blindness. It begins:

When I consider how my light is spent
  Ere half my days in this dark world and
    wide,

and it goes on to express the hope that his

210

Totally blind and defeated in hope, John Milton pressed his three unwilling daughters, rebellious against their father's stern rule, into the labour of taking down the mighty lines of his greatest poem, "Paradise Lost."

affliction may not mean that he can no longer be of any service to his God. He concludes that

They also serve who only stand and wait

Yet even in his blindness Milton did not "stand and wait," but continued with his work. He remained Latin secretary until the Puritan government fell and a king came to the throne again—the son of Charles I, whom Milton had helped to bring to the block. It would not have been at all strange if Milton had himself been beheaded by Charles II. He was at one time actually under arrest. But in the end he was left to himself, and lived out the rest of his life in quiet retirement, poor and blind and in indifferent health, mourning over the defeat of the cause he loved and had championed, but making it immortal in his verse.

Dictating His Great Work

For now the time had come at last for him to remember his old dream of writing some tremendous work which should bring him lasting fame. He could no longer write it himself, but he could dictate it to others— to his daughters, when they did not rebel against the long words he had never taught them to understand; to friends and disciples,

to anyone. One imagines him, awe-inspiring in his lonely genius, rolling out the mighty lines till the scratching pen of the writer was wearied. This is the third and greatest "period" of John Milton's life.

The Glory of "Paradise Lost"

The first poem of this period is "Paradise Lost." There is only one other poem in the world—Dante's "Divine Comedy"—which sweeps us through and beyond all time and space as does this poem—through Heaven and earth and hell, from the infinity before the beginning of the world to the infinite future. It is peopled with vast figures of demons and angels; we listen to the majestic rebellions of Satan, and we hear the pronouncements of God himself. The story tells of the rebellion of some of the angels, who are cast out of Heaven into hell, of the creation of the world, and of the temptation and fall of Adam and Eve. Only very great poetry could embody such a vast story as this. But for stately music, for mighty, awe-inspiring lines, this poetry has never been surpassed.

After "Paradise Lost" had been published, in 1667, Milton wrote a sequel, called "Paradise Regained," which is about the coming of Christ. It is shorter and not so remarkable as "Paradise Lost." He wrote also a dramatic poem called "Samson Agonistes"— the agony of Samson—which takes its story from the Old Testament and something of its form from the ancient Greek drama. In his work, Milton was always combining his love for the old pagan writers with his love for the Hebrew Scriptures.

On November 8, 1674, the great poet died.

Even among the enemies of the Puritan cause to which he had given so many years and the very sight of his eyes, he had already won his fame. "This man cuts us all out, and the ancients too," John Dryden had said when "Paradise Lost" appeared. In all the years since his death there has been no other poet in the world who can be compared with glorious John.

In this little cottage near Bedford lived John Bunyan, the gifted tinker who finally turned preacher and gave to the world that remarkable book of spiritual adventures which we know as "The Pilgrim's Progress." His kindly face is shown in the oval at the right.

Photos by National Portrait Gallery and Rischgitz

An AUTHOR Who WROTE in PRISON

He was a Tinker and He Gave Us a Most Wonderful Book— "The Pilgrim's Progress"

LIKE his father, John Bunyan started out to make his living as a tinker. Wandering about from village to village, he mended pots and pans and did whatever odd jobs he could find. In his spare time he joined in the dancing on the village green, helped the mischievous boys to ring the church bells in the dead of night, and occasionally played at tip-cat. As he himself admits, he even read a novel or two. Now, to us none of that seems so very bad, but to John Bunyan it was very sinful indeed. And even though he went to church every Sunday, and said his prayers regularly,

the poor young tinker's conscience never ceased to trouble him.

At seventeen Bunyan ran away from home. Leaving the little town of Elstow, near Bedford, where he had been born in 1628, he joined the army that was making war against Charles I. A year later he returned home, and soon afterwards he married a young country girl whose only possessions were a few clothes and a small bundle of "godly books." Through her influence and his reading of these books Bunyan was converted. Then his remorse grew so great that it seemed for a time as if he would lose his reason, but at last he devoted himself to preaching. Even then, however, his thoughts were not always as pure as he would have them, and his spiritual struggles were long and serious. But some years later he found the peace that he had so long sought.

Imprisoned for His Faith

So steadfast was he in the Baptist faith that he continued to preach it even in the face of a law forbidding the preaching of any faith except that of the established English Church. He was thrown into jail for preaching, and spent twelve long years in prison. But even there he kept on preaching to his fellow prisoners and poring over his two favourite books—the Bible and Foxe's "Book of Martyrs." To support his family he made shoe laces. When he was offered his freedom if he would agree to give up preaching, the earnest man's answer was always the same: "If you set me free to-day, I will preach again to-morrow."

It was in jail that Bunyan began the writing which was to have more influence than all the sermons he ever preached. When he was released in 1672, he immediately began to preach again. His fame soon spread and people flocked to hear what he

had to say. After three years of successful work he was again sent to prison. In the six months which he spent there, he completed the book that was to make him for ever famous.

"The Pilgrim's Progress," though it reads like the story of a journey, is really the story of a man's spiritual struggles, and as such it remains one of the most remarkable allegories (ăl'ē-gŏ-rĭ) of all time—for an allegory is a tale with a meaning that does not appear on the surface. It has been translated into more languages than any other book except the Bible. It is a forceful and dramatic story, and yet it is so simply told that a child can understand the true meaning of it.

Preaching to the End

When he was set free a second time, Bunyan became one of the most noted preachers of his day. From then on till his death on August 31, 1688, he was happy in the work that he loved. Although he wrote some excellent sermons and several other books, notably "Grace Abounding" and "The Life and Death of Mr. Badman," his name lives chiefly as that of the author of "The Pilgrim's Progress," which will continue to be a classic for many long years to come.

Bunyan's second wife, Elizabeth, scarcely had a happy married life, for her husband was thrown into jail a year after their marriage and, except for a few months, was imprisoned for the next twelve years. Meanwhile the generous woman looked after the four little children who had been left motherless by the death of Bunyan's first wife, and several times petitioned for her husband's release, as she is shown doing above.

FAMOUS *in* SPITE *of* HIMSELF

An Author Who Did His Best to Hide His Great Book from the Public Eye, Only to Have Its Secret Discovered a Century after His Death

ANYBODY might have seen Samuel Pepys (pēps) strutting round London two hundred and fifty years ago, but nobody would have ever dreamed that he would grow famous long after he was dead. He lived to be seventy years of age, and held several important offices, including that of Secretary to the Admiralty. For a time, also, he was a member of Parliament.

When he died in 1703 he left behind him several thick volumes that he had written in a sort of shorthand. For a long time no one could read what he had written, but after a century someone made out part of it and found he had discovered a treasure. In 1825 it was published as "The Diary of Samuel Pepys." Quite recently further portions have been made out and published, and they are most interesting.

But what a different man from the navy clerk is discovered therein! No dull official at all, but a highly interesting being—almost unconsciously humourous, likeable in spite of many a fault, and always amazingly frank.

The son of a gentleman who had married a "washmaid," he was born in 1633 and was educated at Cambridge. At twenty-two, before he could support himself, he married a girl of fifteen. The young people often had to call on their parents for a meal.

At twenty-seven Pepys began his diary. He had worked hard, and already had his foot on the ladder of prosperity. He deserved it, for he was both a competent and a hard worker. But how pleased he was to have money for a little finery! How he pranced about in his new velvets, satins, furs and gold lace! How flattered he felt on first receiving a letter addressed to "Samuel Pepys, Esquire"! By writing down thousands of little incidents like these, he told more about himself than almost any human being had ever told—though, of course, he did not mean us to read it, and never dreamed we should do so.

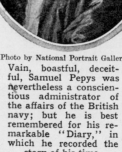

Photo by National Portrait Gallery

Vain, boastful, deceitful, Samuel Pepys was nevertheless a conscientious administrator of the affairs of the British navy; but he is best remembered for his remarkable "Diary," in which he recorded the story of his time.

But he told far more than his own life. He opened a wide window through which we can gaze into the London of his day and see history in the making.

On the throne of England sat the handsome, witty, merry-making Charles II. His court was crowded with beauties and witty courtiers, but hardly with serious statesmen. His every act was applauded by adoring subjects. For it was only ten years since the stern Oliver Cromwell had ruled England, and the people were tired of severity and thirsty for splendour, amusement and excitement.

Pepys did not know the inner workings of the lively court, but he had a keen nose for gossip and he never failed to make a note of any piece of scandal he had heard. He talks of all he knew about the famous persons around him—the clothing they wore, the meals they ate, the houses in which they lived, the plays they saw, their manners, their merry ways, in fact, everything of interest concerning their activities.

What a tragedy that after nine years his eyes failed and he had to give up writing! He never dreamed that he had written a new kind of history, and certainly he would have been greatly astonished—and not a little embarrassed—to think the world would come to know him just as he had known himself.

Amid a gay group of admiring fellow writers the poet Dryden held court at Will's Coffee House. There he and his companions would sit and sip the fashionable beverage, and there they would discuss the latest news or witticism of the day. These coffee houses, scattered about old London, were what clubs are to men of our own time.

A MONARCH Among the POETS
There Have Been Three Great Dictators in English Literature: Ben Jonson, Samuel Johnson, and the One of Whom You Read Here—John Dryden

IF YOU had strolled into the famous Will's Coffee House in London about two hundred and thirty years ago you would have seen an old man seated in the place of honour and surrounded by a number of gay and brilliant young men who hung on his words as he talked about the questions of the day.

In the group around him you might have seen some men who were destined to become famous when he was dead—little Alexander Pope, young Mr. Swift, young Mr. Addison, and Mr. Congreve, with many others who came even more often than these. In the old gentleman himself you would have seen one of the three men who, in their various times, have been dictators over English men of letters. Ben Jonson had held that position before him, and Samuel Johnson was to do so after him. At this moment the dictator was John Dryden.

He had taken part in many a battle and suffered many changes of fortune before attaining his seat of honour. To the present generation he represents little more than a name, for of all the great English poets, Dryden is among the least known and the least honoured.

Dryden was born in 1631, of a good family that took the Puritan side in the war of Cromwell against Charles I. As a boy he began writing verses, and after spending several years at Cambridge University he came to London to win his way as a wit and poet. One way to success was to praise the great Cromwell, and Dryden wrote a poem in Cromwell's honour. But once Cromwell was gone, he could write just as flattering a poem to the gay and frivolous Charles II, who now returned from France to occupy the English throne.

Dryden was rather a turncoat. We are going to see that again. He was not an evil man, but he did seek fortune where he thought it could be found.

Seeking Fortune as a Playwright

The England of Cromwell had been very solemn, and the theatres had all been closed. The England of Charles II was gay and riotous, and the theatres were thrown open to the wildest sort of comedy the land had ever seen. Dryden was hardly one of the born playwrights of the world, but he now sought his fortune in the theatre, and for the next thirty years or so he found it mainly in the long series of comedies that he wrote. Some of them were very fine, and their author became the leading dramatist of the day. His early success was "The Indian Queen," a play which was produced with much splendour in 1664. It was an elaborate affair, with battles on the stage, spirits singing in the air, and the god of dreams appearing through a trap. Then he passed on to such plays as "The Conquest of Granada," "All for Love," and "Don Sebastian." These are among the best-known plays in a long list.

Photo by National Portrait Gallery

John Dryden was the greatest English poet, dramatist, and literary critic of the last quarter of the seventeenth century.

But Dryden was a literary Jack of all trades. After the plague and the great fire of London he wrote a poem, called "Annus Mirabilis" (ăn'ŭs mǐ-răb'ĭ-lǐs), or "Wonderful Year" (1666), about these terrible events. While the theatres were closed on account of the plague he went into the country for safety and wrote the "Essay of Dramatic Poesy," one of the really great pieces of English literary criticism, and one of the monuments in the criticism of Shakespeare.

Above all he proved his genius in satire, or in making savage fun of his enemies in verse. He is one of the three greatest English satirists in verse, sharing the honour with Pope and Byron.

His main satires are "MacFlecknoe," directed against his literary critics, and especially against the poet Shadwell; and "Absalom and Ahitophel." It is in the latter poem that we find the famous lines about the duke of Buckingham:

A man so various that he seemed to be
Not one, but all mankind's epitome:
Stiff in opinions, always in the wrong,
Was everything by starts and nothing long.

Naturally, a man who wrote that sort of thing would have his enemies, and Dryden was no exception. One of them once hired some scoundrels to beat him over the head with cudgels. The rest fought him with their pens, and sometimes wounded him very deeply. The famous "Rehearsal," a dramatic piece by several authors, was written to ridicule him, and there were dozens of other satires against him.

Dryden was a religious poet too, and here again he turned his coat—though how honest he may have been in changing his religion we can hardly tell. While Charles II was still a Protestant king, Dryden wrote his "Religio Laici," on the side of the Church of England. But when James II, a Catholic king, came to the throne, Dryden wrote a beautiful poem called "The Hind and the Panther" in defence of the Catholic faith. In many ways it is a beautiful poem, but it is very little read in our day.

Dryden's Last Years

In his last years as a literary dictator, he did a great deal of miscellaneous work. Chiefly it was in translation—of Virgil, of Ovid, of Boccaccio, and of Chaucer into modern English. Many others of these translations were printed in his fine book of "Fables" in 1700. The same year his vexed life came to an end, and he was laid to rest in the Poets' Corner of Westminster Abbey.

The CREATOR of ROBINSON CRUSOE

Daniel Defoe, Journalist, Novelist and Writer on Many and Varied Subjects, Whose Life was Almost as Adventurous as that of His Famous Hero

ROBINSON CRUSOE . . . Robinson Crusoe . . . What was there about the name that it should have fixed itself in the mind of young Daniel Defoe until, thirty-five years later, he gave it to one of those imaginary characters who are more real to most of us than the people we know? The name was only one of many that Defoe had been spelling out on the old tombstones all day long—to keep his mind off the king's soldiers, who might at any moment ferret out his churchyard hiding-place. For, if they found him, they would drag him away, and the next time he came to a churchyard it would be for his own burial. So here he was reading inscriptions—and somehow taking special notice of the name of Robinson Crusoe.

It was the year 1685, and Defoe, who was twenty-four and aflame with youth and patriotic excitement, had been fighting in the cause of the ill-fated duke of Monmouth. Monmouth had some claim to the throne of England, and when he had taken up arms against the new king, James II, who was a Catholic, many Protestants had flocked to aid him. But the king's forces had met and routed them at Sedgemoor in July, and Monmouth had been beheaded as a traitor. Knowing that a similar fate awaited all others

Photo by Rischgitz

Three times Daniel Defoe had to stand here in the pillory for writing a satire called "The Shortest Way with the Dissenters." In it he apparently took the part of the Church of England against dissenters, though he did so only to make the Church party look absurd. Nevertheless, the work was endorsed by certain churchmen; and when they discovered that it was a hoax they were very angry and at once offered a reward for the arrest of Defoe, describing him as a "middle-sized spare man about forty years old, of a brown complexion . . . but wears a wig; a hooked nose, a sharp chin, grey eyes, and a large mole near his mouth."

who were captured, the unfortunate duke's followers fled in all directions. That was how young Defoe came to be reading names on tombstones until it should be dark enough to come out of hiding and make his escape.

The search for Monmouth's followers went on for some time, but Defoe was so little known that he went unmolested. He did not even have to leave England, but after a while returned to London and began his career as business man, politician, journalist, and writer.

It had never been intended that he should follow any of these occupations. His father, a London butcher, was, above all things, religious, and had wished his son to become a dissenting minister—that is to say, to be a minister of one of the small churches which did not accept the teachings of the Church of England. So Defoe was sent, at fourteen, to a dissenters' academy. There he was given a practical education, quite unlike that of most young Englishmen of his time. Instead of studying Latin and Greek, he studied and wrote English, and learned to do the things he would need most when he grew up. This schooling, which lasted for about five years, really fitted him for the life he was going to lead as well as it would have fitted him for the ministry. Above all, it prepared him to write his own language with ease and grace.

The Soldier Turns Hosier

For a time he had tried to earn his living in various business ventures—his experience in the Monmouth rebellion having discouraged his yearnings towards a political career. His first venture, as a hosier, failed, leaving him some £17,000 in debt, and he had to flee from London to avoid being arrested and put in prison. He became a manufacturer of tiles, and by courage, perseverance and hard work built up a profitable business which enabled him to pay off his debts.

Meanwhile, however, he had returned to politics. King James had fled to France,

Daniel Defoe, the man who wrote one of the world's most famous adventure stories.

and Defoe was an attendant at the coronation of William and Mary. Attired in a handsome uniform and mounted on a spirited horse, he was a member of a royal regiment made up of leading citizens of London. He wrote a poem, "The True-born Englishman," in defence of King William, and was taken into the royal favour.

He began to write political pamphlets in prose. Some of them, like his "Essay on Projects" (1698), are extremely modern in character. He argued, among other things, that women should be educated, that people should not be put in prison for debt, that roads should be improved, and that savings banks should be established.

But the king died, and Defoe soon tumbled from his pinnacle of prosperity. He wrote a clever satirical pamphlet called "The Shortest Way with the Dissenters," and as a result was sentenced to stand in the pillory three times, to pay a fine, and to go to prison for as long as it pleased the new queen, Anne, to keep him there. The first part of this punishment did not prove quite so bad as it was intended to be. Standing in the pillory, the unrepentant Defoe was overwhelmed with flowers and cheers from the people, instead of with the usual jeers and missiles; but spending two years in Newgate Prison was a far worse punishment. When he was free again, he found his business in ruins.

So he turned journalist. He started his "Review," a four-page paper that was to be published for the next nine years and is now regarded as the forerunner of all modern newspapers. He wrote the whole of it himself, more than five thousand pages; he did not even stop work on it during his two long stays in Scotland between 1706 and 1710. At this time he was back in politics, doing government secret-service work, writing and working now for one politician and now for another.

Then in 1719, when he was nearly sixty, he suddenly began to write stories. During the next six years he produced thirteen books of fiction, besides his pamphlets and his journalistic writings. The first and most famous of his marvellous novels was "Robinson Crusoe," named after that unknown man buried in the churchyard where Defoe had hidden from the king's men long before. The story was suggested by the adventures of one Alexander Selkirk, who had been shipwrecked on a South Sea island and had lived there for five years. But most of the adventures narrated are from the author's fertile imagination, although he told them all so carefully and vividly that one feels that they actually happened in just the way in which he describes them. The patient and resourceful Robinson Crusoe and his faithful Man Friday walked straight into the hearts of all lovers of a good tale, and have stayed there ever since.

Perhaps this narrative is a little too meandering to be a real novel, but it was the nearest thing to a novel that had ever been written in English. Some of Defoe's later stories are even more like modern novels—"Moll Flanders," for example, and "Roxana," both tales of adventuresses. There is another book of adventure in a far land, "Captain Singleton," and an account of the great plague in London when Defoe was a mere infant. This is so realistic that people thought at first it could not have been written by anyone who had not lived through the experiences himself. All these stories are still read, and people never cease to wonder at Defoe's ability to make everything seem so real that one cannot help believing every word he wrote as a novelist to be truth.

Defoe did not live to enjoy his fame for long. In 1731 he died. Of his many writings, the one we remember best is the story of Robinson Crusoe—the story, not of the man buried in that old churchyard, but of the hero of those wonderful adventures that took place in the imagination of Daniel Defoe.

Photo by National Portrait Gallery

Jonathan Swift, who is generally regarded as the most brilliant of all the English satirical writers.

The BITTEREST of ENGLISH AUTHORS

It is a Strange Thing that Jonathan Swift Wrote, in "Gulliver's Travels," One of the Best-loved Books of Children without Ever Meaning it for Them at All

IF YOU had been living in London about 1712, you would surely have seen the great Jonathan Swift. Any day you might have caught him in his long black gown and his curly white wig going into the House of Commons or coming out of the office of some important minister of state. Or you might have passed him in the park, where he used to walk a few miles at a brisk rate every day. If it happened to be raining you might hear him grumbling about the British weather and the high cost of a carriage—about how he hated to ride, but how he hated still more to have his new gown spattered with London mud. Wherever you met him, you would have received the impression at once that he was a most important man.

A Keen Mind and a Sharp Pen

For at that period he was about the most important man in England. Not that he held any office; he never did. But during his brief period of glory he was the chief power behind the throne. He had the keenest mind of any man in Britain, and by far the sharpest pen. His opinion was so valuable, and his pen so powerful, that the great ministers of state under Queen Anne could not do without him. He was one of the real rulers of the nation.

Where had he come from? He was born in Ireland in 1667. When only a year old, he had been stolen by his nurse and brought to England. At a very early age he could read the Bible through. He was taken back to Ireland to go to school, and in due time was sent to Trinity College, Dublin, though he does not seem to have shown any sign of genius there. Then he joined the Irish clergy, in a very humble rank, and for about ten years he was in England, serving as a secretary to his distant relative, the famous Sir William Temple, who was living in retirement.

The Greatest Prose Writer of the Age

In those years he did a great deal of writing, both in prose and verse. Nearly all of it he tore up; he was doing it largely for practice. He was connected by marriage to the aged Dryden, monarch among authors of the day; and once when he showed him some of his verses, Dryden shook his head and said, "Cousin Swift, you will never be a poet." The monarch was partly right. Cousin Swift never became a really great poet—he became instead the greatest writer of the age in prose, and the greatest satirist that England had ever seen. But we are going to talk about his satires a little later.

He saved two little masterpieces from the days with Temple and published them in 1704. We still read them and wonder at the genius of their author—"The Tale of a Tub" and "The Battle of the Books." Sir William Temple was now dead, and Swift had gone back to his little parish in Ireland, where he still seemed to have no chance of ever growing famous.

But he soon returned to England, on a mission for the Irish Church, and he had not been here long before the rulers saw that his pen was so mighty that they had need of it in the political war that was going on. In those days a good writer had far more influence than he has now. Swift wielded such an influential pen that any man would tremble if he heard that Swift was going to write a few words against him. So the Tory ministers enlisted the deadly pen of Swift in their bitter struggle with their enemies the Whigs. And for the four years from 1710 to 1714 Swift became the power behind the throne of Queen Anne.

The Famous Journal to Stella

Yet nowadays we do not often read the scathing pamphlets and the biting editorials that flowed from his pen in those years. Although they were so important in their day, they are on matters that are long since dead and buried. We read instead—and how Swift would have been astounded to know it!—a series of letters that he wrote to a girl named Esther Johnson who lived in Dublin. He used to call her "Stella," and these letters form his famous "Journal to Stella."

He just scribbled them to her for fun, often as he lay in bed after he had come home from some great dinner or some weighty council of state, and he little dreamed that they would ever be seen in print. In fact, he wrote them largely in a sort of baby talk, the kind that Stella had spoken when she was a little girl and had been his pupil at Sir William Temple's. So in the letters "Nite, nite" means "good night, good night"; "MD" stands for "my dear"; and "Pdfr" is always Swift himself, for it means "Poor dear foolish rogue."

But the letters were published long after he was dead, and now they are priceless to us. For they are not only highly interesting,

At the country home of Sir William Temple, Jonathan Swift taught little "Stella" her lessons, and in her gentle company spent many a happy hour. Later she became the chief joy in his unhappy life, and the sharer of all his confidences. Many people think he finally married her, though of that we have no reliable evidence.

but they are a matchless record of state affairs and his own hopes and fears during three years of highly important political activity.

The glory was soon over. Queen Anne died, and Swift's friends went out of power. He had thought he would have some great reward, and be made at least a bishop. But he was really too unreliable to be trusted. All the reward that came was an appointment as dean of St. Patrick's cathedral, Dublin. He was very bitter about it, but all he could do was to go back to Ireland— and he hated that so much that he said he was going back to die "like a poisoned rat in a hole."

Tragedy of His Closing Days

Yet he was one of the best friends the Irish ever had, and during the rest of his long life he wrote many books and pamphlets in their cause—some of them even more brilliant and more powerful than anything that he had done for Queen Anne. But the iron bit deeper and deeper into his soul as he kept thinking about the way in which he was neglected and still more about the general folly of the human race in his troublesome time. Finally his mind gave way under the strain, and his dark days ended in 1745, four years after losing his reason. There are few greater tragedies than the life of Jonathan Swift.

What Is a Satirist?

We have said that Swift is our greatest satirist, and he may well be numbered among the greatest of all the world. A satirist (săt'ĭ-rĭst) is one who is so angered with people and things that he lashes them with his words, but at the same time is so witty that he is extremely amusing in the doing of it. The satirist flogs his victim with jest and ridicule. It is not easy to be angry and witty at the same time, and that is one reason why we have very few real satirists. Swift was at once the angriest and the wittiest of men. His greatest rival in this respect was his own friend Pope. If Pope is our greatest satirist in verse, Swift is our greatest one in prose; and all things considered, Swift was the greater of the two.

Swift's best-known satire (săt'īr) is the famous "Gulliver's Travels" (1726-7). That great book has met a very curious fate— as did so much that its author attempted. The book was written for men who had lived in the world a long time and thought about its ways a great deal. For it is a trial and execution of the human race for their sins and follies. There never was a book more savage. But it is a satire, and so it must be amusing; and the amusement comes in when the human race is compared with other and very different races that Gulliver claims to have seen on his travels— little dwarfs an inch high, giants a hundred times as big as ourselves, and strange, horse-like creatures who are so much more sensible than we are. And it is the fun that we all remember, with the strange creatures in the book that give it to us. And so, in a shortened form, the bitterest satire in our tongue has come to be one of the best-loved books of children.

MR. TATLER *and* MR. SPECTATOR

How the Famous Partnership of Steele and Addison Gave Us the Two Most Brilliant Periodicals We Have Ever Had

RICHARD STEELE came from Ireland. He was generous, a little careless, and was often getting into trouble; he was a politician, and he had the gift of words to make him a literary genius: and in those phrases we have painted a great part of his picture.

Born in Ireland, in 1672, he was the son of an attorney. In 1684 he was sent to the famous Charterhouse School in London, where he met Joseph Addison, a meeting which was destined to bring about one of the most famous literary friendships on record. The two went up to Oxford together, though to different colleges; but Steele left Oxford before he had taken his degree, and became a soldier.

Photos by National Portrait Gallery

Joseph Addison (above) and Richard Steele, who were associated in the writing and publishing of the "Tatler" and the "Spectator," famous periodicals of the early eighteenth century.

While in the army he began to write poetry. He wrote some verses to King William which attracted the attention of the colonel of the regiment, who made Steele his secretary and secured for him an ensign's commission. But Steele was disgusted by the conduct of the other officers and fearful of the temptations that beset him, so he wrote a moral book called "The Christian Hero" to try to reform them and prevent himself from yielding to a lower life. Next he wrote a comedy, to prove that he could be as merry as anybody. He called it "The Funeral" (1701), a title which fails to indicate the true character of the play. This was soon followed by "The Lying Lover" and "The Tender Husband," and much later by "The Conscious Lovers."

These are bright and witty plays, and are among the first of the great list of "sentimental" comedies that had a run for nearly a century.

As soon as he had achieved success with his pen, Steele left the army. His first wife having died less than two years after marriage, in 1707 he married again —the widowed lady whom he called his "Dearest Prue" in the hundreds of letters which he wrote to her and which make such delightful reading. He held various offices under the government, including that of gazetteer. In those days the government thought it was safer to own the newspapers, whenever possible, and to publish only what it was safe to let the people know. As gazetteer, Steele had to select the news that the people were to be allowed to read

There is a story that when Joseph Addison lay dying, at the early age of forty-seven, the great man, who had a confident trust in God, sent for his stepson and urged upon him the value of leading a devout religious life.

Once launched as an editor, the idea came to him to produce a paper of his own, and in 1709 he started the famous "Tatler." It was in some degree a newspaper, but in the main it consisted of essays on all sorts of current affairs. It was published at a penny and appeared three times a week.

A Reunion of Forces

Just about this time Addison returned to London, and it was not long before he renewed his association with Steele, and became a contributor to the "Tatler." Addison was a very different man from Steele. He was a great deal less impulsive and reckless, and was so bashful that he often seemed less brilliant in society, but so careful that he never found himself in trouble. He had met with much success in the world, and had held several important offices. Though a very quiet man, he had an even greater literary gift than Steele.

Addison was the same age as Steele. After he had taken his degree at Oxford, he wrote some verses in praise of King William, and as his reward, was sent on a four years' tour through Europe to fit him for a government and diplomatic career. But the king died, and Addison's friends went out of power, so Addison returned to London, where for a time it looked as if he would find nothing to do.

Addison's Good Fortune

He was not idle for very long, however. Addison always experienced good luck. The English general Marlborough had just won a great victory at Blenheim, and the government wanted someone to celebrate the event in a poem. So they sought out Addison and asked him to write the poem. He wrote "The Campaign" (1704), and so assured his future. After that, whenever his friends the Whigs were in power he could always be certain of an office with a good salary.

Steele had started the "Tatler" without telling anyone he was writing it. But in one of the early numbers Addison recognized a remark that he had once made to Steele, and from this he gathered that Steele must be the writer of the paper. In the spirit of friendship he put his pen at the service of Steele, and he received the warmest welcome from his friend. Addison lifted the paper to an even higher level of literature than it had already attained.

Publication of the "Spectator"

It ran for about two years, and then stopped abruptly. There was probably some trouble with the government, for the authors had been treating the party in power to certain criticism. All the same, the paper was followed about two months later by the even more brilliant "Spectator," which ran for nearly two years from March, 1711. The "Tatler" had appeared three times a week, but the "Spectator" came out every day. It was almost equally the work of Steele and Addison, though again the work of Addison is on a somewhat higher plane. It was Addison who gave us the great Sir Roger de Coverley in the paper, though it had been Steele who first suggested the character.

Europe Bows to Steele and Addison

The fame of these two papers was universal. In England and all over Europe, for a century or more, there were hundreds of other papers published on similar lines to the "Tatler" and the "Spectator." But although many of them were excellent papers, none ever came near rivalling the great work of Steele and Addison.

After the "Spectator," Steele published another paper called the "Guardian," in which he still had the support of Addison. Then he wrote a number of other papers, but they were much less successful since they were mostly concerned with his contests and quarrels, political or otherwise.

Steele was elected to the House of Commons as the member for Stockbridge, but soon after he was charged with publishing seditious statements, and was expelled from the House. A little later his friends came into power, and he was again elected to Parliament, and retained his seat for several years, serving also on a number of important commissions. He was rewarded for his labours with a knighthood.

Steele's Last Years

The last years of his life were among his saddest. Although he made much money by his literary and political activities, he had always spent lavishly, and it was not often that he could claim to be free from debt. At length he became so embarrassed financially that he found it desirable to retire from public life and spend the remainder of his days in seclusion at Carmarthen in Wales, the native country of his "beloved Prue." He strove earnestly, however, to pay off his creditors, and was successful in doing so some time before his death occurred in 1729.

Addison the Successful

It was not thus with Addison. Just after the "Spectator" ceased publication, he produced a play called "Cato" which had a run such as hardly any play had ever had before. It was not a play of exceptional merit, though schoolboys still recite its speeches; but it appeared at the right moment in the political strife of the time, and met with remarkable success. Cato was a magnificent patriot, so the Tories thought he must be meant for a great Tory, and the Whigs for a great Whig; and neither party could do too much for the success of the play.

Addison was given the high office of secretary of state, and married the Dowager Countess of Warwick. But he did not live long to enjoy his honour. He died ten years before Steele, in 1719. In the previous year there had even been an unhappy difference between them, but nothing could have been more generous than Steele's forgiveness of his dead friend.

(CONTINUED ON PAGE 319)

What happens at BROADCASTING HOUSE

Photo by British Broadcasting Corporation

This magnificent building is the home of British broadcasting. You must often wonder what actually takes place within its walls—what the many different studios look like; how the orchestras and artists appear before the microphone, and how the various effects are produced. On the following pages some of these secrets are revealed.

Photos by Marcuswell Maxwell

Here are two of the ugliest inhabit ants of tropical Africa. The hippopotamus, which you see in the lower picture, in spite of his bulk and occasional fierceness, is generally mild and inoffensive; but the rhinoceros, seen in the upper picture, possesses an exceedingly bad temper, which makes an encounter with him an experience to be avoided.

The SEVEN WONDERS *of the* WORLD
These are the Things That were for Long Regarded as the Most Marvellous Works of Man

WE LIKE to keep an account of all the records that are broken. We want to know, for example, who ran the fastest hundred yards, who flew the longest distance in an aeroplane, who scored the greatest number of runs, who erected the largest building or the longest suspension bridge. In the same way we often compile lists of the most marvellous things in all the world, and we sometimes try to count seven of them —perhaps because seven has long been considered a sort of "mystic" number.

Now the ancients did exactly the same thing. They also made up lists of the seven most wonderful things in the world as they knew it. Their lists did not always agree, because some of the things that seemed among the most marvellous to one man might not seem so to another. But the most famous list is the one compiled by the poet Antipater (ăn - tĭp′ă - tẽr) of Sidon, about a century and a half before Christ. He is the man who first compiled a list of the Seven Wonders of the World, and this list, slightly altered, is the one that has remained classic to this day.

We may notice that the seven wonders were all things that had been built by man. The list did not include natural objects, for the ancients cared a great deal less about the marvels of Nature than we do.

The Seven Wonders of the World were:
1. The Pyramids of Egypt.
2. The Hanging Gardens of Babylon.
3. The Statue of Zeus (Jupiter) at Olympia.
4. The Temple of Diana (Artemis) at Ephesus.
5. The Mausoleum of Halicarnassus.
6. The Colossus of Rhodes.
7. The Pharos of Alexandria.

Built at a cost of more than £4,000,000 by British engineers, this majestic bridge which spans Sydney harbour may surely rank as a wonder of the world of to-day. Including approaches it measures 3,770 feet in length, and has a main span of nearly a third of a mile. The central roadway, which is 57 feet wide, carries four electric railway tracks, and has two footways, each 10 feet wide. The photograph shows the giant bridge as it appeared just before completion.

All these were certainly marvels from the hand of man in the distant past. About some of them a good deal can be read elsewhere in this work. We have mentioned the great pyramids of Egypt — those monuments of art and engineering in stone that still tower unchanged over the valley of the Nile as they did some five thousand years ago. They seem so eternal that they have given us the Arabic proverb: "Time mocks all things, but the pyramids mock time." There are about seventy-five of them in all; the most famous is the Great Pyramid built by Khufu as a tomb for himself and his queen. There, in a chamber in the heart of the great structure, lay the two bodies in their beautiful cases, concealed as far as possible from any prying eyes. All around ran passages connecting other chambers, and the whole was most marvellously planned. But the care to conceal their treasure by the Egyptians was of little use, for thieves of past ages ransacked the monument and spoilt much of its beauty. It covers some thirteen acres and rises to about 480 feet. Of all the seven wonders of the ancient world, the pyramids alone are left standing for us to see to-day.

We have also referred to the great Hanging Gardens of Babylon—how they are said to have been built about six hundred years before Christ by the famous Nebuchadnezzar (nĕb'-ū-kăd-nĕz'ǎr) for the delight of his queen, who had come from a hilly country and who longed for her native mountains after she came to live in the flat land of Babylon. He built "mountains" for her—the terraces upon terraces of gardens rising three hundred feet into the air and planted with gorgeous flowers and groves.

The ancients who made a list of the Seven Wonders of the World seem never to have realized that Nature can make wonders that man cannot even hope to imitate. But they never knew of Niagara or the Grand Canyon; and if rumour reached them of the Victoria Falls in Africa, they probably thought of it as just another legend.

A Statue of Ivory and Gold

The giant statue of Jupiter, or of Zeus (zūs), as the Greeks called him, dated from about 450 B.C. and was the work of Phidias (fĭd'ĭ-ăs), the greatest of the Greek sculptors and perhaps of all the sculptors of the world. It stood on Olympus, and was a magnificent creation of ivory and gold. But when it disappeared, and how, we do not know. We can well imagine that the barbarians might pull down such a work of art for the precious materials it would contain.

The Temple of Diana at Ephesus (ĕf'ĕ-sŭs) was the greatest and finest of the Greek temples in Asia Minor, and was full of works of the sculptor's art. Only in very recent times have we discovered the spot where it once stood, and found that at least three other temples to the same goddess had been built before it on the same site. The last and most famous of them dated from a little more than three hundred years before Christ.

There is a story that should be told about this temple. It was sometimes called the "Ephesian Dome." There was a man in Ephesus who was very anxious to become famous, but who did not possess the genius to do so. He conceived the idea of setting fire to the great temple of Diana, or of "firing the Ephesian Dome," because he was sure that any man who burnt it down would leave a name behind him. Then, as the centuries passed, the world forgot all about him; but many years later scholars found out his name again, and so he finally had his way—he became famous, in a queer fashion. If you ever hear it said that somebody is trying to "fire the Ephesian Dome," it will mean that he wants to start everybody talking about him.

The Mausoleum (maw'sŏ-lē'ŭm) at Halicarnassus (hăl'ĭ-kär-năs'ŭs) was a great tomb built in Asia Minor about 350 years before the birth of Christ. It was erected by Queen Artemisia (är'tĕ-mĭz'ĭ-ả) as a resting-place for her husband. His name was Mausolus; and for that reason any great tomb since his day has been called a mausoleum.

His own tomb was beautifully decorated, and was surrounded by graceful Ionic columns. Parts of it are still to be seen in the British Museum.

The Hanging Gardens of Babylon may possibly have
looked like this.

We know what the pyramids
look like, for they are
still standing.

The Pharos of Alexandria was reputed to be five hun-
dred feet high.

A reconstruction of the tomb
of King Mausolus. *By courtesy of British Museum.*

The Colossus of Rhodes was seen
by sailors from far
out at sea.

The temple
of Diana of Ephesus
was a mass of gleaming
marble and beautiful sculpture.

The gold and
ivory Zeus at
Olympia was said to
be perfect in every detail.

The Colossus of Rhodes was one of those gigantic statues of the ancient world which **has given** us our word "colossal." It was a great bronze figure of Apollo, the sun god, which stood dominating the harbour of Rhodes, a city on the island of Rhodes, the easternmost of the Aegean Islands—though it did not, as is often thought, bestride the harbour with its legs. It rose about 105 feet, but it did not stand very long. Erected in 280 B.C., it collapsed in an earthquake about sixty years later. Then the bronze giant lay prone for about a thousand years, when the metal was finally sold to a man who is said to have used more than nine hundred camels to carry it away.

A Famous Lighthouse of Old

The Pharos (fär'ŏs) at Alexandria was a famous lighthouse. It took its name from the island of Pharos, on which it stood; and to this day the French call any lighthouse a "phare." The great tower is said to have reached a height of 500 feet, though it is thought to be doubtful if it could have risen as high as this; but whatever its height the fire on top of it could guide the mariners from many miles out at sea into its famous port. It was built nearly three hundred years before Christ, and stood for some fifteen centuries, until it, too, was finally ruined by an earthquake.

Such are the famous seven wonders of the ancient world. And wonders they indeed were—all the more when we remember that they were raised by the hand of man without any of the machinery with which we build our wonders of to-day. We have probably never made anything more beautiful than some of those old buildings and statues. But we have made things far larger and higher, and far more complicated; also far more comfortable. We are surrounded by monuments of stone and steel that would make the ancient Greeks and Egyptians open their eyes in amazement.

And yet the real wonders of our day are not the big things that we can see with our eyes. They are nearly all unseen—they are the secrets of the microscope and telescope, of electric currents that travel over wires and through the air, of thoughts that surge through the mind of man. There are so many of these things that it is futile to try to make a list of seven of them. If you try to compile a list it will run into thousands, but many as they are, you can read about them all in the "Wonderland of Knowledge."

Among the seven wonders of the modern world we might include this great dam on the Upper Murrumbidgee River, in New South Wales, Australia. Situated at Burrinjack, it is 240 feet in height and is capable of storing about 950,000,000 tons of water. This notable engineering achievement forms part of a gigantic irrigation scheme by which 1,500,000 acres of land will in course of time be made more suitable for cultivation.

We TWIST, *We* STRETCH, *and We* CRISS-CROSS

And so We Make Miles of Thread and Yards of Cloth
Out of the Wool of a Single Sheep

IN THE ancient story of the Sleeping Beauty, the princess came upon an old woman who was busy spinning. Of course, the princess wanted to spin too; but she pricked her finger on the spindle, and so fell into a sleep that was to last for a hundred years.

There is little danger that any other girl will ever have the same bad luck. For what girl of our day would even know a spindle if she saw one?

But for many a long century, up to recent times, almost every girl had to learn about spinning, as it was going to be a large part of her work in the world. It is among the oldest of the arts, and we know of no people who did not learn to spin. It has always been mainly the work of women—so much so that to this day an unmarried grown-up girl is called a "spinster."

If you had lived in Egypt long before the Christian era began, you would have seen many a girl spinning; and it was very skilful work, too; it would be no easy thing for you to learn now.

The art of spinning is simply the art of making fluffy wool—or any other fibrous stuff, like flax or cotton—into a single string, or "yarn." To do this, the girl first put some of the wool on the end of a stick which was called a distaff. Holding this under one arm, she twisted the wool into a thread and wound it round a spindle.

The spindle was just another stick of wood. It was thin, or "spindling," and pointed at

This earnest old Italian woman learned as a child the difficult art of spinning with a distaff. The expression on her face tells you how close and exacting the work is. Out of the ball of woollen fluff on the end of the distaff she must twist a long, firm thread. In the oval is a picture of the spindle on which the thread was wound as it left the worker's fingers.

both ends. At one end it had a notch to catch the end of the yarn that was going to be wound up on it. It was made to turn round and round. And in the middle it had a sort of disk, or wheel, heavy enough to make it turn smoothly and evenly. That was all; but it was a clever thing for someone to have thought of centuries before we knew how to read and write. And nothing more ingenious was invented for centuries afterwards.

So the girl held her distaff under her left arm and pulled out some twisted fibres to hook on to the end of her spindle. Then she twirled the spindle and drew out more and more fibres, which she twisted, or "spun," into yarn as they came. Thus she made one long string out of the fluff; and when she had finished, it was all wound up on the spindle ready for the weaver. There are still some primitive people in the world who make their yarn exactly in the same way.

If you think it sounds easy, you might try it if you ever have a chance. It will take some time to learn, and will make you feel as clumsy as any other thing you first tried. Yet those little girls of many centuries ago could do it with flying fingers. And they were highly skilled in making their yarn fine and strong and even. Think of spinning a few handfuls of fluff into a thread a hundred miles long!

But they needed all their speed and skill,

for every piece of cloth has to begin in threads spun out of fluff. And almost down to our own day the girls and their mothers were making the threads in this same way. There were a few inventions to help them; but our great-great-grandmothers still had to do all the work by hand. Think of the toil—the aching backs, the straining eyes, the tired fingers!

It is strange that in an art

By courtesy of the British Museum

so old, and so universal, improvements came more slowly than in almost any other. Not until about four centuries ago did we have a spinning-wheel. This was only a big wheel that made it easier to turn the spindle. It was a great improvement, to be sure, especially after it was made to be turned by foot, for it left both hands free to handle the yarn, and it remained in use down to the time of our great-grandmothers. You may still see a spinning-wheel in a museum, and sometimes in an old attic.

If you had been born round about 1750, you would have found that spinning was a big business. There has always been a great deal of wool in England; and you would have

seen whole towns where nearly all the people did nothing but spin and weave, day and night. The people all worked in their own homes, where the women did the spinning and the men often wove the yarn into cloth.

The spinning-wheel, quaint as it seems to us, was a long step in advance of the distaff and spindle, for it wound up the thread that the spinner's fingers had twisted, and it held the distaff, too. The wheel used by this Dutch peasant woman had to be turned by hand, but the one shown in the oval was operated by a treadle, and so left both hands free to twist the thread. Below is a photograph of models showing how cotton was spun in Japan in the Middle Ages. The Japanese, too, had learned the use of the spinning-wheel, though theirs was somewhat different from ours.

So the towns in which these occupations were carried on were called the "cloth towns."

The Sad Fate of an Inventor

In one of them— at Blackburn—there lived a carpenter and weaver named James Hargreaves. Through an accident he conceived the idea of a spinning-wheel that would make more than a single thread of yarn at once. By

about 1764 he had invented his "spinning-jenny," which spun ten threads instead of one.

It was the first great invention in spinning; but the other workmen thought at first that it was going to take away their work, so they broke into the inventor's house and smashed his machine. He went off to another town, and tried to patent his invention. But he was cheated by the men with whom he had to deal, and a few years after he died, poor and friendless. Meanwhile his machine was coming into use everywhere, and making a fortune for many other men.

The main fault of the spinning-jenny was that it would spin only coarse, rough yarn. So Richard Arkwright began dreaming of

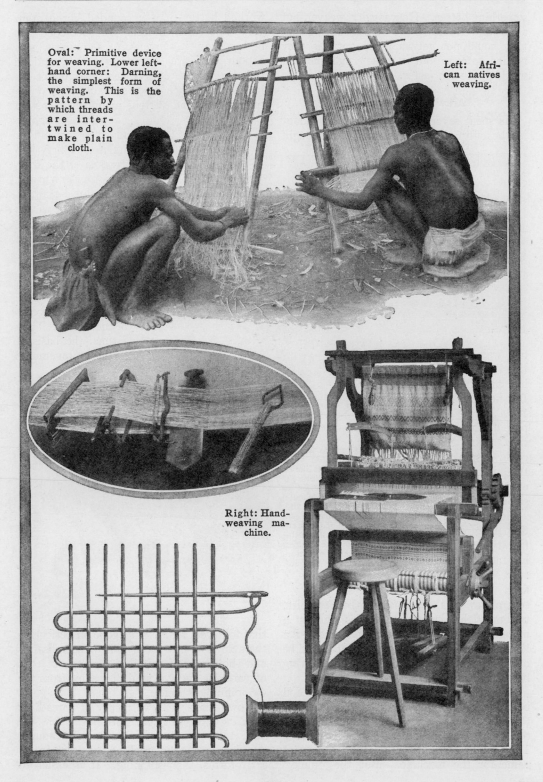

Oval: Primitive device for weaving. Lower left-hand corner: Darning, the simplest form of weaving. This is the pattern by which threads are intertwined to make plain cloth.

Left: African natives weaving.

Right: Hand-weaving machine.

something better. He was not a weaver, but a barber. He heard the weavers saying that they could not get as much yarn as they needed, so he set out to make a machine that would spin yarn faster.

Arkwright's Invention

He spent several years and all his money in the effort. Even his own wife thought he was wasting his time, and once she broke his machine into bits. But he persevered, and by 1769 he had taken out a patent on his invention. His machine could spin many threads at once, and every thread was strong and fine.

He had better luck than Hargreaves. A factory was built for him, and the business succeeded from the first. So in spite of several lawsuits and many other troubles, including the destruction of his mill by a mob in 1779, the inventor had amassed a fortune of £500,000 before he died. And he had become Sir Richard Arkwright, having been knighted in 1786.

But still a third invention was needed before any machine could spin the finest threads. This was made by Samuel Crompton, and was called a "spinning-mule." They might certainly have found a prettier name for the machine. But the "mule"

Below at the right you may see a number of woollen stockings and caps and sweaters, but all unspun. For we must strip the sheep of his coat to get our wool; and then the soft fluff we shear from him must go through many processes before we can obtain the material for making these articles of clothing.

Above, you are shown what the linen in your handkerchief looks like as it comes from Nature's hands. For here is a field of flax, the delicate blue-flowered plant from which linen is made. In the oval is a scene familiar enough in the southern part of the United States when the cotton in the fields is ripe for picking.

worked better than it sounded, for it spun very fine yarn indeed. It succeeded far better than its inventor. Crompton was a poor man who worked in a mill, and he toiled at night for five years to perfect his invention. Then he was unable to find the patent fees, and various manufacturers who adopted his machine failed to pay him for its use. Thirty-two years later the British government made him a grant of £5,000, but this was lost in business ventures and he died in humble circumstances.

These were the three great inventions in spinning, and they all came within a few years of each other. They formed the basis of all the improvements that followed, for we have gone on perfecting them until we now have mills with thousands and thousands of spindles, turning out tons of yarn for every pound that came from the old spinning-wheel.

Now, when we have plenty of thread, or yarn, how do we make cloth out of it? We have to weave it. And, strangely enough, weaving is a simpler thing, at least in its early forms, than spinning. It is easier to

Here are some of the steps in weaving a rug. First, an artist must make the design and paint in the colours on cross-section paper, as shown at the extreme left. Then a machine must stamp the design on cardboard, with thousands of little perforations.

When the design of the rug has been stamped into the cardboard pattern, that pattern is duplicated over and over again on long laced sheets by the machine shown at the right. These perforated sheets, which look very much like the music rolls of a mechanical piano, are what control the pattern in a Jacquard loom, like the one shown below. As they run through the loom the rug is woven, according to their perforated patterns, in every colour known to man.

Right: An American Indian making a rug on the only kind of loom men had for thousands of years.

make our threads into a piece of cloth than it was to make the threads in the first place. So people knew how to weave even before they had learned to spin. For they had plenty of things that could be woven, such, for example, as straw, which we still use in the making of hats.

All we need to do in simple weaving is

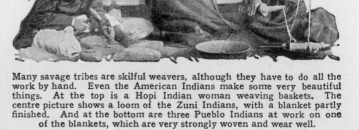

to lace our threads together, in criss-cross fashion, over and under one another, in the way that we string a tennis-racket or make a cane seat. The result is cloth, and we can make it the first time we try; though to make it fine and beautiful we need a great deal of experience.

First we must string out hundreds of threads all running the same way, and as close together as possible. All these threads together are called the "warp." Then we must take another thread and run it straight across and through the threads of the warp—over the first one, under the second, over the third, under the fourth, and so on to the last. Then we double back and run it through the threads again to the side where we first started; and so we go on back and forth until we have woven our cloth. All the threads running across and through the warp are called the "weft" or "woof."

Of course, the closer we can get them together, the stronger our cloth will be. And all this our forefathers knew many hundreds of years ago.

But it was weary work. Just imagine running a thread back and forth thousands of times, pushing it under and over, under and over! At the time of the Egyptians, there was a machine that helped a great deal in the work. It was a "loom."

The first loom merely lowered every other thread of the warp, and lifted every thread in between; so there was a space between the threads of the warp, and the weaver simply ran the thread of woof through the space, without having to lift it up and down all the time. The thread of woof was run through on a stick. When the other side was reached, a turn was given to the machine, and every thread of warp that

Many savage tribes are skilful weavers, although they have to do all the work by hand. Even the American Indians make some very beautiful things. At the top is a Hopi Indian woman weaving baskets. The centre picture shows a loom of the Zuni Indians, with a blanket partly finished. And at the bottom are three Pueblo Indians at work on one of the blankets, which are very strongly woven and wear well.

had been up went down, while those that had been down came up. Then the woof thread was taken back to where it had started; and this time it went under all the threads it had gone over the first time, and over all it had gone under.

234

The first great modern invention in weaving came in 1738, when John Kay, an Englishman, devised the fly-shuttle, without which the power-loom could never have been invented. It was not used until many years later, and then the weavers did not welcome the labour-saving device, as they thought it would take away their work. So in 1753 rioters stormed Kay's house, and the life of the inventor was saved only by the quick-witted plan of his wife, who had him wrapped in a sheet and hurried out of the house in the arms of two workmen. In this picture of the incident, Kay's loom can be seen, with the fly-shuttle on the floor beside it.

In due time the loom was improved, but very, very slowly. Until less than two centuries ago it was always run by hand. The weaver would open the space between the warp threads by pressing on a pedal. Then the woof thread would be carried through on a shuttle. The shuttle was a little wooden case with a spool of yarn inside; and as it passed through it unrolled the thread of woof behind it. Thus it would travel back and forth time and time again. And that is the way in which all cloth was made.

Birth of the Power-loom

At last there came a time when the spinners had progressed far ahead of the weavers. They had found machines that would turn out yarn much faster than the weavers could make it into cloth. So the next thing required was a loom that could work much faster; and it needed steam to run it, for the human hand had already reached its limit. It had to be a "power-loom."

Edmund Cartwright started to experiment. His friends only laughed at him, for he surely had learned nothing about machinery during his student days at Oxford, and since then he had been a clergyman; but he was not to be discouraged, and in 1785 he succeeded in producing the first power-loom. It would press the pedals, open the warp, drive the shuttle back and forth, and even stop working whenever a thread broke. For the yarn of the woof was made to run over a little fork, and if the yarn broke, the fork would slip back and shut off the power.

Cartwright made many improvements on his first machine, but he never prospered from his invention. He had a great deal of trouble with the weavers, who thought his new loom would take away their work. When he had a factory of four hundred looms almost ready to start, someone set fire to it and burned it to the ground. At the age of sixty-six, Cartwright finally received £10,000 from the government; but he had already spent about four times as much in bringing his machine to perfection.

Wonders of the Modern Loom

The machine was a huge success, and since that day many inventors have gone on improving it, making it stronger, faster and more efficient in every way. To-day we have great looms that pull and stretch the cloth exactly as they should, keep all the threads just tight enough, fill the shuttles when the spool inside is empty, roll up the new cloth at just the right speed, and still need so little help that a single weaver can run several machines at one time. How different from the loom of ancient Egypt.

How We Make a Carpet

There are so many special kinds of weaving that we are unable to describe them all. Many of them are unfamiliar to anyone except a weaver.

When you look at a piece of plush, for instance, or a carpet, it certainly does not seem to be a mere set of threads, half of them running one way and half of them the other. It is all velvety with what we call the "pile," and no sort of thread can be seen at all. But underneath the pile is the woven cloth; and what we see, sticking up from it, are only tufts of silk or wool that have been tied into it and cut off smooth to form the pile.

The most wonderful of all weaving machines is the one that puts the patterns into cloth. Everybody knows the marvellous patterns of colour that appear in shawls and dresses, in curtains and in rugs. How can we weave pictures of birds and flowers into cloth if we have nothing but

a thread to go over and under, across and back?

It is a complicated business, but there is a machine that does it all simply and quickly. This machine will pick out any number of coloured threads you wish, and bring them into view on top of the cloth exactly where you want them. Of course, the woof thread in the shuttles has to be changed every so often. So when a fresh colour is needed, to begin a new part of the pattern, the machine stops, and it actually lifts a string to show the weaver what colour is needed next.

Patterns Made With Holes

We have all seen the rolls of paper that are used in mechanical pianos. They are punched full of different kinds of holes, and each hole plays its own kind of note. The weaving machine uses cards punched in the same way, and the cards make the machine do all that is required in weaving the complicated pattern.

It took nearly a hundred years to invent this wonderful machine, and many different people had a share in its making. It was at last perfected in 1801 and the following years by a Frenchman named Jacquard (zhā-kär'), and it is

This is a standard type Hessian loom arranged with individual motor drive. The photograph shows the cloth being woven.

Photo by Urquhart Lindsay and Robertson Orchar, Ltd.

Of quite recent development is this wonderful machine. It is fitted with special automatic shuttle-changing motion and has the advantage over the ordinary loom that one worker can look after any number up to six or possibly eight.

Photo by Urquhart Lindsay and Robertson Orchar, Ltd.

named after him. Jacquard started as a poor workman in a silk mill at Lyons, but he was more fortunate with his invention than were some of his English brethren. For when he went to Paris with his machine in 1806, the government adopted it, gave him a pension, and ordered every mill that used his loom to make him an annual payment. In a little while the land was full of Jacquard looms, and the inventor was a rich man, as he so well deserved to be.

Experiments have been made with a new type of loom which, when perfected, will revolutionize the whole weaving industry. It is a loom without a shuttle—the dream of inventors for more than thirty years. In this machine the work of the shuttle is done by light metal rods, each fitted at the end with a gripper. This draws the weft across the warp until it is met half-way by a rod from the other side, which takes the weft over and completes the journey. This simple process does away with much of the existing heavy and elaborate mechanism, saves time and labour, and enables more colour to be used in the weft, thus giving a greater range of designs.

An Art the Spider Taught Us

In all these ways we have spun and woven many kinds of stuff—wool, cotton, silk, flax and jute. The main idea has always been the same—to twist and stretch the fibres into yarn, and then to criss-cross them into cloth.

But in the past few years we have found a brand-new way of spinning—though it is one that spiders have known all along. The spider spins a thread by squeezing a liquid through a very small hole. And that is just the way in which we now make artificial silk, or rayon. We are going to tell you about rayon in another part of this work, but we ought to say here that the very latest triumph in the art of spinning was the secret of the spider long years before man discovered it.

The HEROIC MIGHT of BEOWULF

Here is the Brave Story Which Our Forefathers Brought to England When They First Came to Our Land, and Which They Wove into an Epic Poem

THE oldest heroic poem in the English tongue was written in a language that no one can speak now and very few can read—the language that the Angles and the Saxons brought to Britain when they overran the country about fifteen hundred years ago. In order to read the poem we have to study Anglo-Saxon, or Old English, just as we have to study Latin to read Virgil; but the few who learn Anglo-Saxon have opened to themselves a door leading into a whole realm of mighty legends.

Of all those legends, the story of Beowulf (bā'ŏ-wŏolf) is the most famous, and the oldest long poem in our tongue is the epic of "Beowulf."

We do not know who wrote this heroic poem, or exactly when it was written. We know that the legend was familiar to the Angles and the Saxons even before they came to Britain, and that is why the scene of the poem is laid in the Scandinavian land from which they had come.

We know how the scalds (skawld), or poet-singers of early days, used to strike their crude harps and chant heroic tales to the warriors gathered in the great bare hall, when they had drunk their mead and eaten their meat, and were eager to hear about the glory of great heroes and the stories of mighty deeds. We know that some time in the sixth century a few of the events recounted in "Beowulf" really happened; and we know that Beowulf's strong grip, like that of a bear, and tales of the dragon that he slew, had grown into marvellous stories, that were frequently told and believed by the people of that period.

Photo by O. Vaering

In a little open boat with curving prow and wind-filled sail the hero Beowulf sets out for Denmark and high adventure. A sea voyage was perilous in Beowulf's day. There was no compass, no chart, no shelter from the storm, no power to drive the vessel except oars and an unruly sail. Yet the bold hero loved his ship, his " timbered vessel," his " well-braced floater," "foamy-necked," " bird-like "—as the poet describes it.

So we must suppose that what happened was somewhat as follows:

Perhaps about A.D. 700 or a little later, when the Angles and Saxons had become more or less civilized, had learned to read and write, and had been converted to Christianity, some great poet wrote down the old stories he had heard of Beowulf. He may have been a monk in one of the monasteries of Northumbria, for these were full of learned men in those days. Whoever he was, he wrote with great fire and force, making his hero very brave and altogether glorious. It is a great pity we cannot hear his very words chanted aloud as they were meant to be; for Anglo-Saxon poetry swings along with resounding accents, like the clashing of shields or the tramp of war-horses. It is impossible to get the same effect in the style of modern English verse.

But we should be thankful that this splendid story has come down to us at all, for when the Danes invaded England in the ninth century they burned down the monasteries and left only scraps of the old poetry to be handed down to our day. We have only one copy of "Beowulf," which was written down about A.D. 1000, and that one was lost for many centuries, and also was nearly destroyed by fire before any copies had been made from it.

Here, then, is the heroic story of the first great poem in English literature—or, for that matter, in the literature of any of the Germanic peoples. It is a genuine epic, because its hero stands for the things the Angles and Saxons held to be noblest in life—loyalty and generous daring, and mighty strength in battle.

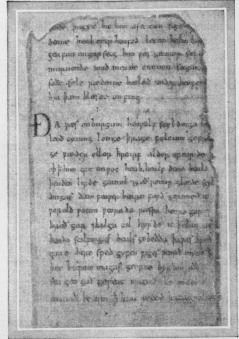

By courtesy of the British Museum

This is a photograph of a page of our only manuscript of "Beowulf." Fragments have been burned off round the edges, as you can see, and this makes it more difficult to read. The precious manuscript is now in the British Museum, and is a sight not to be missed by the student of literature.

The great hall of King Hrothgar (hrŏth'-gär) was desolate. Little had the king supposed, when he fastened over the door the deer's antlers and named his fine hall Heorot (hā'ŏ-rŏt), that he and his queen and his faithful thanes would see it standing thus deserted for twelve long years. But what could be done? Every night the fiend Grendel—that fell monster in human form— would slink across the moors, break into Heorot, and, seizing one of the king's brave thanes as he slept, would greedily devour him. No mortal weapon could pierce the monster's horny hide, and what hero had strength to fight bare-handed with the fiend?

Such a battle was for one hero only. And he did not dwell in Hrothgar's kingdom of Denmark, but far away in Sweden, in Geatland (yā'ät-länd).

But Beowulf, the young hero, nephew of Hygelac (hī'gĕ-lăk), king of the Geats, was as generous as he was daring, and he longed above all things to win fame by mighty deeds. He had heard of the sorrow of good King Hrothgar, and he was eager to test his mettle with this grisly foe. So he called about him fourteen of his noblest comrades, asking if they would share his adventure.

Gaily the bold youths set forth for Denmark, and, having made due offering to Heaven, pushed off in their little viking boat, which floated lightly on the water, its curving prow white with foam.

So they passed across the "whale road," the bright and perilous sea, and arrived in sight of the coast of Denmark. Then came galloping down to the shore King Hrothgar's sentry, shaking his spear fiercely at the strangers.

"No bearers of shields ever tried so coolly to land here!" he cried, warning them.

But Beowulf, strong and handsome in gleaming helmet and corselet of cunningly woven chain-mail, stood up before him in friendly wise, reassuring him. Then the man's manner changed, and he cordially invited the visitors to come before the king. So they strode off, leaving the boat to sway gently about as she lay at anchor.

King Hrothgar stood amazed when he heard the stranger's errand.

"Only let me meet this monster alone," cried Beowulf. "Let no one but the Geats stay to-night in Heorot. With my naked hands will I seize hold of the fiend and battle with him for life—and whoever finds his death may fall knowing it is God's will. If Grendel should overcome me"—and his proud look told Hrothgar that he thought of such a thing as scarcely possible—"let him eat up these my comrades without fear!"

Thus Beowulf boasted, after the manner of the heroes of those days. He asked for no reward should he be successful; but if he should fall, let his helmet and corselet be sent home to his uncle, King Hygelac.

Feasting the Fifteen Warriors

That night Heorot rang once more with the sound of feasting, the shouts and boastings of the warrior thanes, and the brave chants of the scalds. When the feast was over, the Danes passed out of the hall, leaving the fifteen heroes to await what might befall.

When Hrothgar's gracious queen had offered mead to Beowulf, he had answered her, proudly, "I propose to show in this mead hall to-night a princely courage, or pass here my last day."

Now had come the moment to stand fast by his declaration.

The visiting warriors lay down to rest in the gloomy hall. Beowulf, too, lay down. He had put aside his armour and his trusty sword; for the sword was useless against Grendel, nor would the hero deign to use it or to shield himself by helmet and mail against one who neither wore corselet nor understood the art of the sword.

The hero lay waiting in the darkness, hearing all about him the quiet breathing of his sleeping comrades. Suddenly the door of the hall was torn open by some mighty hand, and before Beowulf could raise a finger, one of the sleeping warriors had been seized and devoured by the fiendish monster. Then Grendel strode up to Beowulf himself, ready to destroy him where he lay.

Beowulf's Struggle with Grendel

But the fiend had met his match at last. It was now that Beowulf was grateful for that wonderful grip of his, strong as the grip of a bear. He laid hold on Grendel's arm. Heorot rocked and rang with the mighty struggle that followed. But, for the monster, neither struggling nor wrestling was of any avail. When at last, yelling with rage and pain, Grendel fled to his death over the desolate moor, he left behind him his arm still clutched in Beowulf's terrible grasp.

Great was the joy in Hrothgar's court at Beowulf's victory, and high was the feasting at Heorot. That night the king's thanes would sleep in the great hall without fear.

But, alas, who knew that Grendel had a mother even more terrible than himself! The same night she came stealing over the moor to avenge the death of her son. Breaking into the hall, she seized upon King Hrothgar's favourite thane, Aeschere (ăsh'ĕ-rĕ), and dragged him off to his doom. She took with her, too, the arm of Grendel, which had been hung in triumph on the wall.

Here, then, was another adventure for the hero with the grip of a bear. This time he would not wait for the monster to return, but set off at once to track her to her lair, which, from the blood trail left by Grendel when he had fled from Beowulf, he believed to be a cave beneath the waters of a lake.

Now, Beowulf was a mighty swimmer. He had even boasted of how once he had swum for nine whole days and nights in a match with a youthful rival. As he stood looking at the waters of the lake, he saw the sea monsters and reptiles swimming angrily about as though they remembered how their brothers had fared at his hands in that previous adventure. Listening to their clamour, Beowulf determined not to lay aside his armour but to plunge into the waves just as he was, and fight his way to the cave.

There was feasting once more in Heorot, now that the hero Beowulf had come to do battle with Grendel. All the warriors drank deep of Hrothgar's good mead, and ate of his bounty. There was boasting of heroic deeds done in youth, and the chanting of the bards. Then Hrothgar's queen, Wealtheow, rose, as we see her here, to pass the mead horn to Beowulf in token of her trust in his might. And the hero told her he would not fail.

He plunged, and disappeared from the sight of the anxious watchers. Then blood began to surge up through the waters. Would they ever see their hero again? At last, weary and disheartened, they went homeward, sorrowing.

But Beowulf was not dead. He had fought his way past the sea reptiles and climbed up into the monster's cave, which was a vaulted chamber. There Grendel's mother grappled with him fiercely and threw him down. But in his sore need the hero spied upon the wall of the cave a mighty dagger, and, seizing it, he slew his enemy. It was a magic dagger, or it never could have availed against her charmed life. Then, looking about him, Beowulf saw the body of Grendel lying in the cave. With the magic dagger he cut off Grendel's head, and taking it as a grim trophy, he swam back through the angry waters and returned in triumph to Heorot.

King Hrothgar and his court rejoiced greatly at this amazing victory. The king fell upon Beowulf's neck and kissed him, weeping for very joy and affection. Then, laden with riches pressed upon him by the grateful Danes, the mighty hero set sail with his companions for the land of the Geats.

Beowulf Becomes King

There, King Hygelac, Beowulf's uncle, greeted him joyfully, and listened in admiration as he told of his adventures. So the hero lived at his uncle's court in even more honour than before. And when Hygelac was killed in a raid against the Franks, Beowulf could very easily have made himself king. But he only helped and guarded the boy king, his cousin, until he died. Then Beowulf ascended the throne in all honour.

For fifty years King Beowulf reigned; and he was a good king, a father to his people and a generous bestower of favours. Then, when he had grown old in years and honours, he entered upon his last adventure.

241

Now, you must know that in those days heroes were interred in great burial mounds, and with them were buried treasures of gold and other precious things. To Beowulf's kingdom there came a monstrous fire-breathing dragon which took up its abode in the richest of the burial mounds, guarding the treasure, but a rash thief one night robbed the dragon of a golden cup. In raging fury the fearsome beast sallied forth to seek revenge with fire and slaughter.

The aged king then roused himself for a final battle, that he might save his people from the fury of the monster. Taking with him eleven of his thanes, he approached the dragon's lair. Challenged by Beowulf, the mighty dragon answered by belching forth flames from the mouth of the cave. The cowardly thanes fled in terror—all but the youngest, Wiglaf, who stood by his lord, affirming loyally that death were better than a life of shame.

Beowulf, as fearless as in the days of his youth, attacked the dragon with his sword. But his strength was not what it had once been, and his blade was turned aside by the scaly armour of the foe. Wiglaf rushed forward to help his lord, and though his shield melted like wax in the dragon's breath, he would not retreat. The dragon seized Beowulf by the throat, but even as he felt his death wound, the king thrust at his foe with his short knife, and at the same moment Wiglaf drove his sword into the creature.

In spite of his advancing age, and the scorching flames that burst from the beast's nostrils, Beowulf bravely fought his last battle, against the terrible dragon which was ravaging his kingdom.

Then Beowulf, with a mighty effort, cut the great dragon in two.

But, alas, the hero had struck his last blow and gained his last victory. He lay panting on the ground—dying.

Beowulf bade Wiglaf bring out the treasure that he might see the wealth he had brought to his people before he died. He commanded that when he was dead a great mound should be made on a promontory overlooking the sea, where it might serve bewildered sailors for a landmark. "So shall it be called in days to come the Mound of Beowulf," he said. Last of all, he gave to his loyal young kinsman his corselet and his helmet and the circlet of gold about his neck as a token that he was to be king.

When he had done these things, Beowulf breathed no more. Wiglaf knelt by him, grieving bitterly for the fallen hero.

So it came about that a great mound was raised on a promontory overlooking the sea, and on it was built a mighty funeral pyre. On the pyre the sorrowing warriors hung helmets and bucklers and bright coats of mail. Within the mound, together with the ashes of the heroic dead, they would later lay the dragon's treasure, deeming it too sacred to be used in any other way.

Sadly they laid the body of the hero on the funeral pyre. The fire was lighted and the dense smoke rose up, and the sound of the crackling flames mingled weirdly with the unrestrained weeping of the host of mourners.

Many early peoples had marriage customs that seem very strange to us to-day. This modern picture, called "The Babylonian Marriage Market," illustrates the old Babylonian custom of selling wives—though in later days the "bride price" was handed on to the bride by her father. A father had complete control over his children until they married. He married them to whom he pleased; he could even sell them if he chose. Yet the position of women in ancient Babylon was much better than in other countries at that time.

BABYLON *the* GREAT

The Story of the Wonderful Empires of Babylonia and Assyria, and of Their Speedy Fall

THERE are some words that seem to cast a spell. The sound of them stirs in us all sorts of dim pictures and powerful feelings. Often it is not easy to say just what it is that they make us feel and see; but, nevertheless, we suddenly find ourselves awake in a world that has unexpectedly turned very beautiful and romantic. Now one of these magical words is "Babylon." Few people know much about this ancient city's history. Probably many of us have rather a hazy notion as to where it was built. And yet poets and preachers and painters all use the word because of its amazing power over our minds. What has made the name of that ancient city into a kind of spell?

The story of Babylon (băb'ĭ-lŏn) really begins about 3000 B.C. with a little mud village on the banks of the Euphrates (ū-frā'tēz) River not far from Akkad (ăk'ăd). We may remember Akkad as the home of the great Sargon, who was not only the king of Akkad and Sumer (sū'mĕr), but the ruler of several other countries in addition.

The village of Babylon, which was inhabited by Semites (sĕm'ĭt), a race to which the Hebrews belonged, was not of any importance until the Semitic (sĕ-mĭt'ĭk) tribe called the Amorites (ăm'ŏ-rīt) came there to live about 2200 B.C. The Amorites quickly made Babylon greater and more powerful, and their kings ruled more and more cities until, in about 2100 B.C., there came to the throne a very interesting and mighty king called Hammurabi (hăm'ōō-rä'bē), who made Babylonia (băb'ĭ-lō'nĭ-ȧ) the ruler of all the countries round about. Because he did so many important things, we shall begin our story of Babylonia with Hammurabi, the first great law-maker in history.

Long before peoples grow civilized, they begin to make rules or laws to keep men from doing harm to one another. In old Sumeria the kings were the judges and lawyers, as well as the priests; and we have to-day some of the laws they made and wrote down on their clay tablets. But from the day of Hammurabi there has come down to us a whole collection of laws, the first code in history.

This collection of laws was written—or rather carved—not on soft clay, as were other records of his time, but on a great pillar of hard black stone called diorite (dī′ō-rīt). The pillar is nearly eight feet high, and at the top of it is a picture of Hammurabi receiving his laws from the Babylonian sun-god Shamash (shä′măsh). The writing extends round and round the pillar, and there is thus a great deal of it. This pillar of laws was discovered a long distance from Babylon, which shows how widely the laws of Hammurabi were read and obeyed.

Babylon Four Thousand Years Ago

Besides this code of Hammurabi's laws, we have to-day a collection of fifty-five of his letters, written on clay tablets in the Babylonian language. One of the letters is an order to clear the Euphrates River, which had been blocked up by a flood. Another was written to a man who was in

Thousands of years ago the temple of which this is a model was built in Babylon, and groups of worshippers came and went just as they are doing here. It must have seemed an enormous building to the men of that day, for it was 300 feet high! In plan it was very much like the temples of the earlier Sumerians, whom the Babylonians copied in matters of art.

trouble because he had to attend to two things on the same day—a case in a law court and a religious feast. Hammurabi orders the judge to put off the lawsuit to another time.

Through the letters and laws of Hammurabi we can form a very good picture of what life was like in Babylon over four thousand years ago. We know that women led a very free life and often managed a business or worked for pay, just as did men. The law insisted on justice for the poor widow or for children whose parents were dead.

Perhaps you have read in the Bible about the rule of "an eye for an eye, and a tooth for a tooth." This was the crude notion of justice in the time of Hammurabi. If a man put out another man's eye, whether or not he meant to do it, he must have his own eye put out. And sometimes the rule was even harsher. For instance, if a mud house fell down and happened to kill one man's child, then the child of the man who owned the house might be put to death, even though he had done nothing at all to deserve such a cruel punishment. So we may see that although many of the laws of Hammurabi were very wise, some of them were harsh and absurd.

School Days in Babylon

Boys and girls of Hammurabi's time could go to school just as they do now. But it was much harder to learn to write in the

When Nineveh fell, the king of Assyria set fire to his palace and ended his life in the midst of the flames.

Babylonian cuneiform (kū-nē′ĭ-fôrm) than it is in our own alphabet. For in cuneiform there was a separate sign for every syllable, so that altogether there were about 350 signs to learn. Imagine having 350 hard letters instead of the twenty-six we now learn when we first go to school.

The men who dig up the history of those old countries have found a Babylonian schoolroom of Hammurabi's time, quite complete and showing just how children studied in those days of long ago. Of course, the children had no paper or pencil. Instead, there was a basket of wet clay near the door, and the boy or girl would take a handful and make his own little mud pie on which to write. If he wrote something wrong, he could take a ruler and smooth over the top of the mud pie; then it would be all clear and ready to write on once more. When he finished, he could let the mud pie harden into a tablet, which might even last to our own day.

The writing tool was called a stylus (stī′lŭs), and was made of a reed from the river. One end of it was left round, and the other was whittled to an edge a little like that of a screw-driver. With the round end the child could write down numbers, for these were round marks; with the other end he could put down the marks that made up words.

Learning to Write on Clay

The little Babylonian used to prepare his mud tablet, and then with his reed stylus he would make rows of wedge-shaped marks on it, some up and down, some across and some slanting. He would continue in this way until he could make the wedges well, and then he would be allowed to put the separate wedges together to form letters. To encourage him the teacher might quote a Babylonian proverb or wise saying: "He who is best in tablet writing shall shine like the sun."

Another important advance in Hammurabi's reign was the taming of the horse. The Babylonians did not themselves tame wild horses for use, but they imported them from the mountains to the northeast of Babylonia, and for this reason they called their new creature "the animal of the mountains." The horse was brought down into civilized regions by a wild mountain tribe of men called Kassites, who had themselves received it from other lands to the eastward.

Why was the horse so important for civilization? Already men had donkeys, bullocks, and camels to haul and carry things, to plough, and to ride. But none of these animals could go so fast as the horse. The horse was to the patient donkey what the aeroplane is to the train. He could be harnessed to light chariots for racing or fighting. He could overtake an enemy or help his master to escape from a strong foe. He could draw or carry like the donkey, plough like the ox, and run much faster than either. The horse was therefore a great addition to civilization, and he first galloped into history

The chief god in ancient Babylonia was Shamash, the sun-god, whom you see seated above at the right. In his right hand he holds a staff and circle, emblems of his authority, and on the altar before him is the sun disk, which two attendants are holding up by ropes. Three worshippers are standing in front of the altar, and over them is an inscription which says, "Image of the sun-god, the great lord, who dwells in the temple Ebabbara in Sippar." It was in the ruins of ancient Sippar that this alabaster tablet was found. In that city was built the most magnificent of all the temples of Shamash; it was named Ebabbara, or "the shining house." Because the sun drives away darkness people came to think that Shamash could right wrongs, so he became the god of justice, and could release people from bodily suffering. Hammurabi says that it was Shamash who inspired him to put forth his famous code of laws.

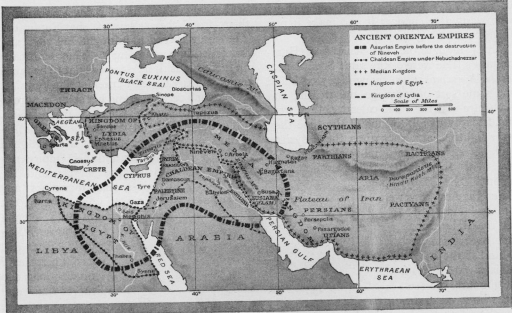

This is the great empire over which the Assyrians ruled. You will notice that it includes all the Fertile Crescent, along which the cities and towns are mostly scattered, and that it also includes the northern part of the Desert of Arabia, to the south. Much of that district was covered with grass during the rainy season, and so supported wandering tribes who obtained a very precarious living by pasturing their flocks and herds.

about 2000 B.C., in the Babylonian kingdom of Hammurabi.

The country which Hammurabi called Babylonia included all Sumer and the land just above Sumer along the Two Rivers— the land where stood the towns of Akkad and Babylon, the capital city of all Babylonia. The old Sumerians (sū-mē′rĭ-ăn) had by now almost disappeared. Their language was no longer spoken or written, and they had so intermixed with the Semites that the two had become one people.

The Kassites' Bad Government

The Kassite tribes who brought the horse to the streets of Babylon saw the riches of this old country and decided to rule it if they could. They did manage to seize the power and govern the country soon after the end of Hammurabi's forty-two-year reign, but their rule was a bad thing for Babylonia. The Kassites were not really civilized people, and they did not know how to govern as Hammurabi had done. They did not care about maintaining the canals and seeing that the laws were properly administered. So the Babylonians were far less happy and prosperous under the new government.

For many hundreds of years after the Kassites seized Babylonia there is little of importance to tell. The people cared less for learning, and left fewer records; and the laws were not so well made or obeyed. Indeed, Babylonia did not write the next chapter in history. She left that to the Assyrians, a people who lived very near, north-westward and upstream along the Tigris River. Do you see how history is broadening and spreading out? First we have only Sumeria, and next Akkad, very near at hand; then Sumeria and Akkad together take the name of Babylonia; and now another neighbouring kingdom, Assyria, comes into view.

A City Between Three Fires

Assyria (ă-sĭr′ĭ-ă) is named after its chief city, Assur. The Semitic people from the desert were living in this town of Assur at about the time when the Amorites came into Babylon (2200 B.C.), but for many hundreds of years Assur was only a small place and by no means strong or rich. In those early days Assur was only about half a mile across, and it was always having to fight off enemies who wanted to conquer it and make it pay them taxes every year.

Even though the Babylonians of Hammurabi's time were of the same Semitic race as the Assyrians; even though they both had the same sort of language and writing and sculpture and the same calendar, they were not friendly at all. Much of the time they were fighting, and very often the Assyrians had to defend the mud-brick walls of their little town against the Babylonians. Often the Assyrians were beaten and had to let the Babylonians rule over them.

And if the Babylonians were bad neighbours, the people who lived to the north and west were much worse. These were wild Hittites from the mountains and from the shores of the Mediterranean Sea. These Hittites would every now and then march through the farming country around Assur and drive the Assyrians out of their fields. They conquered the city of Assur again and again, and held it until they were driven out by the Babylonians.

This lion was unearthed in the ruins of ancient Babylon, where its sturdy strength delighted the hearts of a warlike people.

Why the Assyrians Took Up Arms

After a few hundred years of this sort of thing, the Assyrians became expert fighters. Every boy had to be a soldier, trained to defend his home against the enemy from one side or another. And when people once learn to fight well, they often learn to love fighting.

Perhaps, if the Assyrians had been left alone they would not have grown so warlike. They loved to plough their fields and raise their sheep and goats. But when bands of soldiers kept invading their country to kill the farmers and to steal the sheep and goats, it is no wonder that the Assyrians took to arms and put their trust in war: until by about 1300 B.C. the peaceful Assyrian farmers had turned into terrible warriors.

First they beat the Hittites and drove them from the valley of the Euphrates. Then they turned and fought Babylon, and succeeded in conquering it. They had made up their minds that Assur was not to be taken and taxed any more by cruel foreign kings. It was Assur's turn now, and her soldiers were to go out and conquer all the cities around them.

The victories and conquests of the Assyrians were the greatest that the world had seen so far, and their empire grew to be the largest and the most magnificent of any up to that time, except perhaps the empire of Thutmose III in Egypt. But did their conquests last? Assur was long ago a heap of ruins, and the Assyrian empire was soon to be only a memory. Another empire, started in peace at this very time, lasted much longer; and before you hear of the Assyrian victories you may care to learn something of this peaceful conquest.

The conquest was made by another Semitic desert people called the Arameans (ăr′ă-mē′ăn). Their language was called Aramaic (ăr′ă-mā′ĭk), and it was the very language which Jesus and his disciples later spoke in Galilee. The Arameans came out of the Arabian desert and settled the country from Damascus to the Red Sea, a country later called Syria. Syria was a very different country from Assyria, and the Syrians, or Arameans, very different from the warlike Assyrians of whom we were telling just now.

The Wandering Arameans

The Arameans were in some ways like the Jews of our modern world. They were found among the Hittites, among the Assyrians, the Babylonians, and all the other old peoples. They were great traders and business men, and their language could be heard in many different countries, wherever

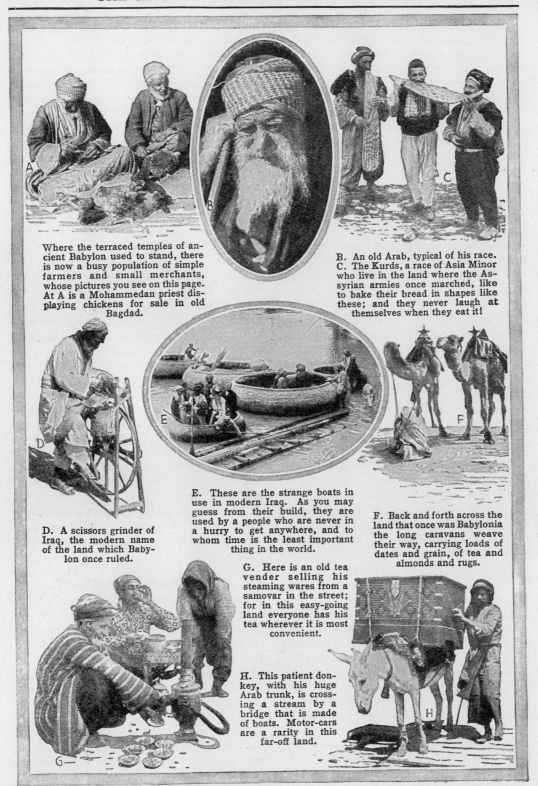

Where the terraced temples of ancient Babylon used to stand, there is now a busy population of simple farmers and small merchants, whose pictures you see on this page. At A is a Mohammedan priest displaying chickens for sale in old Bagdad.

B. An old Arab, typical of his race.
C. The Kurds, a race of Asia Minor who live in the land where the Assyrian armies once marched, like to bake their bread in shapes like these; and they never laugh at themselves when they eat it!

D. A scissors grinder of Iraq, the modern name of the land which Babylon once ruled.

E. These are the strange boats in use in modern Iraq. As you may guess from their build, they are used by a people who are never in a hurry to get anywhere, and to whom time is the least important thing in the world.

F. Back and forth across the land that once was Babylonia the long caravans weave their way, carrying loads of dates and grain, of tea and almonds and rugs.

G. Here is an old tea vender selling his steaming wares from a samovar in the street; for in this easy-going land everyone has his tea wherever it is most convenient.

H. This patient donkey, with his huge Arab trunk, is crossing a stream by a bridge that is made of boats. Motor-cars are a rarity in this far-off land.

trading was carried on. It grew to be very useful for a business man to know the Aramaic language; and since this language was simple and easy to learn, it gradually became a sort of international speech from Egypt in the south to Persia in the north.

The Aramean traders had a great deal of writing to do and many accounts to keep. As clay tablets and cuneiform writing were clumsy and awkward, the Arameans borrowed pen and paper from the Egyptians, and an alphabet from the Phoenicians (fē-nǐsh'ăn), and they taught their sensible and easy ways of writing to the people in the countries where they lived. They spread their alphabet until it was known as far as India in the East and Greece in the West. And it is that very same alphabet which has come down to us and is used to-day.

Proud Damascus

The Arameans never fought if they could avoid it. They always preferred trade to war; but when they had to fight, they were so clever that they learnt to be skilful soldiers. One of their cities, Damascus (dă-măs'kŭs), stood for four hundred years unconquered, while all the other cities around bowed to the Assyrian yoke. Indeed, Damascus is still a Syrian, or Aramaic, city.

But while the Arameans were making their way peacefully, the Assyrians were conquering the world with the sword. And how did they do it? What was it that made the Assyrian armies so terrible in warfare?

First of all, the Assyrian generals made huge machines to use against the city walls in other lands. These machines must have been something like a tank, a steam shovel, a battering ram, and a pile driver, all in one. They were great towers with smaller towers at the top where soldiers could stand and shoot at the men within the town. They had great rams, or arms, which were banged against the brick walls of the towns and battered them to pieces. Few city walls could stand against an attack from the Assyrian war machines.

Secondly, the Assyrians learned from the Hittites to make strong, hard swords and other weapons out of iron. Before this, swords had been made of bronze, a very much softer metal, and most of the old countries still used bronze for swords. An iron sword could cut right through a bronze one.

Thirdly, the Assyrians succeeded in making other people very much afraid of them, and when you are afraid of an enemy he can conquer you far more easily than if you are without fear. The Assyrians had several ways of making people fear them; they did it with their machines and swords, but most of all by their cruelty. They were as cruel soldiers as the world has ever seen. It is not pleasant even to tell of the horrible things they did to their beaten foes, while they were still a living, conquering people. We may be thankful that no Assur exists in the world to-day.

It took Assyria many centuries to grow big and strong enough to conquer what was then thought to be the world, but when Damascus fell, in 732 B.C., the path was open southward and westward for the Assyrian armies, and they swept onward.

The first great war lord of Assyria was Sargon II (722–705 B.C.). That was not his real name, nor was he a king by birth. But when he seized the throne he took the name of that first great Sargon who had ruled Akkad about two thousand years before. Sargon used some of the taxes and plunder which he wrung from unhappy peoples to build himself a magnificent palace near Nineveh (nǐn'ĕ-vĕ). To erect this palace Sargon brought craftsmen from Phoenicia or even from far-away Egypt, for the Assyrians were by no means such good artists as they were soldiers.

Great Babylon Falls at Last

The son of Sargon was Sennacherib (705–681 B.C.). When Babylon tried to revolt against the cruel rule of Assyria, Sennacherib (sĕ-năk'ĕr-ĭb) totally destroyed the old city. His soldiers killed every human being there, battered down the houses, and turned a canal over the ruins. Babylon the great was fallen indeed.

Under Sargon, Sennacherib, and the warrior kings who followed them, war was the main business of the Assyrian state. It was a profitable business, too. Caravans from all the world brought rich trains of tribute to Nineveh, the capital of Assyria, and much valuable plunder was taken in war. Even the Greek cities along the Ionian coast paid tribute to Assyria. All the "Fertile Crescent" was under the Assyrian sway.

The Assyrian kings even wanted to rule Egypt, and Sennacherib sent a vast army to fight the old country along the Nile. In order to reach Egypt the Assyrian army had to pass through Palestine, where the Hebrews were living. You may read in the Bible, and in a famous poem by Byron, the story of what happened. One night the Assyrian host was in camp; the next morning it was gone, its soldiers killed by a terrible plague. But later an Assyrian army did conquer Egypt for a time, and the Egyptians were forced to pay tribute to their conquerors.

One interesting thing the Assyrians did was to build up a post-office system with a regular service of messengers. This post-office went on working for centuries, and some of the clay letters it delivered are in our museums to-day. The Assyrian kings also built up a library of 22,000 clay books. But their works of peace were few beside the sufferings which the Assyrian armies brought upon the world of their time.

With all their fierce fighting and their cruel armies, the Assyrians could not keep their hold upon the lands they conquered. The peoples who had to pay such heavy taxes could not be expected to enjoy their burdens. They revolted again and again, and the Assyrian army had to be increased.

At last there were not enough Assyrians to make up an army large enough, and Hittites and Arameans and other peoples were enlisted as soldiers. But such soldiers were listless fighters, and not so faithful as the Assyrian soldiers had been.

Besides these troubles, savage tribes were beating down upon Assyria from both sides. The Medes and the Persians were attacking from the north, and tribes of fierce desert men called Kaldi from the south. With their farms deserted, their troops unfed, their armies full of foreign soldiers in revolt, the Assyrians saw their war machine weakening and breaking. It was ready to be scrapped when it was scarcely 130 years old. It had grown too big to hold together or to save.

Downfall of Assyria

When the Kaldi, whom we call Chaldeans (kăl-dē'ăn), attacked the city of Nineveh with the help of the Persians, it fell, in 612 B.C., and its fall was the signal for a song of rejoicing from the Nile River, throughout Asia Minor, to the islands of Greece. It was more like a collapse than a mere fall. Assyria simply went to pieces, and her cruel power vanished like smoke. For centuries it had been growing, but in a few brief years it disappeared.

And then the story of history returns for a little while to Babylon, that very Babylon which the Assyrian Sennacherib had so utterly destroyed, but which the Chaldeans were soon busily engaged in rebuilding and making the head of an empire.

Not far from the site of the ancient and magnificent city of Babylon, now just a heap of ruins, stands this interesting building.

Here dark-eyed Arabs come and go, unaware of the echoes from the romantic past, whose relics lie all around them.

Our crane has quite a difficult decision to make. The wolf has been unfortunate enough to get a bone in his throat, and he is pleading with the crane to put his bill down his throat and get it out. What did the crane do?

TANSY and BOBBLES on FABLE ISLAND

Would You Help a Wolf in Distress?   And How Exciting Do You Think it Would be to Go for a Ride on a Goat?

(CONTINUED FROM PAGE 184)

"WHAT can be the matter with the wolf?" cried Bobbles.

Something indeed was the matter, for the wolf was dancing round in the greatest agony.

"Help! Help!" he gasped. But every animal ran away, and none would help.

"What's wrong?" asked Tansy.

"A bone in my throat!" gasped the wolf. "Oh! Oh!"

"Drink at the pond and wash it down," suggested Bobbles.

The wolf thought this a good idea and made for the pond. But, alas, he couldn't drink, and seeing a crane watching him, he pleaded piteously for help.

"You shall have a great reward," he added.

At that the crane, thinking of his wife and family, decided to do the kindness and earn the reward.

So he came close up to the wolf, thrust his head down his throat, and with his long bill pulled out the bone.

"That's better!" gasped the wolf.

"And now the reward," said the crane, eagerly.

"No, indeed!" cried the wolf, pretending to be greatly astonished. "It is reward enough to have put your head into a wolf's mouth and got it out again safely!" and away he ran.

"The vile cheat!" squawked the crane. "I wish I'd never done him the kindness."

"Booh!" said Bobbles.

"You saw what I did and what the wolf did?" demanded the crane, angrily.

"We saw it all," said the fairies. "The wolf was a horrible cheat, but my father says a kindness is no kindness if it is done for a reward."

"Come on!" said Tansy, pulling at Bobbles. "Let's fly off and see what the wolf does next."

Now the wolf, free from the agony in his throat, began to think of his dinner, and as he looked about him he saw a goat feeding high up among a mass of rocks.

"Come down here, my dear goat!" he cried in his sweetest tones; "the grass is far richer and sweeter in the valley."

But Bobbles and Tansy were determined that the wolf shouldn't cheat a second time that day. So they showed themselves to the goat and told him that he mustn't be so silly as to go down to the wolf.

"Be very polite," said Tansy, "but don't go down."

So the goat also put on his sweetest voice and cried, "My lord Wolf! I pray you to excuse me. But I suspect that it is not my dinner of grass you are thinking of in particular, but your dinner of goat's meat that you want."

"I see you—you troublesome fairies!" cried the wolf wrathfully. "You're always at the bottom of mischief."

"Don't mind what he says!" cried the goat. "Jump on my back, and I'll give you the finest ride you've ever had."

So Tansy and Bobbles climbed astride him and held on to his coat—for what a ride it was! All joggles and jumps, upwards and downwards and never once straight. Tansy

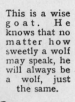

This is a wise goat. He knows that no matter how sweetly a wolf may speak, he will always be a wolf, just the same.

and Bobbles enjoyed every minute of it; for to ride on a goat among the rocks is great fun.

One beautiful moonlight night Tansy and Bobbles were strolling through the woods with Father Fairy when they noticed a dog trotting happily along with a cock perched on his shoulders.

"Don't they look funny," said Tansy. "See!" said Bobbles. "They're off to bed."

And sure enough, the cock flew up into a tree and the dog lay down below, wriggling himself round and round until he felt himself quite comfortable for a night's rest.

"What queer things the Fable Island animals do," said Tansy. "I wish, father, that you'd give us a treat to-morrow and spend the day with us."

"Perhaps I'd better come," said Father Fairy, with a jolly laugh, "or you two will be learning so much that you'll be leaving your father and mother behind."

So early next morning Father Fairy went

off with the children to find out the meaning of things for himself.

They hadn't gone very far before they heard a tremendous crowing.

"That's the cock waking up the dog," said Tansy. "Do let's see them start off on their travels."

"Wait!" whispered Bobbles, for just at that moment a large red fox stopped by the tree, having decided that the cock would make a sumptuous breakfast for his family.

He waited a moment, and then cried out, "Good morning, my handsome bird! Thou art useful indeed, with thy voice. Come down to me, and we will sing together our morning service."

"I do hope he won't come down," whispered Tansy, anxiously.

But she need not have been afraid, for the cock had seen the fox more than once waiting outside the farmyard. So he answered merrily:

"We can't sing our service together until the sexton has rung the bell. Go and call him! You will find him just round the trunk of this tree."

The boar was very fortunate to escape from the hounds which attacked him, and he determined that he would be more cautious in future.

The fox was rather puzzled, but he wanted the cock for breakfast so badly that he ventured round the tree.

But, alas for him! The dog sprang up and killed the fox on the spot.

"Beware, my children," said Father Fairy, "of laying traps to injure others. Who knows but that you may be caught yourselves?"

Just then their attention was attracted by a tremendous hullabaloo, as the huntsmen and hounds came hurrying after a fierce wild boar.

The foremost hound seized the boar by the ear; but, being old and feeble, he was forced to let go, and the boar escaped.

"You miserable old hound!" cried the huntsman, turning savagely to his faithful dog.

"Yes, yes, I know I'm an old hound! That is why my strength failed me. But can't you remember what I once was, and not scorn me for what I am now—grown old in faithful service to you?"

"Yes, indeed!" said Father Fairy sternly. "I shall take your hound from you, and he shall end his days in peace with me."

The huntsman was so amazed at seeing Father Fairy and his children that he couldn't think of a single word to say.

But the old hound staggered up with his tail wagging, and let Tansy put an arm about his neck and lead him away.

Tansy and Bobbles were not going to let their father go until he had been with them a whole day. During the afternoon they heard a tremendous croaking, as though all the frogs were talking at once.

"What can they be doing making all that noise, father?" asked Tansy.

"Well, my dear," he said, "I understand that the frogs have been discontented for a long time, and I have no doubt that they are holding a council."

Neither Tansy nor Bobbles was quite sure what a council was, but they didn't like to ask their father too many questions, for fear he would get tired of them and want to go home.

Evidently a council meant a great deal of chattering, and as they drew nearer, the fairies could distinguish the words that the frogs were all croaking together.

"My lord Jupiter! My lord Jupiter! Give us a king! Give us a king!"

Then, before their eyes, Jupiter descended from the sky and stood by the pond.

"Give us a king! Give us a king!" screamed the excited frogs.

The fairies noticed that Jupiter laughed

The sly old fox is hoping for a nice meal, but there is a very unwelcome surprise in store for him. Wily Reynard had thought to lay a very clever trap for the cock up in the tree, but the tables were turned on him nicely.

as he stooped and threw a mighty log into the pond.

"There is your king!" he cried, and suddenly he vanished.

The frogs swarmed round the log, and presently some of them made bold to spring upon it and dance.

"The log is rather a funny kind of king," remarked Tansy.

"Wait! Wait!" said Father Fairy.

Now as the frogs found that the log never moved and did nothing either to help them or to hinder them, they set up another wild clamouring.

"My lord Jupiter! My lord Jupiter! Send us a more active king!"

So Jupiter appeared again, and again he laughed at them.

"You want a more active king, do you? He is coming towards you now!" and Jupiter disappeared.

In another moment there arrived a great stork with a crown on his head, who cried, "Behold me! I am your king!"

Then he straightway waded into the pond and began gobbling up the frogs as fast as ever he could.

"Oh! how could Jupiter be so unkind!" cried Tansy.

"They must be punished for their folly," said Father Fairy. "Why couldn't they be contented with their natural conditions?"

But neither Tansy nor Bobbles could bear to see the frogs being gobbled up, so they cried to Jupiter to have mercy on the silly animals.

Then Jupiter appeared again, and smiled a wonderful smile as Tansy and Bobbles flew up to him and laid their hands gently on his arms.

"Do, do save the rest of the poor frogs!" they pleaded.

"Very well," said Jupiter. "I will grant your request because I respect your father and mother, and because I like the way in which you are finding out the meaning of things."

So Jupiter called to the stork and told him to take off his crown at once, and instructed him to keep away from their pond in future.

(CONTINUED ON PAGE 347)

These two apprehensive-looking frogs are now wishing that they had been contented with their natural conditions

The butterflies shown here are *Vanessa antiopa*, popularly called Camberwell beauty (top left corner), *Precis octavia* (top right corner), *Agrias claudia godmani* (bottom left corner), *Papilio childrenae* (bottom right corner), *Caligo eurylochus* (centre), *Evenus regalis* (above), *Heodes dispar* (left) and *Argynnis lathonia*, popularly known as the Queen of Spain fritillary (right). The butterfly in the centre of the page is called an owl butterfly, and if you turn the page upside down you will see why.

While he ladles the honey out of the honeycomb, the bee is hard at work storing it up again in those little six-sided wells that it makes out of wax and fits together so neatly. As soon as a well is full it is sealed up as closely as if it had been made all in one piece, and so the precious honey inside keeps in perfect condition.

INSECTS ARMED *With* STINGS

Carpenters, Masons, Miners and Skilled Workers of Many Sorts, the Bees and Wasps All Carry Concealed Weapons

(CONTINUED FROM PAGE 173)

WHEN the winter comes, the insects vanish. Where have they gone? Are they all dead? When summer comes again, will there be no flies or bees in the land? Of course there will; as soon as the warm days arrive, there will be just as many as ever there were, flying and buzzing about.

A great many of the insects die as soon as wintry weather sets in; but some of the hardier ones live through the winter, tucked away in sheltered corners or buried under heaps of rubbish where the frost and bitter wind cannot harm them. A good many spend the cold months of the year sleeping in their cocoons or chrysalis cases, and do not change into perfect insects until the first warm days of spring. And there are heaps of eggs, lying in all sorts of safe places, from which new armies of grubs and caterpillars will hatch out as soon as the fresh green leaves and young shoots appear upon the plants and trees.

So the first days of spring are exciting days. All Nature's children begin to stir themselves and wake up after their long winter sleep.

From under a pile of dry moss, where she has been hiding all the winter, a big black and gold bumble-bee crawls out into the sunshine. Her wings feel stiff and cramped, and she is weak and feeble, poor thing, for she has had nothing to eat since last autumn. But a little rest and a sun bath revive her. She soon cheers up and begins to make her toilet, carefully combing her soft silky hair with the claws on her hind legs, and cleaning and smoothing her delicate wings. Before long she feels able to take some exercise, and so sets off for a short trial flight.

When a Bee Goes House Hunting

At first the bee enjoys a little holiday. She just potters about, visiting the newly-opened flowers, sipping the honey and taking a good look round. She has a big task before her; so she wisely waits for a while until she has regained her strength and is fit to begin her work; but she wastes no time. In a day or two she is bustling about, poking her head into every little hole, pushing her way underneath tufts of grass and examining the ground in every direction, just as if she were looking for something. And so she is. She is house hunting—looking hard for a convenient hole where she may start a home.

If she discovers a deserted mouse hole or a roomy burrow that once belonged to a mole, she will probably take possession of it. But she is very fussy, and if she cannot find an empty house to suit her, she starts digging the foundations of one for herself— under a patch of moss or on a soft bank overgrown with wild plants, where she is well hidden while she is at work.

When her house is ready, she proceeds to furnish it. Backwards and forwards she flies, fetching little bundles of moss, fragments of

This fearsome-looking monster is only a queen bumble-bee as she appears to one of her sisters when they meet face to face.

grass, and fine rootlets. These she dumps on the floor, pulling and tearing the stuff with her strong jaws and sturdy legs to make it soft and comfortable.

Furnishing the Nursery

When she has filled the house with this material, she hollows out a snug little chamber in the middle of the mass. Then

off she goes again to collect honey and pollen, which she brings home and works into a thick, sweet paste.

On the top of the honey she now deposits a few eggs. Then she builds a circular wall of soft beeswax round them, and shuts them in with a neat little lid.

By this time Mrs. Bee must be getting rather tired—but her labours are by no means ended yet. She makes two or three more honey cakes, lays a cluster of eggs on each, and shuts them up in a waxen cell.

Honey for a Rainy Day

Her next care is to gather and store provision for rainy days, or for days when she has so much to do that she cannot possibly leave home. She makes one or two good-sized wax tubs and fills them with honey; then she takes a little rest, sitting on the top of the cells like a brooding hen, so that the warmth from her small body may help to hatch the eggs.

The eggs in the cells soon hatch, and the baby bees find themselves in a neat little nursery. And oh, joy! the floor is actually made of sweet, delicious food. The lucky little things have nothing to do but eat and sleep and eat again.

They are queer little creatures, these bee babies—not a bit like mother. They are tiny white legless grubs, unable to do anything but suck up the food their thoughtful mother has provided for them. She knows when her babies are hatched; and to make sure they have enough to eat, she goes round from time to time and pours a kind of infants' food made of honey and pollen through a small hole in the roof of the nursery.

In about a week's time the bee babies have grown so large and fat that they can eat no more, and each one is sitting in a hole in the honey-cake floor which it has scooped out as it fed. Now the little grubs spin cocoons of white silk, and in these dainty cradles they rest while they are being changed into grown-up bees.

Mother bee is most excited when at last she hears her children moving about in the nursery. She hastens to scrape away the wax that shuts them in and prepares to welcome them.

The new bees are very much like their queen mother, but they are smaller and are called "worker bees." Very trim and smart they look in their fresh, velvety suits of black and orange — after they have once brushed their coats and smoothed the crumples out of their gauzy wings.

The bees have four wings; and on each hind wing is a row of tiny hooks that fasten into a fold on the lower edges of the upper pair. So when a bee flies, the two wings are joined together. This gives the insect a much stronger, swifter flight. The bee needs strong wings to carry her long distances through the air, as she often has to travel for many miles in her search for honey and pollen.

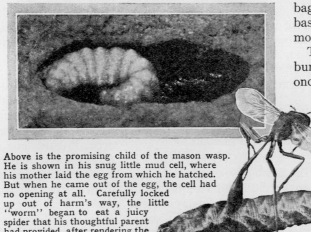

Above is the promising child of the mason wasp. He is shown in his snug little mud cell, where his mother laid the egg from which he hatched. But when he came out of the egg, the cell had no opening at all. Carefully locked up out of harm's way, the little "worm" began to eat a juicy spider that his thoughtful parent had provided, after rendering the creature unconscious by a skilful stab of her sting. In a state of coma the spider lived on in the cell, and all through the autumn, winter and spring the greedy larva continued to eat it, and grew and grew until he was old enough to turn into a fully-fledged wasp. Then he bored his way through his mud prison and came out into the world.

This wasp knows at just what spot to insert her fatal sting in order to paralyse but not to kill the caterpillar. As soon as it ceases to wriggle she will drag it down into her nest, where it will furnish fresh meat for her baby to feed on.

The Bumble-bee's Market Basket

In every way the hard-working bumble-bee is fitted for her busy life. She has a sucking tube to draw up the nectar from the flowers, and a honey bag in her throat in which to carry it home. A strong pair of jaws helps her to bite and mould the wax and building material, and bunches of bristles on all her six legs act as brushes and combs. Her broad hind legs are hollowed out like spoons and fringed with many rows of stiff hairs. They make excellent baskets in which to carry home the pollen when the bee goes marketing. Besides all these tools she has a splendid pair of eyes with which to see; a pair of sensitive feelers on the top of her head with which she touches and inspects everything that comes her way; and, to defend herself, a sharp sting like a bladed sword, with a poison bag at the base to make it more deadly.

The worker bumble-bees at once set to work to help their mother. They go to fetch provisions; they help in building wax cells and honey tubs; and go round with the infants' food to feed the babies. The queen bee now reaps the reward of all her toil and care. Soon she is surrounded by so many willing workers that she is able to leave all the housework to them and content herself with laying eggs.

Who are the Drones?

So the bumble-bee's family has grown larger and more prosperous as the bright summer days pass by. Then, towards the end of the season, a few young queens, exactly like the mother, come from some of the cocoons; and small drones, which are male bees, also make their appearance in the nest. The drones do no work, but fly about with the young queen bees, enjoying the last few weeks of summer weather.

Soon the days grow short and the nights grow cold. The bees cease working and their cheery buzzing is no longer heard. The first winter frosts kill nearly all the busy workers. The old queen mother and the drones die too, and only a few young queens, who sleep through the winter in some sheltered nook, live until the spring comes round again.

The bumble-bees and the honey-bees, who live in hives and make delicious honey for us, are called "social bees," because large numbers of them live and work together in a friendly, social way. Bees that live alone are called "solitary."

Some Bees are Hermits

Solitary bees are quite as interesting in their ways as are the bumble-bees and the hiving bees. There are hundreds of different kinds to be found all over the world, and many of them make the most wonderful and beautiful nests. There are carpenter bees, mining bees, mason bees, leaf-cutting bees and many others.

The big black carpenter bees, found on the continent of Europe, but not in England, are handsome insects, quite as large as bumble-bees. They have very powerful jaws with saw-like edges, and with these they tunnel into great trees, old decaying stumps, and even into dry gate-posts and fences.

It is the lady carpenter who does the hard work. The male carpenter bee is a lazy fellow who does nothing but enjoy himself. So mother bee has to provide for her family without any help from her mate—which is the usual way in the insect world.

How the Nursery is Made

But Mrs. Carpenter does not worry. She sets to work with a right good will and digs out a long, narrow tunnel, about a foot deep, in the wood. Then she divides her tunnel into a number of separate cells, with thin partitions made from the sawdust and chips of wood she has scraped out and mixed with a kind of glue from her own mouth. In each cell the bee places an egg and a nice big cake of honey and pollen and then she proceeds to seal it up carefully.

Here is a bumble-bee's nest, with one of the bees shown in the oval. Some of the brown cells in the nest have been opened in order that you may see the little white grubs that are curled up inside. Some day they, too, will be bumble-bees. This family of bees, which had built their nest in a squirrel's hole, was made up of ten grown bees, three youngsters just hatched, and those well-fed babies which you can see.

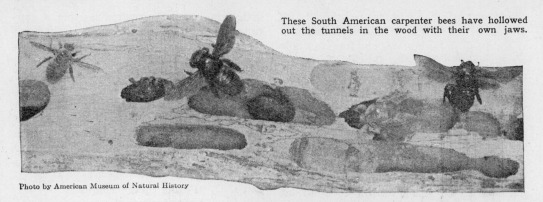

These South American carpenter bees have hollowed out the tunnels in the wood with their own jaws.

Photo by American Museum of Natural History

She makes several of these burrows, each one fitted with about a dozen cells, and then her work is done. She does not wait to see her children, but flies off for her well-earned holiday.

Orphans Locked Up in a Tree

Before long the eggs hatch out and each little bee grub comes out of its shell—to find itself a solitary prisoner shut up in a cell. But the bee grub doesn't mind. It sucks at its cake, and when it has sucked this all away, it spins a cocoon and quietly goes to sleep—to awake in a few short weeks as a splendid carpenter bee.

The bee in the lowest cell is the first one ready to come out—for the egg from which it hatched as a fat little grub was the first one laid by mother bee. It gnaws its way through the floor of its cell and finds itself in a short passage leading to the outside world. At last it is free! One by one the bees in the upper cells now make their escape in the same way. They have only to break through a single thin partition and the way lies open before them.

Entering the World by a Back Door

Don't you think it is clever of mother bee to arrange all these handy little back doors for her children? If she did not do this, and if all the young bees were obliged to leave the burrow by the front entrance, probably none of them would succeed in getting out alive. For those in the lower compartments would have to bite their way through ever so many floors before they reached the top; and in their struggle to get out, they would disturb and hurt all the other poor bees, who would not be ready to leave their cells.

The pretty little blue and green carpenter bees tunnel into twigs, brambles, or any long-stemmed plants that have a soft pith in which it is easy to work. Like the big black carpenter bee, the little mother divides her burrow into a number of separate cells by carefully fitting cross partitions, made from chips of pith, all the way up the hollow shaft.

Good Manners Among the Bees

There are no back doors to these little nests, but the little carpenter bees seem to be so well behaved that they never attempt to push rudely past their younger brothers and sisters. The eldest bee, in the bottom cell, bites a hole in the ceiling and then rests patiently until the next bee is ready to do the same thing. And so they wait politely, one for another, until they are all ready to leave the nest. Then the youngest bee leads the way from the topmost cell, and the others follow in an orderly procession.

Outside the nest, the little bees find their mother ready to welcome them. Instead of flying off as soon as she has sealed up the last cell, like the big carpenter bees, she waits and watches at the top of her nest until her children are grown up. The little family party fly round and enjoy themselves in the sunshine, but they do not spend all their time in idleness. Together the old bee and the young bees set to work to clean out the nest, removing all the broken partitions and making it neat and tidy. Later one of the young bees will take possession of it and fit it up for her own children; but how they decide which is to be the lucky one, nobody can say.

The Clever Leaf-cutting Bee

The stout, fluffy little leaf-cutting bee that we often see bustling about the rose bushes has several interesting tricks. She is a good carpenter and a clever upholsterer, as well as a skilled maker of honey cakes. If she finds a ready-made burrow hollowed out by some other insect, she will take possession of it to save time and trouble; but if not, she will make one for herself.

She bores a long, straight tunnel in a piece of soft wood, rasping away with her jaws and kicking the chips behind her as she goes. Then she walks backwards and pushes all the loose stuff out of the hole.

When her tunnel is finished she bustles away to the nearest rose bush and, using her jaws as a pair of scissors, snips a neat little piece out of one of the green leaves and flies home with it.

All through the hot sunny hours of the day this busy little bee works at top speed, cutting out rose leaves, carrying the tiny scraps home, and stuffing them into her tunnel.

The little leaf-cutting bee is not really as big as this, nor is her dainty little thimble of a nest—which she has been clever enough to make out of a leaf—as large as it is shown in the picture.

When she has collected a little pile of rose-leaf cuttings, the bee stops at home for a time. But she does not rest. She pulls and twists the tiny pieces about with her legs and her jaws until she has made the prettiest little rose-leaf cell imaginable, like a tiny thimble. All the pieces are beautifully fitted together so that they overlap, and each one is fastened with glue from the bee's mouth.

Mother bee uses rather long, oval-shaped pieces of leaf, all the same size, to make her thimble; but when she has half filled it with a soft, pasty honey cake and laid an egg on top, she closes the cell with two or three round pieces which exactly fit the open end of the green thimble.

Filling Up the Tunnel

The bee fills her tunnel with the rose-leaf cells, packing them together one on top of another. She is seldom content with just one burrow, and often makes two or three before she finally ceases from her labours.

Some little leaf-cutters choose the leaves of other plants instead of roses for their thimble cells; and one, the poppy bee, makes hers with little pieces cut from the blooms of scarlet poppies.

Mason bees prefer more solid materials for building. No flimsy rose leaves or poppy petals for them! They make their nests of clay and sand on a firm foundation of rock or stone; or, for even greater safety, they build them in holes in walls, old posts, under the eaves of houses, or inside locks and keyholes.

Several cells are placed side by side like earthen pots or jars; the little mason builds them up, one by one, with tiny pellets of cement made by mixing sand or dry earth and her own natural glue. Using her jaws and her sturdy forelegs as building tools, she pounds and plasters the cement into shape, adding bits of rough gravel or small stones here and there to strengthen the walls of the cell. She carefully smooths the inside of the little pot to make sure there are no rough edges to hurt the tender skin of the little bee grub for whom it is intended. When she has put an egg and a

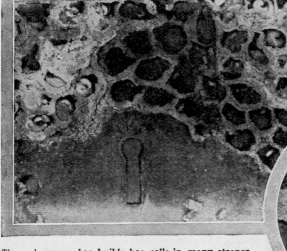

The red mason bee builds her cells in many strange places. Here is a nest built behind a door-lock, and (right) an enlarged view of some cells, showing the bee grubs feeding on their masses of pollen.

supply of food inside the cell, she closes it with a lid of plain cement—without any stones or gravel mixed with it; for the young bee must not be injured when it breaks its way out.

When six or more of these little cells are finished, the mason bee covers them all up with a rough layer of cement. The completed nest is as strong and safe as a fortress, and in appearance resembles a clod of dried mud.

Other Ways of Making Nests

That is how the true mason bees make their nests. Some of their relatives use the gummy resin that oozes from pine trees; others make burrows in the ground, and line them with wool or cotton fibre stripped from the leaves of woolly plants; and one little mason actually uses empty snail shells as nurseries for her babies. There really seems to be no end to the different ways in which these wonderful little solitary bees provide for their children.

There are hundreds of interesting miner bees—some no bigger than flies, others nearly as large as honey-bees. They make their burrows in the ground, often choosing a sandy bank for their mining operations. Although they are called "solitary bees," the little miners are fond of company, and hundreds or thousands live together side by side in underground "towns" and "villages." But each bee in the colony occupies its own home and leaves its neighbours alone. Indeed, it is far too busy to waste time gossiping and playing.

In some of the bee towns every miner has a home of her own, but in others they all live in flats. Each house has a main entrance and a central corridor, which is tunnelled out by several bees working together in friendly fashion, and is the common property of them all. To right and left of the corridor are several passages leading to the private rooms of the bees living in the house. These are entered only by the rightful owners.

Busy Scenes in Bee Town

Miner bees actually live in the burrows, and bring up their children by hand—so to speak—instead of walling them up as do most solitary bees. On a hot sunny day the bee towns hum with life as the busy little inhabitants bustle in and out fetching and carrying food for their young ones at home.

But if the clouds gather in the sky and a few raindrops fall, the cheerful humming ceases. All the little miners hurry indoors, and they will not show a wing above ground until the sun comes out again. To protect their underground towns from being flooded by sudden showers, the wise insects fix funny little crooked chimneys over the entrances to the tunnels. So the rain cannot get in and their houses are always warm and quite dry.

Among all these industrious insects there are a few who do not deserve to be called "busy" bees. They are lazy things who do no work at all; and, more than that, they steal the food and the nests of their hard-working relatives. These are called "cuckoo bees," because, like that bold bird, they make no nests of their own, but expect others to provide for their children.

These cunning paper wasps chose a grey house and then, under the eaves, built themselves a nest out of grey paper, which they have made by chewing up scraps of an old board. No one ever taught them what most of you know—that paper can be made out of wood pulp; but somehow they learned it, many thousands of years ago.

One of these cunning little insects may sometimes be seen loitering about outside the burrow of a leaf-cutting bee. She seems to be examining the flowers near by, or to be busy cleaning her fur coat and her wings. Actually, she is watching the leaf-cutter. When the busy little mother is away from home, cutting out the last small pieces of rose leaves for one of her cells, the sly cuckoo bee slips into the tunnel and lays an egg beside the one already laid in the little green thimble by the rightful owner of the nest. When the leaf-cutter comes back she is in such a hurry to get on with her work that she closes up the cell and never seems to notice the strange egg inside it.

Now, there is not enough food for two in the cell; and the greedy cuckoo grub, either because it hatches first or because it is stronger than its companion, eats nearly all of what there is. So the poor baby leaf-cutter dies of starvation—and it is a cuckoo bee instead that finally comes out of the nest.

Other industrious bees are tricked in the same way by the curious "cuckoos." There is one big lazy bee that actually lives in a bumble-bee's nest. There she lays her eggs and calmly helps herself to food from the honey tubs, without doing anything in return for her board and lodging. She is so like a true bumble-bee in appearance that the busy workers do not seem to notice the stranger among them. Anyhow, the cuckoo bee is not turned out of the nest as she deserves to be.

Wasps are not nearly such popular insects as bees. They look so fierce and carry such horrible little poisoned daggers that many people are terrified by these bold insect warriors in their black and yellow jackets. Yet wasps are really very interesting and busy little insects. To be sure, they are quick-tempered. But they are perfectly harmless if you leave them alone. Wasps will not sting you if you do not frighten them or bother them when they are busy. Even hornets, though they look alarming, are peaceful enough if you don't annoy them.

A City of Industrious Wasps

There are social wasps and solitary wasps —just as there are social and solitary bees. Social wasps make wonderful nests. Some of the nests are so large as to form wasp cities, where thousands of busy workers live together. All through the sunny hours of the summer days constant streams of

This is what a wasp looks like—face to face.

The jaws and other parts of a wasp's mouth have amazing strength, and with them the little creature has to gnaw out and chew up bits of stout wood, to make into paper for her nest. When one thinks of the size of her head, one wonders where she carries the muscles to operate these implements.

Between this wasp's forelegs is stretched a section of a wasp's leg very much enlarged.

Below is a white-faced wasp (magnified) sitting outside its amazing house.

The paper wasp (enlarged) above will not sting you unless you annoy her, but she doesn't like to be disturbed, for she's busy about her nest.

excited "yellow jackets" may be seen bustling in and out of the city gates. These big cities are usually built underground or inside an old hollow tree; but smaller nests, in which little family parties live together, are often hung from the branches of trees or under the eaves of an outbuilding.

The First Paper-makers

Every nest, large or small, is started by a queen wasp who has managed to live through the winter. Alone, she chooses her building-site and lays the foundation of her home. Her first care is to build a few brood cells. These

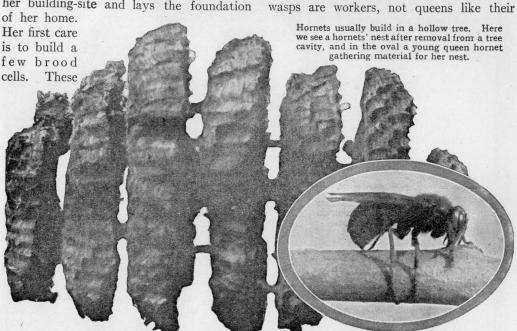

Hornets usually build in a hollow tree. Here we see a hornets' nest after removal from a tree cavity, and in the oval a young queen hornet gathering material for her nest.

as well as paper to make and cells to build. She must go out hunting, too, for the wasp babies need fresh meat if they are to grow up into strong, healthy yellow jackets. So mother wasp darts out of the nest, chasing and catching flies, tearing off their wings and heads and feet, and making them into a kind of fly mash for her young ones.

In a few weeks she is surrounded by many willing helpers. She ought to be very glad to see the first young yellow jackets break through their cocoons! The new wasps are workers, not queens like their

she makes, not of wax, but of paper— and she also makes the paper itself, out of chips of wood torn from an old dry fence or tree stump. She takes tiny fragments in her mouth and gnaws and chews them into a soft pulpy mass that she can easily mould into shape. When it is dry, it makes a kind of tough, waterproof paper. Then the wasp lays her eggs in the cells, which hang downwards from the roof of the nest under a protecting cover like a small paper umbrella. She goes on making more cells and laying more eggs until the first brood of tiny wasp grubs is hatched.

And then the queen wasp has to work harder than ever. She has babies to feed,

mother; and they do not lay eggs, although they share in all the other work of the wasp city. They make paper, build cells, hunt flies, and feed the babies, who open their tiny round mouths like young birds when the nurses come round with their food.

What Happens to Wasps in Autumn

So day by day the city grows, and the workers are kept busy from morning until night. Then, towards the end of the summer, they build some very big cells in which to rear the drones and queens. The drones and young queens soon leave the nest, and as the days grow colder, the workers grow tired and listless. They stop working and stay at home more and more. Since they

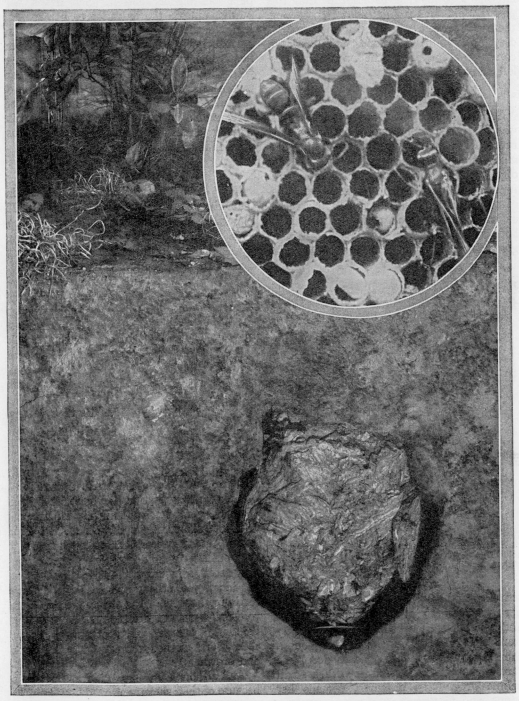

The wasp would seem to have taken a lesson in building from the bee. It is a more blundering workman than its skilful cousin, but it uses the same plan for its mansion containing many six-sided rooms — as the picture in the top right corner will show. There we see two of our touchy friends putting their house in order. Let us pass on quietly! Down below is the safely-hidden underground nest of some yellow jackets.

have no food for their babies, they drag the poor little things from their cells and fling them out of the nest. Then the workers die, for their task is done. When winter comes not one of all the busy throng is left alive in the wasp city.

The Wasp that Lives Alone

Solitary wasps, or "digger wasps," as we call them, live alone like the solitary bees. There are no worker diggers, but only males and females. Each little female wasp digs her own nest and stores it with food for her children. Some diggers make nests of mud and fix them securely under rocks or leaves or the eaves of buildings; others bore tunnels or winding galleries in the ground or in the side of a hill or sandy cliff.

The digger works with furious haste,

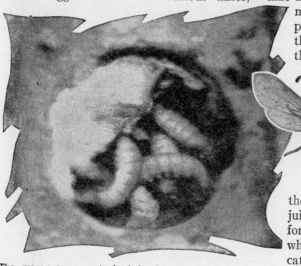

The mason wasp nests in holes in walls and other crevices. Here is the nest of a mother wasp in a bolt hole; it is full of paralysed caterpillars which she has gathered and stored as food for her baby. At the right is the mother wasp herself.

scraping and kicking in the ground with her feet, biting out little lumps of sand and throwing them some distance away from her hole. When she has dug out a short tunnel some three inches deep, she carefully covers up her work with a small pebble or a lump of earth, spreads her wings, and flies away.

A few minutes later she comes back again, clasping tightly a long, limp cater-pillar as big as herself. She drops her burden outside the entrance to her tunnel, removes the pebble, and drags her victim down below. When she has captured from five to ten caterpillars—the number varies with their size—and dragged them into her nest, she lays an egg on top of them and carefully closes the tunnel with pellets of earth and a small pebble, so that there is nothing to mark the spot where her precious egg lies hidden.

Fresh Meat for the Babies

Now, the most wonderful thing of all is that these caterpillars are not dead. If they were, they would be no good to the little wasp grub when it came out of the egg. The little creatures must have meat that is perfectly fresh. So the astonishing mother wasp does not kill the cater-pillars, but only stings them in exactly the right place to paralyse them; so they live on, but lie helpless and motion-less until such time as the wasp grub is ready to eat them.

There are many different kinds of these amazing little solitary wasps. Although they all feed on nectar and fruit juices, they provide fresh animal food for the children that they never see. And while some stock the nursery larder with caterpillars, others store the nests with beetles, grasshoppers, locusts, crickets, flies, cockroaches, or spiders. Some species are very small, measuring less than a quarter of an inch, yet others are as large as the terrifying hornets. And they vary in colour, too, for some are dressed in bright blues, reds and yellows, while others go about their work clothed more soberly in black and brown.

And although we may dislike the wasps because of their sharp, poisoned little swords, we must remember that we are indebted to them for keeping down the numbers of harmful caterpillars and insects.

(CONTINUED ON PAGE 283).

Photo by Alinari

The fifteenth-century Italian painter Carpaccio (kär-pät′cho) has left us this picture of a boy playing the lute. Here the head, with its tuning pegs, was set at an angle with the neck of the instrument in order to increase the tension of the strings and to be handy for tuning during a performance—for lutes had an unhappy knack of getting out of tune. They varied in size, some being as much as six feet in length.

MUSIC *Begins to* SOUND MODERN

How a Great Man Became Famous a Hundred Years after His Death, and How All Paris Fell to Fighting over the Way in Which an Opera Ought to be Written—All of Which Happened in the Days of the Stately Minuet

(CONTINUED FROM PAGE 193)

WHEN the twenty children of Johann Sebastian Bach (yō′hän bäK) practised the little pieces that their gifted father wrote for them to play, they did not know that children two hundred years later would be toiling away at the same little lessons. Those "Two-part" and "Three-part Inventions" of the great man are still the best pieces to help a beginner to learn about that fascinating musical puzzle which we call "counterpoint."

It really is not a puzzle at all, once one knows the secret. It is nothing more than a series of short tunes—two or three or four or more—chasing each other about, in and out and around, all going at the same time and making beautiful harmonies when they meet. If you are listening for a single air, with chords to fill it in—like "Home, Sweet Home" or "Nearer, my God, to Thee"—you will soon be lost in a maze of whirling notes. But once you open your ears and set your wits to work, you will feel that there is nothing in the world more fascinating than trying to disentangle all those charming little tunes and follow the adventures of each.

269

We have already seen that all the music of the Middle Ages was written in this style—before people had learnt to pay so much attention to time or rhythm or key. And we have seen how men gradually evolved those things that seem necessary to music to-day. In doing so, they paved the way for the great Bach (1685–1750). He took all their discoveries and made out of them music so perfect that no one since has been able to equal him in writing counterpoint, or what we call polyphonic (pŏl′ĭ-fŏn′ĭk)—"many-voiced" —music.

And, more interesting still, that music he wrote some two hundred years ago has helped to teach the art to nearly all the great composers since his day. They might write songs or symphonies in quite a different style from his, but they always learnt from him originally what music ought to be, and wrote the better for it. For about a century the public could not understand Bach. Polyphonic music went out of fashion —crowded out by the new love of melody and harmony—and Bach's great works lay almost forgotten. But gradually the more discerning musicians taught the people how beautiful those old masterpieces were, until to-day Bach's name appears on concert

Photo by Luxembourg Museum, Paris

During the eighteenth century and the early part of the nineteenth little girls took lessons upon the clavichord and harpsichord. It is such a lesson that the artist, J. A. Meunier, has shown in this painting, "The Clavichord Lesson."

programmes as often as the names of Beethoven, Wagner and Brahms.

There are still a good many people who do not care for Bach. They say they cannot understand him. But that is usually because they have never learned the secret of following all his little tunes, or "parts," kept going so skilfully together. Unlike those who do understand and care for Bach, they never know the excitement of watching all those parts march on to a triumphant close. Then, too, it is true that if you are to keep track of all those interweaving strands, you must remain wide awake. There is no good way to enjoy Bach and play a hand of bridge at the same time.

The great man wrote music of every kind except opera; but he was a superb organist, and his church music is the finest of all. No one has ever been able to equal him in that form. In Lent, choristers throughout the world sing his "Passion according to St. Matthew," a musical setting of the account of Christ's crucifixion as told in Matthew's gospel. This and an arrangement in B minor of the Mass of the Catholic church are perhaps his two finest works.

He also wrote beautiful short compositions. Many of them were fugues (fūg)—

pieces in which every part, as it comes in, repeats in its turn the musical sentence with which the first part opened the piece. Then they all weave in and out, from time to time repeating that first sentence, or "subject," tossing it about, now high, now low, now this way, now that, until, with a fine air of satisfaction and decision, they all come out

It was a dainty little instrument, with a sweet, soft tone—too soft to be heard except in a small room; but it had one great advantage over its more powerful brother, the harpsichord. Both of them were stringed instruments with keyboards, but the little clavichord was so planned that it was possible to play both loud and soft upon it,

By courtesy of the British Museum

This music is in the hand of the great Bach, and in the upper right-hand corner is part of his signature. It is the first three bars of a prelude from Part II of his "Well-tempered Clavier," which was published in 1744.

together at the end. It is easy to see why the piece took its name from a Latin word meaning "flight" or "fleeing." Many fugues followed very complicated patterns.

The Inventor of Our Modern Scale

But, besides giving us his masterly compositions, Bach did something else for the progress of music which was of the greatest importance. He gave to the clavichord a perfect tuning which enables a scale to be begun on any note in an octave, for among his shorter works is a little collection of preludes (prĕl'ūd) and fugues called "The Well-tempered Clavier."

Now, although so many of Bach's works are played on the piano to-day, none of them was written for it. He had never seen a piano when he wrote those little pieces for the "well-tempered clavier" (klă-vēr'). When he was at home, out of reach of the church organ he loved so well, he would play either upon the harpsichord or the clavichord (klăv'ĭ-kôrd), but he liked the clavichord best.

while all the notes on a harpsichord had just the same volume.

Now, as the great master played more and more upon his clavichord, he grew more and more dissatisfied with the way in which it was commonly tuned. For music written in certain keys, the tuning was almost perfect; but just because it was good for those keys, it was so out of tune for other keys that music written in them could not be played on it at all. The sharps were all too high and the flats were all too low; and that did not please a musician like Bach, who wanted to compose in all the keys.

The Finishing Touch

So he effected a compromise. By tuning his clavichord so that no scale would be quite perfect upon it, he made it possible to play all the scales reasonably well, and so could use it to compose and play music written in all those different keys. That "tempered," or adjusted, scale is the one we use to-day. It is the last step taken by the human race in that long process of

271

developing our present serviceable scale out of the queer little three-toned scales that were the only kind early men could sing. Upon that progress rests all our beautiful modern music.

So sure was Bach that this was the best possible way in which to tune an instrument that he made up his mind to prove it by writing the collection of little pieces for the "well-tempered clavier"—a term that included both harpsichord and clavichord. In his book he was careful to include compositions written in every one of the different keys, in order to show how useful his invention could be.

During all the years in which Bach was doing his great work, he stayed at home in Germany and wrote music for Germans to hear; and although he knew all about the operas the Italians were writing, and the arias they loved so much, he never tried to copy the Italian style. He said what he had to say in his own way, and to the best of his ability. He was too great and sincere a man to do anything else.

George Frederick Handel, the great composer of oratorios.

Italian Opera Introduced into England

Now, only a month before Bach was born, another famous musician had been born in Germany. This was George Frederick Handel (1685–1759) who, next to Bach, was the greatest musician of his day. Early in his life Handel began to copy the Italian music, for he loved opera. He travelled in Italy and met the musicians there, and, when he finally came to England to live, he imported Italian opera and taught the English people to like it. And he himself wrote a large number of very successful operas.

It happened, however, that the tide turned in his fortunes, and he found himself with an empty opera house on his hands during Lent, when operas were forbidden. He was in need of money, so he patched together a kind of sacred music drama, which pleased people so much that he turned his attention to writing "oratorios" (ŏr′ȧ-tōr′ĭ-ō). In construction, these are like operas, but there is no acting and no costumes or scenery. Everything that happens in the story is described and commented on in the songs. The subject and the words of an oratorio are supposed to be taken from the Bible. When the words are not sacred the piece is called a "cantata" (kăn-tä′tȧ).

At last Handel had found his great gift. He wrote twenty-six oratorios altogether, most of them sacred. Many of those great works are sung to-day. All over the world "The Messiah" is given at Christmas time, and there are few lovers of music who have not heard its great Hallelujah Chorus. When it was first sung in London, in 1743, the king and the whole audience rose to their feet as of one accord when those mighty hallelujahs led into the theme, "For the Lord God omnipotent reigneth." And ever since then people all over the world have stood up for the Hallelujah Chorus. This magnificent oratorio was produced by Handel in little more than three weeks, a remarkable feat that has never been equalled in musical composition.

Those oratorios are the work by which we remember Handel. They are full of beautiful, tender melodies, and of noble choruses. Handel knew how to write as the Italians were writing, but he knew how to write fine counterpoint, too—a thing the Italians had almost forgotten how to do. And he never failed to make the most of a dramatic situation, for he had a vivid imagination and the things about which he wrote were very real to him. After he had first heard his own Hallelujah Chorus, he said, "I did think I did see Heaven opened and the great God Himself."

The Greatest Boy Musician

A few years before Handel, a blind old man, was breathing his last in London, another great German musician was first seeing the light of day in far-off Austria.

Photo by Rischgitz
The young Mozart playing before Maria Theresa, Arch-duchess of Austria. When he was only six years old

Mozart made a tour of Europe, and when still under thirty, he was the idol of the gay society in Vienna.

His name was Wolfgang Amadeus Mozart (vôlf'gäng ä-mä'dĕ-ŭs mō'tsärt)—a marvellous boy who was going to crowd into his few years (1756–1791) a great deal more than most men put into a lifetime. This was partly because he began so early. He started composing music before he had learned how to write. He composed a charming and workmanlike symphony at the age of eight, and when he was twelve published four sonatas for the violin. Anyone so gifted beyond his years was sure to do a great deal for the art he loved so well.

When he began writing as a lad he was able to learn a good many things from the work of another gifted Austrian named Franz Josef Haydn (fränts hī'd'n). Haydn (1732–1809) was a good deal older than Mozart, but they became great friends and later Mozart's "Papa" Haydn learned, in his turn, from the music the younger man wrote. Together they did so much to perfect music in various ways that when the great genius Beethoven was born,

he found everything ready to hand for him to write some of the greatest music the world has ever known.

The String Quartet

Mozart and Haydn had shown people how to write for instruments. Haydn worked out the "string quartet," made up of first and second violins, viola (vē-ō'lä), and violoncello (vē'ŏ-lŏn-chĕl'ō)—or 'cello. The viola and the 'cello are larger and deeper-toned brothers of the violin, the 'cello the largest and richest in tone. Both instruments had been brought to perfection by those magicians who had made such wonderful violins in Italy in the seventeenth century.

Instrumental music of this kind—quartets and trios of stringed instruments, or any other combination of a few instruments—is known as "chamber music." We call it that because it is meant to be heard in an ordinary room and not in a great hall or theatre as is an orchestra. It has been said that you can nearly always tell how musical

273

a country is by the amount of chamber music it has. For chamber music is meant to be played at home, and no country can produce great composers unless its people love music enough to want to hear it at home, and to be willing to work in order to learn how to play or sing it there. To listen to music broadcast by the wireless is not enough, though that is a fine way in which to learn what good music is like.

It was during the time of Haydn and Mozart that a new instrument began to supersede the old harpsichord and clavichord. The piano had been gradually growing under the hands of patient, hard-working inventors until at last it had become fit for a musician to play upon. The first pianos had been made as early as 1709 by an Italian named Cristofori (krēs'tō-fô'rē). The spinet, the virginal, the harpsichord and the clavichord had all contributed a little, until at last men had this fine new instrument from which to draw a rich, resounding tone that could be made as loud or as soft as they wished. That was such an achievement that the new device was called by the two Italian adjectives that described its powers—"pianoforte" (pē-ä'nō-fōr'tā), "softloud." We have shortened it to "piano."

This is Joseph Haydn, one of the gentlest, merriest souls that ever expressed his thoughts in music.

Father of the Sonata

Very many composers had already written some fine music for the harpsichord. One of them was Domenico Scarlatti (1685–1757), son of the great Scarlatti (skär-lät'tē). Karl Philipp Emanuel Bach (1714–1788), the gifted son of the great Bach (bäK), was another. He improved a neat little form of composition called a "sonata" (sō-nä'tà) so much that he is sometimes called "the father of the sonata." But Haydn's was the hand that gave the sonata the shape that made it perfect for all kinds of instrumental music. The sonatas he wrote for the piano we still love to play to-day. And Mozart's sonatas are even better.

For a long time people had been writing "sonatas"—for the word merely means "sound piece," and was the term applied to a composition for instruments, just as "cantata," or "song piece," was the name of a composition for the voice. Later a cantata came to be a short oratorio. Haydn's bright, serene mind took all those groping efforts and moulded them to find a good form for instrumental pieces and put the crowning touch on them. Under his hands the sonata took definite "classic" form.

Now, it is very important to know what a sonata is, since it is the style of a great many kinds of musical composition. To begin with, you must bear in mind the fact that "sonata" and "sonata form" do not mean the same thing. Failure to grasp this fact clearly has caused a great deal of confusion in people's minds.

What is a Sonata?

Suppose we discuss the sonata first. A sonata is a long musical composition, usually written for the piano or harp alone, or for a solo instrument—such as the violin, clarinet, 'cello, or oboe (ō'boi)—with a second part for the piano. When the second part is played by an orchestra, we call the composition, not a sonata, but a "concerto" (kŏn-chĕr'tō). Occasionally, though not very often, composers have written double concertos, in which there are *two* solo instruments besides the orchestra. There is no such thing as a double sonata; or rather, there *is* such a thing—two solo instruments and piano—but it is called a trio. When the sonata is played by the orchestra alone, with no solo instruments, we call it a symphony (sĭm'fō-nĭ). When it is written for four single instruments, it is called a quartet (kwôr-tĕt').

Ancestors of the Sonata

Thus you see that the plan of the sonata —remember, that does not mean "sonata form"—is a very important one, and is

The minuet, which the artist Jessie Watkins has shown, was a stately dance in great favour at one time. It is seldom seen now, but the lovely strains to which it was danced still delight audiences in every part of the world.

the foundation of several different kinds of musical composition. Let us see what the plan really is.

You will remember that the gifted Scarlatti wrote overtures—or introductions—to his operas and called them "symphonies." Those little early pieces were the ancestors of our sonatas and symphonies to-day. The form in which they were written was the form everybody was using for all kinds of instrumental music. You will remember, too, that a piece written in that form was divided into three parts, or "movements"— it was really an instrumental "aria da capo." These movements consisted of a lively one, a slow one, and then either a new lively one or the first one over again.

That was the pattern that grew into the sonata of Haydn. Instead of writing the three parts without a break, he made each one much longer, and had them played with a short pause between. But the general plan was what it had been in Scarlatti's day—an opening lively movement, a middle slow movement, and a closing lively move-ment. The last one was always a new movement, not merely a repetition of the opening. Later, when he began to write for the orchestra alone, he added a minuet, or some other dance form, between the second and third movements. This four-movement sonata for orchestra is called a symphony; and to this day composers have written symphonies on that plan.

A Fascinating Musical Pattern

The first movement grew to have an interesting design of its own. It was, and still is, always written in "sonata form." The design might vary in detail, but the general plan was always as here described.

The movement opened with one musical sentence, or "theme"—in other words, with a very short tune. Suppose we call this Theme 1. Theme 1 was played, and re-peated, and perhaps varied a little. Then came a second theme, Theme 2, in another key, which was duly put through *its* paces. Then, after this opening, which is called the "exposition," the two themes were woven in and out, played together and separately, turned backwards and forwards and upside down, through a long passage known as the "development section." At last the composer worked back to the two themes in their original form, and played them both again—but in opposite keys. In other words, he played Theme 1 in the key of Theme 2, and Theme 2 in the key of Theme 1. This section is called the "recapitulation" (rē′kȧ-pĭt′ū-lā′shŭn), or "restatement." Usually he ended the movement with a farewell passage known as a "coda" (kō′dȧ)—which is Italian for "tail"—based on one or both of the themes.

The whole scheme is a fascinating one, for it offers endless opportunities for the composer to show his skill and feeling, and keeps the listener's wits busy following the two themes through their various adventures, and recognizing them in their various disguises.

Curious Form of the "Rondo"

Now you know the difference between a "sonata" and the "sonata form." The first is a name descriptive of the way in which a whole composition is put together; the second is the pattern of a single movement. Not all the movements of a sonata or symphony, however, are written in sonata form. The first movement always is so written, and the last one sometimes—there is no fourth movement in most sonatas. But the second, or slow movement, is often written in the so-called "binary form." If you want to know what that is, look up the description of Scarlatti's "aria da capo." It is the same thing. The minuet, or, as it came to be later, the third or fast movement, is often written in what is known as "rondo" form. In this form there is a first theme, then a second, the first over again, then a third, the first again, then a fourth, then the first, and so on—thus 1, 2, 1, 3, 1, 4, 1, etc.

How the Sonata May Vary in Form

In modern symphonies the form is less strict than it used to be. César Franck's famous Symphony in D major has only three movements instead of four. In Tschai-kovsky's Sixth, or "Pathétique," Symphony, the first movement is in sonata form; the second is a curious sort of tune in five-four time; the third is a march; and the slow movement comes last of all. But we are getting a little ahead of our story. Suppose we go back to the eighteenth century, where, for the time being, we belong.

Mozart a Master of Tone

Both Haydn and Mozart wrote fine symphonies, and taught the world how beautifully the tones of the different instruments in an orchestra could be blended. Mozart in particular, the more gifted and the more artistic of the two, knew even better than Haydn how to combine instruments so as to get an entirely new blend of tone. This is what we call the "colour" of orchestral tone. No composer knows how to get a great many colours from an orchestra unless he realizes that in his vast group of instruments he has something that can be combined by his own ideas into one single instrument, on which the conductor plays just as a pianist plays on a piano. You see, the orchestra by Mozart's time had already grown into something very different from that little group of instruments it had been before.

Opera Becomes More Lively

Mozart wrote charming operas, too, full of lively wit and humour and of exquisite music. We have seen that opera in Italy, the land of its birth, had long ago grown very stale—except for some short comic skits that were set to music and played between the long, tiresome acts of the regular operas. These little operatic pieces were known first as "intermezzos" (ĭn′tēr-mĕt′zō), and later as "opera buffa" (bōōf′fä)—we get our "buffoon" from the same word. They were the one sign of life that Italian opera showed, although the Italian form was considered the correct thing all over Europe and did, it is true, give us some beautiful melodies.

But outside Italy things were very lively indeed. An Austrian named Christoph Gluck (1714–1787) had seen how artificial were all the trills and turns and runs and warbles that the Italian singers had to utter, and had decided that music drama ought

Photo by German National Rlys.

In the days of Mozart there were no great public orchestras, as there are to-day. Noblemen hired bands of trained musicians to live in their castles and give entertainments there, after the fashion shown above.

to be dramatic as well as musical. So he gave expression to his ideas in Vienna when he produced his opera "Orfeo" (1762). The piece seems old-fashioned enough to us to-day, but it was so new and different when it was first performed that the people who heard it were completely mystified. It was the starting-point for our modern operas.

Gluck (glook) did not have much success with his new idea in Austria, so he finally accepted an invitation to go to Paris (1774), where people cared more about such matters. There he had the support of the unhappy Queen Marie Antoinette, whom he had known when she was a little Austrian princess. Immediately he became the centre figure of a little war. For the good people of Paris were already divided into two camps, one favouring the Italian style of opera and one the French style, which was sung in the French language, made use of choruses and dancing, and was a good deal more entertaining.

Gluck at once became a hero to the French party, and his operas were so beautiful that the champions of Italian opera felt that something must be done to uphold their cause. So they urged an Italian composer named Piccini (pĭt-chē'nē), who lived in Paris, to write another opera on the same story of Orpheus. Piccini (1728–1800) did his best, but the French operas were so much better that Gluck and his party were easy victors. Gluck set opera on the right path; and he was, perhaps, the first of all composers to see that every instrument in his orchestra kept its own particular personality.

Composer of Grand Opera at Fourteen

It was while this war was going on that Mozart went to Paris as a young man (1778). He had already, at the age of fourteen, written a grand opera, and now the brilliant youth was not slow to make up his mind about a number of things. When he began to write his next opera, he left the outworn Italian style far behind, and wrote things more or less like the "opera buffa"—a little stiff to us, perhaps, but full of exquisite charm and sprightliness. "The Marriage of Figaro" (fē'gä-rō), "Don Giovanni" (jō-vän'nē), and "The Magic Flute" are the ones that are best known.

Both Haydn and Mozart wrote church music. It seemed to flow quite naturally from Haydn's noble, joyous spirit. In fact, he once said that he "did not think God could be angry with him for praising Him with a merry heart." One of Haydn's best-known sacred works is an oratorio called "The Creation." Mozart's finest piece of religious music is the Requiem Mass he wrote on his death-bed.

(CONTINUED ON PAGE 375)

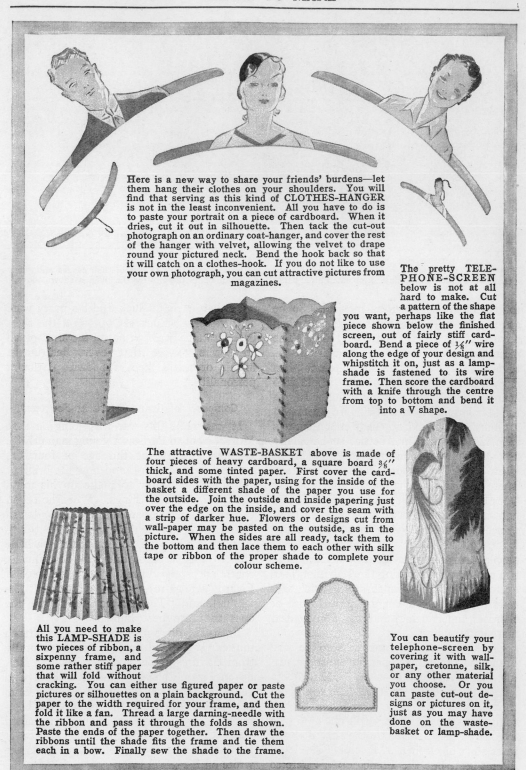

Here is a new way to share your friends' burdens—let them hang their clothes on your shoulders. You will find that serving as this kind of CLOTHES-HANGER is not in the least inconvenient. All you have to do is to paste your portrait on a piece of cardboard. When it dries, cut it out in silhouette. Then tack the cut-out photograph on an ordinary coat-hanger, and cover the rest of the hanger with velvet, allowing the velvet to drape round your pictured neck. Bend the hook back so that it will catch on a clothes-hook. If you do not like to use your own photograph, you can cut attractive pictures from magazines.

The pretty TELEPHONE-SCREEN below is not at all hard to make. Cut a pattern of the shape you want, perhaps like the flat piece shown below the finished screen, out of fairly stiff cardboard. Bend a piece of $\frac{1}{8}''$ wire along the edge of your design and whipstitch it on, just as a lampshade is fastened to its wire frame. Then score the cardboard with a knife through the centre from top to bottom and bend it into a V shape.

The attractive WASTE-BASKET above is made of four pieces of heavy cardboard, a square board $\frac{3}{8}''$ thick, and some tinted paper. First cover the cardboard sides with the paper, using for the inside of the basket a different shade of the paper you use for the outside. Join the outside and inside papering just over the edge on the inside, and cover the seam with a strip of darker hue. Flowers or designs cut from wall-paper may be pasted on the outside, as in the picture. When the sides are all ready, tack them to the bottom and then lace them to each other with silk tape or ribbon of the proper shade to complete your colour scheme.

All you need to make this LAMP-SHADE is two pieces of ribbon, a sixpenny frame, and some rather stiff paper that will fold without cracking. You can either use figured paper or paste pictures or silhouettes on a plain background. Cut the paper to the width required for your frame, and then fold it like a fan. Thread a large darning-needle with the ribbon and pass it through the folds as shown. Paste the ends of the paper together. Then draw the ribbons until the shade fits the frame and tie them each in a bow. Finally sew the shade to the frame.

You can beautify your telephone-screen by covering it with wallpaper, cretonne, silk, or any other material you choose. Or you can paste cut-out designs or pictures on it, just as you may have done on the wastebasket or lamp-shade.

The LAND of the FIRST ASTRONOMERS

Ancient Babylon Rises Out of Its Ruins under a New Name, and Gives Us One of the Greatest of the Sciences

IF SOME wise man or magician had told the Assyrian king Sennacherib, when he was tearing down the walls of Babylon (băb′ĭ-lŏn), that in less than a hundred years the ruins would become a city greater and more magnificent than his own Nineveh (nĭn′ē-vĕ), the king would probably have been very angry, and it might have gone hard with the magician. Yet the story would have been a true one.

The Chaldeans, who helped to destroy Assyria in 612 B.C., loved the old city of Babylon. They worshipped the same gods as the Babylonians, and spoke the same language. When the Chaldeans became the masters of the Fertile Crescent, that much-fought-over strip that sweeps through Western Asia, they rebuilt Babylon and made it their capital city, but they called the country Chaldea instead of Babylonia.

The man who planned most of the rich buildings in the new Babylon was the great Chaldean king Nebuchadnezzar (nĕb′ū-kăd-nĕz′år). He ruled for forty years in Babylon, and he spent all his days of peace in building the great city. When we call one of our cities a "modern Babylon," we are comparing it with the great city of Nebuchadnezzar. The walls of the new Babylon were forty miles round. The streets of houses were three and four stories high. The gate of the goddess Ishtar, the main gate of the city, was known all over the Chaldean empire for its size and beauty. The walls of the street leading to this gate were decorated with pictures of lions and tigers and other wild beasts in coloured brick which gleamed in the sunlight.

But most famous of all the sights of the city were the temple of Marduk (mär′dook),

Great Babylon at last went the way of other ancient cities. The Persians swept down from the north, and amid scenes like the one above, the famous towers and Hanging Gardens became the prize of the conquerors.

This cylinder of baked clay is inscribed with a cuneiform inscription which tells how Nabonidus, the last king of Babylon, rebuilt the famous temple of the moon god at ancient Ur, where it had first been built two thousand years before. Nabonidus was the father of the famous Belshazzar, whose downfall Daniel foretold.

god of war, and the enormous palace of Nebuchadnezzar. The temple had many great towers with sloping paths, or ramps, winding up round the sides to the top. And the palace of the king must have looked like a huge green mountain with palms and trees and grassy lawns growing right on top of it. These were the famous Hanging Gardens of Babylon, which were one of the seven wonders of the old world. There is a story about the planting of them.

Whims of a Median Princess

Nebuchadnezzar had married a princess from the mountains of Media (mē'dĭ-å), a country to the north of Chaldea. This princess did not care for the flat river country around Babylon. She was homesick for the rolling hills of her father's kingdom. To please and surprise her, therefore, Nebuchadnezzar had the high roofs and lofty terraces of his new palace covered over with earth and planted with gardens and groves, just as if the whole thing were a high mountain. Then his queen might see a mountain top from her window, or she might walk in the gardens among running streams of sparkling water. To make those streams Nebuchadnezzar's engineers built

pumping-engines which lifted water up from the Euphrates River far below, and poured it in cascades here and there over the mountain.

Never had the world seen such a palace. And if Nebuchadnezzar was famous as a builder, he was just as famous in his wars, for he ruled almost all the countries which had formerly paid tribute to Assyria. In one of his campaigns he destroyed Jerusalem, the chief city of the Jews, and took many of the Jews as prisoners to Babylon. You may read about this "Babylonian Captivity" in the Book of Daniel in the Bible.

Babylon Looks to the Past

We may remember that just before Egypt fell into decay there was a good time when people looked back to the country's glorious past and tried to make their own time resemble that past as much as they could. Well, this period in New Babylon was very similar. People looked back reverently on the great past of the old Babylon and tried to copy it. Because old Babylon had used clay tablets rather than paper, so must they. Priests and scribes tried to dress and talk as priests and scribes had done in the old Babylon. Men dug about in the ruins of the

A. Bee-hive houses of sun-baked clay built on the site of the Biblical town of Haran.

If the ancient Chaldeans could suddenly come to life, they would find in their land people like the man at B and the others on this page. C and F. In these narrow boats the tribes who dwell in the marshes along the Euphrates pole their way along.

D. Making bricks to-day in the land that was once Chaldea.

Some of the craft one sees along the Tigris River have been in use there since the dawn of civilization.

E. This raft, called a kelak, is made buoyant by goat-skin bladders blown up in the simple way shown here.

old city and eagerly studied the clay books they found there, in order to make their life as much as possible like life in the old days.

And yet the Chaldeans were cleverer in many ways than the old Babylonians. The Chaldeans studied the stars and knew when an eclipse was to come. They knew all the five planets nearest the earth — Venus, Mercury, and the rest. They also understood figures, and divided the circle into 360 degrees and the day into twelve hours. The Greeks learned these things from the Chaldeans, and through the Greeks they have come down to us.

Except for the Egyptians and the Sumerians, all the peoples we have read about in history so far have been of the Semitic (sĕ-mĭt′ĭk) race. Though civilization did not begin with the Semites (sĕm′ĭt), these people did rule the civilized world for very many centuries. But now a new page was turned in history, and a new race of people arose to fame.

But for these restless people from the north the Chaldean empire might have lasted for centuries. As the Semites—Akkadians, Amorites, Assyrians, Chaldeans — had come wandering out of the deserts to the south of the Two Rivers, so these people came sweeping down from the grasslands and pastures to the north. They were Aryan (är′yăn), or Indo-European, in race, and were to be famous for thousands of years to come, just as the Semitic peoples had been for two thousand years before. The first of these Indo-European peoples of whom we know called themselves the Medes

This is part of the far-famed Ishtar gate that stood in Babylon. Its towers still rise to a height of thirty-nine feet, and bear in their rich enamels the gorgeous colour that delighted the eyes of the builders. The uppermost figure at the right is the Babylonian dragon, or "sirrish," coloured a creamy white against an exquisite blue background, with the claws, mane, and tongue done in golden brown. This interesting beast was a serpent provided with a viper's head and forked tongue, a scaly body, a bird's hind legs, and the forelegs of a lion or tiger. It was sacred to the god of war. Below the dragon is the magnificent bull that was sacred to Adad, god of the wind and storm. It was either brown and blue, with green horns and hoofs, or white and blue, with yellow horns and hoofs. This gate in days long past must have been magnificent indeed.

and Persians. They were destined to build a great empire.

Only seventy-two years after the fall of Assyrian Nineveh, the Persians were at the gates of Babylon. The Chaldeans did not fight very hard to keep them out. All the walls and forts of the great city were of little use when the soldiers themselves were afraid and discouraged. With scarcely any fighting the Persians made themselves masters of Babylon, and the brief Chaldean empire came to an end. Little by little Babylon itself crumbled away until it was only a ruin, "one with Nineveh and Tyre."

For, as a ruling race, the day of the Semitic peoples was over. They had done great things for the cause of civilization; they had made great discoveries and had dreamed great dreams. The Hebrew Bible is a monument to their genius that stands even to-day. But for some reason the torch of civilization passed out of their hands, to be taken up by peoples from the north, who were henceforth to press on with it with a greater energy and a greater devotion than the desert races were able to command. The older race by no means passed out of existence; it still survives in the Arabs and Jews and certain other peoples. But its day of empire seems over.

Before we go on, however, with the story of the Persian conquerors, there are two other civilized peoples about whom we must say something. At least one of them was Semitic, and did a great service to the human race, as we shall see. The others were a somewhat puzzling people about whom we shall be glad to know more.

No wonder they stand in amazement! The great mound was heaped up, one grain of sand at a time, by thousands of little ants. To build the Tower of London was an easy task in comparison.

The BUSY LIFE of the ANT

How Thousands of Little Creatures Live in the Cities They Have Built and Keep Pets and "Cows"

(CONTINUED FROM PAGE 268)

DEEP in the quiet woods it often seems so still that we feel all alone in the cool, green world. A roof of leafy boughs is over our heads, and the carpet of leaves and moss under our feet is so soft that we can hardly hear our own footsteps. But if we imagine we are quite alone, we are surely making a great mistake. There are hundreds of little people moving about. They are here, there, and everywhere; but they make no noise and they are so very small that we seldom notice them. All around, too—right under our feet—are model towns and dwellings, with winding roadways leading in every direction—all made by the marvellous little woodland people we call wood ants.

Funny little beings they are, to be sure, clothed from head to foot in a dull reddish uniform. They have queer, flat heads, and long bodies divided into two distinct parts by a thread-like waist with two large knots in the middle of it. Their six jointed legs are very slender, but are long and strong, and the little owners can run about at an astonishing pace.

On their foreheads the ants carry a pair of stout antennae (ăn-těn′ē), or feelers, with a sharp elbow joint in the middle. By means of them they communicate with one another in some way that we do not understand. They are armed, too, with a pair of strong sickle-shaped jaws, which are used as weapons for fighting and as tools for working in a hundred and one different ways. These jaws can be worked quite independently of their other mouth parts, which are used only for eating and drinking.

The Wonders Inside an Ant-hill

These tiny woodland folk live, like the dwarfs and gnomes of our fairy tales, inside a hill or underneath the ground. If you could make yourself small enough to enter and explore one of those ant establishments, you would be astonished at the wonderful way in which it is arranged, and at the orderly manner in which the little inhabitants behave.

From the outside an ant-hill does not seem highly interesting. It looks like nothing but a jumble of pieces of twigs and leaves and pine-needles all heaped up together. But some of the heaps may be over two feet high and several yards round; and when we remember that all the millions of odds and ends of which they are built up have been brought here and twisted into place by such tiny creatures as the wood ants, the building begins to be amazing.

Inside the ant-hill there is perfect order. Many gateways open into long, winding passages—some going up and some going down—where we might easily lose our way unless one of the ant people acted as guide to show us round. There are rooms and halls and galleries in every direction— living-rooms, store-rooms, sleeping-rooms, nurseries, all as neat and tidy as you please. And in and out and up and down, thousands of busy ants are running about, just as throngs of human beings hurry to and fro in a big city.

All the little ant people look much alike. They are all workers, but they are not all busy at the same tasks. Troops of them are hurrying off to their day's work outside the city—some to fetch in fresh supplies of food, others to collect building materials for enlarging or repairing the roof of the nest. Gangs of outdoor workers are busy clearing the roadways of the bits of stick and rubbish which are always falling in the way, or making new paths for the feet of the little people.

The largest British ant is the red wood ant. The winged male (top) and female and the wingless worker are shown here.

Inside the nest the housemaids are busy tidying up the rooms and galleries, while processions of nurses hurry along the passages carrying little white bundles from place to place in their jaws. These little bundles may be cocoons or they may be the ant babies, which are sorted out according to age and kept in special nurseries.

Maids of Honour for the Queen

Besides the swarms of worker ants, in every large ant city there are always several queens. The queens are bigger than the workers. They spend all their days in the nest and never go out for a holiday or a change of air—they are much too busy laying eggs. A little band of workers is told off to wait upon each queen and act as her maids of honour. They follow the queen about wherever she goes, offer her food, attend to her toilet, and stroke her gently with their antennae—an attention which her Majesty seems to appreciate.

As fast as the eggs are laid by the queen, they are picked up by the workers and carried away to special egg rooms. There they are watched and guarded until they hatch, when the new ant babies are at once removed to one of the nurseries.

Ant babies are helpless little atoms, very much like bee grubs to look at, only smaller. And they can do nothing but wriggle their fat little legless bodies and open their tiny mouths to be fed. The nurses take the greatest care of their little charges. They are always feeding them, cleaning them, carrying them about, or stroking them gently with their antennae. At night the babies are carried down to the night nurseries on the lowest floors of the nest, where they are warmer and safer. Then in the morning they are all brought up again to the large, airy day nurseries in the top of the ant-hill. If

The large picture shows an ant nursery. Here are eggs, pupae, and newly hatched ants, all lying on a piece of bark. These are the precious objects that the ant nurses tend so carefully, and carry to safety whenever danger threatens. The oval shows a mountainous ant-hill in Brazil; it is about twelve feet high.

the day is warm and bright the mites are taken out of doors so that they may lie and wriggle in the sun.

Trained Nurses for the Babies

When they are full-grown the ant grubs spin tiny cocoons and go to sleep inside them. But the devoted nurses still keep fussing about with the little things. They are always carrying the babies in their jaws from one place to another, so anxious are they that the sleeping infants shall be neither too hot nor too cold. Then at last, when the magic change is complete and the new ants are ready to leave their cocoons, the nurses hasten to break open the little silken cases and help them out.

The new arrivals in the nest are at first very weak and shaky. But they are well treated by the workers, who assist them to stand up on their thin, quivering legs, give them food, introduce them to their comrades, and show them the way about the city. They do no work for the first day or two, but are allowed to wander about as they please. The young ants, however, have no wish to remain idle. As soon as they are strong enough to work, they take their places with the other workers and share in all the toil.

An Exciting Event in Ant City

So week by week the ant colony increases in size. The little people have plenty to do, enlarging the nest, digging out new rooms, and finding food for the whole population. Then, when work is at its heaviest and the summer sun is still high in the sky, an exciting event occurs in the ant city. Instead of wingless workers coming out of the cocoons, swarms of young ants with four gauzy wings apiece make their appearance. They are "queens," or female ants, and "drones," or males.

The new ants do not begin to work with the other inhabitants of the city, but loiter about getting in the way of the workers—who must find them a perfect nuisance. But the workers are not annoyed. They are very kind and patient. They offer the idlers food and smooth their wings for them. Then on a still, sultry day, when it must be uncomfortably hot indoors with such crowds of ants about, the winged insects grow very much excited, and with one accord they pour in thousands through the city gates and rise together into the air.

The Joyous Wedding Flight

From all the ant-hills round about, swarms of winged ants troop out and join the gay throng. Here and there they drift in little clouds, their wings gleaming with rainbow hues as they dance joyously in the sunshine. For this is the ants' wedding flight. The young queens mate and fly away on a short and care-free honeymoon.

But the happy holiday is soon over. A sad fate overtakes most of the revellers. All the birds in the neighbourhood pursue the dancing ants and gobble them up by hundreds and thousands as they sink to the ground in an exhausted condition.

The queen ants never have another holiday. From now on, like all the other members of the city, they have work to do. They spend the rest of their days laying eggs to maintain a strong and thriving population for the city. And before settling down to her duties, every queen tears her beautiful wings away from her shoulders. She will never fly again!

As for the drones who were not eaten up at once, their fate is certainly a sad one. They are never allowed to go back to the nest. They are of no use to anyone, and the workers will have none of them. The poor things wander about until they die of cold or are snapped up by the hungry birds.

Where Ants Set Up Housekeeping

There are ever so many different kinds of ants. All over the world the determined little insects make their nests and build up their cities, wherever it may suit them. In the woods and in the meadows they raise their hills or tunnel into the ground. Some of them set up housekeeping in old dry

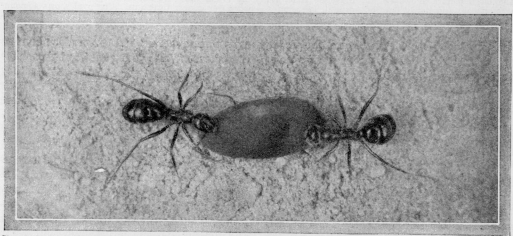

Photo by F. Martin Duncan

Here are two ants carrying a cocoon. It is much larger than they are, and an awkward thing for them to carry.

But if you watch them at their task you will find that they haul it over the ground with amazing speed.

After these adventures, the few young queens who escape the general slaughter seek shelter where they may. Some, with the help of a few workers, soon start new nests of their own. Others creep back into the old home, where they are welcomed and kindly treated by the little citizens.

logs or tree stumps, hollowing them out with their strong jaws. A few make delicate paper nests or live inside bunches of leaves all fastened together with silk; and some invade our houses, where they are a pest.

The little robber ants live, like bandits, by raiding the nests of the industrious tribes

Here is a nest of wood ants, measuring over a yard across and two feet in height. The insect (much enlarged) is a worker in its threatening attitude, ready to spray formic acid at an enemy.

and carrying off the grubs and stores. They are so very small and hard to see in their dull, yellowish suits that they often live and carry on their knavish pranks right inside the nests of the larger ants without being detected and punished as they deserve.

They make narrow, winding passages in the walls of the nest, far too small for the big ants to enter. There they lurk, watching and waiting for a moment when the busy workers will be off their guard. They rush out, seize any grubs and cocoons they can, and scamper back into their holes where the angry workers cannot follow and save their children from being a feast for the bold and wicked bandits.

There is no end to the curious habits and customs of the ant people. Some ants allow strange insects to live in their nests as honoured guests, although they give nothing in return for their board and lodging. Others actually make pets of certain little blind beetles, whom they treat with the greatest kindness and affection. And it is quite a common thing to find large herds of plant-lice kept and tended as domestic animals, or ant cows, by the workers in the ant cities.

Plant-lice— or aphides (ăf'ĭ-dēz)—are those tiresome little insects that swarm in countless numbers on plants of all descriptions, sucking out the juices with their sharp, piercing beaks and draining the life from the plants. They are such greedy little creatures that they suck and suck until their tiny bodies are swollen into balloons and the sweet juice oozes out of them in sticky drops called "honey-dew."

The ants, who love sweet things, are very fond of honey-dew. So they collect large quantities of the little pests and pasture them carefully on suitable plants round their nests. The workers guard their cows from the attacks of other insects, build sheds over them to protect them from the rain, and regularly milk the herds, gently stroking the bulging sides of the insects with their antennae to induce them to yield the sweet, sticky stuff with which they are almost bursting. The ants even collect the eggs of the plant-lice in the autumn and keep them in their nests through the winter. When the eggs hatch in the springtime, the ants take their little cows out of doors to feed on the plants that suit them best.

Honey Pots that are Alive

The honey-ants of North America collect honey from the swellings called "galls" that are made on the twigs of oak trees by small winged insects. A sweet, watery fluid oozes from the galls, and this is lapped up by the ants, who fill their

ants who allow themselves to be used in this extraordinary way for the benefit of their comrades.

There they hang, those strange, long-suffering creatures, clinging to the ceiling by their feet, their hind bodies swollen to the shape of a large currant by the honey with which they are filled. From time to time the other workers visit their living honey-pots and sip the sweet food from their lips. And this is the only way in which the patient insects enjoy the society of their fellows. They never go out of the nest. Indeed, they are too heavy and bloated to walk about; and if they fall from the ceiling, as sometimes happens, the ordinary workers run to their assistance and help the poor things to hang themselves up again.

Several tribes of ants keep slaves to work for them. Well-organized troops of determined little warriors raid the nests of other tribes and, after a desperate fight, carry off the grubs and cocoons in triumph. They certainly treat their little captives well. They look after them as carefully as if they were their own children; and when the prisoners grow up they live in the nests of their owners and work for them quite contentedly.

He so enjoyed eating ants that Mother Nature equipped this lesser ant-eater in the very best way for catching them. He spends most of his time in trees, to which he finds it very easy to cling with the help of his long, powerful tail. This is scaly at the end and may be wrapped right round a limb. His snout is tubular, and from it he can run out that long, agile tongue, which is covered with a sticky saliva. When it is nicely covered with insects he draws it in again and enjoys the catch. In colour he is yellowish white and black; and he lives in South America. He is also called the tamandua.

crops with it and carry it home to the nest. There the honey is stored, for the use of the whole community, in a number of large "honey-pots" which hang side by side from the roof of the nest. And what do you think these honey-pots really are? They are nothing less than worker

In some cases, indeed, the slave owners grow so lazy that they depend almost entirely on their slaves. The captives do all the work, and in the course of time grow so important that they practically rule the city.

The harvester ants that live in large or

All these cows are being milked. Those in the big picture are ants' cows, or plant-lice, which the enterprising ants pasture near their homes and milk for a sweet liquid the queer cows contain.

small colonies on the great western plains of America are wonderfully thrifty in their habits. They gather the grains and seeds of the grasses and store them up for winter, when the supply of food out of doors grows short. They keep their stores in granaries dug out many feet below the surface of the ground; and the soil they excavate is piled up in a large mound over the top of the underground nest. All about the mound the ants cut away the grass, making a large circular clearing. They also cut through the brush broad, straight roads, over which they can carry their loads home instead of having to struggle through a thick mass of tangled scrub.

Two Classes of Workers

There are always two classes of workers in the harvesters' colonies—small ants, called "minor workers," and larger ants with very big heads and huge jaws, called "major workers." It is said that the big-headed "majors" use their strong jaws chiefly to crack the hard grain for their smaller comrades.

There are also major and minor workers among the parasol ants of tropical America, as well as among several tribes of fierce wandering ants called "drivers." The parasol ants construct large underground

towns, crowned by the usual hills, in wood districts or in coffee or orange plantations, where they often make themselves very troublesome by stripping the trees of their foliage. Day after day long processions of the unpleasant insects may be seen making their way over well-worn paths to clumps of their favourite trees. Up the trunks they go, and in next to no time the little wretches are swarming all over the branches, clipping away at the leaves with their strong, sharp jaws.

Parading With Green Parasols

Each ant cuts out a fragment of leaf as big as itself, or bigger. Then, holding this aloft in its jaws, it comes down the tree and marches home with its prize. It is one of the strangest of sights to see these curious little creatures parading home, one behind another, in an almost endless procession, every one of them holding its piece of leaf above its head as if it were carrying a bright green parasol to shield it from the heat of the sun.

All day long the diligent insects travel to and fro between the nest and the trees they are stripping. So there are always two parades going on at the same time, one hurrying out with empty jaws, the other coming back triumphant with the spoils.

The leaves are all torn into fine shreds and packed into large rooms underground. There they are left to ferment and decay till they form a sort of hotbed of rich leaf-mould. On this the ants cultivate a kind of mushroom which they use for food.

The worker minors who stay at home and act as nurses bite off tiny pieces of the mushrooms and pop them into the open mouths of the ever-hungry little grubs. It seems a strange kind of infants' food, but ant babies seem to enjoy it and thrive upon it.

Very different in their ways are the fierce driver ants of Brazil and their equally fierce cousins of the African jungles. Although they usually have some sort of settled home as headquarters, they are very restless creatures, always wandering about and pitching new camps in any convenient spot in which they happen to be when they halt for a rest.

An army of driver ants marching across country is one of the most extraordinary sights of the insect world. First comes a company of major workers, fearsome-looking creatures with huge heads and immense jaws. These are called "soldiers"; but as a matter of fact all driver ants, large and small, are fierce fighters. Behind the advance guard comes rank after rank of minor workers with the baggage of the moving army. Some are carrying the dead insects or grubs which they have seized and borne off from the ants' nests they have raided on the way; others have pieces of stick, leaves, blades of grass, and all sorts of odds and ends that may come in handy on the march. A body of workers follows, bearing the precious babies, which they carry with them wherever they go.

Elephants Put to Flight

On and on come the ants, marching along in close formation, in columns one or two inches wide and sometimes nearly a mile long. They pour like a cataract over every obstacle; nothing but fire or water will stop their progress. Every living creature flees before these terrible insect armies—monkeys, antelopes, even lions and elephants beat a hasty retreat when driver ants are on the war-path. For they would certainly be eaten alive by the angry insects if they didn't get out of the way.

Strange as it seems, these dreaded ants are mostly blind, or nearly so. But that does not seem to cause them any inconvenience. They communicate with one another by touch, and in a very short time can telegraph news up and down the long columns in the most astounding way.

(CONTINUED ON PAGE 331)

Antelopes are about the size of deer, and many, many thousands of times larger than an ant; yet they take to their swift legs with all possible speed when an army of driver ants bears down upon them.

John Cabot and his men thought that it was Northeastern Asia they were claiming for England, but it was really Labrador. Since the forgotten voyages of the Norsemen, no white man had until that day set foot in North America. If Henry VII had only listened to Cabot as Queen Isabella of Spain listened to Columbus, it is possible that English ships under this great explorer might have been the first to find the New World. Even as it was, Cabot laid the foundation of the great British empire that grew up and flourished for long in America.

The FIRST WHITE MAN in NORTH AMERICA

As a Little Boy, John Cabot Lived in the Same City as Columbus, with Never a Thought of the Continent He Would One Day Find across the Ocean

A FEW years before Columbus sailed across the Atlantic Ocean there had come to England an expert Italian seaman named Giovanni Caboto (jŏ-vän'nē kä-bō'tō). The name was rather difficult to pronounce, so he was called John Cabot instead. And as John Cabot he is famous to this day.

He was born about 1450 in Genoa, where Columbus himself had been born about four years earlier. It is possible that when they were boys they may have passed each other in the narrow streets that wind among the tall houses of that city. They little thought in those days that one of them would be the first man to find land on the other side of the great ocean, and that the other was destined to be the first man to see the coast of North America!

At about eleven years of age, Cabot had gone to live in Venice, and had very naturally become a sailor. For Venice, in carrying on trade with Asia, sent many a ship across the Mediterranean. On one of his trips Cabot even sailed as far east as Mecca, the great market city of Arabia to which came the long caravans with their precious loads of jewels, silks and spices. But these caravans had received their goods from other caravans that came from still farther east— perhaps, thought Cabot, even from far-away Cathay (kă-thā'), or China, that wonderful land which another Venetian, the great Marco Polo, had managed to reach nearly two hundred years before.

Now Cabot knew that the earth was round; so, if Marco Polo could reach Cathay by going east over the land, why could not someone else get there by going west across the water? It was the same question that

Columbus asked, and many another man was asking it at the time.

It was with this idea that Cabot had come to England, about 1484, with his wife and three little sons. For many years, in London and in the seaport town of Bristol, Cabot had a hard time trying to persuade anybody to provide him with ships and money for the great venture. But while he was still busy talking about it, the news drifted into Bristol in 1493 that Columbus had sailed across the ocean and found the "Indies"— what everybody took to be the land of Asia.

John Cabot's Scheme Receives the Gracious Approval of the King

Cabot went up to London to see the king. Now King Henry VII was a prudent man, and careful with his money; but when he found that Cabot had amassed enough money for the expedition, and only awaited his gracious permission to carry out his scheme, he soon signed a paper granting to his "well-beloved John Cabot, citizen of Venice, to Lewis, Sebastian and Santius, sons of the said John, full and free authority, leave and power upon their own proper costs and charges, to seek out, discover and find whatsoever isles, countries, regions or provinces of the heathen and infidels, which before this time have been unknown to all Christians." The king was to have one-fifth of any wealth that came out of the venture, and the Cabots should have the sole right to trade with the new countries, without paying any duty on the goods they might find to bring into England.

So one morning early in May, 1497, Cabot set out down the channel from Bristol, with eighteen sailors in a little boat called the "Mathew," to find his way across the ocean. The little ship experienced fine weather, and in less than two months, on June 24, she sighted land, which was probably the northern part of Cape Breton Island.

Here Cabot went ashore and planted the banner of England—and along with it, as a compliment to his own city of Venice, the banner of St. Mark. He thought he had reached the coast of Asia as he cruised along it, landing here and there, naming the capes and islands that he saw, and observing

immense shoals of fish. In fact, the codfish were so plentiful that the sailors had only to let down baskets into the water to catch all they wanted. But Cabot saw no human beings, although he found a few signs of them, such as snares to catch game and some notched or felled trees. He thought he must be fairly far north on the coast of Asia, and that the rich lands of China and Japan must lie to the south. But his provisions were running short, and he was compelled to sail for home.

There must have been great excitement in Bristol on the morning of August 6, when the little ship returned from over the ocean— and a good deal more in London when Cabot arrived to submit his report to the king. The king made him a Grand Admiral and gave him £10—which was then worth considerably more than it would be now.

But Cabot preferred to be a hero on the sea rather than in London, and he persuaded the king to promise him ten vessels for another trip the next spring. By the month of May the number had dwindled to two, but in these he set out with his son Sebastian and about three hundred men. They made for Greenland and then tried to sail on west. But the ice blocked their passage, and they were forced to turn south in search of the islands that we now call Japan. Cabot sailed down the coast of America about as far as Chesapeake Bay, and then had to return home. Shortly after his return he died.

Sebastian Cabot Attempts to Reach China by a Southern Route

His son Sebastian was also a bold mariner. In 1525 he set out from Spain to find his way to China and Japan by a southern route. This took him to Brazil and farther south along the coast. In 1551 he founded the company of merchant adventurers, and in 1553 sent out three ships from England in an effort to discover a north-east passage to the East. The ice prevented them from reaching China, and the crews of two of the vessels were frozen to death. But the commander of the third ship made his way into Russia and established trade between England and that country. It is supposed that Sebastian Cabot died about 1557.

When the brave Breton sailor, Jacques Cartier, finally moored his little ships on the eastern shore of the New World, at the point of land we now call Cape Gaspé, he planted the cross and the banner of France and claimed the fertile soil for his king. And that was the beginning of what later became the colony New France.

LOOKING *for* CHINA *He* FOUND CANADA

And then Jacques Cartier Laid the Foundations of a New France Far Greater in Extent than the Mother Country

HIGH on a granite cliff of Brittany, in France, stands the town of Saint-Malo. The single, slender spire of its cathedral towers above the city walls, soaring upward as though it would pierce the sky. Far out at sea, the sailors catch sight of it before they can discern the town, and so they know that they have nearly completed one more voyage. Now, as always, most of the male inhabitants of Saint-Malo (săN-mä′lō) are sailors, and always they have been renowned as hardy seamen and doughty fighters. So famous have they always been that France's greatest

king would have only Bretons to man his fleets—and only Bretons who were natives of Saint-Malo.

Greatest of all Saint-Malo's sailors, and best remembered by the French, was Jacques Cartier (zhäk kär-tyā′), who sailed from there in 1534 and gave his king a claim on the New World. When only a youth Cartier had made a trip to Brazil. This time, as a seasoned sailor of forty-three years, he did not go southward again, but boldly struck out to the north-west across the Atlantic. He was not seeking new lands, but a sea route to distant China. He sighted Newfoundland, already discovered by John Cabot, sailed along the southern coast of Labrador, and finally moored his ships in a great bay at a point of land which is now known as Cape Gaspé.

Later he wrote that he was spellbound by the beauty of the country, by its fertility, and by the welcome of the hospitable Indians. Here he planted a cross and the banner of France, claiming all the land for Francis I, his great king. This was the beginning of New France.

Discovery of the St. Lawrence

The following year (1536) Cartier set out again from Saint-Malo, this time with a small fleet, for he had some hope of founding a colony. When he once more reached the spot which he had previously visited, his men somehow discovered that the water of this arm of the sea is fresh, not salty. They sailed on westward, and on August 10, Cartier concluded that they were sailing up a great river, and since the date was that of the feast day of Saint Lawrence, he named the river after the saint.

Continuing their course up the magnificent stream, the voyagers came to the point where the city of Quebec now stands, and there they found an Indian village called Stadacona, ruled by a chief named Donnacona. Here they rested for a few days and were entertained by the natives. When Donnacona tried to persuade them not to go any farther, they refused to listen. They sailed on and at last reached a beautiful island lying in the river at a spot where a great hill, towering out of a plain, stands on one bank. Cartier and his men stopped at Hochelaga, the Indian village on the island, and before they left they named the hill Mont-Royal. To this day the isle itself and the city that stands on the site are both called Montreal.

With the arrival of winter, the voyagers decided to return to Stadacona. Unused to such a long cold season, the men suffered great hardships and many died of scurvy. Cartier himself suffered an attack of the disease but was cured by some remedy given him by a friendly and admiring Indian. In the spring of 1537 the ships set sail for France, taking with them Chief Donnacona, who had been treacherously seized despite the many kindnesses he had shown to the sick and suffering sailors.

Cartier's Reward

In 1541 Cartier made his last trip to the New World. The glittering stones that the bold Breton sailor carried back home from this voyage did not prove to bear gold, as he had expected. Nevertheless, his voyages brought him wealth. As a reward for his labours the king conferred on him great farms and a fine home in Brittany, and there the courageous explorer, forgetting the sea and its perils, settled down to write the interesting memoirs that give us a delightful story of his many wonderful adventures. He died on September 1, 1557.

Photo by Rischgitz

Jacques Cartier never found a north-west passage to the East, but he did find the St. Lawrence. Here you see the daring Frenchman and his party sailing for the first time up the great American river, in the year 1536.

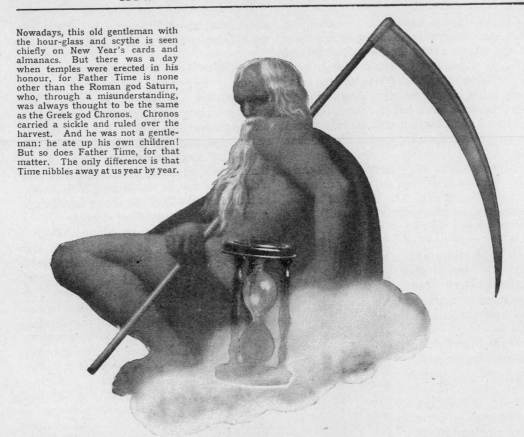

Nowadays, this old gentleman with the hour-glass and scythe is seen chiefly on New Year's cards and almanacs. But there was a day when temples were erected in his honour, for Father Time is none other than the Roman god Saturn, who, through a misunderstanding, was always thought to be the same as the Greek god Chronos. Chronos carried a sickle and ruled over the harvest. And he was not a gentleman: he ate up his own children! But so does Father Time, for that matter. The only difference is that Time nibbles away at us year by year.

How We LEARNED to TELL the TIME

Long before We had Clocks and Watches We Used to Keep Track of Time by Means of Sand, Water, Candles, and Many Other Things

JUST for a minute suppose we try to think of a world without any clocks or watches, or even any sundials. What would things be like? Nobody would know what time it was. Nobody would know when to go to school or to work or to church: the people would all be straggling along at different times. No one could be sure of keeping any engagement. Nobody would know when to start a boat or a train. In fact, the trains would all be running into one another, because they would all be starting at the wrong time. No one would even know when to eat, and many of us would miss our dinners. It would be a sorry, topsy-turvy kind of world in which to live.

Once upon a time, however, such a condition of things *did* exist in this world of ours; but then, of course, nobody cared what time it was. There were no schools or churches to attend, and no trains to start. And as for eating, a man just ate when he was hungry— or rather, whenever he could find something to eat. Nobody ever had to be "on time."

When, therefore, Prehistoric Man set out from his cave, neither he nor anybody else knew when he would be back. He returned when he thought he would, and his friends expected him when they saw him.

After a while, however, he felt he wanted

to let his friends know when he would be back, and eventually he found out a way of telling them. Day after day he had noticed that the shadow of a certain rock or bush beside his cave reached practically the same place at the same time every afternoon. So when he went away he set a stone down at a certain point on the ground. He would try to get back when the shadow reached that point.

Now this man was a genius for his early day. For he had found out a way in which to make the sun tell him the time; he had discovered the principle of the sundial. We have never found anything since that will tell it better. All our clocks and watches are just machines to mark off the time that the sun tells us.

Then this man, or probably some other one, thought of another good idea. If one stone in a certain place would mark the time when the sun reached it every day, then a whole set of stones, placed at certain proper distances apart, would divide up the whole day into fairly equal periods. He would know more or less what time it was when the shadow came to any particular stone. The first stone might mean about what we call six o'clock in the morning, the second seven, the third eight, and so on. Then the man might stick up a sharp-pointed pole to cast a better shadow than the rock or bush; and the first sundial would be complete.

How long ago the first sundial was made we do not know. The earliest mention of such a device is thought to be that found in the Book of Isaiah, xxxviii, 8, which

He must have looked a great deal like this—the genius who first drew a curve to mark the travelling shadow of some rock or tree, and then divided it into convenient sections. That was the world's first sundial—a clock that could never run down.

dates from about 700 B.C.; probably it was an old device even at that period.

When the Sundial was Useless.

For a long time the sundial was far from perfect. It was of no use at night or on a cloudy day, nor was it any use at sea, on an unsteady deck. Moreover, the sun never rises and sets at the same place or time any two consecutive days. So if the shadow reached a certain stone at nine o'clock one day, it would be a little earlier or later the next day; and after a few months it would be seriously out of schedule.

By about 300 B.C., at least, a way had been invented to correct this. A man named Berossus (bĕ-rŏs'ŭs) in Babylon—a priest of the heathen god Baal of whom we hear so much in the Bible—made a hollow hemisphere, like a bowl, with a tiny ball above it to cast a shadow. The shadow of the ball travelled across the curved surface of the bowl once a day; and by dividing its path into twelve sections and then drawing some ingenious curves on the face of the bowl, one could divide every day into twelve equal parts, or "hours."

The days of the year, however, are not of equal length. In the winter the sun may be up for only ten hours, while in the summer it may be up for fourteen. Now, if the shadow of the sun has only a brief time in which to travel through the twelve sections, it will have to hurry, and the "hours" will be shorter; while if it has a long time it will creep more slowly, and the "hours" will be longer. Thus every day would have twelve hours of sunlight, but the hours would be longer in summer than in winter. It is because of this that we cannot reckon the "hemicycle of Berossus," as the sundial of that worthy man was called, to be an accurate instrument for the measurement of time.

His sundial served its purpose so well, however, that it found employment through many centuries in Greece and Rome. Sometimes it was made fairly small, but sometimes it was big enough to fill a whole courtyard. Sometimes it was a dark cavern with one little beam of sunlight coming through a hole in the top.

But the curved dial was an awkward thing. It was hard to read unless it was large, and then it would be hard to make. So the world mostly went back to flat sundials, with the pointer directed due north, and found out ways of making them fairly accurate. Indeed, people made very elaborate and very beautiful sundials throughout the days of ancient Greece and Rome, and throughout the Middle Ages, down to two or three hundred years ago, when clocks and watches began to grow common. After that, the sundial was used mainly for an ornament in gardens, as it still is very often.

Long before, however, men had found out other ways of keeping time—ways in which to tell the time at night, on cloudy days, or on the sea. One of these ways was by means of the famous water clock, or clepsydra (klĕp′sĭ-drȧ). The word comes from the Greek and really means the "water thief."

Telling the Time by Water

At first it was simply an earthenware vessel with a tiny hole in the bottom. When this was full of water, the water would drip slowly away, and one could measure the

By courtesy of the Deutsches Museum, Munich
At the left is the clever water clock of Ctesibius of Alexandria. As water ran out of the container it turned a set of water wheels, and these operated machinery that caused a little figure with a pointer to rise gradually and so to indicate the numbers on an index. Athens is thought to have had a clock of this kind in its famous Tower of the Winds, with the cistern for it in one of the turrets. At the right is one of the familiar forms of sundial. Its shadow at noon points directly north; and as the sun travels down the sky, the shadow travels too, through all the afternoon hours. With the setting of the sun, the dial goes to sleep for the night; but it wakes precisely at sunrise, and proceeds to mark the morning hours that lead up to noon.

time it took for all the water to leak out. Then it would be known that this amount of time would always pass between the first drop and the last drop.

As long as the clepsydra was of earthenware one could hardly tell how much of the water had run out at any moment, or how much time had gone. The next move, therefore, was to make the instrument of glass. Also the water ran much faster when it was full than when it was nearly empty; so the next improvement was to arrange to keep it always full, and measure the water that had run out, into another bowl beneath. But at the best it was an uncertain timepiece. It was too likely to get clogged, and then the orator might go on for ever!

For in Rome men used to time their speeches in the law courts by the clepsydra. The poet Martial tells a story about a nervous and tiresome speaker who kept wetting his lips with a sip of water and who finally said it might relieve him and his hearers if he drank out of the clepsydra!

The clepsydra lent itself to the jeweller's art, and was often very beautiful and very costly. It could be a gift for kings. And sometimes it could be very ingenious. Indeed, a certain Ctesibius (tĕ-sĭb′ĭ-ŭs) of Alexandria, about 140 B.C., made a clepsydra with a system of cogs that caused a pointer to indicate the hours of the day. This was the nearest thing to a clock in ancient days. But the great fault of the clepsydra was that it did not tell the hours—it only told how much time had gone by since it started. Even so it stayed in use for a long while—in France and Italy until about the year 1500—though it sometimes froze in winter!

This last trouble never happened with the

hour-glass. For the hour-glass used sand, or in rare cases mercury, instead of water; and fine sand will trickle through a little hole at a very even rate. The hour-glass was a fat tube pinched in at the waist to leave only a tiny hole. When the sand had run out of the top into the bottom, the glass could be turned upside down to let it run back, or to begin another hour. Of course the glass did not always measure an hour; sometimes it measured only half an hour, and sometimes only a minute.

We do not know how old the hour-glass is, but we have found in Rome a picture of one that dates from about three centuries before Christ. Hour-glasses were still in use until clocks and watches were universally adopted. Preachers used to employ an hour-glass to time their sermons, and to this day there is one in use in the House of Commons. It runs for only two minutes. When there is going to be a vote, the Speaker starts the sand running, and bells are rung—to tell the members that they must be there to vote in two minutes, before the sand is out. Tiny sand-glasses that take three minutes to run out are still employed by some people to measure the time for the boiling of eggs.

There have been many other ways of measuring time, and almost anybody could invent one if he tried. Sometimes it has been measured by a burning candle. For a good candle, well protected from the wind, will burn at a very even rate, and it can easily be marked off into sections an hour long.

But all these devices had their faults, though at their best they were astonishingly accurate. None of them would do to time the running of a train, and none of them except the sundial would tell what time it was—whether six o'clock or twelve o'clock—but only how long it was since they had been started. The sundial

Suppose you found yourself in a land that had neither clocks nor watches, which one of the time-pieces above would you choose? All of them have been used by mankind at some time or other. The flame creeping at steady pace between the equal intervals in a knotted string; water dripping slowly out of a glass vessel with a scale on its side; a candle burning quietly through section after section of its length; a moving sunbeam striking through a hole in a ring and pointing to a number—all these were accurate enough for the needs of the men who used them. But as civilization advanced, time became more and more precious. The burning candle that King Alfred always used was replaced by the lamp clock in the centre of the picture. In it the steady flame on a wick in the little trough-like affair at one side burned up the oil in the glass and made it fall steadily along the scale marked on the strip of metal against the container. Best of all, however, was the hour-glass. The flow of its fine sand was not affected by weather, and it went on at the same speed whether the glass was full or nearly empty.

Photo by Alinari

THE MAN WHO MADE CLOCKS POSSIBLE

It was this great Italian who made our modern clocks and watches possible. Here Galileo is shown in the cathedral at Pisa on that windy Sunday when the swinging lamps taught him the secret of the pendulum.

would tell the hour, approximately at least, but only when the sun was shining. So something better than all these devices was needed, though nothing better appeared until towards the end of the Middle Ages.

Father of All the Clocks

By that time there were a great many big churches and cathedrals. Then some one invented a machine to ring a bell and call all the people to church at the same time. It was not exactly a clock at first; it had no hands or face, and it did not tell the time; it only rang a bell. But it was the father of all clocks, and the very word "clock" in the beginning meant a "bell." It worked with a heavy weight which turned some wheels; and when the wheels reached a certain position, they made the bell ring. Sometimes they made an iron figure of a man, or some similar thing, step out of the machine and strike the bell with a hammer. Such figures were called "Jacks of the clock."

No one knows precisely who made the first clocks or when they were first made; but by the year 1300 they were beginning to be like our modern big clocks, with a face and a hand to tell the time. By 1379 there appeared what has been called the parent of all our modern timepieces. It was then that the king of France called on Henry de Vick to build a clock for the royal palace in Paris. And the clock he made is still standing, although the royal palace has long since become the Palace of Justice. It was driven by a weight of five hundred pounds, and it had only one hand, but it was constructed on the same basic principles as the clocks of our day. For about two centuries afterwards there was no great change in clocks.

Origin of the Pendulum

And then came the pendulum. In 1581 an Italian boy—who was just beginning to study medicine—was sitting in the great, draughty cathedral of Pisa watching the hanging lamps as they swung back and forth in the breeze. Now they would be swinging just a little way; then a gust would strike them and they would swing in a wide sweep. And the boy began to notice something. Since he was the first person in all the world

Expert gardeners often make these floral clocks in which a mechanism hidden inside the mound drives a pair of hands over the surface of a round flower-bed cleverly planted to represent the face of a large clock.

A—In the cathedral at Lund, in Sweden, is this famous astronomical clock, first wound up 500 years ago. It has knights that do battle every day at noon, trumpeters that play a hymn, and Wise Men that bow to the Virgin.

But most remarkable of all is the lower dial, where the movements of the heavenly bodies, the calendar, and certain church festivals are all correctly shown.

B—This quaint old astronomical clock at Prague was built in 1419. It is said that the maker's eyes were put out to prevent his building another. But he stole a part of the works, which no one could replace!

D—The famous clock on the tower of the Metropolitan Life Building, New York City, E — The huge hour hand of the clock for which Big Ben speaks.

C—Big Ben, the most famous bell in the world, announces the hours for this clock on the Houses of Parliament in London.

to notice it, we need not be surprised to learn that he was a great genius—no other than the famous Galileo (gǎl'ĭ-lē'ō).

He noticed that however far the lamp swung, it always took the same length of time in which to come back. If it went a little way, it travelled slowly, and if it made a big swing it went fast; but always it took exactly the same time to complete its swing. And that was an important discovery in science, for since then the pendulum, or swinging weight, has taught us a great deal.

Galileo did not at once put a pendulum into a clock. He merely showed the doctors how they could count pulses with a pendulum. But others soon saw what it would do for the clock, and in 1656 the great Dutch scientist, Christian Huygens (hī'gĕnz), made a far more accurate pendulum clock than the world had ever seen before. He needed it to time the movements of the stars, and ever since then the world has had clocks sufficiently accurate for most purposes. The minute hand now appeared—it had hardly been needed before, because the clocks might easily be many minutes wrong —and finally the second hand came.

Most people even now do not know how a clock works. Of course there are many kinds, and they are often very complicated; but the basic principles are always the same.

First, there must be some power to make the wheels go round. That is supplied by a heavy weight that is always pulling downwards. Then there must be something to keep the wheels from going too fast or too slow—or to make them always keep the same steady pace. That is the pendulum,

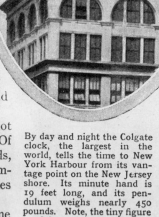

By day and night the Colgate clock, the largest in the world, tells the time to New York Harbour from its vantage point on the New Jersey shore. Its minute hand is 19 feet long, and its pendulum weighs nearly 450 pounds. Note, the tiny figure of the man on the right.

with its never-varying swings backwards and forwards. And finally there must be the network of cogged wheels, all working together at different speeds but all keeping time with the pendulum as they turn the hour hand very slowly, the minute hand faster, and the second hand faster still; for each hand must go sixty times faster than the one behind it.

The weight pulls on a big wheel and makes it turn round slowly; and, through the system of cogs, this big wheel makes all the smaller wheels, of various sizes, turn at their various proper speeds; while the pendulum swings to and fro to keep the big wheel going at exactly the right pace. At the top, the pendulum is attached to a lever catch which works in and out of a set of notches, or "teeth," controlling the "escape" wheel. Every time the pendulum swings back, the catch lets the wheel slip a tooth; and then it holds the wheel still until the pendulum swings back again.

Thus, since the pendulum always swings back in the same time, the "escape" wheel always slips one tooth in the same time, and all the other wheels behave accordingly. But what keeps the pendulum going? Why doesn't it "die down"? Because every time it comes to the end of a swing, it gets a little kick from the lever catch, and so it keeps on. But suppose the whole clock goes too fast or too slow? Then we just make the pendulum a little longer or a little shorter—there is a screw to do this—until we get it exactly right. For the shorter a pendulum, the briefer its swing, and the longer it is the slower. In this way we "regulate" the clock.

That is the main principle of the ingenious

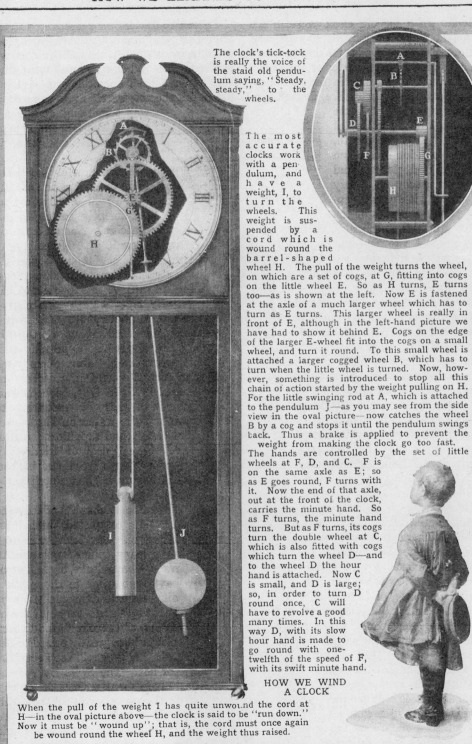

The clock's tick-tock is really the voice of the staid old pendulum saying, "Steady, steady," to the wheels.

The most accurate clocks work with a pendulum, and have a weight, I, to turn the wheels. This weight is suspended by a cord which is wound round the barrel-shaped wheel H. The pull of the weight turns the wheel, on which are a set of cogs, at G, fitting into cogs on the little wheel E. So as H turns, E turns too—as is shown at the left. Now E is fastened at the axle of a much larger wheel which has to turn as E turns. This larger wheel is really in front of E, although in the left-hand picture we have had to show it behind E. Cogs on the edge of the larger E-wheel fit into the cogs on a small wheel, and turn it round. To this small wheel is attached a larger cogged wheel B, which has to turn when the little wheel is turned. Now, however, something is introduced to stop all this chain of action started by the weight pulling on H. For the little swinging rod at A, which is attached to the pendulum J—as you may see from the side view in the oval picture—now catches the wheel B by a cog and stops it until the pendulum swings back. Thus a brake is applied to prevent the weight from making the clock go too fast.

The hands are controlled by the set of little wheels at F, D, and C. F is on the same axle as E; so as E goes round, F turns with it. Now the end of that axle, out at the front of the clock, carries the minute hand. So as F turns, the minute hand turns. But as F turns, its cogs turn the double wheel at C, which is also fitted with cogs which turn the wheel D—and to the wheel D the hour hand is attached. Now C is small, and D is large; so, in order to turn D round once, C will have to revolve a good many times. In this way D, with its slow hour hand is made to go round with one-twelfth of the speed of F, with its swift minute hand.

HOW WE WIND A CLOCK

When the pull of the weight I has quite unwound the cord at H—in the oval picture above—the clock is said to be "run down." Now it must be "wound up"; that is, the cord must once again be wound round the wheel H, and the weight thus raised.

machine. In a big old clock you can see the weight and pendulum for yourself, and watch them work. And some day you may see some of the great clocks of the world that do all sorts of remarkable things. There is one at Strasbourg in France, first built in 1352, which not only tells the hours, but shows the day of the week and of the month, gives the position of the sun and moon and planets, and even predicts eclipses. Every day at noon it shows a procession of the figures of the Twelve Apostles and makes a huge cock on top of a tower ruffle his neck, flap his wings, and crow. In London there is Big Ben of Westminster, with a face about twenty-three feet across and a pendulum weighing nearly 450 pounds, and the Shell-Mex House clock on the Victoria Embankment, the dial of which is twenty-five feet square. In New York there is the great Colgate clock, the largest in the world, with a minute hand nineteen feet long and a pendulum weighing 450 pounds.

The little clocks in your house, however, probably have no pendulums at all, and certainly the watches have none.

Well, once we know how the big clocks run, it is very easy to explain the little clocks and watches. There must still be a power to make the wheels go round, and something to regulate their speed. Now if we just put a spring in place of the weight for power, and a balance-wheel instead of the pendulum for regulator, we have the secret of the little watch and clock. Such a spring and balance-wheel you can see if you open the back of any watch. When the spring is wound up it supplies the same sort of pull as the weight provides, and the balance-wheel does the same kind of work as the pendulum.

This great pointed shaft told time for the Pharaohs in Egypt sixteen hundred years before the birth of Christ. It now stands on the Victoria Embankment, London, and it has a twin in New York. They are known as "Cleopatra's Needles," but the king who set up these two great obelisks as pointers for his sundials lived long before Cleopatra's day.

These two devices were discovered shortly after the pendulum, so, thenceforth clocks could be made smaller and thus watches were evolved. The old clock, named from a bell, had at first been something to which to listen, but the new watch, as its name shows, was something at which to look. The first spring is said to have been made of a pig's bristle.

The names of Jacob Zech (zĕk) of Prague and of Gruet (grü-ā') in Switzerland are prominently connected with the early watches. And an early kind of watch made at Nuremberg in Germany was so fat and round that it was called the "Nuremberg egg." King Edward VI is supposed to have been the first English sovereign to own one, in about 1550. Brass wheels were introduced about that period, and watch-glasses appeared about fifty years later. Minute-hands were not generally used in watches until about 1700. In 1704, Nicholas Facio found out that by mounting the pivots of the watch on hard jewels, like rubies and sapphires, he could save a great deal of friction and keep the parts from wearing out. That is why a good watch has so many "jewels."

Thus the mechanism of the watch was soon completed, and it remained only for later workers to make many minor improvements. Watches and clocks, big and small, have been made in thousands of different patterns, some being very beautiful and very expensive. Many of the old "grandfather's clocks" are greatly prized to-day, whether they still keep good time or not. The Swiss have always been great makers of watches, though many of the most valuable improvements have been due to the inventions of French and English craftsmen.

We have seen that the sundial would not work at sea,

One year is the time it takes the earth to travel around the sun.

One day is the time it takes the earth to turn round on its axis.

Here is the great clock that makes our time. All the little clocks and watches are just machines for dividing into shorter periods the days that the sun tells off for us as he travels across the sky. Those days are always twenty-four hours long, the length of time it takes the earth to spin completely round. And it always takes just the same number of those days for the earth to make its annual march round the sun and so tell off a year. At Greenwich Observatory there is a marvellously accurate clock and also a special telescope by means of which the astronomers can tell from the sun, or from certain stars, exactly how long the earth takes to turn completely round. This enables them to keep the clock exactly right, and twice a day—at 10 a.m. and 6 p.m.—Greenwich Time is broadcast from the Government's high-power station at Rugby.

and that the clepsydra was little better. But the hour-glass worked fairly well. And time is very important on the sea, for by means of it the sailor not only can reckon at what speed his ship is going, but also in what longitude he is sailing.

In the old days the sailor flung overboard a "log," or piece of wood made to resist the action of the waves, with a string tied to it. In the string there was a series of knots, 47 feet 3 inches apart. As the sailor threw over the log and felt the first knot slipping through his fingers, he stamped on the deck. Instantly another sailor turned up the sand-glass, made to run exactly 28 seconds. As the last grain of sand ran out, he gave a signal; then the first sailor clamped his fingers on the string and noted the number of knots or parts of a knot that had run through his fingers. He could then reckon just how fast the ship was going.

For instance, suppose he was just coming to the fifth knot as the sand ran out. Then the ship had gone 5 × 47¼ ft. in 28 seconds. That meant that the ship was travelling at the rate of five knots or five nautical miles per hour. The nautical mile, you must remember, is 6,080 ft., therefore it is longer than the land mile, which is only 5,280 ft. It was made longer in order that it might measure one sixtieth of a degree—and the whole circumference of the earth is 360 degrees.

On the sea the time is kept, not by the hour, but by the "watch." A "watch" is four hours. The first watch is from 8 p.m. to midnight, the second from midnight to 4 a.m., and so on; and a bell is rung every half-hour. "One bell" is struck half an hour after the watch has begun; "two bells" are struck half an hour later, and so on up to eight bells, when the counting starts all over again.

How the Sun Makes Our Time

We have said that the sun makes all our time for us. It marks off our days. From the moment when it is overhead at noon to the next moment when it comes round over-head at noon makes one day. If the sun never moved, but always stayed straight overhead, then it would always be day. It would be noon for ever, and there would be no such thing as time. Now that is something of which most people never think; but the fact is that if there were nothing moving in the universe, if everything stayed still for ever, there would be no time at all. It would always be just "now." Only as we note how long it takes something to move from one place to another can we tell the time that passes. In this respect, time and motion are the same thing.

So the sun makes our day, and then we divide each day into twenty-four hours, each hour into sixty minutes, and each minute into sixty seconds. We might have chosen any other numbers, but these serve

If we reckon our days by the sun, why don't we count from sunrise to sunrise, instead of from noon to noon? It certainly seems to be the logical way, but there is one great objection. The sun never rises at the same time twice in succession; so our days would never be the same length. This is all because the earth is tilted as it travels round the sun; so in winter the sun is directly overhead in the Southern Hemisphere, as is shown at the left, and days in the Northern Hemisphere are short and cold. But as the earth travels on round the sun and gets to the other side of him, the Northern Hemisphere is tilted towards him. The North Pole would now be at A and the South Pole at B, and the sun to people who live in the north would rise early and set late. There is one time in the day, however, of which we can be certain; that is the moment when the sun is directly over a line that would connect the spot on which we are standing with the North and the South Poles. Then it is noon—and from noon to noon is twenty-four hours.

Long ago people used to reckon the day from sunrise. But that did not work well, because the sun keeps rising at different times. So we now reckon from noon, when the sun is at its highest in the sky. From the moment the sun gets there to the next moment it gets there is a solar day

But of course the sun is at its highest at different moments for different places. When it is noon in London it is not noon in New York, and

well enough. Now all our machines for counting time have just been things that made so many *motions* to the hour. The shadow of the sundial creeps just so far in an hour. The water in the clepsydra and the sand in the hour-glass will spill just so much in an hour. The wheels in the clock or watch

There would seem to be nothing unusual about the zigzag line connecting the earth's poles in the picture above, but in reality it is the point at which yesterday turns into to-day and to-day becomes to-morrow. Geographers know it as the International Date Line, or the 180th meridian. It is exactly opposite Greenwich on the earth's surface; so every day whose noon is announced to the world at Greenwich was born twelve hours before on the International Date Line. Or in other words, when it is Sunday on the western side of this line it is Monday on the eastern side. If you could stand on the North Pole and peer down over the side of the earth with Greenwich directly behind you, you would see a sight somewhat like the picture at the right. Round the earth the ships would be travelling in endless procession, and every ship as it crossed the Date Line would gain or lose a day, depending on whether it was going east or west. If it crossed the line going east on December 31st, one end of the ship would be in the old year and the other end in the new. Of course the Date Line is drawn only on maps—and there it is zigzag, in order that it may not cross any land.

Greenwich

when it is noon in New York it is early morning in California. So every place must have its own time. This used to be

will turn just so far in an hour. So time is still motion; and all that we have done to keep better and better time has been to build machines that will keep in step with the sun.

rather confusing, and it would be so still if we had not found a way in which to solve the problem. We can see how hard it would be to run boats across the oceans or fast

It is noon when the sun is directly over an imaginary line connecting the spot on which you are standing with the North and South Poles. Above, it is noon at 12 on the right.

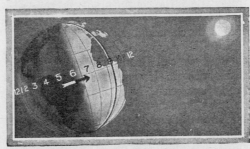

As our globe spins round under the sun, every spot passes beneath it and then leaves it behind. In the picture above, the white line—the meridian of Greenwich—is at 9 a.m.

Now our globe has spun about until Greenwich, which in our first picture was at 6 o'clock in the morning, is now directly under the sun. It is noon there—and morning in America.

Now America, too, is swinging along towards noon, and the International Date Line, where it was midnight when it was noon at Greenwich, has now reached three o'clock in the morning.

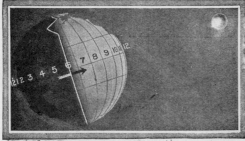

When the International Date Line left midnight behind—shown by the figure 12 at the left—the people along it put a new date on their letters. They were the first to write it.

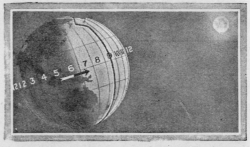

Now all the world you see to the left of the International Date Line is using the new date. But the remainder of the world may not use it until after twelve o'clock at midnight.

By now the Date Line is at noon, and at Greenwich it is midnight. In the United States, on the other side of the earth, day is drawing to a close; it is morning in Asia.

Our old earth will soon have swung completely round. Greenwich has now reached 3 o'clock a.m., and will soon be having her sunrise at 6—her position in the first picture.

trains across the continents if the time were always changing as we swept along. Nobody's watch would ever be right.

Now for years British ships had all run on what we call Greenwich (grĭn'ĭj) time—that is, the time it was at the Royal Observatory, Greenwich, near London. And at last the nations of the world, with a few exceptions, agreed to adopt Greenwich time as their standard—not because it was any better than Paris time or Tokyo time, but simply because it was already followed all round the world at sea. Clocks in countries using Standard Time are set so that the minutes and seconds agree with Greenwich time—only the hour is different.

As you climb the hill to the observatory at Greenwich, you will see a strip of concrete laid down in the road. It marks the path of a line from the North Pole to the South Pole through that point in Greenwich. It is

where longitude begins, and it is where time begins. When the sun gets over that line, it is noon. Anywhere east of there it is later in the day, and anywhere west it is earlier.

Now the whole world is divided up into 360 degrees of longitude. And since a day has twenty-four hours, or 1,440 minutes, we can see by dividing that we have to allow four minutes for each degree. That is the time it takes the sun to pass over one degree. So one degree east of Greenwich it would be four minutes later than at Greenwich, and one degree west it would be four minutes earlier. Fifteen degrees away it would be one hour earlier or later.

If you were travelling west from Greenwich you would therefore have to set your watch back four minutes every time you went one degree; and if you were going east, you would set it forward four minutes. But it would be a nuisance to keep setting your watch

Workmen erecting a new type of clock at Paddington Station, the London terminus of the Great Western Railway. The time is indicated in a form most convenient for passengers, the hour being shown on the left and the minutes past the hour on the right, for example 4.15 or 5.26. The figures are painted on endless moving belts made of steel slats. The right-hand figures change every minute, and the left-hand figures at the end of each hour.

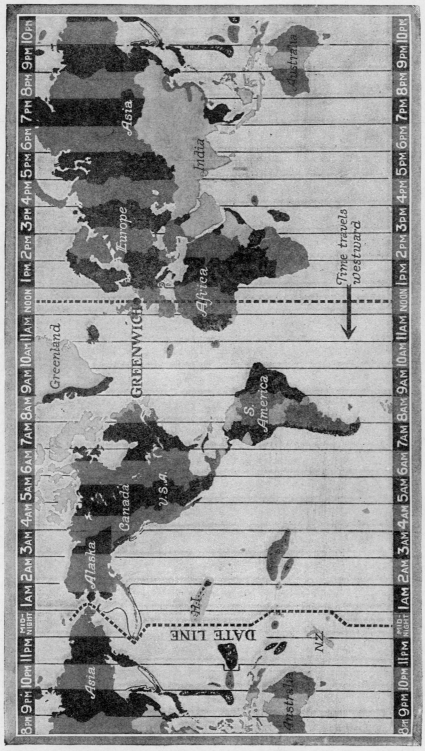

Suppose you could suddenly take the crust off the earth and spread it out flat like this, having slit it from north to south through Eastern Asia. You would still have the whole of the earth's surface, but it would be like a plan. Now let us imagine that lines were drawn north and south just 15 degrees apart. All the places between any two lines will be having the same time, but that time will be an hour earlier or later than the time in the spaces on either side. So if it were noon along the dotted line that passes through Greenwich—that is, if it were noon along the dotted line that passes through Greenwich—that is, if it were noon along the dotted line that passes through Greenwich—that is, if it were noon along the dotted line that passes through Greenwich—that is, if it were noon along the dotted line that passes through Greenwich—that is, the sun were straight above that line—it would be 11 a.m. in the space just west, and 1 p.m. in the space just to the east. The figures at the top and bottom of each zone show what time it will be in that zone when it is noon in Greenwich. But be sure to remember that as soon as you cross the International Date Line, which goes zigzagging north and south across the map at the left, you must step into yesterday if you are going west, and into to-morrow if you are travelling east. For a new day is born every time it is midnight along that line. Countries that are not shaded on the map do not use Standard Zone time; sometimes the time used is an exact number of half-hours different from Greenwich time.

309

every hour or two. So what happens is that everyone agrees to set his watch back once a day; and on a boat going to New York, about the first thing you do in the morning is to find out what time it is and set your watch. How much you set it back depends on the speed of the boat. On the fast ships you will set it back about an hour.

On the land you do not set the watch back every morning, but every time you have

Photo by H.M. Office of Works : by permission of H.M. Stationery Office

This remarkable astronomical clock at Hampton Court Palace was made for Henry VIII in 1540. From the position of the pointer on the dial it is possible to ascertain the hour, the month, the day of the month, the position of the sun, the number of days since the beginning of the year, the various phases of the moon, and the time of high-water at London Bridge. The clock is wound once a week, and it takes about half an hour.

hour. In going from Nova Scotia to British Columbia, for instance, you would set it back four times, and gain four hours. If you were coming the other way, you would set it forward, and lose four hours. The five time belts give us Atlantic, Eastern, Central, Mountain, and Pacific time. Anywhere in one belt clocks show the same time; in the next one they show an hour earlier or later; but in them all it is always Greenwich time—with the proper number of hours added or subtracted.

Now if you kept going west and gaining an hour every so often, you would gain twenty-four hours after a while. You would gain a whole day—and then it would be yesterday! And if you kept going east, it would soon be to-morrow. What would you do when to-day turns into yesterday?

Well, you would simply have to call it yesterday, and let it go at that. And this is exactly what happens. In the middle of the Pacific Ocean, along the 180th degree of longitude and just opposite Greenwich on the world's surface, there is an imaginary line, drawn zigzag to keep it from going through any island. When you cross that line going west, you lose a day. If it is Monday, you just call it Tuesday. And of course if you are going east, you gain a day and call it Sunday. Otherwise an airman who kept going east would soon be back in the middle of last month!

Various countries practise Daylight Saving. In Britain, Summer Time was adopted in 1916. By the Act of 1925, it lasts from the day following the third Saturday in April— or, if that day be Easter Day, from the day following the second Saturday—until the end of the first Saturday of October.

gone a certain distance, or crossed a certain line. For that purpose the whole world is divided into twenty-four time belts, each fifteen degrees wide. As you cross from one into another, you change your watch one

HOW TO MAKE A GOOD SLED

You can get twice as much fun out of winter by making your sporting equipment yourself. Here, for instance, is a sled at which nearly every boy will want to try his hand. For the runners (A) you will need two boards 27 inches long, 5 inches wide, and three-fourths of an inch thick. The two cross supports (C) will take two strips 10 inches long, one and one-half inches wide, and three-fourths of an inch thick. Saw the four braces (B) from a board one and one-half inches wide and one and one-half inches thick; they should each be 3 inches long. Boards three-eighths of an inch thick will make a good top. The notches, hand holds, braces, and runners should be shaped just as they are in the picture. Thin strips of sheet iron nailed on the soles will give speed to the steed. And of course a coat or two of red paint set off with a neat black stripe, as shown at D, will add a touch of style.

BARREL STAVE SKIS

You can make a capital pair of skis by shaving down two ordinary barrel staves till they are 4 inches wide at the point in the centre where the foot rests. Rivet an old slipper on each stave, point the staves slightly at the front end, and sand-paper the bottoms smooth.

THE DUTCH JUMPER

The runner (A) of the jolly affair shown below is 3 feet long, 4 inches wide, and 2 inches thick. The upright support for the seat is 13 inches long, 4 inches wide, and 2 inches thick, and is nailed to the runner 6 inches behind the centre. Two boards 4 inches wide, three-fourths of an inch thick, and 16 inches long will do for the side pieces (B). The triangular braces on the runner are cut from timber 2 inches thick, and are 4 inches wide and 4 inches long. The seat (C) is 6 inches wide, 1 inch thick, and 15 inches long; it, too, is braced with two triangular boards 1 inch thick.

A HOCKEY STICK

Select an elm branch shaped as illustrated. With a spoke-shave, plane, rasp, and sand-paper, finish it to the following dimensions: shaft, 50 inches long, tapering from a diameter of three-fourths of an inch at the handle to five-eighths of an inch at the other end; blade, 12 inches long, two and one-fourth inches wide, three-eighths of an inch thick at the bottom, three-sixteenths of an inch thick at the top.

When Queen Elizabeth ruled over England these were some of the weights and measures her subjects used. Though the workmanship lacked finish, it was substantial and even had a kind of sturdy beauty.

By courtesy of the Science Museum

How BIG Is IT? How HEAVY Is IT?

Here are the Curious and Clever Ways That We Have Found of Weighing and Measuring Things

EVERY one of us has tried hard to find out which of two stones was the heavier by holding one of them out in each hand or by holding both of them out in the same hand, one after the other. And often we have found it very difficult to tell.

Long ago our forefathers had no better way than this of discovering the weight of anything. In due time one of them must have hit upon the happy idea of balancing one stick across another, and of placing the two stones on the two ends of the stick. The stone that sank down would be the heavier, and the genius who thought of this method would have invented the first crude pair of scales.

From that early day down to our own time we have gone on inventing hundreds of methods of weighing and measuring things. And to this day we still have many different ways of weighing and measuring in different countries, or even in various parts of the same country. There are so many of them that they are often confusing, and all but one of them are imperfect. For we have found out only one perfect system of weights and measures, as we shall

see. But first we must mention a few of the curious systems that have grown up in the years that have passed.

The weight of a thing is merely the pull of gravity from the earth upon it. But long before men knew anything about gravity they had invented very good balances for telling how great was the pull, or how much a thing weighed. That was achieved before the dawn of history. For when the curtain of history goes up, we find that the Egyptians already have excellent ways of weighing up supplies and other things—such, for example, as tribute money. They weighed articles by the "uten" and the "kat," just as we weigh them nowadays by the pound and the ounce.

But every other nation has its own weights and measures, often of many kinds, and the situation might be very puzzling for a traveller or trader. To be sure, men had nearly always begun measuring things in much the same way—by comparing them with parts of their own bodies. Thus they very often measured by the "foot," as we do still, though we now call it exactly twelve inches. So they frequently used the "pace," and our own word "mile" comes from the Latin term for a thousand paces—*mille passuum*—though that was really two thousand of our paces, because a pace was one step with each foot. For other measures they took other parts of the body. Thus a cubit was the distance from the elbow to the end of the middle finger, and a span was that from the end of the thumb to the end of the little finger when the hand was spread out. And men also measured by the "finger," or the finger "nail," or the "palm" or "hand." To this very day we always say that a horse is so many "hands" high— though a hand now means four inches.

Measuring with Sticks and Rods

At the very start these measures were far from accurate, because the feet and hands of different men were of such different sizes. A big man always got the best of a bargain. But this trouble was quickly overcome, for it was agreed that a stick of a certain length, or later a metal rod, should be a foot, another one a pace, and so on. These sticks or rods then became the units of measure for everybody; and they have come down to our day, though we still call some of them by the names of parts of the human body.

Why We Write "lb." for Pound

Naturally, any unit of measure that was agreed upon would do well enough for all those who used it. But there were so many units in the different lands, or even in the same land, that at the time when the Roman empire united all lands under one rule the conditions of weights and measures was a very perplexing one. So the Romans settled

By courtesy of W. and T. Avery, Ltd.

Two thousand years before the birth of Christ people were buying and selling in Egypt, and keeping elaborate accounts. We have been able to learn from wall decorations a great deal about the life they led and how they did things, and we know that they weighed their goods in scales like those in this temple. Here a slave is weighing ingots of gold. Notice the fact that his weights have been cast in the shape of cattle.

on a single set of units which would serve for the whole empire—that is, all over the civilized world. They made a certain weight which they called a "libra," or "pound"—that is why we still write *lb.* for "pound"—and a certain bronze rod which they called a "pes," or "foot." They kept them carefully guarded in a Roman temple, and they became the standard pound and foot for all the Roman state. For the first time the civilized world had a single method for weighing and measuring.

But the Roman empire fell, and the method ceased with it. In the Middle Ages people went back to hundreds of different ways of weighing and measuring, such as had existed in earlier days. And we have never managed to get back to any single way since, for we still weigh and measure very differently in England, on the Continent, and in America. If you asked for a "kilo" of beefsteak in Paris, have you any notion how much you would get?

During the Middle Ages, when every little district had its own units of weight and measure, there were many queer results.

How the Measures Varied

Thus in one place a pound might be some thirteen ounces, in another perhaps twenty-four. In one country a foot might be twice as long as in another. On the land a mile might be shorter than on the sea, as it still is to this day. And to mention only one other confusion, a given kind of thing might be weighed in one sort of scale, and another thing in a different sort. Thus gold and certain costly things were weighed in one scale, but meat and other cheaper things in another. And that is why we are still weighing them in different scales to-day—with the result that

By courtesy of the Science Museum

Here is a Roman balance and steel-yard from the first century. The steel-yard, at the right, is a balance in which the two arms are not of the same length. The article to be weighed is hung on the shorter arm, and a weight is adjusted on the longer arm so that the two balance. The longer arm is marked off in a graduated scale, which enables the weight to be read accurately.

an ounce of gold is by no means the same weight as is an ounce of salt or sugar.

Little by little, however, people began to bring order out of this chaos, though often they did it in rather curious ways. When a certain place was a great trading-centre its unit of weight and measure was likely to be followed by the people for some distance around it. Such a place was Troyes, in France, and its unit, of troy weight, has come down to our time as the standard of the jewellers. For all England a yard was fixed as the distance from the nose to the thumb of King Henry I. You may have seen your mother measure a piece of cloth the same way when she had no tape-measure at hand. And in England Parliament settled certain measures of weight and length by so many grains of wheat and barley. Thirty-two grains of wheat made one pennyweight, and three barley-corns laid in a row made an inch. Our way of numbering the sizes of shoes to-day goes back to the crude old method of measuring by barley-corns.

There were many other kinds of measures in England. When a man stretched out his arms on both sides, the distance from finger-tip to finger-tip made a "fathom." The depth of the sea is still measured in fathoms, though a fathom is now always six feet.

What an English "Stone" Weighs

Then there was the "ell" for measuring cloth—the name came from the word for "elbow," but the measure was forty-five inches long in England, though of different lengths in other countries. Another of the early measures was the "stone," which is still used in England for weighing men and

By courtesy of W. and T. Avery, Ltd.

A king in Northern Africa, about 550 B.C., is watching sailors weigh their cargo of asafoetida, a common drug that our grandparents used to wear in little bags hung round their necks to keep the smallpox away.

By courtesy of W. and T. Avery, Ltd.

This Roman butcher, who lived in about A.D. 150, had his shop in the open air and weighed his meat on a steel-yard. One is here shown in use, suspended at the end of the rack on which the meat is hung.

horses. One would rarely say a man weighed 160 pounds, but 11 stone 6 lb.—a "stone" being fourteen pounds.

And when it came to measuring liquids in early times, matters were still worse. There were some eight or ten measuring vessels from which to choose. Of these only the gallon is left to-day, with its division into quarts and pints and gills. But even to-day there are two kinds of gallon: the English one holds ten pounds of water; while the American one, since 1707, has held only eight. And likewise there are two kinds of ton, one weighing 2,000 pounds and the other weighing 2,240. Now, if this used to be the state of things in England, we can imagine the confusion all over the rest of Europe, with each country using its own system or systems of weights and measures. Our weights and measures are still very curious and irregular, and not nearly so easy to understand as the metric system used in France and other foreign countries. The following examples will show how much more difficult is our own system.

Thus *twelve* inches make a foot; *three* feet make a yard; *five and a half* yards make a pole or rod; *forty* poles or rods make a furlong; and *eight* furlongs make a mile—which is 1,760 yards or 5,280 feet —and *three* miles make a league. What a lot of figures to remember!

So much for measuring distance. In measuring area we are no better off. It takes 144 square inches to make a square foot, 9 square feet to make a square yard, 30¼ square yards to make a square pole or

rod, 40 square poles or rods to make a rood, 4 roods to make an acre, and 640 acres to make a square mile.

In solid measure or measure of capacity 1,728 cubic inches make a cubic foot, 27 cubic feet make a cubic yard, and 128 cubic feet make a cord.

In what we call dry measure, 2 pints make a quart, 4 quarts make a gallon, 8 quarts or 2 gallons make a peck, and 4 pecks make a bushel. In liquid measure 4 gills (jĭl) make a pint, 2 pints make a quart, 4 quarts make a gallon, 9 gallons make a firkin, 2 firkins make a kilderkin, 2 kilderkins make a barrel, 3 kilderkins make a hogshead, and 2 hogsheads make a butt.

To cap it all, we have two kinds of weight. In troy weight, as used by the jeweller, 24 grains make a pennyweight, 20 pennyweights make an ounce, 12 ounces make a pound, 25 pounds make a quarter, 100 pounds make a hundredweight, and 20 hundredweights make a ton. But in avoirdupois (ăv'ĕr-dū-poiz') as used by the grocer and others, 437½ grains make an ounce, 16 ounces make a pound, and 2,240 pounds make a ton. And then the apothecary (a-pŏth'ĕ-kā-rĭ), or chemist, uses a kind of weight that is still a little different.

Now we learn all this in school, and then most of us forget a good deal about it. But nobody ever forgets that four farthings make a penny, twelve pence make a shilling, and twenty shillings make a pound. That is because there is not nearly so much to remember. But with our weights and measures the reason we forget is because

By courtesy of W. and T. Avery, Ltd.

If you had lived in England in the year 800, a fish pedlar like this one would have come to your door and weighed out his wares with a curious steel-yard that he held in his hand. It had no movable weights, but the ring by which it was held could be slipped back and forth, and on the beam spaces were marked off by nails driven into the wood. So the weight of an object could be judged by the number of nails between the end of the beam on which the object hung and the spot at which the ring had to be held in order to keep the beam perfectly straight and steady.

not only are they still highly irregular, but also there is a great deal to remember. There is no rule at all about them.

Seeking a Perfect Way to Measure

Nearly a hundred and fifty years ago the king of France decided to have one rule for them all. He chose a committee of French scientists to make the rule; and because he wanted a single rule for all the world, he invited the other nations to send their scientists.

And they might all have come together and agreed but for one trouble. At that time the French Revolution broke out, and it was none too safe for scientists to go to France. Yet the French scientists went on with their work as best they could, and in due time they invented a single rule for all weights and measures. It is the one perfect system that we have already mentioned.

It was no easy thing to invent, as we shall realize if we think about it just a moment. The scientists had to find a single unit by which they could measure every kind of thing in the world, and also weigh every kind of thing. It had to be a unit to measure the length of a line across a room or across a city, the girth of a tree, the circumference of the earth, or the distance from the earth to the North Star. With this same unit they must also measure the area of a building site, or of the land of France; and, furthermore, with it they must measure the volume of any object—a pebble or a mountain, a pail of water or a lake or ocean.

And, finally, with this same unit they must be able to *weigh* everything in the universe—from salt and sugar to the sun and moon. Now how could they find one unit with which

Behind this iron grille is the famous London Stone, which is now set into the wall of St. Swithin's Church, in Cannon Street, London. It is thought that the Romans, when they ruled over Britain, used this stone as a centre from which to reckon distances along their roads.

to measure the distance to the moon, the area of the moon, the volume of the moon, and the weight of the moon? When we have answered that, we shall see that measuring and weighing, as we said before, are really the same thing.

But, before we answer, we must face one other trouble. The very unit that we use, whatever it is, will never remain exactly the same. A metal yard-stick is a little longer in the sunshine than in the shade, in any warm place than in any cold place—because heat expands and cold contracts. Anything that weighs a pound at the Equator will weigh a little more as we take it north or south; that is because the earth is flattened towards the poles, and so the thing will be a little nearer to the centre of the earth, which will therefore pull slightly harder on it. For the same reason, it will weigh rather more at the sea-shore than on a mountain. And it will even be a little smaller—especially if it is a soft thing—at the seashore, because the pressure of the atmosphere is greater there and so presses it together. Everybody knows that water occupies a greater space when it freezes—that is why water-pipes burst. So once we have decided on our single unit, we have to find some way to keep it from varying in size and weight.

All of these troubles, however, the scientists managed to overcome. Let us see how ingeniously they did it.

What Is a Metre?

First they took the distance from the North Pole to the Equator, on a line running through Paris. Then they divided this into ten million equal parts. One of these parts they called a metre, or "measure"; and this metre, which would always be the same, became their unit. The metre is a little longer than our yard; it is 39·37 of an inch.

For shorter measurements they divided the metre by tens—or used the decimal system. Every metre has ten decimetres, a hundred centimetres, a thousand millimetres. For longer things they multiplied the metre by tens. Ten metres made a decametre, a hundred metres made a hecto-metre, and a thousand metres made a kilometre. Whenever they divided they did it in Latin, and whenever they multiplied, to make things easier, they did it in Greek. Thus "millimetre" is Latin for "a thousandth of a metre," while "kilometre" is Greek for "a thousand metres"—or ·621 of a mile—and so on with the other terms.

The picture at the left was based on a scene in a fifteenth century window of stained glass in the cathedral at Tournai. It shows a big pair of scales in use in a French warehouse.

It was easy, of course, to use this same metre for square surface, or area, and cubic contents, or volume. A sheet of paper would simply be so many square decimetres, and the whole country of France so many square kilometres; a pebble would be so many cubic decimetres, and the moon so many cubic kilometres.

Then, instead of pints and pecks they made a measure, for liquids especially out of the same system. They took a cubic vessel exactly ten centimetres on each side, or a thousand cubic centimetres in volume. The amount of water that this vessel would hold was the unit. This they called a litre (lē'tēr). So one thousand cubic centimetres of water made a litre—about one quart. And this they divided by tens into decilitres,

By courtesy of W. and T. Avery. Ltd. Here gold and silver plate is being weighed in a shop in London at the end of the eighteenth century.

centilitres, millilitres and multiplied by tens into decalitres, hectolitres, and kilolitres—words which explain themselves.

But these are all measures. Where do the weights come in? Well, they took the weight of one cubic centimetre of water when water is at its heaviest—just before it freezes, or at 4° Centigrade—and made that the unit. They called it a gramme. So one cubic centimetre of water at this temperature weighs a gramme, or ·0026 of a pound. Then they divided the gramme into decigrammes, centigrammes and milligrammes, and multiplied it into decagrammes, hectogrammes, and kilogrammes.

Such are the main facts about the system which French science gave the world in 1791. It is the famous "metric system"—the only scientific way of measuring and weighing that the world has ever had. Starting with the distance from the North Pole to the Equator, it gave us one invariable unit for measuring and weighing anything from a pinhead to a mountain—and even things far smaller and far larger. Yet it is so simple that anybody who can multiply by ten can learn it in a very short time.

It is now used in nearly every civilized country in the world except England and America. Even in these lands the scientists always employ it, and certain business men are trying to introduce it, for it is much more convenient and so would save time and money. Some day we may adopt it; but "the march of the human mind," as Edmund Burke said, "is slow."

A PIGMY *and His* POWERFUL PEN

Triumphing Over Ill-health and Deformity, Alexander Pope Became the Wittiest and Cruellest of Poets

(CONTINUED FROM PAGE 224)

ALEXANDER POPE was such a small man that he had to sit in a high chair at the table, and so puny that he could not put his clothes on without having someone to help him. He could not even stand up unless he was laced into a sort of corset for support. He felt the cold so much that he had to wear a fur jacket underneath his linen shirt, and was so thin that he used to put on three pairs of stockings to keep his legs from looking like broomsticks. He was a hunchback. In fact, he looked a little like a spider, as he said himself; and he was ill so often

Photo by Rischgitz

For a long time Pope and the famous Lady Mary Wortley Montagu were the greatest of friends. And then one day, so the story goes, he told her he loved her; and she, too ungentle to appreciate the tribute from one of England's greatest poets, burst into laughter at the thought of loving a little dwarf and hunchback like Alexander Pope. He, for his part, never forgave her for the scorn and derision of that refusal.

that he used to describe his whole life as being one long disease.

All the same, the tiny invalid had such a power that many of the mightiest men and women in the land respected him or trembled at his name—lords and ladies, soldiers, statesmen, even kings and queens. And all his power lay in the point of his pen.

For it was one of the sharpest pens that had ever been seen in England, and it left very deep wounds.

He had begun to sharpen it almost as soon as he could hold it in his fingers, for he was an extremely precocious boy. Not that he had much education, for as a Catholic child he could not enter any of the public schools of England in his day. But that made very little difference to a lad like Pope. Unfit for the games of other boys, he buried himself so deeply in his books that he soon knew a great deal more than most boys and girls are able to learn while at school.

In books he found his own game. He loved it better, all his life, than any other pursuit, and he could play it better than any other man about him. It was the game of words. He loved to play with words just as we love to play with bats and balls—to see how many fanciful things he could do with them. So he used to twist and turn them round and round, and try all sorts of tricks to make them say exactly what he wanted, and say it more neatly and more wittily, more skilfully and gracefully, than ever it had been said before.

A Playwright at Twelve

Pope came to be the greatest poet in the land while he was still a boy. Born in 1688, he had written a play before he was twelve, and a long epic poem when fifteen; at twenty-three he was a new monarch in

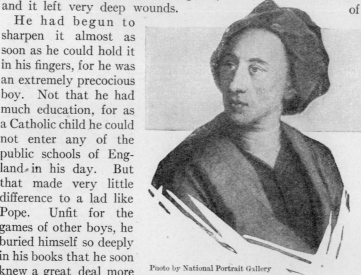

Photo by National Portrait Gallery

Alexander Pope, the "wicked wasp" who was yet one of the greatest poets and one of the tenderest friends among all the English literary men.

English poetry, and he ruled without a rival until his death in 1744. In his dazzling career he had almost every kind of success an ambitious man could want. He even made a good deal of money, which poets rarely do; and with his fortune he retired to a retreat at Twickenham (twĭk"n-ăm), where he planted his beautiful gardens and made his famous grotto, a cave studded with thousands of curious shells and pieces of glass, in which he used to write his poetry and have tea with his friends.

The greatest of his friends was Jonathan Swift. Then there was Dr. Arbuthnot, the queen's physician, who wrote several witty books and who invented for Englishmen the typical name of John Bull. There was John Gay, the lazy, fat poet who wrote many fables and the famous "Beggar's Opera"; and Lady Mary Wortley Montagu, who penned such charming letters and who introduced into England a system of inoculation against smallpox. There were many more, including several statesmen, among whom were the brilliant Viscount Bolingbroke and the earl of Oxford, whose great library—the Harleian collection—is now in the British Museum.

All of these loved Pope, and to all of them he was a kindly friend. But that is about the best we can say for him, for we must now add that he had far more enemies than friends, and for very simple reasons.

For if Pope was like a spider in appearance, he was like a wasp at heart. He was so extremely vain that no amount of fame would satisfy him. Now every vain man has a thin skin, and Pope's was very thin indeed. He would writhe in anguish at the slightest injury, real or fancied; and then he would lie awake at night devising his revenge, and even get his poor old servant out of bed three or four times to put his plots on paper. And the sting of the wasp was terrible.

He fought all his battles with his pen, for it was by far his deadliest weapon. Many of his enemies would have been glad enough to face a sword instead; and since they could not match him with the pen, they often threatened him with other arms. One of them hung up a stout rod in a famous coffee-house and announced that he would use it if Pope ever came there. And at one time there were so many threats that Pope would not go out of his house without a pair of pistols and his big dog Bounce. But his pen never rested. That is why so much of his poetry deals in abuse and ridicule, or is the kind of poetry we call satire (săt′ĭr).

A Writer of Charming Poems Who Could Also Wield a Bitter Pen

He is one of the greatest satirists. His first famous poem was "The Essay on Criticism" (1711), in which he gives much advice to poets and critics, but also a good deal of offence. Then he wrote the daintiest of poems in "The Rape of the Lock" (1712), on the sly theft of a tress of a young lady's hair, though even in this apparently light piece he managed to make a few people angry. After spending ten years on his famous translation of Homer, he set out to pickle all his enemies at once in the long and savage satire of "The Dunciad" (1728). This was followed by several shorter but even more brilliant satires, and by a long poem of philosophy called "The Essay on Man" (1733).

By no means our greatest poet, Pope is still supreme in neat and pointed phrases, in grace and glitter, in polish, and in what we call epigram (ĕp′ĭ-grăm). To say a thing in words so terse and telling, that we are all certain to remember and repeat it, is to make an epigram.

This Play with Words Won Him the Title of the King of Epigram

Pope coined more epigrams than any other Englishman who ever lived, for that was his great aim in his pet game of words. It is not the highest aim in poetry. There is such a thing as being too neat and trim and glittering.

Our greatest poems have no need of glitter, and our real giants must not be too neat and trim. So Pope is not quite one of the true giants. But it is a great achievement to be king of the epigram. Here is one of his epigrams, in his favourite form of verse, the heroic couplet:

Nature and Nature's laws lay hid in night;
God said, "Let Newton be," and all was light.

How the ENGLISH NOVEL was BORN

Samuel Richardson, the Printer, Who Wrote Love Letters for Girls and Made Them into Famous Stories

HERE is the story of the strange way in which the English novel came to be born.

We are apt to think of a novelist as an interesting person who has had all sorts of adventures and who puts them into his books. Many a novelist is like that, but the man we know as the father of the English novel was not that kind of man at all. He was the last person you would ever expect to write a novel He was solemn and methodical, without a romantic spark in his whole being; and as for adventure, he would have run away from it as he would have done from a mad dog—that is, if he had not been too fat to run at all. Yet he is looked upon as the first English novelist, though there were many story-writers before him.

His name was Samuel Richardson, a name that somehow suggests a stolid British tradesman, and that is just what its owner was. When he was born, in 1689, his parents intended him to be a clergyman. That was very suitable, for he was a very good little boy from the start. But he would not play with other boys; he would sit and listen to the old ladies talking. When he was thirteen, the girls used to ask him to write their love letters for them. The letters were full of warmth and maidenly virtue. No one could write such excellent girl's letters as Samuel penned.

This proved to be important, as you are going to see in a moment. Young Samuel learned to look right

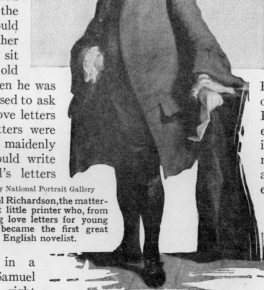

Photo by National Portrait Gallery

Samuel Richardson, the matter-of-fact little printer who, from writing love letters for young girls, became the first great English novelist.

into a girl's heart, and to understand the emotions which he found therein.

Success as a Printer

His parents could not afford to have him trained for the clergy, and he had to go into a printer's office. The perfect young man married the printer's daughter, and settled down to a quiet and happy home life. He took over the business, and made a lot of money out of it. Then he retired from business, a model of virtue, and delighted in giving advice to the young men who he thought should fashion their lives upon his own. So he reached the age of fifty without a single hint of adventure.

And then adventure came to him—nothing exciting, but nevertheless important. Somebody wanted to publish a "Complete Letter Writer," to show young people how they ought to write their letters. It was here that Samuel's youthful experience bore fruit. He composed 173 letters, all very proper and all very dull, from which people could learn to write their own. And yet Samuel got a great idea from them. Why not print them in the form of a story?

He remembered a story of a serving-girl named Pamela (păm'ĕ-lă). Pamela, a simple country girl, is pursued by her young master, who has no thought about marriage, but who eventually comes to regard her with great affection and makes her his wife. And so the virtuous country maiden rides in a "coach drawn by Flanders mares, and is introduced in her blushing beauty to all his great relations." Richardson set out to tell the story in a long series of letters from Pamela to her friends; and it was then that he showed how much he knew about a girl's heart. "Pamela" (1740) was the first full-grown English novel.

That is why so many novels used to be written in the form of letters. For a long time it seemed to be the only way people could think of in which to write a novel.

Novels that Might Cause the Reader to Hang Himself

Pamela was only a serving-girl. Next the author began to write the story of a girl of higher station, and the result was "Clarissa" (1747–1748), another novel in letters, and one of the greatest of eighteenth century novels. After that Richardson wished to write a novel about a perfect gentleman, and so he produced "Sir Charles Grandison" (1753), a lengthy work also written in letter form.

In spite of the fact that they are so long, these novels are really the most absorbing books. They move along so slowly that Dr. Johnson said that a reader who tried to peruse them for the story alone would hang himself. And yet, once started, they hold the reader, for the passions in the hearts of their heroes and heroines cannot be resisted.

A Book that Macaulay Declared He Could Repeat from Memory

Lady Mary Wortley Montagu despised them for their middle-class sentiment, and yet confessed they made her cry "like a milkmaid." A century later Macaulay used to say that if every copy of "Clarissa" were lost, he could give it to the world again from memory. The books became famous in many countries, and the number of novels that have been written on similar lines runs into thousands.

That is the strange story of the printer who so unexpectedly came to be the father of the novel. He lived till 1761, basking in the flattery of his admirers, and expressing his opinions on success and happiness, and how he considered they were best to be attained.

The SECOND Great ENGLISH NOVELIST

Henry Fielding Started by Making Fun of the First Novel by Samuel Richardson, and Ended by Becoming His Chief Rival

UNTIL Samuel Richardson wrote "Pamela," no writer had studied a woman's thoughts and actions so closely and at such length, in a story, as this "twittering" little London printer. He had set a new fashion in writing books. He could claim to be the father of the English novel. But Henry Fielding, a dashing man of the world, thought the story very silly.

It seemed to say, "Just be good, and you can marry far above you and become a lady" —which is not a proper reason for being good. So Fielding set out to poke fun at "Pamela." He wrote a burlesque of it called "Joseph Andrews." His virtuous Joseph is a brother of Pamela, is a serving-man, and is pursued by a terrible lady just as Pamela had been pursued by a terrible man—and amusing situations of all sorts follow close upon each other in the novel.

Before he began this novel, Fielding had done many other things. Born into a well-to-do family, in 1707, he had gone to Eton. Then he had studied for a short time at the university of Leyden, in Holland; but for about fifteen years he had mainly resided in London, where he was known as a gallant wit and a comic playwright. He had written more than a dozen plays, most of them excellent farces. But he had made so much fun of the corrupt government under Robert Walpole that when Walpole had an Act placed on the Statute Book in 1737 requiring a licence for the production of plays, Fielding was unable to obtain one and his career as a dramatist came to an end.

Then Fielding turned to the law for a living, and having a family to support by this time he worked hard at it. He became a barrister in 1740, and set up a practice in Pump Court.

But it was the work he had begun in "Joseph Andrews" (1742) that was to make him famous. He had not progressed very far with that book before he realized that he was engaged on something far greater than on a burlesque on Richardson. So he

From the painting by W. P. Frith, R.A.

Tom Jones, the chief character in Henry Fielding's novel of that name, is here seen showing Sophia her image in a mirror as a pledge of his constancy.

only to make fun of it, became the father of our realistic novel.

All his other novels are of the same character, and they are among the very greatest that we have. "Jonathan Wild the Great" followed his first effort. It is the story of a real criminal who had been hanged in London only a few years before, and is meant to show that a great man is a source of trouble for this world unless he is also a good man. After this came "Tom Jones" (1748), which some readers have called the greatest of all English novels; and less than three years later was published "Amelia," the last novel he wrote.

His career as a novelist was cut short by failing health, brought about chiefly by hard work as a magistrate and as a writer. In 1554 he went to Portugal in a vain effort to regain his health, and there a little later he died.

Fielding was not a prude, like Richardson; indeed he was a man about town. Richardson despised him as a sporting man, and he regarded Richardson as a proud little printer who knew nothing about real life and who filled his novels with womanish sentiment about it. They were both partly wrong in these opinions.

Fielding was a strong, honest man, even if he did see no great harm in a little gambling, and Richardson was far more than a sentimentalist, even if he did love to receive the flattery of adoring young ladies. But we can easily see how we obtained our two main types of novel from these men— the "ideal" novel of sentiment from the dreamy printer, with his clear insight into feminine character, and the "realistic" novel of life from the wide-awake justice of the peace.

forgot "Pamela" and went on to create a new fashion in novels. It is the kind of novel that we call "realistic"—the kind that tries to portray people just as they are. And if Richardson is the father of the "sentimental" novel, Fielding, who had started

(CONTINUED ON PAGE 367)

All along the shores of the Mediterranean these daring Phoenician traders sailed their little barque, and with them they carried something that was more priceless even than all their wares—a sound, serviceable alphabet.

The WORLD'S *First* GREAT TRADERS

To all Parts of the Mediterranean the Little Boats of the Phoenicians Conveyed the Nations' Wares, but the Most Precious Thing They Carried was Always Given Away

WE HAVE already said a word about the Arameans (ăr′à-mē ån) and what great traders, or business men, they were. Their trading was carried on by land, between one city and another. But before ever the Arameans entered history there was a people who were as great traders as they, with one difference—they made many of their journeys by water instead of by land. These people, the Phoenicians (fē-nĭsh′àn), were the greatest sailors of old.

The Phoenicians, like the other Semitic (sĕ-mĭt′ĭk) tribes, came from a wandering life in the Arabian desert to settle down in cities and become civilized. But they happened to settle in a part of the coveted Fertile Crescent—in Asia Minor—which was also on the sea-coast, along the eastern edge of the Mediterranean. On this coast there were several good harbours, and the Phoenicians found these to be the best places in which to build their trading centres—Tyre (tīr), Sidon (sī′dŏn), Byblos (bĭb′lŏs), and others that became great cities.

Most people like the water, but the Phoenicians, desert people though they had been, proved that they had a positive genius for seafaring. They loved boats and the sea better than anything else, and very early in history we hear of them carrying goods to Egypt or to other lands along the Mediterranean coast. At first, probably, they were afraid to venture very far, but soon they grew bolder, until their ships were travelling to Crete, Greece, Italy, and the north coast of Africa; and there is a story that Phoenician traders sailed out even through the Strait of Gibraltar and discovered the British tin mines, long before the Egyptians or the Babylonians even knew that there was such a place as Britain.

Kings Who Preferred to Make Their Conquests by Peaceful Trading

It is pleasant to read about the Phoenicians, because we learn of interesting ideas rather than of kings and battles. The early Phoenician cities each had their kings,

325

one after another; but these kings preferred trading by sea to wars and conquests, and thus are famous for reasons other than mere victories. Byblos had one early king Ahiram (ȧ-hī'răm), whom we remember as the Hiram of the Bible, a friend of David and Solomon, and because his tomb had upon it some interesting writing showing the kind of letters the early Phoenicians used.

The Phoenicians had to fight occasionally against Rameses or Sargon or Sennacherib; but then they fought only to defend their own homes, never to conquer other nations. They preferred to become rich through buying and selling rather than by taking people's wealth by force; and we of to-day would agree that they were wise in this matter.

An Adventurous People Who Wore a Costume Like a Nightdress

None of the early peoples about whom we are learning did more for the world than the Phoenicians. Early in their history they gave the Greeks the kind of dress that Grecian men afterwards wore—a dress which the Greeks called a "chiton" (kī'tŏn) after a Phoenician word "kiton." This dress was like a short shirt or night-gown tied at the waist, very comfortable for a hot country, and also quite attractive in comparison with the heavy, bulky clothes many men have worn since, or with the heavy, shaggy sheepskins which the Greeks had formerly worn.

The Phoenicians, too, were always carrying useful things or works of art in their boats from one country to another. In order to have

more things to sell, workshops were established in the Phoenician cities, and the products of these workshops—combs, ornaments, vases, bowls, jars—are often dug up nowadays in Mediterranean countries. The Phoenician sailors were among the first to carry on an international trade.

Men Who Braved the Dangers of the Seas Three Thousand Years Ago

When did all these things happen? Well, it was probably over two thousand years before our calendar began that the Phoenicians came out of the desert and settled along the coast. They were a newer people than the old Akkadians, for they appeared at about the same time as the Amorites, who first made Babylon a great city. It was not until about 1000 B.C. that the Phoenician ships became very active in trading. Before this the Egyptian and Cretan merchant-sailors did whatever trading there was to be done. It was about 1000 B.C. that the Phoenicians gave the Greeks their chitons, but from this time on for many centuries, the Phoenicians were busily selling things and giving ideas to the world.

Wherever a ship carries goods for trade, it also carries ideas. Perhaps the Phoenician trader-captain may have had among his wares a hollow statue of bronze. A wealthy Greek may have seen and admired this statue, and wondered how it was possible to pour bronze into a mould and yet keep it hollow and of the same thickness. He may have wondered more and more, and finally he may have sent his son back to Sidon with the trader-captain to learn how to cast hollow bronze statues. The Phoenicians had not invented this art or skill. They had learned

In boats like this one the enterprising Phoenician sailors scoured the Mediterranean. They brought about a great advance in the art of ship-building and in navigation, and their vessels were built to carry large cargoes. They were probably the inventors of the bireme and trireme, that is, of ships equipped with two and three tiers of oars.

The fertile coastal plain that was once Phoenicia is now a part of Syria, a country ruled by French mandate. Visitors often ride in seatless vehicles like these at A.

The cedars still grow on the Lebanon Mountains, in Syria, as they did in the days of Solomon; and on the lower slopes mulberries are raised to feed silk worms. At C is a Lebanon boy reeling silk thread.

B. This man of Damascus, in Syria, makes the beautiful inlaid slippers you see on his shelves.

D. Modern Syria has nearly 3,000,000 people, largely Mohammedans. Here is one of them entertaining the country people with his bear. E. Water carriers in the ancient city of Aleppo.

F. In the ancient city of Damascus is this mosque of the howling dervishes, an order of Mohammedan monks who work themselves up into a frenzy in which they eat snakes and live coals and cut themselves with knives.

G. In the court of their home these Syrian women are making bread by a method that their ancestors used hundreds of years ago.

it from the Egyptians. They taught it to the Greek boy, who, going back to his own land, taught it to others there. So an idea was carried, first from Egypt to Phoenicia, then from Phoenicia to Greece, and finally almost all over the world.

The Birth of Our Alphabet

Many such ideas were carried by the Phoenicians to other countries. They were constantly coming across something new, especially in Egypt, which in 1000 B.C. was already a very old country, with great stores of useful knowledge that it had been gathering for some three thousand years. From the Egyptians the Phoenicians learned to weave and

dye linen; to make glass, porcelain, and paper; to hammer and cast and engrave metal. From Egypt they probably took the idea for their alphabet, the greatest idea of all.

Many centuries before—earlier than 1600 B.C.—the Semitic tribes living nearest to Egypt had made an alphabet of their own, on the model of the Egyptian alphabet. The first letter, or picture, in this alphabet was an ox, and it meant the throaty clicking sound which was at the beginning of the Semitic word for ox. They called it *aleph*, or "ox." The second letter was a picture of a house, because it said *b*, the first sound in *beth*, the Semitic word for "house." The third picture, *g*, was a picture of *gimel*, a camel, and, by

Photo by Rischgitz

It is said that the Phoenicians sailed their little crafts as far as the island of Britain, where tin was to be found. Here they are shown offering their tempting wares to the Britons, who have hurried down to the shore to crowd round the boats that these dark strangers have beached there. And marvellous is the cargo to the eyes of the natives—finely engraved dishes of silver and bronze, porcelain bowls of an exquisite blue, delicate perfume bottles from distant Egypt, carved ivory combs, fine jewellery, and woven fabrics dyed with Tyrian dyes to a deep shade of crimson, which was the famous " Tyrian purple " of which we hear so frequently.

the way, our own English word "camel" comes from this word *gimel*.

In all there were twenty-two sound pictures in this old alphabet, and each one carried a sound which was the first sound in the name of the picture. This made the sounds easy to remember. If you saw a camel picture you would naturally say *gimel*, and then you would know that this picture meant the sound g.

By 1000 B.C. these pictures had been so much changed that no one could tell that g was a camel. It was just a mark meaning the sound g. With these marks the Phoenicians kept accounts, and it must have astonished their Greek customers to see the trader-captain write the strange marks with his pen and ink on his sheet of papyrus (pă-pī'rŭs) paper.

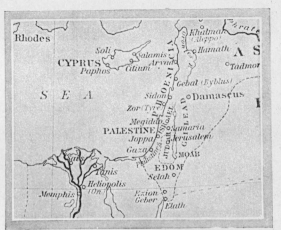

Hugging the narrow coast along the eastern Mediterranean was the little land of Phoenicia, whose enterprising citizens did so great a service to the cause of civilization. Behind them towered the mountains of Lebanon; before them spread the blue of their tideless inland sea. It was always beckoning them to go forth in search of adventure.

At first the Greeks, like the other peoples with whom the Phoenicians traded, were distrustful or even afraid of the queer marks; but the Greeks were full of curiosity. So instead of only distrusting the marks, they asked about them, and learned what they were and the sounds for which they stood.

Forming the Greek Alphabet

And then some intelligent Greek had the idea of using these Phoenician letters to write Greek words. As there were lots of g sounds in Greek words, *gimel*, the old camel picture, would be useful. The trouble was that Greek had some sounds that were not used in Phoenician, and also that Greek had no need for some of the Phoenician letters. In Greek there was no throaty clicking *aleph*, for instance; and in Phoenician there was no picture for *a*.

These clever Greeks altered the Phoenician letters to fit Greek. They made *aleph* into *alpha*, or *a*, the first letter of the Greek alphabet, and they added several letters for their extra sounds. Our own alphabet was founded on that of the Greeks, and the very word "alphabet" is made out of their first two letters, *alpha* and *beta*.

Phoenicians and Greeks must thus divide the credit for the greatest single gift of art to the modern world, the gift of a good alphabet. The Phoenicians also gave us our word "Bible." It is taken from the name of one of their chief cities—Byblos. So much papyrus came from Byblos that the very word itself came to mean *paper*, or *book*, and from that origin we have adopted it as a name for the Book of Books.

It seems a pity that such great carriers of ideas as were the Phoenicians should not have gone on longer enlightening the world through trade and teaching. For many centuries after 1000 B.C. the Phoenicians prospered. They even established colonies at different places along the Mediterranean, and one of these colonies, Carthage (kär'-thāj), on the north coast of Africa opposite to Sicily, became a great kingdom.

It was not until the Persian conquests, about 500 B.C., that Phoenicia began to weaken. Then she lent her ships and men as fighting allies of the Persian kings, and abandoned little by little the trade which had made her so prosperous. Under the Persians, with her ships carrying soldiers and death instead of goods and ideas of her own, Phoenicia could not long remain great.

About 350 B.C. Phoenicia fell from the rule of Persia to the rule of Alexander and Greece; and after that we hear little more of Tyre, Sidon, and Byblos, the three great centres of Phoenician civilization, famous for sailing, for trade, and for the spreading of ideas.

HOW TO MAKE SILHOUETTES

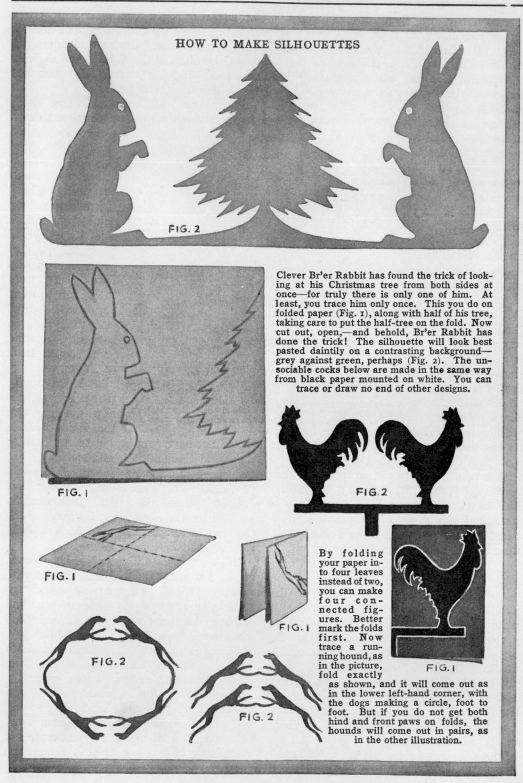

FIG. 2

Clever Br'er Rabbit has found the trick of looking at his Christmas tree from both sides at once—for truly there is only one of him. At least, you trace him only once. This you do on folded paper (Fig. 1), along with half of his tree, taking care to put the half-tree on the fold. Now cut out, open,—and behold, Br'er Rabbit has done the trick! The silhouette will look best pasted daintily on a contrasting background—grey against green, perhaps (Fig. 2). The unsociable cocks below are made in the same way from black paper mounted on white. You can trace or draw no end of other designs.

FIG. 1

FIG. 2

By folding your paper into four leaves instead of two, you can make four connected figures. Better mark the folds first. Now trace a running hound, as in the picture, fold exactly as shown, and it will come out as in the lower left-hand corner, with the dogs making a circle, foot to foot. But if you do not get both hind and front paws on folds, the hounds will come out in pairs, as in the other illustration.

FIG. 1

FIG. 2

FIG. 2

FIG. 1

These beetles come from distant parts of the world. From the top left corner of the page downwards they are *Sagra buqueti*, *Eupholus schoenherri* (New Guinea), *Prepodes vittatus* (Jamaica), *Chrysophora chrysochlora* (Andes), *Stigmodera tricolorata* (Nicol Bay), *Odontobalis delesserti* (Southern India), *Aristobia approximator* (Siam), *Ranzania petersiana* (East Africa), *Trichaptus myrmosarius* (Brazil), *Plusiotis adelaida* (Mexico), and *Demochroa castelnaudi* (East Indies).

The ancient Egyptians worshipped these amusing beetles that they saw trundling great balls of dirt about. We think they are extremely amusing insects, but we know that when a brand-new beetle comes walking out of the ball it is not because the grown-up beetles have created him out of the dirt, but because the mother beetle laid an egg inside the ball.

The QUEER WAYS of the LOWLY BEETLE

Some of These Armoured Insects Are Useful Friends of Mankind, but Others Are Destructive Enemies

(CONTINUED FROM PAGE 290)

IN THE insect world the beetles are a little like the clowns. They are not so beautiful as butterflies nor so intelligent as ants and bees and wasps, but in their way they are interesting insects and some of them are highly amusing.

A solemn old dor beetle slowly plodding along the garden path, or lying feebly kicking on his broad back, does seem rather a dull fellow. But the beetles are not all as slow as a dor beetle, who, if he is so unlucky as to fall over on his back, is too awkward to turn himself right side up again. This position is not only undignified, but is extremely dangerous to the beetle. For if any of the tigerish little ground beetles or a wandering party of wood ants find him in such a helpless state, they will set upon him, cut him up with their strong jaws, and devour him without the slightest twinge of conscience or remorse.

His Suit of Armour

Standing on his six feet the clumsy old dor beetle is much better able to defend himself. His shoulders are protected by a broad shield, and the hind portion of his portly body is covered by a horny sheath— too rough and slippery to be pierced by his bloodthirsty enemies. As a last resort, too, the beetle can always fly away; that is to say, he could fly if this way of escape should occur to his dull wits before he is overpowered by his enemies.

Hiding From the Sunlight

For, with a few exceptions, all the beetles can fly if they choose. But as a rule they prefer to use their legs, and are more often seen running or crawling over the ground than sailing through the air. When we do meet a beetle on the wing it is usually late in the evening. Most beetles dislike broad daylight, and spend the sunny hours under stones, fallen leaves or rubbish heaps; tucked away in cracks in walls and fences; hidden among the roots of plants, beneath the loose bark of trees or in any other dark hole or corner into which they can squeeze. In the cool of the evening they come out to obtain food, and then they sometimes fly round to visit their friends.

Beetles really have four wings, but these are so cleverly concealed when the insect is not using them that many people think they have none. The first two are hard and stiff, and fit together so perfectly when they are closed that the joint is visible only as a fine line down the middle of the back. These curious wings are usually called wing-cases. Their chief use is to provide a protective covering for the "true" wings which are neatly folded up beneath them out of harm's way.

How a Beetle Flies

The other two wings are as fine and transparent as those of a fly, and would very soon come to grief if they were not covered up when the beetle is running about or squeezing into a tight corner.

When about to set off on a flight, the beetle looks for all the world as if it were going to split itself in two. The crack down its back grows wider and wider until the wing-cases stand out stiffly at right angles to its body. Then the gauzy wings are shaken out and, the next thing you know, the beetle has taken off from the ground and is soaring away, high over your head.

Although some beetles are quite at home in the air, many are but poor flyers. They cannot twist and turn about quickly when on the wing, so they are always bumping into things and crashing to the ground. But such accidents seldom seem to do them much harm.

Some beetles have given up travelling by air altogether. Although they have tough, horny wing-cases over their backs, they have no true wings beneath them—or such small ones that they are quite useless for flight. The insects are then doomed to creep upon the ground for the remainder of their lives. A few of them have even lost the power of opening their wing-cases, because they have had no need to open them for so long.

The cockchafer, which hums through the dusk of summer evenings, is a beetle with powerful wings and extremely rapid flight.

This state of affairs has arisen from the lazy habits of the beetles. Their ancestors in olden days had four good wings and flew about with the best of their kind. But as time went on, some of them used their wings less and less, and took more and more to creeping and crawling, until finally they lost the power of flight entirely.

Mother Nature Crops Their Wings

For this is Mother Nature's way. If her children do not appreciate their blessings and make full use of their powers, they are not allowed to keep them.

There are enormous numbers of beetles scattered about the world. They seem to thrive in all climates and under all sorts of conditions. In hot countries, in cold countries, in the water as well as on the land, these hardy insects abound. Many are really splendid creatures clad in purple and scarlet, green and orange, or in glittering suits of gold and silver. But others are quite dull in their plain brown or black coats.

There are beetles so small that they can hardly be seen without a magnifying glass, and there are gigantic fellows with fearsome jaws and horns that may well strike terror to the hearts of all timid insect folk. Yet these alarming giants are usually quite mild, peaceful creatures; their great horns are more ornamental than useful and are seldom employed as weapons.

So, you see, even beetles are not all alike. They vary greatly in their looks and habits. Many are terrible pests. They gnaw the roots of growing crops, strip the foliage from the trees, tunnel into wooden beams and furniture, eat holes in our carpets and furs, get into the flour bins and spoil the flour, and do all manner of annoying things. There is hardly anything they will not eat. Some species of beetle simply revel in red pepper, and thrive on poisonous drugs that would kill us if we ate them for breakfast, dinner, and tea as these queer little creatures do. Some enjoy paraffin; and others think nothing so nice as a good cigar or a cigarette, or dried tobacco of any kind. Most of the damage they cause is done while the beetles are fat, worm-like grubs with hard, horny heads and jaws; but even when they have grown up, the behaviour of some of them is quite shocking.

But there are good beetles as well as bad ones. Some act as dustmen, and do really useful work in clearing away various kinds of decaying rubbish that would poison the air if it were left lying on the ground. Some hasten the decay of fallen trees and old stumps in dense forests by riddling them through and through with tunnels. This helps to

The grooves in this pine wood were not carved with a jack-knife, but were eaten out by the grub of the pine beetle. The eggs are laid in the grooves, between the bark and the wood, and when the youngsters hatch they start eating and eventually kill the tree by girdling it.

make room for fresh young growths to spring up. Others do us good service by hunting down and destroying the harmful insects that devour our crops and spoil our orchards and flower gardens by their greediness.

Our Unpaid Scavengers

Chief among the dustmen are our old friends the dor beetles and their very close relatives, the small black or reddish beetles so often seen flying about pasture land on warm autumn afternoons. These beetles belong to the great "scarab" (skăr'ăb) family, and their principal occupation in life is to scrape up all the filth they can find and bury it out of sight in the ground. It need hardly be said that the beetles do not

undertake this good work for the benefit of the world in general. They are simply engaged in collecting for themselves the food they like best, and in storing up supplies for their future offspring.

Most famous of them is the Egyptian scarab, or the "sacred beetle," as it is called, that lives in Southern Europe and in some parts of Africa. It is an odd-looking insect, with very long hind legs and a funny flat head scalloped all round the edge and finished off with a pair of feelers that spread out at the tips like little red fans.

Hundreds of these queer little scarabs may be seen on sandy slopes in Southern Europe or on the edge of the Egyptian desert, all industriously pushing and tugging and rolling mysterious round balls almost as big as themselves. Some are busy making the balls. They use their flat heads as shovels to scoop up manure and their stout bowed legs to twist and twirl the mass of stuff into a round lump.

The harmless-looking creatures below are known as carpet beetles. Their name reveals their infamous character.

Others are laboriously trundling their property uphill, walking slowly backwards and pushing the ball behind them with their long hind legs. Every now and again one of the beetles will pause for a moment and look round to see if the way is clear. As likely as not, in so doing he lets his ball slip from his clutches. Then away it goes merrily bounding down the slope, with the poor old scarab ambling after it as fast as his odd legs will carry him. If he manages to head it off, he will start trundling it back again with the greatest patience.

Mrs. Scarab Prepares Her Nursery

When the beetle succeeds in rolling his ball home to the hole in the ground already prepared for it, he will sit down and munch away until the last scrap of the feast is finished. Sometimes his mate joins in the banquet, after having first helped to provide and push home the fare. But Mrs. Scarab has frequently a less selfish end in view when she makes and rolls a ball of her own. Right in the centre, in the softest part, she places one of her eggs. Then, having buried the ball, she leaves it to supply plenty of food for the young beetle grub who will be born in due time.

Why the Scarab Was Sacred

Strangely enough, it was the thoughtful care of Mother Beetle that first gave the little scarab its title of "sacred beetle." The old Egyptian priests who dwelt by the waters of the Nile saw the beetles rolling their balls, and also they sometimes saw young beetles breaking their way out, but they did not know anything about the eggs so cunningly hidden inside by Mother Scarab. So they jumped

Photo by F. Martin Duncan
This is the beetle one sees beautifully represented in carvings for rings and necklaces and pins. He is the scarab, or sacred beetle, of the Egyptians, and for centuries received most reverent worship. Now we laugh at him for his amusing antics.

to the conclusion that the beetles actually created others of their kind out of the dust of the earth, and ordered the Egyptians to treat the little scarab with all honour as a sacred creature.

The burying beetles—or sextons, as they are sometimes called—are another family of interesting and useful insects. But instead of helping to keep clean the paths and pastures of the countryside, as the scarabs do, they seek out and decently bury little woodland creatures that have come to an untimely end. They are handsome, sturdy insects, with strong, flat heads, club-shaped antennae, and shiny black wing-cases marked with two broad wavy bands of deep red or orange. They hunt in couples. Soon after the sun has set, Mr. and Mrs. Sexton start off in search of any small furred or feathered creature that lies unburied on the ground.

If a little field-mouse has been killed and left by its slayer—who may have been frightened away before he could devour his prey —the burying beetles scent it from afar and come flying to the spot in the twilight. Two or three couples may come hurrying up to help in the task of burying the little corpse, and all set to work without delay to dig a trench round it. Using their hard heads as spades, they shovel up the earth and throw it out of the trench; they then burrow underneath the mouse, carrying load after load of soil on their heads, until gradually the tiny body sinks lower and lower in the ground. Finally, the beetles crawl out of the hole and, after carefully raking the earth over the mouse and smoothing it with their feet, they open their wing-cases, unfurl their gauzy wings, and fly off.

Born in a Grave

But why do the beetles do this strange thing? It cannot be simply because they are hungry, for they could quite well make a meal of the mouse without going to all the trouble of burying it first. If we carefully watch the gravediggers we shall see that they do not all crawl out of the grave before it is covered over. When their task is done the male beetles fly off, but the females are left behind buried with the corpse. There, hidden in the ground, the mother beetles proceed to lay clusters of tiny eggs; and not until this duty is finished do they push their way up through the loose soil and fly off to join their mates. So

There are more than three thousand different kinds of beetles found in the British Isles alone. A few typical examples are shown above. Beginning at the top left corner and reading across their names are as follows: Ground beetle, cockchafer, burying beetle; trident bearer, great black water beetle (in centre, with wings fully spread), dor beetle; oil beetle, carnivorous water beetle, musk beetle; wasp beetle, summer chafer, pine weevil.

you see the beetles take all this trouble in order to provide plenty of food for their young ones as soon as they are hatched.

Bold and Determined Hunters

The ground beetles, which are very numerous, work in a different way. They are bold, determined hunters, always on the warpath, chasing and killing insects and other small creatures with relentless fury. They attack grubs, caterpillars, and all sorts of harmful insects; so they are a great help to the gardeners and do an immense amount of good without intending it. Even as grubs these beetles are useful, for they burrow just below the ground and feed on insects that destroy the roots of crops.

Ground beetles vary greatly in form. The violet ground beetle is a fine fellow an inch and a half long, with blue-black wing cases shot with violet, and is one of the commonest species. Some are quite tiny things, but they are just as fierce as their bigger cousins. All are distinguished by their flat, smooth bodies, small heads, and the shapely, pointed jaws with which they nip you at once if you interfere with them when they are hunting. Some of the bold hunters fly about very actively. Others have no true wings under their wing-cases, but to make up for the handicap they all have very long legs and can run very fast. One unusually strange ground beetle is the fiddler beetle that lives in Malaya. It looks very much like a violin.

The ground beetles, like so many flesh-

No one needs to be introduced to our great friend the ladybird, though most of us would hardly recognize her when she is a larva, as in the circle, or a pupa, as in the square. We know her as a bright little spotted creature who saves our fruit growers and gardeners thousands of pounds a year by eating the destructive plant-lice.

eating creatures, seldom start hunting until dark; but the tiger beetle, which is every bit as fierce and bloodthirsty, is out in the full light of day, scouring the country for prey. On hot sunny mornings you may find him dashing about on sandy plains or dusty roads, a smart little fellow with a slim, trim, brightly coloured body— usually some shade of green—with contrasting spots of copper or yellow.

The tiger beetle is surprisingly quick both on the wing and on foot—as you will soon find out if you try to catch him. He tears about on his long, thin legs, zigzagging over the ground, and just when you think you have him he whisks round in a flash and is speeding away in the opposite direction as fast as he can go.

A Born Villain

With his sharp jaws and his strong suit of armour the tiger beetle fears no foe. He will boldly attack creatures much larger than himself and hang on to his prey like a bulldog if you attempt to rob him of his prize.

This quarrelsome little insect is just as tigerish in its youthful days, though as yet unable to career about in search of its dinner. Its short, spiny legs are quite useless for running, and its long soft body has no armour to protect it against its natural foes. The young tiger beetle is really a very ugly little grub. It has a hump on its back, a large, flat, horny head, and a terrible pair of huge, sickle-shaped jaws. On the top of its hump are two small curved hooks, and its sides are adorned with little tufts of stiff bristles.

Now the tiger grub is a hungry little grub, and it cannot live without eating; so since it cannot go "a-hunting," it needs must find some other way of getting food. Using its flat head and spiny feet as tools,

The tiger beetles are active carnivorous insects which run and fly about with great rapidity on heaths and moors. Here we see the beetle and (above) its larva in its burrow waiting for prey. Both photographs are enlarged.

the cunning little creature digs out a vertical tunnel, two or three inches deep, in the sandy soil. Then it rests at the top, clinging to the sides of the shaft with its hooks and spines and blocking the entrance with its big head.

There the little tiger grub lies in wait. Sooner or later some unwary insect is sure to pass within reach of those terrible jaws. Then up with a jerk comes the ugly head and the insect is dragged down for the wily little ogre's dinner.

Our Friends the Ladybirds

You would hardly imagine that such tiny things as ladybirds could be of much importance. Yet these pretty little spotted beetles are very useful friends to the farmer and gardener, for they wage constant war against the mischievous little plant-lice and scale insects that do so much harm in our fields and gardens.

The ladybirds creep quietly over the plants infested by such troublesome insects, and lay clusters of tiny eggs here and there on the foliage. Now and then they refresh themselves by eating a few plant-lice, but the ladybird has no great appetite, and it would take a few thousands of the bright little beetles to do much harm to the swarms of lice that crowd in untold numbers on the green leaves and tender young shoots.

How Ladybirds Kill Plant-lice

But when the tiny beetle grubs hatch out from their yellow eggs, they are desperately hungry. They are brisk, energetic little creatures. They run about very fast, clutching the little lice and cramming them into their mouths with their two front legs. It would be hard to say how many of the pests a ladybird grub will account for in the four or five weeks of its active life.

As is usual in the insect world, these beetle grubs are not at all like their parents. They have long, rather flat bodies tapering to a point behind, rough dark skins spotted with red or yellow, and little tufts of bristles down each side. When the time of rest approaches, the little creature does not hide in the ground as do most beetle grubs, but fastens itself by the tail to a leaf or twig, like the caterpillar of a butterfly. Then it shrinks, and, in place of the brisk little grub, behold a hard, round button of a thing, brightly coloured and covered with spots. Even now it does not remain perfectly still all the time. If touched, the funny little pupa springs up with a jerk and stands on its tail in a semi-erect position. This trick no doubt scares away many a creature who might be inclined to eat it.

Every Beetle Has Its Tricks

A ladybird is really a beetle, although it does not look much like one. Under its painted wing-cases two delicate transparent wings are folded away; so it can fly very well, besides being nimble on its feet. Birds do not like these little insects, for they have a most unpleasant smell and a very bitter taste; so, warned by their brightly coloured wing-cases, birds leave them alone.

Beetles are just as cunning as other insects in the tricks they use to deceive their enemies. Some beetles "play 'possum," pretending to be dead at the first alarm; others tuck in their heads and their legs and roll themselves up into hard, slippery balls directly they are touched. Bad-tasting beetles, if they are not decked out in the warning colours of red and yellow, often advertise the fact of their unpleasantness by a very disagreeable smell. Others try to bluff their enemies by pretending to be dangerous creatures, when really they are nothing of the sort. And certain beetles have more than one trick in reserve with which to startle their foes and save their own lives.

The "Devil's Coach Horse"

The rove beetle—sometimes called the "devil's coach horse" or the "cocktail"—is one of these accomplished insects. He is an odd creature with a long black body that he can turn and twist about as he pleases; for his wing-cases come only a little way below his waist, like a short jacket, and do not cover the whole of his back in the usual beetle fashion. Nevertheless, under those wing-cases the rove beetle has a fine, broad pair of flying wings folded away.

If you meet a rove beetle taking a quiet stroll down a country lane, he looks mild and innocent enough; but try to stop his progress by thrusting a stick or a grass stalk in his way, and in a moment he is transformed into a furious little demon. Up goes his head with an angry jerk. He cocks his tail right over his back, brandishing it in a threatening manner, as if he were going to strike like a scorpion. If this does not scare you away, he brings his second trick into action and squirts you with an evil-smelling spray from two little scent tubes in the tip of his tail.

Now, the rove beetle has no sting; and although the scent he squirts is very

Here is one of the funniest little fellows of all the beetle tribe. It is the insect sharpshooter known as the bombardier beetle. Our photographer has caught him clad in his customary uniform of blue and sitting on an oak leaf. He is blazing away with his little pop-gun, which he fires off with a sharp report whenever he is disturbed. Then follows a cloud of smoke which is as bad as poison gas to any insect foe. He would seem to carry only three rounds of ammunition on any given day, for no provocation can induce him to waste his powder further. But after a night's rest his gun is loaded again. Bombardier beetles are rare in Great Britain, but if you suddenly lift a stone or old log as you walk through the damp woods, you may have the luck to see one scurrying away, with a pop-pop-puff of his artillery to cover his retreat. If you catch him and hold him between your thumb and finger you will find that he grows quite hot—just as if he were boiling over with indignation!

nasty, it is not poisonous and does no harm. The behaviour of the bold little creature is sheer bravado; but frequently it has the desired effect of scaring away his enemies.

During the winter, in some countries, the ladybirds hibernate in masses like the ones on these rocks. At that time they are gathered and are kept in cold storage until spring, when they are shipped to regions where their services are needed in destroying plant-lice.

The collection and sale of ladybirds is a thriving business in California, where the orchards would be ruined if it were not for the friendly little beetles. Originally this kind of ladybird was imported from Australia, whence the hated plant-lice had also come.

The "devil's coach horse" has a number of smaller relatives that all act in the same impudent way. Many have bright colours among their attractions, and some are such tiny things that they are often called "black flies." In the western states of America swarms of tiny rove beetles dance like gnats in the air on warm spring evenings. They get into the eyes and make them smart and water, and are really a great nuisance.

Beetle with a Smoke Screen

The funny little bombardier (bŏm'băr-dēr') beetles have even more surprising ways, for they actually use poison gas as a means of defence. Small armies of them roam about the countryside, and if attacked by a more powerful insect, the whole company turn their backs on the foe and discharge a volley of explosive gas bombs full in his face. Then, before the astonished and half blinded enemy can recover himself, the bold bombardiers beat a hasty retreat under cover of the clouds of irritating smoke they have produced.

The gas the beetles use is stored, in a liquid state, in a special gland at the tail end of the insect. When it comes into contact with the air the liquid evaporates and makes little puffs of stinging white smoke.

There are certainly a great many more destructive beetles than useful ones. There are hosts of them doing all they can to destroy timber, grain, fruit, vegetables and crops of every kind all over the world.

The worst destroyer of timber is the death-watch beetle, which plays havoc with the oak beams and woodwork in old buildings.

Many cathedrals, churches and public halls, as well as ancient houses, have suffered severely from the depredations of this beetle, whose activities generally take place unnoticed until extensive damage has been done. The beetle grubs eat away the solid wood until it is nothing but a spongy mass full of holes and tunnels choked with wood dust.

The beetles call to each other by a curious ticking noise, made by tapping on the wood with their heads. In the olden days superstitious people called this the "death-watch," but we now know that this sound has nothing whatever to do with death, but is merely the beetle's love call.

The Skipjack is an Acrobat

The queer little click beetle, or skipjack, is another troublesome offender, although its antics are most entertaining. It is a genuine little acrobat, constantly amusing itself by turning somersaults in the air. If, as it runs about the fields and climbs up and down the grass stalks, the skipjack chances to fall over on its back, the accident does not worry it a bit. Instead of lying feebly kicking its legs, as the dor beetle does, it arches its body so that only its head and the tip of its tail touch the ground. Then with a sudden click the little acrobat jerks itself up in the air, turns a complete somersault, and comes down on its feet, right side up again. It does this trick by means of a kind of notch and catch on the under side of its body. By bending itself backwards it releases the catch, strikes the ground with a sudden jerk, and rebounds into the air.

A Living Piece of Wire

It is while they are grubs that the click beetles do so much harm. They live for two or three years buried in the ground, wriggling their way through the soil and munching the roots of all sorts of useful plants. Whole fields of grain are often ruined by the troublesome little things, which are called "wireworms," because they look more like short pieces of thick, rusty wire than anything else.

The chafers are quite as bad in their ways as the click beetles. They are hand-

The death-watch beetle and its grubs play terrible havoc with the wood of old buildings. The beetle and two of its grubs are here seen busily carrying on their destructive work, burrowing tunnels in the beam of a church.

How different they are—and yet they all are beetles! There are so many members of the tribe that it includes about half of all living insects.

You might well look for cover if you saw this great dragon coming towards you full tilt. It is the male Hercules beetle, six inches long and provided with a pair of pincers that could give one a terrible nip. It lives in Brazil, and is one of the largest of all insects. Here it is shown with its wing cases raised and its flying wings outspread.

The cherry curculio, below at the left, is a wretched little beetle that makes a cut in young cherries when they are about the size of a pea and leaves an egg in the fruit. The picture at the right shows you what happens to a cherry

The demon on the right is the boll weevil, a beetle that has caused the loss of millions of pounds to cotton growers. One pair may have nearly 13,000,000 children in a season, enough to devour a whole crop. In reality the boll weevil is very small, but its size here is quite in keeping with the harm it does.

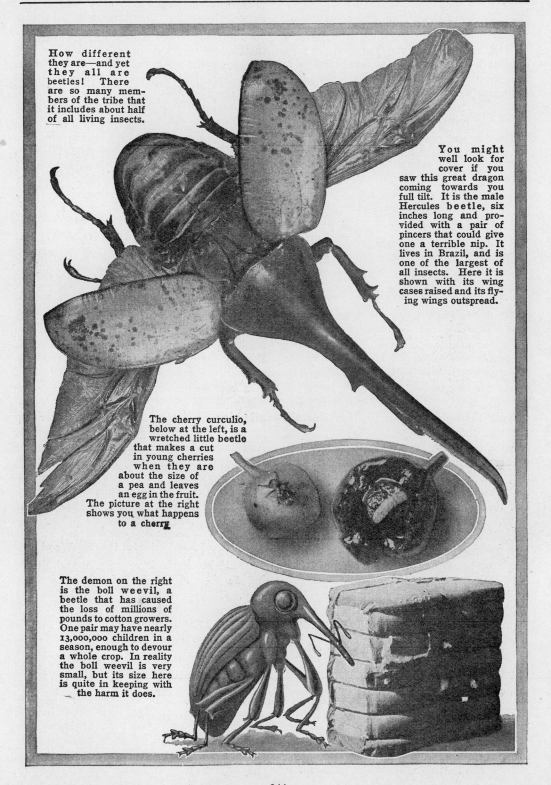

some insects as a rule, and they are all distinguished by their feelers, which have a number of little leaflets at the tips that can be opened or shut like a fan. The male chafers have the finest feelers; Mrs. Chafer possesses a very much smaller fan than her mate.

Grubs Too Fat to Stand Up

The pretty rose chafers, with their golden-green wing-cases, love to feed on roses and the flowers and foliage of the grape-vines. Before they develop into perfect insects they live in the ground and gnaw the roots of grasses and other useful plants.

Their big cousins the summer chafers and the cockchafers, which come whizzing through the air on warm evenings, are even worse offenders. They devour the young green leaves and shoots of trees, often stripping the branches nearly bare; and their ugly white grubs gnaw the roots of grasses and food crops for two or three years before they change to beetles. The young chafers eat so much and grow so fat that they cannot stand up on their six little legs; so the greedy grubs are always obliged to lie curled up on one side. In this odd position they wriggle through the ground, biting at the roots as they go.

Then there are the weevils, or snout bugs —there is simply no end to the damage they can do. They are mostly tiny things, many so small that you can hardly see them; but that makes no difference to their evil ways. These little beetles—and there are thousands of them, each as bad as all the others—may be known by the peculiar shape of the head, which is so drawn out that it looks like a long nose. This nose or beak is Mother Weevil's boring tool. With its aid she pierces the fruit or nut or young bud she thinks her children will most enjoy, and in each tiny hole she lays an egg. The young weevil grubs, when they hatch, have a very good time; but the fruit on which they have been feeding is spoiled and useless, and the nuts from which the weevils have escaped are full of a disgusting pulpy mass instead of sweet kernels.

While the weevil grubs are working away inside the fruit and buds, the full-grown beetles attack the leaves and shoots and flowers and even the tender green bark. But although they may be swarming in thousands over the trees and bushes, the little culprits are not at all easy to see at their tricks. For, besides being so tiny, they are mostly so quietly dressed in brown or grey or dull green that they are practically invisible as they creep about. They are very cunning, too. If you shake the tree they fold up their legs and fall plump to the ground, and there they will lie as if they were dead, hoping to pass unnoticed until the danger is over. Then up they crawl again and continue their destructive attack on the tree.

One of the worst of these little pests is the boll weevil, which deposits its eggs in the buds and pods of the cotton plants, sometimes destroying the entire crop. Another potato pest is the Colorado beetle. Though a native of the United States, this insect has sometimes found its way into Europe, and in 1933 it was discovered in England, but its career of destruction was soon checked.

Giant beetles are not nearly so overwhelming in their numbers as the tiny mischievous imps that swarm over all growing things and give so much trouble. And this is just as well, for if the giant stag beetle, for example, crowded the trees as the weevils do, the branches would break down under the weight of the heavy insects. The giant stag beetle is often two inches long, and has formidable horns.

Baby Stags Thrive on Rotting Wood

These beetles look very fierce and alarming as they move along in their dignified way. Their great jaws, shaped like the antlers of a stag, are slightly raised as if ready to attack all comers. To be sure, if you interfere with one of the big fellows you may get a sharp nip for your pains, but they are really very peaceable creatures.

Stag beetles do not hunt and kill other insects. They love sweet food, and live chiefly on the sap that flows from bruised places in the trees and on the honey-dew formed by plant-lice and scale insects. Their big white grubs live in decayed trees; they thrive and grow fat on the rotting wood,

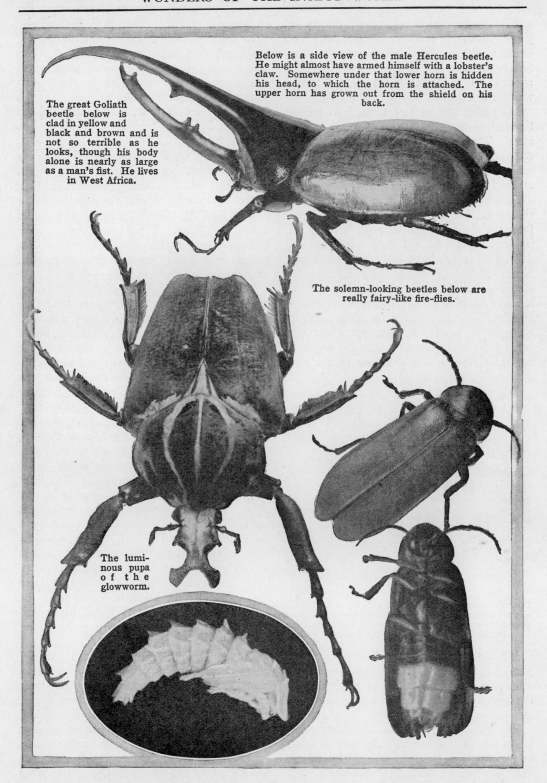

The great Goliath beetle below is clad in yellow and black and brown and is not so terrible as he looks, though his body alone is nearly as large as a man's fist. He lives in West Africa.

Below is a side view of the male Hercules beetle. He might almost have armed himself with a lobster's claw. Somewhere under that lower horn is hidden his head, to which the horn is attached. The upper horn has grown out from the shield on his back.

The solemn-looking beetles below are really fairy-like fire-flies.

The luminous pupa of the glowworm.

343

and do not become perfect beetles for several years. The stag beetle's gigantic jaws are no doubt useful in keeping enemies at a respectful distance, as few creatures would be bold enough to challenge such a well-armed warrior to combat.

Male stag beetles sometimes fight among themselves to gain the favour of a lady stag. Then a tremendous gnashing and clashing of jaws takes place, but the rivals seldom appear to damage one another seriously.

Still bigger than the stag is the curious rhinoceros beetle that has gained its name from the stout, curved horn projecting from its shoulder shield. It measures some two and a half inches in length and is the largest North American beetle. Its cousin, the elephant beetle of South America, is five inches long and carries a long, curved horn—absurdly like an elephant's trunk—on the point of its head. But the great Hercules beats both the rhinoceros and the elephant beetle. It is no less than six inches long

The stag beetle is undoubtedly the finest of British beetles, but only the male possesses the formidable horns. He has a fierce and formidable appearance as he makes his way along. Stag beetles in tropical countries are often brilliantly coloured.

and boasts two enormous horns—one projecting forward from its shoulders, the other rising from the top of its head and curving upwards. Together they form an awe-inspiring pair of pincers.

The giant Goliath is an African beetle. He is four or five inches long, and as stout and portly as a toad; his shoulders are velvety black, strikingly decorated with

stripes and splashes of white or yellow, and the wing-cases are a deep chocolate brown. Although such a big fellow, the Goliath is not so terrifying in appearance as many of the giants of his race. He has only two funny little blunt horns on his head, though he wears sharp spurs on his legs and hooked claws on his feet.

The Largest of All Beetles

These great beetles are not often seen. They live in the dense African jungles, fluttering heavily around the tree tops and feeding on the flowers and juices of the climbing plants. There are also smaller Goliath beetles that are really beautiful insects, with pretty green wing-cases marked with snowy white.

But the giant longhorns of South America are the largest beetles in the world. One member of this distinguished family is said to be nine inches long, and thick and broad in proportion. The long horns are really the beetle's feelers, which in some cases are two or three times as long as the insect itself. Some of these great creatures are called "sawyer beetles," because they have very strong toothed jaws which they use to saw through the bark on the branches of forest trees in order to reach the sap.

In a very old natural history book a writer gives us an amusing picture of one of the sawyer beetles. This is how he describes it:—"It hath a little broad head, great ox-eyes, almost three fingers overthwart in length; it hath a forked mouth, gaping and terrible, with two very hard crooked teeth: with these, while he gnaws the wood (I speak by experience), it doth perfectly grunt aloud like a young pig."

In the struggle for life that is always going on in the insect world, the numerous beetle tribes are well equipped to hold their own. Strong wings and swift feet make many of them equally at home in the air and on the land. They have armour-plated suits to protect them; useful tools and weapons to serve them on all occasions. Beetles knew how to dig and fight long before we did. The lowly little creatures even fore-stalled us in the use of artificial illumination. Ages before man first discovered how to make a light, certain little beetles were already in the habit of lighting up their tiny lamps as soon as daylight failed

In England and in the south of Europe, on soft summer nights, glowing sparks shine out here and there under the hedge-rows like tiny fairy lights. If you touch one it disappears, as if the fairy of the lamp had switched off her light. Nothing is then to be seen but a queer little beetle called a "glow-worm." She is certainly no beauty, for although she is a full-grown beetle, she has no wings or wing-cases, and looks much as she did when she was merely a beetle grub. Like Peter Pan she has never grown up. But no matter. Each summer night she lights her lamp and waits patiently for visitors to come and cheer her; and guided by her beacon, the little males of the species, who have wings, come flying from far and near to pay their court to the "lady with the lamp."

This light of the glow-worm, which is produced from certain cells of fat lying in the hind part of the insect, is of a phosphorescent nature—that is, it gives off light without heat. Thus the lowly little beetle possesses a power which man in all his wisdom cannot imitate; for though we can produce light from gas and electricity we cannot produce it in a heatless form. And some scientists believe that the glow-worm rays possess the same penetrating quality as the X-Rays!

Most wonderful of "living night lights" are the fire-flies of South America and the West Indies. Although they are called flies, the luminous insects are really beetles,

closely related to the skipjacks. On hot sultry nights the dark forests are ablaze with the flashing green lights of thousands of the little insects as they joyously dance and chase one another in the air.

There are fire-flies, too, in North America and in the Far East, while in Southern Europe thousands of small luminous beetles sparkle like diamonds as they cluster on the dark trees and bushes on hot nights, or flash like shooting stars through the air.

Though beetles seem humble enough to us, they are among Mother Nature's favourite children. She has provided for

Here is the fat larva of the dor beetle, the pupa in its earthen cell and finally the newly emerged beetle. The dor beetle is the English representa-tive of the famous sacred scarab.

them so well that they can live everywhere and on anything. It is this marvellous power to survive that one author describes in a melancholy picture of the end of the world

"When the Moon shall have faded from the sky and the Sun shall shine at noonday a dull cherry red; and the seas shall be frozen over, and the ice-cap shall have crept downward to the Equator from either Pole, and no keel shall cut the water, nor wheels turn in mills; when all cities shall long have been dead and crumbled into dust, and all life shall be on the very last verge of extinction . . . then, on a bit of lichen, . . . shall be seated a tiny insect, preening its antennae in the glow of the worn-out Sun, represent-ing the sole survival of animal life on the Earth—a melancholy bug."

(CONTINUED ON PAGE 407)

FUN WITH TRICKS

A GOOD WAY TO BUMP YOUR HEAD

Take a stool and place it next a wall, you yourself standing two stool-widths away. Now bend over and try to pick the stool up.

A NEAT PRACTICAL JOKE

Fill two glasses with water and place them on the backs of a friend's hands, asking him to balance them. He will show you how easy it is to do, and may laugh at such a simple trick; but soon he will discover that he is a helpless prisoner and cannot set the glasses down without assistance.

A FOOT OF LEAD

Stand with the left foot touching the wall and the left arm extended, as you see at the right. Now try to lift the right foot.

A STOOL OF MATCHES

Ask anyone if he can lift thirteen matches with one match. The chances are that he can't. This is the way to do it. Put one match on the table, then set up the twelve others, pointing them in alternate directions, as you see above. Set the thirteenth match on top and lift them all with the match beneath.

A DIFFICULT TASK

It is easy to sit down after first crossing the legs below the knees. But try crossing the legs above the knees, and you will find that sitting down is about as hard as it would be if you had no knees at all.

THE CONTRARY CORK

Try to blow a little cork into a large bottle, first setting the cork inside the bottle neck. The silly cork comes out instead of going in. Now inhale instead of blowing, and the cork goes in with no trouble at all.

THE RESULT IS QUITE A BLOW

Place a paper bag flat upon the table so that the mouth projects over the edge. Now put some heavy books—dictionaries or reference books—on top of it. By blowing into the bag you can make the books tumble over.

PICKING UP THE HANDKERCHIEF

Put a handkerchief directly under the back of a kitchen chair. Lying lengthwise across the chair, try to pick the handkerchief up with your mouth. You may hang on to any part of the chair you like, but you must not tip it over.

THAT FUNNY FUNNEL

Blow straight at a candle with a funnel. The flame can't be made to move, because the air currents are evenly distributed and escape at the base of the candle. If you raise the funnel a little, the currents of air will hit the flame and make it bend.

A QUEER EGG

Put a thin post card on a glass of water and an egg on a plain ring on top of it. Tap the card lightly at one corner and it will slide away, letting the egg and ring fall.

A GAME FOR HALLOWE'EN

Float a candle in a tub of water and try to seize it with your lips and teeth. This can be done only by taking a deep breath and holding it, then ducking into the water and seizing the elusive candle. Keep your hands behind your back all the time.

346

It was not the loss of his tail that made this poor fox ridiculous; it was his foolishness in pretending that he was glad that it was gone. His companions laughed heartily at him, and he hurried away to hide himself in his disgrace.

TANSY and BOBBLES on FABLE ISLAND

Here is the Squirrel's Recipe for Being Always Happy, and the Story of the Grand Visit that the Mouse from the Country Paid to His Cousin in Town

(CONTINUED FROM PAGE 256)

NOW as Tansy and Bobbles hurried off through the woods they noticed a strange thing lying on the ground. It was the brush—or tail—of a fox.

"I wonder which fox has lost his tail in a trap," said Bobbles. "He'll feel terribly disgraced among the rest of the foxes without it."

"Stand back!" said Tansy, and she pulled at Bobbles.

There was the young fox who had lost his tail, making a speech to a number of foxes who had gathered round him.

"Friends!" he cried, "I notice that you are very much surprised at seeing that I have cut off my tail. But you have no idea what a comfort it is to be without the tiresome thing. My tail was always getting in the way, and I really wonder why I have

put up with it for so long. However, here you see me, the first fox without a tail. I now invite you to cut off your own tails and share my happiness."

"Did you cut it off yourself?" asked an old fox.

"Yes, yes!" cried the young fox.

"Ha! Ha!" mocked the old fox. "We may be sure that this youngster would never advise us to cut off our tails if there were any chance of getting back his own."

Then all the foxes began to laugh, and the young fox hurried off in disgrace and dismay.

"Booh!" cried Tansy and Bobbles, as they caught up with him. "What a pity that you lied about it."

But the poor young fox scampered away, wondering where he could hide himself.

347

Presently Tansy and Bobbles stopped short at sight of an old man sobbing and tearing out his grey hair as he stared down into a hole.

How the Miser Lost His Gold

"Has something terrible happened?" asked Tansy sympathetically.

"Terrible! Terrible! I sold my house and garden, and nearly all I possessed and turned them into a lump of gold, which I hid in this hole. Now a wicked thief has stolen it."

"You must be a miser," said Bobbles, seriously. "Fancy trading nice useful things for a lump of silly gold which you can't eat, or wear, or smell, or enjoy at all. See!" and he winked at Tansy as she helped him to roll a great stone down the hole, "pretend that is your treasure. It will be just as good as the lump of gold."

"Look out, Tansy!" whispered Bobbles, "something's going to happen. That careless squirrel has fallen down upon His Sleeping Majesty."

He looks silly and he *is* silly—for he thought that to possess a lump of gold would make him happy.

Certainly the lion, who had been sleeping near by, had roused himself and was showing his teeth to the terrified squirrel, who began to weep and beg his pardon.

The lion, who didn't really wish the squirrel any harm, said that he would let him go if he would explain why he was always merry and gay, while the king of the wood found the days and nights drag so dully.

On hearing this, Tansy flew invisibly to the squirrel, and whispered, "Get safely back into the tree before you dare to speak the truth."

"Oh, sire," replied the squirrel, as he darted up the trunk of the tree, "the truth is that I have a happy conscience. I take no life, but gather nuts for myself and my family. But you, sire, are always wandering about seeking to destroy and devour. You hate and I love; so I am happy and you are miserable," and the squirrel darted out of sight.

"Booh!" said Bobbles, and the lion roused himself from his melancholy.

"No peace in this island from you interfering fairies," grumbled the lion, though indeed he was glad to see them.

"My father says that if we are happy because of the good inside us, we shall always be laughing and joyful."

"I'm not in the mood for a lecture even from your wise father," said the lion. "I want a drink."

"Come on, then," said Tansy, and she flew up and curled herself in the lion's mane, while Bobbles hung on to his tail.

It was terribly hot. As they reached a small fountain, they saw that a goat was in possession. He turned and threatened the lion with his horns for daring to come near the fountain.

"Begone!" roared the lion.

"Begone yourself!" bleated the goat. "I was here first and I have a right to the water."

It looked as if there was going to be a terrific quarrel, but just then Bobbles glanced up into the sky.

"You two silly things," he mocked. "Can't you see that the vultures and the crows are gathering already, waiting to eat up your dead bodies?"

"Yes—quick! quick! Make friends," pleaded Tansy.

"If you will, I will," said the goat.

"If you will, I will," repeated the lion.

So they nodded and made the bargain. The goat stepped back and let the lion drink as much as ever he wanted, and then the lion stepped back and the goat drank as much as he wanted.

And even after they had both quenched their thirst there was plenty of water left when they had finished; so the vultures and crows had to fly away.

This lion wears much the same expression as that worn by people who object to sharing their possessions with other people.

But now all attention was turned to a very funny sight.

A donkey, having dressed up in a lion's skin, came prancing along, frightening the animals and thinking himself very fine.

He was so pleased with the excitement he was causing that he overacted his part, and began to bray loudly.

That set all the animals laughing, until a fox came up to the donkey and said slyly, "I might have been frightened, too, if I hadn't heard your voice."

As for the donkey, when he saw the real lion he dropped his false skin and galloped off for dear life.

This Little Mouse Went Visiting

"Hello! Look where you're going!" exclaimed Tansy, as she sat under a fir tree; for a mouse was running right across her skirt.

"I beg your pardon," cried the mouse, "but I'm so excited because I've a visitor coming, a town mouse, and I fear he'll think my feast of nuts and cheese parings and peas and barley very poor food. Don't stop me! Don't stop me! Here he comes!" and he rushed off.

Tansy and Bobbles watched the two mice trot down into a hole, and waited to see what would happen.

They hadn't long to wait, for the country mouse and the town mouse soon came up, talking eagerly together.

"The town mouse is going to take me to town," cried the country mouse. "He's going to show me all the glories of the feast that he enjoys every night."

"That's a good idea," said Bobbles, "and if you like, my sister and I will take you there in our pockets."

So off they flew to the town. The country mouse poked his head out of Tansy's pocket, and the town mouse looked out from Bobbles's pocket.

When they reached the grand house, the town mouse invited the fairies in. So, making themselves invisible, they gladly accepted the invitation.

They were greatly entertained, as they hovered about in the grand dining-hall, to see the town mouse gathering all the dainties from the banqueting table for his amazed visitor; and the country mouse certainly gobbled as he had never gobbled in his life.

But suddenly the door opened, and in came a number of merry revellers, followed by their dogs.

The dogs made a rush for the mice, and the poor country mouse crouched in a corner terrified, not knowing his way to a hole.

But Tansy took pity on him and picked him up, and off the fairies flew, thankful to be back in the cool night air.

"Dear, dear," said the country mouse, when he got safely back to the wood, "I'd rather enjoy my own quiet home than feast on dainties at the risk of such terrors!" And off he slipped into his hole, to tell his adventures to his wife and family.

The fairies were rather tired and were thinking of returning home, when they heard some pitiful groaning, and found, by the first glimmer of dawn, a poor stag who seemed to be at the point of death.

"Do let us help you," said Tansy.

"Alas!" said the stag, "when I lay down here to recover from my illness, there was abundance of sweet grass all round me. But the friends who came to sympathize with me have eaten it all up, and now I am dying of starvation."

"This is dreadful," said Bobbles fiercely, and he whispered to Tansy.

The fairies disappeared and presently returned with bundles of the daintiest grass from the wood, and they watched with joy as the famished stag revived.

"Now we're going to sleep by your side until the sun is full in the sky," said Tansy; "and then we'll keep guard over you until you are well, and save you from your greedy visitors."

Here is the stag that was almost killed by selfish friends who pretended to be kind.

The stag thanked them, and they leaned up against him and used his soft hide for a pillow on which to sleep until the sun waked them with a big kiss.

"He Steals My Corn," Said the Horse

Tansy and Bobbles liked to make themselves invisible when they went to the farmyard, for it was great fun to say "Booh!" when the creatures there least expected it.

One day they were watching the stableman grooming a horse, when suddenly Bobbles remarked, "How queer that the more he grooms the horse's coat, the less it shines."

"Who spoke?" asked the stable-man, staring around.

"Booh!" said Bobbles.

"Booh!" said Tansy, and there they were.

"How can my coat shine," asked the horse, "when this thief of a stable-man steals my corn? If he'd give me less of his grooming, and more of my corn, you'd soon see how my coat would shine."

"Indeed, you ought to be ashamed of yourself," said Tansy to the stable-man. "How would you like your master to come to your cottage and steal things from your larder?"

The Cock That Crowed Too Soon

Just then two young cocks started a tremendous fight for the right to be master of the barnyard.

They stamped backwards and forwards, pecking in an effort to tear each other's comb with their spurs.

At last one of them, sadly disgraced, crept off defeated.

The other stood up on his toes and crowed his crow of victory, for all the farmyard to hear.

"Look! Look!" whispered Bobbles, as he noticed a mighty eagle hovering above.

The eagle swooped down and carried off the crowing cock; and at that the defeated cock plucked up heart and took possession of the farmyard.

"What's the meaning of that?" asked Tansy.

"Only that one should not crow too soon," said Bobbles. "Come on and we will find a goat to give us a ride."

So off they went; and sure enough, in front of them was a goat cantering off to get a drink. He trotted along at a comfortable pace, and Tansy and Bobbles followed after him a short distance away.

On his way he soon came to a well, and looking down into it he was surprised to see a fox.

If we keep our wits at work we can learn as much from this barnyard as from the most instructive book—and the reason for it is that whenever people are selfish and vain and greedy they behave just as animals do. It is only cocks—and people as silly as they—who cannot keep from crowing over every little achievement.

Now the fox had fallen into the well by accident. But the silly goat did not know that, and he merely asked the fox if the water was fresh and plentiful down in the well.

"Wonderfully fresh, and plenty of it," said the fox. "Jump down and drink for yourself."

So the goat jumped down, and instantly the fox, seizing his opportunity, leaped on the goat's back and scrambled out of the well.

"Oh, dear!" exclaimed the goat, as it dawned on him that he couldn't get out himself, "aren't you going to help me out?"

"Ha! Ha!" laughed the fox, "you can stay where you are. If you'd as much sense as you have beard, you would have looked before you leaped."

He was just cantering off to dry himself when Bobbles shouted "Booh!"

"Oh, it's you," said the fox, looking rather ashamed.

"If your head is so full of brains, how came it that you ever fell into the well?" said Bobbles.

But as the fox couldn't answer that, he galloped off; and Tansy and Bobbles got some branches and pushed them down into the well, so that the goat could climb out.

What a glorious ride he gave them then!

How Jupiter Punished the Bees

"I do wonder how it is," said Bobbles to Tansy, as they lolled in the hot sun on a bed of heather, "that when a bee stings anyone, it dies itself."

"Let's ask one of them," said Tansy. So she put out her finger, and a bee stopped gathering honey and crawled over it.

"How is it that you bees die if you sting anyone?" asked Bobbles.

"Alas!" said the bee, "that was the fault of an ancestor of ours. One morning he took Jupiter a present of honey, and Jupiter was so delighted that he promised him anything he cared to ask. So he pleaded for a sting in order to injure any man who came to get his honey. But Jupiter was angry, for he loves men and thinks our honey is partly for their use.

"'Very well,' said Jupiter. 'You shall have your sting, but he that prays for harm to come to his neighbour shall find harm come to himself.'"

It Always Pays to be Honest

Splash! Up jumped the fairies, forgetting all about the bee.

Running to the edge of a deep river, they found a woodman in great distress because he had dropped his axe into the water. In those days an axe was very valuable, and the woodman was wondering how he could possibly get another, when who should appear, running along the bank, but the god Mercury. He was like a fine, strong young man—and he wore a helmet with two wings on it. He came up to the astonished woodman and listened to his story.

In another moment he had set down his helmet and dived into the river. But he came up quickly, holding a golden axe in his hand.

"Is this your axe?" he cried.

"No, no!" said the honest woodman.

Mercury threw it back into the water, and dived again.

"Is this yours?" and he brought up a silver one.

"No, no!" said the woodman.

Mercury dived again, and this time brought up the plain axe with the wooden handle.

"Is this yours?"

"Yes, yes!" cried the woodman, delighted to see his axe once again.

He thanked the god profusely, and then rushed off to tell his companions what had happened.

Mercury had disappeared, and Tansy and Bobbles were thinking they would look for more adventures, when another woodman came rushing along.

He threw his axe into the deep river and then flung himself down and sobbed and howled in despair.

"He's a cheat; I'd like to tell Mercury," muttered Bobbles, as the god appeared again.

"Mercury will find out for himself," said Tansy. "Wait."

The Reward of Dishonesty

And sure enough, Mercury threw off his helmet, dived into the river, and brought up a golden axe.

"Is this your axe?" he asked the woodman.

"Yes, yes!" cried the woodman, eager to snatch the treasure.

"Ah!" said Mercury, "I see that you are a liar and a cheat. Your axe shall remain at the bottom of the river for ever!"

Mercury rose from the river, took up his helmet, waved it gaily at Tansy and Bobbles, and then disappeared like a mist.

(CONTINUED ON PAGE 451)

MARVELS
of the
MODERN
WORLD

The marvellous Empire State Building in New York—the tallest building in the world—is 1248 feet in height, or more than three times as high as St. Paul's Cathedral, London. It has 102 stories, and the summit is a mooring mast for airships. This photograph was taken from an airship as it was attempting to effect the difficult mooring.

The little boy in the top left-hand corner is a young citizen of Athens, the capital of Greece, and next to him, snugly dressed in a fur suit, is a little Eskimo girl. The dark-skinned girl is a member of the Lambani tribe of Southern India, and the two round-faced children in picturesque costumes on the right belong to mountainous Switzerland.

All these children live in Eastern countries. In the top left-hand picture you see a very young member of a ruling native family of Bombay, arrayed in full ceremonial dress. Next are some Japanese Boy Scouts taking part in a marching display accompanied by song, and below are four Cambodian dancers giving a performance at a fête.

All of these children are dressed in the national costume of the country to which they belong. The two in the upper left-hand corner are Hungarians, and the girl and boy to the right live in the Austrian province of Tirol. Below are a charming little pair from the Basque Provinces of Spain, while on the left is a peasant girl of Latvia.

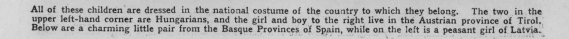

Photo by Rischgitz

Fishermen of the early days of the Iron Age returning with their catch. The Iron Age, which followed the Bronze Age, is so called from the discovery of iron and its use for the making of weapons and other implements.

The MEN With IRON SWORDS
How the Ancient Hittites with the Aid of Superior Weapons Overran Syria and Prevented the Egyptians from Conquering It

AS ONE country after another becomes civilized, we begin to find things happening in the land just south of the Black Sea and north of the Fertile Crescent, between the Aegean Sea to the west and the Caspian Sea to the east. This region is called Asia Minor, and about 2500 B.C. it was inhabited by a people who called themselves Hittites. Some of their modern descendants, the Armenians, still live in this region.

Who those Hittites were is a problem. They seem to have been a mixed race, but they were probably not Semitic like the Assyrians, Babylonians, Phoenicians, and the Hebrews, although they were to have

13   353

some interesting dealings with the Hebrews. We now know that the language they spoke was Indo-European, as were Greek and Persian; and many students of history have believed that the Hittites were themselves of the same race as the Greeks and Persians. But this is very doubtful. They were probably a separate race who happened to learn to speak an Indo-European tongue.

Ancestor of the Double-headed Eagle

When in 2000 B.C. Assur was just a little town and not the famous Assyria it was later to become, the Hittites and the Babylonians ruled it in turn. From the Hittites the Assyrians learned much about the building of palaces and carving in stone. The Hittites had a way of carving two stone animals, perhaps lions, on either side of a palace entrance, and this gave a splendid effect which the Assyrians imitated in their own buildings. One of the figures the Hittites liked to carve was that of an eagle with a double head, one facing each way; and this double-headed eagle is the great-grandfather of the one you still may see on certain coins and other national emblems.

Beginning of the Iron Age

You remember that one of the features which made the Assyrian soldiers so successful was their use of iron swords. The Hittites were among the very first people to know and use iron, and they were the first to work the iron mines along the Black Sea. Iron is very hard, and an iron sword can win easily against a bronze one. With their iron weapons the Hittites pushed southward, until about 1400 B.C. they overran Syria, where the Arameans (ăr'ă-mē'ăn) lived, and stopped the Egyptian kings from conquering the land. Many Hittites went still farther south and settled in Palestine.

In the centuries from 1400 to 1200 B.C., the Hittites were at the height of their power. They did not have little separate city kingdoms, but a single government under one king. The capital of their country was at what is now Boghazkeui (bŏ-găz-kū'ĭ), near the Halys River just south of the Black Sea. They called this city Khatti, which is only another form of the word Hittite.

Even before 1400 B.C. the Hittites and the Egyptians had met one another, in both peace and war. And, as you know, the Egyptians were great makers of pictures and loved to draw whatever they saw of interest to them. In the Egyptian drawings we often see pictures of Hittites, and they are very easy to distinguish by their noses. The Hittite had a nose different from any other nose of the time—a large hooked nose, called an aquiline (ăk'wĭ-lĭn) nose because it is somewhat like the beak of an eagle, and the Latin word for "eagle" is aquila. The Armenians, descendants of the Hittites, have the same type of nose even to-day.

Who Can Read the Hittites' Writing?

In Asia Minor there are some curious pictures carved on stone, having inscriptions in a kind of writing that looks like the Egyptian hieroglyphs (hī'ĕr-ŏ-glĭf). These are old Hittite inscriptions, and the writing is indeed hieroglyphic, but it is built on a different plan from that of the Egyptian hieroglyphs, and no one yet can read what it says, although a few of the signs have been deciphered.

Luckily this picture-writing, which the Hittites fashioned for themselves on the Egyptian model, was not the only one they used. They also wrote in cuneiform (kū-nē'ĭ-fôrm), or wedge-shaped syllables, such as the Babylonians used, though here, too, they made up many of their own signs.

Hittite Writings Deciphered

For a long time we had no way of reading either of these kinds of Hittite writing, but in 1916 an Austrian named Hrozny learned how to read the Hittite cuneiform. The story in these records is fascinating. It tells us something of the great city of Troy, about which we also read in the poetry of Homer, a Greek. It tells us of the Egyptian king, Rameses II, who wrote to the Hittite king to ask for a big shipment of pure iron, and of how the Hittite king answered at once by sending an iron sword, with the rest of the iron to follow later. This was about 1100 B.C., and within a century the "Iron Age" had begun to replace the "Age of Bronze."

This strange haul consists of four divers, sailors in the British Navy being trained at Portsmouth to go down to the ocean's floor. They are receiving instruction in one of the most dangerous of all occupations to follow.

UNDER *the* OCEAN WAVE

How the Bold Diver Goes Hunting in the Watery Depths for Sunken Treasure

IT IS all very fine to take a flying leap off the bank and split the water for ten feet or so—but suppose you had to go down two hundred feet, how would you feel about it?

Down there it would be dark and cold, and the two hundred feet of water over you would be very heavy. And if you started up to the surface for a breath of air, you would drown before you got there. So if you were going so far down, you would need a special sort of suit to keep you alive.

Yet people go down as far as that, and farther still. Sometimes they do it just for fun, or just to see the sights. More frequently they are engaged in salvage work. For on the floor of the sea lies many a gallant ship that went down in a war or as the result of a storm or a collision. In the real depths it will rest in peace, but in shallower waters the divers may reach it. It may still be carrying a great quantity of gold that they can recover, or it may even be brought up from the bottom to sail the sea once more.

Alexander the Great—Diver

For these and other reasons, men have been going down far below the surface ever since ancient times. Alexander the Great once went down to see what it was like, but, of course, he and all the others wore a special kind of diving suit. Yet it was only in the past century that we contrived to make the kind of outfit that is now used wherever the bold divers are at work. What is the outfit like?

In the first place there is the diving-suit. It is like a great baggy set of overalls, made of stout cloth lined with rubber to keep out the water. At the wrists it fits so tightly that no drop can get through. And round the neck it has a metal collar to which the helmet fits.

The helmet is a brass globe with a window of thick glass on each side and in front. When it is screwed down on the collar it is watertight. Inside there is a telephone with a bell button which the diver can press with his chin. And at the back is a stout rubber hose which brings down a supply of fresh air.

On the diver's feet are the heaviest shoes in the world. They are weighted with iron and they weigh about thirty pounds. Over his shoulders are slung two other weights, of some forty pounds apiece, one on his chest and the other on his back. For there is so much air inside his outfit that he would float like a cork if he did not have these weights to take him down below. Indeed, he has a valve in his collar by which he can keep just the right amount of air in his suit; so on the floor of the sea he gets along well enough in his heavy shoes.

He carries down a "life-line" for safety. With this he can signal to the people up above, and can be pulled up again—in a great hurry if he has sent up an urgent signal.

Of course, he is provided with some kind of light, usually a very powerful electric lamp. And finally he takes down any tools that he may need for the particular kind of work he has to do.

And now that he is all dressed, we may lower him beneath the waves. It takes a brave man to go down there all alone. The sea creatures flock around him, attracted by his light, and some of them are anything but pleasant company. And it is lonely work searching for a wreck on the bed of the ocean.

If he finds it he clambers on deck and begins to explore. Is there a door that will open? If so, he must make sure it remains open, and does not cut off his air supply by suddenly closing. In fact, he is going to find it hard enough to drag his air-line and his life-line through the winding corridors of the wreck and still keep them clear.

In a dangerous search he may have a companion, and for a big piece of work he will have several helpers. He may need help to clear away the wreckage and get into the strong room for the gold or valuable papers. But his best help will be an oxy-hydrogen torch that will cut through steel down below just as we often see it doing on land. The diver, therefore, has to be

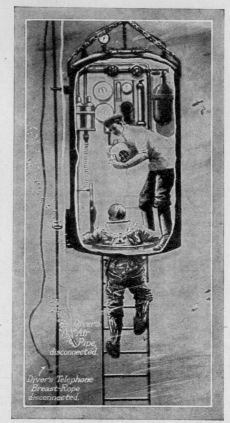

One of the most dangerous features of deep-sea diving is the rising to the surface again. The diver's body becomes accustomed to the heavy pressure of the water overhead, and cannot adjust itself quickly to the lighter pressure at the surface. A man who has been down to a depth of two hundred feet needs to take an hour to come up; otherwise he will suffer from a very painful and fatal disease called the "bends." The device shown above is planned to do away with this danger, and to enable a diver to work 350 feet down. It is called a submersible decompression chamber, and consists of a kind of diving-bell, or small room, which the diver can enter from below on his way up to the surface. He is given oxygen to help in the removal of the nitrogen his system has absorbed at the great depths below, and he does not step out of the decompression chamber into the air at the surface until all danger of illness is past.

Tourist accommodations for deep-sea travelling! At the left is a diving-tube, with a chamber at the end in which one may sit and watch the sea world swim by. To the right of the tube is a diving-bell, which can descend much deeper than the tube. Next is an under-sea tractor, which can travel over the ocean floor, with an observer inside. In the lower corners are a diving-sled and a diver in ordinary deep-sea costume.

an iron-worker, carpenter, and all-round mechanic. In fact, when he is engaged in raising a sunken ship he must also have some knowledge of engineering. For he must tunnel beneath it, and pass chains round it that will enable it to be hauled up. He does his tunnelling with water. A great hose is lowered from above and shoots such a strong stream of water into the mud under the ship that a tunnel is soon cut through.

No diver can stay under the water very long, but the time depends largely on how far down he is. At a depth of two hundred feet the pressure of the water is about eighty-seven pounds to the square inch, and he rarely endures that for more than half an hour. But when he starts to come up, he takes an hour to do it. He goes up a little way and then waits for ten or fifteen minutes; then a little further, with another wait; and so on to the top.

The reason for this is that it takes time for him to get used to the lighter pressure. When the fish from far down in the sea are brought up to the surface they often explode because the great pressure to which they

In the large picture above you see a diver about to make a descent into the ocean's depths. Before he enters the water he will close the door in his helmet, which is made of metal and can withstand a very heavy pressure. In the inset is shown the strange stove-like affair that has been designed for very deep diving. It is fitted with powerful "headlights," and its metal "hands" are operated by mechanism inside the dress.

This is the diving bell invented by Mr. Otis Barton, in which he and Dr. William Beebe, the scientist, went down a quarter of a mile off the Bermudas, then the greatest depth reached. Every square inch of its window of strong quartz glass had to stand a pressure of 650 pounds. In the upper right-hand corner is a diving-bell with open bottom. The water is kept out of it by a heavy air pressure inside the bell. Seats are fixed at the side for the divers.

In oval: Diver uncomfortably seated in one of Father Neptune's coral gardens.

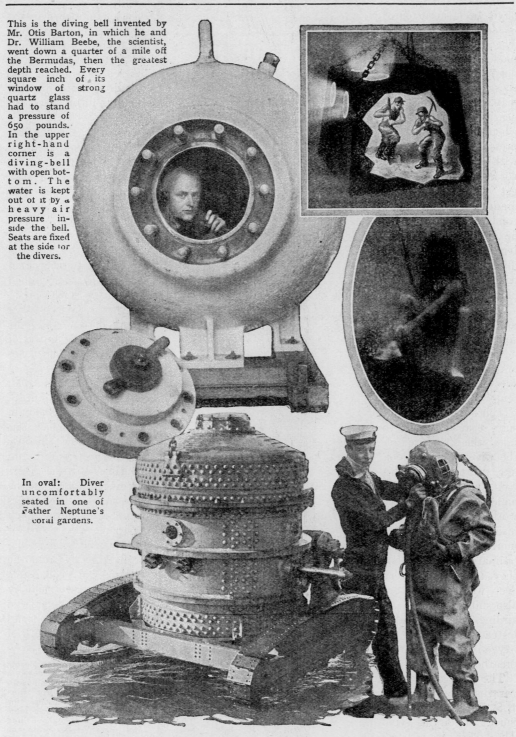

Above is a deep-sea tractor or tank, in which a diver can go exploring in the water world. The portholes enable him to see what is going on around him.

This diver is all ready to take his life in his hands and go down into the sea, where he cannot hope to live for more than five minutes if his apparatus goes wrong.

have been accustomed is suddenly removed. The diver does not explode—he cannot go down as far as where those fish live—but he may suffer something nearly as bad. For when he descends the pressure fills his blood with nitrogen; and as he comes up, he can only get rid of this very gradually. So he must come up slowly. If not, he is likely to get the terrible disease that divers call the "bends," which is always very painful and often fatal.

When he has to come up in a hurry, on account of some accident, he can still be put into a tank under a strong pressure that is gradually removed.

There are steel diving-suits that are built to take the pressure off the diver. They look like great swollen iron men, with clamps for hands, and the diver works the clamps from inside. These suits are more cumbrous than the ordinary diving suit, but they are safer in very deep water. There are also suits that carry no air line, but are provided instead with a tank of oxygen for the diver to breathe.

The new diving apparatus invented by Mr. J. S. Peress of Byfleet, Surrey, is of this type. The dress is a steel cylinder with a dome-shaped top, which is the

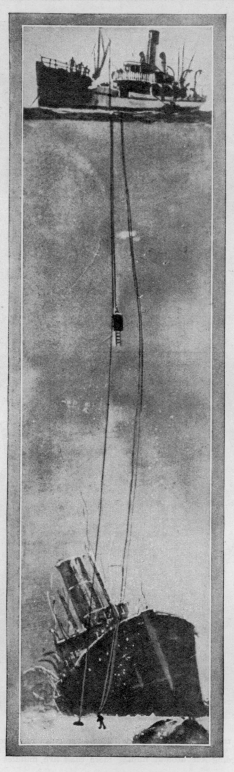

headpiece, to which flexible legs and arms are attached. The arms are furnished with pincer-like claws as hands, and the diver carries his own air supply on his back. With this dress it is claimed that diving can be carried on at much greater depths, and that a man using it can remain below for a far longer period than is now practicable. Flexibility is given to the arms and legs of the apparatus by a cushion of liquid imprisoned within the steel joints.

In the World War many ships went to the bottom at the impact of a torpedo. Sometimes they were carrying a vast fortune in gold. Thus the "Laurentic" sank with £5,000,000 in her strong room. But she went down in only 130 feet of water; and in time British divers recovered nearly all the treasure. Other divers have been down much farther. The record for divers who make a descent directly from the surface in collapsible diver's dress is held by our own naval divers who have at various times descended to a depth of more than 300 feet.

This daring diver is exploring a ship in 350 feet of water, a terrible depth for the human body to endure. But when he ascends, he will enter the decompression chamber some two hundred feet above him, and there recover from the bodily effects of working so long with such an enormous weight of water pressing on him from all sides.

Photos by Siebe, Gorman and Co., Ltd.

Mr. J. S. Peress, the inventor, describing a new diving apparatus with which he claims that diving can be carried on at much greater depths and for much longer periods than is now possible. In the oval is a modern type of diver's helmet, and in the right hand bottom corner is seen a diver getting ready to enter the water.

The Italian divers of the salvage ship "Artiglio"—engaged in the recovery of the £1,000,000 of gold and silver from the "Egypt," which was sunk in a collision off Ushant in May, 1922—were enabled to descend to a depth of about 400 feet by means of a specially invented apparatus. This was a jointed shell of steel, fitted with movable arms and legs, pincer-hands, plate-glass eyes, air-renewing appliances, and a telephone.

Many wonderful salvage feats have been accomplished at different times, not the least remarkable being the raising of a number of sunken German warships at Scapa Flow, in the years following the World War.

A great deal of less heroic, but no less useful, work is done by divers nearer to the surface—twenty or thirty feet below, in harbours and around docks. And a few men have descended to a lower depth than that of 400 feet mentioned previously. But they were not true divers. They went down in a diving-bell, which is a great box or ball of metal. In such a device, in 1930, Dr. William Beebe descended to a depth of 1,426 feet, and in a later effort which he made in 1933 he reached a depth of 2,200 feet. That is only about two-fifths of a mile, but it is the greatest depth that has ever been reached.

The buttons on the back of this man's coat would be really useful if he would button his coat-tails up out of the way. When coat-tails were a little longer than his, men actually did button them up. And some people say that these puzzling back buttons were originally meant to support the belt that held a gentleman's sword.

A *Few* SURPRISES *in* BUTTONS

Even though You Think You Know All about Them, You Will Probably Learn Something New from This Story

YOU would never think buttons were interesting things, would you? And yet have you ever wondered why you wear two or three buttons on your sleeve, where they serve no useful purpose? Or why a man with a long tail-coat has two buttons right in the middle of his back, where he can never use them? Or why men and women wear so many buttons in places where they are never needed?

Not so very long ago a man had to do nearly all his travelling on horseback. He wore a long coat with flying tails, and the coat-tails would get hairy and greasy from flapping against the horse's sides. So he put two buttons on the back of his coat and buttoned up his coat-tails behind him when he started off on his horse. He also wanted his arms as free as possible, especially when he went hunting. So he cut a slit in the end of his sleeve and sewed some buttons along it;

then he could double the sleeves back and button it up on his arm.

Now, man is a strange being. Once he gets accustomed to a thing, he simply will not give it up. Even if he has no use for it any longer, he will keep it at all costs. He never dreams of turning up his coat sleeves now, and he hardly ever wears a coat with long tails. But he still likes to have buttons on the sleeve, and he will not buy a coat without them; while if he does wear a tail-coat, he must still have two buttons on the back of it: it is the same with many of his other buttons. The buttons have a history after all, and this is a portion of it.

When men first began to wear clothes, they had to find a way in which to fasten them on. Doubtless the first fastener was a thorn taken from some sort of bush and used as a pin. Then someone learned how to make his own thorns, by trimming little sticks to a sharp point. These would be better, because he could always have them ready, and in exactly the size he wanted. Later he might punch holes in the skins or cloth he wore, and run laces through them.

That is as far as the Greeks and Romans ever progressed, and to this very day there are people in the world who have never got so far as that —for there are still certain savages

If the shell fishermen below are very lucky, one of them may some day find a pearl. But it is from the mussel-shells themselves that buttons are made. The shells are boiled to get rid of the meat, soaked for a week, and then cut up into disks. Of course, these disks, or "blanks," are going to become buttons — after they have been ground and polished and pierced, as the picture on the left shows.

try, that we have to look for the development of the button trade. Brass buttons were made there in 1689, and in the following century the industry developed rapidly. About 1745, Matthew Boulton introduced a number of improvements in the process of manufacture; and in 1767, his son started a works in Soho. It is interesting to notice that one of the departments specialized in making steel buttons with facets, which sold for as much as 140 guineas a gross.

There are two main classes of buttons—those with a shank, or loop, and those that are pierced with holes for thread to pass

who use nothing but thorns and sharp little sticks for fastening up their clothes. And all of us still use these methods, in our pins and laces, though we now employ buttons more than anything else.

Yet our use of buttons is of comparatively recent adoption. At first they seem to have been used for purposes of ornamentation. In Piers Plowman (1377) we read of a knife with "botones ouergylte" (buttons overgilt), and in a translation of Froissart's "Chronicles" (1525) there is mention of a book bound in crimson velvet with "ten botones of syluer and gylte."

Buttons were first used as fastenings in England in the fifteenth century, but it is to Birmingham, the centre of the button indus-

through. The former were the first used, and were made by needlework with the help of a mould; but about 1807 a Dane named Sanders, who had been ruined by the bombardment of Copenhagen, introduced into Birmingham a better method. This consisted of locking together two disks of metal and enclosing a filling of cloth or pasteboard.

This was a very great improvement on the old method, and in 1825 Sanders's son contributed yet more to the history of buttons

These flat-bottomed boats are loaded with shell-fish. When the fish have been extracted, the shells will be sent to the factory and made into buttons. Hundreds of thousands of our buttons began life as the homes of shell-fish.

when he invented flexible shanks of canvas, or some other material, through which a needle could easily pass. At first, too, buttons had to be made individually, with great care, by skilled workmen who carved or ornamented them, but later machinery came to aid the process and the buttons were stamped out in dies.

A large number of materials are used in the manufacture of buttons, including gold, silver, brass, iron, ivory, horn, bone, mother-of-pearl, wood, glass, porcelain, paper, celluloid and artificial composition, casein of milk and even blood. Of these, ivory buttons are the oldest, although horn buttons were made in Birmingham by 1777. About the middle of the nineteenth century a Frenchman named Émile Bassot (ā′mēl băs′ō) invented a new process which was widely adopted—that of using the hooves of cattle, softened by boiling. Pearl buttons are made from the shells of pearl oysters. They are cut out by tubular drills, and then shaped and polished by machinery. Porcelain buttons were invented about 1840 by a Birmingham man, named Prosser.

As you have seen, the centre of the English button industry has always been Birmingham. But large numbers of buttons are turned out in London, and every kind of button is manufactured in England. The chief buttons we produce, however, are linen, mother-of-pearl, composition, metal and fancy buttons.

A Method of Making Glass Buttons That is Kept a Close Secret

In the same way other countries have their button specialities. Germany, for instance, which has a large button industry, specializes in fancy and galalith (casein of milk) buttons; France in mother-of-pearl and fancy metal; Italy in vegetable ivory, which comes from the South American corozo (kō-rō′zō) nut and can be easily dyed; Japan in several kinds of mother-of-pearl; and Czechoslovakia in glass buttons—of which the secret of manufacture is rigidly kept—china and paste, or imitation jewellery, buttons.

London is the centre of the world's trade in mother-of-pearl shells for buttons, which are brought to England from the colonies—chiefly Australia—and auctioned in their raw state in Mincing Lane.

Buttons are measured in a very novel way. They are reckoned by their diameter, the unit being a "line." It is difficult to imagine a button as small as one line, and indeed none are made as small as that, for ten lines equal a quarter of an inch, and the smallest button measures eight lines. The sizes rise in twos, and there are big buttons measuring as much as a hundred lines, or two and half inches in diameter. This method of measurement is used in all countries except France, where three French lines are equivalent to ten English.

Apart from ordinary purposes, buttons have often been used to mark distinction, social or official. Long ago, rich people used to wear buttons of gold or silver or precious stones, and sometimes they even passed laws forbidding the plain people to wear any buttons at all—for a man's rank was known by the buttons he could wear. He would also decorate his books and knives and swords with handsome buttons.

Nowadays, a Chinese official will wear a button or knob on his hat as a sign of rank, the colour or material of the button denoting his grade. Then many of us have seen costermongers in all their glory of complicated designs in pearl buttons, or "pearlies," sewn on their clothes.

But it is in America that the practice of wearing distinguishing buttons is most widely in force. There the wearing of a button of a particular colour or design, which is usually fastened to a lapel of the coat may denote a decoration, or membership of some political party or order; officials wear them to denote their particular occupation, and children to indicate their class in school or college.

There are a few people in the world who will have nothing at all to do with buttons. They have religious reasons for this. For instance, the Dukhobors (dōō-kō-bôr') in Canada will never wear a button. It is part of their religion never to kill an animal and, since so many buttons are made out of the horns and bones of animals, they do most of their fastening with pins and laces.

Here is a novel use to which pearl buttons have been put. It must have taken many hours of patient sewing to ornament the clothing of these "pearly kings" and their children.

(THE SOLUTIONS TO THESE PUZZLES WILL BE FOUND ON PAGE 388 OF THIS VOLUME)

THE MILKMAID'S PROBLEM
No. 14

The gentleman on the horse would like to buy exactly four gallons of milk, but the milk-maid has only a three-gallon and a five-gallon measure. How does she manage to measure out exactly the four gallons required?

WHAT IS THE RELATIONSHIP?
No. 15

A gentleman in court was asked the name of his nearest blood relative. He replied, "What relation to me is a woman who is my mother's only child's wife's daughter?" What was the relationship?

HOW MANY TRAINS?
No. 16

Every morning at eight o'clock a train leaves Ottawa for Vancouver and every morning at eight o'clock a train leaves Vancouver for Ottawa. If it takes seven days for each of the trains to complete its journey, how many trains will an east-bound train meet on its way to Ottawa. To make the problem simpler we will suppose that there is no change of time between Vancouver and Ottawa.

THE HOUND AND THE FOX
No. 17

If a hound makes twenty-seven springs while a fox makes twenty-five springs of the same length, how many springs will the hound have to make to overtake the fox, which had a start of fifty springs?

BE CAREFUL!
No. 18

What is the difference between twenty four-quart bottles and four and twenty quart bottles? What is the difference between twice one hundred and five, and twice one hundred, and ten? A man was asked how many books he had on a certain shelf. He replied, "If I had as many more, half as many more, and seven in addition, I should have thirty-two." How many had he?

HOW CAN THIS BE?
No. 19

A word I know, six letters it contains;
Subtract just one, and twelve you'll find remains.
What is the word?

THE SNAIL'S PACE
No. 20

A snail climbs up a wall. Every day he manages to pull himself up three feet, but every night he falls back two feet. How long does it take him to reach the top of the wall, which is thirty feet high?

Whenever the great Dr. Johnson was present, everyone else sat still and listened. Here he is seen in
conversation with two of his friends at the Mitre Tavern.
On the left is Goldsmith, and in the centre is Boswell.

SAMUEL JOHNSON: DICTIONARY MAKER

The Son of a Lichfield Bookseller, He Became a Master Mind of His Age, and Founded the Most Famous Literary Club of All Time

(CONTINUED FROM PAGE 324)

HIS face was so scarred and ugly that strangers used to turn and stare after him as he stumped down the crooked streets of old London. His great body would twitch from head to foot as he went puffing along. Sometimes he would be muttering to himself and mysteriously touching the tops of gate-posts; sometimes he would pause to count the steps leading to the next doorway.

These were queer habits, but somehow he could not break them. If it were evening, fashionable ladies might peep out of their sedan chairs to catch a glimpse of him.

They would notice that he carried a club for use against any thieves and ruffians who might be loitering in the dark streets.

This strange person was none other than the great Samuel Johnson (1709–1784), famous all over England for his learning and wisdom. The king once felt honoured to meet him, and he was welcomed at many fashionable dinners, even though his table manners were so rude that they would have disgraced the humblest cottage in the land.

All good people respected him, and his friends loved him dearly. True, he could be haughty when a rich man tried to win his favour; but to the poor he was an angel of mercy. He used to slip pennies into the hands of little waifs whom he found sleeping on cold doorsteps, so that they might wake up with money for their breakfast. For he never forgot his own struggle with poverty in the long years before he became famous.

Johnson's Pathetic Childhood

He had a pathetic childhood. While he was still a baby he suffered from a mysterious disease called "scrofula."

In those days a certain remedy for this complaint was thought to be a touch from the hand of the king or queen, so his poor mother carried her baby to Queen Anne, hoping that in this way a cure might be effected, but, of course, the little one did not improve. The disease made him blind in one eye, twisted his noble features into shapelessness, and left his nerves in such a state that he could not fully control his arms and legs. But his muscles were as strong as iron—and he used to make two boys carry him to school!

One may still go down Wine Office Court, off famous Fleet Street, London, and dine at "Ye Olde Cheshire Cheese," where, it is said, Dr. Johnson liked to dine, in the seat beside the fireplace. At the right is the house in Gough Square, in this neighbourhood, where Dr. Johnson lived for ten years, while he was at work compiling his great dictionary.

In school he learned far more than other boys; for although in those days masters were severe, no whippings could destroy his love of reading. And he never forgot a single thing he read, but could astonish his mother by reciting long passages from books he had skimmed only once.

For two years he browsed in his father's bookshop in Lichfield, until a friend offered to send the brilliant lad to Oxford. At the university the teachers and most of the students admired him greatly, though a few wealthy snobs made fun of his worn clothes.

But Johnson had his share of pride, and when some kindly person left a pair of shoes at his door, he threw the gift away angrily. Asking for no one's pity, he found his greatest pleasure in the books he loved so much. But the money from Lichfield suddenly stopped and his life as a student at Oxford ceased with it.

Then his father died, and Johnson had to earn a living for himself, for his penniless mother, and for the strange woman, nearly twice his age, who soon became his wife.

He tried school teaching, but he was no man to manage children. So he determined to make his way in the great world of London—as an author!

He tramped to London. There he lived in a garret, almost friendless, often half frozen, thankful for every mouthful he could get to eat. But he could not always get the mouthful, and he did not always have even a garret in which to sleep. Young writers in those days could expect nothing better, for books which took months or years to write sold for very little money. Only by gifts from wealthy men could the average author hope to live.

But Johnson was no man to live on wealthy friends. So he had a very bad time. Yet in the end his hard work by day and night, in sickness and health, sometimes in deepest sorrow and despair, brought him decent comfort and extraordinary fame.

He had set his early hopes on a play called "Irene" (1737), but it failed on the stage. His long poems, called "London" (1738) and "The Vanity of Human Wishes" (1749), were praised by critics but brought him little. He is not now remembered chiefly as a poet.

Photo by Tate Gallery

Johnson was a proud man, and he was deeply wounded when the great Lord Chesterfield kept him waiting here in his anteroom and then refused to help him. The picture is from the painting by E. M. Ward in the Tate Gallery.

Photo by Rischgitz

Here is Johnson's famous club assembled at the home of Joshua Reynolds. From left to right they are Boswell, Johnson, Reynolds, Garrick, Burke, General Paoli, Burney the musician, Warton the poet, and Goldsmith.

Many people admired the papers—really short essays published twice a week—which he called "The Rambler" (1750–1752) and "The Idler" (1758). And when, after seven years of toil, he published his great dictionary (1755), he became the literary ruler of his age. A schoolboy would not find the dictionary very helpful, because simple words are so often explained by the hard ones he liked to use himself; as when he defines "network" as "anything reticulated or decussated at equal intervals, with interstices between the intersections."

He was also apt to ridicule anything of which he did not quite approve; so, since he hated the Scots, and since the Scots ate a great deal of oatmeal, he defined "oats" as "a grain which in England is generally given to horses, but in Scotland supports the people."

After the Dictionary came his novel of "Rasselas" (1759), hurriedly written to earn the money to pay for his mother's funeral. The greatest work of all was "The Lives of the Poets" (1779–1781). In these lives we see how widely he had read and how wise he was, even though we may often disagree with his opinions about other famous men.

Photo by National Portrait Gallery

It was the brush of the famous Sir Joshua Reynolds that left us this portrait of his friend Samuel Johnson. More than any other painter he has given us a sense of the wonderful power of the great man's personality.

As he grew older the great man was surrounded by friends, who loved to hear him talk. He was one of the world's best talkers. Often the conversation between him and his friends was magnificent, for they were all remarkable in wit and learning. There was David Garrick, probably the greatest actor of all time; Sir Joshua Reynolds the most famous painter of the day; Edmund Burke the eminent English statesman; Edward Gibbon the great English historian; and Oliver Goldsmith the delightful poet and novelist. With Johnson at their head, these men and others made up the most famous club—the Literary Club—that has ever been known. No other recorded conversations are so wise or so entertaining.

By Johnson's favour a young Scotsman named James Boswell was admitted to the club. He became immortal by writing the famous life of Johnson, which stands without a rival as the best of all biographies. Anyone who reads it may learn much more about Johnson than has been told here; and may see the dear and queer old man just as if he were still alive; and may attend the meetings of his famous club.

The MAN Who FOUND His HERO

He Wrote the Best of All Biographies Because He Had a Genius for Understanding Genius

IN THE days when men wore wigs and took snuff a young Scotsman named James Boswell (1740–1795) came on a visit to London. He was a good-natured, talkative, argumentative sort of fellow, and rather too fond of gay friends. His father, the lord of Auchinleck, insisted on his studying law, but the restless young man thought he would prefer anything else—from entering the army to becoming a priest!

He really did not know what he wanted to do. He loved a good time too well to want to settle down. Still, he had a great deal of common sense and an amazing reverence for men of genius; and above all other things he longed to meet and talk with as many men of genius as he could. They, for their part, were not exactly longing to give up their time to a raw young Scot of whom no one had ever heard, but they

Photo by Rischgitz

It was a great occasion for the young Scotsman, James Boswell, when he was first presented to the famous Dr. Johnson. And it was a great occasion for the world as well, for it led to the writing of our finest biography.

all found that the young Scot was a genius, too—a genius at charming geniuses. So the greatest men in Europe were his prizes—Rousseau and Voltaire among them, and above all the great Dr. Johnson.

Johnson had a heart of gold, but he had no intention of letting the young man from Scotland see it too quickly. He had hated the Scots all his life. So at the very first meeting he threw Boswell into confusion by abusing them and by cutting his new acquaintance short every time he started to say anything. But there was no way of discouraging the young Scotsman, nor any reason for not liking him; and in reality the crusty old philosopher had begun to esteem him. So he wrote long letters to him when he went away again, and Boswell treasured all of them for us to read to-day.

Whenever Boswell returned to London, he sought out Dr. Johnson and followed him like a faithful dog. He soon prepared plans for writing the life of his great idol, and from that time onwards he kept exact notes of the conversation of his hero and of many of the other great men around him—Goldsmith, Garrick, Reynolds, Gibbon, and Burke.

Sometimes, when the talk did not flow quite fast enough, he would make himself ridiculous by asking absurd questions just to goad his hero into speech. Once in a while Johnson would lose his temper over it, as when he cried out, "You have two subjects, sir, yourself and me. I am sick of both." But Boswell would take any slight, and Johnson would soon be asking forgiveness —because he had a good heart and was genuinely fond of his "Bozzy."

Why Mrs. Boswell Disliked Dr. Johnson

In 1766 Boswell was admitted as an advocate, and about three years later he married his cousin and settled down to practise law in Scotland. Mrs. Boswell took a dislike to her husband's hero, for when he came to them he turned down the ends of the candles to make them burn brighter, and let the grease drip all over the carpet. Neither did Boswell's father like his son's great friend. When Bozzy was following

371

at the gruff old doctor's heels on the latter's famous trip through Scotland, his father said that he had often seen a man leading a bear round, but never till then had he seen a bear lead a man.

"The Life of Johnson," published by Boswell in 1791, is the greatest story of a man's life ever written. Even to-day we cannot read it without feeling that we know its hero better than we know most of the people around us. And a multitude of other great men also live in its pages. Few other books contain so many; and no other book tells us so much, and so amusingly, about what its people did and thought and said, the books they read, the plays they saw, the jokes they cracked, the conversations they held—even the dinners they ate.

Photo by L.M.S. Rly.

It was some little Irish village like the one above that Goldsmith had affectionately in mind when he wrote "The Deserted Village." For in his childhood days in Ireland he had played in just such cottages as these.

A POET LOVED *by* EVERYONE

He Often Seemed a Little Foolish among His Great Friends, but When They Left Him Alone with His Pen He Could Surpass Them All

LITTLE Irish children love stories of ghosts and fairies, far-away places and bold adventure. Perhaps that is why they often grow up to be so light-hearted and generous.

When Oliver Goldsmith (1728–1774) was a small boy, about two hundred years ago, he used to listen eagerly to stories of battle and adventure told by the old soldier who was his schoolmaster. From the same man Oliver learned to play lilting Irish melodies on the flute, and liked the music better than the lessons in his books. He never tired of such amusements; all his life he was tender-hearted and imaginative, but never very practical or prudent.

His father was a clergyman, and very poor. When the time came, an uncle had to provide part of the money to send the boy to Trinity College, Dublin. He earned the rest himself by doing a servant's work in the college buildings. Unfortunately, he was sometimes allowed to feel that this was ungentlemanly; and he was already ex-

Photo by Rischgitz

Johnson had received that morning a message from Goldsmith, who said he was in great distress. So the good doctor immediately sent him a guinea, and as soon as possible followed after it. He found that Goldsmith had been arrested at the instance of his land-lady for not paying his rent, but learned that the author had at hand the manuscript of a novel. Dr. Johnson asked to see it, and finally took it to a publisher to whom he sold it for sixty pounds—more than enough to pay the landlady. That novel was "The Vicar of Wakefield."

tremely shy and sensitive, partly because he had been teased so much about his plain looks, for his face was pitted with the ugly scars of smallpox. Yet the students liked Oliver's merry ways, and he got into many a scrape at college by joining in their pranks. Once he ran away because he had been punished, but he returned and finally managed to graduate.

Goldsmith Takes to Playing the Flute to Earn a Living

During the next few years we hear several amusing stories that explain why his relatives were discouraged with him. He was taken to a bishop to study for the Church, but was refused because he wore scarlet breeches. He sold his horse to pay his passage to America, and then managed to miss the boat. He gambled away money that had been given to him by his uncle to help him to become a lawyer. Strangest of all, he went to Holland to study medicine, and then spent most of his time tramping through France and Germany and Italy, playing his flute for a living. He came back to England penniless.

He seldom had any money; and when he did possess any, he would spend it on the gaudy clothes he liked so much, or on expensive presents for his friends. He was never a cautious man, but he was nearly always lovable. And he finally found one way of charming the world—namely, with his pen.

For now he began to earn a meagre living and immortal fame as an author. He has given us many kinds of books, and the best of them are so simply and so charmingly written that people will always love them. It was with "The Traveller" (1764) that he first came into prominence; and the love and praise of rural life and natural scenery that made this poem so beautiful are present in his even greater poem on "The Deserted Village" (1770), in which are the descriptions of the village preacher and schoolmaster that nearly every schoolboy knows.

He also wrote the most delightful novel of his century in "The Vicar of Wakefield" (1766), a tender and amusing story of a country parson and his family that is still read with pleasure and interest.

Dr. Johnson carried the manuscript of this little masterpiece from Goldsmith's lodgings to the publishers, and sold it for enough money to keep "Goldy" out of prison for debt. "The Vicar of Wakefield" assured his reputation as a novelist, and his comedy "The Good Natured Man" (1768) was a stepping-stone to that brilliant dramatic achievement, "She Stoops to Conquer" (1773), which was a comedy so creative of amusement that it is said to have made fashionable again good hearty laughter on the stage.

So in his books and his plays Goldsmith proved that he was a brilliant man after all. Dr. Johnson had known it all along—he had

said that no man was more foolish when he did not have a pen in his hand, or wiser when he did have one. The great actor Garrick said that however Goldsmith may have talked he "wrote like an angel." And their famous friend Sir Joshua Reynolds would have fully agreed with this sentiment.

That is why they accepted Goldsmith in to the celebrated Literary Club that Dr. Johnson founded. And if we want to praise Goldsmith, it is enough to say that the great and kindly Johnson was his closest friend. It was Johnson who said of him, when he was dead, "Let not his faults be remembered; he was a very great man."

You will find his grave in the little round church in the Temple, London, where so many famous men have lived before and since his day. Visitors from every land have paused to look at it. Sometimes they see a child or two playing round it, as Charles Lamb and his sister Mary used to play when they were children in the Temple.

(CONTINUED ON PAGE 402)

This is the way in which Goldsmith earned his travelling expenses during his journey on the Continent. He always loved his flute, and made it a lifelong companion, though he did not often have to rely upon it for bread and butter. We do not know a great deal about this care-free trip. Somewhere or other Goldsmith managed on his journey to obtain a medical degree, but nobody knows just how. And it is said that when he arrived among people whose hearts were closed to the persuasive tones of his flute, the poet would offer to earn a meal by arguing on any subject they might suggest. So Boswell said he " disputed his passage through Europe."

Photo by Rischgitz

In Greece and Rome music played a prominent part in many celebrations. In this painting—"The Vintage Festival"—by Sir Laurence Alma-Tadema, who painted numerous scenes from Greek and Roman life, the processional music is being provided by a pair of tambourines and a trio of pipes called the diaulos (dī-ô′-lŏs), or "double aulos." There was a single pipe called the aulos, but the diaulos was played by the great musicians.

SEVEN GIANTS *of* MUSIC

During the Period of the Romantic Composers, from the Majestic Beethoven to the Graceful Chopin, Music Freed Itself and Greatly Extended Its Scope

(CONTINUED FROM PAGE 277)

IN THE spring of the year 1773, a little three-year-old boy was being taken daily for a walk along the banks of the Rhine. His clothes were poor, and he lived in the shadow of a constant fear, for his father was a violent man and a drunkard besides. The family never saw anything but the direst poverty, in spite of all their mother could do. She was the daughter of the chief cook in one of the neighbouring castles, and had been married to a valet, before she became the wife of the penniless singer who was father to our unhappy little boy.

The squalid home was hardly the place in which one would be likely to look for genius. Yet there it was that Ludwig van Beethoven (vän bā′tō-věn) grew up to be one of the greatest musicians the world has ever known—a man of such lofty gifts and towering grandeur of mind that he forced homage from lords and ladies, kings and emperors, and treated them all as his equals.

The World of Tyranny and Strife into which Beethoven was Born

It was an exciting world into which he had been born in 1770. The revolt in America was not the only one that was going on. In fact, it was nothing more than the edge of a much greater storm that was raging over Europe. For there the French Revolution was soon to sweep away the tyranny that had ground down the French people for so long, and start a great wave of liberty and progress that was to surge over every land on the face of the globe. Timid people were beside themselves with fear. Better keep things as they are, they thought, than run the risk of change that might make them even worse.

A Great Soul and a Great Genius

But Beethoven was not a timid man. He was a great soul as well as a great genius, and he was wise enough to know that the affairs of man have a way of shaping themselves, and that no human power can change their course. "The nobility are good enough in their place," said this man who once refused to take off his hat to the emperor's family when they passed him in the street.

So while the world was being shaken by the clash of arms and of ideas, Beethoven was writing music to voice men's deepest hopes and longings. Disappointment, poverty, and illness never stopped the growth of his genius, or changed his sturdy independence; and great fame and flattery never turned his head. At last he grew so deaf that he could not hear a note he wrote, while at the same time his music had gone so far ahead of his age that people shook their heads at it because they could not understand it. Yet he went on just the same, in poverty and mental anguish, and gave us many of his greatest works. People could applaud or not—he would do the thing in the way he felt it should be done. This is the way of greatness; and it was because of this same greatness that Beethoven had such noble things to express in music

This picture shows the great Beethoven composing. Anyone not versed in the ways of composers might think that they sat at an instrument and tried various combinations until they found one that suited them. But it is just the other way round. Often they will write out a whole composition before they have heard a note of it played anywhere except in their minds.

As we have seen, the knowledge and understanding of music had made such progress that everything was ready for him to set to work. He took the sonata from the hands of Haydn, with whom he studied for a time, and made it express mightier things than it had ever expressed before. He studied all the strange company of instruments that make up an orchestra and wrote for them nine symphonies—"the Immortal Nine"—that stirred men's hearts and minds as no earlier music had ever done: and there has been little since to equal them. For smaller groups of strings he wrote the greatest trios and quartets that had ever been written— and noble concertos (kŏn-chĕr′tō) for solo instruments and orchestra.

Whenever he used the form of the sonata he filled it with meaning. Into its slow second movement, in particular, he put all the sorrow and the passion and the longing of his thwarted life. In place of the minuet, which Haydn and Mozart had used as a third movement, Beethoven always used a very lively one called a scherzo (skĕr′tsō). Its name at first meant "joke" or "plaything" in Italian.

Music that Makes Us Want to Dance

The scherzo had once been a dance, but when it was honoured by being made a part of the sonata it lost the rigid form that music must have if you are actually to dance to it. But it never lost its lively,

This interesting group is made up entirely of musicians who lived in the eighteenth and nineteenth centuries. From left to right their names are Chopin, Handel, Gluck, Schumann, Weber, Bach, Haydn, Mozart, Schubert, Beethoven, Mendelssohn, Wagner, Meyerbeer, Gounod, Verdi, Liszt, Brückner, Brahms and Grieg.

stirring rhythm. It kept that, just as all dances must, even when they are written to be listened to in a concert hall instead of danced to in a ball-room. For real dance music is not necessarily the kind of music to which people dance, but it is always the kind that makes them *want* to dance.

Breaking the Rules of Composition to Give the Sonata Greater Charm

Naturally a man like Beethoven, with so gifted and independent a mind, would not, for long, be satisfied to confine his thoughts within any given mould. The sonata as he used it took on all sorts of shapes. He arranged its movements in every kind of order. Sometimes he increased them to five and sometimes cut them down to only two. He made one movement grow out of another, and so welded the sonata into a firmer whole. You see, he really believed in freedom. "It is a good thing to know the rules so that one can break them," he once said. But in breaking them he always made something finer than had been made before.

One of Beethoven's best-loved symphonies is called the "Pastoral Symphony." In it he describes a visit to the country, which he always loved dearly; for though he spent most of his life in the city of Vienna, he always managed to get away for a time every year. Then he would spend all his waking hours out-of-doors, sometimes hatless, through the fields and woods, with a sketch-book in his hand. And when his ideas carried him away, he shouted and waved his arms in his excitement.

Setting a Summer's Day and a Rippling Stream to Delightful Music

So in this sixth symphony that he wrote he tried to set down all the delightful sensations of a summer's day. The first movement he called "Awakening of cheerful feelings upon arrival in the country"—and it is full of the soft hum and rustle of a summer's day. The next one, "By the Brook," has the gentle ripple of the stream as an accompaniment to the songs of the cuckoo and nightingale and the call of the quail. Next, the scherzo gives us a picture of a "Peasants' Festival," with a funny mimicry of the ridiculous village band and a rough country dance to cap it all. Then the dance is interrupted by a sudden storm, with lightning, thunder, and rain. But the storm passes over, and the symphony closes peacefully with the beautiful "Shepherd's Hymn" of thanksgiving.

Now, all this sound story was a new thing in music. Others had tried it in a small way—Haydn did, for one, in his oratorio, "The Creation"—but Beethoven was the first man to manage it with great success. Of course, there were plenty of people to follow him. And you can see that by and by the events in the story would no longer fit into the old sonata pattern, with its set slow and fast movements. Then composers had a new form in which to work. There

is a great deal of such musical story-telling to-day. We call it "programme music," for the music has to follow a definite series of events, or "programme."

Who are the Romantic Composers?

When Beethoven's great light went out with his death in 1827, there were plenty of lesser lights still burning—and some of them were very bright and clear. All those composers who followed in the path that the great man had begun to tread are called "romantic" composers; and by that we mean that they belong to the amazing age

ROUGET DE LISLE SINGING THE "MARSEILLAISE"

The Romantic period of music was the age of great song writers, and it also produced many great songs by men who were not so great. The picture above shows the dramatic moment when the "Marseillaise" (mär-sä-yāz'), the national anthem of France, was composed by Claude Rouget de Lisle (rōō'zhä dĕ lēl), an officer in the army of the new French republic at the time of the Revolution. One night in 1792, when he was stationed at Strasbourg, he attended a public dinner at which he was moved to a high pitch of patriotic emotion. When the dinner was over he composed, at white heat, the words and music of his famous song, and sang it to a group of friends. At that time he called it "The War Song of the Army of the Rhine," for it was along that river that he and his comrades were stationed. Later, when the Revolutionists stormed the king's palace in Paris and burned it to the ground, Rouget de Lisle's song was adopted by the volunteers who had come up from Marseilles and the country round to take part in the Revolution.

that followed the French Revolution—the "age of romanticism" (rŏ-măn′tĭ-sĭz′m).

What is Meant by Romanticism?

If you think carefully you can realize what that age was like. For it is easy to see that when men have begun to thirst for freedom they will want to find it in all sorts of ways. And when they have grown used to the idea that the ordinary man is worthy to be free, they will respect him a good deal more and take far greater interest in him. So people everywhere will be bursting through old bonds, breaking old rules, and questioning everything they ever believed before. And everywhere deep feelings will be let loose, and come surging up in literature and art and music.

Briefly, you might say that the difference between a romanticist and a classicist is this: the first believes that the material —the musical or literary "idea"—is all-important; while the second believes that the manner, the form in which the idea is presented, is just as important as the idea itself—if not more so.

The best way to understand the chief difference between an exaggerated romanticist and an exaggerated classicist is to think of two cooks. One of them buys the best quality food, and tries to get something new every day, but she either does not bother much about cooking it well, or does not know much about the Art of Cookery. The other is lazy about shopping, and accepts whatever the shopkeeper chooses to offer her, but she takes great pains over her cooking and knows the whole Art of Cookery. The first cook puts better food on the table, but she puts it on neither well nor tastily cooked; the other places very ordinary food on the table, but it is well cooked and very tasty.

During a romantic period people will do lots of stupid things, for there are always plenty of silly people, and if they have a chance they will show just how silly they can be. But there are plenty of fine and earnest people, too; and if you give them a chance they will do fine and earnest things. They will be for ever experimenting, and most of all they will want to express their feelings. You can plainly see that an age of romanticism, no matter what else it may be, will never be dull!

Franz Schubert, who is regarded by many music lovers as the greatest song writer the world has ever known.

Now, if people are trying to express very powerful feelings, one of the first things they will do is to burst into song. You will find that you do so yourself. It is quite natural, then, that this age, when men were thinking so much about their feelings, should have been the age to produce the greatest of all song writers. His name was Franz Schubert (fränts shoo′bĕrt), and he was born in Austria, one of fourteen children. The father was a peasant who had fitted himself to be the village schoolmaster, and the mother had been cook to a family in Vienna. Franz was educated to be a schoolmaster, like his father, but he could no more help writing songs than a bird can help singing. All he needed was a poem to fire his imagination. As soon as he had found that, beautiful music seemed to flow about it in his mind, and all he had to do, it seemed, was to "hurl the notes on to the paper."

Mozart's Short but Busy Life

Like Mozart's, his life was short (1797–1828), but during its thirty-one years of struggle against poverty he wrote some six hundred songs; seven symphonies, besides a famous unfinished symphony; some beautiful "chamber music"—a name given to compositions for just a few instruments— a great number of sonatas and sparkling shorter pieces for the pianoforte; numerous sacred choral works, and seven operas!

But it is for his songs that we know and love him best. Is there anyone who does not know "Hark, hark, the lark" and "Who is Sylvia?"—both of them written on the same day, the first one in a little tavern while he was out for a walk. Like his much greater songs for German words, they are full of the freshest and most sincere feeling. Often he quite gave up the common custom of repeating the same air for each stanza, no matter what feeling the words expressed. Instead, he let the music follow the song— and all great song writers since have done the same. Schubert seemed, too, to care very little for vocal fireworks, such as the writers of Italian opera had liked; and he never wrote songs that went painfully high. Many are for "mezzo-sopranos" (mĕd'zō) — "between" high and low. It was the music that mattered to Schubert, not the singer.

The result is that people who are going to sing his songs well

Robert Schumann, the great German composer, and his wife Clara Schumann, herself a distinguished pianist.

must use their minds and hearts as well as their voices. That means they must be intelligent and very highly trained and the chief result of this was that a good natural voice was no longer at all required to make a good singer.

For although the human voice has been called the most perfect of all instruments, we can be quite certain that for long centuries it was anything but perfect—at least, as people then used it. The first singers lived in Asia, and their manner of singing has been handed down right to our own day in Asiatic countries—to the people of China

and India and Arabia. They will sing their love songs and prayers in voices that we are glad we do not have to hear often. The tones are nasal and, to us, thin and unpleasant.

And that was probably the way the Greeks and Romans sang—and the early Christians. We cannot even be sure that the choristers who sang the mighty music of Palestrina in the sixteenth century had voices to which we should like to listen to-day.

It was not until about two centuries ago that it became possible for a singer to gain a world-wide reputation. The first one who did so was a male soprano, an Italian named Farinelli (fä'rē-nĕl'lē). His teacher, Porpora (pôr'pṓ-rä), trained a great many fine singers at Naples, and for a long time the Italian singers were the best in the world.

But styles in singing have changed a great deal since Farinelli's day, largely because the singer must now put so much more feeling into his songs. And that change has been in part brought about by the exquisite, moving songs of Schubert and the German song writers who followed him. So great was their skill that even in English we often call their pieces "Lieder" (lē'dēr)—the German word for "songs." It is "Lied" (lēt) in the singular.

Another great song writer, a German, was Robert Schumann (shoo'män), one of the greatest composers of the century. His songs are, as a rule, deeper in feeling than Schubert's, although perhaps they are less dramatic where the telling of a story is concerned.

By Schumann's day (1810–1856) people had grown so excited over music that they had begun a kind of war about it. So Schumann established (1834) a musical periodical, "The New Musical Journal," to champion the cause of freedom in music. For he, too, was one of the romantic composers, who did not want his great art to grow stale and dull because people were afraid of doing anything new.

He himself was writing beautiful and original music of many different kinds, but especially for the piano, for he was constantly inspired by his gifted and lovable

a famous pianist and went to live in Paris (1830). During all the unhappy years of his short life he lived for his piano; on it he expressed all those emotions which he felt so keenly. The great Russian pianist Rubinstein called him "the soul of the piano."

It was not strange, then, that he found things to say and ways of saying them that no one had ever found before. By using the curious rhythms and harmonies that he had heard the simple Polish peasants sing, he delighted people's ears with all sorts of new effects. When he died (1849) he left an enormous quantity of every sort of music

By courtesy of the Victoria and Albert Museum

Thomas Webster, a nineteenth century English artist, has left us this charming picture of "The Village Choir." We may laugh at those solemn faces, but it is in just such groups as this that a nation develops its musical talent. To listen to the wireless is not enough. People must make music for themselves and love doing so.

wife, Clara Schumann, who was one of the most distinguished pianists in Europe. When, near the end of his life, he became insane, she supported their children by her playing.

Schumann himself had started his career as a pianist. His piano was always his close friend, on which he could say all that he had to say; and for it he wrote his best music, in many forms, both new and old.

Another great composer for the piano was Frédéric Chopin (shō'păN), who was born in Warsaw (1810) only three months before Schumann. Because he was born in Poland and spent his early years in that country of great artists, the songs of his people always kept ringing in his ears, even after he became

for the piano, much of it in the shorter, newer forms; and he had changed the whole character of piano music.

Still another great name at this time was that of Felix Mendelssohn (1809–1847). He wrote brilliantly and easily, and soon charmed the world with his graceful, clever, and polished music for orchestra, such as the exquisite overture to Shakespeare's "Midsummer Night's Dream." He also composed two fine oratorios (ŏr'ă-tōr'ĭ-ō), "Elijah" and "St. Paul." After Handel's "Messiah," "Elijah" is the most popular oratorio we have.

But Mendelssohn (mĕn'dĕl-sōn), too, was a pianist, and among the works for which we love him most are his lovely little "Songs without Words" for the piano. They were very different from the formal sonatas, which everyone had written fifty years before. Most of them were as like as possible to Schubert's little songs. Mendelssohn just poured out his feelings, grave and gay, and we do not need words to tell us what those feelings were.

A Brilliant Hungarian Pianist Whose Playing Has Never Been Equalled

Both Mendelssohn and Chopin were brilliant pianists, who charmed audiences everywhere in Europe. But the greatest pianist the world has ever seen was Franz Liszt (fränts lĭst), a Hungarian, who during his long life (1811–1886) was probably petted and flattered more than any other musician. In many ways he deserved it, for he was exceedingly generous as well as very gifted, and always lent a helping hand to other less lucky musicians. But so much admiration was not good for him—he was already idolized at the age of twelve—and as a result he grew to need it more and more. Unfortunately, his music suffered sometimes; for he, as a result, wrote what he knew his audiences would applaud, instead of what he himself felt to be beautiful. He was not like Beethoven, who worked steadily on in the best way he knew how, whether people applauded him or not.

So Liszt's compositions are not all so great as those of the other romantic composers, though many of his themes are very fine and full of feeling. He used the wild Hungarian folk songs and gipsy dances as a basis for a certain kind of fiery instrumental composition which he called a "rhapsody" (răp'sŏ-dĭ)—the word had been used in the Greek for a recitation or song. And he wrote songs and some stirring music for orchestra.

His orchestral music was his most important work; for, taking the hint from such compositions as Beethoven's "Pastoral Symphony," he invented an entirely new form, the symphonic (sĭm-fŏn'ĭk) poem. This was nothing more nor less than a re-telling in music of some literary narrative, like "Hamlet" or "Prometheus." In order to do that he had to be a kind of wizard in writing so as to bring out of the different instruments the most beautiful sounds they were fitted to produce.

And herein he was very successful. He had learned a great deal about it from a friend of his in Paris, a fiery Frenchman named Berlioz (1803–1869), a man of bold imagination who had learned to get more amazing effects than anyone had ever got before from the brass and wood and catgut of which an orchestra is composed. His music nearly always told a story, and sometimes a rather wild one. But though Berlioz (bĕr lĭ-ōs') might occasionally be absurd, he was always original, and everyone who wrote for orchestra afterwards had something to learn from his startling experiments.

Now, all these men who followed Beethoven were "romantic" composers; they wanted to put as much feeling as possible into their music and to find new ways of doing it. But there were plenty of people who felt that all this was a mistake. They wanted music to continue in the old way, and to be as much as possible like the music of Beethoven and his age. They were the "classicists" (klăs'ĭ-sĭst), and they were glad enough to welcome a great German composer who more or less agreed with them. His name was Johannes Brahms (yŏ-hän'ĕz bräms), and his music was as good as any since Beethoven.

Symphonies and Songs that Rank Among The Greatest Ever Written

Now Brahms could not help being a product of his age. He lived at a time (1833–1897) when the world was a very different place from what it had been in Beethoven's day, so the music that people wrote had to be different. But he followed the old path, when he could; he wrote symphonies and sonatas for piano, all in the old sonata pattern—with certain changes—and he did not attempt to write "programme music," or music that told a story. His symphonies, his chamber music, and his compositions for the piano are among the very finest that we have, and his songs rank with those of both Schubert and Schumann.

(CONTINUED ON PAGE 459)

382

Photo by Rischgitz

One afternoon in July, 1588, Sir Francis Drake and Lord Howard of Effingham were playing bowls at Plymouth, while all the queen's ships lay at anchor awaiting the coming of the Spaniards. Suddenly up rushed Captain Fleming, gasping out the stirring news that the great Armada had been sighted. Everyone turned to Drake, vice-admiral of the British fleet. He was as calm as if nothing had happened. "There is time to finish our game and beat the Spaniards too," he said. But just the same he had already whispered a quick, efficient order. He not only made everyone as confident as he was of victory, but he ensured victory by his courage and skill. With him as a leader, there was indeed sufficient time both to play bowls and to win.

The BRAVEST of the SEA-DOGS

His Enemies Called Drake a Pirate, but He Broke the Supremacy of Spain and Helped to Lay the Foundation of England's Sea Power

IT WAS in late September, 1580, that a battered and worm-eaten little ship, the "Golden Hind," manned by a handful of bronzed sailors, came limping alone into Plymouth harbour. With four others she had sailed away from that port nearly three years before. Now she was home again, with immense riches in her hold and with the most glorious record ever made by an English ship. For she was the first British boat to sail all the way round the world. Her captain, a red-bearded, sturdy little man, was Francis Drake, returning to his native Devonshire after having penetrated that Golden Sea—the Pacific Ocean. For nearly a century Spain had claimed the ocean as her own, and it had brought her untold wealth. No wonder Queen Elizabeth now sent for Drake to come up to London! There the queen received him daily, and even attended a banquet given in her honour on board his shabby little ship; and there she dubbed him knight. Jealous enemies saw him with different eyes. "Her Majesty's little pirate," they called the daring sea-dog.

Drake was born near Tavistock, in Devon, about 1539. He was brought up by his distinguished kinsman, Sir John Hawkins, and at 18 was purser of a ship trading to Bombay. By 22 he was a captain, and fought gallantly under Sir John Hawkins in the Gulf of Mexico, although he lost nearly all the money he had put into the expedition.

He returned home with a flaming hatred of Spain, his country's bitterest enemy. From now on he was going to live and die fighting against her; so, in two secret voyages, he laid his plans to strike at one of the vital spots in her possessions—the Isthmus of Panama, where the riches from the Golden Sea, silver and gold and jewels, poured across by mule train from the city of Panama on the Pacific to King Philip's waiting ships on the Atlantic side.

Drake Sees the Pacific Ocean

With only two small ships, the "Pasha" and the "Swan," and seventy-three men, Drake set out in 1572 to rifle this treasure chest of the most powerful monarch in Europe. He succeeded in his bold attempt and captured many a rich Spanish ship besides, but only after such struggles and disasters as would have turned back a less dauntless man. When he had finally attained his object and had swept the glittering riches of Spain into his hold, he sped back to England. But he did not start home until, the first of Englishmen to do so, he had seen the mighty Pacific. At sight of its broad waters he fell upon his knees and asked God "of His goodness to give him life and leave to sail once an English ship in that sea."

It was five years later that his prayer was granted, when on December 13, 1577, he set out for the Straits of Magellan. Only one of his ships, the "Golden Hind" commanded by Drake himself, reached the Pacific; but in this he plundered many a rich Spanish settlement, and finally, by way of the Pacific and Indian Oceans, he doubled the dangerous Cape of Good Hope. Drake had now sailed right round the world.

Don Pedro de Valdes, the Spanish admiral, would have fought any other Englishman and gone down with his flag flying. But as soon as he heard that it was Drake who demanded his surrender, he yielded at once, saying that it was an honour to be taken by the greatest seaman in the world. Here he is on Drake's flagship, the "Revenge," giving up his sword. So gallant and courteous was he, and so highly did he compliment Drake's courage and skill, that Drake "placed him at his own table and lodged him in his own cabin." In this way did Drake capture a very large galleon of the Armada and add another name to his list of triumphs.

When Drake returned to England, Queen Elizabeth was at first doubtful how she should receive him, as to recognize his achievements was likely to offend Spain, who demanded his death as a pirate, but at length her stout patriotism triumphed and, as you have already read, she visited Drake on the "Golden Hind" at Deptford and there, on April 4, 1581, he became Sir Francis Drake, while his ship was ordered to be preserved in commemoration of its great captain and his work for England.

It was not long after getting home before the bold captain longed to be at sea again, but the queen wished to keep the daring sailor within reach and refused to allow him to go. He had to be content to serve his country in Parliament and as mayor of Plymouth. That old town still remembers her famous son for the pure water supply he gave it and the flour mills he built there. Then one day came alarming news. Spain was secretly building an immense fleet—the Invincible Armada (är-mä´dä)—to invade England, so England hurried to prepare a fleet of her own. Drake was made an admiral, and with two warships and eighteen cruisers he at once set forth (1585).

Photo by National Portrait Gallery
This is Sir Francis Drake, most famous of the "sea-dogs" of Queen Elizabeth.

First he struck terror along the coasts of Spain. Then he captured and burned Santiago, in the Cape Verde Islands, and the old fortified city of Santo Domingo, in Hispaniola. After he had collected there a ransom equal to some £50,000, "El Draque" —the "Dragon," as the Spaniards called him —suddenly appeared at Cartagena, one of the richest cities on the Spanish Main. Her strong defences crumbled before Drake's skill and daring, the city was stripped of her wealth, and paid many thousands of pounds as ransom. After that Drake touched at Florida, where the town of St. Augustine was plundered and burned, and took aboard Raleigh's discouraged colonists at Virginia, together with the first cargo of tobacco and potatoes that ever crossed the Atlantic. Then he turned towards home. He

had struck a death-blow at the power of haughty Spain.

When Drake reached England, the great fleet that the English were gathering was still far from ready; but there was now no longer any doubt as to Spain's intentions, so, with twenty-three ships, he again put forth, this time bound for Spain, to break up the Armada, if he could, before it formed. After riding out a fierce seven-day gale, he attacked Cadiz, where he had received news that a large fleet was anchored. Twelve thousand tons of shipping in her harbours went up in flames as a result of his visit, and four vessels loaded with provisions were taken, all without the loss of a single English sailor. The incident afterwards became famous under Drake's own title for it. He called it "singeing the king of Spain's beard."

Then the victors set off for Cape St. Vincent, where they captured the castle and later took the greatest of Spanish merchantmen, the "San Felippe."

By this time the Spanish invasion had grown more threatening, and Elizabeth decreed that her fleet should remain in home waters to defend England instead of boldly seeking out the Armada, as Drake had urged for some time. And suddenly the mighty fleet appeared! The English vessels tried to check its progress, but in vain. Day after day it moved steadily up the English Channel and anchored off Calais. There fire-ships were sent among the Spanish fleet, which was forced to cut its cables; the English fleet, under Lord Howard of Effingham, with Drake as vice-admiral, fell upon it at last, and the six-hour battle of Gravelines was fought on July 29, 1588. It left the "Invincible" Armada so badly crippled that a storm shattered it when it was attempting to escape round Scotland.

The country rang with praise of Drake and of his victory. After that, however, Fortune seemed to turn her back upon him, and while on a trip to the New World he died of fever, on January 28, 1596.

BRAVE *and* BRILLIANT WALTER RALEIGH

A Favourite Courtier of Queen Elizabeth, He Planted the First British Colony in America, but Ended His Life upon the Scaffold

WHY should any Englishman desire to leave his own merry land, three centuries ago, and sail hundreds of miles across the sea to live among the Indians in the wilds of North America? Whether he were rich and noble, with a great estate, or poor and humble on a little farm, why should he risk the perils of the waves and forests instead of remaining peacefully at home? There were a good many reasons, and among the chief of them was the love of high adventure that has led so many men to blaze new paths in the world.

And one of the most daring adventurers in England was the man who planted the first British colony across the water. Wit and poet, courtier and scholar and soldier, Sir Walter Raleigh was one of the foremost spirits of his day.

Raleigh was born about 1552 at Hayes, a village in South Devonshire, and came of a good old family. He went to Oxford, where

Photo by Anderson   From the painting by Sir J. E. Millais

When Sir Walter Raleigh was a little boy he must often have sat like this on the seashore in Devonshire and listened to the exciting tales of some old salt till he could hardly wait to grow up and go adventuring himself. For those were the days when every ship brought news of some Spanish galleon robbed of its treasure on the high seas, of some new land discovered or sea explored, of some fresh wonder found in the incredible New World. And when he did grow up this little lad became one of the greatest adventurers of all these men.

his wit and his good looks brought him popularity, but he did not complete his course there. In 1569 he went to France with a party of English volunteers who for some five years fought on the Protestant side with the Huguenots (hū'gḕ-nŏt) in the religious wars. On his return to England he spent some time at the court of Queen Elizabeth, and then in 1578 sailed with his half-brother, Sir Humphrey Gilbert, on what they called a "voyage of discovery." Their real aim, however, was to waylay Spanish ships homeward-bound from America and laden with treasure. Such adventure as this strongly appealed to the daring Raleigh, and also gave him an opportunity to build up a much-needed fortune. For his family had spent their wealth freely and had left little to the son, who was something of a spendthrift on his own account. And Sir Walter's love of luxury, especially of fine clothes—he was the most splendidly dressed courtier of his time—made the lack of money a constant embarrassment to him.

When Raleigh returned from this unfruitful voyage he again became a soldier, this time as captain of some English troops

Photo by National Portrait Gallery

This is Sir Walter Raleigh, about whom so many wonderful stories are told that one could never repeat them all. There is the famous story of his throwing his handsome cloak over a muddy place in Queen Elizabeth's path. There is the tale that once, lying in prison under sentence of death, he asked for one night of freedom to rescue a lady, promising to return—and actually returning. These stories may or may not be true, but he was gallant and high-hearted and witty, of that we may be sure. On the scaffold he felt the edge of the axe with his fingers. "This is sharp medicine," he said, "but it is a sound cure for all disease."

in Ireland. The adventure proved far more profitable than he could ever have anticipated. When, in December 1581, he was sent from the army with letters for Queen Elizabeth, his handsome bearing, sprightly wit, and gracious manner won her favour so completely that she insisted upon his remaining at her court. He soon became one of her favourites. To ensure his fortune she gave him several offices, including licences in the English wine and woollen cloth trades, from which he obtained such a princely income that he could afford to live in the best style of his time and occupy the finest house in London. In 1584 he was knighted.

Having acquired a fortune and established his position at court, Raleigh was now seized with the thirst for adventure, and he began to prepare for another expedition to cross the Atlantic, loot the Spanish ships, and found a settlement in North America. But Queen Elizabeth would not hear of his leaving her court, for she feared to trust her favourite to the perils of the deep and the wilds of America. Yet if he could not go himself, Raleigh could at least send others, and so he did. He fitted out an expedition in

1584 and sent out Philip Amadas and Arthur Barlowe to seek a suitable site. The next year he placed his cousin, Sir Richard Grenville, in charge of seven shiploads of colonists and gave him orders to found a settlement. On an island off the coast of North Carolina they established Roanoke, the first English settlement in America.

Mystery of the Vanished Colony

This first settlement in Virginia—as the lands chosen by Amadas and Barlowe had been named, after Elizabeth the Virgin Queen—did not prosper. After less than a year of hardship and starvation the settlers lost heart and returned to England. But Raleigh was determined to make a further effort, and the following year he sent out a party of a hundred and seventeen men, women, and children, with John White as governor. After a short stay, White returned to England for supplies. When he again reached the settlement on Roanoke Island, he found not a single colonist, but only the half-burned ruins of the houses.

Among the lost settlers was little Virginia Dare, the governor's granddaughter, the first English child born in America. It is now believed that those who were not killed by hostile Indians, were carried off as prisoners or adopted by the tribe. This was the pitiable end of England's first attempt at colonizing the New World. Later colonists, however, wiser and equally courageous, followed Raleigh in planting settlements in this same Virginia, and brought wealth to themselves and to the mother country by growing tobacco, which, with the potato, had been brought back to England by the original settlers at Roanoke.

While Sir Walter's colony at Roanoke was suffering its mishaps, he himself was busy helping to prepare the English fleet which in 1588 was to defeat the Spanish Armada. Shortly after that he married, and lost the favour of his queen. In 1595 he set out for South America in search of the fabled land of El Dorado (ĕl′dŏ-rä′dō), which he believed lay along the Orinoco River. He found little gold there, but he did bring back some mahogany wood, the first ever seen in England, so it is said. After a short rest he joined an English fleet bound for the mid-Atlantic to waylay Spanish treasure ships. This trip took him to the Azores and to Cadiz, in Spain, where as usual he had a hand in some fierce fighting.

In 1603 Queen Elizabeth died and James I came to the throne. This king, who had no friendly interest in the proud and haughty Raleigh, soon began to listen to the many envious courtiers who had long disliked the rich and pampered favourite of Elizabeth. The king was eager to be rid of him. He first deprived him of all the offices and privileges that he had so long enjoyed, and soon after committed him to the Tower of London, where he remained a prisoner for twelve long years. Here he passed his time by writing, among other things, his "History of the World." In 1616 he was at last set free, on his promising to find a gold mine in America for the king.

Still hopeful of finding the El Dorado he had once sought in vain, he immediately set sail for South America again. Making his way up the Orinoco River as before, he arrived at a Spanish settlement, now called Ciudad Bolivar, and there, after some sort of dispute with the inhabitants, he set fire to the place. News of this reached Spain. The Spanish king asked his ambassador in London to lodge a complaint against Sir Walter. King James again gladly listened. Raleigh had assured him that there would be no clash with any Spanish possessions, although he must have realized that this was wellnigh impossible. When he returned to England he was arrested, charged with treason, and beheaded on October 29, 1618.

> ### ANSWERS TO PUZZLES ON PAGE 366
>
> 14—She first fills the five-gallon can with milk. From the five-gallon can, she fills the three-gallon can. She next empties the milk from the three-gallon can into the storage can, and then pours the remaining two gallons of milk from the five-gallon can into the three-gallon can. Next she fills the five-gallon can from the storage can. You will remember that she left the three-gallon can containing only two gallons of milk, so the wise milkmaid now fills it from the five-gallon can, and that leaves exactly four gallons of milk in the five-gallon can. 15—His daughter. 16—13 trains. 17—675 springs 18—56 quarts; there is no difference; ten. 19—Dozens; dozen. 20—The answer is not 30 days. On the 28th day it climbed the three feet as usual and reached the top. The answer is 28 days.

Photo by Rischgitz

We read in the Bible that when God saw the wickedness of the people, He repented that He had made the earth. So He decided to send a great flood and destroy everything upon the earth that He had created. But He warned the just and saint.y Noah of the approaching disaster, and told him to build an ark large enough to hold himself, his fami y, and members of every one of the animal tribes. Noah did as he was told; and when back clouds began to fill the sky, he and his family climbed safely into the Ark. Then the waters descended and covered the face of the earth, but the little Ark weathered the storm. When the rain ceased and the waters passed away, Noah set free a dove which returned to the Ark carrying an olive leaf in its beak. Noah knew then that the earth was again dry, and that he might safely go forth from the Ark.

The STORY of the CHOSEN PEOPLE

This Small and Persecuted Nation Gave Its Mind and Heart to One Great Idea: the Idea of a Single God of Love, Which Became the Religion of the Western World

SOME nations become great because they fight and conquer other weaker peoples, ruling them harshly or kindly until at last the conquerors themselves become weak and are conquered in their turn. Other nations become great because of their wealth in gold, silver, precious stones and other valuable mineral products. And some are great because of the beauty they bring into the world, because they have produced great artists and poets and musicians.

By none of these things do we remember that many-named people commonly known as the Jews. Compared with the Egyptians, the Assyrians, or the Babylonians, their fighting power, even in the days of their highest glory as a nation, is hardly worthy of mention. Compared with the Cretans or the Lydians, their riches were trifling. They produced, in those early days, no great artists or musicians. And yet for three thousand years the world has never been able to forget or ignore this people. Like the Chinese, they have survived, while countless warrior peoples have risen and fallen. They have achieved something no other people ever achieved, the maintenance of a firm bond of union when their numbers were scattered all over the face of the earth, without any national home.

The reason why the Jews hold a unique place in history is easy to see. Thought is one of the greatest human achievements, and the history of the Jewish nation is a history of great thoughts.

Curiously enough, while we know a great deal about Palestine (păl′ĕs-tīn)—the home of the Jews—before the ancient Hebrews came to live in it, we know very little about the coming of those ancestors of the modern Jewish people. Palestine lies in the south-west corner of that Fertile Crescent about which we have heard so much in the stories of Sumeria and Babylonia and Assyria. Situated at a sort of cross-roads between Egypt and Babylonia, and between Greece and Arabia, Palestine had the advantage of being in the centre of things, as well as the great disadvantage of being fought over in nearly every war.

It is a little country, about one-fifth the size of England—the whole length of it, "from Dan to Beersheba," is only about 150 miles. Its green valleys, its one important waterway, the River Jordan, splitting it lengthwise before flowing into the Dead Sea, its parched hills and desert patches, would not seem very attractive to a visitor from broader, greener lands. But strangers who went to Palestine in ancient days came mainly from much more forbidding countries. For they were desert wanderers—the Amorites (ăm′ō-rīt), the Canaanites (kā′năn-īt), the Hittites, the Philistines, and the Arameans (ăr′à-mē′ăn)—who entered Palestine one after another, quarrelling among themselves and appealing to the great nations of Egypt or Babylonia for protection or

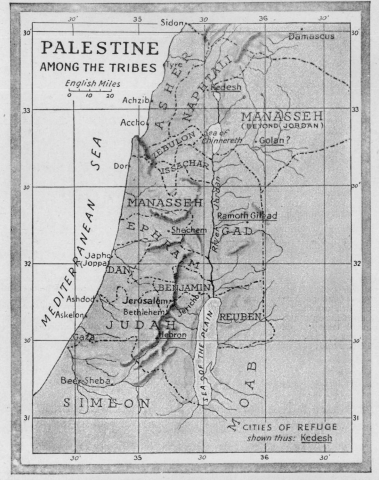

Up and down this little rocky strip of land that we call Palestine warriors from all the nations of the ancient world marched in battle array. For the homeland of the Hebrews was at the cross-roads between Egypt and Asia Minor, and the Mediterranean and lands farther east. It was not an easy country for a nation to hold; but it was an ideal centre for the spread of a religion. Each tribe had its own area.

Jews have always been a nation of thinkers. It was their ideas about God—thoughts dreamed by shepherds under the stars, surging in the minds of kings in stress or danger—which made their early history great. And to-day it is their ideas on every subject —science, trade, religion, history, the arts— that make the Jews a great people. The help. By the time the Hebrews arrived, Palestine was full of these tribes who, with the exception of the Hittites and Philistines, all belonged to what we know as the Semitic (sĕ-mĭt'ĭk) race, to which the Hebrews also belonged.

Who were the Hebrews and whence did they come to Palestine? For all their early history we must go to the Bible. The stories they told of the Creation, the Flood, and other things are curiously like those told in Babylonia, and we know that they once lived among the Babylonians and listened to the stories the Babylonian poets and wise men told. Yet in the Hebrew telling of these stories there is always an important difference: where the Babylonian legends are just stories, those of the Hebrews always teach a moral lesson.

Adam and Eve were sent away from Eden because they were disobedient; Noah was saved from the Flood because he was just, and walked humbly with God. Moreover, where the Babylonians had many gods, the Hebrews —at least after their settlement in Palestine— taught the worship of one God—Yahweh (yä'wĕ), or Jehovah, the all-Father, who made everything good. This idea of one beneficent God was current among the Hebrews long before the beginning of their story as we know it.

We know that the Hebrews lived for a time in Babylonia and heard the stories of the Babylonians, and we are fairly sure that

in the course of their wanderings this little people spent some time in Egypt. Some scholars say that not all the Hebrews, but only a few, lived in the land of the Pharaohs.

Photo by Rischgitz

The Pharaoh of Egypt began to fear the growing number of Hebrews who lived in his land. So he commanded that all the boy babies born to them should be put to death. One mother, hoping that she might save her baby from death, laid him in a basket of bulrushes, made watertight with pitch, and set the tiny craft to float among the reeds by the banks of the Nile. There the Pharaoh's daughter found it when she came to the river to bathe. She adopted the baby and called him Moses, a name which means "taken out of the water."

Others say that no Hebrews were there at all, since no Egyptian records mention them. But many tell us that the Egyptian captivity, when the enslaved people had to labour so cruelly, is history, and that Moses, the great leader who led the Israelites from bondage, really lived.

The law of Moses has to do with three things: God, His people, and His law. It taught that the law was given by God to the people for their preservation; so long as they held to it they were protected from every evil. But God Himself set bounds to the law. He would not help or save a disobedient or rebellious people. To keep the law was man's duty to God.

Unhappily, the Jewish people did not always hold to this magnificent faith in the true God. They were attracted by the Baal (bā'ăl) their neighbours worshipped, by the golden calves of the idolaters, by the loose practices of the heathen peoples around them. All through their history their leaders were trying to bring them back to the pure worship of Yahweh. Perhaps the leaders might have failed in the end had they not been aided by the greatest religious force the Jews have experienced, the force of persecution. For it is very true that a faith for which believers have to suffer often grows stronger just because it is difficult to follow it.

This is how the city of Jericho was conquered, according to the instructions of the Lord. The children of Israel, led by seven priests bearing trumpets made of rams' horns, marched in procession round the city walls. When they had done this seven times, the priests blew a loud blast upon their trumpets, the people of Israel raised a mighty shout, and the walls of Jericho fell down and crumbled at their feet.

The law of Moses was changed and broadened during many centuries, but in the main it was probably first given to the people twelve or thirteen centuries before the birth of Christ, soon after the escape of the Hebrews from Egypt. This escape was followed by forty years of wandering, and then the Hebrews began to flow gradually into Palestine, where some of them had probably already established themselves. They found Palestine a country of little cities, each with its walls and its defences, glaring defiance upon all its neighbours.

Few as the Hebrew wanderers were, they had experienced the hardy desert life to make them strong, and best of all they had one God and one leader. This gave them a great advantage over the disunited and mixed peoples of Palestine. By a long series of petty wars they conquered city after city, sometimes killing and sometimes enslaving the inhabitants. Their heroes — Moses, Joshua, Gideon, Jephthah, and the women Miriam, Jael and Deborah—were more than military chiefs. They were mouthpieces through which the divine voice spoke to the people, telling them of the commands of God. When the Canaanite warrior Sisera (sĭs'ĕ-rȧ) seemed about to overwhelm the Hebrews, and Jael by means of a clever stratagem managed to slay him, the song of Deborah is praise, not to the killer herself, but to the Lord for His avenging of Israel. When Gideon won his battles it was Yahweh who delivered the enemy into his hand. Like a golden thread through the story of conquest runs this reliance upon God and His good will towards the people.

As Palestine fell to the Hebrews, they divided the land into twelve parts, one for each of the twelve divisions, or "tribes," of the people. Beyond these twelve divisions lived the hostile tribes who worshipped many gods, each little settlement having its Baal to manage its harvest, and often its Baalith, or she-Baal, to superintend the important business of fertility.

The Canaanites taught the Hebrews to farm and produce corn, wine, oil and figs. The invaders learned how to make clothes and tools. Even more important, they

When Jephthah returned from his victory over the children of Ammon, his beloved daughter came to welcome him at the door. Then his heart was sad indeed, for he had vowed that if the Israelites were victorious, he would offer up as a burnt sacrifice to the Lord whatsoever should come forth from the door of his house to meet him. Above, you see Jephthah's daughter in the mountains, whither she went to pray. She remained there for two months and then returned to her father to be sacrificed in accordance with his vow.

Samson was the strongest man of his time, and everyone was eager to know in what his great strength lay. Finally his enemies, the Philistines, bribed Delilah, a woman whom he loved, to obtain from him the secret. After much coaxing from her, Samson told her that if his hair were cut off, his strength would then be just the same as that of any other man. And so Delilah sent for a man to cut off Samson's hair as he slept.

learned to read and write—at first only a name or a charm scratched on a sword or a stone, but after a while longer songs and stories. From this time on, the Jews wrote down those stirring tales which are the beginning of their record as a people.

Except for the Philistines (fĭl'ĭs-tĭn) and the Hittites the people then living in Palestine were of the Semitic race. The Philistines, who probably had come from eastern Crete, began to harass the Israelites, burning their cities and plundering their goods. They could not be stopped by the Hebrew captains or by the strong but wayward Samson, who boasted of killing a thousand Philistines with the jawbone of an ass. At the battle of Shiloh the enemy crushed the Hebrew army and carried off the Ark of the Covenant (kŭv'ĕ-nănt) or " Compact "—the most sacred object in their religion.

A hero was needed to save the little nation, and a hero appeared. He was Saul, a young farmer who had become a soldier. Saul led his men through many dangers to victory, and his reward was a crown. Israel, which had been governed by priest-captains, made Saul its first king. But the kingship was an empty honour. Tactless and jealous, Saul turned against himself the priests and the people, who soon forgot the great service he had done in saving the life of the nation. He saw fickle favour turn

to David, a gallant young shepherd with the soul of a poet. Finally Saul fell, slain in desperate battle against the Philistines.

Everyone loves David, the "sweet singer of Israel." The stories tell of him first as a shepherd boy, who early left his flocks and followed a life of stirring adventure. With sling and stone he killed the Philistine champion, Goliath (gō-lī'ăth). Later, exiled by the jealous Saul, he gathered about him a little band of followers, exiles like himself, whom he led in raids not unlike those attributed to Robin Hood. His undying friendship with Jonathan, his chivalrous refusal to kill Saul even to save his own life, his inspiration in the composing of magnificent poetry, all make him at once the most beloved and the most human character in early Jewish history.

Unfortunately David's life was divided into two parts, and the second was by no means so glorious or so admirable as the first. When some ten years after Saul's death, David managed to establish himself as the king of a freed people, with their enemies subdued, he made the kingship a very different thing from what it had been under the simple democratic rule of Saul.

David chose Jerusalem as his capital and the centre of the Jewish religion. He introduced a life of luxury that was hitherto unknown to the Jews. From being a

Here you see the sacred Ark as it was returned to the Israelites after its capture by the Philistines. This was the sanctuary which Jehovah had told Moses to build as a dwelling-place for the Lord among his people. It was made of wood overlaid within and without with gold, according to the Lord's command. Above it was placed the " mercy seat," a slab of gold on which the blood of animals was sprinkled to atone for the sins of the people. A cherub of gold knelt at either end, as the picture shows. Inside were kept the " two tables of testimony, tables of stone written with the finger of God." These " tables " were small slabs of stone which the Lord had given Moses upon Mount Sinai. On them were written the Ten Commandments.

The army of the Philistines and the army of the Israelites were ready to give battle. But instead of attacking, the Philistines sent out a giant named Goliath, who for forty days issued a challenge to the men of Israel, saying that if he were overcome in single combat, he and his people would become the servants of Israel—but that if he should be victorious the Israelites must bow to the Philistines. No one dared fight the Philistine until a shepherd boy named David made up his mind that, with the aid of the Lord, he would go out to meet the giant. Goliath laughed with scorn when he saw his tiny adversary; but David loaded his sling and sent the stone crashing against the giant's forehead, killing him, and thereby saving Israel.

peerless military leader he became something like an Oriental potentate. The people, however, always recognized his charm and honoured him as the true founder of their state.

Under David's son, Solomon, the material kingdom of the Jews reached its brief, glittering noonday. It was he who built the splendid temple in Jerusalem, beautiful with ivory and cedars from the forests of Lebanon, glittering with gold and silver. It is he who lives in story as the shrewd, just judge, so that men speak of a wise man as having "the wisdom of Solomon." It was he whose court was so splendid, according to the story, that the queen of Sheba came to visit him. In truth, Solomon was a great king, and a lover of luxury. We are told that to supply his court he required daily a hundred sheep, thirty oxen, and seven million gallons of flour, besides fowls, wine, and all manner of other delicacies.

This display caused the little Jewish state to be admired and envied by other nations, so that even the mighty king of Egypt sent one of his daughters to be a bride for Solomon.

But the glory was not worth its cost. Foreign wives brought foreign religions into Israel, so that the pure worship of Yahweh became corrupted by all sorts of degrading idolatrous customs. And the heavy taxes that paid for the splendours of the court ground down the common people into bitter poverty. Class distinctions grew; the nobles lounged on couches inlaid with ivory while the poor sweated and toiled in the fields. All this pomp and display attracted the envy of mightier kings, who began to plan wars that threatened to crush and enslave the tiny nation.

Even before Solomon died, the kingdom had begun to break up. Hiram of Tyre secured twenty northern cities in return for the timber and supplies he sent the vainglorious Hebrew ruler. The Edomites, the Moabites and the Arameans, foreign tribes who had been subject to David, revolted successfully. Then Solomon's son, Rehoboam (rē′hŏ-bō′ăm), began his rule by a scornful refusal of a plea for gentler laws and lighter taxes. "My father chastised you with whips," he cried in answer to the complaints, "but I will chastise you with scorpions!"

This was more than his people could bear, and their anger flamed into rebellion. The northern tribes, under Jeroboam (jĕr′ŏ-bō′-ăm), established a separate kingdom (about 930 B.C.). Henceforth the Hebrew nation was to consist of not one, but two little states—Israel in the north and Judah in the south, for ever jealous of each other and quarrelsome. No wonder that the Egyptian pharaoh Sheshonk was soon able to overrun the southern kingdom as far as Jerusalem, robbing the beautiful new temple and exacting a heavy tax.

For hundreds of years the two Hebrew kingdoms lived a troubled life, overrun by many enemies yet never willing to join together for strength and brotherly help. Israel in the north suffered mostly from internal troubles. In thirty-seven years, following the death of Jeroboam, it had six kings, several of whom died a violent death. Only twice did a son succeed his father on the throne.

When the Lord commanded Elijah to hide himself from the people, He did not leave His servant to starve in the wilderness. Morning and evening He sent ravens to carry meat and bread to the prophet. And near at hand was "the brook Cherith," where the man of God might slake his thirst.

The strongest of these Israelite kings were Omri (ŏm′rī) and his son Ahab (ā′hăb), husband of Jezebel (jĕz′ĕ-bĕl). Omri, who ruled in the early ninth century B.C., chose and fortified Samaria (să-mâr′-ĭ-ă) as the capital of Israel. Ahab skilfully managed the trade and foreign relations of his kingdom. And in Judah, the southern kingdom, things were fairly peaceful during this period. Asa (ā′să) and Jehoshaphat (ĕ-hŏsh′ă-făt) were devout kings who ruled for many years according to the faith of Yahweh.

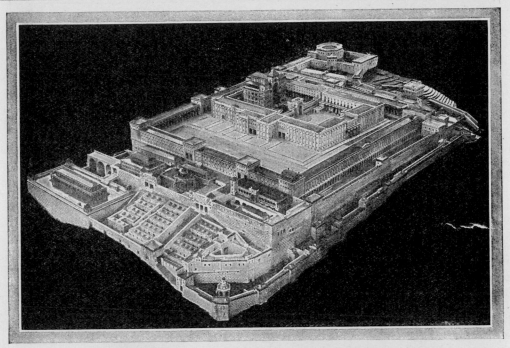

A RECONSTRUCTION OF THE TEMPLE OF THE JEWS AT JERUSALEM

Above is a reconstruction of the temple at Jerusalem as it was rebuilt by Herod. This is the beautiful building of marble and gold which Jesus so often visited. The great gateways at the left led to the Court of the Gentiles, the large open space, which was surrounded by pillared cloisters. Only the Jews could pass beyond it into the inner court, where, in the Women's Gallery, Mary waited while Joseph took the infant Jesus into the court nearest the temple. There no woman might enter. Only priests could go into the temple itself, which held the sacred relics of the Jews. This was the third great temple built in Jerusalem. Almost a thousand years before, Solomon had built his magnificent House of God, which was burned in the time of Nebuchadnezzar. Seventy years later another temple, not so beautiful as the first, was built. This was the one which Herod set himself to rebuild and enlarge, after the plan shown in the model above. It took eighty years to complete the building; and almost as soon as it was finished, it suffered destruction by Titus.

Now there were good kings like these, strong kings like Ahab, in many other of the little states of the Fertile Crescent. There was, for example, King Mesha (mē′shă) of Moab, of whose long reign we know a good deal, because he left behind him a black stone bearing the record of his victories, leaving the defeats to be recounted by other nations. This "Moabite stone" is a precious relic of these early days, and you will find a picture of it elsewhere in this work. But in spite of the Moabite stone and the various records of other kings, we do not remember these rulers as we remember Ahab. Why not? Why should the impotent Hebrews in their two small states interest us more than powerful kingdoms like Tyre and Damascus?

During this period, at least, it is because of the men we know as "the prophets." We remember Ahab, for instance, because it was in his reign that Elijah lived, the lean, hawk-eyed man of God, unrelenting enemy of Baal. Elijah was the first of that long line of preacher-statesmen whose words and acts still flame like fire in the records of history and of poetry.

Elijah's Contempt for Ahab

Elijah scorned the easy-going Ahab and his shrewd, ambitious wife Jezebel, who encouraged the mad worship of Baal, with its sacrifices of children, and its leaping, arm-waving priests who cut themselves with knives in their frenzies. Elijah knew that one steadfast worshipper of the one God was more than a match for all these fanatics, and on one great occasion he put them all to shame. Elijah was saved from the hostility of Jezebel and Ahab, and lived to see Ahab brought home dead—killed in battle by a chance shot from a bow.

Elisha, the pupil and successor of Elijah, was more tactful and gentler in his methods, but he was no less devoted to the single worship of Yahweh, and for this reason he upheld Jehu (jē'hū) in a revolution against Ahab's successor which, for a while at least, put down the worship of Baal in Israel. Neither Elijah nor Elisha wrote down their messages. The story of their lives was written for them by others — students or scribes.

Amos, who lived in the middle of the eighth century B.C., began the long line of prophet - authors in Israel and Judah. A shepherd from the wilderness south of Jerusalem, Amos came to the religious feast at Bethel during a time of careless wealth and ease. His anger was aroused at the sight of so much merriment alongside so much injustice and oppression. He stood in the market-place and began to cry forth the message that he afterwards wrote down: "I hate, I despise your feasts!" God, he said, demanded justice rather than fat sacrifices. A nation corrupt and luxurious could not hope to survive in that welter of little warring nations.

The prophecy of Amos was fulfilled when the king of Israel died (about 745 B.C.) and soon afterwards Assyria swept the land into servitude. A new prophet, Hosea (hŏ-zē'å), now arose to assure the distressed people of God's love and mercy. Though they had

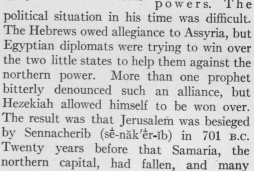

Close to the house of King Ahab stood the pleasant vineyard of a man named Naboth. Naboth was very proud of this vineyard, for it had been in his family ever since the Children of Israel had come into Canaan. And so, when Ahab wished to buy it from him, Naboth refused. Jezebel, the wicked wife of the king, brought about the death of Naboth, and told her husband that he could now take possession of the vineyard. But when Ahab went down to the place he found there the prophet Elijah, whom the Lord had sent to meet him. In the picture Elijah is denouncing Ahab and pronouncing upon him a terrible doom.

sinned, yet God's love could not be turned away: "How can I give thee up, Ephraim; abandon thee, Israel?"

During this time and later, scribes and historians were busy. The law of Moses was rewritten in its final form, and so was the history of the nation, for the purpose of pointing out the hand of God in its affairs. These rewritten codes were then taught to king and people, as they have been taught ever since. This system constitutes the most complete and high-minded moral plan of any ancient people.

And now for over a century prophet after prophet — Isaiah (ī-zī'å), Micah (mī'kå), Zephaniah (zĕf'å-nī'å), Jeremiah— preached in eloquent terms of God's hatred of sin and His joy in repentance. These prophets were often more than preachers. Isaiah, perhaps the greatest of them all, directed the king of Judah wisely in his relations with foreign powers. The political situation in his time was difficult. The Hebrews owed allegiance to Assyria, but Egyptian diplomats were trying to win over the two little states to help them against the northern power. More than one prophet bitterly denounced such an alliance, but Hezekiah allowed himself to be won over. The result was that Jerusalem was besieged by Sennacherib (sĕ-năk'ĕr-ĭb) in 701 B.C. Twenty years before that Samaria, the northern capital, had fallen, and many

From the painting by John Martin

When Belshazzar and his household were feasting and drinking wine from the golden vessels which Nebuchadnezzar had taken from the Temple of Solomon, a hand suddenly appeared, writing on the wall. The king was troubled, and he called in his advisers to tell him what the words meant. All of them failed but Daniel, a captive, who told the king that the writing foretold his downfall, inasmuch as he had displeased the Lord

Photo by Rischgitz

From the painting by Briton Riviere, R.A.

The king of Persia made Daniel a high official, and the other nobles became very jealous. Because he prayed to God and not to the king, they had him thrown into a den of lions. But the Lord took care of His servant, and the next day Daniel was found to be without so much as a scratch, and the king freed him.

Photo by National Gallery, Berlin

Amid such tragic scenes as this, during what is known as the Great Exile, King Nebuchadnezzar carried off the people of Judah into captivity in far-off Babylon, by whose rivers they sat down and wept when they "remembered Zion," the beautiful city of Jerusalem which the Babylonian ruler had razed to the ground.

thousands of its people had been carried away into the bitterness of exile.

In the years which follow we see the two little kingdoms, menaced by constant dangers, and the prophets still exhorting them. During these years, too, the Jews were travelling to far-off lands, to Egypt, Greece and Syria, establishing colonies and carrying on trade. If some fell away from the worship of Yahweh, others remained faithful, so carrying on the traditions of their race.

The Babylonian Captivity

And then (586 B.C.) came the destruction of Jerusalem. A third of the Jews, including the best craftsmen and thinkers, were taken by the Chaldean king, Nebuchadnezzar, to Babylon. Another third emigrated to Egypt, and the starved remnant was left to weep over the ruined cities and the broken walls of their national home. This was the Great Exile, which still lives in Jewish song and

story. For Palestine and for the Jews nothing has ever been quite the same.

Yet it is not the end of the story of the Jews in Palestine. Many sturdy peasants must have stayed on in the country, and other Jews came back as time went on. How Nehemiah (nē′hě-mī′à) rebuilt the walls of Jerusalem, and how these exiles flowed slowly back into Palestine, are stories too long to tell. But gradually Jerusalem and Samaria were rebuilt and the Jews had once more a national home.

Towards the close of the fourth century B.C. there flashed a meteor across the world's sky. Alexander the Great conquered Palestine along with the rest of the Persian Empire. After his death in 323 B.C. its rule was disputed by two of his heirs— Ptolemy (tŏl′ě-mǐ) in Egypt and Seleucus (sě-lū′kŭs) in Asia Minor. At first Palestine was an Egyptian province. Many battles raged over the prostrate land, but finally (198 B.C.) the heirs of Seleucus were successful.

That was a time when Greek manners, Greek ideas, even Greek religious customs, were widespread among the Jews. Not in Palestine only, but in Egypt, in Damascus, in far-away Rome, the Greek worship of beauty and of things of the mind won Jewish followers. It was not the beauty-worship and great thoughts of the true Greeks that were the " abomination of desolation" told of in the book of Daniel. These evils came when Antiochus IV (ăn-tī'ŏ-kŭs), the Syrian king of Palestine, who declared himself a believer in the Greek religion, looted the rebuilt Temple at Jerusalem (168 B.C.), poured out the forbidden swine's blood on the altar, and harshly forbade the ancient Jewish worship. This indeed must have seemed like the end.

But again a leader arose—Mattathias (măt'ă-thī'ăs), an aged priest of Modin (mō'dĭn), a little town north of Jerusalem. Mattathias killed the Syrian officer in charge of the Greek religious rites, together with a cowardly Jew he was about to sacrifice on the Greek altar. Then Mattathias with his five sons—the Maccabees (măk'ă-bē)— escaped to the hills, where they raised a revolution which baffled the mighty but distracted Syrian power. Exactly three years after the Temple had been defiled,

it was cleansed and dedicated again to the worship of Yahweh.

But in the struggle that went on after this, the Maccabees called for aid from the rising power of Rome—and this was to be the last of the world-conquering nations that descended on Palestine in ancient times. Finally, in 64 B.C., Rome the Invincible, represented by the ambitious general Pompey (pŏm'pĭ), besieged Jerusalem, and carried the last barrier on a Sabbath, when the Jews, occupied with their devotions, refused to offer armed resistance. The priests were slain at the very altars, and twelve thousand Jews died in the massacre. Never since that day has there been an independent Jewish state in Palestine — at least not until within the past few years.

After the long sad years of captivity in Babylon, the Hebrews were allowed to return to Jerusalem; and under the leadership of the dauntless Nehemiah, they set about the task of rebuilding the city walls.

But the Jews were already citizens of the world. Their law, in Hebrew, or translated into Greek, was read wherever they congregated, and nearly every good-sized town in any land had its synagogue. Jewish writers, philosophers, and merchants were everywhere prominent. If the little mother country had been stronger—strong enough to keep all her citizens at home—the influence of her culture might have been less widespread. Already the Jews were a moral and intellectual leaven throughout the world.

(CONTINUED ON PAGE 429)

An IMP *Among the* NOVELISTS

The Whimsies of Laurence Sterne are Perhaps the Most Comical That We Can Find in Printed Form

(CONTINUED FROM PAGE 374)

IN ENGLISH literature there are on the one hand many writers who seem each to have a definite rank and whose positions change only as some critic re-interprets the whole range of literature; and on the other there are a few writers who seem to stand outside the main stream, never valued with abiding sureness and always defying critics to produce a measure of their achievements.

Of the second class is Laurence Sterne, the strange Irish clergyman who never published a word until he was more than forty-five years old, and then heard himself hailed as one of the greatest comic geniuses that England had ever known. Even to-day, over one hundred and seventy years after the appearance of "Tristram Shandy," he is still the subject of widely different estimates. To some he is without a superior; to others

Photo by National Portrait Gallery

This strange but intelligent face belongs to Laurence Sterne, the Irish clergyman who wrote some of our most amusing novels.

he is merely dull and affected; there are those who frown on much of his humour; and others, again, who see him as no more than an amusing freak. But—and this is the final test—thousands still read his books and argue about him. His works are read to-day, which is more than can be said of most of the writers of his time.

Sterne's life was almost as fantastic as his books. Born in Ireland, at Clonmel, on November 24, 1713, he spent his first eleven years travelling wherever his father's military duties led, and consequently he had no regular education until at the age of eleven he was sent to Halifax grammar school. Seven years later he went to Cambridge, where he took his B.A., and on leaving the university he was ordained, and was given the living of Sutton-in-the-Forest. He also became a prebendary of York.

For nineteen years he lived in uneventful obscurity with his wife, whom he married in 1741, and, later, their daughter Lydia; and then in 1759, when Sterne was approaching his forty-sixth birthday, a York bookseller published "The Life and Opinions of Tristram Shandy, Gentleman," volumes I and II. In the next year Sterne came to London, had the book published there, and experienced immediate and emphatic success.

With amazing suddenness the middle-aged Irish clergyman of a Yorkshire village found himself commanding the respect of the great men and women of his time—one of the oddest Cinderellas in the history of literature. Seven more volumes of "Tristram Shandy" were received with acclamation, and in 1768 Sterne published "The Sentimental Journey," an account of his travels in France and Italy during 1765. His health, however, which had never been good, had now broken beyond repair, and in March, 1768, he died.

As a writer Sterne is one of the greatest of the splendid line of masters in each phase of comedy that Ireland has produced, a line that includes Jonathan Swift, Farquhar, Sheridan, Wilde, George Bernard Shaw and Sean O'Casey. His style, like his books, is unique and eccentric; he delights to bury a tiny triviality under a tumbling mass of fantastic phrases and sentences; the thread of his story zigzags in every direction, and misses no opportunity of a wild-goose chase; and his original and subtle humour pirouettes delicately through an endless and brilliant stream of words. Whimsical, at times sentimental and over-sweet—perhaps mad!—Sterne yet produced half a dozen great characters, in particular Uncle Toby, who, besides being exquisitely comic, can, like the immortal Don Quixote, win from us a deep and lasting affection.

Perhaps you will find the long sentences or the complicated style rather difficult. If that is so it is best to put Sterne back on the shelf for a year or two. Sooner or later you will catch the infectious spirit of him, and then you may well pay tribute to this strange genius in his own words:

> Every time a man smiles—but much more so, when he laughs it adds something to this Fragment of Life.

The FIRST GREAT NOVELS of the SEA

They Were from the Pen of Tobias Smollett and They Helped to Better the Conditions Under Which Sailors of the British Navy Served

VERY different from Sterne, and yet deriving something from him, was Tobias George Smollett, who was born at Dalquhurn, Dumbartonshire, in 1721. Most of his writings were sombre, rather coarse criticisms of some evil which had roused his wrath, and indeed he himself was a man who went through life with a grievance.

He was easily irritated by misfortune, and unluckily his life seemed to contain one misfortune after another. Smollett's father had died when he was very young, and he was brought up by his grandfather, who himself died when the boy was growing up. Young Tobias, who had been educated for a learned profession, was apprenticed to a Glasgow surgeon for five years, a "deception" which early embittered him.

Unfortunately, a far greater disappointment lay in store for him. He wrote a

Photo by National Portrait Gallery

Tobias George Smollett was a bitter, complaining man, but he left us some brave tales of life aboard ship, the first sea novels in our language.

play, "The Regicide," which he always considered as a great work, and brought it across the Border to England, but no one would produce it, and this remained a life-long grievance. His failure not only enraged the quick-tempered author, but led to his being so reduced financially that he had to accept a position which a friend obtained for him, as surgeon's mate on board the "Cumberland."

While serving on this ship he took part in the ridiculous War of Jenkins's Ear, against Spain, thereby gaining experience of the sea and knowledge of sailors and the appalling conditions under which these men lived. All this he later put into his books, and indeed some scenes in "Roderick Random" led to certain reforms being effected in the navy.

Having returned to England, Smollett married and set up as a surgeon in London, but here again fate was against him. He failed in his profession, and, disappointed in his wife's dowry, he decided to turn his attention entirely to writing. He did a good deal of writing of one sort or another for booksellers, including a complete history of England; and also acted as a sort of literary manager, employing large numbers of minor authors, paying them not too liberally, but feasting them on Sundays with dinners consisting of beef and pudding.

Stories Full of Incident

But it is by his novels that Smollett is remembered. In 1748 appeared "The Adventures of Roderick Random," which was followed in 1751 by "The Adventures of Peregrine Pickle," and, two years later, "Ferdinand Count Fathom."

A great deal in these books was very brutal and coarse, but it must be remembered that the world to Smollett was not a very pleasant place, and he painted the life around him as he saw it, and painted it with fine descriptive skill. On the other hand, he possessed the power of invention, and his stories abound in incident.

Towards the end of his life Smollett suffered much physical pain in one form or another, and lived for some time abroad, but during a partial recovery he wrote "The Expedition of Humphrey Clinker," which is not only his greatest novel but his most pleasant. By this time he had read Laurence Sterne, and his work henceforth contained far more genuine humour and far less brutality. He died in 1771, after a long period of ill-health; and it is good to remember that he wrote in a more kindly vein towards the end.

His Place in Literature

The name of Smollett is usually associated with that of Richardson and Fielding among eighteenth-century novelists, but his work is generally regarded as inferior to theirs. He learned something from them both, as he did from Sterne and a French writer, le Sage, whom he admitted to copying at one time; but at his best he was distinctly himself, and in this way he can claim a place in the history of literature among the more important English novelists.

Edward Gibbon, the great historian, who told us the story of the decline and fall of the Roman Empire.

Photo by National Portrait Gallery

The GREATEST ENGLISH HISTORIAN

Even if We Have Discovered Many Things That Gibbon Never Knew, His Story of Rome Remains a Masterpiece among Histories

ONE day in the autumn of 1764 a young Englishman named Edward Gibbon found himself in Rome and sat "musing amidst the ruins of the Capitol, where the barefooted friars were singing vespers in the Temple of Jupiter." As he dreamed of the glory that had once been Rome and of the ruin into which the proud empire had fallen, "the idea of writing the decline and fall of the city first started" in his mind.

It continued to be the ruling idea in his mind for twenty-three years—until that night in June of 1787 when he completed the last volume of the history that has made him famous. This work, called "The Decline and Fall of the Roman Empire," still ranks as perhaps the greatest history of all time.

Young Gibbon's "Degree of Ignorance"

Edward Gibbon was born at Putney on April 27, 1737. He had poor health, and often had to stay away from school, but he made great progress while he was there, for he was a most studious boy. He says that when he entered Oxford at fifteen, he went up "with a stock of information which might have puzzled a doctor, and a degree of

ignorance of which a schoolboy might have been ashamed."

He always thought his time at Oxford had been wasted, and yet it was at Oxford that he acquired his first real taste for history, and especially for the history of Rome. After fourteen months at college, he managed to get expelled because he declared his belief in the Roman Catholic faith.

A Hard Worker and Deep Thinker

Then his father put him under a Protestant tutor at Lausanne, in Switzerland, and eighteen months later the boy returned to the Protestant faith. From that time on, he spent his time in studying, writing, travelling, and mingling in the social and club life of his time. An unusually plain man, rather given to overdressing and affectation, he was not always popular. But he put so much hard work and so much deep thought into his great history that the world has long since forgiven every fault he possessed in gratitude for the masterpiece he left it.

Hardly any other history is at once so full and true in fact, and so beautiful in literary style. Gibbon's autobiography is also still read. He died in London on January 16, 1794.

405

The SUPREME ORATOR in OUR LANGUAGE

Edmund Burke, Friend of India and America, Has Left Us Speeches That are Read and Admired to this Day

IRELAND must surely have given us more orators than any other nation of its size in the modern world. And Edmund Burke was born in Ireland, in 1729.

He was born into the golden age of British oratory. Never before, and never since, has the House of Commons listened to such masterpieces of eloquence as in his time. From the lips of men like Pitt and Fox and Sheridan fell speeches that were sometimes so dazzling that the reporters were too entranced to be able to take them down. But from the lips of Burke came the finest speeches of all—for, even if they may not have sounded so as he spoke them, they read as the greatest on the printed page to-day. They stamp Burke as our supreme orator.

Oratory is just one form of prose. And because he is our supreme orator, Burke is often said to have given us the greatest prose in all the English language.

A Leading Light of Dr. Johnson's Famous Literary Club

He first went to a Quaker school at Ballitore, county Kildare, and then to Trinity College, Dublin. From there he came to London to study law; he probably mixed with the "bohemian" society of the day, and had ample opportunity for practising the art of oratory; but he wanted far more to be an author than a lawyer, and when this came to the knowledge of his practical father he stopped his son's allowance. There followed a period in Burke's life about which we know very little. He travelled a great deal, and wanted to go to America. He married, and he wrote two books which gave him prominence after 1756. So he came to know many of the great men of his day, among them being the great Dr. Johnson and the members of his famous club. In that club Burke was always a leading light.

He had found his way into politics, first as a secretary and then as a member of Parliament. There he was to spend the rest of his illustrious career. He knew a good deal more than anyone else about the vexing problems that came before the House and he spoke about them far more ably. He astonished Parliament with his knowledge as well as with his eloquence on all the principal questions of the day. Of these there were very many; but the three causes to which he gave chief attention were those relating to America, to India, and to France.

A Loyal Friend of the People Who Strove to Maintain Peace

In the American Revolution Burke was always on the side of the colonists. He protested against the Stamp Act, and against every other effort to oppress the people in America; and he strove hard, though in vain, to keep the peace between the mother country and her colonies. It is well to remember what he said: "Show the thing you contend for to be reason; show it to be common sense; show it to be the means of attaining some useful end."

In the affairs of India Burke took even a firmer stand, and his speech at the opening of the trial of Warren Hastings, the first governor-general of India, who was accused of cruelty to the natives and corruption, is ranked among the greatest pieces of oratory that will endure for all time.

When the French Revolution broke out, it seemed to Burke that the world as he had known it was falling to pieces—as indeed it was, for a time at least. It stirred him to a raging eloquence, a very torrent of oratory, for the world as he had always known it. But this was a lost cause, like most of Burke's great causes. The French Revolution, in spite of all its sins and horrors, was finally going to establish a new régime in France; but Burke could not know this. He could see only the horror that came in the beginning. He died, in 1797, before the dawn of the better day of freedom.

(CONTINUED ON PAGE 505)

Here is a collection of brightly coloured moths. From left to right, beginning at the top of the page, they are *Automeris euryopa*, *Erateina staudingeri*, *Polythysania edmondsii*, *Altha ansorgei*, *Carthaea saturnioides* (centre), *Nevrina procopia*, *Campylotes splendida* (below centre), *Agarista agricola*, and *Cocytia durvillii*.

This old wise doctor is not very well pleased with the behaviour of his crickets. They are crossing antennae, and he wonders if they are saying things in a language he cannot understand.

INSECT FIDDLERS

Little Musicians That Make Merry All Day Long or Sing upon the Hearth at Night

(CONTINUED FROM PAGE 345)

INSECTS may be small creatures but they often make a surprisingly big noise in their own little world.

During the hot days of summer and early autumn we hear them cheerily humming and buzzing, chirping and drumming up and down the countryside. Bees, flies, and beetles all help to swell the merry chorus of busy little creatures rejoicing in the warmth and brightness of the sunny hours. Loud above them all rings the shrill chirping of the grasshoppers and crickets, for these long-legged, acrobatic insects are the most famous musicians of the insect world. All through the day, and through the night as well, the lusty fiddlers keep the concert going.

How Insects Make Their Music

Now, although it seems a strange thing to say, all these noisy insects are really dumb. They do not "sing," for no insect is able to make sounds in its mouth or throat. Locusts, grasshoppers, and their nearest relatives are not choristers but orchestral performers, and their musical instruments are their long hind legs and their stiff wing-cases. Crickets and long-horn grasshoppers perform by raising their wing-cases and rubbing them briskly together. One wing-case has a sharp edge, while the other is like a file; and with this arrangement the little musicians are able to produce a very shrill kind of chirping note.

Playing on a Row of Knobs

The short-horn grasshopper has a more complex instrument of music. On the broad, flat thigh of his long hind leg he has a row of small knobs, like a row of beads. When he is in the mood for a little music, he draws his leg rapidly backwards and forwards across the rough edge of his wing-case, just as if he were playing a fiddle. Only the male insects are gifted in this way; the females

How long do you suppose it would take you to guess that the spot to which the arrow is pointing on this enlargement of a cricket's leg, is really the insect's ear?

have no musical instruments. But they seem greatly to admire the chirping of their mates, who never tire of showing off to attract their attention.

Musical insects have more than one accomplishment. They are the champion long jumpers of the insect world. If we could leap as far, in proportion to our size, as some of the locusts and grasshoppers, we should need no motor-cars or aeroplanes to take us about the country. In a few hops we could cover the ground as quickly as Hop-o'-My-Thumb in his seven-league boots, and be able to bound over trees and buildings with the greatest possible ease.

Most chirping and leaping insects have wonderful flying wings. They are semi-circular in shape, and open and close like a fan. When not in use they lie neatly folded in long, straight pleats under the protecting fore wings, which are much less delicate in texture.

Beautiful Flying Wings

Many of the flying wings are most beautifully coloured and marked in all sorts of startling ways. But the fore wings are less remarkable. They are usually of some shade of green or brown which tones so well with the colour of the soil or foliage on which the insects rest that it is by no means easy to see the cunning little creatures until

they betray themselves by taking a sudden flying leap into the air. Even their shrill chirping does not always give them away, for a cricket or a grasshopper is a clever ventriloquist. He can throw his "voice" in all sorts of directions, and it is often quite a puzzle to tell exactly from whence the queer sound is coming.

The American Locusts

The American locust is a fine fellow, fully three inches long from head to tail, with a reddish-brown body, marked with a yellow stripe all along its back, and clear, transparent hind wings. It sometimes makes itself very troublesome by devouring the crops, but it is not nearly so bad as its terrible cousin, the "migrating locust," of whose destructive ways we shall learn later on. The Carolina locust is another species common all over the United States and Canada. It is nearly two inches long, pale yellowish or reddish brown in colour, and has handsome black flying wings with a broad yellow border ornamented with clusters of

Here is the green locust. Can you make out his musical box, which he always carries about on his back and loves to play on warm summer afternoons? To create its far-reaching sounds he lifts one of his wings just a trifle and vibrates it rapidly against the other.

dusky spots. This locust is fond of hovering in the air a few feet above the ground and making a loud "clacking" noise by scraping the edges of its wing-cases to and fro across the stiff edges of the hind wings.

The coral-winged locust, or "king grass-

hopper," as it is often called, makes a loud, rattling sound with its wings as it flies. It is quite common in the Mississippi Valley, and is a very fine insect indeed, with its bright coral-red wings that gleam splendidly when the light shines through them as the insect is in flight.

He has a knowing look, this grasshopper who is our well-known friend of lawn and field.

Insects, like children, outgrow their clothes. The grasshopper has five different suits in the course of a lifetime. Here are the four old garments that one of them has had to shed.

Other handsome locusts have clear yellow wings, or red and yellow wings with black or dusky marks and borders. But there are a host of dull little grasshoppers all up and down the country who are not so fond of flying and leaping as their more gaily coloured cousins. "Safety first" is their motto. So they hide themselves as much as possible and are never known to show off.

Non-flying Grasshoppers

The short-winged grasshopper of England is more often heard than seen. Being incapable of flight it spends most of its time tumbling and dodging about among tall grasses, where its natural enemies, the birds, cannot easily distinguish its small green body and odd, sharply pointed little face. Other small grasshoppers, less than an inch long, hop and skip about in swampy meadows and on heaths and moors, where their tiny dark bodies are practically invisible among the colours of their natural surroundings.

The Locust Beau Brummel

The most gorgeous as well as the most extraordinary locusts are to be found living in hot countries. Even the tropical butterflies are rivalled by a big South American locust whose body is decked out in light green splashed with black. His wing-cases are pink laced with black, and his flying wings are a blazing scarlet with black borders. As he hurls himself through the air he looks very much like a flower that has taken leave of its stem.

Some of the South African locusts wear a kind of spiked helmet, all covered with spines and prickles; and the head of a tiny Indian species is covered by a huge peaked cap. Strangest of all, perhaps, is a large South African locust that looks exactly as if she were made up for a fancy-dress ball. We say "she" because it is the lady locust which is dressed in this way: her mate is more modestly attired in plain green. The general colouring of this strange insect is a bright apple green, relieved with silvery-white stripes and splashes edged with bright magenta. She has magenta patches on her face, as well as a large number of small white lumps, like tiny pearl beads, each encircled by a mauve ring. Surely if this lady attended a grasshoppers' ball she would be awarded a prize for her startling fancy costume!

Locusts and short-horned grasshoppers belong to the same family, the large ones usually being called locusts. The locust family always have short, stout feelers, while true grasshoppers and crickets have long, wavy ones, often like fine silken threads.

Queer Places for Ears

Grasshoppers, both short-horned and long-horned, do not go through the same wonderful changes as butterflies, bees, beetles and flies. Young grasshoppers are never grubs or chrysalises. When they break through their egg-shells and come out into the big world for the first time, the young are already very much like their parents; but they have no wings. Although they can

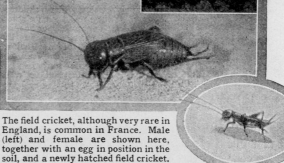

hop and skip about and munch green food with their tiny jaws, they can neither fly nor chirp. But they can listen to the music of their elders, for locusts and grasshoppers can hear very well, though their ears are in the most unusual places, where you would never expect to find them. Locusts have ears on their backs, and long-horned grasshoppers and crickets have ears on their front pair of legs, just below the knee-joint.

The young insects change their skin several times while they are growing up. Then, after the last change, their wings appear in

The field cricket, although very rare in England, is common in France. Male (left) and female are shown here, together with an egg in position in the soil, and a newly hatched field cricket. The two last are much enlarged.

all their splendour; at last they are able to fly and join in the concerts.

The crickets, as a rule, are rather dull-looking insects. The tree crickets are a pale green, but house crickets and field crickets generally have black or brown wing-cases which bend over at the side when closed and cover them like the lid of a box. They have bright eyes and their loud voices are heard chiefly at night. For crickets are shy insects and seldom stir from their homes in the day-time—though the field cricket is fond of sitting just inside the doorway of his underground living-room and chirping away through the warm summer days.

The Cricket on the Hearth

House crickets take up their abode in our dwellings, where they hide away behind stoves and hot-water pipes in the day and come out with a song when it is about time to go to bed.

The mole cricket is quite unlike the other members of the cricket family. He is a large insect, about two inches long, with a broad flat back, and is dressed in a suit of velvety brown. We do not often see him, for, like his namesake the mole, he spends his days below ground; although he often comes up in the evening to sit at the mouth of his burrow and chirp in the true cricket style.

The mole cricket has not such long hind legs as the crickets that live in the upper world, and he crawls about instead of leaping; but he has very sturdy front legs, and his fore-feet, which are shaped like tiny hands,

The lady tree cricket, on the right, is being courted. Her lover, with wings erect, is singing to her in his loudest tones—and they are very loud indeed—while she is listening to him with the ears on her legs.

are armed with sharp claws. This strange cricket lives in damp places where the ground is soft and easy to burrow. He digs his way with his sharp, strong claws through the soil, just as a mole does, throwing up a little ridge of earth as he goes along hunting for earthworms, grubs and the tender roots of plants.

Mrs. Mole Cricket is a good mother. She lays a few hundred eggs in a cosy underground nursery and guards them until her babies hatch out. Even then she stays with her young and feeds them until they have safely shed their first suit of clothes. Then she evidently considers that the children are old enough to look after themselves. The youngsters stray away, and each little mole cricket sets to work to dig a tiny burrow in the ground for itself.

Wings of the Grasshoppers

Grasshoppers are much brighter-looking insects than the sad-coloured crickets. Some have narrow wings and some have broad wings; but they are nearly always of a pretty shade of green or yellow which blends with the leaves and grasses to which the insects cling, and which shields them from the sharp eyes of the insect-eating birds that are constantly on the look out for them.

The wing-cases of great green grasshoppers are so wonderfully like leaves in shape and colour and marking that it is almost impossible to find the insects as they rest among the leaves on bushes and trees. Their hind wings are always clear and delicate. Some of the grasshoppers in tropical lands have pale blue, rosy pink, or bright yellow wings, with a dark brown border. When they are spread out ready for flight such wings look for all the world like pleated dancing skirts.

Insects That Dress Like Flowers

Brighter still are the wings of the strange insects called mantids that live in the jungles of India and in the East Indies. They are so beautifully coloured that they look like flowers as they sway gently in the breeze, clinging to the dark green foliage of the tropical creeping plants. Some are so like rare and beautiful orchids that travellers have actually tried to "pick" them before finding out their mistake.

Other mantids resemble green leaves, or brown and withered ones. To heighten the deception, they have on their legs strange outgrowths that look like fragments of crumpled leaves. Others, again, are so long and thin and brown that they might easily

411

pass for dry twigs. So eager are these insects to escape notice that nearly all of them are fashioned to imitate their surroundings as closely as possible. No matter where they live—in clusters of flowers, among thick foliage, on the bark of trees, or upon tall grasses—the mantids imitate their homes and vary in shape and colour the better to deceive their unwary victims.

A Strange-looking Insect

There is probably no more extraordinary-looking creature or more cunning actor in the whole of the insect world than a mantid, or mantis. The front half of its body is so long and thin that it looks like the neck of a giraffe. It has a queer hammer-shaped head, a triangular face, and absurd bulging eyes. Its two hind pairs of legs are long and spidery, but the front legs are enormous and are always kept doubled up when the

the innocent little insect it would appear to be. Its long forelegs are really horrible traps. The second and third joints have sharp, jagged edges and can be snapped together like the blade and handle of a pocket-knife.

As it rests so quietly, half hidden by the foliage, its queer goggling eyes turn this way and that, watching for some unsuspecting insect to settle near by. Then, slowly and stealthily, like a cat stalking a bird, the cunning mantis creeps up. Out shoots one of those terrible legs, closing with a snap upon its prey, and the poor victim is carried kicking and struggling to the mouth of its captor, who calmly proceeds to bite pieces out of it as if it were a biscuit.

Mantids seem to take a positive delight in their cruel sport. They will go on killing one insect after another, taking a few hasty bites out of the victims, and then dropping them on the ground. They are quarrelsome, too. If two of the creatures happen to meet they are almost sure to start fighting. They lash out viciously with their deadly legs and try their best to cut each other's heads off; and when one succeeds in conquering the other, it at once makes a meal of its vanquished enemy.

The great green grasshopper is the largest of all the British species. It is only to be found along the south coast of England.

insect is sitting down or moving about. It holds them up as if they were arms.

Hour after hour the mantis will sit perfectly still, with its big "neck" raised and its great forelegs held up before its face in an imploring attitude—as if it were trying to say, "Please don't hurt me; I am only a poor, harmless creature."

But the mantis is a humbug. It is not

The lady mantis is just as savage in her ways. She is bigger than her mate, and if she is annoyed with him, she is as likely as not to kill him and eat him on the spot.

One of the most famous of these uncanny insects is the praying mantis of Southern Europe—rather a dull-looking creature about two inches long. In olden days, before its real character was discovered, people be-

By courtesy of the Victoria and Albert Museum

lieved it to be a saintly and highly gifted little creature. When it folded its forelegs it was supposed to be praying; and

If you have ever read Dickens's story of "The Cricket on the Hearth," you will know how faithful the little fellow in the oval can be at cheering an English fireside with his hearty song.

an old monkish legend tells us how the quaint insect sang hymns when ordered to do so by St. Francis Xavier.

The Greeks called it the "diviner," and believed that it could foretell coming events, while the peasant people in many countries declared that if a lost child asked a mantis to tell him the way home, it would raise one of its fore-feet and point out the right direction for him to take.

Live Walking Sticks

Mantids are mostly found in hot countries, where they may sometimes be seen standing motionless in the corner of a window-pane, keeping a hopeful eye fixed on the clumsy antics of a buzzing blue-bottle.

Quite as strange as the mantis, although not quite so barbarous, are the leaf insects and the stick insects—or "walking sticks" as they are often called.

The Mysterious Magical Leaves

Leaf insects are natives of India and other countries in the Far East. They are so amazingly like the leaves on the trees and bushes on which they live and feed that the natives of East India firmly believe they are really leaves which in some magical way have grown heads and legs.

The great green leaf insect is very broad and flat, and in shape and colour is exactly like a large green leaf. Even the markings on its wing-cases imitate the veining of a leaf, while its legs might be small leaflets or broken pieces of leaves arranged round its sides. It is a slow-going, sleepy sort of creature, spending its days peacefully munching the leaves around it and seldom wandering far from home. It never kills and eats other insects—as do the mantids—or interferes in any way with its neighbours. Yet, strange to say, if two leaf insects are shut up in a box together without any real leaves on which to feed, they will often absent-mindedly nibble pieces out of each other's legs and wing-cases instead.

Other leaf insects are brown instead of green, and look crumpled and withered like the dead and dying leaves all about them on the trees. Unless you happened to see one of these leaf actors taking a sly bite at the dry foliage, you would surely never guess that the leaf-like thing was an insect.

While the leaf insects are broad and flat, their cousins, the stick insects, are long and thin—so thin sometimes, poor things, that they seem to be nothing more than skeletons.

Nature's Greatest Mimics

These odd creatures are the most famous actors of the insect world. They mimic sticks and plant stems and twigs in the most extraordinary manner. Those that imitate twigs are bent and twisted just like real twigs; some even appear to have patches of mould or tufts of moss growing on them to make their resemblance to dead twigs

more perfect. Others that live on thorny plants are covered with spikes and prickles.

All the stick insects are timid. They do their very best to escape notice by assuming rigid attitudes and keeping perfectly still from morning until night. But when daylight dies, the sham sticks and twigs suddenly come to life—as if they were enchanted creatures released from a magic spell by the setting of the sun. With slow and cautious footsteps they move like spectres about the trees and bushes, hastily nibbling at the leaves as they go. The poor things are very hungry. And no wonder! They seldom dare to feed in the day-time for fear someone should discover what impostors they are. So they make the most of the hours of darkness to eat all they can, but at sunrise back they all turn to sticks and twigs again.

Most of these strange insects live in hot, tropical lands. In the patches of long grass that are found here and there in the great African forests, you may find the cunning grass-stalk insects. That is to say, you may find them if you can. For although there may be one of them on every other grass stalk, very few travellers in the grassy jungles are sharp enough to discover them. They are so exactly like wisps of dried-up grass that you might take one up in your hand, twist and turn it about, and then throw it away without ever knowing that

Photo by F. Martin Duncan

This is really and truly an insect, one of the many that dress themselves up to look like a leaf.

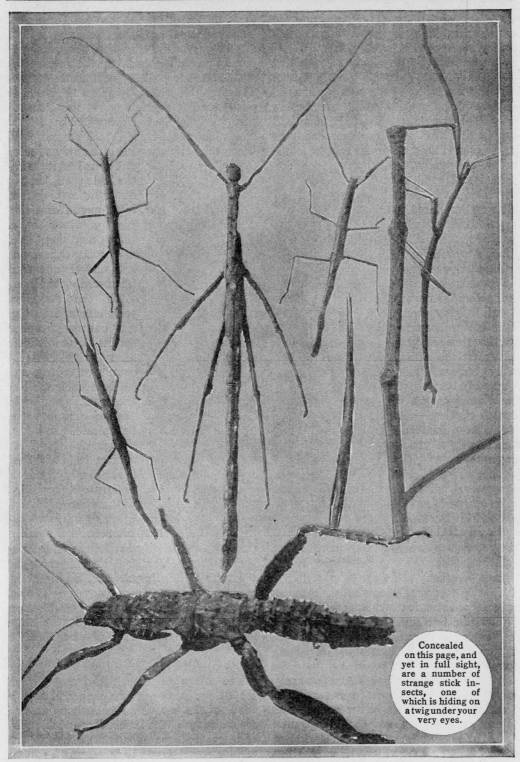

Concealed on this page, and yet in full sight, are a number of strange stick insects, one of which is hiding on a twig under your very eyes.

Photo by F. Martin Duncan

415

it was an insect. The cunning creature will keep perfectly still and never betray itself by moving so much as a leg or feeler.

The favourite pastime of this stick insect is to clasp a tall grass stalk as if it were climbing up a pole—its fore-legs stretched straight out in front of it to form an unbroken line. The four back legs stand out at odd angles, like forks from the grass, and the insect's broad head passes for a knob in the stem. Actually the animal stalk and the vegetable stalk are so alike and so mixed up together that you must be clever indeed to tell which is which.

Another strange thing about these insect actors is the way in which they change their colour according to the time of year. Just after the African rainy season, fresh blades of vividly green grass spring up on the forest clearings—and then all the grass-stalk insects will be vividly green to match. But the hot sun soon dries the grasses and turns them yellow; so the grass-stalk insects turn yellow, too. Later on the grasses are tinged with autumn tints of gold and brown and red; and the insects change to exactly the same colours.

That insects should change their toilets to suit an occasion at first seems most mysterious; but since the queer creatures feed entirely on grasses, it may be that the colour of their food causes the surprising transformation.

In Australia and in South America many stick insects grow to an enormous size. Some are eight or nine inches long and as thick as a man's thumb. Such gigantic "walking sticks" often do a great deal of harm in the Australian forests, where they sometimes strip the gum trees of nearly all

The familiar cockroach is not really a British insect, but was introduced into England many years ago by shipping from the East. This is a larger species—the cosmopolitan cockroach—which was a native of America, but has now spread all over the world.

their foliage. Only a few of the smaller kinds are found in North America; they live mostly on walnut trees and oak trees, and usually pass unnoticed. In the autumn the stick insects drop their eggs upon the ground. The tiny things look just like the seeds of plants, and few people would suspect what they really are. Each egg is like a little box with a close-fitting lid at one end. When the baby stick insect is ready to come out of its box, it pushes the lid open, and a queer little thing that looks more like a tiny piece of black thread than anything else, makes its appearance and staggers about on its absurdly thin legs.

All the American stick insects are wingless, but many tropical species have delicate gauzy wings and fly from tree to tree late in the evening. When the insect is resting in the day-time its wings lie pleated in long straight folds so close against its body that they hardly make a difference in the outline of the "walking stick." These wings are not protected by wing-cases as are the wings of locusts and grasshoppers, for a stick insect's wing-cases are too small to be of much use. However, the outer fold of the flying wings is stiff and strong, and when the wing is closed, covers the more delicate folds, just in the same manner as the outer stick of a fan does.

Classed by Their Wings

The wings of the stick insects—when they have any—are fan-shaped like the wings of the locusts and grasshoppers. So are the wings of the leaf insects and mantids, and for that reason all these insects are classed together. They form a group known as the "straight-winged" insects.

Those unpopular insects, the cockroach and the earwig, are straight-winged insects, too. No one has a good word to say for the cockroach; it really is a most unpleasant creature. As if it knew how much it is disliked, it scuttles away on its long legs in a tremendous hurry whenever it sees anyone coming, and hides its ugly head in the first dark hole or corner it can find. The cockroach is often called a "black beetle." But this is quite wrong. The insect is not a beetle at all, and it is not black, but a dark reddish brown. Although it is such a dingy-looking creature, the common cockroach has some aristocratic cousins living in eastern lands. They are really handsome. They are always dressed in velvety black coats ornamented with large creamy spots or broad orange bands, while a few tropical cockroaches are a pretty pale green.

The earwig is certainly not an attractive insect, but it is quite harmless, and is not so eager to crawl into our ears as some people suppose. The fact is that the ugly little creature very much dislikes the light, and if by chance it finds itself abroad while the sun is shining, it will hurriedly squeeze into any dark hole or crack that is handy—but this hiding-place seldom happens to be a human ear.

What His Pincers Are For

The large, somewhat alarming pincers at the tail end of the earwig's body are no doubt useful in persuading other creatures to treat it with proper respect. But although they are capable of giving a fairly sharp nip, they are chiefly used for packing away the earwig's delicate hind wings underneath its very stout wing-cases. The hind wings are so large that after they are folded length-wise the earwig is obliged to double them up in order to make them fit as neatly as is possible under the other pair.

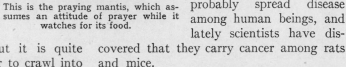

This is the praying mantis, which assumes an attitude of prayer while it watches for its food.

However much we may dislike earwigs we must admit that Mrs. Earwig is a good mother. Unlike almost all other insects, she guards her eggs until they are hatched, and for some time she takes care of the little earwigs like a fussy mother hen with a brood of young chicks.

Both cockroaches and earwigs feed on refuse, and the way to keep a house clear of them is to leave nothing about, even for a few moments, which is likely to tempt them; but it is hard to find anything in the shape of food that will not tempt cockroaches. They have been known to eat blacking and emery paper and other unlikely substances. Such palatable food as they do not eat they render unfit for anyone else by leaving upon it a disgusting odour that comes from a substance secreted by glands on their backs. They probably spread disease among human beings, and lately scientists have discovered that they carry cancer among rats and mice.

The earwig is hated by the gardener as much as the cockroach is by the housewife. For these hungry little creatures can make havoc of a bed of perfect blooms. They gnaw away at the petals with their sharp jaws, and in a very short time the beautiful blossom looks as though some mischievous imp had been at work with a destructive pair of scissors. Nasturtiums seem always to attract them, but especially are they fond of dahlias. If you ever wish to find an earwig, pick up some of the fallen apples or pears in your garden and look inside those which have been attacked by a bird or wasp. You will very likely find Mr. Earwig at home.

Many varieties of foreign cockroaches get introduced by shipping, one of the commonest—a beautiful pale green in colour—arrives in bananas. The American, Australian and Madeiran cockroaches are also frequently brought over in this way.

(CONTINUED ON PAGE 441)

1. Cut a strip of crêpe paper—white, red, pink, or yellow—2½″ wide and 24″ long. Fold it fanwise, making each fold 1½″ wide.

2. On the top fold trace with a pencil the shape of a typical rose petal; then cut with your scissors through all the folds along the traced lines.

3. Hold the tip of each petal between the thumb and forefinger of the left hand. Slowly draw the petal between the thumb of the right hand and the edge of a blunt knife, allowing the thumb to press the petal against the edge of the knife. Repeat this operation until the petal has the desired amount of curl. You had better practise this first on scraps of paper.

4. When your petals are all prettily curled—or, for that matter, when you have curled only four of them, if you prefer to do them a few at a time—you can begin to put your rose together. Spread paste on the uncurled lower end of the first four, and assemble them as in the picture above.

HOW TO MAKE A ROSE

Make a rose? Yes, of course you can. That is, you can make an imitation one that will look like a rose—at least at a distance. In fact, if you have the gift of neatness and patience, you can have a whole garden of delightful paper blossoms. And you will have gained by the way much knowledge of the different flowers. For the expert maker of paper flowers goes to nature for patterns. When that is impossible, however, you can find patterns in pictures, as in our story of flowers. As for material, you need wire, paste, scissors, and crêpe or plain glazed paper in many colours—the best effect is obtained by matching the colours of the real flower. Sometimes you can use odds and ends. A button covered with yellow plush forms a lifelike eye for the daisy—whose name means "day's eye"; coloured silk threads, waxed, make fine stamens; and some flowers, like the pansy, look better tinted with water colour. But now to our rose.

5. Continue building up your rose as described, four petals in each layer. Study the placing of the petals in a real rose, and place your paper petals so as to make them lifelike. Then at last—

6. The rose you have made is finished, except for leaves and stem.

11. Lastly assemble leaves, stem, and rose. Sew the rose to the eye at the end of the stem with a long needle and coarse thread. Make a calyx, or little leaf cup for its base, just as you made the leaves. You must try to imagine the perfume!

10. Next, the leaves. They are green glazed paper pasted on lighter green crêpe paper. Before pasting the layers together, insert a short piece of fine wire between them, allowing it to extend far enough to be fastened to the stem.

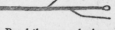

9. Bend the second wire out and continue wrapping to within ½″ of the end. Paste down the end of the paper so that it will not unwrap, and bend the end of the wire into an eye. The wires you left out will carry the leaves.

8. When you have securely wrapped about 4″ of the wire, bend one of the wires out and go on wrapping the remaining two or three for another 2″.

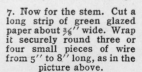

7. Now for the stem. Cut a long strip of green glazed paper about ⅜″ wide. Wrap it securely round three or four small pieces of wire from 5″ to 8″ long, as in the picture above.

This is the gallant Frenchman who helped to bring the Old World over to the New, and to lay the foundations of the splendid land that is now Canada.

The FOUNDER of QUEBEC

He was Samuel de Champlain, One of the Most Adventurous of All French Explorers of the New World

FROM early times the south-west part of France has been renowned for its men of action. There stands La Rochelle, a city whose people have withstood many a siege. There live the restless, talkative, hard-fighting Gascons. There dwelt the Santones, who centuries ago defied Julius Caesar. And from the land of the Santones, or Saintonge (săN'tŏNzh), as it is now called, came Samuel de Champlain (shăm-plăn'), one of the great French explorers and colonizers of America. His name is famous because he had the vision of a New France in the New World.

An Expedition to North America to Found a French Colony

Born in the tiny village of Brouage (broō-äzh') some time in 1567, Champlain sailed, when only a youth, to the Spanish settlements in America. This voyage made him eager to find lands and start colonies for his own country. He even had the idea that a canal ought to be dug at Panama, just about where it was actually built at the beginning of the present century. The French king was impressed by his good sense, and sent him, in 1603, to look for a place to plant a colony in North America. From then until his death in Quebec on

Christmas Day, 1635, Champlain was either busily exploring the New World or living in France and writing accounts of America. Crossing and recrossing the Atlantic many times, he divided his life between the Old World and the New.

On his first expedition Champlain sailed up the Saint Lawrence River as far as the Lachine Rapids, and went some fifty miles up the rushing Saguenay. The following year, at the mouth of a little stream in Nova Scotia, he helped to found the colony named Port Royal—now Annapolis—the first permanent settlement in New France. Still seeking other suitable places for settlement, during the next four years he explored the Bay of Fundy and the coast of New England from Maine as far south as Cape Cod. Meanwhile the settlers at Port Royal were growing ever more dissatisfied, so in 1607 Champlain took them back to France.

The Place Where "Nut-Trees" Grew

The next year he returned with other settlers to America. He sailed up the Saint Lawrence and dropped anchor on July 3 at "a place most proper for a habitation." "No other place," he wrote, "could be more excellent than this, nor better situated, for nut-trees abound here. The point is called

By this single shot from his arquebus, which killed three Iroquois chiefs, Champlain made the powerful Iroquois nation into lasting enemies of France. As a result England and her settlers became supreme in the New World.

Quebec by the Indians." Here Champlain led his followers ashore and started a settlement destined to become the capital of New France.

And now Champlain's activities began in earnest. Forming a league with the neighbouring Huron and Algonquin Indians in 1609, he started war against the Five Nations, a group of war-loving tribes led by the fierce Iroquois. This needless French hostility later caused the Iroquois to become allies of the Dutch and English colonists in their conflicts with New France. While on this expedition into the Iroquois country, Champlain discovered the beautiful lake which bears his name.

His next exploring trips led him into the west and north. In 1611 he established a trading post at Montreal, and in 1613 he sailed up the Ottawa River looking for "a great salt sea" of which he had heard. He returned in a roundabout way, touching the shores of Lakes Huron, Erie, and Ontario, and bringing back much valuable information.

The great western expedition completed, Champlain settled down in Quebec to live quietly and do what he could to promote the welfare of the struggling village. In 1629 the place was attacked by English ships and forced to surrender. Champlain himself was carried to London as a prisoner, but was later released and sent to Paris.

After three years the English gave Quebec back to the French, and at once Champlain set out for his colony with two hundred new settlers. He continued to work there for about two years, dying in 1635 in the prosperous village which he had founded.

SEEKING *a* SEA ROUTE *to* CHINA

While Making One of His Attempts to Find a Passage to the East Henry Hudson Discovered the Site on which New York Now Stands

HERE I am in England and I want to go to China. How in the world am I going to get there? The Turks have closed the only path I ever knew to the East, and now I cannot go that way and get all the silks and spices and precious stones that have always come from that part of the world. I must find another way. How can I go?

A Difficult Puzzle to Solve

That was the puzzle that faced Henry Hudson, the English navigator and explorer, three hundred years ago. He did not know very much about the map, of course. He knew the world was round, and therefore that he could reach China if he could only sail far enough east or far enough west. But if he went east he would have to sail round Africa by the Cape of Good Hope and face all sorts of dangers; and if he went west he must sail round South America by way of Cape Horn.

Could he sail round the north of Europe, and so find a north-east passage? No one had ever done it. Could he sail along the coast of North America? No one had ever done that either, and no one knew how much land or how much ice there would be to block either of these paths. Could he pass right across the North Pole? That would be the shortest way, but were the Polar regions ice-bound? Or could he find a way straight through North America? Nobody knew how wide America was, but perhaps he might be able to discover a water-way and sail across. At any rate, these were the only ways to China of

Aboard the gallant "Half Moon," the little boat in which white men first sailed up the Hudson River. The man on the right is Henry Hudson, the explorer, who made several gallant attempts to find a passage to the East, all of which ended unsuccessfully, but which nevertheless gave much new knowledge to the world.

Farmers such as these Henry Hudson saw along the river that now bears his name. When they wanted a good crop, they put a fish in each corn hill to fertilize the soil. And when they had gathered their grain the women pounded it into meal, as the girl is doing in the picture. Then they baked it without yeast into bread.

which he knew, and so he determined to try them all in turn.

He wanted to find a way to China, and the rich Muscovy Company in England provided the money for his voyage of discovery. He tried all the four ways, and although he never got to China, he found out a great many things in the attempt.

When he first set out, in 1607, he tried to sail across the North Pole. It looked fairly simple, on the map. But the great ice sheet prevented him from getting anywhere near the Pole, and it is a wonder that he ever got back to England alive. He was able to explore several islands on this trip, and he discovered that there were many whales around Spitsbergen.

Then he made another trip and tried to

The Indians had not yet learned to hate the white man when Hudson first landed in North America. This is an artist's impression of the welcome extended by the Indians to Hudson and his brave companions when they landed on North American soil.

go round the north of Europe. There the ice blocked him again. By now he had his own ideas about the way to go, and he started westwards towards America. The winds caught him and drove him out of his course, and he had to return home once more.

But the Muscovy Company were tired of finding money for him. Instead of spending any more time on Hudson, they went in for whaling, and out of that they grew very rich. Then some Dutch merchants sent for Hudson. Hudson told these men wonderful things about his voyages. He said that the way to China lay to the west, either round the north or straight through it somewhere near Virginia. But they ordered him to go round the north of Europe.

So Hudson set out in that direction once more, in 1609. He went in a tiny boat called the "Half Moon," and that boat is now nearly as famous as Hudson himself. It was because he sailed for the Dutch that we sometimes call him Hendrick Hudson, for Hendrick is the Dutch name for Henry.

Once again the ice blocked his passage round the north of Europe. Then he called his men together and offered them a choice. He told them that he intended to go west, and offered them the choice of two routes—one round the north of America and the other straight through the middle of it. His friend Captain John Smith had sent him some maps for that journey. Which way would they go?

They had had enough of icebergs, and they chose the second route.

There was a man on board, named Juet, who kept a log of the whole trip, and parts of it have come down to us. They tell us just what happened on the long voyage. The "Half Moon" lost her mast, and had to put into a bay in Maine to cut down another in the forest.

This is the last sad voyage of the great explorer who discovered the Hudson River. When he was trying to find a passage round the north of America, his rebellious crew set him adrift in this little boat to perish in the bay that bears his name. With him they put his young son and a few sick members of the crew.

One day a man in the crew got an Indian arrow in his throat and died. On September 3 the little ship put into what is now the harbour of New York. Was this the way to China? On the twelfth, Hudson started up the river to find out. He got as far as Albany, before he decided that he would not be able to reach China by way of the Hudson—the river that is now named after him.

Then he had to return home again. It is a curious fact that at Albany he was only about sixty miles away from the great French explorer Champlain, who was just coming down from Canada through Lake George. How surprised they would have been to meet in those wilds!

Trading Along the Hudson River

These events laid the foundation of New York. The Dutch merchants were sorry they had not found the way to China, but they could now send men to trade in furs along the Hudson. A little later they planted a colony there. And that is why there are so many Dutch names round New York to this day, and also so many Dutch customs, like paying New Year's calls and believing in Saint Nicholas.

Henry Hudson made one more trip, in 1610: this time under the flag of England. He tried to reach the East by a route round the north of America. He passed through the strait now named after him, and into the great body of water that we still call Hudson Bay. And there he perished. His men were so angry after a hard winter in that region that they mutinied, and put him, his young son, and a few sick members of the crew into a little boat and left them to their fate.

And now suppose Henry Hudson could see a modern map! How he would laugh to think he tried to reach China by sailing up the Hudson River. Can you imagine anyone taking a ticket for China on a Hudson River boat? But he was striving, as best he could, with the limited knowledge he possessed of the continent, to navigate his ship among its islands and ice-fields. It was all like a gigantic jig-saw puzzle, yet he did a good deal to put it together. But it was too much for any one man to accomplish.

Gipsies have always loved and understood horses; so it is not surprising that every year great numbers of them wander to Epsom Downs for the Derby race-meeting. Here is a happy family encamped and ready to tell the fortunes of racegoers for a piece of silver and wish them all good luck. The races over, they will wander on.

The STRANGEST PEOPLE in the WORLD

Ever Coming, Ever Going, Gipsies are Always the Same; They Have Scarcely Changed At All in a Thousand Years

MYSTERIOUS vagabonds, brown and ragged, sometimes living in caravans —homes on wheels—and sometimes on the plains and in the woodlands like wild creatures. In Great Britain, the gipsies avoid three things: the Church, the sea, and the law courts. They have no business with any government, for custom is their only law, and the chief is their lawgiver.

From village to village and from county to county they travel in their caravans and set up their tents by the roadside: in foreign lands they often cover tremendous distances, going from one country to another; but seldom do they venture to use boats for the journeys. They have no religion at all as we understand religion. They will claim to be Christians or Mohammedans or anything else which may be most convenient for them at the moment; but that is simply make-believe. The only belief they have is in spirits good and bad, supposed to dwell in sticks and stones, in trees and streams, in animals of every kind.

There are some ancient stories that tell us how the gipsies are doomed to wander for ever because they are unbelievers. According to one old tale, a gipsy refused shelter to the Virgin as she was fleeing into Egypt with the Christ Child. Another story says that it was a gipsy who forged the nails for Christ's crucifixion. And for those offences the whole race, according to these legends, was doomed to wander over the face of the earth for ever—like the children of Hagar, the outcast, of whom we read in the Bible.

How the Gipsies Got Their Name

But these are only stories invented by simple folk to explain the strange people who suddenly swarmed into Europe in the early fifteenth century. For several hundred years after their first appearance, nobody was sure who the gipsies were or whence they had come. They did not know themselves, or at least they would not tell. Since they claimed to have come from "Little Egypt"—a land of which nobody had ever heard before—they were popularly called "Egyptians," and in English this word was shortened into "gipsies." The French call them "Bohemians"; and other peoples call them by other names, especially "Czigany," "Zingari," or "Tsigan"—but they call themselves "Rom," meaning simply "men," and their language "Romany" (rŏm'ä-nĭ).

Gipsies roam over almost every part of the world, and it has been impossible to estimate their number; most of them are in Europe, and especially in Rumania, Hungary, and Spain. No matter where a tribe lives, however, in Asia or Europe, in Africa or in Australia, its members all speak a language which in some ways resembles that of all other gipsy tribes. And it was the gipsy language that first gave us a clue as to who these strange wanderers are, and whence they came. Their language also told something of their wanderings, for they had picked up new words from each country that they had visited. About 1850 a German scholar found out a good deal about the history of the gipsies by studying their speech, and from that day to this others who have studied gipsy lore have added information until there is now no doubt that long ago the gipsies came—not from any "Little Egypt"—but from India.

Some time about the year A.D. 1000, a great tribe of swarthy but handsome curly-haired people set out westwards from their home in North-Western India. Nobody knows why they started on this journey. Then as now they loved horses and knew all about them, and they were skilful metal-workers. Even to-day gipsies are frequently tinkers. On reaching Persia the horde separated,

Probably the last place in which we should think of looking for the followers of the "Romany trail" is a great city like London. Yet large numbers of gipsies drift into London and out again. Here are three gipsy girls at a camp pitched on the outskirts of the city.

one part going south-west through Syria and Egypt into Northern Africa; the other north-west into Asia Minor and Greece. There they remained for some four hundred years; in Greece they even had a king. Early in the fourteenth century they started northwards through the Balkans, a wild, sparsely settled region that was to their liking. Here, too, they settled for some time and grew very numerous. From here they streamed into the rich plains of Hungary, and then set out for Western Europe, where some of them have lived ever since.

The gipsies had a fine scheme for their travels through the various lands of Europe. They made use of a story that caused people of both high and low degree to give them a good reception and to help them on their way. The leaders of the first horde that set out from Hungary dressed for their part and played it well. Going on ahead of their ragged and filthy followers, a few men of the tribe who called themselves "dukes," "counts," and even "princes," passed through the cities of Southern Germany about the year 1420. They rode good horses and wore good clothes, somewhat overdecked with gold and silver trinkets to be sure, for then as now the gipsy loved finery and decorations of any kind.

Artful Gipsy Leaders

The leader, who claimed to be some grand person such as Michael, "duke of Egypt," went with his companions before the magistrates of each city, showed a document said to be signed by the emperor Sigismund of

Each tribe of gipsies has its own leader, and many of these are famous in their particular world, and, indeed, often in the world outside. Here you see the funeral of Gipsy Lee, queen of the Kent gipsies, who is said to have foretold the time and manner of her death—a prophecy which was exactly fulfilled. She was well known as a fortune-teller, and her funeral was impressive, as befitted her rank among her own people.

Hungary, and told his tale. Then he asked privileges for himself and for his followers, who were to arrive a few days later.

His people had been Christians, he said, but had unfortunately given up the true religion for a time. They had, however, at last realized their wicked folly and, being very penitent now, had taken a vow not to sleep in a bed for seven long years; to make a pilgrimage on foot to Rome, and there to beg the Pope's forgiveness. He would, of course, have to ask for food for his followers, he said, and for a little money; so he trusted the people of the city would give them those things. And the citizens usually met the gipsy leader's demands, for in those days nobody knew very much about the distant parts of the world, and most people could be easily duped. Besides, nearly everybody was only too eager to believe any tale told by a pilgrim from another country.

Work-shy and Dishonest

But the people were greatly startled when the "duke's" followers swarmed into their city, for they were a ragged, thieving crowd, unwilling to undertake any kind of work, and desirous of making money only by trading and by fortune-telling. It was said that whatever they had to sell was certain to have a fault of some kind; that whenever a gipsy bought anything, he always wanted something else included with it without further payment, but that when he sold, it was only for a price too high. All of them were thieves and liars, it was claimed, and the children were the most cunning of all. Such were the "Egyptians" who had come to Europe on their great pilgrimage.

The Pope Deceived

Although some of the first horde of gipsies finally did reach Rome and secure an audience with the Pope—whom they duped as readily as they had duped the princes—most of them spread out to right and left, and before the end of the century they were in every country of Europe. But a change of scene had brought no change of habits. People soon found out the frauds that the gipies had practised on them, and then they took steps to protect themselves and their belongings.

First in one country and then another the gipsies were outlawed. They were flogged when caught; often branded on the forehead with a hot iron; and sometimes hanged or burned at sight without even being brought to trial. This harsh treatment tended to lessen their numbers in some countries, but in others like Rumania, Spain, and Hungary, where the natives not only tolerate but even show them favour, the gipsies still flourish. In Eastern European countries the metal-working trades—especially blacksmithing and silversmithing—are almost entirely in gipsy hands. Everywhere they are roving menders of pots and pans. Some people think that our English word "tinker" may be only a form of "zigeuner," a German word denoting a gipsy.

The Gipsy Instinct to Wander

But the gipsies are not all metal-workers. In Turkey they are dealers in drugs and precious stones; in Spain they are singers and dancers; in Hungary many are musicians; in Russia they even become entertainers and actors. But wherever they live and whatever they do—whether it be leading a dancing bear through the street of your village or performing before royalty, as they sometimes did in Russia—gipsies do not mingle socially with the "gentiles," as they call all other peoples. They scarcely ever marry outside the tribe; and if a girl does so, she becomes an outcast.

Although gipsies occasionally settle down in one place for a little while, sooner or later they are sure to wander on. In Rumania the government at one time gave every gipsy man a piece of land for his own, thinking that would make them all settle down in a country they seem to love. But the plan did not succeed at all. Some strange instinct lures the gipsy onwards to no particular place, but onwards nevertheless. For that is what it means to be a gipsy.

Life in a Gipsy Encampment

He pitches his tent at the side of the road. In a copper kettle on stones the gipsy woman cooks a favourite dish, a sort of stew made of rice, onions and meat. Gipsy girls clad in a ragged, loose, red garment hardly to be called a dress, plait small scraps of coloured cloth into their raven hair, or care for the half-naked little children who tumble about in the summer grass. Old men and old women—very old, for the gipsy is usually long-lived—smoke their pipes contentedly. The younger men talk of the trading they have done during the day, or they strum guitars and sing in nasal tones age-old gipsy songs. And when night finally comes, the whole community falls asleep under the stars. To-morrow they will move on once more.

A chicken from a neighbouring hen-roost, some odds and ends of vegetables, perhaps a tender young rabbit—anything that is handy goes into the pot to make the gipsies' meal.

If you live where there is good strong ice in the winter-time, you are going to have many hours of thrilling sport when you have finished making the ice-boat described on this page. But since no one can expect ice all the time, and since some of us do not see any of it at all, we have put in two all-the-year-round stand-bys—a whistle and a pop-gun—besides.

HOW TO MAKE AN ICE-BOAT

The framework (A and B) is made from timber 1½″ thick. The seat-board (A) should be 8′ long, 15″ wide, and cut to the shape shown. The cross-board (B) should be 6′ long and 6″ wide. Nail or screw B to the under side of A near the front, as illustrated. To the under side of B, at each end, nail or screw a piece of board 1′ long, 2″ wide, and 2″ thick (D). Clamp a skate to each of these boards just as you would to your shoe. The rudder or steering gear, shown in cross section at C, is a board 15″ long, 3″ wide, and 1½″ thick. Nail or screw a block at each end of this axle at point D and clamp skates to it, as on the cross-piece. Now make the steering-handle (E) fast to the rudder axle by means of a bolt passing through all three boards and secured with lock-nuts. The mast is a straight pole 6′ long, tapering from 3″ to 1½″. The two spars (F, G) are poles 6′ and 4′ long respectively, and each 1½″ in diameter. The sails are strong cotton duck, cut to the shape and proportionate size (H) and securely sewn. You will need rope and several pulleys to operate them.

HOW TO MAKE A POP-GUN

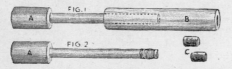

Select a straight stem from an elder tree, and with a ramrod (A) made from a small dowel inserted in a spool, which serves as handle, push out the pith (B). Smooth the rod with fine sand-paper or a piece of glass. To smooth the inside of the barrel wrap sand-paper round the ramrod and push it to and fro. Now find two corks (C) that fit the barrel snugly but can be pushed through it with the ramrod. Rubbing the outside of the corks with wet soap will make them slip through more easily. Now fix one of them in flush with one end of the barrel, fit the other in the opposite end, and push the second one through with the ramrod—quickly. Pop! goes the first cork; and who knows what bear or lion it may bring down? If you want to turn your pop-gun into a syringe gun that will throw a stream of water several feet, burn a small hole with a hot wire through one of the corks and place the cork in the tube. Wrap some woollen yarn round the end of the ramrod (Fig. 2). The water will shoot out through the hole in the cork.

HOW TO MAKE A WHISTLE

Select a straight branch of willow, about 5″ long and free from sprouts or knots. Cut a ring round the bark through to the wood (Fig. 1, A), cut the other end at an angle (B), and make a small notch in the bark opposite the beginning of this angle cut, as illustrated (C). Now tap the bark carefully all round, between A and B, until you have loosened it and can draw it off whole (Fig. 2). Now cut a long narrow notch in the wood as shown at D. Remove a few shavings between notch D and the end of stick to permit air to pass from the mouth into the notched chamber at D. Finally slip the bark on again, put the slanting end in your mouth, and blow. You will have a fine whistle—maybe. If it does not work well, it is because either the notch in the bark or the one in the wood is too large or too small and so too much or too little air can enter. Only persevering with these things until you get them right will make you a good whistle maker.

This ancient wall in Jerusalem has heard the prayers and laments of the Jewish people for many centuries. It is called the "Wailing Wall" because, since it is one of the few relics of their ancestors remaining to the Jews, it has become a holy place to which they go to pray in time of deep trouble. It has been the cause of many bitter differences between the Jews and the Moslems. Not long ago a special commission was formed by the British government to decide the question of ownership. They came to the decision that the wall belonged to the Moslems, but that the Jews should be allowed to carry on their worship there at all times.

The WANDERER Among the NATIONS

Persecuted and Driven to the Ends of the Earth, the Jews are the Only People Who Have Kept Their Race and Faith Pure Throughout the Ages

(CONTINUED FROM PAGE 401)

FEW stories in history are as strange as that of the people called the Jews.

For nearly two thousand years they have been wanderers without a national home. They have suffered more persecution than any other people since the beginning of time. And yet they have remained one people, and have kept all their national traits and ideals. They have also produced many of the world's greatest artists, scientists, writers, and industrial leaders.

What has kept the Jews a single race, while the Babylonians, the Assyrians, the Romans, and many other peoples have disappeared from history? It is mainly the Jewish religion, a religion with a central idea which has grown in beauty and power through the ages. Jewish worship centres about one God, who is a Father. The fundamental principle of the faith is what is known as the "Shema" (Deuteronomy vi. 4, 5): "Hear, O Israel: The Lord our God is one Lord: and thou shalt love the Lord thy God with all thine heart, and with all thy soul, and with all thy might." This Jesus called the first commandment; and this belief in the oneness and fatherhood of God, along with all the laws and customs and rites of worship which grew up about it, has given the Jews, wide-scattered as they have been, a strong bond to hold them close to one another and apart from others.

Strange and Sad Story of the Jews

The story of the Jews is as sad as it is strange. For it is the story of hideous cruelty dealt out to them in mistaken zeal for One whose second commandment was that we love one another. Jewish history since the time of Christ is a long record of cruel oppressions visited upon them by the peoples of many other races.

Even before the time of Jesus, the quarrelling factions in Palestine had felt the power of Rome, and the tiny kingdom had been swallowed up by the enormous Roman Empire. But if it had been unpleasant to receive the Romans, it was a tragic error to have urged the Roman governor, Pontius Pilate, to allow the crucifixion of Jesus of Nazareth. It was this crime of their ancestors that was later used as a reason for most of the hatred of the Jews. Both Jew and Christian forgot that Jesus Himself and all His early followers were Jews. At first the apostles had even objected to admitting any Gentiles (jĕn′tĭl), or non-Jews, to their fellowship. It was the wisdom of Paul that carried the gospel to all the world.

Meanwhile, the Roman governors and their Jewish subjects did not agree very well. The Romans could not understand the Jews.

Photo by Alinari

When Jesus was brought before Pontius Pilate, the Roman governor judged Him innocent. Leading Him out before the crowd which had assembled below, Pilate said, "Behold, I bring Him forth to you that ye may know that I find no fault in Him. Behold the man!" But the Jews insisted that Jesus be crucified. When Pilate asked what evil Jesus had done, the multitude merely cried, "Crucify Him! Crucify Him!"

Why should they be so devoted to their laws and customs? Why should they think it a shameful thing to eat the flesh of pigs? Why did they refuse to worship the great emperors of Rome, who had been declared to be gods? For their part, the Jews neither understood the Romans nor liked them. Misunderstanding developed into armed clashes, until in A.D. 66 the Jews revolted openly against Roman rule.

Rome sent two of her best generals, Vespasian (věs-pā'-zhǐ-ăn) and Titus, to put down the rebellion. It was not an easy task, for the Jewish patriots fought with great stubbornness. Starving, wounded, desperate, they contested every inch of the way, in the midst of horrors such as the world has seldom seen. But in A.D. 70 the upper part of Jerusalem fell, the sacred Temple was burned, and the Jewish state was no more.

The design on the front cover of the Talmud, a great digest of Jewish civil and religious law, reproduced from the copy in the British Museum.

We are told that more than a million Jews died in the siege of Jerusalem. But if every Jew in Palestine had fallen, it would by no means have put an end to this hardy race, for the people were already scattered far and wide in many lands. At Alexandria, in Egypt, there was a large settlement; into Greece, Persia, Rome itself, Jews had travelled as traders and settlers. Moreover, there had been in Jerusalem a rabbi (răb'ĭ), or teacher, named Johanan ben Zakkai, who had foreseen that the sacred city would fall. This rabbi went with his books to the Roman general, begging permission to establish a little school at Jabneh, on the coast of Palestine. This little school, which the Romans did not think it worth while to forbid, now became the centre of the Jewish religion. The Great Sanhedrin (săn'-ĕ-drĭn), the supreme Jewish council, consisting of seventy-one learned men, did its work there, and Jewish thoughts and beliefs and ways of living were there preserved from destruction.

For Jewish troubles were just beginning. Persecutions under various Roman emperors led finally to the second destruction of Jerusalem in A.D. 135, after which the Romans placed a swine's head over the city gate and forbade any Jew to enter. But Christians might enter; and this act marks a clear separation between the two faiths.

The persecution extended to the school at Jabneh; so the rabbis fled to Usha, in Galilee, where they hoped their school would be safer. Then from Usha the centre moved to one town after another— Shearam, Beth Shearim, Sepphoris, Tiberias —until finally it moved out of Palestine and established itself in Babylonia.

In all these centres of Jewish learning, the rabbis set themselves to study and interpret the law of Moses. The greatest of these interpreters was Rabbi Judah, sometimes called simply "Rabbi." This great teacher lived in Palestine in the second century; his book is called the Mishna, and all the rabbis who came after him based their work more or less upon it. Finally, the learning of many scholars in the Jewish schools of Babylonia was gathered together into another book,

THE HISTORY OF THE JEWS

called the Gemara (gĕ-mä′rȧ). These two books, the Mishna and the Gemara, together make up the Talmud (tăl′mŭd), a great digest of Jewish thought and opinion.

The Talmud lays down rules about almost every little act of every day: that on the Sabbath one shall not read by lamplight; that separate dishes must be used for cooking meat and milk, and separate cloths for cleaning such dishes; that it is doubtful whether a Jew may eat an egg laid on the Sabbath. But along with such little rules there are many moral sayings of great beauty, teaching the great virtues of charity, kindliness, and temperance in all things.

Persecution by the Romans

After the second destruction of Jerusalem, the Roman Empire had treated the Jews much better; but when the emperors became Christians, it was another story. During the fifth and sixth centuries there was persecution almost everywhere. In 425 the emperor Theodosius (thē′ō-dō′shĭ-ŭs) forbade the Jews to have any "patriarch," or leader. One "Prince of the Exile," as their leader was called, was crucified, and another was hanged. Things were better again for a time after the barbarians overran the empire, for the teachings of the form of Christianity in which these tribes believed

did not differ greatly from the teaching of the Jewish religion. But by the seventh century some countries were making laws against the Jews, and nowhere quite so fiercely as in the Gothic kingdom of Spain.

Yet it was in Spain that the Jews were to have a few centuries of rest from the worst of their troubles. For soon after A.D. 700 Spain was conquered by the Moors, who were Mohammedans, and the Mohammedans did not persecute the Jews.

It had not been so at first. Mohammed himself, who taught in the early part of the seventh century, had taken much of his new religion from Jewish teachings, but he soon quarrelled with the Jews and ordered his followers either to convert this stubborn race or butcher them. After a time, however, the Mohammedan rulers decided to let the Jews buy toleration by paying a regular tax. Thenceforward, in the East, the Jews throve and prospered, and began to show their skill in the sciences and the arts.

"Golden Age" of the Jews

When the Mohammedan hordes conquered Spain, the Jews, made wise by experience, settled there in large numbers. And now for four hundred years (900–1300), this persecuted people enjoyed a "Golden Age." Poets, the greatest of them Judah

Before Nebuchadnezzar, king of Babylonia, captured Jerusalem and burned the temple of Solomon to the ground, the city, as seen from the north-east, probably looked very much as the artist has shown it above.

432

Photo by Rischgitz

If you have read Scott's "Ivanhoe," you will probably have formed a clear impression of how badly the Jews were treated in the days of the Plantagenets. To plunder a Jewish home, after the manner shown in the picture above, was not an unusual practice among people who nevertheless called themselves Christians.

Halevi, began writing beautiful Hebrew verse. Scientists, especially physicians, made new discoveries. Philosophers speculated on deep matters. Perhaps the greatest figure of this Golden Age was Moses ben Maimon, or Moses Maimonides (mī-mŏn'ĭ-dēz). In his thought and writings Maimonides tried to put the Jewish faith on a rational or scientific basis, freeing it from the shackles of superstition or of mere tradition.

This Golden Age did not extend beyond the Mohammedan Empire. In the Christian countries during the Middle Ages the Jews were persecuted bitterly, not by the Pope himself so much as by the people and their kings. Often a Jew was given the choice of leaving the country or being baptized as a Christian. Thousands were not even allowed to choose, but were baptized by force—as if such a baptism could change their religion! Hundreds of thousands were exiled. Thousands were massacred. The crusaders in Palestine included the Jews in the ranks of their enemies. Even when there was no killing in the mass, many a Jew, especially if he were a rabbi, suffered burning or crucifixion.

But religion was not the only cause of trouble for the Jews. Another was money. Since the Christian Church sternly forbade usury (ū'zhŭ-rĭ), or the lending of money for interest, the Jews, who were forbidden to engage in farming or industry, were allowed to become money-lenders. Many Jews made huge profits at this trade, since they asked enormous rates of interest, because lending money often resulted in considerable loss to the lender.

The wealth which the Jews gained in money-lending now became a danger to them. A Jew had little protection in law or in custom, and it was easy to murder or rob the money-lender and seize all he had. Some districts would now and then order all Jews to leave, then seize their property, and after a time permit them to return to make more. Torture, too, seemed a simple way to force money from a Jew. It is said that King John of England seized one Jew reputed to be wealthy and ordered a tooth to be pulled out each day until the unfortunate man should yield up the sum the king asked. And every Jew had to wear a special badge or mark, so that everyone should know him for a member of the hated race.

This regulation did more to break the Jewish spirit than any of their torments. The ghettos, or Jewish quarters, which now grew up in many cities of Europe, were always situated in the ugliest and dirtiest parts. And besides the dirt, there was the terrible crowding, for the ghettos were seldom large enough to make decent homes for the thousands crowded into them. Moreover, the enemies of the Jews now knew exactly where to find them. A band of ruffians might at any time bring fire and sword

The history of the Jews is the history of a persecution which, beginning in Egypt, has lasted throughout the ages. Here we see the people of Zion driven from their ruined city to be sold into slavery at Babylon. Scenes like this, differing only in detail, have been enacted over and over again during the long history of these homeless wanderers on the face of the earth.

against the people of the ghetto without much fear of punishment. Small wonder that the Jews hated a religion whose followers had strayed so far from the doctrines of its Founder.

Cruel tales, which were lacking in truth, had come to be believed about the Jews, and turned many simple and naturally kindly people against them. One of the most horrible—and also most absurd—was the accusation of "ritual murder." Someone started the hideous story that a certain Jewish religious ceremony was not complete without the blood of a Christian child, and that each year a child would disappear, murdered by the Jews for this rite. For centuries people believed this foolish lie, and many were the stories of child martyrs they told in connection with it. Indeed, difficult as it is to believe, a Jew named Mendel Beilis was put on trial to answer such a charge in Russia as recently as 1913. Happily he was acquitted by an all-Russian jury.

It is hard to see how the lot of the Jews in Europe could have been worse than it was during the late Middle Ages and the early modern period. Edward I expelled them completely from England in 1290, and soon other countries followed England's example. In 1394 France not only expelled them for the third time, but made it a crime worthy of death for a Christian to protect or even talk to a Jew. In Germany many towns, although not the country as a whole, drove them out. Finally Spain, now Christianized, turned savagely upon them and expelled them in 1492.

In dress, manners, even language, the Jew was a marked man. Spanish Jews began (about 1200) to speak Ladino (lä-dē'nō), a mixture of Spanish and Hebrew. German Jews spoke Yiddish, a dialect made up of fourteenth century German and Hebrew. Yiddish has survived to our own times, and many books and newspapers are still written in that language. It is not Hebrew, but anyone who knows German and the Hebrew alphabet can read it.

Kicked, lashed, and subjected to other forms of ill-treatment, the Jews huddled together in any land which would tolerate them. To be sure, if a Jew was willing to become a Christian, then he might remain where he was; and in Spain many a Jew, desperate at the prospect of losing all his posses- sions, did accept baptism. These con- verted Jews were called Maranos (mä - rä′nō)— "accursed." Generations later, when persecution had died down, many of them re- turned to the old faith of their fathers.

In spite of all this brutal persecution the Jews held to their Law. To be sure, as time went on, it became a little mixed with the doctrines of the cabala (căb′ā-lā), a queer system of magic and incantations which grew up in eleventh-century Spain. And they tended to add a surprising number of little laws to the bigger and more important ones. In 1555 Joseph Karo drew up a system of rules for Jewish practice regulating everything possible —even to which shoe to put on first. The system has ever since been in great favour among strict Jews. If it was narrow and bigoted and rather un- reasonable, it at least gave the Jews something definite to hold to, and helped them to keep their faith, and their race with it, from dying out.

Martin Luther, the great German religious reformer of the sixteenth century, was at first friendly towards the Jews, but later he turned against them. He is here seen preaching one of his impressive sermons.

But most Jews took the hard road of exile and poverty. Poland and Turkey were the countries most ready to receive them, and by hundreds of thousands they sought refuge in those lands. The Spanish Jews, or Sephardim (sĕ-fär′dĭm), preferred Turkey; the other Jews, or Ashkenazim (ăsh′kĕ-năz′- ĭm), generally chose Poland.

To this day there is a distinction between these two great branches of the Jewish race, and the Sephardim consider them- selves to possess purer blood in their veins.

The Protestant Reformation, which began when Martin Luther first openly questioned Catholic doctrine, did not at once help the Jews. Luther, at first friendly and tolerant, suddenly turned hostile and declared that if he could he would pull every Jewish tongue out by the roots.

But new forces and new ideas were abroad in the world, and new lands were being opened up, too. In some of the European

A. Just married! A Bedouin bride and bridegroom photographed in Palestine.

D. A sheikh and his wife from Ramleh, the modern name of an ancient town where Nicodemus and Joseph of Arimathea are said to have lived.

B. A woman of modern Jericho baking unleavened bread.

C. This is a scene in modern Bethlehem; but the well from which the women are drawing their water is the one which the people of Bethlehem used at the time when Christ was born.

E. Measuring out grain into an apron in Palestine.
F. In Central Palestine there is an ancient Jewish sect known as the Samaritans. These people claim to have lived in the Holy Land since the time of Moses. This is Aaron, their high priest. G. This young woman of modern Bethlehem is doing some work in mother-of-pearl.

A. This street vendor in modern Jerusalem is doing a thriving business. His specialities are cakes and home-made sweets. B. Seated before the tomb of Ezekiel in Babylon, these scribes look much as their ancestors must have looked. Thousands of years ago the scribes of Egypt sat in the same cross-legged fashion.

C. The little maiden stroking a lamb is a native of Bethlehem. There she tends her flock just as the shepherds of the Bible did.

D. Here are two natives of modern Palestine, with their patient beast of burden.

E. What can this street vendor of Jerusalem be pouring from the odd contrivance he carries about with him?—goat's milk, or coffee? No, it is just refreshing home-made lemonade.

countries the clouds began to lift. Holland, defender of freedom, offered a refuge. Oliver Cromwell permitted Jewish immigration into England, and Denmark also opened her doors. Although permitted few rights and privileges, the Jews nevertheless found in these countries an escape from the bitterness of persecution. And there was the New World. All through the seventeenth century a steady stream of Jews was flowing towards freedom—either across the Atlantic Ocean or into the more hospitable of the European lands, especially Holland.

During all these centuries the Jews had never ceased to look with hope for the Messiah, the divinely anointed leader of whom they believed the prophets had spoken. And many false Messiahs appeared, among them Solomon Molko, of Portugal, and Sabbatai Zevi, of Turkey, both of whom had astounding adventures. In Lithuania, about 1700, lived another leader, called Baal Shem Tov, or "the Good Master of God's Name." He never called himself a Messiah, but he started a Jewish sect known as the Chassidists—from the Hebrew word for "righteous"—which still survives.

The Dawn of Liberty

The next century saw the first real signs that the Jews were to be considered as worthy of having rights like other people. The doctrine of "Liberty, equality, fraternity" in France and America applied to Jew as well as to Gentile. Although in Austria the empress Maria Theresa had tried (1744) to exile all Jews by royal decree, she failed, and nearly forty years later (1782) her son Joseph II announced his famous Edict of Toleration, which abolished the poll tax and the "badge of shame" that was still worn by all Jews. He even permitted Jewish students to enter the universities. Three years later revolutionary France revoked every anti-Jewish law of the land.

Everywhere in Europe the walls of prejudice were beginning to crumble. And, as might be expected, the Jews themselves, strong and restless in their new freedom, not quite so absorbed in merely being Jews, began to murmur against the harsh restraints of their own ancient Law. Moses Mendels-

sohn (měn'děl-sōn) actually dared to publish the Hebrew Scriptures in the German tongue, with comments which paid little respect to the wilderness of mere forms that had been growing up during the centuries. He became the founder of a liberal movement which has led to the formation of the Reformed Judaism (jū'då-ĭz'm) of the United States. These liberals began to write, in the classic Hebrew of the Bible, many poems, and other works.

Scientists, Musicians, and Poets

As another natural result of the increased freedom, many Jews, formerly held by persecution to their faith, began to desert it for irreligion, for philosophy, even for Christianity. In the nineteenth century universities opened their doors to Jews, who also won the vote and the right to hold office. Then Jewish men and women began to plunge with ardour into the stirring life of their time. They became scientists, musicians, poets, writers, statesmen. Sometimes they abandoned the whole of their ancient faith; sometimes they clung to it all; and sometimes they held only to the spiritual truths which they felt lay behind the Law.

Only in the East was there little or no change. In Russia and Poland the Jews were still herded into ghettos, still massacred now and then in horrible anti-Jewish outbreaks called pogroms (pŏ-grŏm'). And in Western Europe, although so much progress had been made, there was still among non-Jewish people a strong sentiment known as anti-Semitism (sĕm'ĭ-tĭz'm). It was now whispered that the Jews were preparing to conquer the whole of the world and subject it entirely to Jewish domination.

The New Birth of a Great People

All this time it was occurring to many far-seeing Jews that a good way to solve their problem might be to set up a Jewish state, preferably in Palestine, the ancient homeland of the Jews. Several books on this "Zionist" movement appeared, but the one which attracted most attention was "The Jewish State," by Theodore Herzl (hĕrtz'l) of Budapest, in Hungary.

The World War (1914–1918) brought both joy and sorrow to the Jewish world. All the war years and those that followed were stained by fearful atrocities in the East— in Russia, Poland, Rumania, Hungary. There were ghastly massacres in which thousands of Jews perished.

On the other hand, the British government (1917) announced its intention of making Palestine a national home for the Jewish people, thus raising the hopes of the Zionists. And their hopes were partly realized. In 1922 England secured from the League of Nations a mandate to govern Palestine, and at once the work of immigration and re-organization began. In 1925 the Earl of Balfour opened the Hebrew University at Jerusalem as a permanent centre for the Jewish world of scholarship.

Not all Jews are Zionists, just as not all are liberals in religious matters. Many Jews feel that for their race to confine itself to a single strip of land would be a great mistake. They are loyal members of the various nations in which they are now citizens, and are convinced that their greatest service to the world can be rendered as members of those nations. Moreover, Palestine would not now support the whole Jewish race, and for them to attempt to live there in any great numbers would mean a great loss in physical and intellectual vigour.

Broadly speaking, there are now three main groups among the Jews: the Spanish or Sephardim, Jews, a small but illustrious group; the German Jews; and the Russian or Eastern Jews, the most numerous of all. The last group have suffered bitter persecution, from which they are just beginning to escape; while the Jews in Germany have had many of their rights and privileges withdrawn by the Nazi government.

It is unnecessary to question the future of the Jewish people. Its members have already proved their qualities and abilities. It is pleasant to remember that their mental and spiritual vigour and inspiration have at last been set free to work for the progress of man.

These picturesque Arabs have pitched their tents along the grassy slopes of a hill overlooking the beautiful city of Jerusalem, whose walls and towers rise like a mirage of the desert. First occupied by the Egyptians, the city next became the stronghold of the Israelites, and here David built his citadel, and Solomon raised his magnificent temple. Assyrians, Babylonians, Macedonians, Romans, Mohammedans, Crusaders and Turks have all struggled for its possession, and its fortifying walls have risen and fallen with the tides of conquest.

1. A PASSEPARTOUT frame is just what you need to set off your favourite snapshot, sketch, or print. First get a piece of glass the right size, and trace round it on mounting-paper and on a piece of cardboard.

2. Then cut mounting-paper and cardboard backing to the exact size of the glass.

3. The right and left borders of the picture must be exactly equal; that below should be a trifle wider than that above. Place the picture in one corner of the mounting-paper and measure to the edges with a piece of paper.

4. Now cut the piece of paper where you have marked it and fold it double. This will give you the width of one of two equal borders.

5. Lay the paper which gives the width of the side borders on the mounting-paper and make a slight mark near the points where each corner of the picture will be. Adjust the height of the picture to suit your eye and mark.

6. Now you are ready to mount the picture—a most important procedure, as the slightest lopsidedness or the smallest smear of paste on the mounting-paper may spoil the effect. Just a touch of paste at each corner of the picture should be enough.

7. With its corners on your marks, press the picture down. Another way is to cut out the mounting-board along the markings and paste the picture face down on the back of the mount.

8. Whichever way you have mounted your picture, here it is, ready for the frame.

9. Now take your passe-partout binding and cut four strips, two of them an inch longer than the width of your glass, two of them an inch longer than its length. Crease each lengthwise down its centre.

10. Moisten the gummed side of one longer strip and glue it the length of the glass, with the crease exactly at the edge. Repeat with the other side.

11. Lay the mounted picture and backing on the glass, turn the passe-partout over the edge, and gum down carefully.

12. You have already trimmed off the ends of the first two strips. Now apply the shorter strips in the same way and trim the ends neatly.

13. A piece of heavy paper slightly smaller than the glass makes a neat protective finish for the back of your picture.

14. Then you will need one or more ring hangers, which you must be very careful to fix exactly in the centre.

15. And if you have worked neatly and tastefully, you will have something that you will always be able to admire.

Kill him! Kill him! He is the terrible house-fly, as he looks in a greatly enlarged model. He and his kind cause thousands of deaths every year. He can keep the germs of typhoid alive in his body for a period of twenty-eight days, and carries on his filthy legs the germs of many another deadly disease.

The HORRIBLE HOUSE-FLY

A Harmless-looking Creature That Kills More Men than All the Lions and Tigers in the World

(CONTINUED FROM PAGE 417)

WHEN is a fly not a fly? Perhaps you will say, "When it is a fire-fly." But those little beetles are not the only creatures that are wrongly called "flies." So that answer won't quite do.

No, the best answer to the riddle would be, "When it has four wings."

Fire-flies, butterflies, dragon-flies, May-flies, and caddis-flies, for example, all have four wings; so they are not true flies. True flies never have more than two.

Flies are the only insects that have only a single pair of wings, although beetles and bugs use their first pair merely as wing cases to protect the hind pair. Where we might expect to find a second pair of wings, a fly has two small knobs fixed on the top of short, slender stalks that look like two little pins stuck into its back. These curious objects are called "balancers"; and although

they do not look as if they could be of any use, they are really most necessary to the insect, for if they were clipped off it would not be able to fly.

There are hosts of these two-winged insects dancing and buzzing and crawling about all over the globe. Although some of them are friendly and useful, most of them are anything but good for us.

The common house-flies that buzz up and down the window-panes and fall into uncovered milk jugs and jam dishes are not the harmless little insects they were once supposed to be. They are really dangerous creatures, and behave so badly that we must not allow them to make themselves at home in our houses. They make trouble wherever they go by carrying the germs of typhoid fever and several other infectious diseases on their feet and their hairy little bodies.

Fortunately, it is not difficult to get rid of the little pests. They thrive in dust and dirt and all unclean things. So if our houses and streets are kept as they should be, and no dust or decaying rubbish is allowed to accumulate, house-flies and various other harmful little creatures soon begin to die out.

If only two or three flies contrive to establish themselves anywhere, the place will soon be swarming with these troublesome things unless prompt measures are taken to destroy them. For every female fly may lay five or six batches of eggs in a single season, each batch containing over a hundred eggs. From these eggs, in a few hours, tiny white legless grubs are hatched. They feed and grow, turn to pupae (pū′pē), and come forth as winged flies, all in the short space of ten or twelve days. The new flies lay eggs in their turn—and so the tale goes on. So quickly do these insects multiply that before the summer is over every female house-fly may be a great-great-grandmother and have more descendants than we could count if it were possible to collect them together.

A fly has no jaws, so it cannot chew. It sucks up its food through a queer li tle trunk, or proboscis (prŏ-bŏs′ĭs). On the end of its trunk is a cushion-like sucker. When you see a fly working away with this sucker at a grain of sugar, it is really engaged in dissolving the sugar—turning it into syrup in order to lap it up.

When the fly has finished its meal it proceeds to "clean up," for it is most careful about its toilet. It rubs its fore-feet briskly together as if it were washing its hands, smooths

Here are pictures of the house-fly at four stages in its death-dealing career. In the little round circle are six of its eggs, greatly enlarged. They are always laid in some kind of filth—the worse the better. In from eight to twenty-four hours the disgusting little grub, or maggot, shown enlarged in the rectangle, has hatched and begins to gorge itself upon the filth. As it grows it casts its skin twice. At the end of some five days it is ready to seek a drier place and turn into the pupa which is pictured enlarged in the oval. In warm weather it will be able to step into the world in three or four days, a full-grown fly. In the picture it is magnified, but nothing could magnify the harm it can now do. It eats all kinds of filth, lays countless eggs, and has a disgusting way of vomiting up its food so that it may eat the more. It is literally crammed with poisonous germs. It may carry at least 7,000,000 of them about with it, and leave 700,000 in every footprint on our food. It is one of the greatest distributors of disease throughout the world.

its wings, and brushes its eyes with the tufts of fine bristles on its slender little legs. It twists and twirls its head about in the most astonishing manner, just as if the head were set on a pivot—for the short neck that joins the fly's head to its shoulders is no thicker than a fine thread, and is just as flexible.

Another remarkable thing about the fly is its enormous eyes. They are so big that they almost meet on the top of its head, leaving only a narrow strip of a face. No wonder it is so hard to catch one of the quick little creatures!

The burly blue-bottle has just as bad a

SOME FLIES THAT YOU MAY OFTEN SEE

Here are some British flies. Starting at the top of the page, and reading from left to right, they are the mosquito, great hawk fly, bee parasite, snipe fly, hornet fly, common hawk fly, clegg, great gadfly, pellucid bee fly, bumble-bee fly, autumnal gadfly, blue-bottle fly, drone fly, caterpillar parasite, and grey carrion fly.

character as its cousin the house-fly. It invades the larder at every opportunity and lays its eggs on any meat not put away in the safe, loudly buzzing all the time in the most impudent way as if it knew it was spoiling the food. The stable-fly and the horse-fly are no better. They worry horses and cattle by piercing the skin of the poor animals and sucking their blood, often making them quite ill.

There are other flies that spoil cheese and ham and bacon, causing the loss of thousands of pounds every year. Still worse are the flies whose horrid little grubs devour onions, sugar-beets, cabbages, and useful plants of all kinds. But worst of all is the dreaded Hessian fly, a tiny blackish insect only a tenth of an inch long—but the smallest insects often do the greatest damage. Mother Hessian Fly lays her eggs on young wheat, and when the tiny grubs hatch they drain away the sap of the growing plants, often ruining completely the entire crop.

Then there are the mosquitoes. No one has a good word to say for them. They are out to suck your blood whenever they get the chance, and raise painful bumps on your hands and face. Worse still, in tropical lands they infect their victims with the disease known as malaria.

The Mosquito that Causes All the Suffering

It is the female mosquito that does all the harm. Her long sucking tube is armed with a set of sharp, needle-like lancets; with these little instruments she punctures the skin of her victims before sucking their blood.

The little male is harmless. He lives on nectar and the sap of plants, and never attempts to drink your blood. You may know him by his beautiful feelers, which are like thick, bushy plumes, while those of his mate are simple threads with only a few

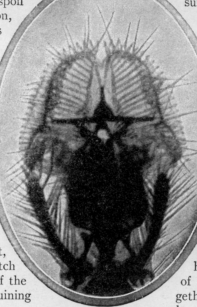
The curious tongue of a blue-bottle fly as seen through a microscope.

short hairs upon them arranged in little circles.

There are many different kinds of mosquitoes, and they are not all dangerous, blood-sucking insects. The harmless ones are usually called gnats. They have shorter sucking tubes, live on the juices of plants, and do not hurt anyone, though they often make a nuisance of themselves by dancing wildly round your head on warm summer evenings.

The life story of a gnat or a mosquito is like a real fairy story. Very early on a bright summer morning, with a shrill "ping! ping!" the little quick-winged gnat comes flying down to a quiet pool. Lightly she rests upon the surface without even wetting her dainty feet, and quickly she lays one tiny egg after another right on top of the water. She works very fast, and before the sun is up she holds between her feet a mass of eggs all carefully glued together in the form of a tiny boat-shaped raft.

Her work done, Mother Gnat darts up into the air to spend the rest of the summer day in merry dancing, leaving the cluster of eggs to float on the water.

The tiny raft is waterproof, and so well shaped that it cannot sink or overturn. Each little egg in the cluster has a pointed top and a little trap-door which is kept tightly shut to prevent the water from flowing in.

All day long the tiny craft floats lightly on the water. Then, early next morning, the trap-doors open and all the gnat babies come tumbling out of their fairy boat. But what odd little babies they are! They are not in the least like Mother Gnat. They have long bodies, no legs, big heads and shoulders with stiff bristles sticking out like long whiskers all round, and funny forked tails with one fork longer than the other.

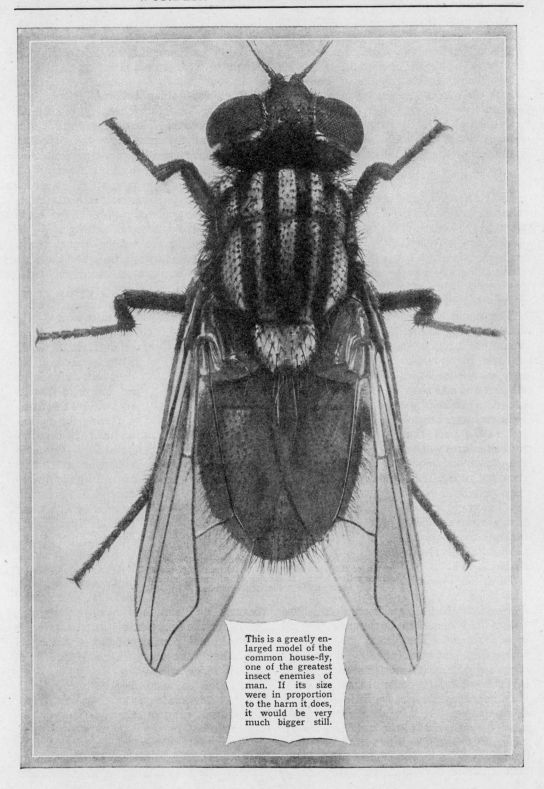

This is a greatly enlarged model of the common house-fly, one of the greatest insect enemies of man. If its size were in proportion to the harm it does, it would be very much bigger still.

These queer little "wrigglers" spend most of their time hanging head downwards in the water, all bunched up together as close as can be. The tips of their tails—which are really breathing tubes—are pushed just above the surface of the pool to take in oxygen from the air. The little creatures jerk themselves about like acrobats, as they lash the water with their whiskers, sweeping invisible particles of food into their mouths.

Frightened by a Shadow

They are timid little beings. If so much as a shadow passes overhead, they all dive down to the bottom of the water, where they plunge and wriggle about in a state of the wildest commotion. As soon as the trouble passes, they all come up again to crowd together, upside down, at the top of the pool, just as before.

The queer gnat babies grow very fast. Like all young insects, they cast their skins from time to time—each time coming out a little bigger than they were before. If all goes well and they are not gobbled up by some hungry monster of the pool, the little creatures will be full-grown in about ten days' time. Then they cast their skins once more; but this time when they change their coats they change their shape as well.

The long-bodied, fork-tailed "wriggler" disappears. In its place is an absurd little object that seems to be wearing a huge diver's helmet. The young gnat has, of course, become a pupa (pū'pȧ). But instead of resting quietly, as most insects do, while its final and most wonderful transformation is taking place, the strange little thing is as active as ever. It bobs about in the water and constantly rises to the surface to take in a supply of air through two trumpet-shaped horns on the back of its helmet. The funny little creature does not feed any more; it

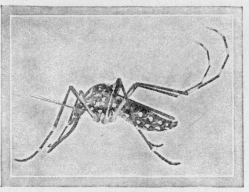

This model from the Natural History Museum shows the female of the anopheles (ă-nŏf ĕ-lēz) mosquito, which carries yellow fever. It is enlarged, of course, but not in proportion to the harm it can do.

cannot. The big helmet, which entirely encloses its head and shoulders, is tightly sealed up; so it would be quite impossible for the pupa to eat, even if it wanted to.

This stage in its life soon passes. Within that clumsy-looking helmet the head, the gauzy wings, and the slender legs of the little gnat are growing. The time is near when the ugly water baby must leave the dark pool where it has passed its infant days and rise, as a winged insect, into the sunlit air.

When the thrilling moment of its escape arrives, the pupa rises for the last time to the top of the pool and pushes its big helmet clear above the surface of the water.

As it dries in the air the helmet cracks and splits, and through the rent the little gnat appears and stands, weak and trembling, poised on its old pupa skin.

The quick-winged gnat doth make a boat
Of his old house wherewith to float
To a new life.

But all is not yet safe. If it slips, the little gnat will be drowned, for it is no longer a "water baby." It stands quivering for a while on its old house while its wings dry and stiffen in the warm air. Then, taking courage, it darts aloft to join its sisters and brothers in a merry dance.

Numberless little midges and other tiny flies that whirl in millions over the pastures and meadows have been water babies for the first part of their lives, living in pools and ponds, puddles and ditches until they were ready to take the air as perfect winged flies.

Although so many insects live in fresh water or pass some part of their lives there, they do not care for salt water and hardly any are to be found in the sea. An exception to the rule is the queer little long-legged tide-rock fly that runs about on the wet rocks on the seashore in California. It does not seem

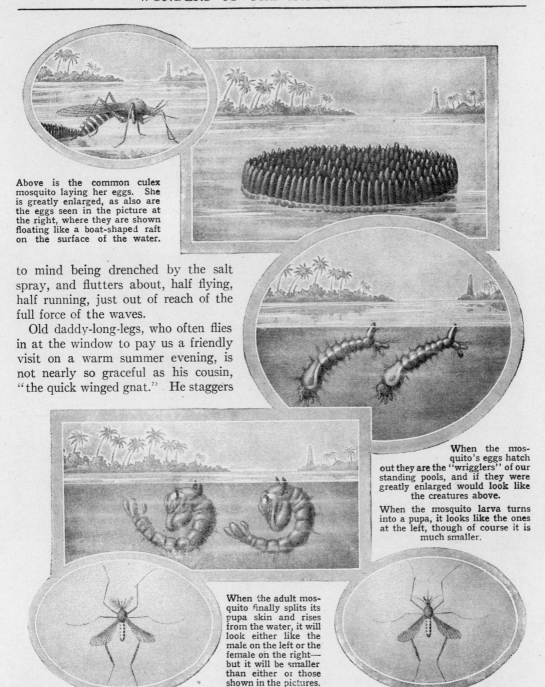

Above is the common culex mosquito laying her eggs. She is greatly enlarged, as also are the eggs seen in the picture at the right, where they are shown floating like a boat-shaped raft on the surface of the water.

to mind being drenched by the salt spray, and flutters about, half flying, half running, just out of reach of the full force of the waves.

Old daddy-long-legs, who often flies in at the window to pay us a friendly visit on a warm summer evening, is not nearly so graceful as his cousin, "the quick winged gnat." He staggers

When the mosquito's eggs hatch out they are the "wrigglers" of our standing pools, and if they were greatly enlarged would look like the creatures above.

When the mosquito larva turns into a pupa, it looks like the ones at the left, though of course it is much smaller.

When the adult mosquito finally splits its pupa skin and rises from the water, it will look either like the male on the left or the female on the right— but it will be smaller than either of those shown in the pictures.

about on his absurdly long legs, tries to scorch his wings in the gas, bumps into things, and flops over in the most ridiculous way. Yet "daddy" is quite a harmless person—although some people are terrified at the sight of the big, clumsy fellow. He neither bites nor stings. His trunk, which looks like a very long nose, is intended only for lapping up the juices of plants, and not for the purpose of sucking your blood.

The daddy's long legs seem very awkward to manage, and they are so delicate that they break off at the slightest touch. Strange to say, this does not appear to distress the curious fly; for if you catch a daddy by the leg he will fly off leaving it in your hand and dance away quite as merrily without it. That is why one so seldom sees a daddy-long-legs with his six legs all complete.

But a daddy's long legs are not designed for dancing on window-panes. They are in-

Daddy-long-legs is one of the crane-flies. He has a great many relatives, some so small that they may easily be mistaken for midges; but you may always know a crane-fly by the curious V-shaped mark on its shoulders.

The giant crane-fly is the most distinguished member of the tribe. He can boast of being one of the largest of all British flies. He measures two inches in length and over four inches across his outspread wings; and as for his legs, three finer pairs are seldom to be met with in the insect world.

The bright and graceful little flower-flies that hover like tiny humming birds over the flowers all through the hot sunny hours of a summer's day—now poised almost motionless in mid-air, now darting away swift as a lightning flash—are welcome visitors to orchards and gardens.

Some of these flies, in their black and yellow banded suits, are so like small wasps that you might easily be

The giant crane-fly is a relative of the daddy-long-legs. Here we see the eggs laid by one crane-fly, the "leather-jacket" grub, and the empty pupa case. Only the fly is of natural size.

tended for walking over grass, where they are really quite convenient. There "mother-long-legs" lays her eggs, stabbing little holes in the earth with her sharp egg-laying tube and leaving an egg in each hole.

The Harmful "Leather Jackets"

In their young days, it must be said, daddies are not so well-behaved as when they are grown up. They are strange-looking worm-like grubs called "leather jackets" on account of their very tough skins; and they do a great deal of harm in valuable pasture lands by gnawing the roots of the grasses.

deceived by their looks if you did not notice that they had only a single pair of wings—which shows at once that they are true flies. Others are very like bees, and they hum and buzz and crawl in and out of the flower cups like real bees.

Flower-flies—or hover-flies, as they are sometimes called, from the way they hover in the air—feed on nectar and honey. So they act as pollen carriers, helping the flowers to form their seeds. But it is while they are tiny fly grubs that they are most useful, for then they feed on troublesome little plant lice—just as the ladybird grubs do. The flower-fly grub is a soft, pale-green little creature, shaped like a pear, with a tiny round mouth at the small end. It moves about, stretching and drawing up its little body in a slug-like way, seizing on the plant lice, sucking them dry, and dropping their empty skins. The tiny creatures feed day and night for ten days before they rest from their labours and turn to pupae. Since it takes them only a moment to devour a plant louse, you can imagine how many of the tiny pests each baby flower-fly must destroy.

The bee-flies are even more like bees, with their plump velvet-coated bodies and black and amber colouring. Some of them mimic bumble-bees, others hiving bees. Even a spider is sometimes deceived by their looks, and hesitates to tackle them when they come blundering into his beautiful web.

He Breathes Through His Tail

Most curious of all is the big drone-fly that goes buzzing about just as if it were a real bee. It will sometimes pay us a short visit in the autumn, if the weather is dull or cold, and stay in the house buzzing about for two or three days. Since it does no harm, we need not object to our uninvited guest.

The drone-fly starts out in life as a queer little grub with a very long tail. It is then called a "rat-tailed maggot." It lives in muddy puddles or stagnant water, and keeps its tail well up in the air. For, as you probably have guessed, its "tail" is really a breathing tube through which the little creature draws in its breath.

The flower-flies and the bee-flies are all well-behaved, peaceful insects; but the big,

hairy, ferocious-looking robber-flies bear a very different character. They are bold bandits of the insect world, who live by hunting and killing other insects in the most savage way. They lie in wait on the ground or on some low-growing plant. Then with a fierce "buzz" they fly up and chase their victim through the air, pouncing on him and stabbing him in the back with their stout horny beaks. So bold and fearless are the robber-flies that they will even attack and kill wasps, dragon-flies, and fierce tiger-beetles.

Fly Which Spreads Sleeping-Sickness

One of the most terrible members of the fly family is the dreaded tsetse (sĕt′sĭ) fly of tropical Africa. It carries germs of a disease known as tsetse fly disease, or nagana, which it gives to animals, and of the dreaded sleeping-sickness which it transmits to man.

It is an inconspicuous dark-coloured fly, with a pair of wings that it folds one on top of the other lengthwise along its back. Its sharp sucking tube sticks straight out in front of its head, and is inserted into living creatures to draw the blood which is the fly's only food. Sometimes it gorges itself to twice its own weight; and if its victim is suffering from one of the diseases just mentioned, it carries the germs to the creatures it bites within the next few days.

Some varieties of tsetse fly carry nagana, others sleeping-sickness. These flies are interesting in that the female does not lay eggs, but every two or three weeks bears a grub that digs its way into the earth and turns to a pupa. Finally it emerges as a mature fly, and starts immediately upon its deadly work.

(CONTINUED ON PAGE 481)

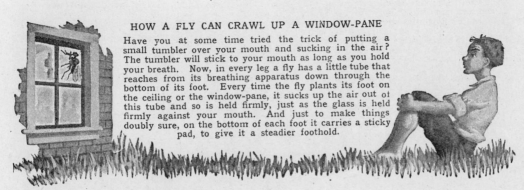

HOW A FLY CAN CRAWL UP A WINDOW-PANE

Have you at some time tried the trick of putting a small tumbler over your mouth and sucking in the air? The tumbler will stick to your mouth as long as you hold your breath. Now, in every leg a fly has a little tube that reaches from its breathing apparatus down through the bottom of its foot. Every time the fly plants its foot on the ceiling or the window-pane, it sucks up the air out of this tube and so is held firmly, just as the glass is held firmly against your mouth. And just to make things doubly sure, on the bottom of each foot it carries a sticky pad, to give it a steadier foothold.

MAGICAL CUPS

For this trick, besides the quick hand a conjurer always needs, you must have two handleless cups, with straight sides and bottoms sunk about ¼″. Turn them upside down, and on the sunken bottoms glue some bird-seed. The cups will then look as if they were right side up and full. When doing the trick, have a bag of the same seed. Show your audience that the cups are empty, but do not let anyone come dangerously near you. Now dip one cup in the seed as if to fill it, but instead turn it upside down, so as to show the glued seed. Now put it under a hat, but as you do so dextrously turn it right side up again. Now place the other cup, which is empty, under another hat, but turn this one upside down, so it will look full. Finally say some magic words, remove the hats, and show the people that the cups have changed places.

MAGIC

THE OBEDIENT KEY

This trick requires an extraordinarily strong magnet, a little preparation beforehand, and the faithful help of a friend. Make a large frame, taller than your friend, and cover it with paper as you would a screen. Then set the screen up in such a way that your friend can hide behind it—with the magnet. When the audience has gathered together, draw on this screen a picture of a nail or hook. Then borrow a key or a key-ring from someone—it must be something that a magnet will attract—and offer to hang it on the nail you have drawn. This is easy to do, provided that your friend holds the magnet just behind the "nail," where it can attract the key through the paper.

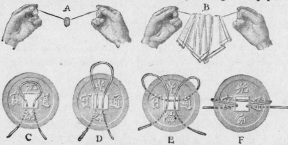

THE TRAVELLING COIN

Find a hair from 10 inches to a foot in length. On each end place a dab of magician's wax and stick each dab to a separate button on your waistcoat—this is no trick, you see, for a girl! Borrow a coin from the audience, and secretly press it against one dab of wax so that the wax will come off the button and stick to the coin. Now drop the coin in a goblet. Making magical passes to distract attention, slowly move the goblet away so that the unseen hair draws the coin up the side.

CHINESE COIN TRICK

Any kind of coin with a hole in it will do, but you must have two exactly alike. Palm one coin, that is, conceal it in your hand. Pass the other, and a piece of string, round for inspection. Ask a spectator to slip the string through the hole and hold it, an end in each hand (A). You promise to take the coin off the string while he holds it so; but it is a dark Chinese trick and you must work under cover. So borrow a handkerchief and throw it over the string (B). Under it move the coin a little to the left. Then attach the palmed coin to the centre of the string as shown in the pictures: draw a loop of string through the hole (C, D), slip the loop over the edge of the coin (E), and draw it taut (F). The string has to be rather slack for this. But now ask the spectator to tighten it, at the same time closing your hand over the first coin. Pretending that he is not doing it right, take the left end of the string, as if to show him, and as you hand it back slip your hand off the left end with the first coin in it. Now take off the handkerchief. The string across the coin will look like a knot you have been tying to make it all the harder to remove the coin. With a flourish, grasp the coin in one hand, slip the loop back over its edge—and the trick is done.

The eagle has stolen a cub from his friend the fox and is going to feed his young with it. And his wife, sitting by, is doubtless thinking how successful and efficient her husband is. But in a moment she will change her mind. For the eagle is not nearly as clever as she believes; he is just short-sighted and selfish and cruel.

TANSY *and* BOBBLES *on* FABLE ISLAND

The Exciting Adventures of the Fox and the Eagle, the Reed and the Oak, the Wolf and the Lamb, and the Marvellous Goose

(CONTINUED FROM PAGE 352)

EVERYONE knew that the eagle and the fox had formed a strange friendship with each other.

The eagle had his nest at the top of a very high rock, and the fox lived with his wife and cubs in a hole at the bottom.

Tansy and Bobbles loved to see the cubs romping and rolling one another over, and sometimes they said "Booh!" and joined in the fun.

But they were horrified early one morning to see the eagle make a swoop and carry off one of the poor little cubs to his nest.

The father fox was away on his travels, but the mother and the other cubs made a terrible outcry and besought the eagle to have mercy and restore the cub.

The eagle, however, thought that the nest was too high for the fox to catch him, and that he was safe in his wickedness.

At this Bobbles and Tansy were so filled with wrath that they flew up to the nest and cried "Booh!"

"Well," said the eagle, looking rather awkward, "what do you want?" But he had already guessed why they had come.

"Aren't you ashamed of yourself?" said Bobbles. "That cub belongs to your friend."

"I don't care," answered the eagle savagely.

"Oh, don't you!" replied Bobbles.

"And listen to the poor mother and brothers and sisters crying down below!" pleaded Tansy.

"They can't get up here," said the eagle, triumphantly.

But just then the fairies saw that the fox had returned. The minute his wife told him what had happened he rushed to an altar, seized a brand of burning wood from it, and began to set fire to the nest.

"Oh, my dear, my dear," screeched the mother eagle. "Now all our eaglets will be burned alive!"

"Quick! Quick! Give me that cub!" cried Tansy; and she flew down with it safely in her arms.

"You see," said Bobbles sternly to the eagle. "You may despise the cries of those you've injured, but you can't make yourself safe from their revenge."

Now it happened that evening, as the fairies were going

This is the dog that was willing to wear a bell all day long if only it would attract attention to himself.

along by a stream, wading in the cool water, that they came upon an angler who had been fishing all day and had caught nothing except one tiny fish, which was now struggling in his hand.

"Spare me! Spare me!" cried the fish. "I'm such a tiny little fish. Throw me back into the stream and in a month's time I shall be big and worth catching."

But the angler gave a laugh.

"Ha! ha!" he said, as he shook his head. "You are in my hand now, but if once I let you go back into the water, you'll change your ideas. You'll be calling to me, 'Good angler, pray catch me if you can!' A fish in the hand is worth two in the stream." And with that, he killed the fish and put it in his basket, to take home for his supper.

"Oh dear, dear," said Tansy, "what heaps and heaps of things we are finding out."

"That's true enough," admitted Bobbles. Then he added wisely, "But we mustn't get so conceited that we swell and swell and burst, like poor Mother Frog."

And the fairies laughed as they took to their wings and flew home.

Some People Are Like This Dog

"Do you hear that bell?" asked Tansy, as she and Bobbles passed invisibly towards the market-place of the town.

"It's the tradesman's mischievous dog," said Bobbles. "The tradesman had to put a bell on the dog's neck to give warning to the people that the dog was there."

"There he is," cried Tansy. "Do look at him shaking his head. I believe he's really quite proud of his noisy bell."

"Booh!" said Bobbles and Tansy, and the mischievous dog stared at them.

"If I were you," said Bobbles, "I wouldn't ring that bell so loudly."

"But why?" asked the mischievous dog. And he shook his head till the bell rang louder than ever.

"You may think that bell was given to you for glory, but really it was given to you for disgrace," said Bobbles.

But the mischievous dog showed his teeth, and, raising the hair on his back, trotted off in disgust.

"He'd rather they would all notice him for his mischief than not notice him at all," said Bobbles, looking almost as wise as good Father Fairy himself.

The Goose that Laid the Golden Eggs

They hurried on to find out what was happening at the egg dealer's stall, round which the people were crowding.

It appeared that the dealer had a wonderful goose, who laid a golden egg every day.

The people came from all over the island to buy these eggs, and the egg dealer couldn't supply them fast enough.

So, not satisfied with his present luck, and

growing daily more greedy and money-grubbing, he thought of a splendid idea.

If he killed the goose, then he would get all the eggs at once and grow rich much faster.

"He's killed his goose!" cried the people, as Bobbles and Tansy came up.

"And she's nothing but a common goose after all," said an old woman.

The old woman was right, for there lay the goose, cut open on the bench; and all the man now had was a goose to roast for his supper.

"It's easy to know the meaning of that," said Tansy. "But come along, Bobbles; I'm tired to death of this noisy town."

The Oak that was Too Proud

So away they flew to the wide moor, and startled the peewits and the larks by crying "Booh!" Presently they reached a giant oak. Here they perched themselves on a branch and reached out for acorns with which to pelt the squirrels.

A gentle breeze was blowing, and below them a reed was bending and bowing backwards and forwards with the breeze.

"Why do you bow before a breeze?" asked the oak irritably. "I wish you'd keep still, as I do."

"I must bow, for I'm only a poor reed," came the modest reply.

"I'm an oak!" cried the tree proudly. "I never bow!"

"Booh!" said Bobbles. "Pride, you old oak, may bring you to the ground even yet."

This goose is pleased with herself because she has just done quite a distinguished thing. She has laid an egg of solid gold.

"Ha! ha!" laughed the oak. "You can't count how many storms I've weathered."

But just then the storm, as if it had heard the proud boast, roused himself to battle.

"Look out, Tansy," cried Bobbles, and he helped his sister to a sheltered spot behind a rock which lay close by.

The storm blew and blustered, and the oak refused to bow, though the reed sank to the ground.

But when at last the storm had passed and the fairies peeped out, they saw that the oak was torn up by the roots, though the reed was standing calm and upright.

"Alas! poor oak," said the reed, pityingly. "We were always the best of friends."

Mother Lark Moves Her Family

"I do love the harvest field," said Tansy, as she and Bobbles played hide-and-seek among the standing grain and poppies.

They could do no harm, because they were fairies. Presently they came upon a nest of young larks, whose mother was away looking for food.

Tansy and Bobbles knelt down by the nest, and Tansy asked whether they were not afraid that the reapers would destroy their home now that the grain had ripened.

The young larks explained that they had been afraid, but that their mother refused to move.

"We told her," said the eldest lark, "that we'd heard the farmer say he must send for his neighbours to cut down his grain, but mother said, 'Pooh! there's no fear of the neighbours doing that for him.'"

"And we told her," piped up the eldest daughter, "that we'd heard the farmer say that he must send for his uncles and nephews and cousins to reap his harvest, but mother said, 'Pooh! His relatives will never help him.'"

Just then the mother returned, and nodded towards the fairies.

"Have you heard anything more, children?" she asked.

"Yes, yes, mother," cried the youngest lark. "We've heard the farmer say that the grain is now so ripe that he will have to reap it himself."

"Dear! dear!" cried the mother lark. "We must move at once. If the farmer is going to work himself, he means business."

"Let us help you to move," cried Tansy.

So Tansy and Bobbles carried off the nest and the young larks, and put them in a safe place in another field.

"Good-bye! Good-bye!" cried the young larks. "When we are grown up we will sing you beautiful songs."

"And we will fly races in the sky with you," said Bobbles.

Then they heard the sound of a scythe. The farmer was beginning to reap his grain. "Only just in time," said the mother lark, with a contented sigh of thankfulness.

Unkindness Never Pays

As the fairies went off along the high road, they noticed a horse coming along with a light load on its back, while behind there was a donkey very heavily laden.

"Please, please," moaned the donkey to the horse, "do take some of this heavy load, or indeed I shall die under the weight of it."

"What have I to do with your load?" said the horse. "I don't want to hear your complaints. Just get on with your work."

But suddenly, to the horror of the fairies, the poor donkey fell dead.

"You see what you've done!" said Bobbles angrily.

The horse turned, and saw the dead donkey.

"It's none of my business," he said.

But now the master came rushing up, and unloosed the load from the donkey, piling it on the horse. Then he lifted the donkey's carcass and laid it on the top, so that the horse had now to carry, not only the donkey's load, but the donkey too.

"You see what comes of refusing to share your neighbour's burden," whispered Bobbles in the horse's ear.

"Alas!" agreed the horse. "If I'd taken my share, I shouldn't now be punished by having to bear all."

Tansy and Bobbles had been fast asleep under a spreading beech when they were gradually wakened by the sound of a low, grumbling voice.

On sitting up they saw a sleek, well-fed donkey standing near them in the shade and waiting till the woodcutters had collected a load for him.

"Booh!" exclaimed the fairies. "What has gone wrong with you?"

"Don't worry me," grumbled the donkey, "but look yonder at that pampered puppy of my master's."

No wonder the horse looks dismayed. He has found out too late that shirking one's work does not pay.

He looks an uncommonly intelligent and well-behaved donkey, but he has a bad time ahead, for he has allowed himself to feel envious of his master's little dog, and no one can be envious and happy at the same time.

The fairies looked and saw that the master was amusing himself with the gambols of a tiny dog who pranced about him, climbed on his knee, licked his face, and nestled against his arm.

"Well," said Tansy, "he's just a puppy; you're a strong, sober donkey."

"Oh, indeed," scoffed the donkey. "I carry wood, and help to turn the mill; but though I look well fed and prosperous, I'm tied up in the stable at night while that silly dog has meals at my master's table and sleeps at the foot of his bed."

"But you wouldn't like to frolic about like that puppy," said Tansy. "And you'd be very uncomfortable in your master's dining-hall." And she laughed merrily.

"It's nothing to laugh about," said the donkey, gloomily. "But you come to the house at midday and you will see that even a donkey can strike for his rights!" Then the donkey stopped talking, for the men had come to load the wood on him.

At midday Bobbles and Tansy could not resist going to the house to see what the foolish donkey would do. Making themselves invisible, they popped in at the window of the dining-hall, and swung their legs from the ledge.

The master sat down to a fine dinner, and, true enough, the pet dog had a chair by his side.

But suddenly there was a tremendous commotion. The donkey had broken loose and came dancing and prancing into the room, standing on his hind legs, grinning from ear to ear, swishing the crockery from the table, breaking the furniture in his gambols, and finally going up to his astonished master and trying to lick his cheeks and caress him with his hard, iron-shod hoofs.

"Out! Out!" cried the master. "Have you gone mad?" and he rang a bell, while the puppy escaped into a corner and barked violently.

"No, no, Master! I would have you love me as you love your pet dog," brayed the donkey; and again he tried to climb on to his master's lap.

But in rushed the servants, and seizing the donkey, they beat him off with such terrible blows that in a few moments he was lying in the stable yard, groaning in pain.

"We are so sorry," said Bobbles and Tansy, as they knelt beside him.

"Alas!" he groaned, "why couldn't I be satisfied to be a donkey? Why did I want to imitate a puppy?"

The fairies wandered off, feeling rather sad that such a punishment had befallen the donkey, because of his foolishness. So they decided to relieve their feelings by going down to the sea and having a swim.

It was a glorious, hot afternoon, and the sea gave them a sparkling welcome.

"One! Two! Three!" shouted Bobbles, as he and Tansy tiptoed on a rock. Then off they dived into the sea.

"Oh, there's the wolf!" grumbled Tansy to Bobbles one glorious morning. "I wanted to be jolly all the day, and now I'm sure I can't, for I do so dislike the wolf."

"Oh, but you must be fair," said Bobbles. "The wolf can't help being a wolf. He can't help his nature.'

"Still I wish father hadn't said we must be polite to all the people and creatures on the island," sighed Tansy.

No one could feel miserable on such a day, however, so Tansy cried "Booh!" and ran up to the wolf to wish him a good morning.

"It's no good morning for me," grumbled the wolf. "I've had a fine night of it, I can tell you."

"Do tell us!" said Bobbles.

"Why, in that house over there I heard a nurse say to her crying child, 'If you don't stop crying, I'll throw you to the wolf.' So, as the child went on crying, I waited and waited, for he would have been a choice morsel for me and my family. But by and

This is a deeply disappointed wolf. He has been waiting for someone to throw the baby out to him for his supper, but nothing has happened.

by there was silence, and then I heard the nurse say, 'Good child! Good child! That wicked, wicked wolf shall never get you. If he tries, we'll drive him off and kill him.' Now what do you make of that?"

"Well," said Bobbles, "I suppose it's no use listening to people who say one thing and mean another."

"Liars! Liars!" cried the wolf wrathfully. "Oh dear, I'm so thirsty that I'm off for a drink at the stream."

Now, as the wolf was lapping the cool water, he noticed a stray lamb wading about in the stream, some way down.

"Ha! ha!" thought the wolf. "He will make up for that child I lost!" So he hastily planned an excuse for killing the innocent lamb.

"How dare you make my stream muddy," he called, "when I want to drink!"

"Indeed," cried the terrified lamb, "I'm far below where you are drinking."

"That may be," said the wolf, dashing towards her, "but a year ago I heard you call me shocking names."

And he looked very fierce.

"Indeed," cried the lamb, "I wasn't born a year ago!"

"Don't argue with me!" stormed the wolf; and without more ado he seized the helpless lamb and carried her off.

"Now, Bobbles!" cried Tansy, indignantly, "what can you make of that?"

"I've heard father say that a bully will always find an excuse for doing anything which is wrong," said Bobbles, rather sadly. "But come on. Let's talk to the stag."

An old stag was resting on the grass under

the shade of a tree, and a fawn was skipping about near him.

"Booh!" cried the fairies, and the fawn put her soft nose into Tansy's hand.

"Let's have a game," said Tansy. So the fawn chased Tansy and Bobbles, and then Tansy and Bobbles chased the fawn, until at last they flung themselves down to rest by the old stag.

Our wolf is hardly an agreeable-looking fellow—and his sides seem very hollow. But it is safe to prophesy that they will not look hollow much longer.

"What a fine, strong-looking creature you are," said Tansy to the stag.

"Ah!" sighed the fawn, "he *is* very strong; but though he has horns and can run faster than a hound and can keep his breath for miles, he flies for his life the moment he hears a hound bay."

"I know, I know," said the stag. "Although I always resolve to be brave, when I hear the hounds my courage fails me."

"Hark!" cried the fawn.

"Hounds!" exclaimed Bobbles.

The old stag jumped to his feet and darted away, followed closely by the young fawn.

"You see," said Bobbles, "habits soon become a second nature."

Crows are Conceited but Clever

"Do look, Bobbles, at that clever crow," said Tansy, joyously.

Indeed, the crow was very much pleased with himself.

Being terribly thirsty, he had been very glad to find a pitcher. But alas, the water was so low he couldn't reach it.

In his first disappointment he had tried to break the pitcher, but he wasn't strong enough, so he decided that this was a very silly scheme. He was therefore picking up pebbles and dropping them one after another into the pitcher, until at last the water rose within his reach.

"Booh!" cried the fairies.

"Did you see what I did?" asked the crow; "my skill and my patience have won the day!" And off he flew.

"He's a conceited old bird," said Bobbles. "Still, as father would say, 'Necessity is the mother of invention.'"

Just then the fairies heard sounds of splashing, and they hurried off to find some boys swishing flat stones along the surface of the pond, in a game of "ducks and drakes." But in their sport the boys were actually killing some poor frogs.

"Stop! Stop!" cried a courageous frog, as he stood up on a stone and faced the thoughtless boys. "What may be fun to you is death to us."

The boys laughed, but Bobbles and Tansy made themselves invisible and began flying round the boys, pulling their hair and pinching their cheeks until the air rang with their cries.

"Oh! oh!" squealed the boys. But the more they tried to dart away, the more the fairies pinched them and the more they pulled their hair.

"You don't like it! You don't like it!" mocked Bobbles.

Then suddenly the fairies cried "Booh!" and ordered the boys to gather round them in a circle.

The terrified boys obeyed, and listened to the stern lecture which Bobbles gave them; and they promised, by every hair in their heads, that they would never again hurt frogs or any other harmless creatures.

How Crafty Mr. Fox Played a Practical Joke On Poor Old Mr. Stork

So the fairies made themselves invisible again and flew off. And presently, as they were walking down a sheltered valley, they noticed that a fox was giving a dinner to a stork.

"I don't think the stork is getting much to eat," whispered Tansy, who was rather amused at the strange party.

And he certainly was not, for the fox had provided a number of shallow dishes of soup, which he could lap up easily, while the stork, with his long bill, could only get a few drops.

The stork, being the guest, was very polite to the rude fox. But Bobbles suddenly thought of a good way for the stork to get even.

He perched on the stork's shoulder and whispered something to him. As the stork rose and thanked the fox for the delightful meal, he invited him to come next day to dinner—a very special dinner.

Mr. Stork's Queer Dinner Party Teaches Mr. Fox a Much-needed Lesson

The fox gladly accepted. And next day Tansy and Bobbles had the joy of seeing the dismay of the fox when he found that the stork's dinner of delicious minced meat was served in a narrow-necked jar. The stork could eat plentifully, but the fox could only lick up a few drops of the sauce which trickled down from the top of the jar and feed off the few stray scraps which fell from the stork's beak.

"Now you know how it feels to have a bad host," whispered Bobbles to the fox.

The fox looked round, and guessed who was there, for he had met the fairies once or twice before and knew that they possessed the happy knack of being able to turn up at very awkward moments.

"Good stork," said Tansy, "I trust you have enjoyed your dinner better than the one you had yesterday."

The fox was turning away grumpily when Bobbles added, "It isn't fair to play a joke unless you can take a joke in return."

(CONTINUED ON PAGE 543)

Our friend the fox thought he was very clever, but he was not quite as clever as he thought. In fact, sly people rarely are—and the reason is easily discovered. If they were really clever they would never need to be sly, but would have the sense to know that they could get along better by using their wits without making enemies.

John Callcott Horsley, the well-known painter, has caught in this picture the humour of a situation common in many a family that owns a budding musician. He has named his work "The Rival Performers." Every musician will remember an occasion when, as a beginner, he poured his whole heart into his effort—only to find that no one was paying the least attention.

By courtesy of the Victoria and Albert Museum

MIGHTY MUSIC *for Our* MODERN AGE

From the Time of Wagner, That Great Forger of Musical Thunderbolts, Down to the Gifted Men of the Nations of To-day, Modern Composers have been Trying to Make Music Tell a Story, Sing a Song, and Paint a Picture

(CONTINUED FROM PAGE 382)

THERE are some men who always seem to live in the midst of a storm. This usually is because they have loftier, larger ideas than the men among whom they dwell, and so, like a tall mountain, they always have the lightning playing round them. For if there is anything that ordinary people hate, it is to be told that there is a better way to do a thing than the way in which it has always been done. To change anything means thinking about it—and many people find thinking very hard work indeed!

All this is true in music, as in other things.

Nearly every great musician has had to fight his way against all the people who did not like his music because it was different from the kind to which they were accustomed. So some of the noblest music the world has ever known was actually hissed the first time it was heard.

During the nineteenth century there was an especially bitter war carried on between the new and the old, and the man who was the central figure in this struggle was Richard Wagner (väg′nẽr). Fortunately, he lived longer (1813–1883) than most of his fellow musicians, and so was able to see the day when he was honoured and famous. But even then there were large numbers of people who thought of him as a kind of musical savage.

He belonged to a family of German actors, so it was natural that when he began to write music he should want to write music dramas. But he did not want his operas to be like those the Italians wrote—a long string of songs without action. He wanted them to be real dramas, with the music a necessary part of the action, and the words a necessary part of both.

It was a hard task that Wagner set himself, but he succeeded in it, and was the first man ever to do so. For always before, either the music had swamped the drama, as with the Italians, or the drama had swamped the music, as with the French. Wagner had to be a great genius in many ways in order to do a thing that was so difficult. He had to know how to build up a thrilling drama; he had to be poet enough to know how to write fine words—or what we call the "libretto" (lĭ-brĕt'ō), the "little book"; and he had to write music that would be beautiful and yet, at every moment, reflect as vividly as possible all the thoughts and feelings and actions of his characters.

Like many later writers of opera, he was able to learn a good deal from Carl Maria von Weber (fŏn vā'bĕr), a man who had preceded him by a short time (1786–1826) and had written the first real German opera. Previously, operas, even though they might have been written by Germans, had copied the Italians or the French. But Weber was great enough to strike out in a new direction, and when he produced "The Marksman" (Der Freischütz) (1821), people were delighted. It was a beautiful and melodious

The German composer, Richard Wagner, one of the greatest writers of opera of all time.

music drama built up round an old German legend, and it was in German. Later he came to England and wrote another charming opera round an English story of the king of the fairies. It was called "Oberon" (ō'bĕr-ŏn).

So Wagner, too, built up his operas round German characters and German myths— the doings of the old German gods, of the mastersingers, of the knights of the Holy Grail. And instead of having nothing but solo melodies, or arias (ä'rĭ-ȧ), with long chanted prose explanations between them— called recitative (rĕs'ĭ-tȧ-tēv')—he went back to the music of the great Bach (bäK), and wove together a number of separate short tunes, all of which he kept going at the same time. That is what we call counterpoint; and the use of it made the music of Wagner's operas very much fuller and richer than the older operatic music had been.

But, more interesting still, he gave every one of those separate tunes, or "motives," a special meaning. He made it stand for a particular character or idea in the opera, and so whenever its own especial character appears or is mentioned, you begin to hear the theme that belongs to him weaving in and out of the music. In Wagner's last opera, "Parsifal" (pär'sĭ-fȧl), which tells the story of a knight of the Holy Grail, there are some especially beautiful themes belonging, for instance, to Parsifal, to his sword, and to the Grail. Whenever a theme is given this special meaning it is called a "leitmotif" (līt-mō̆-tēf'), or "leading motive," and it is always in keeping with the character or idea it represents—grave or gay, evil or holy.

Above all, the very story of the opera usually has an inner, hidden meaning. Its characters and their deeds tell, in one way or another, of the trials and the adventures of the human soul—the clash of good and evil,

In this scene from Wagner's opera, "The Twilight of the Gods," we are shown Siegfried, in the course of the hunt, as he is about to be slain by one of the followers of the treacherous Gunther, the brother of Kriemhild.

the effects of sin and the way of redemption from it. You can see why Wagner's operas, even though they are so German in subject matter, have a strong interest for people of every nation and every age.

The Scandalous Scene at the First Performance of a Powerful Opera

As Wagner worked, his powers increased. His first great opera was "The Flying Dutchman" (1843). The next was the beautiful "Tannhäuser" (tän′hoi-zēr), which contains the Pilgrims' Chorus that everybody loves. Yet when "Tannhäuser" was first performed in Paris (1861), the audience received it with hisses and jeers and made a scandalous scene that was not forgotten for many years. Other great works followed, all of them masterpieces—"Lohengrin" (lō′ĕn-grĭn), with its famous Wedding March; "Tristan and Isolde" (ē-sōl′dĕ), based on an old love tale; "The Mastersingers," Wagner's only comic opera, and the one that contains the well-known Prize Song; and, perhaps, greatest of all, the four operas that make up what is known as "The Ring of the

Nibelungs" (nē′bē-lŏŏngz)—or as it is often called, "The Ring."

The operas in the Ring cycle are, in order, "The Rhinegold," "The Valkyrie" (văl-kĭr′ĭ), "Siegfried" (sēg′frēd), and "The Twilight of the Gods"—and one must hear all four in order to know the whole story of the famous ring made out of gold stolen from the Rhine maidens, who had been set to guard it deep in the waters of the river. This ring brought magic power to its owner, but it brought a curse as well, and the working out of the curse is the story of the four great music dramas.

Critics Who Ridiculed Wagner and Jeered at His Wonderful Work

Wagner became so famous that before his death he was able to see one of his great dreams fulfilled, when the Festival Playhouse was opened (1876) at Bayreuth with the production of "The Ring." The new opera house was intended to work out Wagner's ideas of what opera should be.

But how Wagner was hated, just the same! A well-known writer said he could make music just as good as Wagner's by letting his cat walk up and down the piano keys. Rossini, the greatest composer of Italian opera at the time, held "Lohengrin" upside down and said he couldn't make head or tail of it. One distinguished critic said it was nothing but "blubbering baby talk," another called it "opera without music"; and even the generous Clara Schumann, wife of Robert Schumann, said that "Tristan and Isolde" was "the most repulsive thing" she had ever seen or heard in her life. One German writer has actually collected and published a whole "Schimpf-lexikon"—or "abuse dictionary"—consisting of nothing but the uncomplimentary and abusive things that people said about Wagner and his music.

And yet, now, there is a whole army of critics who would agree that Wagner was one of the greatest geniuses the world has ever produced.

Richard Strauss (strous) is the leading composer in Germany since Wagner's day. He was born in Munich in 1864, and is still writing his brilliant and amazing symphonic poems and songs and operas. One of his best-known works is the opera "Salome" (sä-lō′mē), which stirred up almost as much fury as had some of Wagner's operas. For Strauss, too, trod a new path. He uses an enormous orchestra with more than a hundred performers and all sorts of contrasted instruments to give new kinds or textures of sound. He works for startling effects. Another of his operatic masterpieces is the well-known "Der Rosenkavalier," or "The Cavalier of the Rose."

His greatest contributions to modern music, however, lie in his magnificent symphonic poems: "Till Eulenspiegel's Merry Pranks," "Don Juan," "Death and Transfiguration," "Don Quixote," and "A Hero's Life" are among the best known. In these he has developed the form of the symphonic poem far beyond the point at which Liszt left it, and has written music that has no equal for the vividness with which it imitates natural sounds, or paints a picture for the mind to see.

Quite recently a new group of composers has

The lovely Jenny Lind, known as "the Swedish nightingale," was the idol of musical audiences in the middle of the nineteenth century. She sang many famous operatic roles, both in Europe and in America, and was unexcelled in oratorio.

sprung up in Germany. Like Strauss and Wagner before them, they are trying to make music say more than it has ever said before. Among them are Arnold Schönberg (shĕn′bĕrg), Paul Hindemith (hĭn′dĕ-mĭt), and Alban Berg (bĕrg). Like so many other modern composers they are startling the world with music that is not written in any key. It all sounds very terrible and bewildering to most of the people used to the ordinary harmonies, but many skilled critics think very highly of it.

In other countries besides Germany opera has grown more and more beautiful and interesting. For a long time Italy clung to her old habit of making the song the whole thing and the action nothing at all, until finally her writers of opera began to go to France. That brightened up their work at once, and Rossini (rŏs-sē'nē), whom we remember for his comic opera, "The Barber of Seville" (1816), and for "William Tell" (1829); Donizetti (dō'nĕd-zet'ē), whose "Lucia (lōō-chē'ä) di Lammermoor" (1835) contains the famous Sextette that all barrel-organs used to play; and Bellini (bĕl-lē'nē), all wrote music that people have hummed and whistled for a century.

But much greater than these was Giuseppe Verdi (jōō-sĕp'pä vär'dē), who always stayed at home in Italy, where, as a tiny boy, he loved to dance along behind the village organ-grinder. His operas are still among the most popular that we have. Everyone knows the famous Anvil Chorus from "Il Trovatore" (ēl trō'vä-tōr'ä), the Triumphal March from "Aïda" (ä-ē'dä), and a host of other airs from his tuneful works. His finest operas, "Otello" and "Falstaff," were written towards the close of his long life (1813–1901), when he had learned much from the great work of Wagner.

Photo by Elliott and Fry

The Great Puccini

Since Verdi's day Italy has given us Puccini (pōōt-chē'nē), who died as lately as 1924. He was worthy of the great men who had gone before him, and his chief successes, such as "La Bohème" (lä bō-ĕm'), "Tosca," "Madame Butterfly," "The Girl of the Golden West" and "Turandot" have provided some of our most famous singers with rôles.

Frenchmen, too, were hard at work in

opera during the nineteenth century. They were headed by a German named Meyerbeer (mī'ĕr-bâr), who went to live in Paris and produced his pompous historical operas there —such as "The Huguenots" (1836), "The Prophet" (1843), and "The African" (1838–1865). And after him came Gounod (gōō'-nō), whom we have to thank for "Faust" (foust), one of the most popular operas ever written. He gave us some beautiful sacred music too.

Another French opera that people never seem to tire of hearing is "Carmen," by Bizet (bē-zā'). Baritones love to sing its stirring Toreador Song—just as contraltos love to sing the famous aria from "Samson and Delilah," by the Frenchman Saint-Saëns (săN-säNs). During a very long life (1835–1921) Saint-Saëns wrote charming, graceful music that one often hears to-day.

But the greatest of all the modern French musicians was Claude Debussy (klōd dĕ-bü-sē'), who, besides his opera "Pelléas and Mélisande" (pĕl-ā-äs' mā-lē-sôNd'), set modern music on a new path with his amazing orchestral works, such as "L'Après-midi d'une Faune" ("The Afternoon of a Faun"), and his piano compositions "Gardens in the Rain," for instance, or "Reflections in the Water." Debussy (1862–1918) has been called an "impressionist," for the effects that he produces are all vague, subtle and dreamy. They awake all manner of powerful feelings in us, but nothing is ever very clear-cut or definite, although his work is always fine and restrained. He tries to arouse in the listener the same feeling that he would have if he were actually looking at a rain-washed garden or at the mysterious shadows in a pool.

Two famous operatic composers of the nineteenth century: at the left, the Italian Puccini, whose best-known work is "Madame Butterfly"; below, the German Meyerbeer, author of many historical operas.

Photo by J. and W. Chester, Ltd.

Debussy had studied the new music that was being written in Russia. He often used an unusual scale—one made up of six whole tones—and that produced the most amazing harmonies. Many people could see nothing but senseless noise in his music, but to-day he is considered one of the great modern masters. His influence on the younger composers has been very great.

Among them is Maurice Ravel (rá-věl'), a talented Frenchman who follows the lead of Debussy in many ways. Everyone who listens to music over the wireless has heard

in the Paris Conservatoire. He, too, struck out for himself, and shocked many musicians of his day; but his fine, thoughtful, serene spirit produced magnificent sacred music, several striking works for the piano, and some excellent compositions for orchestra—especially his masterpiece, the Symphony in D minor, which one may often hear.

His pupil, the French composer d'Indy (dăN-dē'), said of him: "The foundation of his character was gentleness, calm and serene goodness. He had high ideals and lived up to them. He never sought honours or distinctions, but worked hard and long to give of the best that was in him."

Now, it may have occurred to you that during all the centuries since the time of the Greeks, music has seemed to be in the hands of just three countries—Italy, Germany, and France—with a reference to England now and then.

Does this mean that the other nations of the world had no ear for music at all?

No, indeed! There never

Photo by Rischgitz

The charms of music have given rise to many legends. Such is the Greek story of the sirens, whose exquisite singing lured unfortunate sailors to destruction. And such is the German tale of the Lorelei (lōr'ě-lī), a maiden believed to inhabit a cliff overlooking the Rhine. There she sat and sang, and by her beauty and the unearthly loveliness of her music she lured sailors to their death on the treacherous rocks below.

his "Boléro," that exciting dance which makes it difficult for a listener to remain seated.

Another great French composer of the nineteenth century was César Franck (sā-zär' fräNk), who was a Belgian by birth but spent the greater part of his life (1822–1890) in Paris, as church organist and teacher

was a people yet who did not love music. But it does mean that other countries were imitating the great composers of their neighbours and had not learned to appreciate the beautiful folk songs that the humble people were singing at home. For no nation has ever produced great music till it learned

Photo by Swedish State Rlys.

It is by simple folk such as these inhabitants of Sweden that music is kept alive in every nation, for no people can possibly produce great music until the common man has learned to put his deepest emotion into song.

to voice its own musical thoughts, and not just echo the thoughts of some foreign country.

About 1850 Russia awoke to the fact that her own unhappy peasants were singing songs as lovely and moving as any in the world. At that time a group of five talented men, none of them professional musicians, started to write music that should be thoroughly Russian. A composer named Michael Glinka had already shown them the way with an opera called "A Life for the Tsar" (1836), which had aroused the greatest excitement everywhere in Russia. So when The Five began to preach Russian music for the Russians, people were ready to be convinced—and Russian music soon came to be a thing of great beauty and power.

A Masterpiece which Caused Annoyance to the Critics

The greatest of them was probably Modest Moussorgsky (mō′dĕst mōō′sôrg-skĭ), whose masterpiece was "Boris Godounov" (bŏ-rēs′ gô′dōō-nôf′). When it was produced (1874), many critics were enraged, just as they had been by "Lohengrin." But we now know that it is one of the grandest operas ever

written, and count ourselves lucky if we can hear Chaliapine (shäl-yä′pēn), the greatest singer of the twentieth century, sing the rôle of the mad king who is its hero.

Another famous member of The Five was Nicholas Rimsky-Korsakov (rĭm′skĭ-kôr′så-kôf), who is much better known than any of the rest. His two best operas are "The Golden Cockerel" and "The Snow Maiden." But on the wireless we often hear the fascinating music from his "Scheherazade" (shĕ-hä′rå-zä′dĕ). It is an orchestral suite (swēt)—that is to say, a series of "movements," or detached pieces in different moods.

The Russian who is best known of all is the famous Peter Ilyitch Tchaikovsky (chī-kôf′skĭ), who did not belong to The Five at all. Because he wrote music more or less as the other Europeans were writing it, he was much easier for the world to understand. His life (1840–1893) was not a happy one, and his music reflects its tumult and sadness; but his symphonies are among the most popular music that we possess. You will frequently hear the strains of his delicate Nutcracker Suite on the wireless.

17

It is only in recent years that the world has discovered all this beautiful Russian music, which has come to have such a tremendous influence on all our present-day composers. A few years ago Igor Stravinsky (ē′gôr strä-vĭn′skĭ) astonished the world—and enraged a part of it—by his compositions for orchestra. They are often written without any key, and show the author's liking for courageous discords, his clever imitations of the sounds of everyday life, and his deep understanding of how to play on the human emotions. He is still at the height of his powers—he was born in 1882—and is probably having as much influence on the course of music as any composer to-day. His best-known works are two orchestral pieces called "The Fire Bird" (1909) and "The Rite of Spring" (1911).

These are two of the greatest modern interpreters of music. Above is Ignace Jan Paderewski (pä′dĕ-rĕf′skĭ), the great Polish pianist, who has also served his country as its premier. At the right is Fritz Kreisler, the famous Austrian violinist.

The Russians were not the only people who were beginning to find their inspiration in the airs they heard at home. Composers in other lands were also weaving into their works echoes of the simple folk-songs they had learned to sing as tiny children. For every race has its own particular genius when it comes to the music that humble people make to cheer them while they work, or when they gather for a wedding or some special festival.

No one knows whence this folk-music comes, any more than we can tell how the wild flowers that spring up along a country road were sown. Some simple ploughman, some country fiddler, some busy mother humming at her work devised a little tune

and others heard and liked it. Finally it was tossed about from mouth to mouth, people improved upon it as they sang it, and no one could remember where it came from.

But it is those simple tunes that sing themselves through the works of nearly every great composer, for they have been born in the very heart of the race—and every race has its own particular airs, as different from the songs of other races as an Irishman is different from a Swede. Just hum over to yourself the tune of "Loch Lomond," from Scotland, and of "Holy Night," from Germany. They are both folk melodies—yet how different they are!

So the Norwegian composer, Edward Grieg (1843–1907), built up his exquisite music for orchestra or voice or piano by using

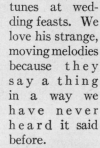

echoes of the wild or gay songs that he had heard among the fiords or in the pine-clad mountains of his native land, and more especially, perhaps, tunes made up by fiddlers they hire in Norway to play dance tunes at wedding feasts. We love his strange, moving melodies because they say a thing in a way we have never heard it said before.

Antonin Dvořák (1841–1904), a Czech, also made good use of the songs of his native land. Americans should be especially grateful to Dvořák (dvôr′zhäk), for he lived three years in their country as head of a conservatory of music in New York, and at that time wrote his beautiful symphony, "From the New World." Into this noble work the Bohemian butcher's son wove the Negro melody, "Swing low, sweet chariot"—and echoes of various other negro melodies. But we know him even better for the popular

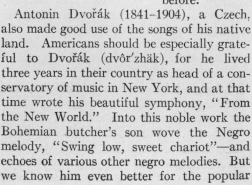

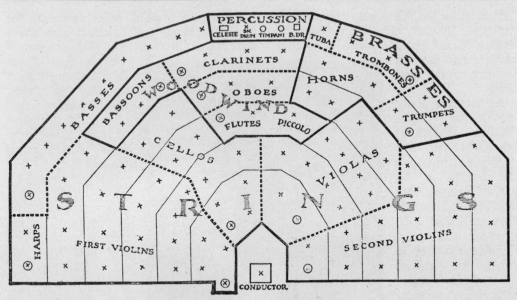

Above is the diagram of a common plan for seating the players in a large orchestra. You will notice that the string instruments, "the soul of the orchestra," are placed at the front of the stage, nearest the conductor.

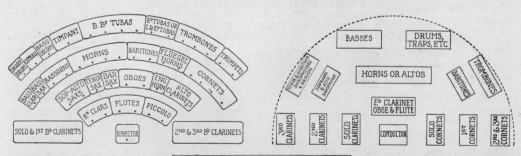

Above is the seating arrangement for a symphonic band. This large band, as you can see, has quite a different arrangement from that of the smaller band of thirty-six pieces or less, shown at the right.

A concert band, usually consisting of not more than thirty-six pieces, is seated more or less as we have shown above. Here you see the cornets and clarinets at the front, and the saxophones and bassoons at the left.

| B♭ CLARINETS |
| OBOES·ENGLISH HORN·BASSOONS·B♭ CLARINETS |
| ALTO & BASS CLARINETS   ALL SAXOPHONES |
| E♭CLARINETS CYMBALS BASS DRUM 2 SNARE DRUM PICCOLOS |
| CORNETS, TRUMPETS, & FLUEGEL HORNS |
| E♭ TUBA HORNS OR ALTOS BARITONES E♭ TUBA |
| 2 BB♭TUBAS TROMBONES 2BB♭TUBAS |

DRUM ● MAJOR

A marching band usually lines up in the order shown above, with an imposing drum-major at the head, to set the time with his baton. You will notice that a band has no strings, but has certain other instruments instead, such as saxophones, cornets, and one or two additional clarinets.

"Humoresque," which he also wrote while in America. He had "Way down upon the Swanee River" in mind when he wrote it, and the two can well be sung at the same time.

At the close of the last century Jean Sibelius (sĭ-bā′lĭ-ŭs) began to put into mighty sombre music the picture of his native Finland, "the land of a thousand lakes and islets." His symphonic poem "Finlandia" (1894) so stirred the patriotic spirit of the Finns— who were then under the heel of the tsar of Russia—that the Russian authorities forbade its being played.

In England, since 1700 down to the time when Elgar, now Sir Edward Elgar, became famous through performances of his "King Olaf" and his oratorio "The Light of Life" (1896) we have had no musicians who have been thought worthy to compare with the great Continental composers.

From somewhere between 1400 and 1420, when an Englishman, John Dunstable, who is thought by many to have been the inventor of counterpoint —because he was the first to give to each voice an independent part in his compositions—England led the world in music (in spite of Flemish rivalry) until 1560, from which date to 1722 it was the

Copyright: Elliott and Fry

Sir William Schwenk Gilbert, the English playwright and humorist, whose light operas are world famous.

Copyright: Elliott and Fry

Sir Arthur Seymour Sullivan, who wrote most of the music for Sir William Gilbert's light operas.

Italians who excelled other nations. The great Palestrina (pä′lā-strē′nȧ) gave them their start. From 1722 to 1833, however, it was the turn of the Germans, when Bach invented the "tempered" scale; and they remained supreme until the death of Richard Wagner.

An Irishman, John Field (1782 – 1837), deserves mention, for he invented a new form in musical composition. This was the "Nocturne," which Chopin soon after was to render immortal. Field was thought to be the most expressive player on the piano the world had ever heard.

A little later William Sterndale Bennett (1816–1895) raised great expectations. Both Mendelssohn and Schumann greatly praised him. But, already, in 1842, Sterndale Bennett seemed to have lost his originality, and became a musical drudge.

During the next twenty years England had nothing original to show in musical composition, but in 1862 Arthur Seymour Sullivan (1842–1900) wrote some promising music to "The Tempest." It was not this, however, nor his opera "Ivanhoe," but the music he composed for W. S. Gilbert's plays which made his name known throughout the world.

His melodies were graceful and his harmonies refined, and whilst the world delighted in his tunes and the perfect way they fitted the words of Gilbert's plays, skilled musicians admired the neat workmanship of his compositions. In the Gilbert-Sullivan operas Sullivan had to invent a style of music very different from any then known, and this he did in a thoroughly artistic manner.

As Gilbert's plays were very wittily written, Sullivan was obliged to take care that all the words should receive a proper share of the attention of the audience; consequently, although he took great pains to compose charming music, he never made the music so fascinating that it might have prevented people from giving due attention to the words. The best-known of all these operas are "The Mikado," "The Gondoliers," and "The Yeomen of the Guard."

Photo by Swaine

For fifteen years after Sullivan no young composer came forward except F. H. Cowen. A little later three appeared about the same time. These were C. Hubert H. Parry, C. Villiers Stanford, and A. C. Mackenzie. These three, with Sullivan, remained for some time at the head of English musicians, but they had very little fame outside England.

Of the three, Parry produced the best composition, and that was his first oratorio "Judith." Villiers Stanford showed, in "Shamus O'Brien" (1896), great talent for light opera, but he also composed some beautiful sacred music. Mackenzie, Parry, Cowen and Villiers Stanford all received the honour of knighthood. But already their works are being forgotten.

In Sir Edward Elgar, however, England may justly boast she has a composer many of whose works will for very long be known and liked throughout the world. His knowledge of orchestration (how to write in the way best suited to the different instruments and how to blend them) is generally believed to be unsurpassed by any composer. "The Enigma Variations" and his "Violin Concerto" are known in every musical country.

Edward German (German Jones) was born in 1862, and after Sullivan he is our best writer of artistic light music. Granville Bantock, born in 1868, has tried to invent, and perhaps succeeded in inventing, a new technique or style of writing choral music. He sought to get the same variety of tone

out of a chorus of voices as other composers had obtained from orchestras. "Vanity of Vanities" and "Omar Khayyám" are his principal big choral works.

Arnold Bax is now famous abroad as well as in England. His music is severe and scholarly yet poetical.

Photo by People's Concert Society
Sir Edward German (left) and Sir Edward Elgar, two of the best-known modern English composers.

Of Vaughan Williams, Frederick Delius and Gustav Holst it may now be safely said that their genius has been fully recognized, and that their place in the Temple of Fame is assured for all time. Rutland Boughton, York Bowen, Benjamin Dale, and Frank Bridge have written comparatively little music, but they have all shown outstanding originality and fine feeling. Among women composers Dame Ethel M. Smyth stands first, and much is expected from Dorothy Howell.

There are so many young composers to-day in England who seem to us at present of nearly equal merit that it must be left to future generations to decide their rank.

One, however, William Turner Walton (born 1902), has been acclaimed by all our critics far beyond the others. His principal works, "Façade" and "Belshazzar's Feast," have brought him European fame. Constant Lambert set all England talking with his "Rio Grande," but, unfortunately, he has since then not quite fulfilled his early promise. Arthur Bliss is considered by many of the foremost critics to be one of the most original and serious-minded of our composers.

A Composer Who Was Inspired by the Songs of the American Indians

In the United States of America, Edward MacDowell (1861–1908) took the songs of the American Indians and wove them into an orchestral suite (1896), which became a landmark in American music. Deems Taylor is perhaps the best-known American composer. He has written two operas— "The King's Henchman" and "Peter Ibbetson." His best-known orchestral suite is called "Through the Looking-glass."

Charles Tomlinson Griffes (1884–1920) gave special attention to Japanese music and composed "Five Chinese and Japanese Songs" (1916–17) written in pentatonic and hexatonic scales (scales of 5 and 6 notes). His career was brief, but his talent was decidedly original. John Alden Carpenter (born 1876) has written many striking songs and the orchestral suite "Adventures in a Perambulator." Leo Sowerby (born 1895), besides musical composition, has done important work as a writer on musical subjects. Arthur William Foote (born 1853) shows novelty and strength of construction, and

Edward MacDowell, whose portrait is shown here, was probably the greatest American composer. He was the first to see the beauty in the strange wild music of the American Indians.

has written important works on the theory of music.

A name better-known in England is that of Percy Aldridge Grainger, born in Australia in 1882; he is claimed both by Australia and America. Of his many folk-song settings, most, however, are English. One of his pieces, "Zanzibar Boat Song," is written for three pianists, all to play at one piano! In 1906–1907 he was very friendly with Grieg, and his playing of Grieg's music is thought to be the best yet heard. There is something fairy-like and something puckish in his music. In England we know him best by his "Molly on the Shore" and "Shepherd's Hey."

Ernest Bloch (blŏK), Charles Martin Loeffler (lĕf'lĕr), and Edgar Varèse (vȧ-rĕz') all went to America after having received their musical training in other countries. Bloch represents better than any other composer the genius of Hebrew music. Edgar Varèse has sought especially in "Hyperprism" to bring out the hidden music in "noise." His compositions please very few. C. M. Loeffler sprang into fame with his Requiem for Kiel.

As you have already been told, there was a time when all new music was badly received. To-day there appears to be a tendency to welcome most new music, and this may be because we are less critical than our forefathers were, and are more easily pleased with what we hear. The great test, however, is the lasting popularity of music. There are many people who believe that in a hundred years' time very few of our most startling modern composers will be found amongst those who have been called to the Temple of Fame. And yet, even those who are destined to be forgotten will have helped the progress of Music. For new works stimulate new interest.

Photo by Anderson

Over the grassy plains of Western Asia and through the sharp defiles that led from valley to valley, our far-off ancestors drove their herds and flocks. They were always moving on, for grass was as necessary to their lives as the air itself, and whenever the pastures grew bare the people packed their scanty household goods and pushed on to greener lands. But these men from north of the Caucasus had one great advantage over the men of the south: they had tamed the horse, and could press him into service to fetch and carry.

The LAND of the THREE WISE MEN

In Ancient Persia There Grew Up One of the Greatest Empires of Early History, and One of the Most Beautiful of Religions

EXCEPT for the Egyptians, the Sumerians, and the Hittites, all the people about whom we have talked so far in history were Semites (sĕm´ĭt). The birthplace of this great Semitic (sē-mĭt´ĭk) race was probably the grassland on the outskirts of the Arabian Desert, where tribe after tribe led a wandering shepherd life until it decided to leave the desert and settle down in one place. These Semitic peoples settled Babylonia—later called Chaldea—Assyria, Syria, Phoenicia, and Palestine, all the countries in the Fertile Crescent, in Western Asia; and their colonies dotted the southern coast of the Mediterranean. Because these countries are to the south of those we shall now tell you about, we may call the Semites a southern race.

Where Did the Great Aryan Race Have Its Original Home?

Now began the history of a northern race, the people we call Indo-European or Aryan (är´yăn), one of the greatest branches of the white race. Some historians believe that this race began its career in the country north of the Caucasus Mountains, in Western Asia. Others put the first home of the Northern Race east of the Caspian Sea. But wherever it was, it was a grazing country in which men drove their flocks and herds from place to place in search of good pasture. It was a fairly small country and there could not have been many people in it; yet, to-day, the descendants of this Northern Race occupy more of the earth than any other people.

Before 2500 B.C. these northern wanderers were roaming about the pasture-lands with their flocks and herds. As they had no way of writing they were not yet civilized enough to leave us records of their life. They had no iron, and possibly not even copper; but they had tamed the horse, and had learned to raise barley and perhaps other grains as well. Thus they were clever and teachable, even though they had not yet learned the art of reading and writing,

After a few centuries, these northern tribes had spread over a much larger area than the one in which they first lived. They had crossed into Persia and perhaps had even reached India in the east, and they had also spread south and west towards Asia Minor, Greece and Italy. Wherever they went they mixed with other races, so that their language became very different in Persia from what it was in Greece or Asia Minor.

The peoples began to differ, too, in looks and in customs, so that it is only lately that students have found that all those northern peoples were really related to one another.

Where the Persians Came From

This Northern Race of people made its home mainly along the north coast of the Mediterranean, as the Semites had settled to the east and south. And from now on many of the wars in history are conflicts between the Southern and the Northern Races—the Semites and the Indo-Europeans. Until the Medes and Persians came on the scene, the Semites had things all their own way, and fought mostly among themselves. The first northern conquerors were the Medes and Persians.

It was about 2000 B.C., or perhaps a little earlier, that one group of Indo-Europeans wandered south-east into the country now called Persia on the maps. Those wanderers split into two groups, one of which went on to India, possibly about 1800 B.C. The other group remained in Persia. One of its tribes, the Medes, settled in the western hills of Persia; and another, the Persians themselves, settled in the central part, especially the country bordering on the Persian Gulf, almost as far as Sumeria. The Medes and the Persians were really the same people, with the same language, religion, and ways of living. A different people, the Elamites (ē'lăm-īt), lived between the Persians and the Sumerians.

What a Persian Boy Was Taught

Herodotus (hē·rŏd'ō-tŭs), a Greek historian who lived many hundreds of years after the beginning of Persia, says that every Persian boy was taught three things—to ride,

This is the far-flung empire that belonged to ancient Persia, a country that at first covered only a small territory east of the Persian Gulf, but finally conquered most of the then known world. It is one of the few ancient nations that has lasted down to our own day; but its people are no longer interested in progress. Entrenched on their lofty plateau, with its barren deserts and romantic rose-clad vales, the Persians carry on an extensive trade in silks and rugs and perfumes, and jealously guard the rich and coveted deposits of oil.

Photo by Anderson   From the painting by Fr. Juan Bautista Mayno

THE WISE MEN PAY HOMAGE TO THE INFANT CHRIST

These are the Three Wise Men who were led by a star to Bethlehem, carrying with them rare gifts for the infant Christ. It is thought that they came from Persia, where the priests were students of the heavens, and worshipped a God very much like the God of the Hebrews. Later, the legend arose that the Wise Men were three kings of the East—Caspar, Melchior, and Balthazar—and that one of them was of negro origin.

to shoot, and to tell the truth. From the very beginning, the Persians had loved horses, and there is evidence that they were skilled in horsemanship, a form of exercise which helped to make them strong and hardy.

As for telling the truth, that too, was a quality of the Persians. They tried very hard to be good, for they had a very beautiful and inspiring religion given to them by the prophet Zoroaster (zō'rŏ-ăs'tēr). This religion taught that there is a group of good spirits or forces, of whom the greatest is Mazda or Ahura-mazda (ä'hoō-rȧ-mäz'-dȧ), which means "Lord of Wisdom." These good spirits are always being opposed by evil spirits, with Ahriman (ä'rĭ-mȧn) at their head. But good is always triumphant, and hence it is best to join with the good, or we also will be beaten with the rest of evil.

Mithras (mith'-räs), or Light, was one of the great good spirits, and hence light in the shape of fire entered into the worship of the Persians. But it is not exactly true to call them "fire worshippers." The fire was not itself a god to these people, but an image or symbol of light and truth. The Three Wise Men who brought gifts to the infant Christ were probably followers of Zoroaster.

Origin of the Word "Magic"

This simple, beautiful religion took the place of an earlier religion in which the priests were "magi" (mā'jī), a name which has given us the word "magic." This older religion was not nearly so beautiful and pure as the religion Zoroaster taught.

Croesus, a rich king of Lydia in Asia Minor, is receiving Solon, the great Greek law-giver who, as the story goes, once came to pay the monarch a visit. When Croesus made an effort to impress the wise man with his wealth, Solon eloquently rebuked him, and in doing so pronounced the famous phrase : "Call no man happy until he is dead." It was a timely warning, for later Croesus fell before the power of Persia.

When the exciting part of Persia's history begins, about 600 B.C., the Medes were more powerful than their cousins the Persians, and every year the Persians had to pay them tribute. Naturally, the Persians did not like being a subject race.

Cyrus, whom we call Cyrus the Great, was born in Persia about 600 B.C. Stories say that he was the grandson of Astyages (ăs-tī'ȧ-jēz'), king of the Medes, but this is not certain. Some of the stories say that when Cyrus was very young Astyages dreamed of him with great wings which enfolded the whole of Asia. That dream came near to being realized in later days.

Cyrus was at first king or chief of a little district called Anshan, in Elam, in the south of Media. When he was about fifty years old he gathered soldiers about him and defeated Astyages, making himself master of all Media as well as Persia. One conquest led to another. In 546 B.C. Cyrus captured Croesus (krē'sŭs), the wealthy king of Lydia, on the Aegean Sea. Then he began to lay his plans for conquering Babylon, where, you may remember, the Chaldeans were ruling in great luxury, with the Jews in captivity under them.

As it happened, Cyrus came to the throne at a favourable time. Babylon had a weak king who was quarrelling with the priests; and the captive Jews were looking for someone to free them from their slavery and let them go home to Palestine. A city or state quarrelling within itself is always easier to defeat than one which is united ; and the records say that Cyrus did not even

Photo by Rischgitz

Darius the Greek, who ascended the Persian throne in 521 A.D., was a strong and active ruler, who greatly reorganized the empire. He set up his seat of government at Susa. Here he is seen being carried in triumph after a battle.

have to fight his way into Babylon, but took possession of its magnificent palaces and temples almost in peace.

This conquest in 539 B.C. made a great empire of Persia, with Cyrus at its head. But, like many another great empire builder, Cyrus did not know when to stop. He never paused to wonder whether the other countries would like being conquered any better than did Persia when she had been under the the rule of Media. He just went on fighting and conquering until he died, in 529 B.C. No one knows how Cyrus died, except that it was in battle.

The Noblest of the Persians

In spite of all his wars and fighting, most people loved Cyrus. His people called him "father," and the Bible spoke of him as the "anointed of the Lord," and "His shepherd." The Greeks, although they fought to escape the power of Cyrus, still admired him greatly.

This was partly because the Persian rule was much gentler than any other foreign

rule had been. Cyrus did not destroy whole cities with hideous tortures, as Sennacherib the Assyrian had done. He did not carry off numbers of people into captivity, as Nebuchadnezzar carried off the Jews. He was a wise and kindly prince, and the Northern Race may well be proud of its first emperor

How the Persians Ruled Their Empire

Cyrus and the Persian kings who followed him made their capital at Susa (soo'så), in Elam, near Cyrus's own district of Anshan. But they also owned palaces at Persepolis (pĕr-sĕp'ó-lĭs) and Pasargadae (pȧ-sär'gȧ-dē), and sometimes they lived in the palace at Babylon. From those palaces they ruled their great possessions more wisely than former conquerors had done.

These Persian kings—Cyrus, Cambyses (kăm-bī'sēz), Darius (dȧ-rī'ŭs), Xerxes (zûrk'sēz), Artaxerxes (är'tăk-zûrk'sēz)—divided their countries into districts which they called satrapies (sā'trȧ-pĭ). Over each district was placed a satrap (sā'trăp), or governor, responsible for seeing that the country was rightly governed and that taxes were sent regularly to the king. This system of district governors was used ever afterwards in the management of empires, and is still in use to-day.

Many Persians had learned to read and write in cuneiform (kū-nē′ĭ-fôrm) long before Cyrus the Great conquered the world, but when they had a world to manage they needed writing much more than before. The Persian scribes accordingly worked out a cuneiform writing of their own. It had forty-one letters, one for every sound. In other words, the Persians invented an alphabet in cuneiform, and did not use the Babylonian syllable signs which were so much clumsier and more awkward.

A Famous Historical Puzzle

The account of the way in which we learned to read this old Persian writing is a fascinating story. Of course, it would be much easier to read Old Persian with only forty-one sound pictures, than Old Babylonian with over three hundred syllable pictures. Persian writing was finally read by a man named Grotefend (grō′tē-fĕnt), who worked it out in much the same way as Champollion (shôN-pŏl-yŏN′) did the Rosetta Stone, that is, from the names of kings which it contained. You see, if a king wrote an

inscription anywhere it would be fairly certain to begin with his own name, and there are dozens of these inscriptions in Persia and Mesopotamia.

The Key to Babylonian History

There is a famous inscription at Behistun (bā′hĭs-tōon′); it is cut into the face of a huge rock in the side of a deep gorge or craggy gully in a tall mountain, three hundred feet above the ground. It bears a huge picture of the great king Darius, and standing in front of him a row of false kings who had claimed his throne. At his feet lies the worst of the rebels, Gaumata by name. Below these pictures are the same words in three different languages—the Old Persian, the Elamite and the Babylonian.

This enormous rock is the key to the Old Babylonian language, and the solution of its puzzle was begun by Sir Henry Rawlinson, a British officer stationed in Persia. In 1844 he climbed the dangerous rocks to the dizzy height and succeeded in making copies of all three inscriptions. He not only copied all the inscriptions but, quite unaided, succeeded in reading the Old Persian, which was difficult enough, and the Old Babylonian, which seemed almost impossible. It is to Sir Henry Rawlinson that we owe our

The picture below shows King Cambyses, son of Cyrus the Great, charging across the field at the siege of Pelusium, in which he overcame the Egyptians and so was finally able to bring their land under his sway. To annoy his enemies, Cambyses ill-treated all animals which they regarded as sacred. Eventually he was forced to yield to a usurper, and thereupon took his own life.

The male members of a family belonging to the "black tent dwellers", a wandering tribe of Persians.

C   This beautiful gate, which seems to be made of gold, is one of twelve in the wall that encircles the city of Teheran, capital of modern Persia. It is a fine example of Persian art, which is always extremely rich in design and colour.

B. This Persian woman has almost finished the beautiful rug upon which she is working. It will bring a high price, but she herself will get very little for her labour.
D.   Traffic moves but slowly in a Persian city. If it did not, the driver of this donkey would never be able to stop in the middle of the highway for a smith to come and put a new shoe on his four-footed friend.

On this page are scenes from modern Persia, the ancient land that proud Darius once ruled.

A. This typical family of modern Persia consists of eight tattered boys. But though they are ragged they are glowing with health, for they live mainly on fruit, cheese, and coarse rye bread.

C. Some ten miles from Tabriz, the second city of modern Persia, stands this famous Mohammedan mosque, built on top of a mountain 4,000 feet high. The only descendants of the ancient Persians who are still Zoroastrians are the Parsees, a people of India who left Persia in the 8th century.

B. In Teheran, the capital of Persia, the shoe "shops" walk about on two legs. But none of the lads who furnish the motor power ever seems to sell enough goods to get a pair for his own feet.

E. A Persian mullah, or teacher of the Mohammedan law, who is judge, jury, and legal adviser for the whole village.

D. This upper-class Persian woman guides her donkey by pressure of the toes.

knowledge of Babylonian cuneiform writing. as well as of the writing of Darius and the other Persian kings.

For two hundred years the Persian empire continued in peace and prosperity. On the whole the Persian kings were better than any others of whom we know in ancient times, except perhaps the Egyptian kings of the great Middle Kingdom. Darius says, in the Behistun inscription: "I was not wicked, nor was I a liar, nor was I a tyrant, neither I nor any of my line. I have ruled in righteousness."

But, little by little, too much wealth and power made the Persian kings soft and weak. The Persian empire fell into decay, and finally in 323 B.C. it passed to the great Alexander, of whom we shall have much to tell a little later.

Persia herself, however, has never been tossed about from one conqueror to another as many of the weaker nations have been. For three thousand years Persia has been ruled by Persians, and her Peacock Throne, though many different lines of kings have occupied it since the days of Cyrus, has not for long been under foreign rule. In A.D. 651 an Arabian conquest exchanged the religion of Zoroaster, as a state or national religion, for that of Mohammed, which has remained ever since the national faith of Persia. In 1162 the Mongolian (mŏng-gō'lĭ-ån), or yellow race, under the great Genghis Khan (jĕn'gĭz kän) swept over Persia and conquered it for a time.

The great thing to remember about the Persians is that about 550 B.C. they first established the power of the Northern Race, which for over two thousand years since has continued to grow more and more powerful. To-day the members of the Northern Race —English, French, German, Scandinavian, Italian, Russian and others—have developed a civilization which covers a great part of the earth.

Decrees of Persian Kings that are Recorded in the Bible

This civilization, with all its faults, is kinder and more just than were the earlier civilizations. And the Persians began this progress by being better governors than the rulers who came before them. If you would like to read some of the kind decrees which the old Persian kings made, open your Bible at the sixth and seventh chapters of Ezra and you will find two of them recorded there.

Apart from this, the Persians did not give the world so very much. They were not great inventors or great artists, though they had a deep appreciation for beautiful things. They made no great discoveries in metals. But they are the oldest of the Indo-Europeans.

Here is the unhappy family of King Darius kneeling before Alexander, their conqueror, and beseeching him for mercy. For it was the custom, in those more savage times, for the conquered to be taken as slaves or put to death. Modern warfare is the worst the world has ever known, but those old cruel customs are gone.

Here are some more animals, with cages for them, which you can draw to scale, as explained in pages 26-31. They will do splendidly for your circus or menagerie. The boy with an inventive turn of mind can build a Noah's Ark, and make two of each kind of animal to put into it. He can also attach the heads and legs and tails of his pets in such a way as to make them perform some amusing antics when they are drawn across the floor.

From the top left-hand corner reading across the page the names of these butterflies are *Lycaena arion* (large blue), *Vanessa cardui*, *Lymanopoda samius*, *Papilio bachus belsazar*, *Heliconius doris delila*, *Argynnis paphia* (silver-washed fritillary), *Heliconius doris aristomache*, *Chlorippe lavinia*, and *Vanessa io* (peacock).

He hardly needs to be afraid of this one insect. But, you see, he once saw an army of millions of them devouring everything in sight, and he knows that where there is one, there will be others to follow.

INSECT ARMIES

Sometimes They are Big Enough to Hold Up a Railway Train and to Turn Daylight into Darkness

(CONTINUED FROM PAGE 449)

THERE is a great story of a brave little band of men and women who long years ago founded beautiful Salt Lake City in the midst of the towering Rocky Mountains.

For many a weary month they had journeyed all the way from the Atlantic coast, right across the great plains of North America, with their children, their tools, and their household goods in great covered wagons—for there were no railways in those far-off days.

They climbed over the top of the first ranges of mountains and settled in a wonderful valley surrounded by hills on every side. There they hastily built huts and cabins in which to live through the coming winter. Men, women, and children all set to work with a will to raise crops of wheat and vegetables so that they should not starve when the provisions they had brought with them were all gone.

They tilled the ground, sowed the good seed they had carried safely for so many hundreds of miles, watered the dry land, and waited patiently for the coming of spring.

At last their labours were rewarded by the sight of the first green blades pushing their way up through the dark earth, and soon the fields were covered with tender young plants.

Then one day, when everything seemed bright and hopeful, a terrible thing happened. Down the mountain sides a ravening army of hungry locusts came hopping and crawling. Before the people realized what was happening, the enemy was swarming over the beautiful fields and greedily eating up all the precious green shoots.

The men shouted and rushed about, trying to beat off the locusts; but it was of no use. On and on the creatures came, like the waves of the sea. When they were attacked in one place, fresh battalions would march down on the fields from other sides. There seemed to be no end to the pests.

The people were in despair. All hope of saving their crops seemed gone. Then suddenly a sound of beating wings was heard overhead and an army of great white birds came flying to the scene. The gulls of Great Salt Lake, which lies like an inland sea at the foot of the western hills, had come to the rescue. With shrill, excited cries and tremendous flapping of wings they swooped down upon the locusts and started gobbling them up by the thousand. Seldom had the birds had such a glorious feast. They ate and ate until they could eat no more; then they flew heavily back to rest. But fresh companies of gulls kept flying up to carry on the good work, until at last the enemy was fairly routed. Hardly a locust was left alive to tell the tale, and so the crops were saved.

Now this all happened early in the nineteenth century; but it was not the first nor the last time that an army of those destructive insects descended on the crops in North America. Unfortunately, flocks of friendly gulls have not always been at hand to eat them up; and on many occasions the insect armies have been so overwhelming in their numbers that if all the birds in the neighbourhood for miles around had flocked to the rescue, they could not possibly have destroyed the locusts—no matter how hungry they were and how fast they ate.

Time and again have the rich grain fields of Africa, Asia and America been raided by flying squadrons of the dreaded locusts.

This monument in Salt Lake City, U.S.A., was not raised to man or woman, but to a flock of gulls that once saved the place from complete destruction by eating an army of attacking locusts.

The hungry insects travelled by air all the way from their strongholds on the plains and plateaux among the mountain ranges, perhaps a thousand miles away. High overhead they swarmed in countless numbers, like silvery clouds in the sky as the sunlight glinted on the millions of fluttering gauze wings. Then down they swooped as lightly and gracefully as a flight of aeroplanes, covering the ground for miles; and when the invaders rose and flew on their way, not a green blade was left in the once smiling fields and meadows. As the prophet Joel wrote of the locusts in Palestine so many hundreds of years ago: "The land is as the garden of Eden before them, and behind them a desolate wilderness."

Fortunately for America, such terrible insect invasions no longer occur in that country. Now that there are so many farms and ranches on the great north-western plains, the eggs of the locusts are turned up and destroyed by the plough. Although the insects are still very troublesome, they no longer have things all their own way. Since 1876 the "migrating locusts," as they are called, have made no very serious raids on the green fields of the Mississippi Valley.

But in Asia and in Africa plagues of locusts occur even now from time to time, just as they did in the days of the Pharaohs—though fortunately at fairly long intervals.

Here is the first line of defence in a war against an army of locusts in the Holy Land. Bedouin Arabs are repairing a wall of zinc plates that has been stretched across the desert in front of the advancing hordes. Beside the wall a good-sized trench is dug, into which the insects fall. They are then destroyed.

These insects are larger than the Rocky Mountain locusts and are even more difficult to fight. They breed and multiply unchecked in the vast uncultivated tracts of the East, and when they have stripped the land of every green thing, they set off in search of fresh feeding grounds.

The young locusts, before their wings have grown, set out on their adventures on foot. Driven from home by hunger, they move over the land like a living flood, destroying all vegetation in their line of march. They often travel several miles in a day, hopping, leaping and scrambling along in a dense mass, marching straight forward regardless of any obstacle that may bar their triumphal progress.

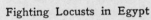
This locust is laying her eggs in the earth.

How Armies of Locusts Are Checked

If they arrive on the banks of a stream, the water will not stop them. The whole army plunges in, struggling and pushing and clutching at floating leaves and straws, and climbing on top of one another till they form a floating bridge from bank to bank right across the stream. Some of them are drowned, but most of the army finally lands safely on the opposite side of the stream and continues to march onwards.

The advance of marching locusts can sometimes be checked by digging trenches across the route that the insects are expected to follow and lining them with oilcloth; for locusts cannot keep their footing on anything slippery. When they meet such a barrier, thousands upon thousands of the creatures slip and slide and tumble on top of one another, crushing those underneath; and their triumphant march is broken.

But if the army is on wings you cannot stop it in this way. Clouds of flying locusts will sometimes appear, darkening the sky as they pass high overhead. When they are known to be on the way, everyone prays that the wind will change and blow the insects out to sea, or that violent rainstorms will arise to destroy them before they alight and destroy the crops and leave the land a barren waste.

Fighting Locusts in Egypt

For several years a country will be fairly free from migratory locusts. Then suddenly, when people are beginning to forget all about them, the appalling insect armies again make their appearance and are just as bad as ever. As late as 1930 a plague of locusts swept over Arabia and North-western Africa. Although fifteen hundred tons of the insects were killed and two hundred tons of eggs collected in Egypt, the damage done was terrible. An army of large red locusts came flying over the country. Their ranks were twelve miles long. Here and there a regiment paused and settled on a green spot,

No wonder Pharaoh and his people were disturbed when Moses brought the plague of locusts upon them! This picture will give you some idea of what things were like in Africa and Arabia when the locusts came in 1930. The camera which they seem about to devour was being used to take pictures of the havoc they caused, and the motor-car they are so resolutely attacking was carrying one of the officials in charge of the work of extermination.

used to fight invading armies of locusts, poison being sprayed on them while in flight.

Although they have never been quite so bad as the migratory locusts, the "seventeen-year cicadas" (sĭ-kā′dă) were at one time a most terrible plague to American farmers. From their habit of suddenly appearing in enormous numbers and fairly eating up the land, cicadas are often called "locusts." But this is quite wrong. A cicada is a bug, not a straight-winged insect as is a locust.

The name "bug" rightly belongs to a particular kind of insect that has a sharp, piercing beak and can only take liquid food. There

leaving the ground bare when they rose again. In some places swarms of the locusts were three feet deep upon the ground. They actually held up the progress of trains by settling in masses on the railway tracks.

Attacked with Flame-Throwers

Everything possible was done to fight the plague. As many as 75,000 men were sent out to attack them, armed with 200 tons of liquid destroyer and 140 flame-throwers. The battle raged between the men and the insects for weeks before the invaders were finally routed; and the battle-fields, when the fight was over, were indeed a sorry sight. In recent years aeroplanes have sometimes been

are a great many of these creatures in the insect world, living on the land and in the water; many of them are very tiny and most of them are troublesome. They do no end of mischief by sucking the sap of plants and trees in farms, orchards, and meadows; and others weaken our domestic animals by piercing their skin and sucking their blood.

But to go back to our seventeen-year cicada—one of the largest and most entertaining of the bug tribe, which is peculiar to

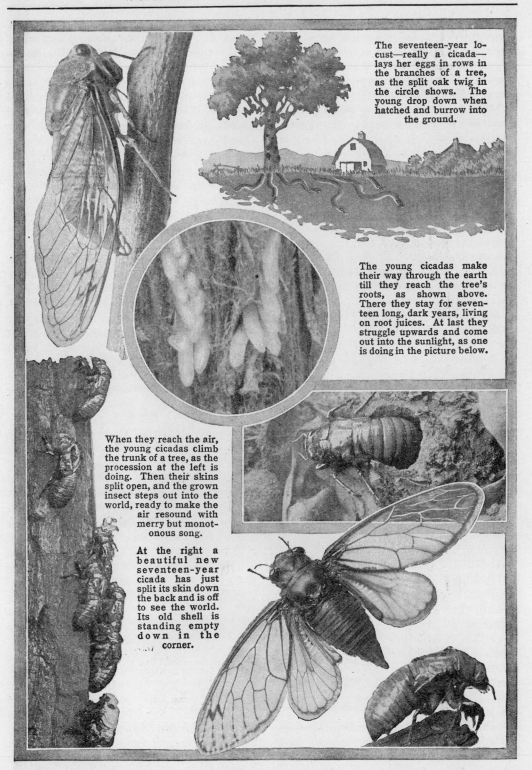

The seventeen-year locust—really a cicada—lays her eggs in rows in the branches of a tree, as the split oak twig in the circle shows. The young drop down when hatched and burrow into the ground.

The young cicadas make their way through the earth till they reach the tree's roots, as shown above. There they stay for seventeen long, dark years, living on root juices. At last they struggle upwards and come out into the sunlight, as one is doing in the picture below.

When they reach the air, the young cicadas climb the trunk of a tree, as the procession at the left is doing. Then their skins split open, and the grown insect steps out into the world, ready to make the air resound with merry but monotonous song.

At the right a beautiful new seventeen-year cicada has just split its skin down the back and is off to see the world. Its old shell is standing empty down in the corner.

America. This insect has gained its curious name from its habit of turning up in overwhelming numbers, in the same district, once in every seventeen years—"and that is once too often," as a farmer once remarked after one of their rare and unwelcome visitations.

The cicada is a big, stout insect with the usual sharp, piercing beak with which all bugs are armed. Its four transparent wings are arranged over its back like the slanting roof of a cottage. Two great bulging eyes, set sideways on the head, somehow make the cicada look as if it were squinting at you, while in the centre of the forehead are three tiny simple eyes that glint like coloured jewels, the one beauty the lumpy-looking creature possesses.

However, although they are not beautiful, the cicadas, like the locusts and grasshoppers, are first-rate musicians. At least, the male cicadas are. But instead of playing the fiddle they perform upon the drum, and are said to be the noisiest insects in the whole world.

The cicada's musical instrument is part of his anatomy. Underneath his body is a hollow cavity partly covered by two sounding-plates. The cicada does not beat his drum. He makes it vibrate by working the strong muscles attached to the plates, and produces a loud booming, chirping sound that some people admire, though others say it reminds them of the whistle of a steam-engine, the noise made by a distant threshing-machine, and the croaking of frogs all going at the same time Sounding-plates inside the insect's body increase the noise and broadcast the "music" far and wide over the still countryside.

The female cicada has no musical instrument, but she has a remarkable egg-laying tube armed with a saw-like instrument. With this handy tool she makes a number of neat little grooves in living twigs on trees and bushes, and packs a dozen eggs or so in each one. As Mother Cicada arranges four or five hundred eggs in this way, she has plenty to do through the long sunny days without playing the drum or indulging in other foolishness.

The eggs in the twigs soon hatch out. But the cicada grubs do not stay in their snug little nests. They drop to the ground, push their way into the soil, and disappear from view. And for seventeen long years the strange little creatures are neither seen nor heard.

Buried deep in the soil, the young cicadas live all that time in perpetual darkness, slowly worming their way through the ground and sucking the rootlets of the trees and plants. But at last, when their seventeenth birthday is approaching, the cicada grubs creep up towards the light once more and begin to make preparations for leaving the dismal underground world. They change their skins and alter their appearance slightly, but they do not spin cocoons. They are still able to move about, and at this stage in their lives are usually called "nymphs."

Sometimes the nymphs make funny little chimneys of earth, which stick up two or three inches above the ground. There they spend a day or two until it is time to come right out into the open. Others do not make chimneys but just hide away under stones and sticks

Many of you know the tent caterpillars, which live under a beautiful silken web thrown over the branches of a tree. They are as ravenous as an army, and will come out of their tent to devour every vestige of foliage on the tree. Here a cluster of young caterpillars is shown attached to a walnut tree.

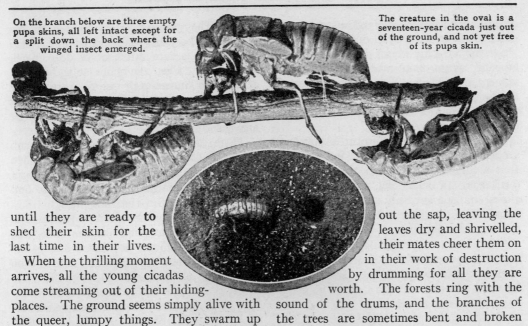

On the branch below are three empty pupa skins, all left intact except for a split down the back where the winged insect emerged.

The creature in the oval is a seventeen-year cicada just out of the ground, and not yet free of its pupa skin.

until they are ready to shed their skin for the last time in their lives.

When the thrilling moment arrives, all the young cicadas come streaming out of their hiding-places. The ground seems simply alive with the queer, lumpy things. They swarm up the trees and bushes all around, and cling to the twigs and branches as if they were dazed and dazzled by the strong light—as well they may be after spending years in the dark.

The Grown-up Cicada Throws Off His Uncomfortable Suit of Armour

They must feel very uncomfortable, too, poor things, for their skin hardens in the fresh air, so that each of them finds itself enclosed in a stiff shell; but they have not long to wait in this condition. The hard skin cracks all down the back, and the cicadas, quite grown up at last, squeeze their way out of their old shells.

Pale, ghostly things they look at first; they are almost colourless, and their wings hang limply down as the insects crowd together, clinging to the leaves and twigs and the bark of the trees. Gradually they darken in colour; their wings grow firm and stiff; and in a very short time the cicadas are ready to fly and play their drums and enjoy their new-found liberty.

And enjoy themselves they certainly do, in their own peculiar fashion. They take complete possession of the woods and plantations all around, and gather together in hundreds and thousands upon the branches of the trees. And while the females dig their beaks into the green leaves and suck

out the sap, leaving the leaves dry and shrivelled, their mates cheer them on in their work of destruction by drumming for all they are worth. The forests ring with the sound of the drums, and the branches of the trees are sometimes bent and broken by the weight of the insects.

This does not often happen now, and America may well be thankful. Much of the land in which the cicadas bury themselves for the first seventeen years of their lives has been built over; still more has been brought under cultivation; and the perky little English sparrow—who was introduced into the country some years ago to wage war upon the insect pests—has done its best to reduce the strength of the destructive armies. The drumming of the cicadas is still heard in the land in the early summer, but the insects no longer assemble in such enormous swarms as they did before.

A Warrior in the Wheat Field

The cicadas do not all take so long in growing up. The thirteen-year cicada of the southern states spends thirteen years underground, while the big black and green dog-day harvest fly, which is another member of the cicada family, comes up to the light and changes to a perfect winged insect when it has been only two years down below. The shorter-lived members of the cicada family are found in all warm climates.

Another troublesome insect, known as the army-worm, often plays terrible havoc in the grain fields of Canada and the United States. It is not really a worm, but a black caterpillar, with green and yellow stripes; and he finally becomes a small dull-brown moth.

Swarms of army-worms sometimes attack growing wheat and nibble almost every young green blade. Then, having done all the mischief they can in one field, they march off in detachments to another one and spoil that too.

There is another army-worm in Southern Europe that is quite a different kind of insect. It is a tiny thing, not more than a quarter of an inch long, with an almost transparent body and a tiny round black head, which gives it rather a knowing look.

This little army-worm does no harm. It is even rather useful, as it lives and feeds on decaying leaves. Millions of the tiny creatures often swarm under the trees in woodland districts, though they are so small that they are scarcely noticed among the fallen leaves. But when the time comes to change into chrysalises, the quaint little things collect together in hundreds of thousands. They form ranks, sixty or seventy abreast, and march through the woods in a long, straggling line that winds in and out of the roots and the trunks of the trees like a great grey snake.

Suddenly the army halts, and the insects all roll themselves up together into a big round ball. For some time this tangled ball of wriggling grubs lies on the ground. Then, in some mysterious way, it begins to shrink. None of the insects breaks away from the ball, yet slowly and steadily it grows smaller and smaller, until at last, just as if it had vanished into the air, the ball completely disappears. Whatever can have become of those thousands of grubs? Well, the artful little creatures have not melted

away. They are all safely hidden in the ground. The army had halted and rolled itself up on a nice soft spot of deep, black leaf mould. Then the grubs at the bottom of the ball immediately set to work to dig in, and one after another all the others followed in regular order until not a single army-worm grub was left above ground.

There, in the darkness, each little grub turns to a mummy-like pupa; and when their transformation is complete, a swarm of tiny black midges rises from the ground and dances gaily in the sunlight.

The flying squadrons of locusts, the regiments of drumming cicadas, and the battalions of marching caterpillars are only too plainly to be seen when they choose to invade the land. But in some countries there are enormous hidden armies of insects that cannot bear to appear in public, and never show themselves in the open if they can possibly avoid it.

These unseen insects are termites (tûr'mīt), strange little creatures often called "white ants." But they are not ants. They are quite a different race of insect folk, and not related to the little ant people in any way—although they live together in large communities very much as ants do.

Some termites live inside the trunks and branches of dead trees. Some live outside living trees, but are always under cover just the same, for they plaster the trees with clay or chewed wood pulp, making huge shapeless nests and long covered ways that shelter them from observation.

Other termites live in deep underground cities where living-rooms, store-rooms, nurseries, and great vaulted halls have been hollowed out in all directions, and are connected by main roadways and numerous winding passages. Over the chief entrance to their cities the termites often raise great mounds of earth, called "ant-hills,"

Termites, or "white ants," build nests of many kinds, both inside trunks of dead trees and on the outside of living trees. This one from tropical America is attached to a small limb of a living tree.

Surveyors for the Cape to Cairo railway in Africa built their look-out station on top of a termites' nest. The walls of such great "ant-hills" are very solid, as is shown by the series of steps that have been cut into this one.

with the soil they have dug out. These also contain many chambers, galleries, and communicating passages.

In the heart of Africa acres and acres of dry, sun-baked land are covered with such "ant-hills," some rising singly like tall towers twelve or fifteen feet high, others grouped together like tiny mountain ranges. They are so firm and strong that you may climb all over them without breaking them down. Yet, although the hills and the ground under our feet are teeming with the strange little insects, never a termite is to be seen—only by their work do we know they are there.

In every big hill or underground city there are several kinds of termites; a king and a queen, a small army of soldiers, and a large number of ordinary workers, besides quantities of babies and children of all ages. The babies are not legless grubs like true ant babies. When they come out of the egg they are tiny things, with heads, feelers, and six legs all complete. They look like small editions of the workers. Of course, the little creatures can do nothing for themselves for some time after they are hatched; so they stay in the nurseries, and the workers bring them food until they are old enough to take their places among the grown-up termites in the great city.

The workers are very ugly little creatures. They have soft, flabby bodies, like dirty-white crumpled sacks, and their heads and shoulders are a dark, oily brown. They do all the work of the city—care for the children, collect food, attend the king and queen, build the mounds and tunnel out the chambers and roadways underground. They must really have quite enough to do to keep everything going.

The soldiers are larger than the ordinary workers. They have big, queer-shaped heads

These locusts were tired of flying, so they settled on a great bough of a tree. If the bough had been slender they would surely have broken it.

and huge jaws like scythes. It is the soldiers' duty to guard the colony; so while the workers are busy, the soldiers march up ready to fall upon any daring creature who attempts to interfere with them.

Their Silent Language

Strange to say, both the soldiers and the workers are usually blind. But they are not deaf. They have ears on their front pair of legs, just as grasshoppers have, and appear to talk to one another by jerking their heads and shoulders in a very curious way. It is supposed that by moving the back of its head against its shoulders, a termite makes little sounds which its companions can hear and understand—although the sounds are much too faint for our ears to catch.

The king is quite an ordinary-looking termite, though a good deal bigger than the workers. But the queen—well, she is simply enormous and just like a sausage or a white bolster, with a tiny head and shoulders on one end and six feeble legs. Few people have seen a queen termite, for she spends her life hidden in the royal apartments deep down in the earth, where she does nothing but lay eggs all day long at the rate of sixty a minute. Both the king and queen have eyes, but as they always live in the dark their eyes can hardly be of much use to them.

At certain times of the year the nurseries in termite cities are suddenly filled with troops of royal children. It is not until they are nearly full-grown that they can be distinguished from the ordinary children of the colony. Then four pretty gauzy wings appear upon their shoulders to prove that they are real princes and princesses, who may, at some future time, become the kings and queens of termite cities of their own.

This great termites' nest is only one of many at Elizabethville, in the Belgian Congo, Africa. Half of it had to be cut away to make a road, but there is very little danger of its caving in. It is too solid to do that.

We say "perhaps," for it is really most unlucky to be a prince or princess in the insect world. They nearly always come to an untimely end, for with one or two exceptions the chances are that all the royal termite children will be dead a few hours after they have gained their wings.

They do not know this, and all the royal youngsters are in a hurry to leave their old home and try their wings. So out they all come and fly off in a great swarm. But the moment they show themselves out of doors, all the insect-eating creatures from far and near are after them. Birds chase them through the air, rats and reptiles pounce upon them and gobble them up by thousands when they alight upon the ground. When the excitement is over, nearly all the termites are gone, and the greedy birds have eaten so many they can hardly close their beaks.

Only a few royal couples manage to escape the general slaughter; and as soon as they settle on the ground they shed their wings and look about for shelter. If they are near a termite city where a king and queen are wanted, some of the workers will come out and fetch them in; if not, they may start a new colony for themselves. But once they are safely underground they will never come out again. The workers feed them and look after them generally, and the queen grows bigger and bigger until she becomes so ungainly that she is perfectly helpless and cannot even move about the royal apartment.

This strange turret, photographed in West Africa, is only one of the queer shapes that a termites' nest may take.

Dead Wood is Their Favourite Dish

Some termites cultivate different kinds of fungus in the underground cities to make a sort of "mushroom cake," most of which is given to the children. The favourite food of the grown-up insects is wood—dead wood—which they chew and chew again until there is nothing more to be got out of it. Decaying trees, old stumps or posts, any sort of wood will serve them so long as it is dry enough. To get the wood the termites are obliged to leave their homes. But as nothing will induce them to show themselves above the ground, they take the ground along with them, building little tunnels of earth as they go, so that they always move from place to place under covered ways. The strange little insects will carry their tunnels right up a tree twenty or thirty feet high in order to reach a dead branch at the top.

The earth is carried grain by grain, twisted about in the workers' jaws until it is soft and sticky, and firmly rammed into place at the end of the tunnel. But the cunning little masons never show themselves. They work always on the inside. In some of the African forests, nearly every other tree is plastered with the winding tunnels of termites.

Now, so long as the termites just eat the fallen tree trunks and the rotting stumps and branches, they are really doing good work. For the forests would soon become impassable if the dead wood were not cleared away. But when they invade houses and destroy property, it is quite a different story. And if there is a house within reach of a termite colony, it is almost impossible to keep the little pests out of it, for they, like the locusts, are persistent creatures.

The mischief they do is appalling. Telegraph poles, musical instruments, books, clothes, wooden houses, furniture, anything that comes in their way they will devour.

In spite of their small size and timid ways, they are one of the terrors of the Tropics.

(CONTINUED ON PAGE 501)

Above you may see a plan of the inside of a termites' nest. Such a city may be more than twenty feet high, and has ventilation and sewerage. The big room at the top is for storing air. In the room below, the youngsters are probably kept. The king and queen live in the smaller one near the bottom, with cells for their servants all around them, and store-houses for food for the half million inhabitants. You can see where the eggs are kept, in the oval is a larger picture of them. The sewers are at the bottom of the nest.

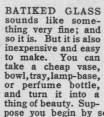

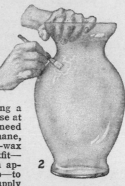

BATIKED GLASS sounds like something very fine; and so it is. But it is also inexpensive and easy to make. You can take a cheap vase, bowl, tray, lamp-base, or perfume bottle, and turn it into a thing of beauty. Suppose you begin by selecting a graceful colourless glass vase at a sixpenny store. You will need also some coloured cellophane, a paint-brush, some sealing-wax paint, and a sealing-wax outfit—sticks of coloured wax, an applier, and an alcohol lamp—to be bought at any artist's supply store.

1. Of course you can make up all sorts of designs. This one is going to be very modernistic, with geometric shapes of cellophane in different colours stuck on just as the fancy strikes you. First, then, cut out triangles, rectangles, and circles.

2. Then, starting at the top of the vase, apply a generous coating of collodion glue. 3. Over this area pat into place the piece or pieces of cellophane you have decided will look best there. Press the cellophane down firmly to avoid air bubbles. Keep on spreading glue and patting patches neatly into place until you have covered the whole surface. The success of this style of design will depend a good deal on how true an eye you have for attractive combinations of colour and line.

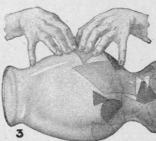

4. Next, with melted wax in your wax applier, follow the outline of each piece of cellophane. Build up the outlines to a good thickness. Black wax usually sets the many-coloured patches off best, but wax of other colours, especially bronze, may be attractive, too. 5. When all the outlines have been built up, give the vase time to dry thoroughly. Then paint it with transparent amber sealing-wax paint, applied rather thickly. This transparent finish keeps the cellophane from peeling off. 6. And now the vase is completed. If you have done your work well, it should be pretty enough to fill you with pride. Perhaps you will want to start at once on a bowl or tray, if only to try some other colour scheme or design.

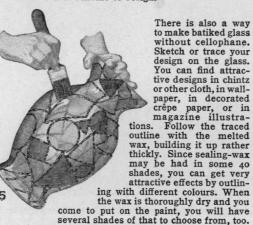

There is also a way to make batiked glass without cellophane. Sketch or trace your design on the glass. You can find attractive designs in chintz or other cloth, in wallpaper, in decorated crêpe paper, or in magazine illustrations. Follow the traced outline with the melted wax, building it up rather thickly. Since sealing-wax may be had in some 40 shades, you can get very attractive effects by outlining with different colours. When the wax is thoroughly dry and you come to put on the paint, you will have several shades of that to choose from, too.

A MAN *the* RED INDIANS LOVED

That is Why They Told Him So Much about What He Could Discover All Along the Upper Mississippi River

IT WAS noble blood that ran in the veins of Jacques Marquette (zhäk mär′kĕt′). The king of France had conferred fresh honours on his father; and the father may have been a little sorry when his youngest son, born in 1637, wanted to become a Jesuit (jĕz′ū-ĭt) priest and a missionary to the Red Indians instead of carving out a great career in France. Yet Jacques was going to make a name that would outlast those of all his kinsmen.

He began his studies as a Jesuit monk when he was only sixteen. Known for his gentle disposition and his skill in languages, he made rapid progress; and when his training was over he settled down as a teacher in the Jesuit college. But the quiet life there did not suit him. From time to time he read the stories that were received from the Jesuit missionaries of New France, or Canada, and with every letter he grew more impatient to join them in the wilds of the New World.

At last, when he was twenty-nine, he was sent over to Quebec. For a little while he remained there, and then he was sent into the western forests to a region known as the Country of the Upper Lakes. He spent some time at a mission on Chequamegon Bay, on Lake Superior, and then went back to the rapids in the Saint Mary's River, where he started a mission at the place now called Sault Sainte Marie. After some months he opened another mission farther south at Michilimackinac (mĭ-chĭl′ĭ-măk′ĭ-năk on Mackinaw Strait. And it was there that his great adventure began.

In 1672, Count Frontenac (frŏN′tĕ-näk′), the governor of New France, sent out Louis Joliet (zhō-lyā′), a skilful woodsman and

Gentle Father Marquette, an early French missionary to the New World, succeeded where others were to fail. For he carried with him a magic key which unlocked all hearts—the key of kindly words and deeds. The picture above shows the Jesuit explorer first entering the broad waters of the Mississippi River in 1673.

SIMPLE SIMON

Simple Simon met a pieman
Going to the fair;
Said Simple Simon to the pieman,
"Let me taste your ware."
Said the pieman unto Simon,
"First give me your penny!"
Said Simple Simon to the pieman,
"Indeed, I have not any."
He went to catch a dicky bird,
And thought he would not fail,
Because he had a little salt
To put upon its tail.
He went to ride a spotted cow
That had a little calf;
She threw him down upon the ground,
Which made the people laugh.
Then Simple Simon went a-hunting

For to catch a hare;
He rode a goat about the street,
But could not find one there.
Simple Simon went to town
To buy a piece of meat;
He tied it to his horse's tail
To keep it clean and sweet.
Simple Simon went a-fishing
For to catch a whale,
And all the water he had got
Was in his mother's pail.
He went to take a bird's nest—

'Twas built upon a bough;
A branch gave way, and Simon fell
Into a dirty slough.
He went to shoot a wild duck,
But the wild duck flew away;
Said Simon, "I can't hit him
Because he will not stay."
Once Simon made a great snowball,
And brought it in to roast;

He laid it down upon the fire,
And soon the ball was lost.
He went to slide upon the ice,
Before the ice would bear;
Then he plunged in above his knees,
Which made poor Simon stare.
Simple Simon went to look
If plums grew on a thistle;
He pricked his finger very much,
Which made poor Simon whistle.
He washed himself with blacking ball,
Because he had no soap;
And then said to his mother,
"I'm a beauty now, I hope."
He went for water in a sieve,
But soon it all ran through.
And now poor Simple Simon
Bids you all adieu.

Photo by the Autotype Fine Art Company

Bearing the precious thread and the sword with which he had just slain the Minotaur, Theseus emerged from the labyrinth to greet the waiting Ariadne, to whose love and clever foresight he was indebted for his life.

The LAND of the MINOTAUR

How the Existence of an Ancient People Who Lived on the Mediterranean Island of Crete was Brought to Light

SIXTY-FIVE years ago boys and girls who studied Greek history were told that it began with the first Olympic games in 776 B.C. Before that time we knew nothing but what was legend or myth. But in 1870 a German business man named Heinrich Schliemann (shle'män) spent a great deal of his money in digging into a hill which he thought covered the ancient city of Troy. Few people believed that there had ever been a Troy, or a Trojan War—but Schliemann proved that both of these were true. For he found the ruins of a city, and signs that it had been sacked as Homer had said, about 1200 B.C.

That discovery put the beginning of Greek history back more than four centuries, and people believed this for another thirty years.

But in 1893 an English scholar, Arthur Evans, believed that by digging in another place he could tell whether another legend was true, the legend of Theseus (thē sūs) and the Minotaur (mǐn'ǒ-tô). He, too, was successful, for he found the ruins of a great palace on the island of Crete. The palace was so large and had so many rooms and halls that it was very much like the labyrinth (lăb'ǐ-rǐnth), or maze, through which Theseus groped his way.

But what was the meaning of the story of the Minotaur, the bull of Minos, a creature half-man, half-bull? On the walls of the palace had been painted pictures, and in the ruins were some little ivory figures which answered the riddle. They showed that in order to amuse King Minos (mī'nǒs) young

19

men and women were put into a small space with a bull. When the bull charged, the young people dodged, or jumped over the bull's back. A single slip, a single error, meant the end of that performer. No wonder that Minos had to obtain fresh victims every year, and no wonder that some one —it may have been Theseus—finally killed a bull with a concealed dagger and probably killed the king as well.

After this discovery of the palace at Cnossus (nŏs'ŭs), men began digging all over the island and in many other places round the shores of the Mediterranean. The authors of Greek histories had to correct their old books, or to write new ones, until now we read that long before the Assyrians or the Greeks or the Hittites became famous, Crete was a thriving and civilized kingdom, with ships for trading and workshops for making useful and beautiful objects like cups and jars and rings. Indeed, in some ways Crete was the most modern of all the ancient countries. But to tell the story of all this we must go back to about 3000 B.C.

Long before the Indo-European, or Northern race, as it is called, began to spread and to conquer, people were living on the shores of the Mediterranean Sea, especially on the north shore. These people could neither read nor write, and they had no metal tools; they were not civilized, but barbarians. They lived in Spain, Italy, Greece, and the many islands of the Aegean Sea, including the southernmost of the Greek islands, which we call Crete. To-day the descendants of those Mediterranean people are so mixed with the Indo-Europeans that we do not classify them separately.

In the year 3000 B.C., as you remember, Egypt was a civilized land. Menes had united Egypt into one country, and the age of pyramid building was soon to begin. Egyp-

As far back as the Stone Age the people of Crete were making fine pottery, and by 2500 B.C. their vases and bowls had become very beautiful and substantial. They liked to paint their handiwork in colours on a shiny black ground, or in black on a buff ground. By 1500 B.C. they had reached a higher degree of skill in vase painting than was attained by anyone again for nearly a thousand years. At the left above is a Cretan jug made about 1800 B.C., and at the right is a Cretan vase made of soapstone and carved, in the lively fashion the Cretans loved, with scenes from a wrestling match and a bullfight.

tian boats and ships, which at first merely rowed up and down the Nile, were beginning to explore eastward and westward from the mouth of the river, and even to cross the great sea to obtain curious th ngs from the barbarians for the princes of Egypt, and to exchange Egyptian goods for them. And as you will see from the map, Crete was one of the first places upon which they would be sure to come.

As Egyptian ships came more and more frequently to Crete, the Cretans began to learn many things from the Egyptians. First of all, they obtained copper, and knives and tools made from copper were much better than those chipped from stone. They secured jars and dishes from Egypt, and the Cretan workmen soon began to copy these, often very skilfully indeed.

Above all, the Cretans were able to borrow from Egypt the sound pictures which we call hieroglyphs (hī'ĕr-ŏ-glĭf); these made a kind of alphabet. At first the Cretan signs were almost exactly like the Egyptian. Later, as people learned better how to write and wanted to write quickly, another set of letters developed, but no one has yet succeeded in reading this Cretan writing. To write it down the Cretans used clay tablets like those of the Sumerians.

Life in a Cretan Palace at Cnossus More Than 3000 Years Ago

It must have been a gay life in the great palace at Cnossu in Minoan times—we call this period, from about 2000 to 1500 B.C., "Minoan" (mĭ-nō'ăn), from "Minos," the name of the kings. The palace had great halls and open courts, and the wall were covered with beautiful paintings or glazed work showing scenes from Cretan life—bullfights, crowds

The people of ancient Crete were gifted artists, and loved to decorate their walls and vases with realistic pictures from daily life. This picture shows how the gay designs were painted on a vase after the clay had hardened. A vessel of this shape was commonly used for the storage of liquids, grain, honey, and other foods.

of people, ships sailing, and many other things. The Cretan palace had no thick walls for defence against enemies, for no enemies could come by land; but against sea foes there were fighting ships. And in the palace many store-rooms were filled with weapons of bronze, for the use of the Cretan guardsmen.

The Cretan ladies of quality wore dresses that had long full skirts with flounces and ruffles, as we can see from the pictures and statues. Some of the Cretan dresses would not look at all out of place to-day at a fashionable dinner party. So far as we know, life on this island was happy and peaceful, with the nobles fishing, boating, bullfighting, and generally enjoying themselves, and the artists and skilled workmen creating beautiful things to use at home or to send abroad.

For the Cretans became the great seafaring nation of their day. The farmers cultivated the fertile land outside the palace city and raised olives, grapes, and grain as food for the people.

One interesting thing about the great palace at Cnossus is that it had drainage and bathrooms. The pipes were made of pottery. In Egypt copper drain-pipes had been used long before, but those at Cnossus show how civilized Crete, too, had become; for bathrooms are certainly a sign of civilization.

The end of Cretan civilization came suddenly, and we do not yet know for certain what caused it. Perhaps, after Theseus killed the bull king, the Greeks sailed to Crete and overran the island, laying waste the fields and carrying the people into slavery. Perhaps the enemy who swept down about 1450 B.C. was not a Greek race but another Mediterranean group. It could scarcely have been the Egyptians, or we should have a record of it; the probability is that the invaders were the Greeks.

All we do know is that almost fifteen hundred years before our year one, the palace at Cnossus became desolate and empty, and the civilization of Crete, which had lasted over a thousand years, came to an end. But meanwhile this gifted people had learned to make many useful and beautiful things and had advanced a long step in the onward march of civilization. We should remember them with gratitude and keen admiration.

The Cretans were always interested in nature. In their later period, between 1700 B.C. and 1500 B.C., they became fascinated by the plants and animals of the sea as well as by those on land ; so the octopus began to thrust his clammy tentacles round the plumper vases, and star-fish and shell-fish peeped from behind clusters of seaweed.

Long before the people of Crete had learned to make the painted clay vases you see here, they were making vases of stone. These were very plain but very beautiful because of their simple shapes, which were sometimes borrowed from Egypt, and because of the high polish which was given to the jewel-like, colourful stone. Later workmen perfected their crude clay pots until, in 1800 B.C., or the middle period of Cretan history, they had reached the stage of making stencil-like designs, such as you see below.

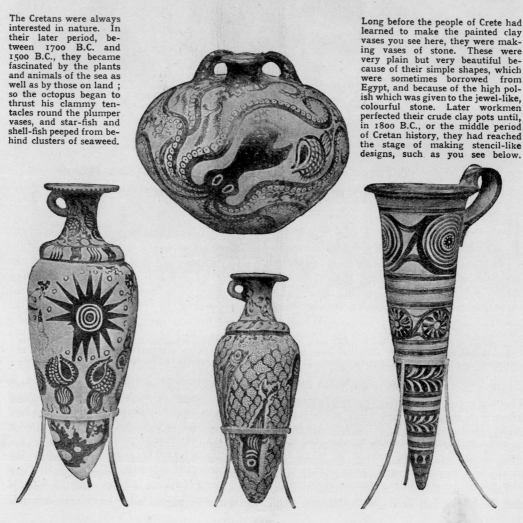

Two fearsome creatures are threatening the poor little man and he has every reason to be afraid. The insect ogre at the left is the caterpillar which hatches into the swallowtail butterfly. The other is the stag beetle, which is ready to meet all comers.

OGRES *of the* INSECT WORLD

Tiny Creatures That are a Terror to All the Other Little Insects within Reach

(CONTINUED FROM PAGE 492)

IF WE keep our eyes open and look about as we walk through the fields or woods on a summer's day, we may perhaps find one of the most lovely insects in the insect world. It will be moving slowly and quietly over the smooth green leaves or flying about. It is hardly an inch long, and a pretty clear green in colour. Its wonderful eyes are of shining gold, and its four lovely wings seem to be made of the finest lace which has been woven by fairy fingers.

A Pretty Insect to be Admired but Not to be Touched

This beauty of the fields is the lace-wing fly. It is not a rare insect. It loves the fields and meadows, and often comes into our gardens to visit the flower beds. But the lace-wing is a quiet little creature, and

its green colouring makes it so inconspicuous that we often pass it by.

If you ever see a lace-wing fly, stop and admire its delicate wings, its long feelers, and the way in which its big golden eyes change colour and flash like jewels in the light. But do not touch the pretty insect, whatever you do, for it will cover your fingers with a disgusting smell, and you will be obliged to scrub them again and again before you can get rid of it. This, of course, is only the way in which the little lace-wing protects itself from its enemies. There probably are not many insect-eating creatures that would care to meddle with it.

As she walks over the green leaves the lady lace-wing deposits, here and there, a little cluster of tiny creamy eggs. Each egg is fixed separately right at the end of a long slender stalk. So when the baby lace-wing hatches out, it finds itself swinging in the air—like the "baby on the tree top." But it does not stay there. The tiny creature climbs down its egg-stalk and lands safely

In the oval on the left, each one placed at the top of a tiny thread, are the eggs of the golden-eyed lace-wing fly. It is a wise arrangement, as it keeps the first-born from eating up the other eggs that are not yet hatched.

ingly fierce and bold for their size, and although "hunting the aphis," or plant louse, is their favourite sport, they will attack and devour caterpillars and other insects several times larger than themselves. They suck the eggs of any insects they can find; and one strongly suspects that Mother Lacewing fixes hers on the ends of those long stalks to prevent her children from eating them—which they would certainly do if they could.

The aphis lions prowl about, sucking eggs and aphides and killing all the small insect folk they can clutch with their sucking spears. At last they are quite "fed up." Then they creep away under a leaf or

Below is the golden-eyed lace-wing fly. It is of great value in destroying enemies of valuable plants.

on the broad leaf to which it is attached.

The babies of the lace-wing fly are not at all pretty. Their small flat bodies bristle with short stiff spines, and they are armed with long slender jaws that have very sharp points—sucking spears with which they pierce and suck their food.

These queer little grubs are called "aphis lions"; you can guess from their name how they amuse themselves. They are surpris-

Magnify the cocoon of the lace-wing fly and it will look like this—a charming little silken casket with a neat round lid attached to the top. The beautiful fly has been caught in the very act of emerging into the world, all ready to devour the millions of green plant lice on which it will live.

into a crack in a stalk, and there each little "lion" spins a small cocoon of glistening white silk and shuts itself up inside it. The cocoon is like a tiny round box, fitted with a circular lid; and after the little creature inside has rested for a while, it cuts round the lid with its jaws, pushes it up, and comes out as a lovely golden-eyed lacewing fly instead of an ugly little aphis lion.

The ant lion, in its young days, is even more ferocious than the aphis lion. When it is a grown-up insect it is not unlike a dragon-fly, with four big gauzy wings and a long slim body; but while it is in the grub stage it is a horrible little ogre and the terror of the small insects that come within its reach.

An uglier little creature than a young ant lion you could hardly imagine. Its dull-coloured, clumsy-looking body is shaped like a flattened egg, with a row of warty lumps covered with tufts of black bristly hair all down each side. Its legs are ridiculously small and feeble; its head is square and flat; and its long, curved, sharply-pointed jaws look frightful enough to scare the life out of any small timid creature that may cross its path.

Photo by F. Martin Duncan

This is the remarkable larva of the ant lion. Its merciless habits make it a terror to all small insects.

An Insect That Walks Backwards

Now the young ant lion is no bold hunter. He is much too slow and awkward to catch anything. You see, his legs are so very weak, and are fixed to his sides in such a curious way, that he is obliged always to walk backwards. So since he cannot go hunting, the ant lion has to find some other way of procuring his dinner. And this is how he does it.

First he chooses a nice dry spot, where the soil is loose and sandy, and makes a circle on the ground, marching solemnly round in a ring, backwards, and making a shallow furrow by ploughing up the sand with his broad flat body. Stepping inside the ring, he now scoops up the sand with one of his forelegs, shovels it upon his big flat head, and with a sudden jerk sends the load flying over the border.

He plods away all round the ring until he has made a neat circular trench; then he sets to work to make another trench just inside the first one. This is hard work. And since the leg on the inside of the circle has all the shovelling to do, the ant lion will give it a rest now and then by turning round and working in the opposite direction.

Round and round he goes, ploughing the sand, shovelling it upon his head, and flinging it as far away as he can outside his excavations. At the end of each round he draws nearer to the centre of the circle; and when at last he arrives there, the persevering little creature has scooped out a round, funnel-shaped pit about two inches deep and three across, with steep, sloping sides.

Well, there the little monster is, down at the bottom of his pit. And very tired and hungry he must be. For unless some silly insect walked right into his jaws, which is not likely, he can have had nothing to eat all the time he has been working so hard. But the ant lion's task is finished now. There is nothing more to do. So he shuffles himself down into the sand at the bottom of the pit and waits for his dinner with all the patience at his command.

The Ogre in His Lair

He seldom has long to wait. For whenever you find an ant lion's pit, you may be quite sure that there are some ants' nests not very far away. Now ants are very inquisitive insects. As they hurry to and fro, all very busy about one thing or another, one of them is sure to spy the little pit in the ground and stop to have a look at it. She runs up and peers over the edge. There, down at the bottom, she sees a terrible pair of jaws sticking up from the ground. Not liking the look of this, she turns to go. But the loose sand gives way under her feet, and before she knows what is happening, the inquisitive ant is slipping and sliding down the sloping sides of the pitfall.

The hungry ant lion grows very much excited when he sees his dinner coming. He shovels up the sand with his flat head and flings it up in showers, which fall upon the struggling ant and knock her back again every time she tries to scramble up to the top. And so the poor thing slips farther and farther down the hill and rolls right into the cruel jaws of the horrid little ogre waiting below.

The ant lion has plenty to eat. Not only ants, but flies and little beetles and insects of all kinds are always falling into his pit. He sucks his victim dry, much as a spider does; then, putting the empty skin on the top of his head, he jerks it as far from the pit as he can. In this way the ogre keeps his pit clear, and there is nothing to frighten careless or inquisitive insects away from the deadly trap.

Building a Home with Sand and Silk Before Going Out into the World

The ant lion lives for quite a long time in his pit before he changes to a pupa. But at last his appetite fails. He then sets to work to make a round ball of sand, fastening the grains together with fine silken threads—which he spins from a spinneret at the tail end of his body. The ball is hollow and lined with silk to make it soft and comfortable inside. In this curious cocoon the ant lion rests for a time. Then, when this transformation is complete, he comes forth and flies away as a graceful winged insect.

But although he is so changed in every way, the ant lion does not change his name.

He is still called an ant lion, though he no longer lives in a sand pit and devours unwary ants. The ant lion is now a hunter and chases his prey on the wing. But he is rather shy and timid and does not fly about in the sunny hours of the day like bold dragon-flies. He spends most of the day resting among the leaves on trees and bushes, and comes out in the dusk to hunt the moths and flies that flutter about in the twilight.

Like the " Devil's Darning Needle " but Not Nearly as Handsome

The ant lion is much the same shape as the dragon-fly—or "devil's darning needle" —but is not nearly such a beautiful insect. Its long body is almost black and its wings are usually spotted with dull brown. Ant lions are found, too, in hot, dry, sandy districts, while dragon-flies haunt the streams and pools and seem for ever on the wing.

From early morning until quite late in the evening they dart backwards and forwards over the water, flashing in the sunlight with wonderful changing colours of shining blue and green, copper and purple. For a moment they rest, clinging to the reeds and rushes with their long, slender legs. Their great eyes gleam like lamps of copper and gold. Then off they go again, twisting and turning so swiftly in the air that our eyes can hardly follow them. They are the boldest of hunters, and they catch and even eat their prey without pausing in their flight.

The lovely dragon-flies were not always such bright and airy creatures. In their early days they crept about in the mud at the bottom of the pond; there they lurked among the water weeds and pounced upon small water folk that swam by. Slow, dull, ugly creatures they were then; you would hardly think it possible that they could ever be changed into glorious dragon-flies.

But the insect world is full of such wonders. The woods, the meadows, the ponds and streams all have marvellous tales to tell. In a later volume you will read about insects that haunt ponds and streams.

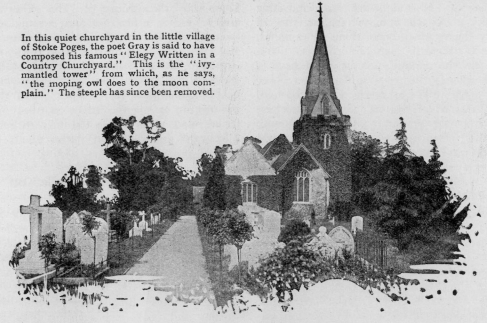

In this quiet churchyard in the little village of Stoke Poges, the poet Gray is said to have composed his famous "Elegy Written in a Country Churchyard." This is the "ivy-mantled tower" from which, as he says, "the moping owl does to the moon complain." The steeple has since been removed.

Photo by G.W.Rly.

WHICH *is the* BEST-KNOWN POEM?

Possibly it is Gray's Famous "Elegy," of Which Nearly Every Line is a Familiar Quotation

(CONTINUED FROM PAGE 406)

THOMAS GRAY wrote what is perhaps the best-known poem in the English language. It has been reprinted hundreds of times, translated into almost every language of which we can think—even into Latin, Greek, and Hebrew — and quoted, imitated, and parodied until we almost wonder why it has not been spoiled for us altogether. Yet we never tire of its lines:

The curfew tolls the knell of parting day,
    The lowing herd winds slowly o'er the
        lea . . .

The paths of glory lead but to the grave . . .

Full many a flower is born to blush unseen,
    And waste its sweetness on the desert
        air . . .

Far from the madding crowd's ignoble
    strife . . .

These and many other familiar quotations all come from the same famous poem, Gray's "Elegy Written in a Country Churchyard."

It is strange that the man who wrote this poem, now known all over the world, nearly two centuries after it was written, wrote so little else. He wrote some very fine odes, which you may read some time, and he was a great letter writer in an age when writing letters was not a lost art, as some say it is to-day. But he really wrote very little in either prose or verse; and now he is mostly remembered for his great "Elegy."

Thomas Gray was born in London in 1716, the son of a money-scrivener, or as we would say to-day, a money-lender. His father was a brutal, jealous, selfish man, who made life miserable for his family. His mother, who had been a milliner before her marriage, continued with her work and thus provided for herself and her son. It was her money which enabled young Thomas to go to school.

At Eton, the famous school to which his mother sent him when he was eleven, Gray was too delicate to take part in sports as the other boys did, and thought his own reading more interesting than the regular work of the school. He found three true friends there, and with them he formed a "quadruple alliance" which became one of the most important features in his life. Later, when he went up to Cambridge, he corresponded with these other young men. Their letters were not ordinary letters, but were written in Latin or French; or, if in English, they were frequently in verse. All the young men were scholars, though as time went on Gray was to become much more learned than any of the others.

Yet he did not like studying at Cambridge any more than he had liked it at Eton, though he gave much attention to the subjects that interested him. It is said that his fellow undergraduates, with their taste for sport, regarded him as a fop. He left the university without taking a degree, and went back to London to study law in order to earn his living.

There soon came a pleasant interruption. In 1739 he set off for the "grand tour" of the Continent with his best friend of the "quadruple alliance." This was Horace Walpole, later to become known as a famous lover of the arts and as a wit. They travelled in France, Switzerland and Italy, and Gray, in his careful scholarly way, made notes of everything he saw. They had adventures, too. They crossed the Alps, a feat almost unheard of in those days, and in one wild and dangerous pass a wolf dashed down and carried off Walpole's little lap dog. Yet they revelled in the wild scenery of the mountains—a taste in which they were ahead of their time, for it had not yet become fashionable to look upon mountain-climbing as a sport.

In Italy, Gray and Walpole quarrelled, and Gray returned home alone. He was back in

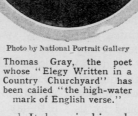

Thomas Gray, the poet whose "Elegy Written in a Country Churchyard" has been called "the high-water mark of English verse."

London by the autumn of 1741. Shortly afterwards his father died, and his mother took a house at Stoke Poges (stōk pō'jĕs), a village in Buckinghamshire, and Gray returned to Cambridge to take a degree in law. At this time, Richard West, another member of the "quadruple alliance," died. Gray was melancholy by nature, and the death of his friend was a great shock, and left him with a feeling of despair and loneliness.

Very little else happened to Gray during the rest of his life. He drifted away from the study of law, but he stayed on at Cambridge. He did not like it any too well, but living there was cheap, and it was convenient to be near the libraries. For he was soon deep in the study of Greek, and all his life he continued to study and become more and more learned, until there were few, if any, men of his time with a greater store of knowledge. When it was not Greek, it was the dark corners of the history of English literature that he was exploring, or studying Icelandic and Celtic verse. Once in a while he ventured forth on a visit to Stoke Poges or to London, or went to see Walpole, with whom he became friends again after a time. Walpole loved to receive his friends in his splendid mansion at Strawberry Hill; but Gray was shy and studious, and spent most of his life among his books.

The Most Modest of English Poets

Occasionally he would write a poem. Some of the most famous of his poems, such as "The Bard," were inspired by his studies of old Celtic or Norse lore; Gray had a great deal to do with the growing interest in these subjects. The "Elegy," however, is not concerned with these studies, but the meditations, mournful and yet somehow sweet, which come to him as he sits on a gravestone in a country burial-ground. At Stoke Poges they will show you the exact gravestone on which he sat when he wrote the poem, and point out the very yew trees which cast their "mournful shade" over him as he wrote. But others say he wrote the poem in a church-yard in Cambridge—or somewhere else—and there are others who say that he did not really write it in a churchyard at all.

Shy as he was, Gray did not seek fame. He refused an honorary degree from the university of Aberdeen, and also the office of Poet Laureate. Only once could he be per-suaded to take any money for his poems. But when he died in 1771 he had come to be known as a great poet. And his best-known poem is possibly the most familiar and the most quoted in our language.

A BOY GENIUS *and a* FORGER

Of All Literary Forgeries, Those of Chatterton are the Most Brilliant and the Most Famous

THIS is the story of one of the most brilliant boys that ever lived, and one of the most pitiable. The boy was a genius in poetry, and also a forger.

Thomas Chatterton was born at Bristol in 1752. For a long time his ancestors had been sextons at the beautiful old church of St. Mary Redcliffe. At first the boy did not seem to be able to learn how to read and write. But when he found some old music scores and manuscripts in the ancient church, he soon taught himself his letters out of them. That good fortune was also his downfall, as we shall see.

Before he was in his teens, Chatterton began to write poems, and it was his one desire to be a poet. Just about this time many people were becoming interested in the older poetry of England—in ballads and other poems that had been sung and written in the Middle Ages and had been forgotten a long time since. People were going about the land collecting these old forgotten poems and printing them, and there was a vogue for them with the public.

Chatterton had no old poems, but he knew he was a poet him-self. He had found out a good deal about the ancient English language from his old music scores and manuscripts, from reading Chaucer and other of the old authors. He conceived the idea of writing some poems of his own in this old style and passing them off on the world as manuscripts that had sur-vived from the Middle Ages and which he had discovered in the old church at Bristol.

He carried out this idea, and he deceived a good

In this fine old church of St. Mary Redcliffe, in Bristol, young Thomas Chatterton found a world of dreams so much more enchanting than the world around him that he ceased to live the life of a normal boy. His family had been sextons in the church for nearly two hundred years, and he in turn made friends of the stone images stretched upon its tombs and pored over the ancient manuscripts lying forgotten in its archives. When he came to write his strange poems he pretended that they were the work of one Thomas Rowley, an imaginary monk of the fifteenth century, who had been befriended by Master William Canynge, one of the ancient dead whose tomb is in the church.

many people. He deceived a poor pewterer named Burgum into believing that he was descended from an aristocratic family named "de Bergham," by forging a pedigree. Next he hoaxed the good people of the city with a description from an "old manuscript" of the opening of the 13th century bridge across the Avon. Then he tried for higher game. He wrote to a publisher in London with a request to have his supposed discoveries published, and even to the great Horace Walpole, who was captivated and completely deceived until better informed friends showed them to be forgeries.

Then Chatterton, though still a boy, came up to London to make fame and fortune with his pen. He had some little success there with the brilliant poems and short dramatic pieces written in his own name. But he could not make a living, and it was not long before he found himself without money and food. In desperation he shut himself up in his garret, and ended his life by taking poison, in 1770, before he was eighteen years old.

It is a pathetic story, and after his death it attracted widespread attention. His poems were then published, and they occasioned much discussion. They have since set a standard for many poets, like Keats, who were even greater than Chatterton. His life has often been written, and plays and novels have been founded on it, but he never tasted the fame that was to come years after he was laid to rest in a pauper's grave.

A GLITTERING WRITER of PLAYS

Richard Brinsley Sheridan was One of the Most Brilliant of All Wits and One of the Most Moving of All Orators

EVERYTHING was dazzling in the life of Richard Brinsley Sheridan. He did so many things well, and all he did was on such a generous scale, with such a grand and sweeping gesture. He was the idol of the play-going public, and ever since his death his comedies have been more popular than those of any other English dramatist except Shakespeare. He was the idol of "high society," and the most intimate adviser of the gay young Prince of Wales. He was one of the most brilliant orators who ever spoke in Parliament. Even his debts were heavy enough to be romantic.

Sheridan started to do spectacular things before he was twenty. He was born in 1751, in Dublin, of a very clever family—his father being a distinguished actor, his mother a novelist. After going to school in Dublin until he was

Photo by National Portrait Gallery

Richard Brinsley Sheridan, the famous dramatist, orator and wit.

eight, he left Ireland for ever, to follow his parents to England. At nineteen we find him running off to France with Elizabeth Linley, daughter of the composer Thomas Linley. He escorted her to a nunnery in France, whither she was going to escape the attentions of another suitor; she changed her mind, however, and decided to marry Sheridan instead. The girl's father followed her and brought her back to England and Sheridan had to fight two duels with the disappointed admirer of his beloved, and both fathers sternly forbade the match. Nevertheless, the young people did eventually marry, Sheridan having secured the consent of the bride's father, although that of his own father was withheld.

Meanwhile, Sheridan had been studying to become a lawyer; but he never practised. He had been doing a good deal of

When his family removed to Bath, Sheridan made the acquaintance of Thomas Linley, the composer, and two years later married Elizabeth, one of his gifted daughters. It was Linley who set to music Sheridan's "Duenna."

writing, too, though he had published nothing under his own name. Now suddenly, in 1775, a comedy of his was produced at Covent Garden Theatre, and has been playing somewhere or other almost ever since! This was "The Rivals," one of the most famous of English comedies.

Within the next five years Sheridan wrote all the plays he was ever to write, except one patriotic melodrama long ago forgotten. Besides "The Rivals," the most famous of them are "The Critic" and "The School for Scandal." "The Critic" is a very clever satire on the kind of plays popular at the time. "The School for Scandal," one of the wittiest plays in the language, makes delightful fun of all sorts of absurdities in higher society. It is as popular to-day as it was when first presented to the public.

The author of these sparkling plays had become the admiration of his audiences and a power in the theatre. In 1776 he became manager and part owner of Drury Lane, and he was connected with this most famous of London playhouses for the rest of his life. In the literary world, his fame brought him an invitation to join the Literary Club of the great Dr. Johnson. Yet Sheridan did not devote himself entirely to literature and the writing of plays, for after 1779 he turned his overflowing energies to politics.

Here he speedily won glory as great as he had achieved in the theatre. He entered Parliament in 1780, and was active in the affairs of government until four years before his death. He became the devoted friend of Charles James Fox, leader of many liberal and reform movements in Parliament. Sheridan defended the American colonists in the quarrel which led to their independence; the Continental Congress wished to send him a thank-offering of twenty thousand pounds, but he gracefully declined. He defended the French Revolution, too, at a time when it took a great deal of courage to do so. He stood also for the freedom of the press, although he admitted in his old age that his own life had been made miserable by lies about him in the papers.

When Lord Rockingham was prime minister for the second time, he appointed Sheridan under-secretary of state for foreign affairs; and when a coalition ministry was formed, the playwright was made secretary of the treasury. Sheridan was a terrible person to meet in a debate, for he had a genius for discovering the weak spots in his opponent's armour and planting a shaft of good-natured ridicule in every one. No verbal weapon is more deadly.

Sheridan Denounces Warren Hastings in a Brilliant Five Hours' Speech

He was one of the greatest of parliamentary orators. Between 1787 and 1794 there was a long drawn-out impeachment trial before Parliament of Warren Hastings, a former governor of India, who was accused of cruelty and dishonesty. Sheridan's first speech against Hastings lasted for more than five hours; when he sat down the House was so moved that it broke into a tumult of applause, for the first time in history expressing its approval by the clapping of hands. Voting on the report Sheridan had brought in had to be put off until the members' emotions had abated. Later in the trial he spoke for several hours on each of four days, the whole making really one mammoth address which stands among the most notable speeches of the British Parliament. At the end, he sank exhausted into the arms of that even greater orator, Edmund Burke, saying, "My lords, I have done."

In 1791 Drury Lane had to be rebuilt, and Sheridan tried to shoulder all the debts involved. To make matters much worse, the new theatre was burnt down in 1809. When this happened, the House of Commons voted to adjourn as an expression of sympathy with Sheridan in his misfortune. That was an honour indeed!

But after that Sheridan's finances were in a bad way. Once he was arrested for debt. During the illness which preceded his death, in 1816, he was forced to sell pictures and other possessions to pay off his creditors. When stories found their way into the papers that he lay dying in poverty, offers of help poured in. But as a matter of fact, he had every care that money or affection could bring him. Even the debts he left were paid by his family. To this day he lives on in legend and in his immortal comedies. Actors still delight to play the rôles of his creation.

A WOMAN WRITER *of* GREAT CHARM

Jane Austen was Just a Village Girl Who Wrote of Village Life—a World in Miniature

JANE AUSTEN knew a magic way of finding a pearl in every oyster. The dullest thing would shine when she looked at it.

Jane was just a pretty English girl with pink cheeks, gay and sprightly with a little touch of mischief in her, but she could see so deep into the hearts of the people of her little country village and find such roguish secrets to disclose about them that thousands of people enjoy them even now, more than a hundred years after her death.

She was born, in 1775, in the sleepy little village of Steventon, in Hampshire, where her father was the rector of the church. In her forty-one short years she seldom travelled far from Steventon, where no one else had ever seen anything of outstanding interest, or anything that could be made the basis of a story. But when Jane died, in 1817, she left us six novels, and in those novels we can find the wisdom and the folly, the heroism and the frailty, and above all the humour, of all the Steventons in the world. We can find them as we find them in other books conceived in a far larger world.

When we read those novels we soon realize that we know the people in them a

Photo by Southern Railway

This is a little English village of the kind Jane Austen knew so well. In and out of picturesque houses like the ones above her characters came and went, and through those tiny panes peeped out at passers-by. No cinema, no gramophone or wireless, no train or bus or motor-car interrupted the uneventful, drowsy summer afternoons or long winter evenings. The little handful of people were thrown upon themselves for all their diversion and amusements; and any seeing person could hardly fail to learn to know them intimately.

great deal better than we know the people all round us, even our friends and relations. This is because Jane could see right through them and tell us what she saw. Many a man has lived a long time in a Steventon without ever seeing very much in its people, until he read what Jane had to say about *her* Steventon; and then the seemingly dull people in his own world began to excite his interest because of their resemblance to her own characters.

Every one of her characters produces this effect—we feel that we have long known them all. An excellent example is Mr. Collins. He is just a pompous visitor who is always talking about the fine "bread and butter" letter he is going to write when he gets back home. But he is so real, and so ridiculous, that to this day a bread and butter letter is still referred to as a "Collins."

And who was the creator of these every-day characters leading an everyday existence? Just a happy country girl—so happy at home that it is said she never wanted to marry. She was the baby in a family of seven—five boys and two girls—the other girl being the Cassandra whom she loved so dearly. Jane had plenty of good looks and gay spirits; and she was such a sweet girl that everybody used to say that Cassandra kept her temper well but Jane had none to keep.

She had very little education—she just found out that she knew how to write. It was not her custom to tell people that she was writing novels, and when her stories were printed she used to love to hear her friends trying to guess the name of the great author. Whoever it was, they often said, he had more wit and more common sense than anybody else in England.

The titles of her six novels are. "Sense and Sensibility," "Pride and Prejudice," "Northanger Abbey," "Emma," "Mansfield Park," and "Persuasion." "Pride and Prejudice" and "Emma" are possibly the best.

Jane called them "little bits of ivory two inches wide." But Sir Walter Scott taught us the value of her miniatures when he said: "That young lady had a talent . . . which is, to me, the most wonderful I ever met with. The big bow-wow strain I can do myself like any one going; but the exquisite touch . . . is denied me."

(CONTINUED ON PAGE 531)

A GREEN ALLIGATOR

This fearsome beast is really no more terrible than the runner bean from which he is made. Notch his back with a knife and run a wire through him lengthwise so that he may be bent into shape. A slit at one end forms an expressive mouth, and two cloves make baleful eyes. Smaller beans cut in half and strung on wire—a hairpin will do—can be bent to look like legs. Put a pair of legs on one wire run crosswise through the body.

IN ESKIMO LAND

You may have an Arctic scene on the hottest summer day if you make your igloos out of egg-shells instead of ice. Block them off with a pencil, and surround them with a snowdrift of cotton-wool.

ALGERNON PEA-NUT, M.D.

Here is old Doctor Pea-nut. His tall hat is a cork, with cardboard brim. His arms and legs are of wire run through the pea-nut and bent into the right position. They will look more elegant if you cover them with cloth, but slender runner beans will also make them quite life-like. The feet are made of slices of cork in which the wire legs are inserted, and the cane is a match-stick. You will have to make the eyes and nose and mouth with ink. And as for the bag, we leave it to you!

AN EDIBLE KANGAROO

To the small end of a pear fasten the tip of another pear, using a match-stick to attach it. Good ears can be cut out of cardboard, and a tail and legs are made from runner beans strung on a wire, as described above. Grains of rice make bright eyes. Your jumping kangaroo—and your whole zoo, for that matter—will look a good deal more savage if you paint the lips and mouth.

THE FAMOUS DODO BIRD

Few of your friends will have seen a Dodo bird, so they'll take your word for this one. The body is a large carrot, and the head a small one attached by a match-stick. Run a wire through the large carrot to hold it in shape. Dodo's tail is the carrot top, and the legs are two four-inch lead pencils stuck into the halves of a potato. Her eyes are shoe buttons, and her wings are single feathers.

THE WONDERLAND OF KNOWLEDGE

Specially painted by CHARLES ROBINSON, R.I.

GE IS POWER

Frontispiece to The Wonderland of Knowledge, Volume I